Artificial Intelligence in Education - Creating an Equitable, Creative, and Effective Learning Environment

Edited by Seifedine Kadry and Balasubramaniam S.

Published in London, United Kingdom

Artificial Intelligence in Education - Creating an Equitable, Creative, and Effective Learning Environment
http://dx.doi.org/10.5772/intechopen.1008616
Edited by Seifedine Kadry and Balasubramaniam S.

Contributors
Ahmadov Tarlan, Alina Bârgăoanu, Ameed Inam, Anh Thu Le, Asif Iqbal Kawoosa, Chandan Kumar Sah, Christina Costa, Christine A. Royce, Damola Olugbade, Deepak Prashar, Dev Aditya, Eginiwin E. Joseph, Funda Örnek, G. Michael Bowen, George Hanshaw, Gila Kurtz, Hua Shen, Hussein Chaitani, Jai Prakash Pandey, Joseph O. Ukoba, Juan Pablo Valenzuela Barros, Jyoti Suhag, Kumar A N Veerendra, Kumar V Sampath, Laud C. Ochei, Laura Albrant, Leo C. Ureel II, Li Zhang, Maria Luisa Arancibia Muñoz, Mariluz Henshaw, Matthew Montebello, Meital Amzalag, Meredith Sanders, Michael Pin-Chuan Lin, Michelle Jarvie-Eggart, Mihnea Ioan Nicolescu, Okengwu A. Ugochi, Osman Aksit, Pauldy C.J. Otermans, Priya Soni, Raquel Ritchie, Renato Essenfelder, S.M.F.D. Syed Mustapha, Sage Arbor, Sebastian Fitzek, Tafline Arbor, Tony Xu, Verena Van Fleet, Victor Martinez-Luaces, Wolfgang Gerstlberger, Xiaoli Lian, Xiaoxue Du, Yasemin Gulbahar, Ying Cheng

First published in London, United Kingdom, 2026 by IntechOpen
IntechOpen is the global imprint of INTECHOPEN LIMITED, registered in England and Wales, registration number: 11086078, 167-169 Great Portland Street, London, W1W 5PF, United Kingdom

For EU product safety concerns: IN TECH d.o.o., Prolaz Marije Krucifikse Kozulić 3, 51000 Rijeka, Croatia, info@intechopen.com or visit our website at intechopen.com.

British Library Cataloguing-in-Publication Data
A catalogue record for this book is available from the British Library

Artificial Intelligence in Education - Creating an Equitable, Creative, and Effective Learning Environment
Edited by Seifedine Kadry and Balasubramaniam S.
p. cm.

This title is part of the Artificial Intelligence Book Series, Volume 44
Topic: Applied Intelligence
Series Editor: Andries Engelbrecht
Topic Editor: Vladimir Robles-Bykbaev

Print ISBN 978-1-83635-545-8
Online ISBN 978-1-83635-544-1
eBook (PDF) ISBN 978-1-83635-546-5
ISSN 2633-1403

If disposing of this product, please recycle the paper responsibly.

IntechOpen Book Series

Artificial Intelligence

Volume 44

Aims and Scope of the Series

Artificial Intelligence (AI) is a rapidly developing multidisciplinary research area that aims to solve increasingly complex problems. In today's highly integrated world, AI promises to become a robust and powerful means for obtaining solutions to previously unsolvable problems. This Series is intended for researchers and students alike interested in this fascinating field and its many applications.

Meet the Series Editor

Andries Engelbrecht received the Masters and Ph.D. degrees in Computer Science from the University of Stellenbosch, South Africa, in 1994 and 1999 respectively. He is currently appointed as the Voigt Chair in Data Science in the Department of Industrial Engineering, with a joint appointment as Professor in the Computer Science Division, Stellenbosch University. Prior to his appointment at Stellenbosch University, he has been at the University of Pretoria, Department of Computer Science (1998-2018), where he was appointed as South Africa Research Chair in Artifical Intelligence (2007-2018), the head of the Department of Computer Science (2008-2017), and Director of the Institute for Big Data and Data Science (2017-2018). In addition to a number of research articles, he has written two books, Computational Intelligence: An Introduction and Fundamentals of Computational Swarm Intelligence.

Meet the Volume Editors

Seifedine Kadry holds a Bachelor's degree from Lebanese University (1999), an MS degree from Reims University (France) (2002), an MS degree from EPFL (Lausanne) (2002), a Ph.D. from Blaise Pascal University (France) (2007), and an HDR degree from Rouen University (2017). His research currently focuses on Data Science, education using technology, system prognostics, stochastic systems, and applied mathematics. He is an ABET program evaluator for Computing and for Engineering Tech. He is a Fellow of IET, a Fellow of IETE, and a Fellow of IACSIT. He is a distinguished speaker of the IEEE Computer Society. He is a Professor of Data Science at the Lebanese American University in Lebanon.

Dr. Balasubramaniam S. is an Assistant Professor at the School of Computer Science and Engineering, Kerala University of Digital Sciences, Innovation and Technology, Digital University Kerala (DUK), Thiruvananthapuram, Kerala, India. Prior to joining DUK, he was with the School of Computer Science and Engineering at Vellore Institute of Technology (VIT), Chennai, where he served as a senior associate professor. He has around 15+ years of experience in teaching, applied research, and industry. He holds a Ph. D degree in Computer Science and Engineering from Anna University, Chennai, India, in 2015. He has published more than 30 research papers in reputed SCI/WoS/Scopus-indexed Journals. He has been granted one Australian patent and two Indian Patents and has also published two additional Indian patents. He has presented papers at conferences, received a best paper award, contributed 40 chapters in edited books, and served as an Editor for 15 books published by international publishers. His research and publication interests include machine learning, deep learning, federated learning-based healthcare and security applications, cloud computing security, Generative AI, and Agentic AI. He is serving as an Editor in Scientific Reports, Springer Nature, and Frontiers in Medicine Journals.

Contents

Preface

Artificial Intelligence (AI) has rapidly shifted from a specialized technological domain to a pervasive force reshaping every facet of education. Across early childhood learning, K–12 schooling, higher education, and professional training, AI now influences how learners engage with content, how teachers design instruction, and how institutions envision the future of equitable and inclusive learning. However, despite its transformative potential, AI introduces profound pedagogical, ethical, and societal questions that demand critical inquiry. This book emerges from that intersection of promise and responsibility.

The chapters collected in this book present a rich, multidimensional exploration of AI in education. They examine not only the power of AI to personalize learning, generate insights, enhance assessment, and extend access, but also the challenges of bias, equity, transparency, and the preservation of human agency. Together, they invite educators, researchers, technologists, and policymakers to reflect on what it truly means to teach and learn in an era shaped by intelligent systems.

The volume begins with investigations into AI-powered learning management systems, intelligent tutoring, and adaptive feedback mechanisms, illuminating how these tools support student engagement and early detection of learning difficulties. Studies from dental education, science education, and data mining reveal both instructional benefits and the pressing need for ethical guidelines, AI literacy, and institutional readiness. Parallel research illustrates how generative AI is already embedded in students' academic routines, bringing forth new dilemmas around accuracy, privacy, and academic integrity.

Several chapters extend beyond the classroom to examine systemic transformations in curriculum design, assessment, and teacher preparation. Contributors analyze the integration of AI into preservice teacher training, classroom personalization, activity-based pedagogy, competency-based assessment models, and large-scale online learning environments. Case studies, from Chile to Africa, Turkey to India, highlight how diverse educational contexts shape the challenges and opportunities of AI adoption.

A central thread running through the book is the insistence that ethical and human-centered design must accompany technological innovation. Critical AI literacy, fairness evaluation frameworks, and reflections on neurodiversity, cognitive diversity, and inclusive intelligence underscore the imperative to ensure that AI augments, rather than diminishes, human flourishing. Several chapters call for a reimagining of personalization: not as automated optimization, but as a collaborative process that protects dignity, fosters creativity, and honors cultural and pedagogical diversity.

The breadth of topics, ranging from generative AI in statistics and programming education to early learning companions to medical assessment generation to global perspectives on equity, reveals the complexity of AI's role in shaping the future of education. This book does not offer simple solutions; instead, it provides a nuanced, research-informed foundation for dialogue, innovation, and thoughtful action.

Ultimately, the chapters collectively affirm that AI's place in education cannot be defined solely by its technical capabilities. It must be evaluated through the lenses of ethics, equity, pedagogy, and humanity. As we move toward an increasingly interconnected and AI-augmented educational ecosystem, this volume serves as a guide and a provocation, inviting all stakeholders to engage critically, responsibly, and imaginatively with the possibilities ahead.

We extend our deepest appreciation to the authors whose scholarship and perspectives make this book possible. Their contributions reflect a global commitment to building educational systems that are not only technologically advanced but also just, inclusive, and fundamentally human.

Seifedine Kadry
Lebanese American University,
Beirut, Lebanon

Balasubramaniam S.
Digital University,
Kerala, India

Section 1

Foundations & Conceptual Perspectives on AI in Education

Chapter 1

A Conceptual Framework for the Effective Use of Generative AI Tools in Learning Programming and Data Mining: A Case in the Context of Education

Yasemin Gulbahar

Abstract

As generative artificial intelligence increasingly becomes part of the wider teaching and learning process, the question of how these tools can be utilised more effectively becomes paramount. As educators, we need to explore, adopt, and be fully able to utilise today's innovative pedagogical approaches within our individual educational contexts. As such, the aim of this research study was to develop a conceptual framework for the effective use of AI tools by students to support their learning of data mining concepts. Based on qualitative and quantitative data collected from students via a survey approach, the study's findings revealed an organisational level need to define standards for the ethical use of AI tools and the establishment of appropriate guidance policies. Additionally, suitable training should be developed and delivered to both educators and learners on the fundamental topic of AI literacy. The findings of this study also make it clear that both educators and instructional designers need to rethink AI-supported pedagogies, especially in terms of student assignment reliability. The research was aimed not only at informing readers about the instructional design of relevant courses from a pedagogical perspective but also at shedding light on the learning processes pertinent to students seeking help from AI tools in the form of personalised intelligent tutoring.

Keywords: learning analytics, AI tools, pedagogy, ethical use, conceptual framework

1. Introduction

The use of AI tools, specifically generative AI (GenAI), has attracted interest from many educators and researchers, resulting in diverse and conflicting discourse in the current literature. For example, whilst concerns have been expressed about the potential pitfalls and negative impact of AI usage on assessment integrity [1–3], others have openly encouraged its integration within teaching and learning processes [4–7]. This presents evidence that a significant gap still exists in the current literature about how students can utilise AI tools within their education, how to ensure they benefit appropriately and ethically in doing so, and how teachers can best integrate these tools into their teaching practices. When discussing technology integration, it is usually the case that teachers are trained first in order to effectively teach their students how best to use the technology. However, recently, due to the predominance of easy and open-access policies associated with these technologies, the integration of AI tools has effectively started simultaneously on both sides, that is, by both educators and students alike.

1.1 Educational technology and humans

Technology integration not only concerns educational technology and humans as end-users (i.e., teachers and students), but also encompasses academic research on how established and contemporary pedagogy may be affected. The study conducted by [8] presents a good example of this interdisciplinary approach, whereby the researchers considered a wearable, real-time awareness tool for teachers working in AI-enhanced K-12 classrooms as a learning analytics tool and also explored the iterative co-design, development, and classroom evaluation of the whole learning analytics system. Their study underlined the need to involve every level of stakeholder within the design and development process due to the inherently challenging structure and complexity of today's learning analytics systems.

Some of the published research has focused on teachers' perspectives and initiatives for incorporating AI tools into teaching processes. In a study by [9], a structural equation modelling approach was employed to investigate teachers' continuance intention to teach with AI. The research tested 10 hypotheses regarding anxiety (AN), self-efficacy (SE), attitude towards AI (ATU), perceived ease of use (PEU), and perceived usefulness (PU). The researchers not only concluded that 'teachers' SE would positively influence their PEU and ATU about adopting AI technologies, and it could further affect PU through PEU' (p. 124), but also mentioned that 'teachers' PEU would positively affect their PU as well as their attitude toward applying AI technologies to support teaching' (p. 125).

In a research by Lu et al. [7], GenAI was incorporated into the training of pre-service teachers to consider the potential positive impact of cultivating their higher-order thinking and self-efficacy as teachers. The study developed a supportive method of GenAI usage to aid the practical training of pre-service teachers in their teaching skills and investigated the potential impact through educational experiments. Having explored the effects of generative AI-assisted pre-service teaching skills training on pre-service teachers' self-efficacy and higher-order thinking, the study concluded that GenAI can be effective in supporting teachers' professional development.

In a research by Pham et al. [10], an AI-assisted learning flow was developed, aimed at encouraging students and instructors to integrate ChatGPT into their teaching and learning processes. The researchers repeatedly validated and assessed a variety of exercises, tutorial tasks, and assessment-based questions, and also evaluated generative responses through a self-rating system. The findings concluded that 'ChatGPT has significant potential to assist students; however, there is a necessity for training and offering guidance to students on effective interactions with ChatGPT' (p. 1).

Of course, students can independently try to learn about the potential benefits of using AI tools out of personal curiosity and then reflect on the various challenges and opportunities that AI-technology presents. In a study by Delcker et al. [11], the relationship between first-year students' knowledge, skills, and attitudes was examined, together with their use of AI-tools as part of their existing learning process. The study concluded that attitudes towards AI significantly explained the intended use of the tools, leading the researchers to call for instructional designers and other higher education stakeholders to become role models in providing 'best-practice examples of how AI-tools can be used to positively influence learning processes if they want to facilitate the usage of the respective tools' (p. 1).

In a study by Chan and Hu [1], university students' perceptions of GenAI technologies were studied within the higher education context, and the findings revealed a focus on familiarity, willingness to engage, potential benefits and challenges, and effective integration. The researchers concluded that students have an awareness of the potential of AI tools used for personalised learning support, for writing and brainstorming assistance, and for the purposes of research and analytical work. However, they also shared concerns regarding the accuracy and ethical usage of AI tools.

In order to discuss and support the development of hybrid human-AI learning technologies as well as pedagogies [12], the detect-diagnose-act framework was used to describe the function of AI's use in education. In search of a common language, the researcher suggested a six-level automation model aimed at considering the roles of AI, learners, and teachers within educational applications. The study formed an important step towards new pedagogical models 'to support a coordinated development of an interdisciplinary dialogue between quadruple helix stakeholders, to build on the combined strength of human and artificial intelligence' (p. 641).

Recently, there has been notably increased attention from professionals and scholars regarding the collaborative use of GenAI [13, 14]. Some literature now suggests that GenAI can help improve how educational content is taught and learnt [15, 16], as well as having a positive effect on students' drive, emotional state, and ultimately their academic grades [17, 18].

1.2 Instructional design and practices

The published literature regarding the use of GenAI and its associated practices presents varying insights into specific cases, leading to controversial issues being raised in some instances. In a study by Li et al. [6], the effects of 'human-human' and 'human-machine' collaborative learning approaches were investigated through an exploratory quasi-experimental study with a focus on critical thinking, learning performance, and cognitive load as a means of revealing student teacher performance. Their findings indicated that student teachers who used ChatGPT exhibited higher critical-thinking systematicity, task completion efficiency, and experienced lower cognitive load, whereas student teachers paired with in-service teachers slightly outperformed their peers in the final teaching design proposal, which evidenced the changing potential and strengths of humans versus machines.

In an article titled 'Designs and practices using generative AI for sustainable student discourse and knowledge creation' [5], the authors addressed how emergent technological advancements, such as GPT, can be incorporated into designs for sustainable student discourse and knowledge creation. The researchers also examined the potential effects and repercussions of technological utilisation and misuse to reveal GPT's role in diverse settings. In research by Davy Tsz Kit Ng et al. [19], a framework for AI literacy/competence in education was suggested to address certain pedagogical concerns of AI usage as well as instructional design considerations. Their framework extended beyond technology-related competency by underlining a holistic understanding of the ethical, safe, and appropriate use of AI tools [20, 21]. The proposed model offered insights to encourage meaningful interventions to foster 'students' AI competencies via four processes: 1) teachers' professional engagement; 2) instructional support; 3) content choices across disciplines; and 4) students' learning competencies [19] (p. 153).

In a study conducted at Temple University in Pennsylvania, United States of America [22], both students and lecturers considered GenAI tools helpful when used in creative tasks (brainstorming, coding, feedback) on computing courses. GenAI was also seen as capable of improving time management through the automation of basic tasks, allowing for greater focus on software design. The participant students viewed GenAI as a personalised teaching assistant, whilst some of their instructors saw errors made by GenAI tools as opportunities to develop their students' critical thinking, requiring them to evaluate and improve AI-generated content rather than just writing reports [22]. Similarly, a survey of 399 students in Hong Kong by Chan and Hu [1] revealed positive student attitudes towards GenAI, with perceived benefits including round-the-clock personalised support, writing and brainstorming aid, tailored feedback, and improved research. It was considered particularly helpful for non-native English writers. The students also noted GenAI's ability to help with workload reduction and assist with research tasks, although concerns were raised regarding AI's accuracy and the ethical implications of its usage within educational contexts. The study went on to suggest that the participant students were open to the use of GenAI, appreciated it as a utility and for its ease of use, and linked positive views of learning with deeper engagement [1]. On the other hand, a study of 74 university students in China [23] explored GenAI learning experiences and revealed that initial enthusiasm had given way to mixed views (optimism, doubt, pragmatism). Students reported that GenAI fostered deep reflective learning and empowered them as accountable learners with agency over their AI tutor.

Similar to the previously mentioned research on the benefits of using generative AI, a study by Rasul et al. [24] involving 10 researchers from Australia, Brazil, and India argued that ChatGPT can deliver tailored learning experiences with personalised feedback that builds upon what learners already know. Their study also pointed out AI's value in conducting research, data analysis, literature reviews, text summarisation, and translation tasks. Furthermore, the authors suggested that ChatGPT could help educators automate certain tasks and facilitate the creation of innovative assessments that promote creativity and critical thinking. In another study by Darvish et al. [25], researchers assessed the effectiveness of an AI assistant, traditional checklists, and a combination of both with 1,625 University of Queensland students in Australia. Their study's results affirmed the significance of teachers and established methods. While students who received AI support initially outperformed their peers, their performance dropped off considerably once the AI tools were no longer available. The researchers interpreted this as an indication that the students depended too heavily on the technology instead of developing their own learning strategies. In contrast, students who only used traditional checklists displayed the greatest self-regulation and retention abilities [25].

The position paper of [26] argued that GenAI can help boost productivity, especially for lower-skilled individuals (e.g., those with writing skill deficiencies), leading to more equitable outcomes with higher quality and faster output. They advised a balanced view, urging universities to offer AI education and ethics, and called for research-based policies to be established. Another developing potential of GenAI's usage within education concerns the customisation of open-source LLMs for specific educational purposes. For example, Sarčević et al. [27] developed an AI chatbot for first-year programming students that used fine-tuning and retrieval-augmented generation (RAG), allowing the LLM to access current external data. The study found RAG to be more effective than fine-tuning in the generation of accurate answers.

A review of 64 publications and a study of 112 students by Saúde et al. [28] explored GenAI's benefits in higher education. Overall, 28% of the students saw it as mainly beneficial, while 10% found it to be unfavourable. The top perceived benefits included resolving uncertainties, promoting autonomy, aiding tasks, saving research time, improving information access, easing educator workload, and enabling the introduction and application of new and contemporary teaching methods. The participant students had concerns about AI-usage dependency, apathy, plagiarism, reduced levels of critical thinking, and weakened student-teacher relationships. The research highlighted GenAI's potential to plagiarise and the need for teachers to adapt accordingly to using AI in their teaching practices [28]. In a study by Johnston et al. [29], it was reported that 2,555 students showed support for clear AI regulations to be introduced in order to address concerns about unfair competition between student cohorts. While views on AI misuse varied by tool and usage amounts, Grammarly was the most favoured over ChatGPT for essay writing. Students with high levels of writing confidence were less inclined to use or support GenAI use by others. The study noted challenges evident in banning the use of GenAI tools for certain student groups. Suggestions included GenAI-proof assessments or universities incorporating GenAI into their teaching and learning practices.

As a summary, a rapidly evolving era of AI-related innovations has been witnessed in the educational context. As mentioned in [30], in the theory of diffusion of innovations (DOI), new implementations and technologies can spread through a population or social system in quite diverse fashions due to the varied characteristics of individuals. Whilst some may be called innovators, early adopters, or even the early majority if they are more open and ready for change, others are grouped as the late majority or laggards if they show resistance. As such, individuals all go through the same steps but with different timing. Thus, according to [30], there are five stages in the DOI process: awareness, interest, evaluation, trial, and adoption, where an individual might reject an innovation at any time during or after the adoption process. The current limited literature shows us that those researchers who have published in this area are in the adoption process based on their trials.

Based on the background highlighted in the literature, the current study aimed to understand students' usage patterns and motivations for employing generative AI. It also investigated their reported experiences – both positive and negative – with these tools in their academic endeavours. Furthermore, the current study explored their perspectives on the ethical implications, output quality, and potential future of generative AI. Finally, the study aimed to define the scope of a conceptual framework for the effective integration of GenAI tools within educational settings and thereby address these four research questions:

1. What are students' behaviour patterns and reasons for using generative AI?

2. How do students explain their experiences (positive or negative) when using AI tools in their academic work?

3. What perceptions do students hold about GenAI tools regarding their ethical aspects, output quality, and future directions?

4. What should be the scope of a conceptual framework for the effective use of GenAI tools within educational contexts?

2. Methodology

2.1 Research method

Use of both qualitative and quantitative approaches was preferred for the current research, in which survey-type questions were employed. Quantitative questions were used to gather demographic data about the study participants, whilst qualitative questions were aimed at revealing deeper insights into the participants' usage of GenAI tools [31, 32].

2.2 Participants

This case study was conducted within a specific context with postgraduate students of a 'Learning Analytics' programme. Out of 64 active students taking the programme, a total of 23 voluntarily participated in the study, representing a participation rate of 36%. The demographic features of the study group were explored in terms of their age, gender, background, daily Internet usage, awareness of AI tools and their possible usage, years of experience using computers for research and academic purposes, and their previous use of AI tools.

Of the 23 participating students, 9 were aged 22–23 years, 8 were aged 24–25 years, 1 student was aged 28–29 years, and 5 were older than 30 years. In terms of gender, there were 10 male students, 12 female students, and one student identified as non-binary.

As an interdisciplinary field, learning analytics programmes generally attract students from diverse backgrounds. In the current study, there were four students each studying economics and psychology, three studying business, education, and statistics, two from the mathematics department, and one student each from the departments of administration, information technology, sociology, cognitive science, liberal arts, management, and science.

Regarding the participants' daily Internet usage, one student stated using the Internet for more than 13 hours, 6 students mentioned using the Internet for 10–12 hours each day, 9 students for 7–9 hours, 6 students for 4–6 hours, and one student used the Internet for less than 3 hours daily. Of the 23 participating students, 22 mentioned that they did have prior awareness of AI tools and their possible usage, whilst one student mentioned having only some level of prior awareness.

The students were also asked about their experience using computers for research and academic purposes. Of the 23 participating students, 4 had more than 17 years of experience, 5 had 7–9 years, 9 had 4–6 years, and 5 students had less than 3 years of experience using computers in their academic work. When asked, 'Did you use AI tools as a support to your academic work (bachelor's thesis, preparing a report, course project, research for an assignment, etc.)?', all 23 of the students answered affirmatively.

2.3 Data collection and analysis

Data on the use of AI tools by the participating students was gathered via a survey administered as a Google Form. The survey consisted of 21 questions, including six multiple-choice questions, six check-box type questions allowing for more than one selection, two Likert-type items, one short-answer question, and six open-ended questions. Descriptive analysis was used to analyse the students' demographic information, whilst inductive coding was used to analyse their open-ended question responses.

3. Findings

3.1 Quantitative measures: Student population demographics

A total of eight questions were posed to the participants in order to understand their intentions and preferences for using GenAI tools.

When the participants were asked about their preference for using various AI tools, it was clear that almost all of them (n = 22) had used ChatGPT, followed by DeepL, Bard/Gemini, and GPTZero (see **Figure 1**).

Among the reasons given by the participants for avoiding the use of AI tools, trust was the most mentioned concern, along with other reasons (see **Figure 2**) that mostly indicated a lack of knowledge, which underlines the importance of achieving 'AI literacy'. Notably, some of the students were against the use of AI tools in academic settings.

Besides the students having certain trust issues regarding the use of AI tools in their education, they provided several reasons as to why they still used them (see **Figure 3**). The reason most frequently mentioned was to develop ideas (n = 16), followed by getting feedback on their own text (n = 15), to summarise text (n = 15), and for program/code development (n = 15).

3.2 Quantitative measures: Students' preferred approach to using AI tools

The participants' perceptions varied in terms of their perceived usefulness of AI tools used in specific activities (see **Figure 4**). The most mentioned perceived usefulness was gaining different insights and learning new information (n = 15), whilst half of the participants stated that AI tools were useful for learning new

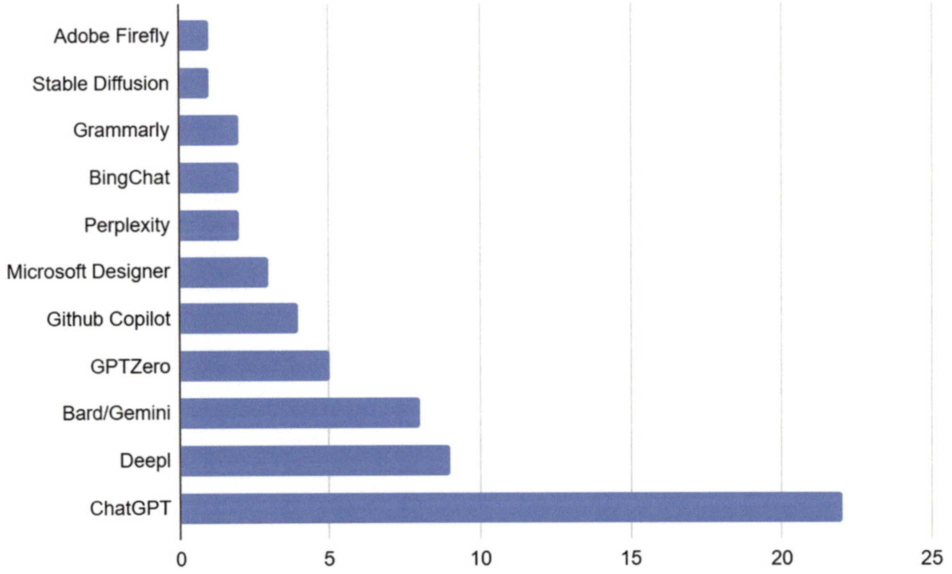

Figure 1.
AI tool usage.

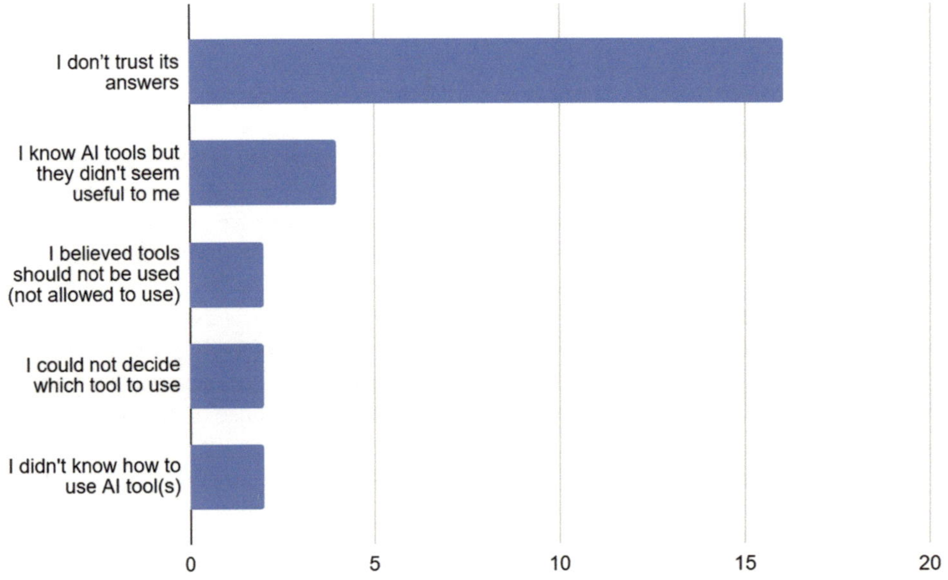

Figure 2.
Reasons to avoid the use of AI tools.

information, program/code development (n = 14), the development of ideas, and for the purposes of text summarisation (n = 13).

When the participants were asked about their feelings toward the usability of AI tools based on a Likert-type scale ranging from one (difficult to use) to five (easy to use), most of the participants mentioned ease of use, while two remained neutral.

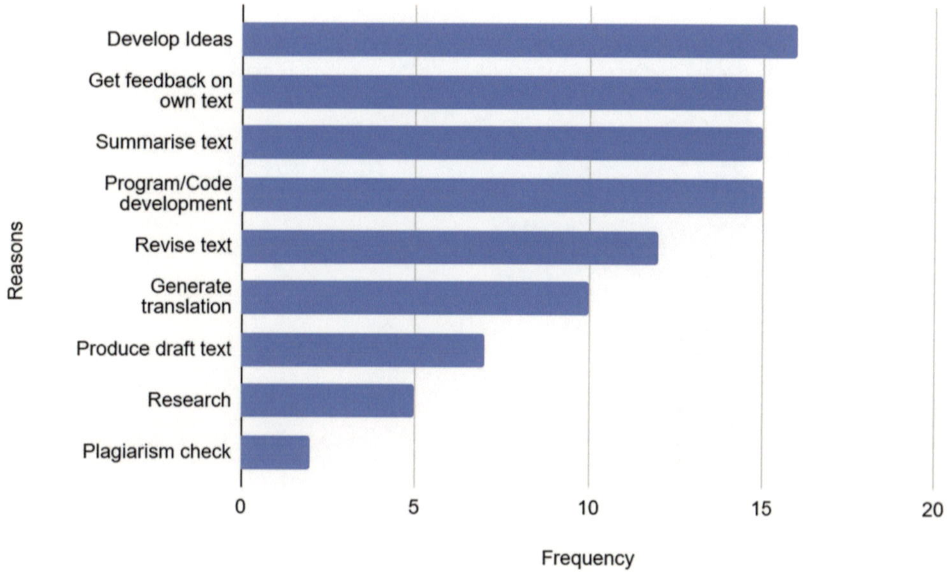

Figure 3.
Reasons to use AI tools.

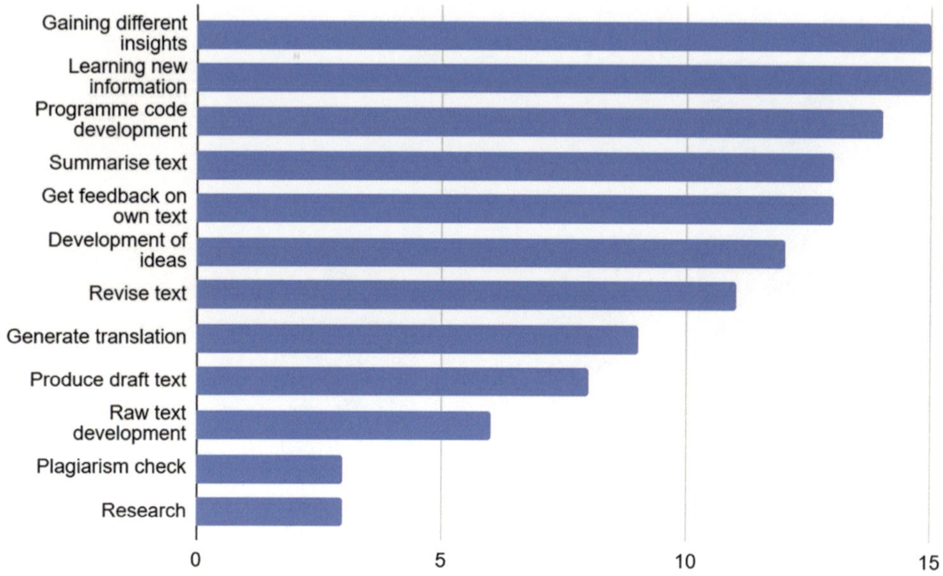

Figure 4.
Perceived usefulness of AI tools.

Similarly, with regard to possible time savings from using AI tools, on a Likert-type scale ranging from one (significant time loss) to five (significant time saving), 19 of the participating students were positive, whilst four responded neutrally.

When questioned about the source of their AI literacy (see **Figure 5**), the majority of the students mentioned peer learning (n = 11), whilst just over half mentioned

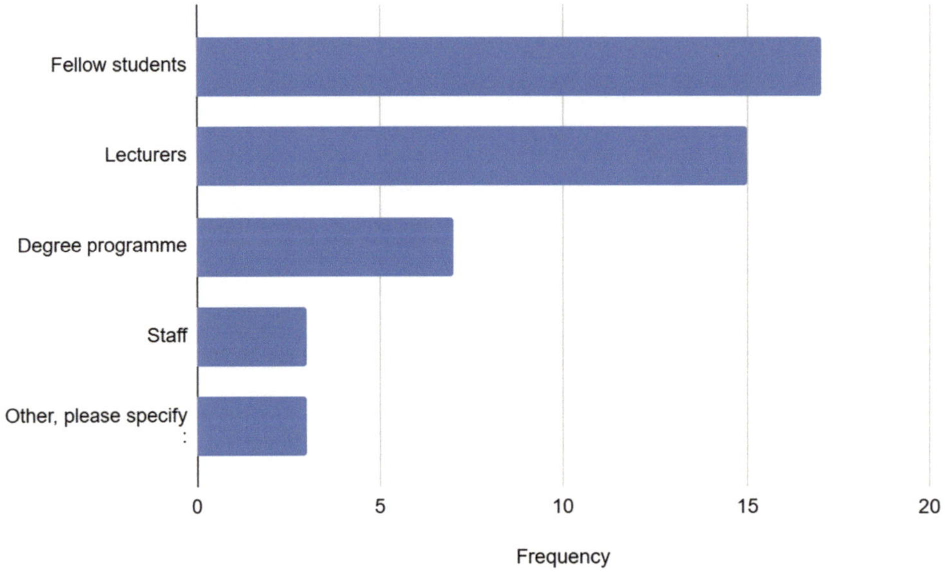

Figure 5.
Information sources for gaining AI literacy.

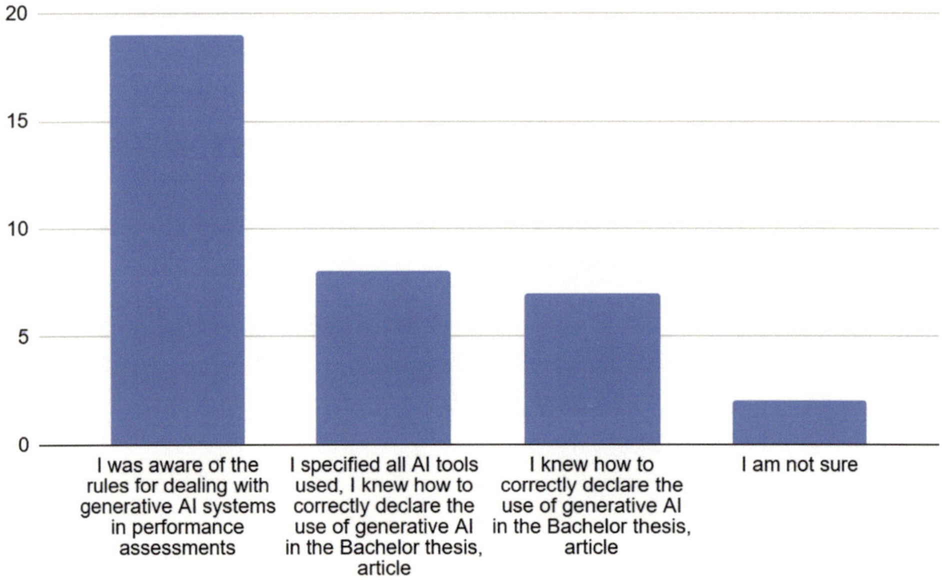

Figure 6.
Self-awareness about AI literacy.

their lecturers ($n = 8$) as the source of instruction and information on the use of AI tools in their academic work.

Lastly, when the students were asked about their self-awareness regarding their own use of AI tools (see **Figure 6**), most stated that they were aware and used AI tools (n = 19), whereas two students mentioned being unaware of the tools or not using them frequently.

3.3 Qualitative measures: Experiences of using AI tools in academic work

Of the six open-ended questions, findings from the first three questions are summarised as follows in order to answer the study's second research question.

Answers to the question 'What has been your most positive experience of using AI tools in academic work?' were analysed, revealing four themes: 'improving language' (n = 10); 'getting insight or innovative ideas' (n = 8); 'assisting code writing' (n = 7); and 'error detection in code' (n = 5). Under the theme of 'improving language', students mentioned cases such as instant proofreading and editing rough-drafted text, improving written text, learning to use language in better ways, obtaining an overall idea of an assignment (to save time), supporting a better understanding of a concept or process, searching for titles when writing a report, and translating textual matter. For the theme of 'getting insight or innovative ideas', the students pointed to having used AI tools to generate new ideas, look for new perspectives, get help in being creative, and seek inspiration. Students' usage of AI tools for writing program code, code development, and seeking relevant examples was merged under the theme of 'assisting code writing'. One student commented, 'I use AI to help my programming projects, debug, and to revise my reports', while other students mentioned having used AI tools to better understand their areas of weakness in terms of knowledge mastery, save research time, create outlines, and elicit feedback. One student said that 'It become easier for me to find information I want' by focusing on the tutor role of AI tools', and another mentioned that:

> *'I tend to use them to revise my written paragraphs and to check my homework answers. In terms of the former, AI can rewrite my sentences more concisely, from which I can pick up common but unfamiliar phrases and expressions. For home-work, it can help ensure that my answers are correct and indicate where my weaknesses lie in terms of knowledge mastery.'*

Contrarily, when the students were asked about negative experiences with using GenAI tools, most of the answers given concerned inaccurate output. They underlined incorrect answers received in terms of statistics and numbers, false information, hallucinations (i.e., made-up or fictional information like fake references), as well as inefficient or suboptimal outcomes. Three of the students also mentioned the limited understanding of the context and limited creativity of some AI tools. On this, one of the students mentioned that,

> *'If I am entirely unaware of the research topic that I am looking up, there is some level of suspicion I have with the information generated. I personally wouldn't use AI to research a topic I knew nothing about. I would first do my own research and then use AI to supplement that research, if at all.'*

Other students revealed concerns based on their own negative experiences while searching for references, summarising documents, or editing work based on AI-edited text. On this, one student mentioned that, 'Sometimes, the capabilities of AI tools may not align well with the specific needs or objectives of a research project, leading to inefficient or suboptimal outcomes', while another shared their concerns about individual skills, saying that, 'I realised that my writing ability and critical thinking went down as I became more reliant on using AI tools'. The potential negative consequences of using AI tools in learning were stated as a heavy reliance upon the veracity of generated responses and the inherent dangers in directly copying/pasting AI-generated output into academic work.

Another question posed to the participants was, 'What else would you like to tell us about AI use in the context of your work (e.g., wishes for your university with regard to AI tools, lessons learnt, problems accessing AI tools, etc.)?' Of the 23 participant students, nine responded by saying, 'Teach us how to effectively leverage AI tools in education!' whilst three urged that their university 'have a consistent policy on AI usage across all courses'. Four students expressed their willingness to benefit from and learn about AI, whilst one mentioned the need for assignments to be redesigned, and another requested that processes and workflows be more automated. Some of the students' comments were as follows:

- 'I think the university should teach students how to use AI and develop its own AI tools to facilitate student learning.'

- 'I think universities should offer more courses on how to use AI correctly because the development of this technology is irreversible. Everyone knows that it is easy to use and saves time, but how to use it without violating morals and ethics is an issue.'

- 'Institutions should have strict guidelines on how to use AI tools and integrate detection tools to identify AI-generated work in order to better promote academic integrity.'

- 'Institutions should provide training for their students and faculty members on how to properly and efficiently use AI tools. We live in the era of technology, but must also remember that while AI doesn't master the world, people need to know how to use it.'

- 'AI should be used as a resource, but should not be generating all of a student's work. Many of my classmates solely rely on AI tools as if they were their own brain. They can't even brainstorm or write a paragraph on their own without using an AI tool, and that is troubling.'

- 'I wish the university would re-think what they should teach students in the area of AI. A lot of skills can be undertaken by AI, now which makes it pointless to learn such skills. For example, should we still need to learn programming languages if now ChatGPT can do it fast and accurately?'

- 'AI is often useless or even harmful if you don't understand the scope of usage and fundamental principles.'

3.4 Qualitative measures: Ethical issues, output quality, and future directions

Of the six open-ended questions, findings from the last three are summarised as follows in response to the study's third research question.

DOI: http://dx.doi.org/10.5772/intechopen.1012778

3.4.1 Ethical issues of using AI tools

The extent of using AI tools to support academic work was generally reported as ethical if students perceive its role to be only that of a supportive tool. On this point, the participants mentioned various cases where AI usage could be deemed 'ethical':

- 'You cite [AI] tools [used] and provide prompts';
- '[AI] is used for the adjustment and improvement of the quality of your work';
- 'You seek support, and ask [AI] simple things';
- 'You are searching for or sorting information';
- 'You treat AI essentially like another tool, such as the ability to use calculators in a maths exam';
- 'you are seeking feedback'; or
- 'You ask [AI] for summary points and seek help to find bugs in your code'.

One student mentioned the following as a supportive argument: 'Using AI ethically means treating it as a supplementary resource rather than a substitute for critical thinking, and properly citing AI-generated content when it influences academic work.'

With regards to the ethical use of AI tools for the public good, one student stated, 'AI tools can democratise access to information, providing students and researchers with resources that might otherwise be unavailable due to geographical or financial constraints', whilst another shared that, 'I believe you shouldn't use AI tools to generate ideas with the objective of copying down information or use them to generate work from zero based on your research question; but to just use them to adjust and improve your work; that is ethical usage.'

In terms of the unethical usage of AI tools, one student stated that:

> *'Using AI to finish academic work fully is not at all ethical, which I oppose to the highest extent since it is a violation of academic integrity and is unfair to those who spend tons of time developing their own thoughts.'*

Additionally, another student stated that, 'I think that students will really lose out on the educational experience if they rely upon AI tools as their main source of information.'

3.4.2 Satisfaction and future expectations from using AI tools

Of the 23 participant students, 20 mentioned that using AI tools had met their expectations, and all of them mentioned ChatGPT as being the primary AI tool that they used (a finding consistent with **Figure 1**). On this, one student commented that:

> *'To be honest, ChatGPT has greatly exceeded my expectations. I am used to asking it directly instead of Google for some unfamiliar knowledge. Even though I know that it also searches from the Internet, it can sort out knowledge very logically.'*

Overall, 16 of the students mentioned that ChatGPT had helped them while writing code/programming, in debugging code, and in providing clues to improve their work and enrich their understanding, whereas 5 of the students stated that they were satisfied with using ChatGPT for proofreading and text editing tasks, for correcting grammatical errors, and helping to improve their word selection skills; basically, to help with reading and writing proficiency. Related to this, one student said that 'Claude2 and ChatGPT helped me save time on summarising and to reduce my cognitive load in reading and writing.' Two other students addressed the use of ChatGPT in analysing data and for uploading files in order to have materials summarised. The remaining three students were, however, less satisfied with their experience of using AI tools in their studies. Additionally, expressing a different point of view, one of the students said that 'Yes, ChatGPT has met my expectations. I not only use it to study and help me summarise data, it can also help as my mental health therapist.'

3.4.3 Potential of using AI tools

With regards to the potential of AI tools usage reshaping the process of their academic work, 17 of the 23 students expressed positive thoughts, whilst 4 were negative or unsure. On not realising the potential of using AI tools, one student mentioned that AI is just a tool and that it cannot go beyond being thought of as a similar tool to that of a calculator or a personal computer, whilst another mentioned that AI tools can only assist learners but cannot reshape learning itself. Additionally, one student mentioned that the use of AI tools 'cannot just change our responsibility to learn more'. In summary, the participant students believed that the potential of using AI tools may bring about numerous changes, but that it would not be enough to reshape the whole teaching and learning process. There were also some significant concerns raised which counter the potential benefits of AI usage, such as focusing on human critical thinking, the ease of overusing such tools, and the necessity to re-think the criteria and processes involved in evaluating student output (greater focus required on the students' thinking process and individuality).

On the other hand, in terms of the potential that AI tools can offer learners, the participants recognised the changing nature of today's learning and educational environments and underlined the importance of addressing more critical thinking and evaluative thinking components in academic assignments, noting that certain assignments need to be re-designed in line with the use of AI tools by students. Other potential contributions of using AI tools in academic studies were as follows:

- 'To shape our reading ability (due to usage in summarisation)';
- 'To shape how students work on their assignments and coursework';

- 'To provide support in gaining creative and comprehensive views';
- 'To guarantee the quality of students' work output';
- 'To save time in reviewing';
- 'To enable a more personalised learning experience';
- 'To re-shape academic work by streamlining the research process';
- 'To help make students' preparation processes more efficient';
- 'To change learning processes through the integration of simple tasks';
- 'To improve efficiency in undertaking research and analysing data';
- 'To eliminate unnecessary content contained within instructions';
- 'To promote more complex thinking and support dealing with matters of increased complexity';
- To promote personal cognitive development while competing with AI-generated results'.

4. Discussion and conclusion

As a contribution to the ongoing public discourse on AI's position within contemporary education, the current study's findings revealed a number of potential applications as well as some notable concerns that will be of interest to all stakeholders.

Concerning the use of GenAI tools within teaching and learning contexts, the study's findings were analysed and categorised under six dimensions: ethical concerns, use cases, individual level, challenges, organisational level, and teaching and learning, as illustrated in **Figure 7**.

Based on the study's findings, it is clear that using AI tools to gain new insights, improve or justify existing ideas, or further develop knowledge and skills not only provides multiple perspectives and comprehensive outputs, but also helps foster cognitive engagement and development in learners. This result can be interpreted according to the DOI theory, as set out in a study by Rogers [30], in that this may affect students at almost all educational levels and stages. This highlights an urgent need to formulate global, national, and local guidelines and regulations on the usage of AI tools by both educators and students, since the use of such tools could do as much harm as good if misused or used inappropriately. Frameworks for integrating GenAI in education were discussed in a study by Kurtz el at. [33], in which the importance of training educators and students to use these tools optimally and ethically was emphasised and where student-educator partnerships were highlighted as key components of a successful teaching-learning process. Additionally, an educator-led partnership focused on ethics and

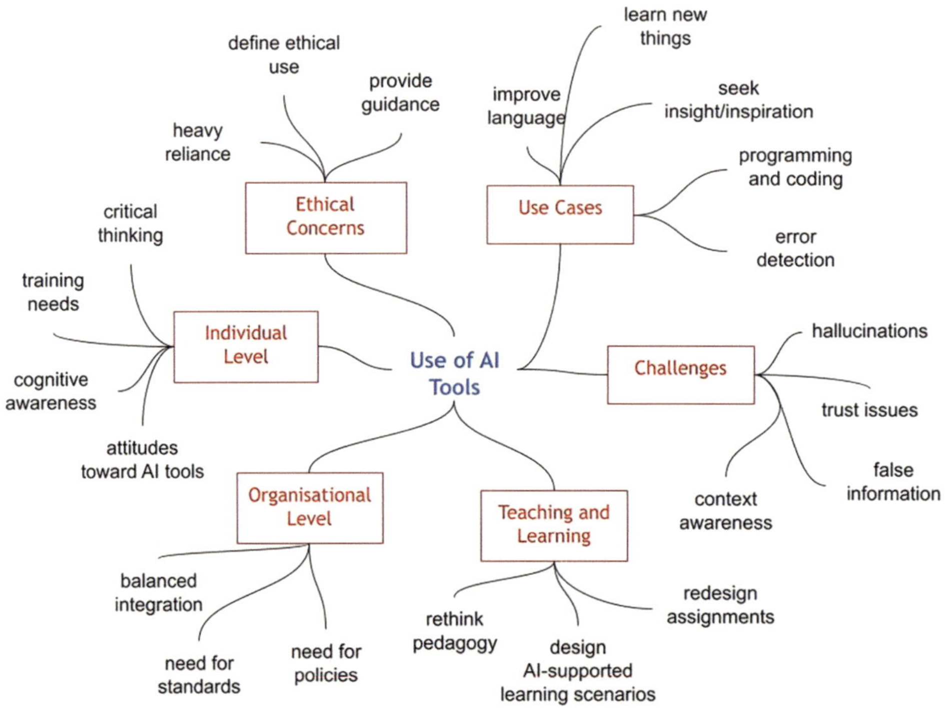

Figure 7.
Dimensions for the effective use of AI tools.

skill-building was proposed in the study by Kurtz el at. [33] as a key component for all higher education curricula.

Based on a study by Lee et al. [5], the use of know-build-critique (KBC) was suggested to navigate the use of GenAI for the purposes of knowledge building and to sustain student discourse, where GPT was promoted to learn about AI (know), improve ideas with AI (build), and evaluate AI output (critique). This suggestion also directly applies to the findings of the current study, as use cases of students were seen to be significantly related to the learning of new ideas, the improvement of ideas, and the assessment of AI output, similar to that of a mentor's role. On the other hand, the participant students' experiences were found to be quite diverse, addressing important needs in terms of providing related learning opportunities [12], as well as the setting of standards and policies, which can be directly interpreted as students being in need of official and trusted guidance on AI usage in their academic work. A study by Fawns et al. [34], consisting of 20 online focus groups and involving 79 students from four Australian universities, revealed that any lack of clarity on the appropriate use of GenAI tools could lead to student apprehension. Similar concerns were also mentioned by the participant students in the current study, where it was revealed they held fears regarding heavy reliance upon AI tools as part of the learning process, the potential loss of critical-thinking skills [35], and decreased motivation to learn new things, which can just as easily be accomplished by AI tools in today's digital era. Thus, based on the current educational landscape, it is paramount that all students have the ability to both leverage the benefits of AI tools and apply critical thinking responsibly when such tools are used.

The lack of, or the limited scope of, guidelines for GenAI tools' usage is considered an area of significant concern [36]. Although many universities are announcing their own perspectives on this issue, most guidelines have a different focus in terms of the respective institutional priorities. Hence, higher education establishments may need to reconsider their current regulations in order to find the middle ground between the prevention of academic dishonesty and fostering innovation and open inquiry in their educational processes and academic environment. Similarly, Raman et al. [37] pointed out several ethical issues that GenAI raises in terms of its application within academic settings, such as decreased creativity, academic dishonesty, overdependence, and reduced intellectual engagement. They also raised the ongoing challenge of defining the boundaries between appropriate, inappropriate, and excessive use of GenAI in educational contexts. Thus, in order to deal appropriately with today's challenges, educational institutions and organisations need to clearly define what constitutes the ethical use of AI tools in the educational context, set appropriate standards, and establish coherent policies in this critical area. Moreover, establishments need to provide continuous support and training on all such relevant issues to all types of AI users (i.e., both educators and learners). On the other hand, once equipped with the necessary knowledge and skills, educators should work to re-design their respective teaching and learning environments and processes, as well as existing student assignments, in order to provide a more democratic environment for each and every student. Hence, researchers should continue to explore the role of hybrid human-AI use cases and envision accompanying roles for learners, teachers, and AI, in order to come up with effective instructional strategies and pedagogical approaches [12]. Exploring student behaviour and usage patterns, as well as their willingness and concerns regarding the use of AI tools, will help support educators to better understand and integrate AI technologies into teaching-learning processes, thus ensuring that they complement and enhance traditional teaching methods [1] rather than hinder the evolution of educational practices.

The context of the current research was 'learning analytics', in other words, the use of educational data for analytical purposes to ensure its usage is deemed beneficial. Looking back to when spreadsheets were used to make computations using formulae and even manually clean data, we have since switched to easier and more comprehensive software such as SPSS and SAS. This journey is now undergoing a new transformation with the use of programming languages (e.g., Python, R) in collaboration with machine learning algorithms, where we no longer need to deal with variables but with models. Thanks to special libraries established for specific purposes, this makes the process that much easier, but the question now is: what if AI is doing all of these data analysis steps for you?

Hence, conducting research about AI tool usage within educational settings is like attempting to solve equations with several unknown variables. Educators need to teach through and with AI, using suitable teaching tools and pedagogical support by shifting their focus away from technology-oriented designs to a more interdisciplinary approach [19]. In a study by Walter [38], it was argued that education needs to shift from traditional methods in order to fully leverage GenAI for personalised learning and support. The researchers emphasised AI literacy as central to modern-day education, including skills like prompt engineering, computational thinking, and critical thinking, to enhance learning and appropriately prepare students for the future environment in which they will undertake their respective careers. This represents a huge innovation that will transform and change society with all of its components, where we have to regularly and urgently deal with uncertainty and increased levels of complexity.

To summarise:

- Educational organisations should define standards for the ethical usage of AI tools and establish coherent policies.

- Related units should provide the necessary training on AI literacy to both educators and students.

- Educators and instructional designers should rethink AI-supported pedagogies and assignment reliability.

Despite the findings of the current research on the use of AI tools within the learning analytics context, there are three notable limitations of the current study that suggest the need for further empirical research. First, although the number of participants represented 36% of the target sample, this relatively small sample size may lead to under-representation of the discipline. In this respect, future research should broaden the study scope to include a much larger sample size in order to be able to generalise the findings. Second, the nature of the survey approach prevented the researcher from continuing with more in-depth interviews on the phenomenon. Hence, future research could seek to reach deeper insights with a longer data collection duration and the use of varied data collection approaches. Finally, only the context of the learning analytics curriculum was considered in the current study; hence, it is recommended that future research investigates the use of AI tools in a broader context in terms of educational levels and discipline areas.

Author details

Yasemin Gulbahar
Teachers College, Columbia University, Manhattan, United States.

*Address all correspondence to: gulbahar@tc.columbia.edu

References

[1] Chan CKY, Hu W. Students' voices on generative AI: Perceptions, benefits, and challenges in higher education. International Journal of Educational Technology in Higher Education. 2023;**20**:43. DOI: 10.1186/s41239-023-00411-8

[2] Dwivedi YK, Kshetri N, Hughes L, Slade EL, Jeyaraj A, Kar AK, Baabdullah AM, Koohang A, Raghavan V, Ahuja M, Albanna H, Albashrawi MA, Al-Busaidi AS, Balakrishnan J, Barlette Y, Basu S, Bose I, Brooks L, Buhalis D, Wright R. "So what if ChatGPT wrote it?" multidisciplinary perspectives on opportunities, challenges and implications of generative conversational AI for research, practice and policy. International Journal of Information Management. 2023; **71**:102642. DOI: 10.1016/j.ijinfomgt.2023.102642

[3] Ivanov S, Soliman M, Tuomi A, Alkathiri NA, Al-Alawi AN. Drivers of generative AI adoption in higher education through the lens of the theory of planned behaviour. Technology in Society. 2024; **77**:102521. DOI: 10.1016/j.techsoc.2024.102521

[4] King S, Prasetyo J. Assessing generative AI through the lens of the 2023 Gartner Hype Cycle for Emerging Technologies: A collaborative autoethnography. Frontiers in Education. 2023; **8**:1300391. DOI: 10.3389/feduc.2023.1300391

[5] Lee AVY, Tan SC, Teo CL. Designs and practices using generative AI for sustainable student discourse and knowledge creation. Smart Learning Environments. 2023;**10**:59. DOI: 10.1186/s40561-023-00279-1

[6] Li T, Ji Y, Zhan Z. Expert or machine? Comparing the effect of pairing student teacher with in-service teacher and ChatGPT on their critical thinking, learning performance, and cognitive load in an integrated-STEM course. Asia Pacific Journal of Education. 2024;**44**(1):45–60. DOI: 10.1080/02188791.2024.2305163

[7] Lu J, Zheng R, Gong Z, Xu H. Supporting teachers' professional development with generative AI: The effects on higher order thinking and self-efficacy. IEEE Transactions on Learning Technologies. 2024;**17**:1279–1289. DOI: 10.1109/TLT.2024.3369690

[8] Holstein K, McLaren BM, Aleven V. Co-designing a real-time classroom orchestration tool to support teacher–AI complementarity. Journal of Learning Analytics. 2019;**6**(2):27–52. DOI: 10.18608/jla.2019.62.3

[9] Wang Y, Liu C, Tu Y-F. Factors affecting the adoption of AI-Based Applications in higher education: An analysis of Teachers' perspectives using structural equation modeling. Educational Technology and Society. 2021;**24**(3):116–129. DOI: 10.30191/ETS.202107_24(3).0009

[10] Pham T, Nguyen TB, Ha S, Nguyen Ngoc NT. Digital transformation in engineering education: Exploring the potential of AI-assisted learning. Australasian Journal of Educational Technology. 2023;**39**(5):1–19. DOI: 10.14742/ajet.8825

[11] Delcker J, Heil J, Ifenthaler D, Seufert S, Spirgi L. First-year students AI-competence as a predictor for intended and de facto use of AI-tools for supporting learning processes in higher education. International Journal of Educational Technology in Higher Education. 2024;**21**:18. DOI: 10.1186/s41239-024-00452-7

[12] Molenaar I. Towards hybrid human-AI learning technologies. European Journal of Education Research, Development and Policy. 2022;**57**(4):632–645. DOI: 10.1111/ejed.12527

[13] Fui-Hoon Nah F, Zheng R, Cai J, Siau K, Chen L. Generative AI and ChatGPT: Applications, challenges, and AI-human collaboration. Journal of Information Technology Case and Application Research. 2023;**25**(3):277–304. DOI: 10.1080/15228053.2023.2233814

[14] Kangiwa BI, Abubakar NS.Awareness and utilization of ChatGPT among academic staff of Federal College of Education (Technical) Bichi. International Journal of Educational Research and Library Science. 2024;**4**(8):196

[15] Johri A, Katz AS, Qadir J, Hingle A. Generative artificial intelligence and engineering education. Journal of Engineering Education. 2023;**112**(3):572–577. DOI: 10.1002/jee.20537

[16] Ouyang F, Zheng L, Jiao P. Artificial intelligence in online higher education: A systematic review of empirical research from 2011 to 2020. Education and Information Technologies. 2022;**27**(6):7893–7925. DOI: 10.1007/s10639-022-10925-9

[17] Huang G, Liang X Generative AI Research of Education from 2013 to 2023. In: Proceedings of the 6th International Conference on Computer Science and Technologies in Education (CSTE); April 19-21, 2024; Xi'an, China. New York: IEEE; 2024. pp. 125–130. DOI: 10.1109/CSTE62025.2024.00030

[18] Chiu TK. A classification tool to foster self-regulated learning with generative artificial intelligence by applying self-determination theory: A case of ChatGPT. Educational Technology Research and Development. 2024;**72**(4):2401–2416. DOI: 10.1007/s11423-024-10366-w

[19] Ng Davy Tsz Kit, Leung JKL, Su J, Rcw N, Chu SKW. Teachers' AI digital competencies and twenty-first century skills in the post-pandemic world. Educational Technology Research and Development. 2023;**71**(1):137–161. DOI: 10.1007/s11423-023-10203-6

[20] European Commission. Report on the safety and liability implications of Artificial Intelligence, the Internet of Things and robotics. 2020. Available from: https://eur-lex./eu/ropa./eu/legal-content/EN/TXT/PDF/?uri=CELEX/:52020DC0064 [Accessed: 2025-November-4]

[21] DTK N, Lee M, Tan RJY, Hu X, Downie JS, Chu SKW. A review of AI teaching and learning from 2000 to 2020. Education and Information Technologies. 2023;**28**(7):8445–8501. DOI: 10.1007/s10639-022-11491-w

[22] Zastudil C, Rogalska M, Kapp C, Vaughn J, MacNeil S. Generative AI in computing education: Perspectives of students and instructors. ArXiv. 2023; DOI: 10.48550/arxiv.2308.04309

[23] Yang Y, Luo J, Yang M, Yang R, Chen J. From surface to deep learning

approaches with Generative AI in higher education: An analytical framework of student agency. Studies in Higher Education. 2024;**49**(5):817–830. DOI: 10.1080/03075079.2024.2327003

[24] Rasul T, Nair S, Kalendra D, Robin M, Santini FO, Ladeira WJ, Sun M, Day I, Rather RA, Heathcote L. The role of ChatGPT in higher education: Benefits, challenges, and future research directions. Journal of Applied Language Teaching. 2023;**6**(1):29. DOI: 10.37074/jalt.2023.6.1.29

[25] Darvish A, Khosravi H, Sadiq S, Gašević D, Siemens G. Impact of AI assistance on student agency. Computers and Education. 2024;**210**:104967. DOI: 10.1016/j.compedu.2023.104967

[26] Okaiyeto SA, Bai J, Xiao H. Generative AI in education: To embrace it or not? International Journal of Agricultural and Biological Engineering. 2023;**16**(3):285–286. DOI: 10.25165/j.ijabe.20231603.8486

[27] Sarčević A, Tomiči I, Merlin A, Horvat M Enhancing programming education with open-source generative AI chatbots. In: Babic S, et al., editors. Proceedings of the 2024 MIPRO Conference; 20-24 May 2024; Opatija, Croatia. New York: IEEE; 2024. pp. 2367–2372. DOI: 10.1109/MIPRO60963.2024.10569736

[28] Saúde S, Barros JP, Almeida I. Impacts of Generative Artificial Intelligence in Higher Education: Research Trends and Students. Perceptions. Social Sciences. 2024;**13**(8):410. DOI: 10.3390/socsci13080410

[29] Johnston H, Wells RF, Shanks EM, Boey T, Parsons BN. Student perspectives on the use of generative artificial intelligence technologies in higher education. International Journal for Educational Integrity. 2024;**20**(1):2. DOI: 10.1007/s40979-024-00149-4

[30] Rogers EM. Diffusion of Innovations. 5th ed. New York, London: Free Press; 2003

[31] Cohen L, Manion L, Morrison K. Research Methods in Education. 8th ed. London: Routledge; 2018

[32] Creswell JW, Creswell JD. Research Design: Qualitative, Quantitative, and Mixed Methods Approaches. 5th ed. Los Angeles: Sage; 2018

[33] Kurtz G, Amzalag M, Shaked N, Zaguri Y, Kohen-Vacs D, Gal E, Barak-Medina E. Strategies for integrating generative AI into higher education: Navigating challenges and leveraging opportunities. Education Sciences. 2024;**14**(5):503. DOI: 10.3390/educsci14050503

[34] Fawns T, Henderson M, Matthews K, Oberg G, Liang Y, Walton J, Corbin T, Bearman M, Shum SB, McCluskey T, McLean J, Shibani A, Bakharia A, Lim L-A, Pepperell N, Slade C, Chung J, Seligmann A. Gen AI and student perspectives of use and ambiguity: A multi-institutional study. Abstract from Annual Conference of the Australasian Society for Computers in Learning in Tertiary Education 2024. Melbourne, Victoria, Australia: 2024. pp. 132–134. DOI: 10.14742/apubs.2024.1218

[35] Kenedy RA.The challenges of critical thinking in the era of Artificial Intelligence. European Journal of Multidisciplinary Studies. 2024;**9**(2):19–36

[36] Silva ADO, Janes DDS. Artificial Intelligence in education: What are the opportunities and challenges? Review of Artificial Intelligence in Education. 2023;**5**:e018. DOI: 10.37497/rev.artif.intell.educ.v5i00.18

[37] Raman R, Kowalski R, Achuthan K, Iyer A, Nedungadi P. Navigating artificial general intelligence development: Societal, technological, ethical, and brain-inspired pathways. Scientific Reports. 2025;**15**(1):8443. DOI: 10.1038/s41598-025-92190-7

[38] Walter Y. Embracing the future of Artificial Intelligence in the classroom: The relevance of AI literacy, prompt engineering, and critical thinking in modern education. International Journal of Educational Technology in Higher Education. 2024;**21**(1):15–29. DOI: 10.18559/ebr.2023.2.743

Chapter 2

Artificial Intelligence, Ideology, and Literacy: A Multilectal Framework for Empowering Criticality in Adult Education

Hussein Chaitani

Abstract

Literacy has been associated with greater economic prosperity and is considered a key component of the corporate approach to human resource development. A more critical perspective is Paulo Freire's banking education concept that removes criticality from a learner's repertoire and facilitates alignment with the prevalent liberal education and its hegemonic objectives. Drawing on the concept of banking education, it is suggested that this approach trains marginalized learners to accept the dominant social structures imposed upon them. To develop as critical readers, writers, and most importantly, critical thinkers, learners must be able to recognize and navigate the ideological nature of literacy and understand how it contributes to the creation and exercise of power. With Big Tech, market-logic literacy has just become much more powerful. With the rise of Big Tech and cloud capital, precaritization of the masses and further serfitude is inevitable. The focus of this chapter is on multilectal or multilevel literary criticality across different cultures and ideologies. Multilectal criticality has become a necessity and needs to become a key component of Adult Education.

Keywords: AI in education, adult education, social system, lifeworld, communicative action, ideology, neoliberalism, cultural hegemony, democratic agency

1. Introduction

Literacy is a socially situated construct shaped by prevailing power structures and institutional interests, in which individuals actively engage in literacy as part of broader cultural and social processes. While globalization has structurally unified societies through economics and technology, it has not produced a unified global culture or civilization, as colonial legacies continue to impose binary and hierarchical discourses that disrupt indigenous lifeworlds and epistemologies [1, 2].

To better understand literacy as a socially situated construct, an examination of the social system is necessary. A social system can be understood as a network of interdependent actions that achieve functional integration through communicative processes ([3], p. 118). These systems encompass institutions such as markets, educational organizations, and bureaucracies, which are primarily coordinated through strategic action and instrumental planning. Unlike communicative action, which seeks mutual understanding, strategic coordination within the social system is often driven by systemic mechanisms such as money and power, reflecting a logic of efficiency and control rather than consensus. The lifeworld constitutes the implicit horizon of shared cultural knowledge, habitual practices, and normative attitudes through which individuals interpret and engage with their social reality.

Interdependent actions are linked through communicative actions that flow through the social system as discourse. To better examine the hierarchical discourses at all levels, a multilevel framework is necessary: the macro-, meso-, and micro-levels. At macro-, meso-, and micro- levels, literacy is shaped by complex social, cultural, and institutional forces. The macro-level reflects broader ideological and historical structures such as globalization and colonial legacies [1, 2], while the meso-level encompasses community institutions and policies that mediate literacy practices. At the micro-level, individuals engage in literacy as socially embedded, purposeful activities that reflect their lived experiences and cultural contexts [4].

Culture operates across macro-, meso-, and micro-levels, shaping individual lifeworlds through shared values, beliefs, and institutional practices. Hofstede's widely cited framework conceptualizes culture as the "collective programming of the mind" that differentiates groups, with national cultures rooted in enduring values and institutional cultures shaped by modifiable practices ([5], p. 1). At the macro-level, dominant ideologies, such as neoliberalism, encode cultural norms through communicative media, influencing institutional control at the meso-level and shaping individual behavior and meaning-making at the micro-level.

Scholars such as Althusser, Thompson, Eagleton, and Freeden have emphasized ideology's role in structuring belief systems and legitimizing power relations, while Hofstede's cultural framework illustrates how shared mental programs condition responses to social environments. Through communicative media – oral, print, digital, and multimodal – ideological discourse flows from dominant macro-level structures into meso-level institutions and micro-level practices, embedding power and control within everyday meaning-making and literacy [3, 6, 7].

Dialog and communicative action, central to adult education traditions such as study circles and tutorial classes, foster humanization through problem-posing education, continuous learning, and critical reflection [8, 9]. Technofeudalism describes the transformation of capitalism into a system where digital platforms and Big Tech corporations exert feudal-like control over data, labor, and markets through algorithmic governance and monopolistic infrastructure. This shift is marked by the commodification of personal data, behavioral manipulation via digital nudging, and the erosion of democratic agency, reinforcing structural inequalities across education, labor, and society at large. As AI becomes embedded in educational ecosystems, its integration can either extend human cognition and creativity or reinforce hegemonic paradigms that diminish intellectual diversity and agency [10]. These dynamics challenge adult educators to resist algorithmic control and neoliberal institutional processes by cultivating critical literacy and democratic pedagogy.

This chapter critically examines the role of technology in education, arguing that educational technologies must be evaluated not only for their instructional utility but also for their influence on ideological discourse, institutional governance, and learner agency across macro-, meso-, and micro-levels. Using Habermas's framework of the system and the lifeworld as an organizing lens, the chapter explores how literacy, culture, ideology, and adult education are shaped by and respond to technological integration within educational contexts.

2. Theoretical framework

2.1 Habermas's system and lifeworld

The Habermasian framework offers a comprehensive, multidimensional view of the interaction between societal structures and their institutions. "The lifeworld is the background environment of competences, practices, and attitudes representable in terms of one's cognitive horizon" ([3], p. 124). According to [11], "Habermas employs a conception of society as a lifeworld" (p. 62) "in which participants are immersed and which they reproduce in a characteristic way" (p. 61) with "communicative action as the type of interaction that is coordinated through speech acts and oriented to reaching understanding" ([3], p. 86). Through communicative action, participants reaffirm shared cultural values, social norms, and personal identities, maintaining coherence and continuity of the lifeworld and ensuring it remains a living context for meaning-making and social coordination. Cultural continuity, the sustenance of social relations, and socialization are key elements that keep the lifeworld coherent (Sitton).

Reproduction of the lifeworld "revolves around the three structural components of culture, society, and personality." "A social system is a complex of interrelated actions that are functionally integrated through the medium of communication" ([3], p. 118). The social system is composed of institutions, markets, schools, and bureaucracies that are coordinated through strategic action and planning, often influenced by money and power rather than mutual understanding. While the lifeworld is oriented toward meaning and consensus, the social system is focused on process, efficiency, and control. Both operate independently but are dynamically linked. The health of modern society depends on maintaining a balance where systemic efficiency does not undermine communicative rationality.

A hegemonic dynamic is established when systemic power infiltrates the lifeworld, subordinating individual agency and communicative rationality to institutional imperatives. This encroachment reflects Habermas's theory of colonization, where the logic of bureaucratic and economic systems overrides the normative structures of everyday life, thereby distorting democratic discourse and critical engagement [3, 12]. In healthcare, medical decisions are increasingly influenced by insurance companies and administrative protocols. In education, standardized testing and bureaucratic oversight dominate educational priorities. In the public sphere, commercial media prioritize advertising and ratings over public deliberation [13]. Lifeworld implications include less patient centric healthcare, teaching for performance rather than critical thinking in education, and public discourse shaped by advertising rather than democratic engagement. Commercial interests intrude into spaces where communicative action takes place, including family, social norms, and identity, colonizing the lifeworld and leading to the loss of meaning-making [3].

2.2 Literacy as social practice

Literacy is situated and always exists in a social context. Social practice does not transfer unproblematically across contexts but needs to draw from a variety of literacies. Barton and Hamilton [4] argued that reading and writing are embedded within social structures, with literacy practices "reflecting the general cultural ways of utilizing written language" (p. 7). However, values, attitudes, feelings, and social relationships are processes internal to the individual; at the same time, literacy practices are the social processes that connect people with one another, including shared cognitions represented in ideologies and social identities. Social rules shape practices and regulate the use of texts, bridging the gap between individual and social worlds. Literacy practices are more fully understood "as existing in the relations between people, within groups and communities, rather than as a set of properties residing in individuals" (p. 8) and cannot be wholly contained in observable activities and tasks.

Literacy is not the same in all contexts, and within a given culture, there are different literacies. Socially powerful institutions, such as education, tend to support dominant literacy practices visible in discourse formations and institutionalized configurations of power and knowledge [4]. The focus on standardized testing forces educators to reduce time spent on meaningful engagement with students' cultural and experiential knowledge, marginalizing diverse literacies and identities [14]. Neoliberal accountability policies focus educators on testable content to prioritize efficiency, measurement, and control, reducing the discursive space of dialogic, critical, and multimodal practices. This leads to curricular narrowing and the marginalization of diverse literacy forms [15]. Educators are not able to adapt literacy instruction to students' cultural contexts and lived experiences of diverse student populations in their classrooms. Bureaucratic control and neoliberal education reform, based on commercial interests, undermine culturally sustaining pedagogy [16].

As a social construct, literacy cannot be seen outside of the powerful interests and forces that seek to shape it in particular ways. It is no longer linear that people follow a hierarchical pathway but rather a web that cannot be taught without consideration of the social and ecological context [17]. People are active in what they do, and "literacy practices are purposeful and embedded in broader social goals and cultural practices" ([4], p. 11). Culturally constructed literacy practices have their roots in the past and, at the macro-level, are nuanced by ideology, culture, and traditions and are as fluid, dynamic, and changing as the lives of which they are a part.

Globalization, through economics, politics, communication, transportation, and technology, has become a unifying element among global societies. Such global unification is structural. The same cannot be said about culture or civilization [1]. The world system has been based on European dominance as a global unifying system, but cultures and civilizations have not become a holistic world civilization. Binary and hierarchical discourses constructed via colonial structures through capitalism, nation-states, the Enlightenment, science, patriarchy, evangelism, and White supremacy have destroyed beliefs, symbols, values, and epistemologies of the colonized [2]. The lifeworld of indigenous populations has been disrupted. On the macro-level, politics and power, as discoursed through media, propagate a particular worldview. Educational systems of the more powerful colonizer were added to and supplanted earlier systems of learning. The broader macro-level describes the ways in which whole communities use, interpret, and understand literacy. The detailed micro-level refers to several participants sharing, evaluating, meaning-making, and creating more than their individual practices.

3. Multilectics in education

Multilectics in educational contexts takes a multiperspectival or dialogic approach to knowledge, emphasizing the coexistence and interaction of multiple literacies, epistemologies, or discourses. A useful framework to describe different levels of analysis across education is to use the terms macro, meso, and micro. Each level offers a distinct lens for examining phenomena. At the macro-level, large-scale social structures, social systems, and ideologies are examined. Multilectics engages with how neoliberal education reforms, standardized testing, and global discourses shape literacy ideologies [15, 16]. At the meso-level, institutions, organizations, and communities are examined. The meso-level bridges the micro- and macro-levels. Multilectics at the meso-level examines how school systems, curriculum design, and teacher practices mediate macro-level policies and micro-level learner experiences [4, 14, 18]. At the micro-level, individual personal experiences, behaviors, small group interactions, and meaning-making processes are examined within specific contexts. Multilectics focuses on learner identities, classroom discourse, and community literacies. It values students' lived experiences and cultural knowledge as central to literacy learning [19–21].

Social life is complex. Understanding social life and learning to appreciate multiple contexts is even more so. Multilectics values the intertwined relationship between multiple perspectives, lenses of perception, modes, meanings, and voices. The objective is to discover the "truth" of ideas by discussion and logical argument in the context of a hermeneutic circle, with the learner engaging in a procedure of transforming one's understanding of the context, its component parts, and the whole through iterative recontextualization. Social life needs to be examined consciously in ways that cohere with our life experiences, that is, as a multilectic experience of macro-, meso-, and micro-fields [22]. A teacher's classroom practice (micro) is shaped by school curriculum mandates (meso), which are, in turn, influenced by national policy (macro). In turn, innovative classroom practices can inform institutional change or policy reform when documented, scaled, and not stymied by power imbalances. In other words, literacy needs to be understood at all levels: individual, group, community, and social levels.

4. Culture and ideology

4.1 Cultural dimensions

Cultural practices can be national or institutional, thus operating at the macro- and meso-levels and forming the context of individual lifeworlds at the micro-level. On a more macro-societal level, no agreement exists among social scientists on a universal definition of culture [23]. While the definitions of culture are diverse, most stress the values, beliefs, and attitudes that differentiate one group of people from another [5, 24, 25]. Hofstede [5] defined culture as the "collective programming of the mind which distinguishes the members of one group or category of people from another" (p. 1). A more refined definition states, "Culture consists of shared mental programs that condition individuals' responses to their environment" ([26], p. 6). A review of 180 empirical studies published between 1980 and 2002 that used Hofstede's cultural dimensions concluded that it remains one of the most influential and widely used models in culture research [27].

Hofstede's research focused mainly on organizational settings. Differentiating national and corporate culture, Hofstede [5] noted that while national culture related primarily to values, corporate culture related to practices. Values hardly changed, but practices, with the institutional management's attention, can change or be modified. Hofstede concluded that shared practices, not shared values, hold a multinational organization together. At the meso-level, organizations and institutions use management theories to organize tasks, activities, processes, and departments. Hofstede's research demonstrated that the socio-cultural characteristics of the cultural settings were reflected in management theories [28].

A larger meta-analytic study of 598 empirical articles, master 's and doctoral theses, conference presentations, and unpublished studies from the period between 1980 and 2009 confirmed the enduring relevance of Hofstede's definition of culture and its influence on individual and organizational outcomes [29]. Specifically, cultural values "can predict certain organizational and employee outcomes similar to, or even stronger than, other individual differences such as personality traits" (p. 410). Here, the micro-individual level constructs, such as personality traits, have been shown to be directly linked to the more macro-cultural value dimensions, conceptualized as shared mental programs, when it comes to certain organizational outcomes.

Institutions, at the meso-level, are devised by human beings to shape interaction within society and act as a constraint on behavior [30]. The more powerful "code" of the culture, as per Hofstede's definition, the "collective programming of the mind distinguishing one group of people from another," can take place. A neoliberal ideology at the macro-level provides the language for the coding that, through communications media, provides the shared mental programs the more powerful use to set institutional control at the meso-level, set direction, and maintain control of individuals at the micro-level. At the top, the macro-level, sits the dominating power, the coding language that programs the meso-level elements and shapes the lifeworld at the individual micro-level.

4.2 Ideological structures

The concept of ideology has been extensively theorized across disciplines, yet remains contested in meaning and scope. Althusser [31] conceptualized ideology as the imaginary relationship individuals have to their real conditions of existence, emphasizing its role in shaping subjectivity. Thompson [32] framed ideology as the mobilization of meaning to legitimize and reproduce asymmetrical power relations, thereby sustaining domination. Eagleton [33] argued that ideology is both complex and contested, encompassing structured belief systems and mechanisms of social legitimation. Freeden [34] defined ideology as a patterned set of ideas, beliefs, and values held by significant groups that compete to influence public policy, aiming to justify, contest, or transform the social and political arrangements of a political community. More broadly, Bloor and Bloor [35] defined ideology as "a set of beliefs or attitudes shared by members of a particular social group" (p. 11). Appleman [36] defined ideology as "a system of values and beliefs that help create expectations for individual behavior and for social norms," Furthermore, it is "a social and political construct, one that subtly shapes society and culture" (p. 179).

When an ideology becomes embedded in the shared consciousness of a group and gains social significance, it becomes increasingly resistant to critique. Ideologically constructed beliefs and attitudes may not be apparent to individuals and thus may be difficult to question, thereby becoming hegemonic. As Hofstede et al. [26] describe culture as "shared mental programs that condition individuals' responses to their environment" [p. 6], this conditioning reflects how individuals' lifeworlds at the micro-level are shaped by institutional structures at the meso-level, which are themselves guided by dominant ideologies at the macro-level. This recursive influence results in the programming of cultural norms and individual cognition, reinforcing ideological conformity and limiting critical reflection.

Flow from macro to meso to micro occurs through communicative media. Communicative media refer to the channels and technologies through which communication is transmitted, shaped, and interpreted. These media include oral language, print, digital platforms, visual media, and multimodal forms that integrate text, image, sound, and interactivity. Habermas [3] identifies communicative media as central to the coordination of social action, distinguishing between media that facilitate communicative action (oriented toward mutual understanding at the micro-level) and those that support strategic action (oriented toward control and efficiency at the meso- and macro-levels). Kress [6] argued that different media afford distinct possibilities for meaning-making, and that the transition from print to digital media transformed how literacy is practiced and understood.

Technology has transformed literacy as a social practice embedded in everyday life, shaped by the norms, values, and tools of digital culture. Digital media have redefined literacy as a participatory, multimodal, and socially embedded practice, emphasizing collaborative meaning-making and challenging traditional, hierarchical conceptions of literacy. Lankshear and Knobel [7] highlighted how digital media foster participatory, networked, and multimodal forms of communication, reshaping literacy into a socially situated and technologically mediated practice. Through networks, users are not just consumers but co-creators of meaning across global contexts, enabling collective knowledge production. Text, image, sound, and interactivity are integrated and multimodal, leading to an expansion in the ways meaning is constructed and communicated [7].

Regardless of the medium used or the definition adopted, discourse is ideologically based and can be so deeply ingrained in thought patterns and language that it is taken for granted and unrecognized. From a cultural studies perspective, Marxist variants of ideology concepts as exploitative and misleading dominate [37], with the exploitative system of social relations leading to a "false consciousness" (p. 97) and worldview. Gramsci's writings further supported the Marxist account of ideology as being exploitative and misleading by noting that ideology "is grasped as ideas, meanings, and practices which, while they purport to be universal truths, are maps of meaning that support the power of particular social classes" ([37], p. 97). Thus, capitalist belief systems can be taken for granted, naturalized, with work in the interest of one group at the expense of another, normally a marginalized group, taking place.

Flores [38] conceptualizes banking education as a global mechanism that sustains hegemonic power structures, where ideological rigidity can blind policy-making and provoke resistance that may escalate into violent extremism. In this framework, banking education functions to indoctrinate the oppressed into preserving the dominant social order, reinforcing the values and interests of the oppressor rather than fostering critical consciousness and transformative agency [38]. Banking education ensures that discussions on an issue are bounded within "proper limits," and debate can be tolerated ([39], p. 147). Without close contact with other cultures, individuals tend to adopt the established values or ideology of their own social groups without questioning such values [35].

Such assumptions may be challenged when individuals interact with different cultures. Discourse will then be challenged because the underlying assumptions of the ideology are different. Understanding and analysis of the discourse will require investigation "with a fresh and open mind" ([35], p. 19). Kawalilak and Groen (2021) [40] argued on the importance of contextualization and relationality (relational learning), given that adults are embedded in many complex systems in a world that is multifaceted, interconnected, nonlinear, and often experienced fortuitously. Roland [30] indicated the close evolutionary relationship between culture, technology, and scientific knowledge. Both culture and technology evolve slowly and continuously at varying paces [30]. Over the last two decades, the owners of Big Tech, the new social elite, have dramatically increased the pace of technological evolution and, with it, power and control over society.

5. Technofeudalism and AI

5.1 Technofeudalism defined

The power of technology could deepen hegemonic control of society. Yanis Varoufakis defines technofeudalism as a new form of economic and social organization where digital platforms and Big Tech are able to exercise control over markets, data, and labor in ways that resemble feudal power structures. Instead of owning land, as in traditional feudalism, technofeudal lords control digital infrastructure and user data, leveraging algorithmic control and monopolistic practices to extract value [41]. Gramsci [42] explained that the method by which a capitalist state maintains control and power over its citizens occurs through the dominance of cultural aspects, processes, and norms. The ideology of the elite becomes subtly and overtly accepted by ordinary citizens, who normalize the ideology through their daily engagement and practice. Historically, feudalism morphed into capitalism, which is morphing into technofeudalism. The current elite are the owners of Big Tech.

5.2 AI as an ideological instrument

Artificial intelligence (AI) is not an apolitical or universally objective computational tool. It is deeply embedded within social, political, cultural, and economic structures, shaped by the values, priorities, and institutional contexts of its developers and deployers [43, 44]. At the macro-level, technology can function as a hegemonic force when its design, deployment, and governance reflect and reinforce dominant ideologies, institutional interests, and power structures, thereby shaping social relations and limiting democratic agency [43–45]. At the meso-level, AI systems are designed through processes that reflect and reinforce existing hierarchies, often encoding discriminatory classifications that mirror societal biases [46]. At the micro-level, and when implemented in domains such as law enforcement, healthcare, education, and the judiciary, these systems can perpetuate and intensify structural inequalities rather than mitigate them [47, 48]. By design, AI technologies are frequently developed to serve the interests of powerful institutions, states, corporations, and bureaucracies at the meso-level. Institutional goals include profit maximization, surveillance, and control [43, 44]. In this sense, AI functions as an instrument of power, reflecting broader economic and political imperatives and respective ideologies at the macro-level.

5.3 Data colonialism and surveillance capitalism

With Big Tech, society is more challenged than ever. According to economist Yanis [41], since the Industrial Revolution, capitalism has evolved from putting a price on things that were self-produced and had no price (land, labor, bread, wine, clothes), to efficiently manufacturing things that people craved (post-Industrial Revolution), to the skillful manufacture of desire (since the 60s and 70s), to something he calls cloud capital. Krasulja et al. [49] argue that many of the risks of the liberal market have been shifted from digital platforms to workers, with workers having little influence on the "new economy" and work precariousness increasing. "Governance incursions and social harms such as control over AI or rampant disinformation are too frequently seen as distinct crises and siloed, each with its own specialists and prescriptions, rather than understood as organic effects of causal economic operations" ([50], p. 1).

Big data practices have become a new form of colonialism, shifting land and labor extraction, characteristic of classical colonialism, to data colonialism, with data as the raw material to be extracted from human life [51]. At the macro-level, domination, exploitation, and asymmetrical power embedded in the design and operation of data systems continue the evolution and transformation of colonialism. Digital platforms serve as digital infrastructures that mediate between users, services, and data. These platforms extract value by controlling access and aggregating user activity, positioning themselves as indispensable intermediaries in various sectors. In business, the platforms extract and monetize user data, relying on network effects to increase usage and value, ultimately creating monopolistic conditions [52]. In education, platform-based learning systems or learning management systems may replicate similar dynamics, centralizing control, commodifying learner data, and influencing pedagogical practices.

Fuchs [45] noted that digital media are not apolitical but ideological, shaping consciousness and social relations. Aligned with capitalism, digital platforms at the micro-level promote individualism, competition, and consumerism, undermining collective agency. At the macro-level, data colonialism reinforces structural inequalities, policies, and procedures by concentrating power in the hands of a few tech corporations. Users produce content and data that are commodified by platform owners, reinforcing capitalist exploitation in the digital sphere [45]. In educational settings, educational technologies increasingly function as surveillance systems, collecting extensive data on student behavior and performance, which can undermine learner autonomy and reinforce standardized norms [53]. Users often have limited understanding or control over how their data is used, undermining informed consent and democratic agency. At the micro-level, social relations are transformed, with human experiences turned into quantifiable inputs for algorithmic processing, affecting how people relate to institutions, each other, and themselves. Algorithmic decision-making in these platforms may embed biases that marginalize diverse learning styles and perpetuate educational inequalities [54].

Digital platforms serve as tools for surveillance capitalism, commodifying personal data as a raw material for profit. Unlike traditional capitalism, which commodifies labor, surveillance capitalism extracts behavioral surplus from digital interactions to predict and influence future behavior. Big Tech platforms use predictive algorithms to respond to user preferences, providing interface usability and accessibility and, in the process, actively shaping user preferences. By curating content, advertisements, and social interactions, these platforms create feedback loops that condition users to desire what is most profitable for the platform, thus manufacturing desire [44, 45].

5.4 Algorithmic control, behavioral nudging, and ethical use

Subtle design features on digital platforms, such as layout, wording, default settings, and visual cues, can influence decision-making without restricting choice. Digital nudging is defined as "the use of user-interface design elements to guide people's behavior in digital choice environments" ([55], p. 433). Varoufakis argues that platforms engage in digital nudging, using data-driven insights to subtly steer user behavior toward predefined outcomes. This is achieved through interface design, recommendation systems, and real-time personalization, which function as tools of behavioral control [56, 57]. Examples include default settings (nudges toward a choice), using progress indicators (encourages task completion), social proof, "most popular choice" (leverages social norms to guide behavior), and visual emphasis (using color or size to steer users toward preferred options).

The logic of behavioral prediction and modification shifts the locus of control from individuals to algorithmic systems governed by corporate interests. Power is exercised through algorithmic control. "Concentration of economic power produces collateral concentrations of governance and social powers" (p. 1). Crucially, unlike traditional markets, power is not accountable to democratic institutions, creating asymmetries in knowledge and control between corporations and individuals. In education, the platforms collect data, predict learning behavior, and shape educational experiences that may not align with pedagogical or democratic values [58].

In the workplace, digital platforms have transformed traditional employment by enabling freelance work and facilitating the transition to flexible, short-term work arrangements. This remote work arrangement presents substantial challenges, including insecurity, algorithmic control, and inadequate worker protections. Digital platforms frequently control access to work, dictate wage structures, and retain ownership of employees' data [49]. Through machine learning, neural networks, and algorithms capable of reinforcement learning, we are enjoying the services of algorithms, with no option but to cut a Faustian deal with the owners of Big Tech [41].

For personalized services, anything from driving an electric Tesla car to listening to music or commanding Alexa, cloud-based command capital is turning users into serfs, aided by users and user's unpaid labor to enrich the owners of Big Tech.

While critics argue that the concept of technofeudalism may oversimplify the systemic complexity of contemporary digital capitals [49], there is no denying that Big Tech owners wield immense power. The business model is based on the harvesting of our data, tracking our activity, and the invisible curating of our data, giving the Big Tech owners immense power – the power to predict our behavior, guide our preferences, influence our decisions, change our minds, and keep mining our information, shaping our identities and patterns of behavior that sustain and increase cloud capital's power by training Big Tech's algorithms. The new digitized economy is underpinned by the financialization of economies, algorithmic control, and political complicity. With limited worker influence, technofeudalism represents a modern form of domination through control of digital spaces while maintaining inequality through privileges such as tax breaks and monopolies over data and technologies such as artificial intelligence [41].

There is a need to find the right balance between the positive and negative aspects of technology and its impact on humanness. Resisting exploitative data practices and supporting equitable learning environments requires fostering critical data literacy and promoting participatory, transparent data governance in education, which are essential [59]. Part of humanness is having values, from physiological to self-actualization needs and desires, and criticality with liberation through cognitive acts. Championing material needs and using media to influence and commercialize the masses enable the ruling elite to control the masses using the collective monetary power of the system [60]. Clark [10] suggested the need for careful integration of AI into human cognitive ecosystems, supported by education, infrastructure, and ethical oversight.

Technology can potentially enhance human cognition and creativity if used ethically and responsibly. AI tools could extend human cognition by integrating with biological and environmental systems, forming what Clark calls hybrid thinking structures. AI could enhance creativity through the exploration of unthought-of possibilities. AI tools, in specific contexts, could provide efficient cognitive assistance and decision-making. By using AI to perform lower-order thinking tasks, users can focus on higher-order thinking. Finally, reasoning and problem-solving can be enhanced when human–machine ecosystems engage in tackling complex challenges [10]. Key threats of AI include the reinforcement of dominant paradigms (entrenching existing norms, processes, and methodologies), the reduction of cultural and intellectual diversity (the influence of AI on cultural transmission may lead to the homogenization of ideas), the erosion of human creativity (creativity becomes obsolete when users rely uncritically on AI-generated content), cognitive offloading and dependence (overreliance on AI may diminish internal cognitive capabilities), and epistemic vulnerability (not recognizing that AI outputs can be misleading or inaccurate). To support the conceptual clarity of the chapter, **Figure 1** illustrates the multilevel framework through which ideology, technology, and literacy interact within adult education. It is structured across macro-, meso-, and micro-levels, showing how dominant ideologies and technological infrastructures influence institutional practices and individual learner experiences. The figure also reflects the recursive nature of educational multilectics, where bottom-up resistance can reshape institutional norms and challenge hegemonic paradigms [3, 4, 22].

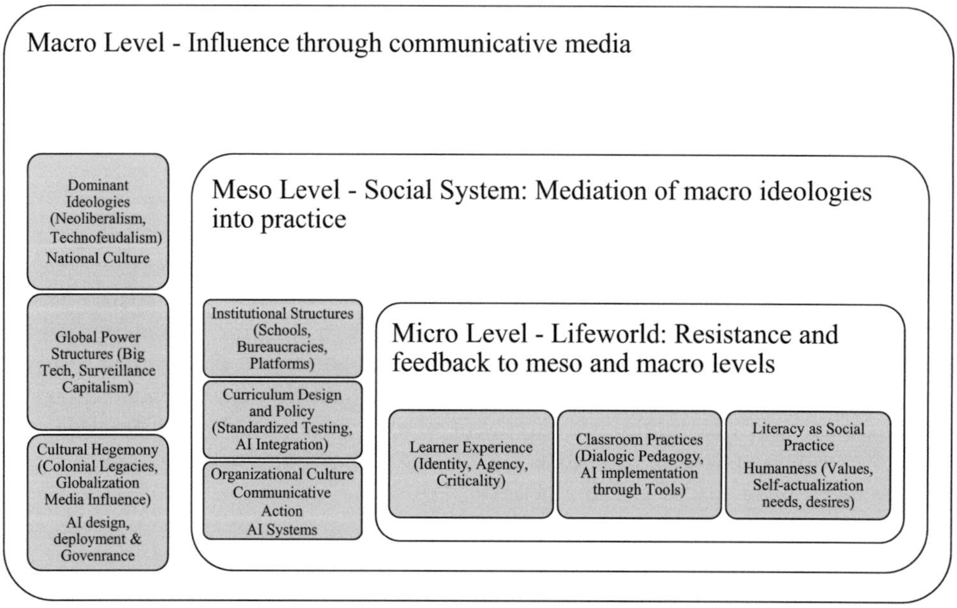

Figure 1.
Multilevel framework on the structural dynamics of AI, literacy, and ideology in adult education.

6. Implications for adult education

6.1 Freirean pedagogy and criticality

Dialog and communicative action oriented toward reaching a consensus in an uncoerced and free exchange (study circles, tutorial classes) have historically been pivotal to the adult education movement. Humanization, according to Paulo Freire, requires: 1) a problem-posing education, 2) continuous learning, and 3) a continuous criticality, with liberation occurring through cognitive acts [8]. Such a problem-posing approach, in which students are challenged about their relationship with the world, requires a dialogical setting and an interrogation of complex problems that intersect in several specializations: psychological, political, theological, and social [9], in other words, complex problems within the Habermasian social system and the individual lifeworld at all levels – the macro, meso, and micro – in a hermeneutic context.

6.2 Risks and opportunities of AI

With AI, depending on its integration into human–machine ecosystems, technology can be used actively as a mind-extending resource to enhance creativity, reasoning, and decision-making. Conversely, if used passively, a reduction in thought, critical thinking, and reinforcement of hegemonic paradigms ensues. In the classroom, hegemonic paradigms could be reinforced by using AI-enhanced learning platforms, reducing intellectual diversity. Conversely, personalized tutoring systems can have the opposite effect. Students using generative AI to brainstorm ideas or visualize concepts may expand creative thinking but risk becoming passive curators and losing original thought. AI-generated feedback on student assignments can guide improvement but may also be accepted without critical evaluation and understanding. Too much reliance on AI may weaken comprehension and retention. Teacher guidance to ensure balanced use in the classroom context may result in AI supporting inquiry-based learning, but curricula need to be adapted [10].

Advancing the interest of reason may be limiting if reason is captured in static institutional processes, so that processes must be followed and stakeholders of those processes are left without individual agency to contribute. Individual agency is further compromised when the stakeholder is an algorithm that can learn to predict our behavior, guide our preferences, influence our decisions, change our minds, and keep mining our information, shaping our identities and patterns of behavior. This new hegemony is tied to the established institutional processes. With the new digitized economy, the financialization of economies, algorithmic control, and political complicity, adult education is challenged further.

6.3 Counterhegemonic pedagogy

Championing material needs and using media and increasingly advanced technology to influence and commercialize the masses enables the ruling elite to control the population through the collective monetary power of the system. The key to successful counterhegemonic cultural research involves: 1) the ability to link the production of representations, images, and signs of hyperreality to power in the political economy; and 2) the capacity, once this linkage is exposed and described, to delineate the highly complex effects of the reception of these images and signs on individuals located at various race, class, gender, and sexual coordinates within the web of reality [61]. Built-in neutrality is part of the institutional processes at universities, described as "an ideological phantom, meant to create complacency" [62, p. 247]. Universities and learning institutions could be seen as part of Habermas's system – an institution that generates graduates who meet employers' needs and are programmed to contribute commercially. Formal and nonformal learning are both intentional and based on organized educational activities, with formal learning leading to a credential and nonformal learning sponsored by organizations, agencies, and institutions [40]. Algorithmic control enhances complacency and stymies criticality to ever-increasing levels. Powerful literacies must be oppositional to expose and counteract institutional processes [17].

Adult educators have to reconstruct the learning and teaching process and base their pedagogy on issues of social justice, equality, and democracy rather than use "banking education," which primarily addresses the needs of the economy. The dominant "market-logic literacy" (p. 7), driven by the neoliberal ideology, is structurally powerful and ubiquitous. Literacy education should enable people to interrogate claims made on their behalf and unshackle individuals, groups, and communities. The role of adult educators is to point out all aspects of the literacies – a discursive moment's six elements [63] – in an issue at hand: (a) discourse/language, (b) power, (c) social relations, (d) material practices, (e) institutions/rituals, and (f) beliefs/values/desires. The commodification of that moment results in information fitting into a discursive space that is critically dialogued between learners.

Becoming critical learners may enable readers and writers to detect and handle the inherently ideological dimensions of literacy. Giroux [64] believed that educators must be free to explore the hidden curriculum, uncover assumptions, and interrogate culture because education is both embedded in society and influences social practices and mores. Critical pedagogy is vital to maintaining democracy by developing students into engaged citizens who question practices, people, and policies, and affirm the value of diverse knowledge and opinions.

Literacy has been linked to economic prosperity as part of the corporate model of human resource development, and its distribution by and to different social groups is not something that happens neutrally [17]. Literacy is embedded in an infrastructure of power relationships and is "deeply and inescapably bound up with producing, reproducing, and maintaining unequal arrangements of power" (p. 2). Universalisms used in educational institutions need to be disentangled to include how knowledge about the less powerful "other" is expressed, understood, and valued [2].

Apple and Beane [65] challenged educators worldwide to implement transformative education to nurture epistemological spaces essential to freedom, democracy, and social justice. They reminded educators to maintain their movement toward critical consciousness while confronting issues of power, including algorithmic power and privilege. These issues need to be repositioned in an evolving criticality; the capitalist and increasingly techno-feudal "yoke" must come off. Reductionist objects created by the media and algorithms are taken at face value; superficial understanding does not promote the learning of complexity, so that focus on following systems, set processes, and objectivity leads to a failure in in-depth understanding.

Criticality and the insights generated therefrom would return agency to the lifeworld. Some members of the social system do not agree with society and the power of the state–corporate complex. The discursive space does not permit criticality. Agency is taken from some citizens and controlled by institutional processes, such as legalese influenced by power; in a sense, they feel shut out of an unjust, hegemonic society. Humanity needs to be cultivated more effectively and must go beyond a neoliberal binary of "us versus them" or the objectivity of "right and wrong." Literacy, as a communicative resource for members of a community, is influenced depending on its location in relation to mass media and new technology. Lack of criticality among citizens may result in hegemony taking hold of them through the discursive sphere being controlled by the media, Big Tech, corporate money, and the power of the state-corporate complex. Large areas of the lifeworld, such as the public sphere, education, and citizenship, have been "mediatized" and are increasingly being "technotized."

7. Conclusion

In conclusion, this chapter has examined how literacy, ideology, and technology intersect within the structures of the social system and lifeworld. Drawing on [3], the theory of communicative action, it is evident that systemic mechanisms – such as markets, bureaucracies, and educational institutions – operate through strategic coordination driven by money and power, often at the expense of mutual understanding and democratic agency. Literacy, as a socially situated practice, is shaped by macro-level ideologies, meso-level institutional policies, and micro-level lived experiences, all of which are influenced by cultural norms and communicative media [4–7].

DOI: http://dx.doi.org/10.5772/intechopen.1013545

The rise of technofeudalism and algorithmic governance has intensified these dynamics, transforming education and labor through data commodification, behavioral manipulation, and surveillance infrastructures. These developments challenge the foundational principles of adult education, which historically emphasized dialog, criticality, and humanization [8, 9]. As AI becomes increasingly embedded in educational ecosystems, adult educators must resist hegemonic paradigms and neoliberal institutional processes by fostering critical literacy, promoting democratic pedagogy, and reclaiming the lifeworld as a space for emancipatory learning and collective agency.

Author details

Hussein Chaitani
University Canada West, Vancouver, Canada

*Address all correspondence to: hussein.chaitani@ucanwest.ca

References

[1] Tibi B. The Challenge of Fundamentalism: Political Islam and the New World disorder. Berkeley, CA, USA: University of California Press; 1998

[2] Hanson C, Jaffe J, Rocco TS. Decolonizing Adult Education. The Handbook of Adult and Continuing Education. 1st. New York, NY, USA; London, UK: Routledge; 2021. 341–349. DOI: 10.4324/9781003447849-42

[3] Habermas J. The Theory of Communicative Action: Lifeworld and System, a Critique of Functionalist Reason. Boston, MA, USA: Beacon Press; 1987

[4] Barton D, Hamilton M. Literacy practices. In: Barton D, Hamilton M, Ivanic R, editors. Situated Literacies: Reading and Writing in Context. 1st ed. London, UK: Routledge; 2000. p. 7–15

[5] Hofstede G. Culture's Consequence: Comparing Values, Behaviors, Institutions, and Organizations across Nations. 2nd ed. Beverly Hills, CA: SAGE; 2001

[6] Kress G. Literacy in the New Media Age. London, UK: Routledge; 2003

[7] Lankshear C, Knobel M. Part 2 - New Literacies: Some Everyday Practices. In New Literacies: Everyday Practices and Social Learning. Maidenhead, UK: McGraw-Hill Education; 2011

[8] Freire P. Pedagogy of the Oppressed, 30th ed., Bergman Ramos M, Trans. London, UK; New York, NY, USA: Continuum; 2005. Original work published in 1970

[9] Chaitani H. Towards a more critical cognizant learning model. International Journal of Adult Education and Technology. 2024;**15**(1):1–19

[10] Clark A. Extending minds with generative AI. Nature Communications. 2025;**16**(1):4627

[11] Sitton J. Habermas and Contemporary Society. New York, NY, USA: Palgrave Macmillan US; 2003

[12] Fraser N. 1990. Rethinking the public sphere: A contribution to the critique of actually existing democracy. Social Text. **25**(26):56–80. DOI: 10.2307/466240

[13] McCarthy T. Lifeworld and system in Habermas's theory of modernity. Philosophy & Social Criticism. 1990;**16**(3):1–19

[14] Compton-Lilly C. Confronting Racism, Poverty, and Power: Classroom Strategies to Change the World. Portsmouth, NH: Heinemann; 2004

[15] Au W. 2007. High-stakes testing and curricular control: A qualitative metasynthesis. Educational Researcher. **36**(5):258–267. DOI: 10.3102/0013189X07306523

[16] Lipman P. High Stakes Education: Inequality, Globalization, and Urban School Reform. New York, NY: Routledge; 2004

[17] Hamilton M, Tett L. More powerful literacies: An introduction. In: Tett L, Hamilton M, Crowther J, editors. More

Powerful Literacies. 1st ed. Leicester: National Institute of Adult Continuing Education; 2012. p. 1–12

[18] Cope B, Kalantzis M, editors. Multiliteracies: Lit learning. Routledge. 2000. DOI: 10.4324/9780203979402

[19] Heath S. Ways with words: Language, life, and work in communities and classrooms. Cambridge University Press; 1983

[20] Dyson AH. Writing superheroes: Contemporary childhood, popular culture, and classroom literacy. Teachers College Press; 1997

[21] Gutiérrez KD, Rogoff B. Cultural ways of learning: Individual traits or repertoires of practice. Educational Researcher. 2003;**32**(5):19–25

[22] Tobin K, Ritchie SM (2012). Multi-method, Multi-theoretical, Multi-level research in the learning sciences

[23] Chokar J, Brodbeck F, House R. Culture and Leadership across the World: The GLOBE Book of In-depth Studies of 25 Societies. New York, NY: Lea's; 2008

[24] Kuran T, Sandholm W. Cultural integration and its discontents. Review of Economic Studies. 2008;**75**(1): 201–228

[25] Pryor F. Culture and economic systems. The American Journal of Economics and Sociology. 2007;**66**(4):817–855

[26] Hofstede G, Hofstede GJ, Minkov M. Cultures and Organizations: Software of the Mind. 3rd ed. New York, NY, USA: McGraw-Hill; 2010

[27] Kirkman BL, Lowe KB, Gibson CB. 2006. A quarter-century of culture's consequences: A review of empirical research incorporating Hofstede's cultural values framework. Journal of International Business Studies. **37**(3):285–320. DOI: 10.1057/palgrave.jibs.8400202

[28] Rees C, Althakhri R. Organizational change strategies in the Arab region: A review of critical factors. Journal of Business Economics and Management. 2008;**9**(2): 123–132

[29] Taras V, Kirkman BL, Steel P. 2010. Examining the impact of culture's consequences: A three-decade, multilevel, meta-analytic review of Hofstede's cultural value dimensions. Journal of Applied Psychology. **95**(3):405–439. DOI: 10.1037/a0018938

[30] Roland G. Understanding institutional change: Fast-moving and slow-moving institutions. Studies in Comparative International Development. 2004;**38**(4):109–131

[31] Althusser L. Ideology and ideological state apparatuses (notes towards an investigation). The Anthropology of the State: a Reader. 2006

[32] Thompson JB. Ideology and Modern Culture: Critical Social Theory in the Era of Mass Communication. Stanford, CA, USA: Stanford University Press; 1990

[33] Eagleton T. Ideology : An Introduction. London, UK; New York, NY, USA: Verso; 2007

[34] Freeden M. 1998. Is ideology still relevant? Political Studies. **46**(5): 748–765. DOI: 10.1111/1467-9248.00165

[35] Bloor M, Bloor T. The Practice of Critical Discourse Analysis: An Introduction. London: Hodder Arnold; 2007

[36] Appleman D. Critical literary theory in a literature methods class. In Reclaiming English Language Arts Methods Courses, New York, NY, USA; London, UK: Routledge; 2015. 34–51

[37] Barker C. The SAGE Dictionary of Cultural Studies. London, UK; Thousand Oaks, CA, USA; New Delhi, India: SAGE; 2004

[38] Flores Y. The Pedagogy of Violent Extremism. New York, NY, USA: Peter Lang, International Academic; 2017

[39] Chomsky N. Necessary illusions: Through control in democratic societies. In Chomsky N 1999, Essential Classics in Politics Noam Chomsky. London, UK: Pluto Press Electric Book; 1989a

[40] Kawalilak C, Groen J, Rocco TS. Adult Learning. The Handbook of Adult and Continuing Education. 1st. New York, NY, USA; London, UK: Routledge; 2021. p. 73–80. DOI: 10.4324/9781003447849-10

[41] Varoufakis Y. Technofeudalism: What Killed Capitalism. Brooklyn, NY, USA; London, UK: Melville House; 2023

[42] Gramsci A. Selections from the Prison Notebooks. In: Hoare Q, Smith GN, editors. London, UK; New York, NY, USA: Continuum International Publishers; 1971

[43] Crawford K. Atlas of AI: Power, Politics, and the Planetary Costs of Artificial Intelligence. New Haven, CT, USA: Yale University Press; 2021

[44] Zuboff S. The Age of Surveillance Capitalism: The Fight for a Human Future at the New Frontier of Power. New York, NY, USA: PublicAffairs; 2019

[45] Fuchs C. Towards a critical theory of communication as renewal and update of Marxist humanism in the age of digital capitalism. Journal for the Theory of Social Behaviour. 2020;**50** (3):335–356

[46] Benjamin R. Race after Technology : Abolitionist Tools for the New Jim Code. 1st ed. Cambridge, UK; Medford, MA, USA: Polity; 2019

[47] Eubanks V. Automating Inequality: How High-tech Tools Profile, Police, and Punish the Poor. New York, NY, USA: St. Martin's Press; 2018

[48] Noble SU. Algorithms of Oppression: How Search Engines Reinforce Racism. 1st. ed. New York, NY, USA: NYU Press; 2018. DOI: 10.18574/9781479833641

[49] Krasulja N, Ilic D, Radosavljevic D, Mihajlovic A. 2024. Interdependence of digital platforms, development of technofeudalism and work precariousness in the Gig economy. Journal of Economic Development, Environment and People. **13**(4):1–11. DOI: 10.26458/jedep.v13i4.867

[50] Zuboff S. Surveillance capitalism or democracy? The death match of institutional orders and the politics of knowledge in our information civilization. Organization Theory. 2022;**3**(3). DOI: 10.1177/26317877221129290

[51] Couldry N, Mejias UA. 2019. Data colonialism: Rethinking big data's relation to contemporary capitalism.

Television and New Media. **20**(4): 336–349. DOI: 10.1177/15274764187 96632

[52] Srnicek N. The challenges of platform capitalism: Understanding the logic of a new business model. Juncture. 2017;**23**(4):254–257

[53] Williamson B. Learning in the 'platform society': Disassembling an educational data assemblage. Research in Education. 2017;**98**(1):59–82

[54] Prinsloo P, Slade S (2017, March). An elephant in the learning analytics room: The obligation to act. In Proceedings of the seventh international learning analytics & knowledge conference (p. 46–55)

[55] Weinmann M, Schneider C, Brocke JV. Digital nudging. Business and Information Systems Engineering. 2016;**58**(6):433–436

[56] Pasquale F. The Black Box Society: The Secret Algorithms that Control Money and Information. Cambridge, MA, USA: Harvard University Press; 2015

[57] Zawacki-Richter O, Marín VI, Bond M, Gouverneur F. Systematic review of research on artificial intelligence applications in higher education–where are the educators? International Journal of Educational Technology in Higher Education. 2019;**16**(1):1–27

[58] Zuboff S. Big other: Surveillance capitalism and the prospects of an information civilization. Journal of Information Technology. 2015;**30** (1):75–89

[59] Andrejevic M. Automated surveillance. In Routledge Handbook of Digital Media and Communication, London, UK; New York, NY, USA: Routledge; 2020. p. 242–253

[60] Chaitani, H. Neoliberalism and Adult Education: Taylor, Habermas, Freire, and the Precaritization of the Masses. In Facing Precarity in Adult, Community, and Vocational Education: Role of Meaningful Work. IGI Global Scientific Publishing; 2026. p. 85–112

[61] Kincheloe J, McLaren P. Rethinking critical theory and qualitative research. In: Denzin N, Lincoln Y, editors. The Sage Handbook of Qualitative Research, 6th ed.). Thousand Oaks, CA, USA: SAGE Publications Inc.; 2023

[62] Kincheloe J, McLaren P, Steinberg S, Monzo L. Critical pedagogy and qualitative research. In: Denzin N, Lincoln Y, editors. The Sage Handbook of Qualitative Research. Thousand Oaks, CA, USA: SAGE Publications Inc.; 2018

[63] Chouliaraki L, Fairclough N. Discourse in Late Modernity: Rethinking Critical Discourse Analysis (Critical Discourse Analysis Series). Edinburgh, UK: Edinburgh University Press; 1999

[64] Giroux HA. Theory and Resistance in Education: Towards a Pedagogy for the Opposition. Westport, CT, USA: Bergin & Garvey Publishers Inc.; 2001

[65] Apple MW, Beane JA. Democratic Schools. Portsmouth, NH, USA: Heinemann; 2007

Chapter 3

Beyond Personalization: Cultivating AI-Augmented Human Flourishing in Education

Joseph O. Ukoba, Okengwu A. Ugochi, Eginiwin E. Joseph and Laud C. Ochei

Abstract

This chapter argues for an expansive vision of artificial intelligence (AI) in education, moving beyond the current focus on personalization to a model of AI-augmented human flourishing. While personalization offers benefits, it often overlooks AI's potential to foster holistic student development, which includes physical, psychological, social, and spiritual well-being. Using a conceptual analysis methodology, we deconstruct flourishing and analyze how AI can strategically support its various dimensions, such as emotional intelligence, creativity, and critical thinking. The chapter discusses ethical considerations, like data privacy and algorithmic bias, advocating for a human-centered AI design that prioritizes fairness and a values-driven integration. We conclude by proposing a comprehensive framework with practical recommendations for educators, policymakers, and developers to harness AI's full potential for a more equitable and enriching educational future.

Keywords: AI in education, human flourishing, personalized learning, ethical AI, equitable learning

1. Introduction

The rise of artificial intelligence (AI) in education largely focuses on personalization, adapting content and pace to individual student needs, or streamlining administrative tasks [1, 2]. While beneficial, this approach often overlooks AI's potential to foster comprehensive human flourishing – a state where individuals balance inner needs and external demands, optimizing physical, psychological, social, and spiritual well-being [3–6]. Specifically, current personalization-centric AI literature suffers from a notable gap in empirical evidence demonstrating its ability to cultivate social and emotional competencies [7]. As Zawacki-Richter and Latchem note, many claims about AI's benefits are theoretical and not yet backed by robust, large-scale studies [8]. Furthermore, existing frameworks often fail to integrate AI tools in a manner that supports students' holistic well-being beyond academic metrics, a point underscored by

Popenici and Kerr, who argue that personalization often overlooks crucial social, emotional, and cultural factors [9]. Flourishing encompasses purpose, positive relationships, emotional mastery, and continuous growth.

This chapter champions an expansive vision: AI as a catalyst for comprehensive flourishing, nurturing not only just cognitive skills but also emotional intelligence, creativity, and critical thinking, fostering equitable learning [10, 11]. Using a conceptual analysis methodology, we first pinpoint the limitations of current personalization-centric AI. Subsequent sections explore flourishing's dimensions – physical, mental, emotional, and social – and how AI can strategically support them, empowering both students and teachers. The discussion then shifts to ethical considerations: promoting fairness, avoiding bias, and ensuring AI enriches human experience. We advocate for human-centered AI design, prioritizing the "why." Finally, we propose a framework for cultivating AI-augmented human flourishing, offering practical recommendations for educators, policymakers, and developers to unlock AI's full educational potential. The insights from this work can be used to inform the design of future AI educational systems and influence policy recommendations for integrating AI into teacher training curricula to better support student well-being.

2. Methodology

This chapter employs a systematic literature review methodology, drawing on the rigorous guidelines proposed by [12] to explore the evolving role of AI in education, specifically moving beyond personalization to the cultivation of human flourishing. This structured approach ensures a systematic process for identifying, selecting, critically appraising, and synthesizing relevant studies on the potential of AI to foster human flourishing in education. The process, as depicted in **Figure 1**, was divided into three distinct phases: Planning, Selection, and Extraction & Execution.

2.1 Planning

The initial planning phase involved clearly articulating the scope and objectives of the review. The primary research questions guiding this review were defined as: (a) What are the limitations of current AI personalization models in supporting holistic student development? and (b) How can AI be strategically integrated to augment the various dimensions of human flourishing in educational settings?

To ensure a broad and relevant search, a comprehensive search strategy was developed. This strategy utilized a combination of keywords and their variations, including "Artificial Intelligence," "AI in education," "personalized learning," "human flourishing," "well-being," "holistic development," "affective computing," and "critical thinking." These keywords were strategically combined using Boolean operators (AND, OR) to maximize the breadth and relevance of the search queries across selected databases.

2.2 Selection

The selection phase focused on identifying and filtering relevant studies from a wide array of sources. The search was primarily conducted across major academic

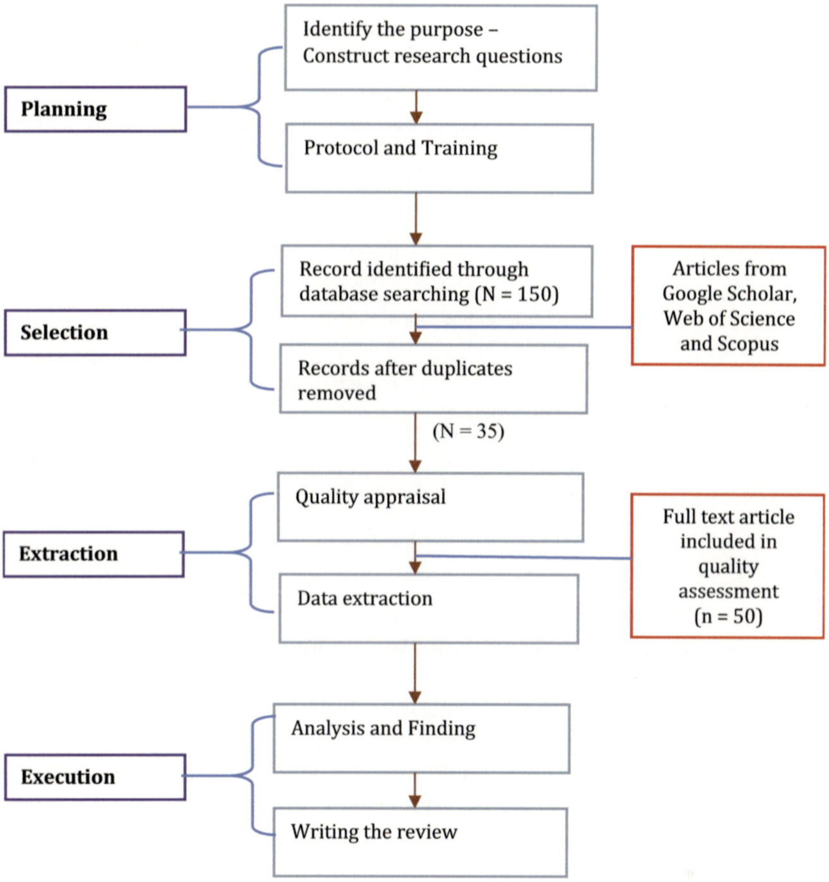

Figure 1.
The SLR process: adapted from [12]

databases, including Scopus, Web of Science, and Google Scholar. This diverse selection aimed to capture a wide spectrum of scholarly work.

Strict inclusion and exclusion criteria were applied during this phase to ensure the quality and relevance of the included studies. The inclusion criteria mandated that studies must be peer-reviewed journal articles, conference proceedings, or reputable book chapters published in the English language. They also had to be directly relevant to AI applications in educational contexts and address concepts of human flourishing, well-being, or holistic development. Conversely, the exclusion criteria led to the removal of non-peer-reviewed sources, publications not in English, studies focusing purely on technical AI development without an explicit educational application, and duplicate publications. **Table 1** provides the criteria used for the literature search.

2.3 Extraction and execution

The final phase involved the systematic extraction of pertinent data and its synthesis. Data from the selected studies were meticulously extracted, with a focus

Inclusion criteria	Exclusion criteria
Peer-reviewed journal articles, conference proceedings, and reputable book chapters.	Non-peer-reviewed sources, such as blog posts, news articles, or popular science magazines, should only be used when providing foundational definitions or widely accepted conceptualizations.
Publications in the English language.	Publications not written in the English language.
Content directly relevant to AI applications in educational contexts.	Studies focusing purely on technical AI development, without explicit educational applications or human-centric considerations.
Content addressing concepts of human flourishing, well-being, or holistic development in education.	Redundant or duplicate studies.
Publications discussing ethical implications, societal impacts, or frameworks for AI in education.	Publications are not available in full text.

Table 1.
Inclusion and exclusion criteria for literature search.

on key themes. The themes included the limitations of AI personalization, the conceptual components of human flourishing as defined in the literature, specific AI applications that support these components, and identified ethical considerations (e.g., data privacy, algorithmic bias).

The extracted data were then thoroughly synthesized to identify overarching trends, common findings across different studies, and significant gaps in the existing literature. This thematic synthesis facilitated the development of a comprehensive framework for "AI-augmented human flourishing in education," which forms the basis for this chapter's conclusions and recommendations.

3. Review of literature – thematic analysis

This review of literature provides a comprehensive overview of AI's role in education, transitioning from the current dominant model of personalization-centric AI to a more expansive vision of AI-augmented human flourishing. It critically examines the established applications and benefits of personalization while also highlighting its limitations and ethical concerns. Subsequently, the review deconstructs the concept of human flourishing and maps how AI can be strategically leveraged to support its various dimensions, moving beyond a narrow focus on academic outcomes.

3.1 The dominant paradigm: Personalization-centric AI in education

The prevailing approach to integrating AI into education is centered on personalization, tailoring learning experiences to individual student needs, preferences, and pace [1, 2]. This model aims to optimize learning outcomes by providing customized content, adaptive assessments, and targeted feedback. Key applications define this paradigm, including adaptive learning platforms that adjust content in real-time based on student performance; intelligent tutoring systems (ITS) that offer personalized guidance and feedback [2, 13]; content curation that recommends resources based on student interests; automated assessment that provides instant feedback; and learning analytics that use predictive modeling to identify at-risk students [1, 2, 13, 14].

These applications offer significant benefits, such as increased student engagement due to tailored content and immediate feedback [14, 13]. They lead to improved learning outcomes by addressing individual learning gaps [14] and enhance accessibility by providing support for diverse learners [3]. Furthermore, personalization-centric AI increases efficiency for educators, automating administrative tasks and freeing up teachers for higher-level pedagogical tasks and human interaction [14, 13].

3.2 Limitations and critical perspectives

Despite its advantages, the personalization paradigm faces notable limitations and ethical challenges that have been rigorously critiqued by scholars like Neil Selwyn and Audrey Watters, who caution against a simplistic "techno-optimism." A primary concern is data privacy and security, as these systems collect extensive student data, necessitating robust safeguards [13, 15]. Algorithmic bias is another critical issue, as biased training data can perpetuate and amplify existing societal inequalities, leading to unfair outcomes for certain student demographics [13, 15].

There's also a risk of over-reliance and diminished critical thinking. Excessive dependence on AI-provided answers could hinder students' development of independent problem-solving and analytical skills [16]. Furthermore, AI cannot fully replicate the human touch, risking a dehumanized learning experience that could impact students' social-emotional development [16]. Academic integrity is also challenged by generative AI, raising concerns about plagiarism [16]. Finally, scalability and equity of access remain hurdles, as robust AI systems require significant resources, potentially widening the digital divide [16, 17].

3.3 From personalized learning to human flourishing: A conceptual shift

Given these limitations, the future of AI in education requires a conceptual shift from merely adapting content to fostering holistic student development. This evolution aligns with the concept of human flourishing, which encompasses a state of well-being that goes beyond academic metrics to include physical, psychological, social, and spiritual well-being [3–6]. Flourishing involves dimensions such as physical and psychological well-being, cognitive growth, purpose and personal growth, socio-emotional intelligence and positive relationships, emotional mastery, and continuous growth as illustrated in **Figure 2**. Understanding these dimensions is crucial for moving toward an AI-augmented model that supports the whole student, rather than just their cognitive performance.

3.3.1 Mapping AI's potential to the dimensions of human flourishing

Artificial intelligence can directly contribute to fostering the various dimensions of human flourishing.

(1) **Augmenting physical health and psychological well-being**
Artificial intelligence (AI) tools can assist in monitoring students' physical well-being by analyzing behavioral patterns in online learning environments

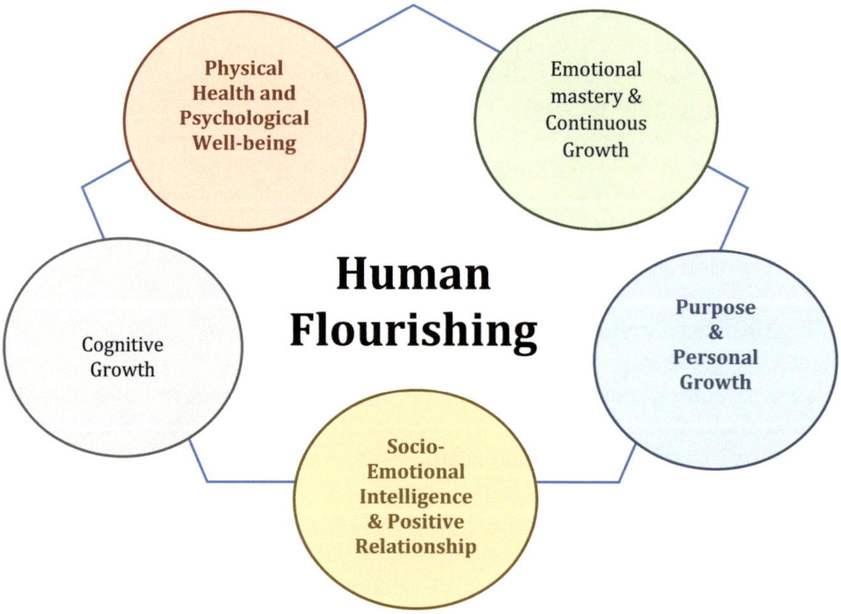

Figure 2.
Dimensions of human flourishing.

or promoting healthy habits through timely nudges [4, 5]. Similarly, AI can play a supportive role in mental health by identifying potential signs of distress through sentiment analysis, offering mindfulness exercises, or providing access to mental health resources [4, 5].

(2) **Fostering cognitive growth: Critical thinking and creativity**
Artificial intelligence can be leveraged to develop higher-order thinking skills. Instead of merely assessing knowledge, it can facilitate debates, present conflicting viewpoints, or analyze student arguments to strengthen critical thinking [13]. Furthermore, generative AI tools can serve as a creative partner, inspiring new ideas and assisting in the iterative process of creation, allowing students to explore novel solutions and express unique capacities [14, 13].

(3) **Cultivating social-emotional intelligence and positive relationships**
Artificial intelligence can facilitate collaborative learning environments, connect students with shared interests, and analyze group interactions to provide feedback on communication and teamwork skills. While human interaction remains paramount, AI can support the development of empathy and social awareness by curating diverse perspectives or facilitating role-playing scenarios.

(4) **Guiding purpose in life and supporting personal growth**
Artificial intelligence can help students identify their interests, aptitudes, and values by analyzing their learning patterns and preferences. It can provide personalized career guidance or suggest pathways for continuous skill

development aligned with individual purpose, fostering a sense of meaning in their educational journey.

(5) **Supporting environmental mastery and autonomy**
Artificial intelligence can provide students with greater control over their learning environment and pace, fostering autonomy. By offering adaptable resources, choices in assignments, and personalized feedback, AI empowers students to manage their learning process, adapt to challenges, and optimize their engagement with educational content.

4. AI augmenting human capacities in education

Artificial intelligence serves not as a replacement but as an augmentation of human potential, enhancing both the student and educator experience.

4.1 Empowering students: Enhanced agency and deeper engagement

Artificial intelligence technologies, by personalizing content and providing immediate feedback, significantly increase student engagement and motivation [13, 15]. Furthermore, by offering adaptive learning pathways and enabling self-paced study, AI fosters greater student agency, allowing learners to take more control over their educational journey and adapt to their individual learning styles.

4.2 Supporting educators: Streamlining tasks and enriching pedagogy

Artificial intelligence can significantly reduce teachers' administrative burden by automating tasks like grading, attendance tracking, and scheduling. This frees up valuable time for educators to focus on more complex pedagogical decisions, individualized mentoring, and fostering deeper human connections with their students [13, 14].

4.3 Innovative pedagogical approaches with AI as a collaborative partner

Artificial intelligence enables new teaching methodologies, moving beyond traditional lecture-based models. Teachers can leverage AI to create highly interactive simulations, immersive virtual reality environments, and adaptive problem-solving scenarios. Artificial intelligence can act as a "thought partner" for both students and teachers, facilitating complex project-based learning and inquiry-based approaches.

4.4 Cultivating skills for an AI-driven world

Beyond subject-specific knowledge, AI in education is crucial for developing "future-ready" skills. Students exposed to ethically designed AI tools in their learning environment will naturally develop AI literacy, understanding its capabilities, limitations, and ethical implications. This prepares them to navigate and contribute to an increasingly AI-driven society and workforce.

5. Ethical considerations and human-centered AI design

The successful integration of AI for human flourishing in education hinges on a robust ethical framework and a steadfast commitment to human-centered design. This section outlines the critical ethical principles that must guide the development and deployment of educational AI to ensure it serves the best interests of students and educators.

5.1 Data privacy, student agency, and consent

The collection and analysis of student data, while beneficial for personalization and insights, raises significant privacy concerns. Protecting student information requires robust safeguards and transparent policies. Educational institutions must adhere to strict regulations, such as the General Data Protection Regulation (GDPR) and the Family Educational Rights and Privacy Act (FERPA), which mandate specific protocols for data handling. Beyond compliance, a focus on student agency is crucial. This involves providing students and their guardians with clear, accessible information on what data is being collected, why it is being collected, and how it will be used. Explicit consent must be obtained, and students should have the right to access, correct, and even request the deletion of their personal data.

5.2 Mitigating algorithmic bias and ensuring fairness

Artificial intelligence algorithms, if trained on biased data, can perpetuate and even amplify existing societal inequalities. This is a critical ethical challenge in educational technology, as biased algorithms can lead to unfair outcomes for specific student demographics. Developers and educators must work collaboratively to audit and mitigate algorithmic bias, ensuring equitable access and outcomes for all learners, regardless of their backgrounds or characteristics. This requires the use of diverse datasets for training and continuous monitoring of AI system performance.

5.3 The imperative for transparency and explainable AI

For AI to be trustworthy and effectively augment human capabilities, its decision-making processes should be as transparent as possible. This section emphasizes the importance of Explainable AI (XAI) in education, allowing students, teachers, and parents to understand how AI tools provide recommendations or assessments. Transparency helps build trust and empowers educators to critically interpret AI-generated insights rather than blindly accepting them.

5.4 Maintaining human agency and teacher oversight

While AI can automate tasks and provide insights, the ultimate decision-making authority and human connection must remain paramount. This section discusses the critical role of human teachers in interpreting AI data, providing emotional support, and fostering social development. Teachers must be seen as the ultimate leaders in the classroom, ensuring AI acts as a tool, not a replacement for meaningful human interaction.

5.5 Prioritizing the "Why": A values-driven AI integration

The core principle for integrating AI in education should always be its contribution to human flourishing. This section advocates for a values-driven approach, where the "why" behind AI adoption – to enhance human potential and create a more equitable, engaging, and enriching learning experience – guides all design and implementation decisions. This perspective is reinforced by emerging ethical frameworks that provide a blueprint for responsible AI development, such as the OECD AI Principles, which emphasize human-centered values and public benefit, and UNESCO's AI Competency Framework, which promotes the ethical use of AI in education. Similarly, the IEEE Ethically Aligned Design framework provides a practical guide for building AI systems that prioritize human well-being from the outset, ensuring technology is designed for the benefit of humanity.

6. Framework for cultivating AI-augmented human flourishing in education

The proposed framework is a model for cultivating AI-augmented human flourishing in education. It is not a rigid, single-step plan but rather a comprehensive, multi-stakeholder framework built on a set of core principles and actionable recommendations for different groups. The framework's structure and key components are:

6.1 Core principles

The framework is founded on a set of fundamental principles that guide the design and implementation of AI in education. These principles include the following:

(1) Human-centricity: Prioritizing the human experience and well-being in all AI design and integration decisions.

(2) Ethical by design: Building AI systems with ethical considerations, such as fairness and privacy, embedded from the outset.

(3) Equity and inclusion: Ensuring AI tools promote equitable access and outcomes for all learners.

(4) Holistic development: Focusing on AI's potential to support cognitive, emotional, social, and ethical growth – not just academic achievement.

(5) Teacher empowerment: Using AI to support educators and freeing them to focus on high-impact pedagogical tasks.

(6) Continuous evaluation: Regularly assessing AI tools to ensure they align with the goals of human flourishing.

6.2 Recommendations for key stakeholders

The framework provides practical guidance tailored to specific groups involved in the educational ecosystem:

(1) For educators, actionable strategies for teachers on how to leverage AI tools to foster critical thinking, creativity, socio-emotional learning, and personalized support in the classroom.

(2) For policymakers and institutions, guidance on the systemic changes required to support this vision, such as curriculum development, funding for ethical AI research, teacher training programs, and establishing clear regulatory guidelines.

(3) For technology developers, guidance on designing tools that are inherently ethical, transparent, user-friendly, and aligned with the principles of human flourishing. It encourages collaboration between developers and educators to ensure the tools are fit for purpose.

7. Conclusion

The "Framework for Cultivating AI-Augmented Human Flourishing in Education" is not merely a technical guide but a philosophical roadmap. It fundamentally argues that the successful integration of AI into educational systems hinges on a human-centric approach. This means AI should serve as a powerful tool to amplify human potential, rather than a force that automates or diminishes the unique qualities of learners and educators. The framework prioritizes core psychological needs, such as autonomy, competence, and relatedness, as the guiding principles for AI-powered educational design. By doing so, it moves beyond a focus on efficiency and data to a more profound goal: using technology to create more meaningful, engaging, and purposeful learning experiences that genuinely support individual growth and well-being.

Ultimately, the framework's conclusion is that the future of education is a collaborative one, where human and artificial intelligence work in concert. It calls for a paradigm shift from viewing AI as a solution to all educational challenges to seeing it as an enabler of a more humanistic and flourishing learning environment. This approach suggests that the true measure of AI's success in education will not be found in improved test scores or streamlined administrative tasks, but in its ability to help students discover their passions, develop a deeper sense of purpose, and cultivate the critical thinking and creativity needed to navigate a complex, AI-infused world. The framework serves as a vital blueprint for ensuring that, as we embrace technological change, we do so in a way that respects and elevates the inherent value of human flourishing.

Author details

Joseph O. Ukoba[1*], Okengwu A. Ugochi[2], Eginiwin E. Joseph[1] and Laud C. Ochei[2]

1 Federal Polytechnic Orogun, Orogun, Nigeria

2 University of Port Harcourt, Port Harcourt, Nigeria

*Address all correspondence to: ukoba.joseph@fepo.edu.ng; ukobajosephorode@gmail.com

References

[1] Baker RS, Siemens G. Educational data mining and learning analytics. In: Spector JM, Merrill MD, Elen J, Bishop MJ, editors. Handbook of Research on Educational Communications and Technology. 4th ed. New York: Springer; 2014. p. 253–264

[2] Woolf BP, Lane HC, Chaudhri VK, Kolodner JL. AI grand challenges for education. AI Magazine. 2013;**34**(4): 66–84. DOI: 10.1609/aimag.v34i4.2490

[3] Piñeiro-Cossio J, Fernández-Martínez A, Nuviala A, Pérez-Ordás R. Psychological wellbeing in physical education and school sports: A systematic review. International Journal of Environmental Research and Public Health. 2021;**18**(3):864

[4] Sakellari E, Notara V, Lagiou A, Fatkulina N, Ivanova S, Korhonen J, et al. Mental health and wellbeing at Schools: Health promotion in Primary Schools with the use of digital methods. Children 2021;**8**:345

[5] Zhang Y, Mavoa S, Zhao J, Raphael D, Smith M. The association between green space and adolescents' Mental Well-being: A systematic review. International Journal of Environmental Research and Public Health. 2020;**17**(18):6640

[6] Chen W, Gu X, Chen J, Wang X. Association of cardiorespiratory fitness and cognitive function with psychological Well-being in School-aged children. International Journal of Environmental Research and Public Health. 2022;**19**(3):1434

[7] Das A, Malaviya S, Singh M. The impact of AI-driven personalization on learners' performance. International Journal of Computer Science and Engineering. 2023;**11**(8):15-22. DOI: 10. 26438/ijcse/v11i8.1522

[8] Zawacki-Richter O, Marín VI, Bond M, Gouverneur F. Systematic review of research on artificial intelligence applications in higher education—where are the educators?. International Journal of Educational Technology in Higher Education. 2019;**16**(1):39. DOI: 10.1186/s41239-0 19-0171-0

[9] Popenici SA, Kerr S. Exploring the Impact of Artificial Intelligence on teaching and learning in higher education. Re-conceptualising the Role of Teaching and Learning in an Age of Emerging Technology. 2017;**12**(22):45–60

[10] Luckin R, Holmes W, Griffiths M, Forcier LB. Intelligence Unleashed: An Argument for AI in Education. London: Pearson; 2016

[11] Siemens G. Learning analytics: The emergence of a discipline. American Behavioral Scientist. 2013;**57**(10): 1380–1400

[12] Okoli C, Schabram K. A guide to conducting a systematic literature review of information systems research. Sprouts: Working Papers on Information Systems 2010;**10**(26)

[13] University Canada West (UCW). Advantages and disadvantages of AI in education [Internet]. 2024 Jul 19 Available from: https://www.ucanwest.ca/blog/education-careers-tips/advantages-and-disadvantages-of-ai-in-education [Accessed: 2025-June-22]

[14] Abuhassna H, Al-Rahmi WM, Yahaya N, Abumandil M, Alyoussef I, Kian P, et al. The role of artificial intelligence in personalizing educational content: Enhancing the learning experience and developing the teacher's role in an integrated educational environment. Current Educational Technology Research 2025;**1**:21

[15] Johri M. The Impact of AI on student engagement and learning outcomes. International Journal of Teaching, Learning and Education. [published online ahead of print] 2025. Available from: https://www.researchgate.net/profile/Manjari-Johri/publication/391463951_International_Journal_of_Teaching_Learning_and_Education_IJTLE_The_Impact_of_AI_on_Student_Engagement_and_Learning_Outcomes/links/6819a5fdbd3f1930dd6cac6d/International-Journal-of-Teaching-Learning-and-Education-IJTLE-The-Impact_of_AI_on_Student_Engagement_and_Learning_Outcomes.pdf [Accessed: 2025-June-22]

[16] Afzal A, Khan S, Daud S, Ahmed Z, Butt A. Addressing the digital divide: Access and use of technology in education. Journal of Social Sciences Review. 2023;**3**(2):883–895. DOI: 10.54183/jssr.v3i2.326

[17] Bozic V. Strengthening EFL learners' autonomy: Exploring the Voscreen app and its impact on encouragement and engagement in technology-based language learning. Language Education & Technology (LET Journal). 2023;**3**(2):96–109. Available from: https://langedutech.com/letjournal/index.php/let/article/view/53/42

Chapter 4

Bidirectional Human – AI Alignment in Education for Trustworthy Learning Environments

Hua Shen

Abstract

Artificial intelligence (AI) is rapidly reshaping education, offering new possibilities for personalization, adaptive assessment, and institutional decision-making. Yet alongside these opportunities arise significant risks related to equity, privacy, transparency, and student agency. This chapter advances the framework of bidirectional human–AI alignment in education, arguing that trustworthy learning environments require more than embedding human values into AI systems. Instead, alignment must be understood as a dynamic, reciprocal process in which AI systems are designed to reflect shared educational values, while educators and learners develop the literacy and agency to interpret, critique, and guide AI technologies.We first clarify what must be aligned—core ethical principles, substantive educational goals, and human–AI interaction norms. We then outline three complementary pathways for achieving alignment: (1) human-centered and value-sensitive technical design, (2) ethical, legal, and governance frameworks, and (3) continuous evaluation and adaptive feedback mechanisms. The chapter further traces AI's evolving role from support tool to collaborative partner and interactive tutor, examining its impact on teacher practice, student autonomy, assessment, and educational governance.By reframing AI adoption as an ongoing process of mutual adaptation rather than one-way control, this chapter offers actionable recommendations for policymakers, developers, institutions, and educators. Ultimately, bidirectional alignment provides a roadmap for ensuring that AI enhances human flourishing, strengthens trust, and advances the deeper aims of education rather than undermining them.

Keywords: AI for education, Bidirectional Human–AI Alignment, Trustworthy Learning Environments, evolving AI roles in education, Educational AI Governance

1. Introduction

Artificial intelligence (AI) is rapidly becoming woven into the fabric of education [1, 2]. From adaptive learning platforms and automated assessment tools to intelligent tutoring systems and predictive analytics, AI technologies promise to reshape how students learn, how teachers teach, and how schools make decisions [3, 4]. These innovations hold the potential to address long-standing challenges – personalizing learning at scale, reducing administrative burdens, and generating timely insights to support both teaching and student progress.

Yet alongside this promise lie significant risks. Without deliberate attention to ethics, inclusivity, and transparency, AI systems may amplify biases, erode student privacy, or diminish teacher autonomy. They can also disrupt the delicate social dynamics of classrooms, altering power relationships between students, educators, and technology providers. In this sense, the introduction of AI into education is not merely a technical shift but a cultural and normative one [5].

Building on the "Bidirectional Human-AI Alignment" framework [6, 7], this chapter proposes a bidirectional approach to human – AI alignment in education – one that treats alignment not as a one-way imposition of human values onto machines, but as a dynamic process in which both humans and AI systems co-adapt. On one hand, AI must be designed and deployed to reflect shared educational values such as equity, trust, and student agency [8, 9]. On the other hand, educators and learners must also develop new literacies, skills, and mindsets to engage productively and critically with AI systems [10]. Only through this reciprocal relationship can AI enhance, rather than undermine, the human goals of learning. The chapter unfolds in five major parts:

- **What needs to be aligned**: We begin by unpacking the foundations of alignment in education: shared values and ethical principles, clear learning goals, and well-defined interaction norms between humans and AI systems.

- **Pathways to achieving alignment**: We explore technical design strategies, ethical and legal frameworks, and mechanisms for continuous feedback and adaptation that sustain alignment over time.

- **Evolving roles of AI in education**: We trace AI's trajectory from a support tool to a collaborative partner, focusing on adaptive learning, personalization, and enhanced assessment.

- **Impacts of AI on the educational ecosystem**: We examine how AI affects teachers' roles, students' agency, classroom safety, and the broader capacity to interpret and critique algorithmic decisions.

- **Moving forward: Actions and recommendations**: We conclude with practical steps for policymakers, educators, and developers and identify key areas for future research and innovation.

By weaving these threads together, the chapter aims to provide a roadmap for designing trustworthy learning environments where human and artificial agents work in concert. Our goal is not simply to safeguard against harm but to actively cultivate a culture of mutual trust, transparency, and shared responsibility – ensuring that AI enhances the human dimensions of education rather than eroding them.

2. What needs to be aligned?

The promise of AI in education hinges on alignment – ensuring that technologies support, rather than distort, the aims of teaching and learning. Alignment is not a single dimension; it is a multi-layered process spanning values, goals, and norms [6]. Before technical solutions or policy frameworks can be implemented, we must first clarify ***what*** should be aligned [11]. This section identifies three foundational elements: (1) core values and ethical principles, (2) educational goals and desired outcomes, and (3) human–AI interaction norms and boundaries.

2.1 Core values and ethical principles

Trustworthy learning environments are grounded in shared values and ethical principles [12, 13]. Drawing on human value theories from social science and psychology (e.g., Schwartz's theory of basic values [14, 15]), core principles such as equity, inclusivity, privacy, transparency, accountability, and respect for human dignity should serve as the "north star" for designing and deploying AI in education [16–18]. Without an explicit commitment to these principles, even well-intentioned technologies risk reinforcing biases, commodifying learning, or eroding student agency [19]. I elaborate below on several key values that are particularly important for AI in education.

Equity and inclusion. AI systems should reduce, not exacerbate, disparities in access, achievement, and representation. This requires diverse training data, inclusive design processes, and ongoing monitoring for unintended discrimination.

Privacy and data protection. Given the sensitivity of student data, privacy safeguards and transparent data governance are non-negotiable.

Transparency and explainability: Educators, students, and parents should be able to understand how AI systems arrive at their recommendations or decisions.

Accountability. Clear lines of responsibility must be established so that when systems err, human actors – not algorithms – are ultimately answerable.

Articulating and embedding these principles early in design can provide a moral compass for developers and institutions, ensuring technology supports the flourishing of learners rather than merely optimizing measurable outcomes.

2.2 Educational goals and desired outcomes

Aligning AI with ethical values is only one part of the equation; it must also align with the substantive goals of education itself [20]. Educational systems are built not only to deliver content but to nurture critical thinking, creativity, collaboration, and lifelong learning. AI should, therefore, be evaluated not just on efficiency gains but on its contribution to these broader aims. Integrating AI into education requires careful consideration of its effects on curricula, pedagogy, and learner development. Key dimensions include:

Curricular alignment. AI should reinforce intended learning objectives rather than introduce incentives that distort student focus. Systems that reward superficial engagement risk undermining deeper understanding and conceptual mastery.

Skill development. Beyond academic knowledge, AI should support higher-order skills such as problem-solving, creativity, digital literacy, and ethical reasoning. Tools that simulate real-world challenges or collaborative projects can foster these transferable skills.

Student agency. Effective education empowers learners to set goals, make choices, and reflect on progress. AI can facilitate this through adaptive pathways and meaningful feedback, while avoiding approaches that encourage passive consumption.

Holistic development. Education extends to social-emotional learning, well-being, and civic responsibility. AI should support these dimensions – for example, by prompting reflection, fostering empathy, or promoting collaborative civic projects – rather than marginalizing them.

By making desired outcomes explicit, we can better judge whether an AI product is a true pedagogical asset or merely a novelty. True pedagogical alignment requires moving beyond efficiency gains to support multidimensional growth, ensuring AI serves as a partner in human development rather than a substitute for the essential human elements of education.

2.3 Human–AI interaction norms and boundaries

Aligning AI with educational goals requires clear norms and boundaries for human–AI interaction. These define expectations for transparency, consent, roles, and the appropriate limits of automation, ensuring AI supports rather than undermines teaching and learning.

Transparency of roles. Students and educators should clearly understand when they are interacting with AI, what data is collected, and how outputs are generated. Transparency fosters trust and informed engagement.

Human oversight. Decisions with significant consequences – such as grading, placement, or disciplinary actions – must remain under human review to preserve fairness, contextual judgment, and accountability.

Boundaries of influence. AI should augment, not replace, teacher judgment or peer interaction. Well-defined limits prevent over-automation, which could erode essential human relationships in learning.

Norms of conduct. Ethical and respectful behavior applies to both humans and AI systems. Tutors, chatbots, and other AI tools should model constructive, respectful communication.

Reciprocal learning. As AI adapts to learners, students and teachers must also develop the literacy to critique, guide, and influence these systems, fostering a two-way learning process.

Establishing these norms and boundaries creates a shared framework of trust, clarifying which aspects of teaching and learning can be safely automated and which must remain inherently human.

Together, these three elements – core values, educational goals, and interaction norms – define the foundation for bidirectional human–AI alignment. Without clarity in these areas, even sophisticated technical or policy measures risk addressing symptoms rather than causes.

3. Pathways to achieving alignment

Clarifying what needs to be aligned is only the first step [21]. The next challenge is to translate those principles, goals, and norms into practice [22]. This section outlines three complementary pathways – technical approaches and design strategies, ethical/legal/policy frameworks, and ongoing evaluation with feedback and adaptation – that together create an ecosystem for trustworthy AI in education.

3.1 Technical approaches and design strategies

Embedding alignment into AI systems begins at the design stage [23]. Rather than treating ethics or usability as add-ons, they must be integral to the development lifecycle.

- **Human-centered design**: Engage educators, students, and parents early and throughout the design process to ensure the system reflects real-world needs and values.

- **Value-sensitive design**: Translate ethical principles – fairness, privacy, transparency – into explicit technical requirements. For example, using explainable models where interpretability is critical.

- **Bias mitigation and inclusive data**: Curate diverse datasets, conduct fairness audits, and employ algorithmic techniques to detect and reduce biases that could harm marginalized groups.

- **Personalization with guardrails**: While adaptive learning systems tailor content to individual students, they should also respect boundaries, avoid over-surveillance, and maintain curricular integrity.

- **Transparency features**: Dashboards, explanations, and open documentation can make it easier for teachers and students to understand why a system recommends a particular action.

Technical strategies alone cannot guarantee trustworthy systems, but they provide the "hardwiring" that makes alignment feasible at scale.

3.2 Ethical, legal, and policy frameworks

Technical fixes must be supported by institutional and societal safeguards [24–26]. Ethical, legal, and policy frameworks provide the rules of the road that guide both developers and users [27, 28]. Corresponding to the core alignment objectives mentioned above, I discuss potential frameworks that are valuable for embedding values into AI systems.

Codes of practice and standards indicate that professional associations and education ministries can publish clear standards on responsible AI use, data governance, and transparency.

Privacy and data protection laws emphasize that strong regulations around data collection, consent, and retention (e.g., GDPR-like policies) help ensure student data is handled ethically.

Procurement and certification show that schools and governments can require third-party audits or certifications of AI products before adoption, much like safety checks in other industries.

Accountability mechanisms require policies to define who is responsible when AI systems err – vendors, schools, or both – and establish processes for redress.

Equity mandates enable policy frameworks that can explicitly require equity impact assessments to prevent exacerbating digital divides.

These frameworks not only protect stakeholders but also create predictable conditions for innovation, allowing developers to build with confidence and schools to adopt with trust.

3.3 Ongoing evaluation, feedback, and adaptation

Alignment is not a one-time achievement but a continuous process [29, 30]. As classrooms evolve and AI systems learn, the conditions under which they operate also change. Continuous evaluation ensures systems remain fit for purpose.

Monitoring and auditing. Regular audits of performance, fairness, and privacy compliance can identify issues before they escalate.

Feedback loops. Provide clear channels for teachers, students, and parents to report problems or suggest improvements, and ensure those inputs feed back into system updates.

Adaptive governance. Policies and norms should be revisited periodically to reflect new research, technologies, and societal expectations.

Impact studies. Longitudinal research on AI's effects on learning outcomes, student agency, and teacher roles can inform future design and policy.

Professional development. Equip educators with ongoing training to understand updates, interpret outputs, and integrate AI tools responsibly.

This iterative approach mirrors how learning itself works – testing, feedback, and revision – ensuring that alignment remains robust over time.

Together, these pathways create a resilient infrastructure for bidirectional human–AI alignment in education. Technical design, governance frameworks, and continuous evaluation form a mutually reinforcing system: each supports the others to ensure AI remains trustworthy and responsible to human needs.

4. Evolving roles of AI in education

AI in education has moved beyond experimental pilots to widespread adoption in classrooms, administrative systems, and educational platforms [31, 32]. As these technologies mature, their roles evolve from simple tools to complex partners in the learning process [33, 34]. This section traces that trajectory, highlighting how AI can (1) transition from a support tool to a collaborative partner, (2) enable adaptive and personalized learning, and (3) enhance assessment, feedback, and learning analytics.

4.1 From support tool to collaborative partner to interactive tutor

AI in education has evolved from performing narrowly defined, transactional tasks – such as grading multiple-choice tests, scheduling classes, or delivering drill-and-practice exercises – toward becoming a more relational and collaborative presence in learning environments [35]. This evolution reflects a continuum in AI's role, from support tool to collaborative partner to interactive tutor (**Table 1**).

Support tool. In its initial form, AI primarily handled administrative or repetitive tasks, providing efficiency and freeing educators to focus on higher-level instructional work.

Collaborative partner. AI increasingly engages educators in shared decision-making. Systems can assist in designing lesson plans, identifying at-risk students, and differentiating instruction, transforming teachers into co-pilots rather than passive

Role	Primary function	Typical features	Implications for educators & students
Support tool	Automates routine or administrative tasks	Grading multiple-choice tests, scheduling, drill-and-practice exercises	Frees educators to focus on higher-level instruction; limited relational interaction with students
Collaborative partner	Assists teachers in decision-making and planning	Lesson design, identifying at-risk students, differentiated instruction, teacher dashboards, analytics	Enables co-piloting with AI; supports teacher collaboration and data-driven interventions; requires trust and understanding of AI recommendations
AI tutor	Provides adaptive, personalized learning support directly to students	One-on-one dialog, adaptive hints, tailored explanations, co-creation of exercises and simulations	Offers individualized guidance; enhances student engagement and learning; requires clear boundaries and oversight to preserve human judgment

Table 1.
Roles of AI in education: Functions, features, and implications.

users. AI-powered dashboards and analytics further facilitate teacher collaboration, enabling data-driven interventions and coordinated instructional planning.

Interactive tutor. Advanced AI systems now simulate one-on-one tutoring, engaging students in adaptive dialog, asking probing questions, offering hints, and tailoring explanations to individual learning responses. Some platforms even support the co-creation of learning content, generating exercises, simulations, or multimodal experiences that blend human creativity with computational power.

This progression – from tool to partner to tutor – raises important considerations regarding trust, transparency, and autonomy. As AI assumes more relational and pedagogical roles, educators and students must establish clear expectations about responsibilities, boundaries, and oversight to ensure AI enhances learning without undermining essential human judgment.

4.2 Enabling adaptive and personalized learning

A central promise of AI in education lies in its ability to deliver personalized learning at scale – an aspiration that remains challenging for even the most skilled educators managing large, diverse classrooms. AI-driven personalization can enhance engagement, accelerate learning, and support students' individual needs through several key mechanisms:

- **Dynamic content delivery**: AI systems can adjust lesson difficulty, sequencing, and modality (e.g., text, video, or simulation) to align with a learner's current knowledge, skills, and preferences.

- **Real-time feedback**: Adaptive platforms provide immediate feedback, hints, or scaffolding, helping learners remain within their "zone of proximal development" and optimize growth.

- **Individualized learning pathways**: By recommending enrichment opportunities or targeted remediation, AI ensures that advanced learners are challenged, while those requiring support receive tailored interventions.

- **Multimodal accessibility**: Personalization extends beyond content pacing, incorporating language support, assistive technologies, and culturally relevant materials to promote inclusivity and equity.

While AI can substantially enhance personalization, its implementation must be carefully balanced with considerations of equity and learner autonomy. Systems that are overly prescriptive, opaque, or deterministic risk constraining students to fixed learning trajectories, potentially limiting exploration and self-directed growth. Educators play a critical role in maintaining oversight, fostering metacognitive awareness, and helping students understand the rationale behind personalized recommendations, thereby preserving agency and promoting deeper learning.

4.3 Enhancing assessment, feedback, and learning analytics

Assessment and feedback are central to the learning process, yet traditional approaches are often slow, resource-intensive, and limited in scope. AI has the potential to transform this landscape by providing more timely, nuanced, and actionable insights. For instance, AI systems can extend beyond grading multiple-choice or essay items to evaluate complex learning activities such as problem-solving processes, collaborative discussions, and oral presentations.

AI also enables continuous, low-stakes feedback through embedded micro-assessments. These assessments provide students with ongoing guidance throughout the learning process, reducing the pressure associated with high-stakes examinations while supporting incremental improvement. By aggregating data across learning activities, AI-driven learning analytics can reveal patterns and trends at the classroom, school, or district level, thereby informing targeted interventions and guiding the strategic allocation of educational resources.

Predictive analytics further enhance instructional decision-making by identifying students who may require additional support before traditional performance indicators signal concern. Coupled with well-designed dashboards and visualization tools, these analytics empower teachers, students, and parents to engage with data in a meaningful way, closing the feedback loop and making insights actionable rather than abstract.

Despite these benefits, the use of AI in assessment and analytics raises important concerns around privacy, consent, and interpretability. Data must always be contextualized, and analytics-driven recommendations should complement, rather than replace, the professional judgment and nuanced understanding that educators bring to their students' learning needs.

Together, these evolving roles highlight AI's dual nature in education – as a transformative enabler and a potential disruptor. By treating AI as a partner rather than a substitute, and by embedding transparency and human oversight, schools can harness these new capabilities to enhance rather than diminish the human experience of learning.

5. Impacts of AI on the educational ecosystem

As AI tools become more embedded in classrooms and educational institutions [36, 37], their influence extends beyond instructional delivery to the very structure of teaching, learning, and governance [38, 39]. These changes affect not only what students learn but also how educators work, how decisions are made, and how agency is distributed [40]. This section explores four critical dimensions of AI's impact: (1) the human capacity to interpret and critique AI decisions, (2) AI's role in promoting safety and well-being, (3) shifts in pedagogical practices and teacher roles, and (4) effects on student autonomy, agency, and motivation.

5.1 Human capacity to interpret and critique AI decisions

For AI to be trustworthy in education, teachers, students, and administrators must be able to interpret, question, and critique its outputs. Without this capacity, AI risks becoming a "black box" authority.

- **Algorithmic literacy**: Educators need professional development to understand how algorithms work, where biases may arise, and how to contextualize recommendations.

- **Transparency tools**: Clear explanations, confidence scores, and data visualizations can help stakeholders understand why an AI system produced a particular output.

- **Critical pedagogy**: Students can be taught to question automated feedback and recommendations, integrating digital and algorithmic literacy into curricula.

- **Shared decision-making**: Systems should be designed so that human users can override or appeal AI recommendations, reinforcing human judgment as the final authority.

Building this interpretive capacity is essential for maintaining accountability, avoiding blind trust, and fostering a culture of informed skepticism rather than passive compliance.

5.2 Shifts in pedagogical practices and teacher roles

AI in education does more than automate routine tasks; it fundamentally reshapes pedagogical practices and the role of teachers. As AI systems increasingly deliver personalized content, the traditional focus on content transmission shifts toward facilitation. Teachers can devote more time to mentoring, project-based learning, and supporting students' social-emotional development, emphasizing the human dimensions of education that AI cannot replicate.

Real-time analytics provide educators with actionable insights, enabling data-informed instruction. Teachers can adjust lesson pacing, groupings, and targeted interventions responsively, tailoring learning experiences to meet diverse student needs. This shift necessitates the development of new professional competencies, including data literacy, ethical oversight, and technological fluency, ensuring that educators are prepared to navigate AI-enhanced classrooms effectively.

In this evolving landscape, teachers increasingly function as orchestrators who collaborate with AI tools – much like pilots supervising an autopilot system. AI can provide scaffolding, suggestions, and monitoring, while teachers make nuanced judgments and maintain human oversight. However, without careful implementation, there is a risk of de-skilling, as reliance on AI for core instructional tasks may erode professional expertise. Schools must, therefore, ensure that AI augments, rather than replaces, teacher practice.

When integrated thoughtfully, these shifts empower educators to focus on the uniquely human aspects of teaching – empathy, mentorship, and creativity – while maintaining autonomy and professional judgment. Effective training and institutional support are essential to realizing the full potential of AI in reshaping pedagogy.

These shifts can empower teachers to focus on the uniquely human aspects of education – empathy, mentorship, and creativity – if they are supported with training and autonomy.

5.3 Effects on student autonomy, agency, and motivation

One of the most profound impacts of AI in education is its influence on students' sense of control, motivation, and identity as learners.

Enhanced agency through personalization. Adaptive systems can let students progress at their own pace, choose learning modalities, and receive tailored feedback – fostering ownership.

Risks of over-scaffolding. At the same time, there are risks associated with over-scaffolding. If AI systems become overly directive, they may reduce opportunities for struggle, experimentation, and self-regulation – skills that are critical for lifelong learning.

Motivational dynamics. Similarly, gamified or algorithmically optimized environments can increase engagement, but they may also create a reliance on extrinsic rewards, potentially undermining intrinsic motivation.

Transparency and choice. To mitigate these risks, students should understand the rationale behind AI-generated content and recommendations, and they should be empowered to adjust or opt out of suggested learning paths.

Developing metacognition. Educators play a crucial role in leveraging AI feedback to cultivate metacognitive skills, guiding students to reflect on their learning strategies, build self-awareness, and develop resilience.

The challenge lies in striking a balance where AI empowers rather than constrains, amplifying students' intrinsic motivation and supporting self-directed learning.

Together with changes in pedagogy and assessment, these developments illustrate that AI's impact on education is both systemic and deeply personal. By anticipating these shifts and shaping their implementation proactively, policymakers, schools, and developers can ensure that AI enhances – rather than diminishes – the human capacities that are central to meaningful learning experiences.

6. Moving forward: Actions and recommendations

The preceding sections have demonstrated that AI in education carries both transformative potential and significant risks. Realizing its benefits while minimizing harms requires deliberate, coordinated action by policymakers, educators, institutions, developers, and researchers. This chapter concludes with practical recommendations under three broad areas: (1) policy guidelines for responsible AI integration, (2) best practices for educators, institutions, and developers, and (3) key priorities for future research and innovation.

6.1 Policy guidelines for responsible AI integration

Robust policy frameworks can establish a foundation of trust and accountability that enables innovation while safeguarding learners. Transparency and accountability should be central: educational authorities and technology providers need to disclose the purposes, data sources, and performance metrics of AI systems in ways that are accessible to the public. Stronger privacy and data protection laws are essential to safeguard student information, including strict limits on data retention, sharing, and commercial exploitation.

Ethical and equity impact assessments should become standard practice before large-scale deployments, ensuring that AI systems do not inadvertently exacerbate disparities. Governments and accrediting bodies can also create certification schemes for AI education products – analogous to safety or accessibility ratings – so that schools can make informed purchasing and implementation decisions.

Interoperability and open standards are equally important. By promoting platforms that enable data portability and integration across multiple tools, policymakers can reduce vendor lock-in and allow for holistic oversight of students' learning data. Finally, stakeholder engagement must be embedded into policy design. Regular consultation with teachers, parents, and students can ensure that regulations remain responsive to real-world needs and inclusive of diverse perspectives, rather than imposed from the top down.

6.2 Best practices for educators, institutions, and developers

While policy frameworks provide the foundation for responsible AI use, day-to-day practices within schools and development teams determine how these technologies actually affect teaching and learning. Educators, institutions, developers, and students each play a crucial role in ensuring AI tools enhance, rather than diminish, educational quality.

For **educators**, the priority is to integrate AI thoughtfully into pedagogical practice. Teachers should treat AI as a complement to – not a replacement for – human expertise. This means maintaining active oversight of AI recommendations, fostering students' metacognitive skills, and using data insights to inform rather than dictate instruction. Professional development is essential: training in data literacy, ethical oversight, and technological fluency can help teachers navigate AI-enhanced classrooms with confidence.

Institutions can support responsible adoption by creating clear governance structures and ethical guidelines for AI use. School leaders should ensure transparency with parents and students about how AI systems work, what data they collect, and how that data will be used. Institutions can also invest in digital infrastructure that prioritizes security, interoperability, and accessibility, thereby enabling educators to experiment with AI tools without compromising privacy or equity.

Developers, meanwhile, should design AI systems with the educational context in mind. This includes building transparent interfaces, offering meaningful user control, and testing for bias or unintended consequences before deployment. Collaboration with educators and students during the design phase can produce tools that align with real classroom needs rather than imposing rigid technological solutions.

For **students**, responsible use of AI involves cultivating digital literacy, self-regulation, and a critical awareness of how AI systems shape their learning. Learners should be encouraged to view AI as a tool to support – not substitute – their own thinking, and to question or adjust recommendations when appropriate. Educators and institutions can foster this agency by explicitly teaching students how to interpret feedback, manage data privacy, and reflect on their learning strategies. When students understand how AI systems operate and develop the confidence to use them judiciously, they are better equipped to take ownership of their education and to transfer these skills to future workplaces and civic life.

Taken together, these practices create an ecosystem in which AI strengthens teaching and learning. When educators retain agency, institutions provide safeguards, developers prioritize ethical design, and students develop the skills to use AI responsibly, the technology can serve as a catalyst for innovation while upholding the values of equity, inclusion, and human development at the heart of education.

6.3 Key areas for future research and innovation

Beyond immediate policy and practice, the next decade of AI in education will be shaped by targeted research and sustained innovation. Several areas merit particular attention if AI is to enhance – not diminish – human potential in learning environments.

First, researchers should deepen our understanding of how AI affects learning outcomes, equity, and student well-being over time. Longitudinal studies can illuminate not only academic gains but also impacts on motivation, agency, and social-emotional development. This evidence base is critical for moving beyond anecdotal claims and toward empirically grounded policy decisions.

Second, there is a need for more transparent and explainable AI systems tailored to educational contexts. Innovations in interpretable models and user-friendly dashboards can help educators, students, and parents understand why certain recommendations are made, strengthening trust and enabling informed decision-making.

Third, future development should prioritize inclusivity and cultural responsiveness. This involves building systems that work across languages, learning differences, and socio-economic contexts, while actively testing for and mitigating bias. Collaborative research between technologists, educators, and communities can ensure that tools are designed for diverse learners rather than assuming a single "typical" user.

Finally, the field would benefit from new paradigms that blend human and artificial intelligence in genuinely complementary ways. This includes co-creative learning environments, adaptive assessment models that foster metacognition, and hybrid teaching roles that emphasize empathy, mentorship, and creativity while drawing on AI's data-processing strengths.

By investing in these areas, policymakers, institutions, and developers can help steer AI in education toward a future that prioritizes human flourishing. Research and innovation should not simply chase technical possibilities but actively shape systems that embody educational values, safeguard equity, and cultivate lifelong learning.

7. Conclusion

This chapter has examined the foundations, pathways, and impacts of bidirectional human–AI alignment in education. We began by identifying what must be aligned – core values and ethical principles, educational goals, and human–AI interaction norms. We then mapped the pathways to achieve alignment through technical design strategies, ethical and legal frameworks, and ongoing evaluation. We traced AI's evolving role from support tool to collaborative partner, explored how personalization and analytics can transform learning, and reflected on the implications for teacher practice, student agency, and institutional systems.

The central insight is that alignment is not a one-time act but an ongoing process. It requires translating principles into design, embedding safeguards into policy, and cultivating human capacity to interpret, critique, and improve AI systems. When done well, alignment enables AI to expand human potential, strengthen trust, and advance education's deepest aims. When neglected, it risks undermining privacy, equity, and autonomy.

Looking ahead, the goal is not simply to "fit AI into schools" but to reimagine schools as spaces where humans and intelligent systems learn, adapt, and improve together. This vision frames AI not as a substitute for educators but as a collaborator that augments teaching, supports student growth, and creates new opportunities for creativity and critical thinking. Such synergy depends on mutual adaptation: AI systems designed for transparency, fairness, and inclusivity, and human actors equipped with the literacy and agency to guide, challenge, and improve those systems.

Achieving this vision demands collective action across all stakeholders. Policymakers must create clear guardrails and incentives for responsible innovation. Educators and institutions must develop new competencies, governance structures, and professional cultures. Developers must embed human values into the technical core of their products. Researchers must produce evidence and new models to anticipate risks and inform practice. And students themselves must be engaged as active co-designers and evaluators of the tools shaping their learning experiences.

By working together across these boundaries, we can create trustworthy learning environments where technology enhances – rather than diminishes – the human experience of education. This is the promise, and the responsibility, of bidirectional human–AI alignment: to ensure that as AI grows more powerful, education grows more equitable, empowering, and humane.

Author details

Hua Shen
NYU Shanghai, New York University, Shanghai, China

*Address all correspondence to: huashen@nyu.edu

References

[1] Ma Q, Shen H, Koedinger K, Wu ST. How to teach programming in the ai era? using llms as a teachable agent for debugging. In International Conference on Artificial Intelligence in Education; Cham: Springer Nature Switzerland; (2024, July). 265–279. DOI: 10.1007/978-3-031-64302-6_19

[2] Harry A, Sayudin S. Role of AI in education. Interdiciplinary Journal & Hummanity (INJURITY). 2023;**2**(3): 260–268. Available from: https://radensa.ru/wp-content/uploads/2024/05/Role_of_AI_in_Education.pdf

[3] Sajja R, Sermet Y, Cikmaz M, Cwiertny D, Demir I. Artificial intelligence-enabled intelligent assistant for personalized and adaptive learning in higher education. Information. 2024;**15**(10):596. Available from: https://www.mdpi.com/2078-2489/15/10/596

[4] Demartini CG, Sciascia L, Bosso A, Manuri F. Artificial intelligence bringing improvements to adaptive learning in education: A case study. Sustainability. 2024;**16**(3):1347. Available from: https://www.mdpi.com/2071-1050/16/3/1347

[5] Muthukrishna M, Dai J, Panizo Madrid D, Sabherwal R, Vanoppen K, Yao H. AI can revolutionise education but technology is not enough: Human development meets cultural evolution. Journal of Human Development and Capabilities. 2025;1–11. DOI: 10.1080/19452829.2025.2517740

[6] Shen H, Knearem T, Ghosh R, Alkiek K, Krishna K, Liu Y, . . . Jurgens D. Position: Towards Bidirectional Human-AI Alignment. In: The Thirty-Ninth Annual Conference on Neural Information Processing Systems Position Paper Track. 2025. Available from: https://openreview.net/forum?id=PgA9rZoMY8

[7] Shen H, Knearem T, Ghosh R, Liu MX, Monroy-Hernández A, Wu T, . . . Hearst M. Bidirectional Human-AI Alignment: Emerging Challenges and Opportunities. In: Proceedings of the Extended Abstracts of the CHI Conference on Human Factors in Computing Systems; (2025, April). 1–6. DOI: 10.1145/3706599.3716291

[8] Shen H, Knearem T, Ghosh R, Yang YJ, Mitra T, Huang Y. Valuecompass: A framework of fundamental values for human-AI alignment. arXiv Preprint. 2024; arXiv:2409.09586. Available from: https://arxiv.org/abs/2409.09586

[9] Tsai YS, Perrotta C, Gaševi D. Empowering learners with personalised learning approaches? Agency, equity and transparency in the context of learning analytics. Assessment & Evaluation in Higher Education. 2020;**45**(4):554–567. DOI: 10.1080/02602938.2019.1676396

[10] Prabhudesai S, Kasi AP, Mansingh A, Das Antar A, Shen H, Banovic N. "Here the GPT made a choice, and every choice can be biased": How Students critically engage with LLMs through end-user auditing activity. In: Proceedings of the 2025 CHI Conference on Human Factors in Computing Systems; (2025, April 1–23); DOI: 10.1145/3706598.3713714

[11] Gabriel I. Artificial intelligence, values, and alignment. Minds and

Machines. 2020;**30**(3):411–437. DOI: 10.1007/s11023-020-09539-2

[12] Land S, Jonassen D. Theoretical Foundations of Learning Environments. Routledge; 2012. Available from: https://lchc.ucsd.edu/People/MCole/theoreticalfoundations.pdf

[13] Lleo A, Ruiz-Palomino P, Guillen M, Marrades-Pastor E. The role of ethical trustworthiness in shaping trust and affective commitment in schools. Ethics & Behavior. 2023;**33** (2):151–173. DOI: 10.1080/10508422.2022.2034504

[14] Schwartz SH. A theory of cultural values and some implications. 1999. Available from: https://books.google.com.hk/books?hl=en&lr=&id=mnNZxPa68IC&oi=fnd&pg=PA23&dq=+Schwartz%E2%80%99s+theory+of+basic+values&ots=3TUYdHejf5&sig=-e-KhtFZtQAfAj4LWfg1X8-960I&rediresc=y#v=onepage&q=Schwartz%E2%80%99s%20theory%20of%20basic%20values&f=false [Accessed: 1999-February-23]

[15] Schwartz SH. An overview of the Schwartz theory of basic values. Online Readings in Psychology and Culture. 2012;**2**(1):11. Available from: https://scholarworks.gvsu.edu/orpc/vol2/iss1/11/

[16] Khan WN. Ethical challenges of AI in education: Balancing innovation with data privacy. AI EDIFY Journal. 2024;**1** (1):1–13. Available from: https://researchcorridor.org/index.php/aiej/article/view/238

[17] Alawneh YJJ, Radwan ENZ, Salman FN, Makhlouf SI, Makhamreh K, Alawneh MS. Ethical considerations in the use of AI in primary education: Privacy, bias, and inclusivity. In: 2024 International Conference on Knowledge Engineering and Communication Systems (ICKECS); IEEE 2024. Available from: https://ieeexplore.ieee.org/abstract/document/10616986/

[18] Lata P. Towards equitable learning: Exploring Artificial Intelligence in inclusive education. Issue 5 International Journal of Law, Management and Human. 2024;7:416. Available from: https://heinonline.org/hol-cgi-bin/get_pdf.cgi?handle=hein.journals/ijlmhs31section=35

[19] Monett D, Paquet G. Against the Commodification of Education—if harms then not AI. Journal of Open, Distance, and Digital Education. 2025;**2** (1). Available from: https://ojs.uni-oldenburg.de/journals/ojs2/ojs/index.php/jodde/article/view/47

[20] Holmes W, Persson J, Chounta IA, Wasson B, Dimitrova V. Artificial Intelligence and education: A Critical View through the Lens of Human Rights, Democracy and the Rule of Law. Council of Europe; 2022. Available from: https://books.google.com.hk/books?hl=en&lr=&id=RM-lEAAAQBAJ&oi=fnd&pg=PA5&dq=Aligning+AI+with+ethical+values+is+only+one+part+of+the+equation%3B+it+must+also+align+with+the+substantive+goals+of+education+itself&ots=gddYIs-ez-&sig=83xOlUQighxnUQxfGY2CYo58bc&rediresc=y#v=onepage&q&f=false

[21] Gabriel I, Ghazavi V. The challenge of value alignment. The Oxford Handbook of Digital Ethics. 2022. 336–355. Available from: https://books.google.com.hk/books?hl=enlr=id=2bjiEAAAQBAJoi=fndpg=PA336dq=what+needs+to+be+AI+aligned+is+only+the+first+stepots=ijasVqkvE8sig=aHUBA4RVzwu2ludn-

HcENEvMZIsredir_esc=y#v=onepageq f=false

[22] Ji J, Qiu T, Chen B, Zhang B, Lou H, Wang K, . . . Gao W. Ai alignment: A comprehensive survey. arXiv Preprint. 2023;arXiv:2310.19852. Available from: https://arxiv.org/abs/2310.19852 [Accessed: 2026-February-23]

[23] Ramachandran M. AI ethics by design with AI reference architecture: Embedding ethics by design in AI architecture. In: Engineering Ethics of AI by Design: Principles, Practices, and Frameworks for Responsible Artificial Intelligence. Singapore: Springer Nature Singapore; 2025. p. 409–464. DOI: 10.1007/978-981-95-2909-4_9

[24] Smuha NA. Beyond the individual: Governing AI's societal harm. Internet Policy Review. 2021;**10**(3). Available from: https://papers.ssrn.com/sol3/papers.cfm?abstract_id=3941956

[25] Cath C. Governing artificial intelligence: Ethical, legal and technical opportunities and challenges. Philosophical Transactions of the Royal Society A: Mathematical, Physical and Engineering Sciences. 2018;**376** (2133):20180080. DOI: 10.1098/rsta.2018.0080

[26] Cheong I, Caliskan A, Kohno T. Safeguarding human values: Rethinking US law for generative AI's societal impacts. AI and Ethics. 2025;**5**(2):1433–1459. DOI: 10.1007/s43681-024-00451-4

[27] Shneiderman B. Bridging the gap between ethics and practice: Guidelines for reliable, safe, and trustworthy human-centered AI systems. ACM Transactions on Interactive Intelligent Systems. 2020;**10**(4):1–31. DOI: 10.1145/3419764

[28] Ryan M, Stahl BC. Artificial intelligence ethics guidelines for developers and users: Clarifying their content and normative implications. Journal of Information, Communication and Ethics in Society. 2021;**19**(1):61–86. Available from: https://www.emerald.com/jices/article/19/1/61/213924

[29] Shen H, Ma Z, Ghosh R, Knearem T, Liu MX, Wu T, . . . Li Y ICLR 2025 Workshop on bidirectional human-AI alignment. In: ICLR 2025 Workshop Proposals. Availabe from: https://openreview.net/forum?id=HcTiacDN8N [Accessed: 2026-February-23]

[30] Shen H, Gordon M, Kalai AT. Tutorial: Human-AI alignment: Foundations, methods, practice, and challenges. Available from: https://hua-shen.org/assets/files/neurips_2025_tutorial.pdf [Accessed: 2026-February-23]

[31] Pedro F, Subosa M, Rivas A, Valverde P. Artificial intelligence in education: Challenges and opportunities for sustainable development. 2019. Available from: https://repositorio.minedu.gob.pe/handle/20.500.12799/6533 [Accessed: 2026-February-23]

[32] Schiff D. Out of the laboratory and into the classroom: The future of artificial intelligence in education. AI & Society. 2021;**36**(1):331–348. DOI: 10.1007/s00146-020-01033-8

[33] Chen L, Chen P, Lin Z. Artificial intelligence in education: A review. IEEE Access. 2020;**8**:75264–75278. Available from: https://ieeexplore.ieee.org/abstract/document/9069875/

[34] Kayyali M. The evolution of AI in education from concept to classroom. In: Navigating Barriers to AI

Implementation in the Classroom. IGI Global Scientific Publishing; 2025. p. 325–368. Available from: https://www.igi-global.com/chapter/the-evolution-of-ai-in-education-from-concept-to-classroom/382086 [Accessed: 2026-February-23]

[35] Ahmed ZE, Hassan AA, Saeed RA, Eds. AI-Enhanced Teaching Methods. IGI Global; 2024. Available from: https://books.google.com.hk/books?hl=enlr=id=l-UEEQAAQBAJoi=fndpg=PR1dq=AI+such+as+grading+multiple-choice+tests,+scheduling+classes,+or+delivering+drill-and-practice+exercisesots=jqCx5h9vQhsig=nl03Jvr3YEaOJXx2TenbE7dp1U4redir_esc=y#v=onepageqf=false [Accessed: 2026-February-23]

[36] Filgueiras F. Artificial intelligence and education governance. Education, Citizenship and Social Justice. 2024;**19**(3):349–361. DOI: 10.1177/17461979231160674

[37] Mariam G, Adil L, Zakaria B. The integration of artificial intelligence (ai) into education systems and its impact on the governance of higher education institutions. International Journal of Professional Business Review. 2024;**9**(12):13. Available from: https://dialnet.unirioja.es/servlet/articulo?codigo=9868422 [Accessed: 2026-February-23]

[38] George B, Wooden O. Managing the strategic transformation of higher education through artificial intelligence. Administrative Sciences. 2023;**13**(9):196. Available from: https://www.mdpi.com/2076-3387/13/9/196 [Accessed: 2026-February-23]

[39] Schiff D. Education for AI, not AI for education: The role of education and ethics in national AI policy strategies. International Journal of Artificial Intelligence in Education. 2022;**32**(3):527–563. DOI: 10.1007/s40593-021-00270-2

[40] Selwyn N. Should Robots Replace Teachers?: AI and the Future of Education. John Wiley & Sons; 2019. Available from: https://books.google.com.hk/books?hl=enlr=id=wcm1DwAAQBAJoi=fndpg=PT6dq=s+AI+tools+become+more+embedded+in+classrooms+and+educational+institu-+tions,+their+influence+extends+beyond+instructional+delivery+to+the+very+structure+of+teaching,+learning,+and+governance.ots=KJzF4A-5m1sig=72YKsB1tM69VaNnQCmRSOyMJVkAredir_esc=y#v=onepageqf=false [Accessed: 2026-February-23]

Chapter 5

From Enchantment to Responsibility: Cultivating Ethical Action through Critical AI Literacy in Education

Renato Essenfelder

Abstract

This chapter addresses the ethical and epistemological challenges posed by the integration of artificial intelligence (AI) into educational environments. While AI tools are increasingly promoted as solutions for personalization, efficiency, and learning optimization, their use often leads to a reduction of pedagogical complexity and a shift toward epistemic passivity. Students are encouraged to accept machine outputs without question, while teachers are repositioned as facilitators of opaque systems whose inner workings they do not understand. Drawing on a critical theoretical framework and building on the distinction between ethical form and ethical action (Essenfelder et al., 2023), the chapter proposes an approach to Critical AI Literacy that moves beyond technical skills to include reflexive, ethical, and interpretive competencies. It presents four pedagogical strategies designed to foster this literacy: *Debunk the Bot*, *Algorithm Audits*, *Ethical Simulations*, and *Prompt Criticism*. These interventions are meant to help students interrogate algorithmic outputs, understand systemic biases, and reclaim authorship in AI-mediated contexts. The chapter argues that AI should not be rejected outright, nor adopted uncritically, but engaged with as a socio-technical system that shapes what counts as knowledge, learning, and agency. Ultimately, the goal is to cultivate students' capacity for ethical action in technologically mediated environments and to reassert education as a space of dissent, deliberation, and epistemic responsibility. Critical AI Literacy, we suggest, is not an optional enrichment but a necessary condition for preserving the democratic and humanistic ethos of education in the age of intelligent systems.

Keywords: education, AI Literacy, ethics, epistemology, algorithmic bias, artificial intelligence, AIEd, automation in education

1. Introduction

In recent years, artificial intelligence (AI) has undergone a profound shift, moving from research laboratories and speculative fiction to school curricula, teacher dashboards, and student essays. What was once a distant technological horizon has become an everyday presence, often presented as a "neutral" solution to the most pressing challenges in education: personalizing learning, reducing dropout rates, and streamlining assessment. The promise is alluring, the vocabulary is seductive, and perfectly aligned with the core values of late capitalism: "efficiency," "adaptivity," and "scale." Yet, beneath the surface of these promises lie deep, unresolved ethical questions related to AI in general that cannot be addressed by metrics alone – questions that are especially dangerous when we consider all the complexity and vulnerabilities of our learning environments.

Essenfelder et al. [1] remind us that the question is not whether AI *is ethical* in the abstract sense, but whether its adoption in education enables conditions for *ethical action* – a notion grounded in lived experience, concrete dilemmas, and relational responsibility. They argue that in the educational field, what matters is not the mere alignment of AI systems with predefined ethical "forms" or universalized principles (that may even look perfectly solid and correct at a distance), but the capacity of these systems, and of those who deploy them, to support contextualized decisions, reflexivity, and human autonomy.

Ethical action, in this sense, emerges not from regulatory compliance or techno-legal correctness but from the recognition that classrooms are spaces of ambiguity, vulnerability, and negotiation, where learning is not merely cognitive but ethical and social.

Rather than asking whether AI technologies conform to a set of idealized standards (like: "*Is it fair?*" "*Is it unbiased?*"), the more urgent pedagogical question becomes: What kinds of relationships, responsibilities, and subjectivities are being formed through the massive use of these systems? In a context where machine outputs are increasingly taken as truth and algorithmic judgment as neutral, the move toward ethical action is not rhetorical but necessary. It requires educators and students alike to confront the ways in which technological tools participate in shaping what can be known, said, and done, and to reclaim agency within those processes.

What we see emerging in classrooms is not only the presence of AI but also its growing *authority*. As students interact with large language models (such as ChatGPT and Gemini), adaptive tutors, and predictive dashboards, they are subtly trained to trust machine outputs, often without understanding how those outputs are generated or what assumptions they encode. This phenomenon, widely described as "automation bias," undermines one of the most fundamental aims of education: to form autonomous subjects capable of critical reflection.

This erosion of critical distance in student–machine interactions echoes the automation bias [2]: the tendency to favor suggestions from automated decision-making systems and to dismiss contradictory arguments and information that were humanly developed or presented, without recourse to automation, even if it is correct.

In educational settings, this bias manifests not only in the uncritical acceptance of machine-generated content but also in the gradual reconfiguration of epistemic authority itself, from human inquiry to statistical plausibility. Automation can increase user complacency and reduce vigilance [3], especially when the system performs sufficiently well most of the time. The pedagogical implications are significant: If learners are habituated to trusting algorithmic outputs without interrogation, they may lose the disposition to engage in epistemic struggle, which is the very process through which critical thinking and ethical discernment are cultivated. In this sense, automation bias should not be read merely as a technical vulnerability; rather, it is an educational liability. To resist it, educational environments must actively foster habits of doubt, verification, and interpretive agency – skills that are foundational to any democratic conception of learning.

When faced with exhausted or underprepared teachers, instead of doubt, students are encouraged to accept. Instead of exercising creativity, critical authorship, or imaginative construction, they are increasingly positioned as curators, simply assembling and adapting machine-generated outputs.

The problem of AIEd, then, is not mainly technological (i.e., "*What are the best tools*?"). It is epistemological and pedagogical. AI does not merely offer instruments; it reorganizes relationships with knowledge and recalibrates what counts as "thinking."

Most AI systems in use today are not designed to emulate human reasoning but to be "efficient" within bounded, data-driven constraints. Their outputs may be coherent and fluent, but coherence is not the same as truth, and fluency is not the same as understanding. As Chomsky et al. [4] argue, systems such as ChatGPT are best understood as "pastiche machines" – capable of mimicking linguistic form but fundamentally incapable of generating meaning or engaging in genuine reasoning.

In a similar vein, Marcus [5] has referred to large language models as "stochastic parrots," which means statistical engines that recombine existing linguistic patterns without understanding their meaning or consequences. While these systems can produce text that appears coherent, even eloquent, their outputs are fundamentally disconnected from the cognitive and ethical structures that ground human thought and responsibility.

Faced with this scenario, educators are placed in a difficult (yet vital) position. If they are to resist the uncritical adoption of AI, they must be equipped to mediate its use ethically, pedagogically, and politically. In this sense, this chapter argues that one of the most urgent tasks of education today is to develop what we call Critical AI Literacy: a pedagogical approach that empowers students to interrogate algorithmic systems, identify their biases, understand their limitations, and make better decisions about when to trust, when to challenge, and when to disengage.

To that end, this chapter unfolds in three movements. Firstly, we examine the limitations of ethical frameworks in the AI and education discourse, particularly their disconnection from everyday classroom realities. Secondly, we analyze how uncritical interactions with AI systems can foster epistemic passivity and diminish student agency. Thirdly, we propose a set of pedagogical practices, ranging from Algorithm Audits to error-based learning exercises and simulated ethical dilemmas, that aim to restore space for ethical action in AI-mediated educational environments.

The goal is not to reject AI outright, nor to idealize human judgment. Rather, it is to defend a space, which is fragile and increasingly rare, where students can learn not just to use intelligent systems but to be able to think with, or even against, them.

2. Epistemological passivity

The field of artificial intelligence in education (AIEd) is expanding rapidly. In their comprehensive bibliometric analysis, Durak et al. [6] examined a curated corpus of 1,726 academic articles on AIEd, published between 2013 and 2023 and indexed in the Web of Science database. Their findings confirm a rapid growth in the field, with the United States and China emerging as the dominant contributors in terms of volume and citation impact.

At first glance, this explosion of research may signal a maturing field, but sheer volume does not equal depth. A closer look reveals a paradox: As the language of ethics becomes more prevalent in institutional discourse, its practical translation into classroom life becomes more elusive.

The mainstreaming of AI in educational contexts has been strongly reinforced by leading strategic documents in the field. According to the Horizon Report 2023 [7], the two most significant technological drivers shaping the future of education are as follows: (a) AI-enabled applications for predictive personal learning and (b) generative AI.

This emphasis not only reflects a growing institutional interest in automation and personalization but also consolidates a pedagogical imaginary centered on prediction and production. Under this framework, students are no longer seen as active agents in open-ended learning processes but rather as data profiles to be optimized and nudged. The promise of personalization, while rhetorically appealing, often disguises a deeper shift toward prescriptive learning paths and standardized outputs, raising important questions about creativity, agency, and the narrowing of epistemic horizons, as Essenfelder et al. [1] states. As such, the Horizon Report functions less as a neutral diagnosis than as a technopolitical artifact: It shapes expectations, orients funding, and codifies which futures are desirable and which are not.

From corporate guidelines to UNESCO reports and European frameworks, the field has produced dozens of documents listing ethical principles for AI, such as transparency, accountability, nonmaleficence, fairness, and privacy [8]. These principles are important but insufficient. They function as ethical forms, with some moral orientation but no pedagogical agency. Ethical forms suggest that ethics can be ensured through design; ethical action, by contrast, recognizes that the classroom is not a neutral container but a living space of asymmetries, judgment, conflict, and care.

This tension is particularly stark in the context of AI technologies. Despite growing recognition that AI is a socio-technical artifact, shaped by data choices, institutional agendas, and political economies [9, 10], educational technologies are often presented as intelligent, neutral, and objective. The language itself participates in the myth: We speak of systems that "learn," "decide," or "understand," when, in fact, they configure, calculate, and correlate. As Holmes [10] points out, this anthropomorphism feeds a form of "automation enchantment," making it difficult for educators and students alike to question the authority of the machine.

The result is widespread confusion between ethical design and ethical engagement. A learning platform may be GDPR-compliant (in Europe), avoid discriminatory data, and offer algorithmic explainability, but still suppress student agency, flatten complexity, or encourage epistemic passivity. As Durak et al. [6] note, most implementations of AI in education prioritize optimization over reflection and prediction over pedagogy. In such contexts, ethics becomes a matter of compliance, not transformation.

Moreover, these frameworks are frequently disconnected from the lived realities of classrooms, which poses a relevant threat. Ethics in education must begin not with abstract principles but with situated action – the concrete ways in which

DOI: http://dx.doi.org/10.5772/intechopen.1012997

teachers and students negotiate power, meaning, and responsibility in learning environments. Ethical literacy, in this view, is not an external condition to be "added" to AI systems, but an internal disposition to be cultivated in practice.

The critical question, then, is not (only) whether AI is aligned with ethical principles, but whether it enables ethical practices in the everyday life of education. Does it foster discernment and critical authorship? Or does it outsource decisions to systems whose logic remains opaque and whose outputs remain unchallenged? The latter scenario appears to be increasingly common – and increasingly dangerous.

When AI systems are accepted uncritically, taken at face value, without interrogation, they risk reshaping educational subjectivity itself. Students become less likely to question and more likely to delegate. Instead of cultivating epistemic agency, we risk producing a generation of passive curators of algorithmic output. It is precisely this shift – from decision to delegation, from action to adherence – that demands renewed attention to pedagogical ethics in the age of AI.

One of the most insidious effects of uncritical AI adoption in education is epistemological: It fosters a mode of engagement in which students are gradually trained to just accept things as they are, rather than question. This is what we refer to as "epistemic passivity," a condition in which the perceived authority of the algorithm silences the uncertainty of inquiry. What is at stake here is not merely the accuracy of machine outputs, but the formation of the learner as a subject of knowledge.

This shift is particularly evident in the use of generative AI tools for writing, summarization, and language processing. When a system produces a coherent answer, students are often left with few cues to evaluate its validity, especially if the text is syntactically plausible. The danger is not that students will be misled by occasional errors, but that they will stop asking whether the text means anything at all.

The classroom, under the increasing influence of AI, risks becoming a site of epistemic outsourcing – a space where judgment is delegated to algorithms and interpretation is replaced by automation. As Holmes et al. [9, 10] point out, many AI systems operate under the rhetorical guise of personalization, yet function primarily as instruments of standardization and control, structured by logics of efficiency and predictive modeling. Far from fostering individualized learning, these tools often delimit the scope of what can be known or done.

Prediction, as an epistemological mode, is inherently conservative: It extrapolates from past data to infer future outcomes, thereby naturalizing historical patterns and reinforcing biases [11]. This process is described as the "datafication of education," where complex learning processes are reduced to measurable inputs and outputs, reconfiguring students as statistical subjects [12]. It is further argued that such developments are rarely pedagogically driven; rather, they reflect managerial imperatives that prioritize scalability over meaningful engagement [13]. Additionally, the EdTech industry frequently cloaks these tendencies in mythic narratives of disruption and innovation, obscuring their effects on teacher autonomy and educational purpose.

Together, these critiques reveal that the expansion of AI in education is not merely a technical development but a political and epistemological shift, demanding urgent scrutiny and pedagogical resistance.

In such a setting, the role of the learner shifts from one who helps to construct knowledge through dialog and reflection to one who selects from preformulated possibilities. The educational process risks becoming a choreography of responses, where the space for ethical action collapses into functional decision trees.

The amount of data may be huge, the predictions may be (eventually) precise, but the pedagogical horizon narrows. As Zawacki-Richter et al. [14] observe, the teacher's role in this scenario often becomes secondary, reduced to a facilitator of systems whose logic they did not design and whose assumptions they may not fully understand. This delegation of authority results in a gradual erosion of epistemic autonomy, masked by the rhetoric of innovation.

In that sense, the bibliometric mapping of AIEd [6] documents a striking expansion in the number of studies published over the past decade, but few studies interrogate the underlying assumptions of the technologies being deployed or critically engage with their impact on the student experience. The risk is that we are building a field that knows how to implement but not how to reflect.

If education is to reclaim its critical function in the age of AI, it must resist this tendency toward epistemic outsourcing. It must create interruptions in the automated flow of information, spaces where students can doubt, contest, and re-signify what the machine delivers. As we will argue in the next section, this requires not only technical knowledge but also pedagogical courage: The courage to make visible what the system obscures, to ask what the algorithm ignores, and to restore the learner as a thinking subject, capable not just of using AI, but of thinking with, without, and even against it.

3. Pedagogies of Critical AI Literacy

If, as we have argued, the uncritical use of AIEd gives huge incentives to epistemic passivity and algorithmic dependence, then the task before educators is urgent: to design pedagogical practices that preserve or restore critical judgment and epistemic autonomy. This means moving beyond the question of how to use AI in the classroom and asking instead how to teach students to think beyond the systems they encounter.

In that sense, what follows is not a definitive curriculum but a set of replicable interventions, rooted in dialog and reflexivity, that aim to cultivate Critical AI Literacy as a lived practice in classrooms.

These pedagogical interventions were piloted and refined through classroom practice in higher education institutions in Portugal, where the author teaches across undergraduate, master, and doctoral levels in the fields of Communication Sciences and Psychology. Implemented over multiple semesters between 2022 and 2025, these exercises proved not only feasible but intellectually challenging, offering students structured opportunities to interrogate the assumptions embedded in AI systems and to reflect critically on their own patterns of trust, delegation, and judgment. Specifically, they were implemented in courses focused on scientific methodology, cyberculture, contemporary economy, and contemporary politics – disciplines where the relationship between knowledge, power, and technological mediation is continuously examined.

Activities such as *Prompt Criticism* and *Algorithm Audits* resonated strongly with students, particularly in their ability to reveal the epistemic and political implications of everyday interactions with so-called *intelligent* systems. Rather than treating AI as a neutral layer of technical enhancement, these interventions positioned it as an object of inquiry, inviting students to engage with it as both users and critical analysts. The exercises thus contributed not only to digital and ethical literacy but to the formation of epistemically autonomous subjects – an outcome that is increasingly vital in educational landscapes shaped by automation and algorithmic authority.

3.1 Debunk the Bot

One of the simplest yet perhaps most effective strategies to initiate critical engagement is to invite students to challenge the authority of the machine. In a "Debunk the Bot" exercise, students are presented with AI-generated outputs, such as summaries, direct answers, intricate arguments, or translations, and tasked with verifying, refuting, or revising them. These texts may contain factual errors, biased assumptions, logical inconsistencies, or stylistic flaws, many of which are difficult to detect at first glance.

The objective is not to dismiss the utility of the machines but to train the students' attention and critical skills: What is being claimed by the algorithm? What is missing? What assumptions are embedded (can we spot any biases)? What is the source, and can it be trusted? This activity turns the students from passive recipients into active examiners, restoring space for doubt and evaluative judgment.

Such practices echo what Chomsky et al. [4] describe as the need to distinguish between surface plausibility and semantic depth. They also resonate with Marcus's [5] critique of "stochastic parrots": systems that excel in linguistic form but falter in meaning.

This technique was particularly effective in a session on contemporary politics (focused on a class for a master's degree in communication sciences) centered on the global rise of far-right populism. Students were prompted to use generative AI tools to produce short essays or summaries answering the question: *"What explains the recent rise of far-right movements in Europe and Latin America?"* The AI-generated responses, while grammatically polished, often reflected uncritical syntheses of mainstream discourse, frequently reducing complex political phenomena to vague notions of "economic anxiety" or "cultural backlash," while omitting critical dimensions such as historical fascism, structural racism, the power of ideology, algorithmic amplification, or media manipulation. Through close reading and discussion, students identified not only factual omissions and logical simplifications but also subtle ideological framings – for instance, the tendency to neutralize moral judgment by equating far-right populism with generic "political discontent."

The classroom became a space of *epistemic disruption*, where the authority of the machine was not rejected wholesale but placed under scrutiny. Students brought in alternative sources, proposed missing analytical lenses, and reflected on the implications of algorithmically generated narratives in shaping public opinion and historiography – maybe in the same way we would have done years ago, even before the Internet, comparing different mediatic approaches to a political event.

The pedagogical value of the exercise resided precisely in its capacity to restore interpretive agency: Students moved from consuming content to actively contesting it, and from trusting outputs to interrogating the assumptions that produce them. In doing so, they not only learned about far-right movements but also enacted a form of critical engagement that is indispensable for democratic life in the age of AI.

3.2 Algorithm Audits

Another layer of Critical AI Literacy involves exposing, as thoroughly as possible, the operational logic of the tools themselves. Many educational platforms use recommendation engines, predictive scores, or automated feedback systems whose internal workings are opaque to both teachers and students. However, Algorithm Audits, conducted at a classroom level, can help to understand how these systems sort, prioritize, or evaluate learners.

Students might compare the outputs they receive based on different input variables (e.g., prompts, grammar choices, metadata) and reflect on what changes, what remains stable, and what this reveals about the system's embedded logic [9, 10]. It emphasizes that such opacity is not a technical accident but a structural feature of algorithmic governance. By demystifying the tool, the audit becomes an ethical act: It returns agency to the learner and repositions the teacher as a mediator.

This strategy also aligns with what Zawacki-Richter et al. [14] call for: greater involvement of educators in understanding and critically engaging with educational AI, rather than merely facilitating its use. When students and teachers jointly interrogate how a system works, and for whom, it becomes possible to reimagine its function not as a neutral arbiter, but as a political actor within the pedagogical process.

This approach proved especially fruitful in a scientific methodology course taught in the psychology program, where students were learning how to formulate research questions, assess the validity of sources, and construct robust scientific arguments. As part of a module on literature reviews and hypothesis building, students were invited to use LLMs (ChatGPT, Claude, and Gemini) to generate short research proposals on a given topic, such as the relationship between social media use and anxiety in adolescents, a subject with a massive amount of data available today. They were then asked to submit variations of the prompts, altering keywords, syntactic structure, or disciplinary framing (e.g., "clinical psychology" vs. "neuroscience").

What emerged from this collective exercise was a striking pattern of algorithmic preference: Certain framings consistently led the system to reproduce behaviorist interpretations, while others prompted more neurobiological or diagnostic perspectives. Few prompts yielded proposals that incorporated critical theory, qualitative methods, or sociocultural frameworks, revealing not only the training data's dominant paradigms but also the system's ideological bias toward positivist epistemologies. Students were asked to analyze the implications: What kinds of science are being made possible, and which are being rendered invisible? How does the system's output shape their understanding of what counts as a valid research question?

By treating the tool not as a neutral assistant but as an epistemic filter, the exercise enabled students to connect methodological rigor with ethical responsibility. The audit process thus deepened their understanding of scientific reasoning itself, not as a linear technique but as a contested and contextual practice. It also reinforced the role of the teacher not as a transmitter of correct procedure but as a guide in the negotiation of complexity, ambiguity, and power within the research process.

3.3 Ethical simulations

While much of the discussion around AI in education focuses on efficiency and outcomes, what is often missing is the space to deliberate on ethical dilemmas.

Critical AI Literacy also involves the ability to reflect on consequences, imagine alternatives, and reason morally within technological systems.

In ethical simulations, students are presented with realistic scenarios involving AI use in education: For example, a peer submits a paper generated by ChatGPT without citation; a learning platform flags a student as "at risk" and suggests intervention; and a teacher relies on an AI tool that subtly penalizes nonstandard language varieties. Students may be asked: What would you do? What values are in tension? Who is accountable?

These exercises serve to restore ethical action as a central goal of education, as proposed by Essenfelder et al. [1]. They position students not merely as users or regulators, but as moral agents capable of judgment and pressing for transformation. In this way, Critical AI Literacy becomes not a skill set but a key mode of subjectivation, a broad ethical orientation toward technology and the world.

If AI threatens to automate decision-making and flatten difference, then pedagogy must respond by reopening those spaces: for doubt, for dissent. What these three interventions share is a commitment to disruption – disruption of the output, and also of the illusion of neutrality. They insist that to learn with AI, one must also learn to say no to it, to interrogate its frames, to reframe its outputs, and to reassert the human perspective as fundamental.

3.4 Prompt Criticism

A fourth pedagogical strategy to cultivate Critical AI Literacy lies not in challenging the output of generative systems but in scrutinizing the conditions that produce it – at least the conditions that we can still have some agency over: the prompts. This is the work of Prompt Criticism, a collective classroom exercise that asks students to interrogate and deconstruct the prompts themselves.

Most educational uses of generative AI begin with a seemingly innocuous instruction: "Write a persuasive essay on. . .," "Summarize this article in 100 words. . .," "Generate a multiple-choice quiz on. . .." Such prompts appear neutral, yet they encode assumptions about genre, authority, discourse, and audience. As Noble [15] argues in her study of algorithmic bias, technological systems reflect the hegemonies of the societies that produce them. In this light, prompts are not mere queries; they are acts of framing, delimiting what counts as relevant, valuable, or even intelligible to the machine.

In this activity, students are asked to examine a set of standardized prompts and reflect on the values they embed: What is being asked? In what tone? What perspectives are privileged or excluded? They then rewrite the prompts with the intention of subverting their default assumptions, introducing alternative voices, destabilizing fixed genres, or posing open-ended, ambiguous tasks that resist proceduralization. For instance, a prompt such as "Summarize the causes of the French Revolution" might be reworked into "What perspectives are typically omitted when AI summarizes the French Revolution, and why?"

The exercise culminates in a comparative analysis of the outputs produced by the original and reimagined prompts. The pedagogical goal is twofold: first, to make visible the performative role of language in shaping algorithmic reasoning [8], and second, to return to students the authority to shape the communicative frame and to author not only responses but the very questions posed to the system.

While both *Algorithm Audits* and *Prompt Criticism* involve critical engagement with AI systems through language-based interactions, they operate at distinct levels of analysis and pedagogical intent. *Algorithm Audits* focus primarily on the systemic behavior of the AI, seeking to uncover how different inputs are processed, categorized, or weighted by the underlying model. The goal is to illuminate the internal logic and biases of the system itself, often through comparative testing and reflection on hidden parameters such as genre preferences, disciplinary framings, or linguistic norms. *Prompt Criticism*, by contrast, turns the analytical gaze toward the *human framing* of the interaction, examining how the way we phrase prompts encodes ideological assumptions, epistemic constraints, and discursive power. Whereas "audits" ask, *"How does the machine work?"*, "Prompt Criticism" asks, *"What are we asking of the machine – and why?"*

Together, these exercises form complementary dimensions of Critical AI Literacy: One aimed at demystifying the algorithm, the other at reclaiming the human act of intentional question design.

Besides that, Prompt Criticism, as with the other exercises listed in this chapter, is not about rejecting AI use *per se*, but about reclaiming intentionality and epistemic agency in the process. It insists that the locus of creativity and responsibility lies not in the machine, but in the way we name, describe, and direct our engagement with it.

Taken together, these four exercises (Debunk the Bot, Algorithm Audits, Ethical Simulations, and Prompt Criticism) form a constellation of pedagogical interventions aimed at cultivating not just technical fluency, but ethical, epistemic, and discursive agency. When implemented consistently and dialogically across the academic year, they can help students develop skills that are not incidental but foundational to higher education: critical thinking, ethical reasoning, reflective judgment, and the capacity to act meaningfully in uncertain and contested knowledge environments.

As Barnett [16] argues, the role of higher education is not merely to deliver knowledge but to foster the student's capacity to live purposefully in a world of uncertainty and change. In this sense, Critical AI Literacy should not be treated as a peripheral digital competency but as a core educational imperative in an age increasingly mediated by algorithmic systems. It is through this kind of literacy, rigorous and reflective, that students may reclaim their place not only as users of intelligent technologies but as thoughtful interlocutors and responsible cocreators of the futures these systems help shape.

4. Conclusion

This chapter has argued that the integration of AIEd, far from being a neutral or inevitable process, raises deep pedagogical, ethical, and epistemological challenges. While the rhetoric surrounding AI in education often highlights its potential to personalize learning and optimize outcomes, we have shown that such promises are not without cost. When deployed uncritically, AI systems risk producing what we have called epistemic passivity: a condition in which students outsource judgment to algorithms, accept outputs without scrutiny, and reduce learning to procedural consumption.

To counter this tendency, we proposed a pedagogical framework rooted in Critical AI Literacy, understood not as a set of technical skills but as a form of epistemological, interpretive agency. Drawing on the distinction between ethical form and ethical action [1], we argue that students must be empowered not only to use AI systems but also to interrogate and reframe them. This demands a deliberate effort to reintroduce friction and dissent into educational spaces increasingly shaped by automation.

The four pedagogical strategies explored – Debunk the Bot, Algorithm Audits, Ethical Simulations, and Prompt Criticism – are examples of how such literacy can be cultivated in practice. These exercises are designed to disrupt the illusion of neutrality, expose the ideological framings embedded in algorithmic systems, and restore the learner's capacity for critical authorship and ethical judgment.

Ultimately, our claim is not that AI should be excluded from education, nor that human judgment is always and inherently superior. Rather, we insist that education must remain a space where technologies are questioned, interpreted, and contested, and not merely applied. As Barnett [16] reminds us, the true purpose of higher education is to prepare individuals to live and act in a world marked by uncertainty, complexity, and contestation.

In this spirit, Critical AI Literacy is not an elective enrichment; it is a condition for preserving the ethical and democratic integrity of education in the age of intelligent machines.

Author details

Renato Essenfelder
University Fernando Pessoa, Porto, Portugal

*Address all correspondence to: ressenfelder@ufp.edu.pt

References

[1] Essenfelder R, Araújo DLD, and César TC. Da forma ética à ação ética: Riscos na adoção da inteligência artificial em sala de aula. In: Educação E Tecnologias: Formação Docente, Inteligência Artificial E Humanismo Em Tempos de Desafios. Lopes, Luis Fernando, and Cavazzani, André Moscaleski São Paulo: Editora Bagai; 2023: 113–130. DOI: 10.37008/978-65-5368-316-7.07.12.23.6

[2] Parasuraman R, Riley V. Humans and automation: Use, misuse, disuse, abuse. Human Factors: The Journal of the Human Factors and Ergonomics Society. 1997;**39**(2):230–253

[3] Cummings ML. Automation bias in intelligent time critical decision support systems. In: Decision Making in Aviation. London: Routledge; 2017. p. 289–294

[4] Chomsky N, Roberts I, and Watumull J. The false promise of ChatGPT. The New York Times. Available from: https://www.nytimes.com/2023/03/08/opinion/noam-chomsky-chatgpt-ai.html. [Accessed: 2023-March-8]

[5] Marcus G. Artificial general intelligence is not as imminent as you might think. Scientific American. 2022;1 Available from: https://www.scientificamerican.com/article/artificial-general-intelligence-is-not-as-imminent-as-you-might-think1/

[6] Durak G, Çankaya S, Özdemir D, Can S. 2024. Artificial intelligence in education: A bibliometric study on its role in transforming teaching and learning. International Review of Research in Open and Distributed Learning. **25**(3):219–244. DOI: 10.19173/irrodl.v25i3.7757

[7] Pelletier K, Brown M, Daniel B, Chalmers D, and Specht M. EDUCAUSE Horizon Report: Teaching and Learning Edition. EDUCAUSE. 2023. Available from: https://library.educause.edu/resources/2023/4/2023-educause-horizon-report-teaching-and-learning-edition [Accessed: 2023-March-17]

[8] Jobin A, Ienca M, Vayena E. The global landscape of AI ethics guidelines. Nature Machine Intelligence. 2019;**1**(9):389–399

[9] Holmes W, Persson J, Chounta IA, Wasson B, and Dimitrova V. Artificial intelligence and education: A critical view through the lens of human rights, democracy and the rule of law. Council of Europe. 2022. Available from: https://unesdoc.unesco.org/ark:/48223/pf0000377074 [Accessed: 2023-March-30]

[10] Holmes W. AI and education: A critical studies perspective. In: Utilizing AI in Developing Education Systems. UNESCO 2021. Available from: https://discovery.ucl.ac.uk/id/eprint/10186094/

[11] Williamson B. Big Data in Education: The Digital Future of Learning, Policy and Practice. London: SAGE Publications; 2017

[12] Selwyn N. Should Robots Replace Teachers? AI and the Future of Education. Hoboken: John Wiley & Sons; 2019

[13] Watters A. Teaching Machines: The History of Personalized Learning. Cambridge: MIT Press; 2023

[14] Zawacki-Richter O, Marín VI, Bond M, Gouverneur F. Systematic

review of research on artificial intelligence applications in higher education – Where are the educators? International Journal of Educational Technology in Higher Education. 2019;**16**(1):1–27

[15] Noble SU. Algorithms of Oppression: How Search Engines Reinforce Racism. New York: New York University Press; 2018

[16] Barnett R. University knowledge in an age of supercomplexity. Higher Education. 2000;**40**(4):409–422

Chapter 6

Rethinking Pedagogy and Assessment in the Age of Generative AI

Matthew Montebello

Abstract

Generative artificial intelligence (GenAI) is emerging as a transformative force in higher education, disrupting long-standing pedagogical models and assessment practices. Far from being a threat, GenAI represents a necessary catalyst for updating academic practice to match the realities of a digitally saturated, socially networked, and innovation-driven world. Drawing on survey data from academics who participated in two sequential workshops – first on GenAI for teaching and assessment, and then on GenAI for academic research and writing – this chapter explores evolving perceptions, adoption patterns, and ethical considerations in academic contexts. It examines the dual role of GenAI as both a productivity amplifier and a source of pedagogical challenge, highlighting AI tools that can support both students and educators, from content generation and research synthesis to feedback and creative production. The discussion addresses the implications for instructional design, academic integrity, and student engagement, advocating for an intentional shift towards inquiry-based, creativity-oriented, and authenticity-driven teaching and assessment models. By proposing re-skilling pathways and institutional frameworks, the chapter offers a roadmap for harnessing GenAI's potential while safeguarding educational values and equity.

Keywords: generative AI, pedagogy, assessment, academic integrity, authentic learning

1. Introduction

The accelerating integration of generative artificial intelligence (GenAI) into higher education represents one of the most significant pedagogical turning points since the advent of the internet. Tools such as ChatGPT, Microsoft Copilot, Google Gemini, and Perplexity AI are not merely incremental innovations; they are transformative technologies capable of reshaping how educators design, deliver, and assess learning experiences [1, 2]. Rather than viewing GenAI as an existential threat to academic integrity, this chapter positions it as a necessary disruptor, a catalyst for rethinking long-entrenched pedagogies and aligning educational practice with the realities of a digitally networked, socially mediated, and AI-driven world [3–5].

In an era where students are adept at navigating multimodal, algorithmically curated content streams, traditional lecture-and-exam formats increasingly appear disconnected from learners' lived experiences [6, 7]. The convergence of social media culture, pervasive digital innovation, and the creative affordances of GenAI demands that educators adjust, adapt, and re-skill to remain relevant [8, 9]. This entails not only technical competence in AI tools but also a renewed focus on fostering critical thinking, creativity, and authenticity – competencies that cannot be outsourced to machines [10, 11].

Empirical data from the two workshops that underpin this chapter, first on *GenAI for Teaching and Assessment, followed by GenAI for Academic Research and Writing*, reveal a complex academic landscape. Participants ranged from early adopters who actively experiment with AI in teaching and scholarly work to cautious sceptics concerned with plagiarism, privacy, authorship transparency, and ethical use [12, 13]. Yet, across this spectrum, there is growing recognition that GenAI can enhance productivity, democratise access to resources, and stimulate pedagogical innovation [14, 15]. In this chapter, we respond to that recognition by contextualising GenAI within the broader history of educational technology disruption, while mapping the attitudes, experiences, and ethical concerns of academics through recent survey findings. We also showcase AI tools that support both educators and students in research, writing, and assessment contexts as we analyse implications for instructional design, academic integrity, and student engagement. Finally, we propose pedagogical and assessment models that embrace AI as a partner in learning while safeguarding educational values and equity. The argument builds on decades of research into adaptive learning, personalisation, and AI-enhanced pedagogy [16, 17], reframing GenAI not as an end in itself but as an enabler of richer, more authentic, and more inclusive learning environments. The challenge and opportunity lies in navigating the tension between innovation and tradition, automation and human judgment, speed and reflection. It is within this tension that the future of academic practice will be forged.

2. The disruptive nature of GenAI in higher education

The arrival of GenAI in higher education marks a transformative moment, not merely because of its technological capabilities but because of the scale and speed with which it challenges deeply embedded assumptions about teaching, learning, and scholarship [11, 18]. GenAI tools, such as OpenAI's ChatGPT, Anthropic's Claude, Google Gemini, Microsoft Copilot, Perplexity AI, and a growing ecosystem of AI-enabled research assistants, are already altering the academic landscape. These tools are capable of generating coherent essays, synthesising literature, producing programming code, generating visual artefacts, translating across languages, and designing interactive content, often within seconds. Such capabilities fundamentally challenge the idea that certain forms of academic production are uniquely human – a premise that has underpinned assessment design, authorship conventions, and pedagogical approaches for centuries [1, 2, 11].

2.1 From technological enhancement to pedagogical disruption

Disruption in higher education is not new. The introduction of the printing press in the fifteenth century transformed the accessibility and dissemination of knowledge [19], breaking the monopoly of handwritten manuscripts and altering the relationship between learner and text. Similarly, the rise of the internet in the late twentieth century redefined the boundaries of the classroom, enabling remote and asynchronous learning, while learning management systems (LMSs), such as Moodle, Blackboard, and Canvas, facilitated new models of course delivery and student engagement [6, 20]. In each instance, the technology not only improved efficiency but also forced a reconsideration of pedagogical norms and institutional structures.

However, the emergence of GenAI represents a qualitatively different form of disruption. Earlier technologies often served as conduits for information retrieval and distribution, whereas GenAI tools generate novel content on demand. This means that tasks historically used as proxies for learning, such as summarising an article, writing an essay, creating a data visualisation, or generating problem sets, can now be completed by an AI system with minimal human input. This shift undermines the validity of traditional assessment formats and challenges educators to reconsider what constitutes evidence of learning [12, 13].

Christensen's [4] theory of disruptive innovation provides a useful framework for understanding the impact of GenAI. Disruptive innovations often enter the market by serving the needs of non-traditional users or providing a 'good enough' alternative to established products. Over time, they improve in quality and performance, eventually displacing incumbents. In the context of higher education, GenAI has already crossed the threshold from 'novel curiosity' to 'mainstream utility', being adopted by both students and academics to enhance productivity, creativity, and efficiency. The challenge for institutions is to adapt proactively rather than reactively, integrating AI in ways that preserve educational values while leveraging its transformative potential.

2.2 The social and cultural drivers of disruption

The disruptive potential of GenAI is amplified by its alignment with broader cultural and social trends. Today's learners are 'prosumers', simultaneously consumers and producers of content, operating within ecosystems shaped by social media platforms such as TikTok, YouTube, and Instagram [21]. In these spaces, multimodal communication, rapid content remixing, and algorithmic personalisation are the norm. GenAI tools mirror these affordances, enabling instant creation of tailored, context-sensitive outputs in text, image, audio, and video formats.

For educators, this means that students' out-of-classroom digital experiences may already be more interactive, personalised, and creative than what they encounter in formal academic settings [7, 9]. This mismatch creates what might be called a 'pedagogical relevance gap', a disconnect between institutional practices and the lived digital literacies of learners. GenAI, far from being an external threat, can serve as a bridge between these two worlds, enabling the adoption of more authentic, inquiry-driven, and creative approaches to learning [6].

2.3 Pedagogical and ethical tensions

The integration of GenAI into higher education introduces a series of pedagogical and ethical tensions. On one side, the technology offers opportunities to enhance personalisation, accessibility, and inclusivity. Adaptive GenAI tools can generate learning resources tailored to individual reading levels, language preferences, or disciplinary contexts, potentially reducing barriers for students from diverse linguistic and cultural backgrounds [16, 17]. AI-driven translation tools and multilingual content generators can support more equitable access to course materials, aligning with UNESCO's goals for inclusive education [1].

On the other side, GenAI raises questions about academic integrity, authorship, and the nature of original thought. If a student uses ChatGPT to draft an essay or Perplexity AI to summarise a reading, where does the student's intellectual contribution begin and end? The European Union's Artificial Intelligence Act [21] emphasises transparency, traceability, and accountability in AI applications – principles that higher education must also adopt. Yet, enforcing such principles in educational contexts is challenging, particularly given the speed of GenAI adoption and the limitations of AI detection tools [13].

These tensions require a shift from policing AI use towards designing assessments that integrate AI in pedagogically meaningful ways. Instead of banning AI-generated content, educators can require students to document their interactions with AI, critique the outputs, and demonstrate how these informed their final work. This aligns with a 'process-over-product' approach to assessment, which not only mitigates plagiarism risks but also encourages metacognitive awareness of the tools' capabilities and limitations [22].

2.4 Threats to traditional academic practices

The threat that GenAI poses to traditional academic practices is multi-faceted. First, it challenges the centrality of memorisation and reproduction as markers of mastery. If AI can produce correct answers or coherent essays faster than humans, the value of recall-based assessment diminishes. Second, it raises concerns about the erosion of disciplinary identity. Disciplines that rely heavily on written assignments, such as the humanities and social sciences, may feel particularly vulnerable to automation, while fields like computer science must now contend with AI-generated code that can rival novice programmers' work [11].

Third, GenAI risks widening the digital divide between students who are proficient in leveraging AI tools and those who lack the skills or resources to do so effectively. Without institutional support, this could exacerbate existing inequalities in academic achievement and post-graduate opportunities [9]. Addressing this requires embedding AI literacy into curricula, ensuring that all students, regardless of background, can engage critically and effectively with these technologies.

2.5 Opportunities for renewal and innovation

While the threats are real, the opportunities for renewal are equally significant. GenAI can reduce administrative burdens for faculty, freeing up time for higher-value teaching activities. It can support rapid prototyping of learning materials, generate multilingual versions of resources, and enable real-time feedback loops for students [14, 15]. In research contexts, tools like Elicit, Scite, and ResearchRabbit can automate literature searches, summarise findings, and suggest relevant citations, accelerating the pace of scholarly inquiry without compromising rigour when used appropriately.

Moreover, GenAI opens possibilities for truly personalised learning pathways. By combining AI-generated content with adaptive learning systems, educators can create responsive curricula that adjust to each learner's progress, preferences, and needs. This aligns, as shown in **Figure 1**, with long-standing calls for personalised education and represents a practical means of implementing such approaches at scale [17].

2.6 GenAI as a catalyst for professional re-skilling

Perhaps the most profound aspect of GenAI's disruption is its impact on academic professional identity. Instructors who have taught the same way for decades may find their methods rendered obsolete almost overnight. This can be unsettling, but it also presents an opportunity for re-skilling and pedagogical growth. The ability to critically evaluate AI outputs, design AI-inclusive assessments, and guide students in ethical and effective AI use will become core competencies for educators in the coming decade [8]. Institutions that invest in continuous professional development and foster communities of practice around AI integration will be better positioned to harness the benefits of these tools while mitigating their risks.

2.7 Navigating the duality of disruption

The dual nature of GenAI, simultaneously threatening and enabling, means that higher education must adopt a balanced, proactive approach. Reactive measures, such as banning AI tools or relying solely on detection software, are unlikely to succeed in the long term, as the technology will continue to evolve. Instead, institutions should focus on embedding ethical guidelines, transparency requirements, and pedagogical strategies that turn GenAI into an ally rather than an adversary. This approach reframes disruption not as a destabilising force but as a driver of necessary transformation, pushing academia towards more authentic, equitable, and creative learning environments.

In this sense, GenAI is not simply another tool to be added to the educator's repertoire. It is a mirror reflecting the evolving realities of the digital age, compelling institutions to reassess what, how, and why they teach. For those

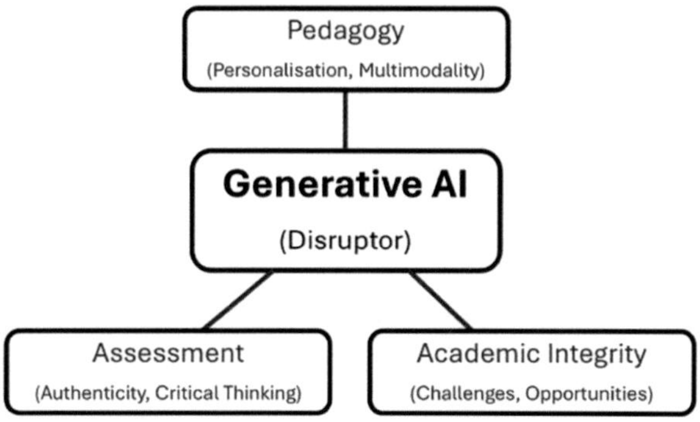

Figure 1.
GenAI Healthy DIsruption.

willing to engage with its complexities, GenAI offers an unprecedented opportunity to align higher education with the skills, literacies, and ethical sensibilities required in the twenty-first century.

3. Insights from the academic workshops and survey

The disruptive nature of GenAI, outlined in the previous section, is best understood not only through theoretical frameworks but also through empirical evidence that captures how educators themselves are encountering and responding to the technology in practice. This section draws on data collected from two consecutive workshops delivered to academics at the University of Malta. The first workshop, GenAI for Teaching and Assessment, focused on the pedagogical integration of AI tools into instructional and evaluative contexts. The second, GenAI for Academic Research and Writing, explored AI's role in scholarly production, literature synthesis, and writing support.

By surveying participants after their exposure to both the workshops, the study sought to capture a snapshot of evolving attitudes, adoption patterns, and concerns among academics from diverse disciplines. The data, while representing a specific institutional context, provides valuable insight into how faculty navigate the opportunities and tensions inherent in GenAI adoption. It also illuminates a wider point from the literature: the trajectory from initial curiosity towards informed, critical engagement is neither linear nor uniform across academic communities [5, 13]

3.1 Participant profile and context

The respondents represented a cross-section of faculties, including humanities, social sciences, physical sciences, and professional disciplines. This diversity is important, as the literature suggests that disciplinary culture strongly shapes both the pace and the mode of technological adoption [23, 46]. Fields with long traditions of text-based assessment, such as the humanities, may feel more directly challenged by GenAI's capacity to generate coherent written prose. In contrast, disciplines like engineering or computer science may initially approach AI more as a technical resource or a productivity enhancer than as a threat to core pedagogical practices [11].

It is also significant that the workshops were delivered in a post-pandemic higher education environment, where many educators had already undergone a period of rapid digital upskilling in response to the emergency shift to online teaching [24]. This prior experience with educational technology may have lowered the barrier to experimenting with GenAI, but it also means that participants entered the workshops with an acute awareness of both the promises and the pitfalls of rapid technological adoption.

3.2 Patterns of adoption and frequency of use

Survey results show that the majority of respondents had already integrated some form of GenAI into their professional workflows by the time of the second workshop. Seven participants reported using GenAI tools daily or regularly, with another five indicating occasional weekly use. Only three described their engagement as rare or non-existent. These figures align with wider trends in early-adopter research, which show that a core group of faculty tends to adopt emerging technologies at higher rates, often serving as internal champions or informal mentors to colleagues [3, 25].

Those who used GenAI more frequently often cited clear, tangible benefits: efficiency in drafting teaching materials, improved clarity in research communication, and the ability to quickly explore alternative ways of framing complex concepts for students. This echoes findings by Ding, Dong, and Grewal [15], who reported that educators using GenAI for preparatory work saved time that could be reallocated to direct student interaction and feedback.

Conversely, the small group of non-users identified several barriers to adoption. Some had not engaged with GenAI prior to the workshops and felt they needed more guided practice to apply it effectively. Others perceived a lack of relevance to their immediate teaching or research contexts. This hesitation is consistent with earlier research on the diffusion of innovation, which emphasises that perceived relative advantage and compatibility with existing practices strongly influence adoption rates [25]. In many cases, non-adoption was less about rejection and more about a readiness gap – a gap that targeted professional development could help close.

3.3 Use cases and creative applications

The variety of reported use cases suggests that participants were already exploring GenAI's potential in creative and discipline-specific ways. Examples included lecture and presentation design with the use of tools like Microsoft Copilot and ChatGPT to create PowerPoint slides, draft lecture outlines, and generate illustrative examples. Additionally, it was used in text editing and language improvement for tasks like refining grammar, simplifying complex texts, or improving fluency for non-native English audiences. Similarly, assessment design by generating formative assessment questions, developing scenarios for case-based learning, and creating rubrics featured as another top example. Others included research synthesis to summarise journal articles, suggest alternative perspectives on a topic, and identify key concepts from large reading lists, as well as creative production by using visual GenAI tools such as DALL · E to create images for teaching materials or for stimulating creative student projects.

These uses mirror global academic practice as documented in recent studies. For example, Haniya et al. [26] note that AI tools are increasingly employed for 'content scaffolding', providing initial structures that educators then refine and contextualise. Perkins et al. [13] similarly observed that academics often use AI for 'idea sparking' and initial drafting rather than for producing final outputs, reflecting a hybrid human–AI workflow.

3.4 Ethical concerns and reservations

Despite the breadth of experimentation, the survey revealed a near-even split between those who expressed no concerns about student use of GenAI (55%) and those who did (45%). The concerns articulated by the latter group were strikingly consistent with themes emerging in international debates on AI in education: risks to academic integrity, over-reliance on AI-generated material, and questions of authorship transparency [9, 27].

Plagiarism was the most frequently cited issue, with participants worried that students might submit AI-generated work without adequate disclosure. Others expressed concern that reliance on GenAI could short-circuit the cognitive and metacognitive processes that assessments are designed to cultivate. As Montebello, Cope, and Kalantzis [28] argue, the educational value of an assignment lies not only in the final product but also in the process of analysis, synthesis, and reflection that leads to it. If students outsource too much of that process to AI, the opportunity for deep learning is diminished.

Interestingly, a smaller subset of concerns was related to equity and access. Some academics noted that students with better digital skills or personal access to premium AI tools could gain an advantage over peers, reinforcing the digital divide. This aligns with the caution by Williamson and Eynon [9] that, without deliberate intervention, educational AI could exacerbate existing inequities rather than alleviate them.

3.5 Shifts in attitudes between workshops

A particularly valuable dimension of this study is its sequential design. Because participants attended two workshops months apart, it was possible to capture not just a static snapshot but an indication of attitudinal change. While the survey did not quantify this change with pre- and post-workshop measures, qualitative feedback suggested a gradual reframing of GenAI from a novelty or threat to a practical, if still cautiously used, tool.

This mirrors the 'exposure effect' documented in educational technology adoption literature [29], where hands-on interaction with a new tool, combined with opportunities to discuss its implications with peers, tends to increase both confidence and perceived value. Several respondents explicitly noted that the workshops provided not just technical demonstrations but also a safe space for ethical debate and reflection, which, in turn, influenced their willingness to experiment.

3.6 Readiness and professional development needs

The survey findings suggest that while many academics are eager to explore GenAI, there is a pressing need for structured institutional support. This support must go beyond technical training to include, among others, four basic needs, namely: AI literacy required for understanding how GenAI models work, their limitations, and their potential biases [30]; pedagogical integration required for designing activities and assessments where AI use is transparent, purposeful, and aligned with learning outcomes; ethical frameworks for establishing clear policies on disclosure, acceptable use, and authorship attribution [27]; and equity considerations for ensuring that access to AI tools is not restricted to those who can afford commercial subscriptions.

These needs reflect broader recommendations from bodies such as UNESCO [1] and resonate with findings from other higher education contexts [11], where institutions that invest early in faculty development see more effective and ethical integration of AI into teaching and research.

3.7 Interpreting the data through the lens of disruption

Viewed through the lens of disruptive innovation theory, the survey results capture a faculty cohort at multiple stages of adoption, from innovators and early adopters to those still at the margins of engagement. Importantly, this variation is not purely attitudinal; it is shaped by factors such as disciplinary fit, prior exposure to educational technology, perceived workload pressures, and institutional policy clarity.

The data also illustrate a paradox noted in Section 2: GenAI's potential to both destabilise and enrich academic practice. For some, its capacity to automate traditional tasks creates anxiety about the erosion of core scholarly skills. For others, the same capacity frees time and cognitive resources for higher-order activities, creative exploration, and more personalised student support. The decisive factor in determining which of these trajectories predominates will likely be the intentionality with which institutions and educators design their AI integration strategies.

3.8 Implications for the remainder of the chapter

The insights from this survey will inform several later sections of this chapter. First, they will help ground the discussion of AI tools in Section 4 in lived academic practice rather than abstract capability lists. Second, they provide empirical support for the argument in Sections 5–7 that instructional design and assessment strategies must evolve to harness GenAI productively while safeguarding integrity and authenticity. Third, they underscore the need for Section 8's focus on re-skilling, as the readiness gaps and equity concerns identified here point directly to the areas where faculty development should be concentrated.

Ultimately, the workshops and the survey demonstrate that academic engagement with GenAI is not a binary of use or non-use. Rather, it is a dynamic spectrum of exploration, adaptation, and critical reflection. This finding aligns with the broader claim of this chapter: that GenAI, far from being an optional extra, is now a central feature of the higher education landscape, and that the question is no longer *whether* to engage with it, but *how* to do so in ways that are equitable, creative, and pedagogically sound.

4. AI tools for students and educators

The survey results presented in the previous section reveal a community of academics already experimenting with GenAI across a variety of tasks, ranging from lecture design and research synthesis to image generation and language refinement. This section expands on those practical accounts by situating them within the wider ecosystem of AI tools currently available for educational purposes. It examines not only their functional capabilities but also their pedagogical implications, ethical considerations, and potential to transform instructional design, assessment, and research practices.

The discussion is organised into five broad categories of tools: text-based, multimodal, research-oriented, creative production, and educational design, reflecting both their dominant mode of output and their primary use cases in academic contexts. Within each category, I draw on examples reported by workshop participants alongside tools documented in the literature [1, 11, 15] noting affordances, limitations, and points of caution.

4.1 Text-based GenAI tools

4.1.1 Large language models (LLMS) for writing and communication

The most widely reported tools among survey respondents, ChatGPT and Microsoft Copilot, belong to the class of LLMs, which can produce human-like text in response to prompts. These models are already used by educators to assist them with numerous chores like drafting lecture notes, lesson plans, and assignment briefs; suggesting alternative phrasings or explanations for complex concepts; and providing grammatical corrections and stylistic refinements for both academic and public-facing writing.

From a pedagogical perspective, these uses correspond to what Haniya et al. [31] term 'scaffolding functions', supports that help educators focus on the substantive aspects of teaching while delegating mechanical or preliminary tasks to the AI. For students, such tools can provide on-demand language feedback, act as a brainstorming partner, or offer accessible summaries of challenging texts [13].

However, these benefits come with limitations. LLMs can generate plausible but inaccurate information (often referred to as 'hallucinations'), fail to provide verifiable sources, and reproduce embedded biases present in their training data [32]. For these reasons, educators must explicitly teach critical evaluation of AI outputs, incorporating fact-checking as a core learning activity.

4.1.2 Multilingual and translation support

Several respondents highlighted the value of AI in improving language clarity or translating material for multilingual audiences. Tools such as DeepL Write, Google Translate (enhanced with neural machine translation), and ChatGPT's translation capabilities can help both educators and students access academic material in multiple languages.

This has profound equity implications. In multilingual classrooms, AI-assisted translation can reduce linguistic barriers, fostering participation and inclusion [16]. Yet, caution is warranted because literal translations can miss disciplinary nuance, and over-reliance on AI translation may prevent students from developing their own academic language proficiency.

4.2 Multimodal AI tools

4.2.1 Image generation and visual communication

Workshop participants mentioned using tools such as DALL · E and Canva's AI Image Generator to create custom visuals for teaching materials. This aligns with the shift towards multimodal learning design [6], which recognises that learning is enhanced when content is presented in multiple modes: textual, visual, auditory, and interactive. Visual GenAI can create culturally relevant imagery for case studies, generate conceptual diagrams not readily available in stock libraries, and support creative student projects that blend disciplines (e.g., combining data analysis with visual storytelling). However, as Fajt and Schiller [12] warn, image generation tools can also reproduce stereotypes or create ethically questionable outputs if prompts are not carefully constructed. Integrating these tools into coursework should, therefore, include critical media literacy components.

4.2.2 Audio and speech synthesis

Although not widely reported in the survey, AI-driven audio tools such as ElevenLabs, Murf, and Microsoft Azure Speech Studio are increasingly being used for producing accessible audio versions of reading materials, creating voice-overs for instructional videos, and supporting language learning through accent modelling and pronunciation feedback. For visually impaired learners or those who process information better through auditory channels, these tools can be transformative. As with text generation, however, accuracy and clarity must be verified, particularly when working with technical terminology.

4.3 Research-oriented AI tools

4.3.1 Literature discovery and synthesis

A number of participants described using AI to summarise academic articles or extract key points from lengthy documents. Beyond ChatGPT's general capabilities, dedicated academic tools such as Elicit, Scite, ResearchRabbit, and Connected Papers can help educators and students identify relevant literature from large databases, map relationships between publications, and summarise research findings with citations. These tools address a perennial challenge in both teaching and research: the cognitive overload associated with information abundance. They allow educators to stay updated in their field while providing students with entry points into complex topics. Yet, their reliance on available datasets means they may miss significant literature outside indexed databases, necessitating traditional search strategies as a complement [3].

4.3.2 Data analysis and visualisation

GenAI-powered platforms such as ChatGPT, Code Interpreter (Advanced Data Analysis), Wolfram Alpha, and Tableau's AI features can assist in data cleaning, statistical analysis, and generating interpretive visualisations. For students, these tools can democratise access to analytical methods that previously required advanced programming skills, enabling them to focus on interpretation rather than manual computation.

Still, there is a pedagogical trade-off. Although automation can accelerate analysis, over-reliance risks bypassing the learning process associated with data literacy. As Yuan and Hu [11] suggest, educators should frame these tools as *assistants*, not replacements, embedding reflective checkpoints where students explain their analytical choices.

4.4 Creative and generative production tools

4.4.1 Video generation and editing

Although not as frequently cited by survey participants, AI video tools such as Synthesia, Pictory, and Runway are becoming popular for creating explainer videos, lecture introductions, or visual abstracts for research outputs. These tools can save production time for academics creating MOOCs (massive open online courses) or online resources, enable students to present projects in creative, multimodal formats, and support flipped classroom models by producing short pre-class instructional videos. However, issues of authenticity arise when synthetic avatars are used to represent human speakers, raising questions about disclosure and audience trust.

4.4.2 Interactive content and gamification

GenAI can also contribute to interactive learning environments. Platforms like Kahoot! AI Quiz Generator, Quizlet Q-Chat, and ChatGPT plug-ins can rapidly create quizzes, simulations, or branching scenarios. In line with Montebello's [8] emphasis on adaptive and gamified learning, these tools can make engagement more dynamic and personalised.

The risk lies in overusing gamification as a surface-level motivator, rather than integrating it meaningfully into the learning design. AI can generate the scaffolds, but educators must ensure alignment with learning objectives.

4.5 Educational design and instructional support

4.5.1 Curriculum and assessment design

Several survey respondents used GenAI to create formative assessment questions or generate policy frameworks for course delivery. Tools like Magicschool.ai, Eduaide.AI, and Learnosity AI offer structured environments for educators to align learning outcomes with activities and assessments, generate variations of assessment items for diverse learner needs, and produce rubrics with clear performance criteria. From an instructional design perspective, these affordances can accelerate course development while promoting consistency in evaluation. Yet, as Perkins et al. [13] stress, AI-generated assessments must still undergo rigorous human review to ensure validity, fairness, and cultural relevance.

4.5.2 Student support and feedback

AI chatbots embedded within LMS platforms (e.g., Moodle AI assistants, Canvas Studio) can provide students with just-in-time responses to frequently asked questions, freeing instructors to focus on higher-level interactions. These bots can easily clarify administrative details, provide reminders for deadlines, and offer generic study tips or guidance on resource use. Although such systems enhance accessibility, they also risk depersonalising the student experience if overused. A hybrid model, where AI handles routine inquiries and educators engage in personalised mentorship, appears to offer the best balance [14].

4.6 Ethical, pedagogical, and strategic considerations

The survey findings confirm that tool adoption is not merely a technical decision but one deeply entangled with ethical and pedagogical judgments. Across all categories, four themes emerge, namely: transparency, whereby students should know when AI has been used to generate materials or feedback; critical literacy, where both educators and learners need skills to evaluate AI outputs for accuracy, bias, and relevance; equity of access, where institutions must ensure all students can access and learn to use AI tools effectively, avoiding a two-tiered learning environment; and pedagogical alignment, where AI tools should enhance, not replace, the intellectual and relational work of education. The literature underscores that, without intentional design, AI adoption can reinforce existing inequities and even erode trust in educational processes [9, 27]. The challenge is to move from ad hoc experimentation towards a coherent institutional strategy that aligns AI tool use with core educational values.

4.7 Integrating tools into authentic learning and assessment

One of the strongest implications from the workshops and the survey is that AI tools are most powerful when embedded into authentic learning experiences. For example, instead of forbidding students from using ChatGPT for essay drafting, an instructor might require them to generate an AI-assisted draft, annotate sections where they accepted, modified, or rejected AI suggestions, and even reflect on how AI shaped their thinking and identify its limitations. Similarly, in research training, students might use Elicit to assemble an initial reading list, then manually cross-check results against disciplinary databases, learning in the process about coverage gaps and the importance of triangulating sources.

Such assignments embody the 'critical integration' model advocated by Montebello, Cope, and Kalantzis [22], where AI becomes a catalyst for higher-order cognitive work rather than a shortcut to bypass it.

4.8 Building institutional capacity for AI-enhanced education

If GenAI is to fulfil its potential as an enabler of equitable, creative, and effective learning environments, institutions must provide a supportive infrastructure that includes curated lists of approved AI tools evaluated for compliance with data protection and accessibility standards, faculty training programs that integrate technical skills with pedagogical design principles, policies that address intellectual property, authorship, and responsible disclosure of AI use, and student workshops on AI literacy, ethics, and critical evaluation. Such measures align with UNESCO's recommendations [1] and with emerging national policy directions [27], ensuring that AI adoption is both strategic and value-driven.

5. Implications for instructional design

The rapid integration of GenAI into higher education has significant implications for instructional design. As the preceding sections have demonstrated, educators are already deploying a wide range of AI tools for purposes as diverse as lecture preparation, assessment creation, research synthesis, and creative production. While these applications provide tangible efficiencies and new creative possibilities, their real transformative potential lies in how they compel a fundamental rethinking of learning design, assessment practices, and the role of the educator. This section examines these implications through a pedagogical lens, considering how AI can be embedded into instructional design in ways that promote critical thinking, creativity, authenticity, and equity.

The starting point for any analysis of AI's impact on instructional design must be the recognition that traditional pedagogical structures, particularly those relying heavily on recall-based or text-production assessments, are increasingly misaligned with the realities of an AI-saturated environment. When students can generate an articulate, grammatically correct essay on a given topic within seconds, the act of producing text alone can no longer serve as a reliable proxy for learning. This is not to suggest that writing or production skills are obsolete, but rather that the educational value of such tasks now lies less in the mechanical act of generating output and more in the intellectual processes of framing, critiquing, and refining ideas. Consequently, instructional design must shift towards learning activities and assessments that cannot be meaningfully completed by AI in isolation, but which require students to demonstrate human judgment, contextual knowledge, and reflective insight.

One of the clearest implications of this shift is the need to design for process transparency. In an AI-enabled learning environment, instructors can no longer rely solely on evaluating final products; instead, they must create structures in which the development process itself becomes an assessable component of learning. This might involve requiring students to submit iterative drafts accompanied by reflective commentaries on how they used AI tools, what prompts they employed, and how they evaluated the outputs they received. The value here is twofold: first, it preserves opportunities for formative feedback during the creation process; second, it provides insight into the student's critical engagement with AI, rather than their ability to passively accept machine-generated content. Research by Montebello, Cope, and Kalantzis [22] supports this approach, noting that metacognitive awareness – thinking about one's own thinking – is a crucial skill in an era where content generation can be automated.

Designing for transparency also demands a re-evaluation of how originality is defined and assessed. Traditional academic integrity policies are often predicated on the assumption that originality equates to producing all work independently, without external generative assistance. In the context of AI, such definitions risk becoming both impractical and pedagogically limiting. A more constructive approach, advocated by Perkins et al. [13] and echoed in the feedback from workshop participants, is to shift the emphasis from whether AI was used to how it was used. In this model, originality is not about eschewing AI entirely but about the originality of the thought process, interpretation, and synthesis that the human brings to the AI-assisted task. Instructional design, therefore, needs to include assessment criteria that explicitly value the student's capacity to direct, critique, and integrate AI outputs into a coherent, contextually appropriate response.

The use of AI in instructional design also intersects with the long-standing aspiration for personalised and adaptive learning. AI systems can, in principle, create customised pathways through course material, offering resources at varying levels of complexity or in different modalities to match individual learner profiles. The workshops revealed examples of this potential in practice, with academics using AI to reframe explanations for students who struggled with certain concepts or to generate multilingual summaries for international cohorts. However, without deliberate pedagogical framing, personalisation risks becoming superficial, merely a matter of rewording content rather than genuinely adapting the learning trajectory. Effective instructional design in the GenAI era will require more than just customising outputs; it will require rethinking the sequencing, pacing, and scaffolding of learning activities so that AI becomes an enabler of deeper engagement rather than a shortcut to surface-level comprehension.

Another significant implication concerns the development of critical AI literacy as a learning outcome in its own right. As Bender et al. [32] and Williamson & Eynon [9] argue, the ability to critically evaluate AI-generated information, assessing its accuracy, bias, and contextual appropriateness, is now an essential component of digital literacy. This literacy extends beyond technical familiarity with AI tools to include ethical awareness, such as understanding when disclosure of AI use is appropriate or recognising the implications of data privacy in AI-mediated learning. Instructional design that embeds AI literacy should, therefore, create opportunities for students to interrogate AI outputs, compare them with authoritative sources, and reflect on the differences. This aligns closely with inquiry-based learning approaches, where questioning and analysis take precedence over rote reproduction of information.

The design of AI-inclusive learning activities must also address issues of equity and access. Survey respondents raised concerns that unequal access to advanced AI tools could exacerbate the digital divide, privileging students with greater technological literacy or financial means. From an instructional design perspective, this underscores the importance of either providing institutionally supported access to AI tools or designing activities that rely only on freely available resources. Equity considerations also extend to ensuring that AI-generated content is culturally responsive and inclusive, avoiding stereotypes or linguistic biases that could alienate certain learners. Such concerns are not merely technical but deeply pedagogical, as they affect the inclusivity and relevance of the learning environment.

Importantly, the integration of AI into instructional design must also grapple with the evolving role of the educator. In a traditional model, the instructor is often the primary source of authoritative knowledge and feedback. In an AI-enhanced model, much of the 'content delivery' function can be delegated to automated systems, freeing educators to focus on higher-value activities such as facilitating discussion, guiding inquiry, and mentoring students in the ethical and strategic use of AI. However, this shift is not automatic; it requires conscious redesign of learning activities to ensure that human–AI collaboration is purposeful and pedagogically grounded. Without such intentionality, there is a risk that AI tools will simply replicate existing content delivery models rather than catalysing deeper forms of engagement.

A related challenge is that of maintaining student engagement in an environment where AI can perform many of the routine tasks traditionally assigned in coursework. If students perceive that AI can do 'the work' for them, motivation to actively participate in the learning process may decline. Instructional design must, therefore, prioritise tasks that are inherently participatory, requiring students to apply knowledge in contexts that demand personal judgment, creativity, or interaction with others. This might involve collaborative projects where AI is used as a shared resource, but where the primary value comes from the group's negotiation of ideas and division of labour. Such activities can also foster the social dimensions of learning, which are less easily replicated by AI and remain central to the educational experience.

In rethinking assessment, AI's disruptive influence becomes especially pronounced. The workshop survey revealed both enthusiasm and caution among faculty, with concerns about plagiarism and over-reliance on AI emerging as recurring themes. One instructional response is to design assessments that explicitly integrate AI use while embedding safeguards against academic dishonesty. For example, students might be tasked with using AI to generate multiple solutions to a problem, then critically compare and refine them based on criteria discussed in class. This approach transforms AI from a potential source of misconduct into a tool for developing evaluative judgment, a skill that is increasingly valued in professional and academic contexts.

The assessment of creative and higher-order thinking also benefits from multimodal task design. Rather than relying solely on written essays, educators can invite students to demonstrate understanding through podcasts, videos, or interactive presentations, many of which can incorporate AI-generated elements. The key, however, is to assess the student's curation and interpretation of these elements, rather than the mere inclusion of AI-generated content. This aligns with the argument by Cope and Kalantzis [20] that, in a multimodal learning environment, meaning-making involves orchestrating diverse resources into coherent narratives or arguments. AI can supply some of these resources, but the intellectual labour of orchestration remains a distinctly human contribution.

Furthermore, AI's capacity to provide instant feedback creates opportunities for more iterative and reflective forms of assessment. Students can use AI to test ideas, receive immediate suggestions, and then revise their work before formal submission. Instructional design that leverages this capacity might, for instance, incorporate AI-mediated peer review, where students critique both the AI's and their peers' feedback, thereby deepening their evaluative skills. Such practices also align with formative assessment principles, emphasising learning as an ongoing process rather than a one-time performance.

The integration of AI into instructional design also invites a reconsideration of curriculum coherence and alignment. As Ding, Dong, and Grewal [15] note, AI tools can accelerate the development of learning materials, but without careful design, the result can be a disjointed collection of AI-generated fragments rather than a cohesive educational experience. Curriculum mapping, where learning outcomes, activities, and assessments are aligned across a program, becomes even more critical in an AI-rich environment. This ensures that AI is employed in ways that support the overarching pedagogical goals of the course or program, rather than as a series of isolated interventions.

From a strategic perspective, the effective integration of AI into instructional design requires institutional policies that balance innovation with ethical responsibility. Clear guidelines on acceptable AI use in coursework, transparent communication about data privacy, and support for faculty professional development are all essential components. The workshops demonstrated that faculty are eager for such guidance, both to clarify expectations for students and to ensure that their own use of AI aligns with institutional values. This policy environment must remain adaptive, given the rapid evolution of AI technologies, but should be anchored in enduring educational principles such as fairness, inclusivity, and the promotion of critical thinking.

Ultimately, the implications of GenAI for instructional design are far-reaching, touching on every aspect of the learning experience, from the design of individual tasks to the structuring of entire curricula. At its most transformative, AI can serve as a catalyst for pedagogical renewal, prompting educators to shift from content transmission towards the cultivation of skills and dispositions that will serve students in an AI-augmented world. These include the capacity to frame meaningful questions, critically evaluate diverse sources of information, engage in creative problem-solving, and navigate the ethical complexities of technology use. Achieving this transformation will require not only new technical competencies but also a willingness to experiment, reflect, and adapt – qualities that are as much about pedagogical mindset as they are about technological proficiency.

6. Implications for academic integrity

The integration of GenAI into higher education brings with it a complex and evolving set of challenges for academic integrity. As the survey results discussed in Section 3 clarified, concerns about student misuse of AI were among the most frequently expressed reservations by faculty participants. Eight respondents indicated no specific worries, whereas seven highlighted issues such as plagiarism, unauthorised use of AI in assessments, and the erosion of critical thinking skills. These concerns echo those voiced in global discourse [9, 13, 32], where AI's capability to produce polished, human-like work within seconds has been described as a 'paradigm disruptor' for established models of academic honesty.

To address these concerns, it is important first to understand the nature of the disruption. In traditional academic integrity frameworks, copying another person's work without attribution has been the primary threat. Detection tools and institutional policies have evolved accordingly, focusing on text-matching software, citation requirements, and penalties for misconduct. GenAI complicates this picture because the work in question is not copied from another human but generated *de novo* by an algorithm trained on vast datasets. This means that plagiarism, in its conventional sense, is often not applicable, even though the underlying ethical concern – misrepresenting the source and process of the work – remains.

As a result, institutions face the challenge of redefining what constitutes academic misconduct in the AI era. Several commentators [33, 34] have suggested that, rather than framing all AI use as inherently suspect, policies should distinguish between permissible and impermissible uses based on the context and learning objectives of a given task. For example, using AI to brainstorm ideas for a research project or to check grammar in a draft might be acceptable if disclosed, whereas using AI to generate a complete essay for submission without any human refinement would likely violate academic integrity principles. This shift from a binary prohibition model to a context-sensitive model aligns with the survey's evidence that many faculty members are willing to see AI as a legitimate academic tool, provided its use is transparent and purposeful.

Transparency, therefore, becomes a cornerstone of academic integrity in the GenAI context. One practical implication for assessment design, as noted in Section 5, is that students should be required to document their interactions with AI tools, including the prompts they used, the outputs they received, and the ways in which they modified or integrated those outputs. This process not only deters unethical 'black box' usage but also develops students' metacognitive awareness of AI's affordances and limitations. From an instructional perspective, such reflective documentation can itself be assessed, shifting the evaluative focus from the product to the process.

An additional complexity arises from the detectability, or lack thereof, of AI-generated content. While some tools claim to identify AI-produced text, studies have repeatedly demonstrated that these detectors are unreliable, producing false positives that can unfairly penalise students [35]. Reliance on detection technologies alone, therefore, risks undermining trust between students and educators. A more constructive approach is to design assessments that are resistant to unauthorised AI completion, such as tasks requiring personal reflection, contextualised application of knowledge, or in-class components that allow educators to observe the student's reasoning in real time.

However, the move towards AI-integrated assessment design also raises equity questions. As respondents in the survey noted, not all students have equal access to AI tools or the digital literacy required to use them effectively. This creates a potential two-tier system in which more technologically adept students can leverage AI's capabilities to enhance their performance, while others may be disadvantaged. Addressing this disparity requires institutions to ensure that all students have both access to appropriate AI tools and the training needed to use them responsibly. This approach aligns with UNESCO's [1] call for AI policies in education that balance innovation with fairness.

A related equity issue concerns linguistic and cultural bias in AI outputs. Research has shown that LLMs often reflect the dominant linguistic and cultural patterns of the data on which they were trained [32]. For students from underrepresented linguistic or cultural backgrounds, this can lead to outputs that misrepresent or marginalise their perspectives. From an academic integrity standpoint, it is important to acknowledge that integrity is not only about avoiding misconduct but also about ensuring that the tools used in learning and assessment do not structurally disadvantage certain groups. Instructional designers and faculty should, therefore, encourage students to critically interrogate AI outputs for bias and to integrate their own disciplinary, cultural, and contextual knowledge into their work.

The ethical use of AI in academic work is also intertwined with questions of authorship and attribution. If a student uses ChatGPT to generate a paragraph in an essay, how should that be acknowledged? Current citation standards are still evolving on this point, with some style guides (such as APA) recommending that AI tools be acknowledged in a manner similar to software, specifying the version and date of use. Institutions may need to adopt or adapt such guidelines to ensure consistency. More importantly, they must make students aware that transparency about AI use is part of the scholarly conversation, reinforcing the idea that integrity involves giving an accurate account of the origins of one's work, regardless of whether those origins are human or machine.

Faculty training is another critical component of upholding academic integrity in the AI era. The workshops conducted for this study provided a forum for discussing the pedagogical and ethical implications of AI use, and survey responses suggest that such discussions can shift faculty perspectives over time. Instructors who understand both the capabilities and the limitations of AI are better positioned to design integrity-friendly assessments, interpret student work in context, and guide students in ethical usage. As Dawson [34] notes, academic integrity is as much a cultural practice as it is a set of rules, and that culture is shaped by the values and behaviours modelled by educators.

From a broader strategic perspective, integrating AI into the academic integrity framework requires a whole-institution approach. Policies must be clear but flexible, acknowledging that AI technologies are rapidly evolving and that pedagogical best practices will change accordingly. Student orientation programs should include AI literacy and ethics as core components, ensuring that new entrants to the academic community understand both the opportunities and the responsibilities that come with AI use. Faculty development initiatives should equip educators not only with technical skills but also with strategies for embedding integrity into course and assessment design.

The institution must also decide on its stance towards different categories of AI tools, distinguishing between those that support learning in acceptable ways and those that circumvent essential learning outcomes. This categorisation should be grounded in pedagogical principles rather than in blanket restrictions. For instance, AI-based grammar checkers may be considered acceptable aids, akin to spell checkers, while end-to-end essay generators might be restricted unless their use is part of a guided learning activity. Such distinctions should be made transparent to students, reducing ambiguity and the risk of unintentional misconduct.

Perhaps the most far-reaching implication of AI for academic integrity is that it challenges educators to move beyond a purely policing mindset towards a developmental one. Rather than focusing solely on catching misconduct, the emphasis should shift to cultivating students' ethical reasoning and professional judgement. This is particularly important given that AI tools are already pervasive in many industries; preparing students for the ethical use of AI in their future workplaces is therefore an extension of higher education's broader mission to foster responsible citizenship and professional competence. The survey responses suggest that faculty are already aware of this dual responsibility: to uphold academic standards while preparing students for the realities of an AI-augmented world.

Ultimately, safeguarding academic integrity in the GenAI era will require rebalancing of trust, transparency, and accountability. Trust is maintained when students feel that integrity policies are fair, relevant, and consistently applied. Transparency is achieved when both students and educators are open about how AI is being used and for what purpose. Accountability is ensured when policies and assessment designs create clear expectations, and when violations are addressed through processes that are educative as well as disciplinary. Achieving this balance will not be easy, but it is essential if AI is to be harnessed in ways that enrich, rather than undermine, the educational experience.

7. Implications for student engagement

The introduction of GenAI into higher education is not simply a matter of enhancing instructional efficiency or innovating assessment practices; it fundamentally reshapes the dynamics of student engagement. Engagement, as defined in the higher education literature, extends beyond mere attendance or participation to encompass the cognitive, emotional, and behavioural investment that students make in their learning [36, 37]. In the context of GenAI, this investment is being renegotiated in real time, with both opportunities and risks that demand careful instructional and institutional responses.

The survey results presented earlier offer a snapshot of this evolving landscape. Many faculty respondents reported using GenAI tools such as ChatGPT, Microsoft Copilot, and DALL · E to design materials, refine language, and create visual resources – applications that can enrich the student learning environment by diversifying resources, offering multimodal stimuli, and enabling more rapid feedback cycles. Yet, the same survey revealed persistent faculty concerns about student misuse of AI, particularly in ways that might short-circuit the deep cognitive engagement traditionally sought through academic tasks. This tension between enrichment and erosion captures the central challenge of fostering meaningful student engagement in the age of AI.

One of the most direct ways GenAI can enhance engagement is by increasing the immediacy and relevance of learning materials. Faculty in the workshops reported using AI to produce context-specific case studies, translate complex concepts into accessible language, and generate examples aligned with students' disciplinary or cultural backgrounds. Such practices resonate with self-determination theory [38], which identifies relevance and autonomy as key drivers of intrinsic motivation. When students encounter learning materials that feel tailored to their contexts and needs, they are more likely to invest emotionally and cognitively in the task. GenAI can facilitate this tailoring at scale, allowing educators to adapt resources for diverse learners without incurring prohibitive time costs.

However, this adaptive potential comes with caveats. If students perceive that AI has done the substantive work of creating examples, summarising readings, or generating solutions, the sense of ownership over the learning process may diminish. As Chickering and Gamson [39] observed long before the advent of AI, active engagement requires students to 'talk about what they are learning, write about it, relate it to past experiences, and apply it to their daily lives'. In AI-mediated contexts, the instructional challenge is to ensure that these active components are not bypassed. For example, rather than providing AI-generated summaries outright, educators might require students to compare AI outputs with their own, analyse discrepancies, and discuss which version better meets disciplinary standards. In this way, AI becomes a catalyst for engagement rather than a substitute for it.

The cognitive dimension of engagement is particularly susceptible to being undermined if AI is positioned as an answering machine rather than a thinking partner. The literature on productive struggle [40] underscores the value of grappling with complex problems before receiving solutions. If students turn to AI too early in the problem-solving process, they may miss the formative benefits of this struggle. Instructional design can counteract this tendency by structuring activities so that AI is introduced at specific points in the learning cycle, perhaps after initial brainstorming or preliminary analysis, thereby preserving the opportunity for independent reasoning.

Emotionally, GenAI can both support and threaten engagement. On one hand, students who experience anxiety around academic writing, public speaking, or tackling unfamiliar disciplinary genres can use AI as a confidence-building tool, generating first drafts, outlines, or practice responses that reduce the fear of failure. On the other hand, over-reliance on AI for these functions may lead to a kind of learned dependency, where students feel less capable of performing without technological assistance. Faculty in the workshops expressed ambivalence here, recognising that AI could lower barriers to participation but worrying that it might also erode students' sense of competence. This aligns with Bandura's [41] findings on self-efficacy: confidence built on unsupported performance is fragile and easily undermined when the assistive technology is removed.

Behavioural engagement, manifested in class participation, assignment submission, and time-on-task, can also be reshaped by GenAI. AI tools can streamline routine academic tasks, potentially freeing students to invest more energy in higher-order activities. Yet, if students use AI primarily to minimise effort, behavioural indicators may show surface compliance rather than genuine engagement. Here again, the solution lies in designing tasks where AI use is integrated but not sufficient for completion. For example, collaborative projects that require negotiation, critique, and synthesis of multiple AI-generated drafts can ensure that behavioural participation remains tied to cognitive and social investment.

The social dimension of engagement, often overlooked in discussions of AI, is particularly important in higher education. Peer interaction is a significant predictor of persistence and success, and collaborative learning has been shown to enhance both achievement and satisfaction [42]. GenAI has the potential to reshape these interactions in complex ways. On one hand, shared use of AI tools can become a site for collaborative exploration, as students work together to craft prompts, interpret outputs, and apply them to authentic problems. On the other hand, if AI becomes a solitary shortcut, it may reduce the frequency and depth of peer-to-peer exchange. Survey responses suggested that faculty are still exploring ways to integrate AI into group activities, but examples such as co-editing AI-generated case studies or jointly critiquing AI-produced solutions point to promising directions.

Another implication for engagement is the need to cultivate AI literacy as a shared competence within the learning community. When students understand how to operate AI tools as well as how they function, what biases they contain, and how to evaluate their outputs, they are better positioned to engage critically and creatively with the technology. Embedding AI literacy into curricula can turn AI from a passive resource into an active stimulus for discussion, debate, and co-construction of knowledge. This aligns with constructivist theories of learning, where meaning is built through interaction with both the material and the community [42].

Equity concerns, already discussed in Sections 5 and 6, have a direct bearing on engagement. Students without reliable access to AI tools or the digital skills to use them effectively may disengage if they feel disadvantaged as compared to their peers. Both institutional provision of AI access and targeted support for digital literacy are, therefore, essential not only for fairness but also for sustaining inclusive engagement. Moreover, culturally responsive use of AI, ensuring that examples, case studies, and generated content reflect diverse perspectives, can help maintain relevance and belonging for all students, which are key predictors of sustained engagement [43].

The role of assessment in shaping engagement cannot be overstated. As the survey data indicated, faculty are aware that students' strategic use of AI is often driven by assessment demands. If assessments reward only the final product, students may see little value in engaging deeply with the process. Conversely, if assessments explicitly recognise process, critical reflection, and integration of AI use, students are incentivised to engage in more substantive ways. Assessment thus becomes a lever for aligning AI use with the deeper forms of engagement valued in higher education.

From a strategic standpoint, fostering engagement in the GenAI era requires a deliberate shift in institutional culture. Workshops like those described in this study can be expanded to include students, creating shared spaces for discussing the ethical, practical, and creative dimensions of AI use. When engagement with AI is framed as a collaborative exploration rather than a covert or contested activity, trust between students and faculty is strengthened, and technology can be harnessed in ways that serve shared learning goals.

Ultimately, the implications of GenAI for student engagement are neither wholly positive nor wholly negative; they are contingent on design, framing, and institutional context. When integrated thoughtfully, AI can personalise learning, lower barriers to participation, and stimulate creative problem-solving. When adopted uncritically, it risks fostering passivity, dependency, and disengagement. The challenge, and the opportunity, for higher education lies in steering AI adoption towards the former using engagement as both a design principle and a measure of success.

8. New pedagogical strategies and assessment models

The adoption of GenAI in higher education necessitates not just incremental adjustments to existing teaching practices but a substantial reimagining of pedagogy and assessment (**Figure 2**). As earlier sections have shown, AI's capabilities disrupt established norms in content delivery, learning activities, and evaluation methods, creating both opportunities for innovation and challenges to foundational academic values. In this section, I propose a set of pedagogical strategies and assessment models that respond to the realities of an AI-saturated environment while preserving – and in some cases strengthening – core educational goals such as critical thinking, creativity, authenticity, and equity.

The first imperative is to shift from a product-oriented to a process-oriented conception of learning. Traditional assessment models have often placed a disproportionate emphasis on the final artefact – a completed essay, a solved

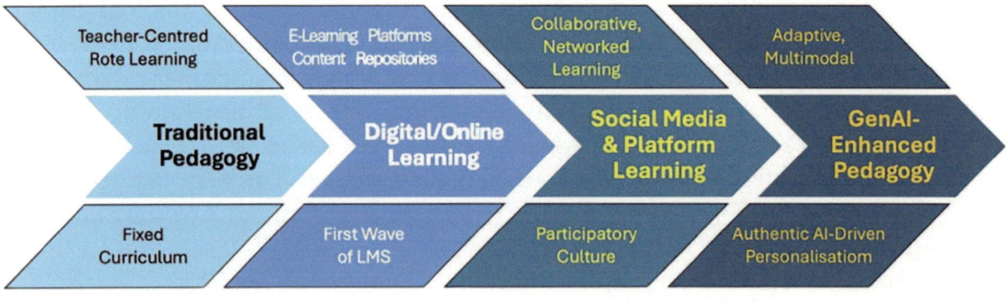

Figure 2.
GenAI-Enhanced Pedagogy.

problem set, or a finished project – while treating the process of arriving at that product as invisible or secondary. In the context of GenAI, where a polished product can be produced with minimal human input, such an approach is increasingly untenable. Process-oriented assessment foregrounds the steps students take in generating ideas, evaluating information, integrating feedback, and refining their work. This requires students to maintain transparent records of their engagement with AI tools, including the prompts used, the outputs generated, and the decision-making process by which these outputs were accepted, modified, or rejected.

One model that operationalises this shift is the AI Use Portfolio, an assessment format in which students compile artefacts from their interaction with AI across the semester, accompanied by reflective commentary linking these artefacts to learning outcomes. The portfolio might include screenshots of AI prompts and responses, annotations explaining why certain outputs were discarded or adapted, and reflections on how the use of AI influenced the student's understanding of the subject matter. Such portfolios turn AI from a hidden shortcut into an explicit site of learning, aligning with constructivist principles that emphasise metacognition and self-regulation [44].

A complementary strategy is the integration of comparative analysis tasks that position AI outputs as objects of critique rather than as final solutions. In such tasks, students might be given an AI-generated essay or problem solution and asked to evaluate it against disciplinary standards, identify inaccuracies or biases, and propose improvements. This not only develops critical thinking and evaluative judgment, skills identified by Perkins et al. [13] as essential in an AI-mediated academic environment but also models the professional reality that AI-generated work often requires expert oversight.

GenAI also invites a rethinking of the boundaries between formative and summative assessment. AI's capacity for instant feedback means that students can engage in rapid cycles of iteration, testing ideas, and refining them before final submission. To harness this potential, assessments can be designed with staged deliverables, each incorporating AI-supported feedback alongside peer and instructor input. This approach echoes Sadler's [45] vision of formative assessment as a process of closing the gap between current performance and desired standards, but it extends that vision by embedding AI as one of multiple feedback sources. The role of the educator becomes one of guiding students in weighing and synthesising these feedback streams, reinforcing the human skills of discernment and judgement.

In creative disciplines, where originality and innovation are paramount, AI can serve as a provocative partner in ideation. Here, assessment models might explicitly require students to use AI to generate unconventional ideas, which they then develop into unique outputs that bear the imprint of their personal style and disciplinary sensibility. For example, in a design course, students might use AI to produce a range of initial visual concepts, but the assessment would focus on how they select, adapt, and refine these concepts into a coherent final piece. Such models encourage risk-taking and creative experimentation while making it clear that the human contribution lies in curation and transformation, not merely in generation.

Collaborative assessment models also stand to benefit from AI integration. Group projects can incorporate AI as a shared resource, with teams collectively deciding how to deploy it and documenting their decision-making process. This mirrors the collaborative use of AI increasingly seen in professional contexts and creates opportunities for students to negotiate ethical and strategic considerations with peers. Importantly, such projects should assess both the collective product and the collaborative process, ensuring that all members engage substantively with the AI-mediated work.

Another pedagogical strategy is the design of AI-resistant tasks, not in the sense of trying to 'outsmart' AI, but in creating activities where AI can only play a partial role and where meaningful completion depends on uniquely human capacities. These might include tasks requiring personal experience, situated fieldwork, real-time interaction, or integration of local data not available to AI systems. For example, a public policy assignment might require students to interview local stakeholders, analyse AI-generated policy briefs in light of these interviews, and produce a final report that synthesises both sources. Such designs preserve the relevance of human-centred inquiry while recognising AI's potential as a supplementary tool.

The ethical dimension of pedagogy in the AI era cannot be overlooked. New assessment models must embed explicit learning outcomes related to AI ethics, including issues of bias, transparency, authorship, and societal impact. This can be achieved through scenario-based assessments in which students confront ethically complex situations involving AI use, deciding, for instance, whether and how to disclose AI assistance in a grant application or how to respond to biased outputs in a cross-cultural research project. By situating ethical reasoning within authentic disciplinary contexts, these assessments prepare students to face professional realities beyond the university.

Importantly, any pedagogical innovation involving AI must be accompanied by deliberate scaffolding of AI literacy. This includes not only operational skills (how to craft effective prompts, how to verify AI outputs) but also critical literacies that enable students to interrogate AI as a socio-technical system. Instructional activities might involve tracing the provenance of AI-generated information, comparing outputs from different AI tools, or exploring the ways training data shape AI's capabilities and limitations. Assessment models can incorporate these literacies by requiring students to explain the rationale behind their AI use and reflect on its appropriateness for the task at hand.

Equity considerations must also inform new pedagogical strategies. As discussed in Sections 5 and 7, disparities in access to AI tools and digital skills can create uneven learning opportunities. To mitigate this, institutions can provide centrally supported AI platforms, integrate AI literacy into orientation and study skills programs, and design assessments that do not disadvantage students who are new to the technology. In some cases, this may mean limiting the range of permissible AI tools to those that are freely accessible and institutionally vetted, thereby ensuring a level playing field.

The implementation of these strategies requires a reconfiguration of the educator's role. Instructors must act not only as subject-matter experts but also as AI mentors, helping students navigate the practical, ethical, and creative dimensions of AI use. This expanded role underscores the need for ongoing professional development, enabling faculty to stay abreast of emerging tools, pedagogical models, and ethical debates. Faculty training should itself model the principles of AI-integrated pedagogy, offering hands-on opportunities to experiment with AI tools, design AI-inclusive assessments, and critically reflect on their implications.

DOI: http://dx.doi.org/10.5772/intechopen.1012982

Institutional policy and infrastructure play a crucial role in supporting these pedagogical shifts. Clear guidelines on acceptable AI use, integrated into course syllabi and assessment briefs, can reduce ambiguity and set shared expectations. Assessment moderation processes may need to be adapted to account for AI-mediated work, with reviewers considering both the appropriateness of AI use and the quality of human oversight. Investment in learning technologies, including AI literacy resources and secure, privacy-compliant AI platforms, can further enable the effective integration of new assessment models.

The ultimate goal of these pedagogical strategies and assessment models is not to police or prohibit AI use but to channel it towards the development of higher-order capabilities that will remain essential in an AI-augmented world. These include the ability to ask meaningful questions, evaluate and synthesise diverse sources of information, engage in creative and ethical problem-solving, and communicate effectively across modalities and contexts. By designing learning experiences that make AI use visible, purposeful, and critically examined, educators can harness its transformative potential while reinforcing human capacities as a hallmark of higher education.

9. Future directions

The emergence of GenAI represents one of the most significant inflection points in the history of higher education. Across this chapter, we have explored its disruptive potential, its implications for instructional design, academic integrity, and student engagement, and the pedagogical strategies needed to ensure that this disruption leads to innovation rather than erosion of core academic values. What emerges from this analysis, supported by both the workshop survey results and the wider literature, is a clear and urgent message: higher education cannot afford to treat GenAI as a peripheral curiosity or a short-term challenge to be 'managed' until it fades away. It is, and will remain, a transformative force that demands systemic pedagogical, ethical, and institutional adaptation.

The position advanced here is that GenAI is not a threat to be contained but a catalyst for the renewal of academic practice. Like other major technological shifts – printing press, internet, learning management system – its integration into higher education will be uneven, contested, and at times uncomfortable. Yet those institutions and educators willing to adapt, experiment, and re-skill will not only preserve their relevance but also open new pathways for creativity, equity, and effectiveness in teaching and learning.

The survey results from academics attending the two workshops at the University of Malta illustrate both the promise and the pitfalls of GenAI adoption. On one hand, faculty are already using AI tools to enhance their own research and teaching, generating ideas, summarising publications, and creating tailored learning materials. They recognise AI's potential to streamline routine tasks, free up time for higher-value pedagogical work, and offer students new kinds of feedback and resources. On the other hand, concerns remain about plagiarism, erosion of critical thinking, unequal access to technology, and the possibility that students might rely on AI as a substitute for genuine intellectual effort. This duality, the co-existence of enthusiasm and caution, is mirrored in the broader global discourse on AI in education [9, 13, 33].

If the disruptive power of GenAI is to be harnessed constructively, higher education must engage in three simultaneous transformations.

First, we must transform pedagogical design. As outlined in Sections 5 and 8, assessments and learning activities must evolve from product-focused to process-focused models, making visible the reasoning, decision-making, and ethical considerations involved in AI use. This entails valuing transparency over prohibition and designing for authenticity, creativity, and critical engagement. The integration of AI portfolios, comparative analysis tasks, staged feedback cycles, and collaborative AI-mediated projects are concrete steps towards this transformation. Such designs do more than accommodate AI; they actively teach students how to think with it, about it, and beyond it.

Second, we must transform academic integrity frameworks. As debated in Section 6, integrity in the AI era is less about detecting prohibited behaviours and more about defining, communicating, and supporting responsible use. This requires institutional clarity about acceptable AI practices, reliable access to approved tools, and embedding of AI ethics into curricula. Integrity must be reframed not as a compliance with static rules but as a living practice of intellectual honesty, shaped by evolving technologies and contexts.

Third, we must transform professional roles and capacities. Faculty are no longer simply content experts and assessors; they are mentors in AI literacy, curators of learning experiences, and ethical guides in technology-rich environments. As the workshops demonstrated, faculty development is critical. Educators need both the technical confidence to use AI tools effectively and the pedagogical vision to integrate them in ways that serve learning outcomes. This is not a one-time training exercise but an ongoing professional learning journey, supported by peer exchange, institutional resources, and engagement with research.

Looking forward, several key developments are likely to shape the trajectory of GenAI in higher education.

One is the evolution of AI capabilities themselves. As models become more multimodal, capable of seamlessly integrating text, images, audio, and video, educators will have unprecedented opportunities to create rich, immersive, and accessible learning environments. This will require rethinking curriculum design not only at the course level but across programs, ensuring that students graduate with the capacity to critically and creatively operate in multimodal, AI-enhanced professional contexts.

Another factor is the emergence of regulatory and policy frameworks at national and international levels. The European Union's AI Act, for instance, will influence the permissible uses of AI in education and research, shaping institutional policy in areas such as transparency, bias mitigation, and data protection. Universities will need to navigate these frameworks while also articulating their own pedagogical and ethical principles for AI use. The challenge will be to comply with regulatory requirements without stifling innovation.

Equally significant is the potential for AI to narrow or widen equity gaps. If institutions take proactive measures to provide equitable access to AI tools, train all students and staff in their effective use, and ensure that AI-generated content reflects diverse perspectives, the technology could be a powerful force for inclusion. On the contrary, if access and literacy are left to individual initiative, the benefits of AI will accrue disproportionately to those already advantaged by digital resources

DOI: http://dx.doi.org/10.5772/intechopen.1012982

and cultural capital. Equity, therefore, is not an incidental consideration but a central measure of success in AI integration.

Finally, there is the question of cultural change within higher education. The integration of GenAI will not succeed if it is framed solely as a technical upgrade or an academic integrity challenge. It must be understood as part of a broader cultural shift towards more open, collaborative, and adaptive forms of learning. This requires building trust between students and faculty, fostering a shared language for discussing AI use, and positioning AI literacy as a core graduate attribute alongside critical thinking, communication, and ethical reasoning.

In practical terms, the future direction of AI in education will depend on a cycle of innovation, evaluation, and refinement. Pilot projects, whether in assessment redesign, AI-supported learning analytics, or multilingual content generation, should be systematically studied, with findings shared across the institution and the sector. The dual-workshop approach by the University of Malta offers a promising model here, combining hands-on exploration with structured reflection and peer exchange. Scaling such initiatives and connecting them with global networks of practice can accelerate the development of effective and ethical AI pedagogies.

In conclusion, GenAI challenges higher education to move beyond defensive postures and towards proactive, principled engagement. The technology is a disruptor, but disruption need not mean de-stabilisation. Managed wisely, it can be the spark for a renewal of pedagogy, recalibration of academic integrity, and deepening of student engagement. The work ahead is not about containing AI's influence but about shaping it, so that the values of higher education – from intellectual honesty to inclusivity and creativity – are not only preserved but reimagined for the twenty-first century.

The future will belong to those institutions and educators that are willing to embrace this reimagining. By anchoring AI integration in pedagogical purpose, ethical clarity, and a commitment to equity, we can ensure that the GenAI era will not be remembered as the moment of academic integrity collapse, but as the moment when higher education rose to meet a profound technological challenge with imagination, resilience, and vision.

10. Conclusion

GenAI is no longer an optional add-on in higher education but a disruptive force that compels institutions, educators, and students to rethink the purposes and practices of teaching, learning, and assessment. Throughout this chapter, we have examined how GenAI has already begun to reshape pedagogy, from its capacity to support content generation and feedback to its potential to challenge long-standing assumptions about academic integrity. The workshop survey revealed that academics are simultaneously intrigued and cautious, embracing the productivity benefits of GenAI tools while voicing concerns about plagiarism, superficial learning, and ethical ambiguity. This duality reflects the broader global discourse: AI is both an opportunity and a risk, depending on how higher education chooses to engage with it.

The path forward requires universities to act decisively, not defensively. Pedagogical design must emphasise authenticity, creativity, and process, rather than rote reproduction of knowledge. Academic integrity frameworks need to be reframed around transparency, responsible use, and ethical literacy. Faculty must re-skill continuously, guiding students in navigating AI-rich learning environments while safeguarding equity and access. If institutions meet this challenge with imagination and principled leadership, GenAI will not erode the values of higher education but re-animate them for a new era. The conclusion is clear: the future of education will not be defined by whether AI is present, but by how courageously and thoughtfully we choose to integrate it.

Author details

Matthew Montebello
University of Malta, Msida, Malta

*Address all correspondence to: matthew.montebello@um.edu.mt

References

[1] Bandura A. Self-efficacy: The Exercise of Control. NY: W H Freeman/ Times Books/ Henry Holt & Co.; 1997

[2] Bender EM, Gebru T, McMillan-Major A, Shmitchell S (2021). On the dangers of stochasticparrots: Can language models be too big? In: *ACM Conference on Fairness, Accountability, and Transparency*. DOI: 10.1145/ 3442188.34459222

[3] Brusilovsky P, Milla E. User models for adaptive hypermedia and adaptive educational systems. In: Brusilovsky P, Kobsa A, Nejdl W. eds. The Adaptive Web. Heidelberg: Springer; 2007. pp. 3–53

[4] Camilleri V, Dingli A, Montebello M. AI in education – A practical guide for teachers and young people. Msida: University of Malta; 2019

[5] Chengzhi Z, Magerko B. Generative AI literacy: A comprehensive framework for literacy and responsible use. Human-Computer Interaction. 2025;**40**:171–194. DOI: 10.48550/ arXiv.2504.19038

[6] Chickering A, Gamson Z. Seven principles of good practice in undergraduate education. New Directions for Teaching and Learning. 2006;**39**(7):63–69. DOI: 10.1002/ tl.37219914708.

[7] Christensen C. The Clayton M. Christensen Reader. Boston: Harvard Business Review; 2015

[8] Cope B, Kalantzis M (2017). *Scholar's New Analytics App: Towards Mastery Learning*. (Common Ground) Available from https://cgscholar.com/community/community_profiles/new-learning/community_updates/54189

[9] Cope W, Kalantzis M. e-Learning Ecologies. New York, USA: Routledge; 2017

[10] Cotton DR, Cotton PA, Shipway JR. Chatting and cheating: Ensuring academic integrity in the era of ChatGPT. Innovations in Education and Teaching International. 2023;**61** (2):228–239

[11] Dawson S, Joksimovic S, Mills C, Gašević D, Siemens G. Advancing theory in the age of artificial intelligence. British Journal of Educational Technology. 2023;**54** (5):1051–1056

[12] Deci E, Ryan R. Intrinsic Motivation and Self-determination in Human Behavior. New York: Plenum Press; 1985

[13] Ding M, Dong S, Grewal R. Generative AI and usage in marketing classroom. Customer Needs and Solutions. 2024;**11**. DOI: 10.1007/s40547-024-00145-2

[14] EC. *Regulation (EU) 2024/1689 Laying down Harmonised Rules on Artificial Intelligence (Artificial Intelligence Act). Official Journal of the European Union, L1689*. Brussels: European Parliament & Council of the European Union; 2024

[15] EC, "*Proposal for a Regulation Laying Down Harmonised Rules on Artificial Intelligence (Artificial*

Intelligence Act)". (2021). Available from https://artificial-intelligence-act.eu/. [Accessed: 2025-October-1]

[16] Eisenstein E. The Printing Press as an Agent of Change. Cambridge: Cambridge University Press; 1980

[17] El-Soussi A. The shift from face-to-face to online teaching due to COVID-19: Its impact on higher education faculty's professional identity. International Journal of Educational Research Open. 2022;**3**:100139

[18] Ertmer P, Ottenbreit-Leftwich A. Teacher technology change: How knowledge, beliefs, and culture intersect. Journal of Research on Technology in Education. 2010;**42**:255–284. DOI: 10.1080/15391523.2010.10782551

[19] Fajt B, Schiller E. ChatGPT in academia: University Students' attitudes towards the use of ChatGPT and plagiarism. Journal of Academic Ethics. 2025;**23**:1363–1382. DOI: 10.1007/s10805-025-09603-5

[20] Freeman T, Anderman L, Jensen J. Sense of belonging in college freshmen at the classroom and campus levels. Journal of Experimental Education. 2007;**75**:203–220. DOI: 10.3200/JEXE.75.3.203-220

[21] Haniya S, Tapping R, Ferguson D. Integration of multimodality and critical clinical thinking approaches in medical education: A futuristic perspective. In: Montebello M. ed. Handbook of Research on Promoting Next-Generation Learning Environments through CGScholar, Hershey, Pennsylvania, USA: IGI-Global; 2023. pp. 187–205.

[22] Haniya S, Tzirides O, Georgiadou K, Montebello M, Kalantzis M, Cope B. Assessment innovation in higher education by integrating learning analytics. International Journal of Learning and Teaching. 2020;**6**(1):53–57

[23] Haniya S, Tzirides O, Montebello M, Georgiadou K, Cope B, Kalantzis M. Maximizing learning potential with multimodality: A case study. World Journal of Educational Research. 2019;**6**(2):260

[24] Hasanov Z, Panayiotis A, Garayev V, Elchin S. The impact of behavioural, cognitive and emotional dimensions of student engagement on student learning: The case of Azerbaijani higher education institutions. International Journal of Knowledge and Learning. 2021;**14**(10). DOI: 10.1504/IJKL.2021.10037816

[25] Jenkins H, Clinton K, Puroshotma R, Robinson A, Weigel M. Confronting the Challenges of Participatory Culture: Media Education for the 21stCentury. Chicago, Illinois, USA: The MacArthur Foundation; 2006

[26] Johnson D, Johnson R, Smith K. Cooperative learning: Improving university instruction by basing practice on validated theory. Journal on Excellence in College Teaching. 2014;**25**(4):303–333

[27] Kapur M. Productive failure. Cognition and Instruction. 2008;**26**(3):379–424

[28] Knox J. Artificial intelligence and education in a postdigital era. Postdigital Science and Education. 2020;**2**(2):247–265

[29] Kuh G. The national survey of student engagement: Conceptual and empirical foundations. New Directions for Institutional Research. 2009;**141**:5–20

[30] Liu D, Son S, Cao J. The determinants of public acceptance of telemedicine apps: An innovation diffusion perspective. Frontiers in Public Health. 2023;**11**. DOI: 10.3389/fpubh.2023.1325031

[31] Miao M, Holmes W. Guidance for Generative AI in Education and Research. Paris, France: UNESCO; 2023

[32] Montebello M (2016a). *Personalised e-Learning*. Sheffield, UK: Ed.D. Thesis

[33] Montebello M. AI-Injected e-Learning - the Future of Online Education. Switzerland: Springer; 2018a

[34] Montebello M. "I Am the Institution," In *Handbook of Research on Digital Learning*. Hershey, Pennsylvania, USA: IGI-Global; 2020. pp. 291–310

[35] Montebello M (2021). "Smart Education through AI," In: *2nd International Conference of the Journal Scuola Democratica "Reinventing Education"*. Rome, Italy: Sapienza University of Rome

[36] Montebello M (2025). Transforming Assessment Paradigms - The Role of Generative AI as a Disruptive Force in Higher Education. In: *The Thirty-Second International Conference on Learning*. Granada, Spain

[37] Montebello M, Cope W, Kalantzis M, Searsmith D, Amina T, Tzirides A, et al. (2018). Critical Thinking through a Reflexive Platform. In: *17th IEEE International Conference on Information Technology Based Higher Education and Training*. Olhao, Algarve, Portugal: ITHET

[38] Montebello M, Kalantzis M, Cope W (2018). Evolving Pedagogical Artefacts. In: *Proceedings of the 3rd. IEEE International Conference of the Portuguese Society for Engineering, (CISPEE 2018)*. Aveiro, Portugal

[39] Perkins M, Roe J, Vu B, Postma D, Hickerson D, McGaughran J, et al. Simple techniques to bypass GenAI text detectors: Implications for inclusive education. International Journal of Educational Technology in Higher Education. 2024;**21**. DOI: 10.1186/s41239-024-00487-w

[40] Rogers EM. Diffusion of Innovations. *5th* ed. New York, N.Y: Simon & Schuster; 2003

[41] Sadler DR. Formative assessment and the design of instructional systems. Instructional Science. 1989;**18**:119–140

[42] Vygotsky L. Mind in Society: The Development of Higher Psychological Processes. Cambridge: Harvard University Press; 1978

[43] Wang Y, Yang N, Wang L, Wei F. Examining false positives under inference scaling for mathematical reasoning. Computation and Language. 2025. DOI: 10.48550/arXiv.2502.06217

[44] Williamson B, Eynon R. Historical threads, missing links, and future directions in AI in education. Learning, Media and Technology. 2020;**45**(3):223–235

[45] Yuan B, Hu J (2024). Generative AI as a Tool for Enhancing Reflective

Learning in Students. *Human-Computer Interaction*, https://arxiv.org/abs/2412.02603 [Accessed: 2025-October-1]

[46] Zawacki-Richter O, Marín VI, Bond M, Gouverneur F. Systematic review of research on artificial intelligence applications in higher education. International Journal of Educational Technology in Higher Education. 2019;**16**(1):1–27

Chapter 7

The Transformation of Education: Artificial Intelligence Replacing Traditional Classroom Teaching

Asif Iqbal Kawoosa and Deepak Prashar

Abstract

Over the past two decades, artificial intelligence (AI) has transformed the educational landscape, emerging as a disruptive force in the classroom for both teachers and students. AI-driven technologies enhance the accessibility of learning environments, optimize administrative procedures, and facilitate personalized learning experiences, thereby enhancing their inclusivity and success. AI is employed to investigate its impact on higher education in several significant domains, including adaptive learning platforms, intelligent tutoring systems, automated grading, and AI-enhanced virtual classrooms. It explores the application of AI in data science, computer-aided design, and skill-based learning, illustrating how these technologies facilitate the acquisition of competencies beneficial in the professional realm. The chapter discusses the application of AI in accordance with India's National Education Policy (NEP) 2020, which emphasizes bilingual education, vocational training, and interdisciplinary learning. The role of AI in research assistance, career guidance, and continuous education is also examined. Simultaneously, critical subjects are addressed, including data privacy, digital disparities, equity, ethical challenges, and the significance of human interaction in education. The chapter anticipates a future in which AI continues to innovate educational methodologies in collaboration with human educators, ensuring outcomes that are equitable, ethical, and student-centered.

Keywords: artificial intelligence, education, teaching, techniques, tools

1. Introduction

The Evolution of Teaching in Higher Education: Since the beginning, the foundation of higher education has been traditional classroom instruction. One-way delivery, in-person lectures, and teaching strategies that are universally applicable form the foundation of this approach to education. Despite the fact that it is appropriate for many, it is susceptible to a number of limitations, including the following. Due to the lack of customization, it may be challenging for students with varied learning styles and paces to keep up with the speed of the class.

Predetermined hours and locations reduces the amount of freedom and accessibility available to non-traditional students. The availability of the teachers, along with their level of expertise and teaching style, significantly influences the learning process. AI's emergence in the educational sector adds a number of innovations, including adaptive learning platforms, intelligent tutoring systems (ITSs), and automated grading systems[1–5]. These technological advancements offer solutions to the shortcomings of traditional methods, which pave the way for the creation of an educational framework that is more dynamic, inclusive, and effective. The learning management system [6], shown in **Figure 1**, remains available to the students 24 × 7.

2. Applications of AI in education

Personalized learning experiences: AI has greatly improved education, especially in individualized learning. Using AI, instructors and students can access personalized tools and platforms, making learning more effective and interesting. SWAYAM, Unacademy, Coursera, Khan Academy, and Open English [7–11] demonstrate how AI-driven platforms are changing education. These systems tailor materials and learning courses to each student using clever algorithms.

AI's capacity to assess learning styles and preferences is a major advancement in education. Tracking a learner's material engagement, identifying strengths and shortcomings, and evaluating progress are exceptional advantages of using AI. Learners are supplemented with visual materials such as films, graphs, or infographics, and textual learners are provided with reading material to ensure that every student gets the help they need to succeed, as shown in **Figure 2** and **Figure 3** below.

AI does a great job of tailoring information and tasks. It can match topics and activities to a learner's skill level based on performance assessments. For instance, if a learner is having difficulty with a math concept, the site may provide additional practice problems or lessons. This personalization allows students to overcome problems without being swamped by hard information or bored by trivial chores.

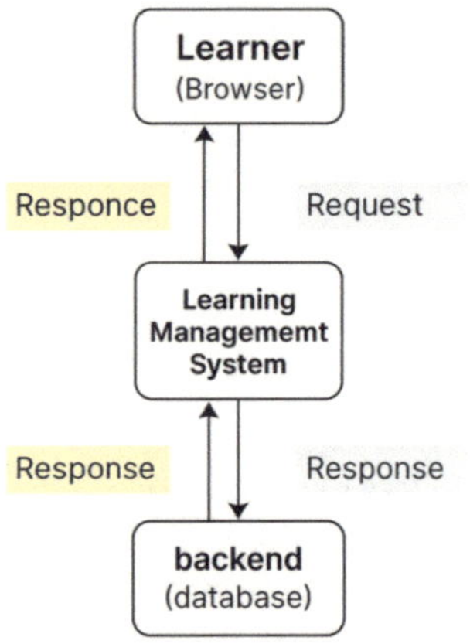

Figure 1.
Learning management system.

DOI: http://dx.doi.org/10.5772/intechopen.1012993

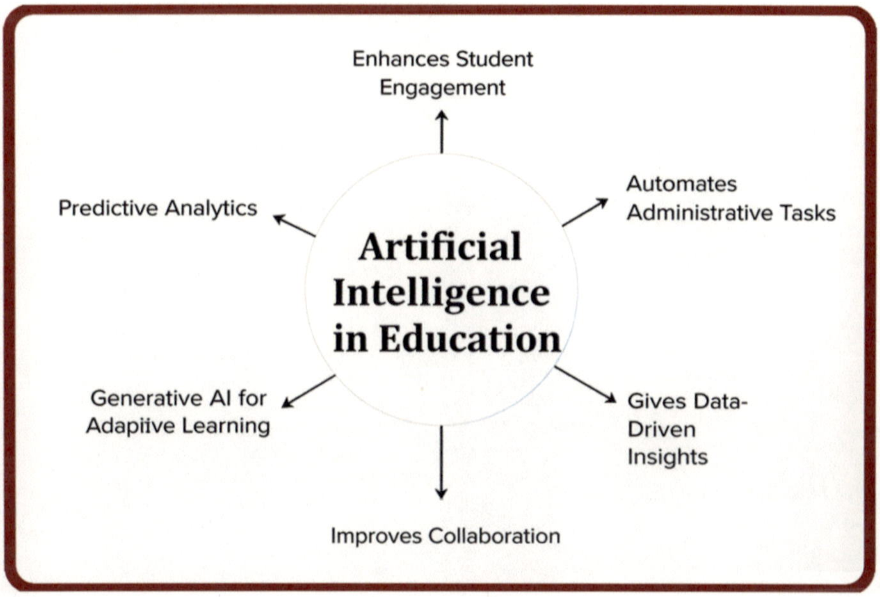

Figure 2.
Features of AI in education.

The second is language learning by using language-learning platforms like Open English, and so on, to engage and interact. Speech recognition and natural language processing (NLP) [11–14] provide learners with real-time feedback on pronunciation, grammar, and vocabulary. It can also teach people new languages and cultures through cross-language conversation. This learning extends the goal beyond the classroom. Advanced learning systems can help students, college students, and working professionals upskill. SWAYAM and Coursera offer industry-specific courses so that professionals can learn at their own pace. Khan Academy also provides all school-level material for various disciplines and ages. It gives student performance insights to instructors. Data-driven reports enable teachers to monitor the progress of students and identify their needs. More effective teaching tactics can thus be formed in this manner. Hence, the learning environment is enhanced by the partnership between AI systems and instructors. AI has much more potential to democratize and improve learning as technology advances. Personalized learning systems like SWAYAM, Unacademy, Coursera, Khan Academy, and Open English [7–11] have transformed learning, making education interesting, efficient, and global, while adjusting to individual preferences, offering personalized information, and aiding in language learning.

Assess progress and recommend areas for enhancement: AI assesses student progress and suggests areas for improvement. Since each student learns at a different speed and comprehends at different levels, AI-based applications bring about more engagement and retention. The students are motivated to learn more as they continue to achieve their goals in academics more effectively.

Intelligent Tutoring System (ITS): ITS is one of the major AI-based education breakthroughs, developed to replicate human tutor capabilities. Such systems personalize guidance and support to cater to the needs of individual learners. The

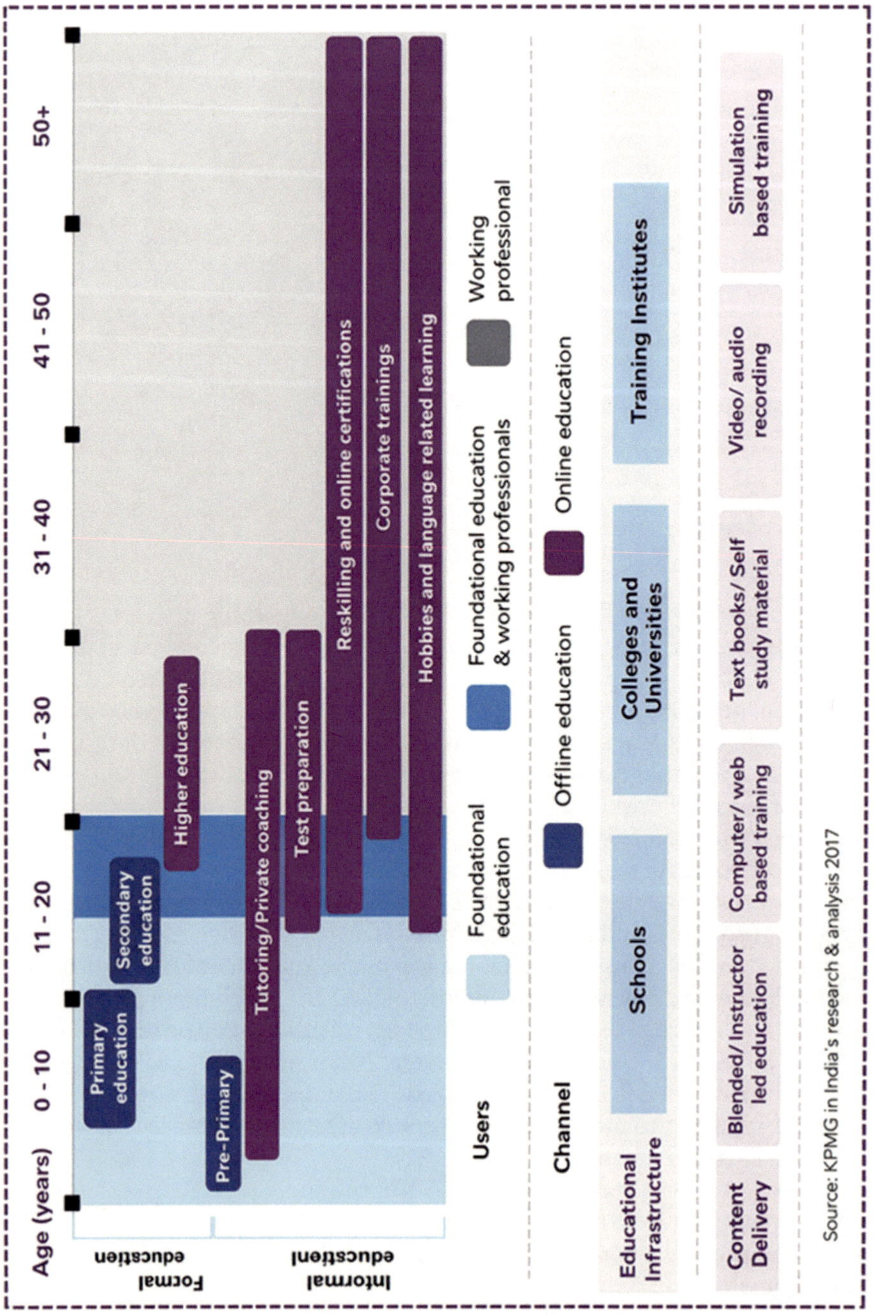

Figure 3.
Online, offline and blended learning in India. Source: KPMG in India's research and analysis, 2017.

best examples include BYJU'S, Toppr, Carnegie Learning, and Socratic by Google [5, 15–17] which implement ITS in the practical world through systematic instruction, considering the user's progress. They not only track performance but also review student comments for points of clarity. For instance, associated conceptual gaps are identified, and suitable interventions are directed at a student who consistently makes numerous mistakes on a particular type of arithmetic problem. These systems usually present step-by-step explanations, resources, or exercises for targeted practice in addressing challenges that students face. ITS also adds value for learners who need additional support outside of regular hours, offering supplementary assistance to ensure that he or she can understand the material well.

Apart from changing the way students learn, it has optimized many administrative tasks that used to take up a significant amount of time for teachers. Automated administrative functions enable educators to focus more on mentoring and instruction rather than routine paperwork.

One of the most impactful features of AI is the automated assessment and grading of students. Tools like Gradescope, Quizizz, Grammarly, Turnitin, and ChatGPT [12, 13, 18–20] streamline the evaluation process by grading assignments, identifying instances of plagiarism, and providing constructive feedback as per teachers' instructions. These systems save time and maintain consistency in evaluation, which is crucial for large classes or institutions.

One of the revolutionary advancements of AI is attendance monitoring using facial recognition and geo-location. These systems automatically track attendance, reduce manual work, and ensure accuracy as shown in **Figure 4**. They have almost eliminated the traditional method of taking attendance by calling roll numbers in class. Teachers can now dedicate this time to actual teaching. AI assistants like IBM Watson chatbots, Google Dialogflow, and Microsoft Azure Bot Service [14, 21, 22]

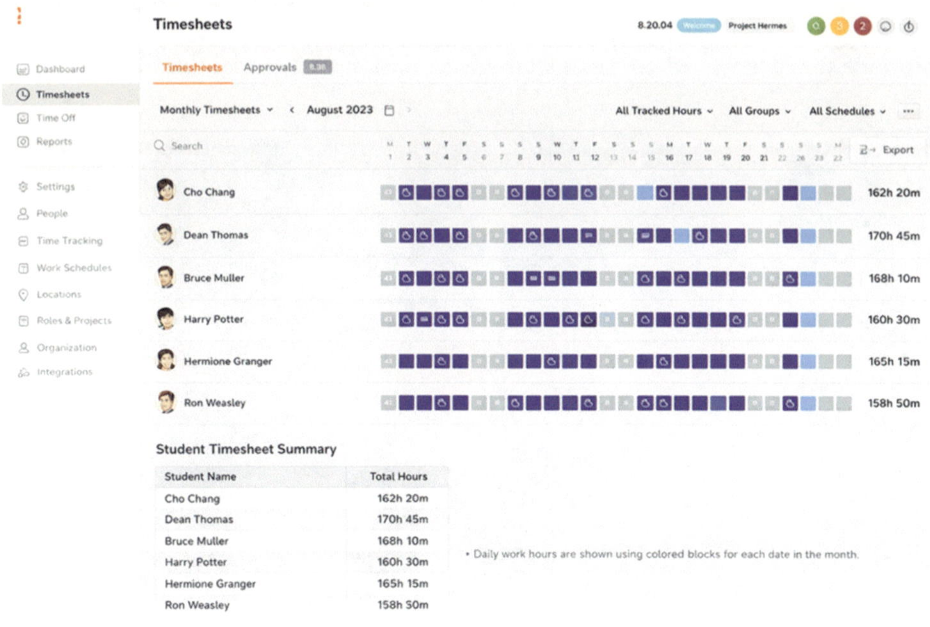

Figure 4.
Online attendance tracker. Source: Internet

have streamlined scheduling and the management of inquiries. They schedule timetables, set reminders for tasks due on deadlines, and manage frequently asked questions (FAQs) by students or their parents. Therefore, efficiency in the workflow of handling administrative affairs improves through timely responses to queries or issues. Besides streamlining tasks, AI has also promoted an educational environment that acts more responsively. Teachers gain back time to focus on meaningful activities, develop innovative ideas for teaching, nurture students, and collaborate with colleagues who are also working to improve the curriculum. From this perspective, AI can be integrated into education in areas far beyond individualized learning. These technologies address issues on both academic and operational levels, ensuring that the overall educational experience for all parties becomes more effective, stimulating, and supportive. As they evolve, these technologies will become even stronger aspects in shaping the future of education.

3. Virtual classrooms and AI-enhanced content distribution

The rise of virtual classrooms has changed the nature of higher education by enabling easy interaction between students and faculty from around the world. Applications like Zoom, GoogleMeet, GoogleClassroom, and Microsoft Teams [23–26] are some of the common platforms for carrying out learning. They enable institutes to bridge the gap and conduct teaching through distance methods. AI integration into the virtual classroom as can be seen in **Figure 5** has further transformed it and has been instrumental in the learning process, as it makes learning efficient, engaging, and interactive.

One of the most important applications of AI for virtual classrooms relates to the immediacy of recording and interpreting lectures. With this, students who have hearing deficiencies or language proficiency issues can use AI-powered tools to get real-time captions during classes. The content transcribed then becomes a potential resource for reviews, where such students can listen to material that they may not

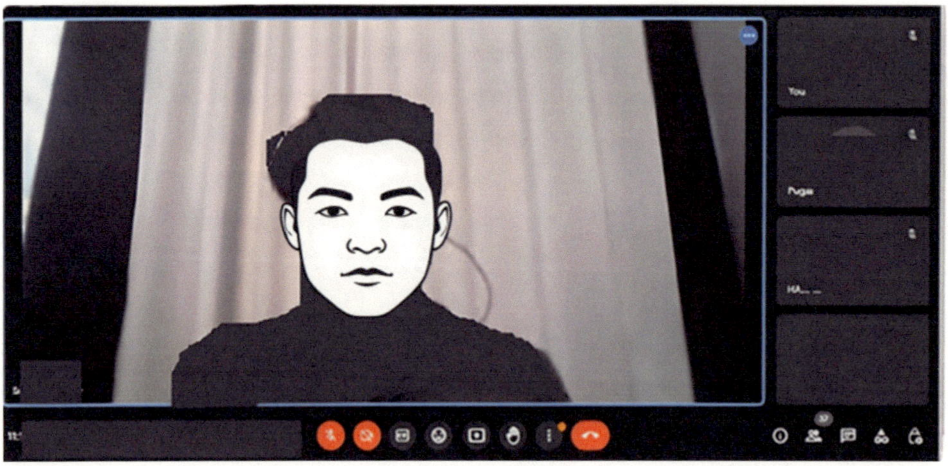

Figure 5.
Virtual classroom (googlemeet).

have understood. In addition, AI can analyse lecture content, summarize key points, and generate concise notes to support efficient learning. AI also enhances virtual learning environments through interactive quizzes and surveys [6]. These tools allow educators to measure the level of understanding in the class in real time, thus enabling active participation. For instance, a machine can generate a set of test questions about the topics covered and, after a lecture, provide students with an opportunity to assess their knowledge as well as receive immediate feedback. The use of interactive surveys can gather opinions and spark discussions meant to build community in a virtual classroom.

Yet another important benefit AI brings to virtual education is student engagement monitoring and analysis. Techniques, such as sentiment analysis [27], allow AI to analyse the student's facial expressions, tone, and other behaviours during virtual class sessions. That information provides insights into students' levels of interest, motivation, and understanding. Teachers may use this knowledge to identify the disengagement of their students and implement remedies, such as changing teaching styles or providing supplementary support.

Figure 6 illustrates the model of a virtual classroom used for learning. AI-driven technologies have helped with administrative tasks by allowing educators to focus on teaching and jobs like grading assignments, managing attendance, and organizing sessions for group activities. These efficiencies not only save time but also enhance the overall learning experience. With the variety of benefits in teaching pedagogies, the potential of AI in virtual education is long and arduous.

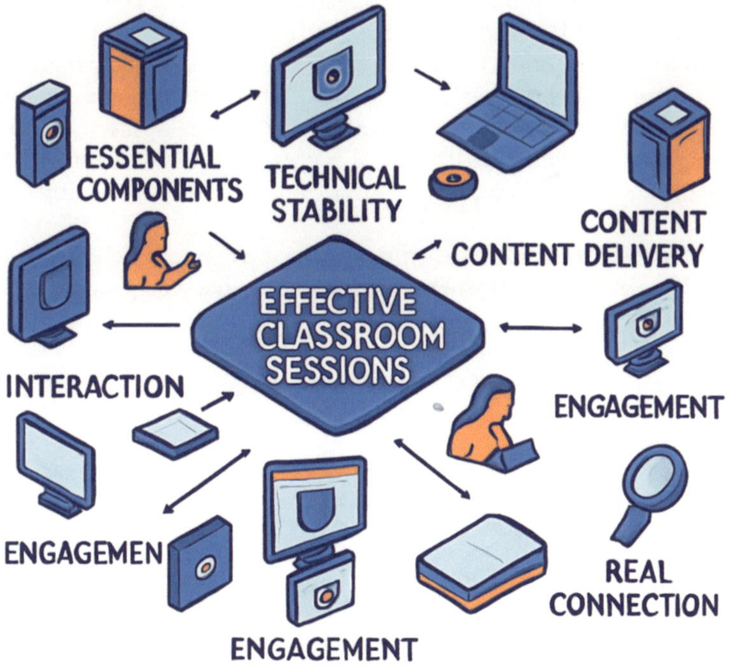

Figure 6.
Essentials of virtual classroom learning.

Ensuring data privacy, addressing technical glitches, and bridging digital divides [28, 29] are issues that still need to be resolved for equitable learning. However, with continued innovations in AI technology, the future seems bright for virtual and hybrid learning. Platforms such as Zoom, Google Meet, Google Classroom, and Microsoft Teams, equipped with AI-driven tools, have revolutionized the teaching–learning process. Lectures transcribed by AI, interactive quizzes created by AI, and analysis of student engagement and learning experiences make virtual learning dynamic and impactful.

4. Skill education

Skill-based education is another opportunity to acquire new skills through innovative experiential learning. This is more evident in disciplines such as Programming, Graphic Designing, Photo/Video Editing, Digital Marketing, Business and Management, Public Speaking, Academic and Business Writing, Electronic Mechanics, Dress Making, Fashion Design Technology, Cosmetology, Office Management, and technical competencies, which require practical experience for mastering skills. AI-driven platforms such as LinkedIn Learning, Udacity, Codecademy, Khan Academy, edX, Skillsoft, DataCamp, and Skillshare [8, 30–36] empower students to acquire industry-relevant expertise in a flexible, self-paced environment.

The most significant contribution of AI in skill-based education is its ability to design an interactive and immersive learning experience. This is quite distinct from the traditional approach, which gives academic knowledge more weight than practical experience presented above in the **Figure** 7. In a web programming course, we can see students creating real-world websites or genuine apps, and the AI tools instantly offer comments and ideas for development without human intervention. In robotics, students may also create, test, and improve their creations using simulations and virtual environments without relying on any costly hardware.

Platforms like Udacity, Codecademy, edX, and Skillshare do cater to the many demands and preferences of learners. With subjects like web programming, graphic

Figure 7.
Skill education learning.

design, data science, and machine learning, such platforms provide courses at several levels – from basic introductions to advanced specialties. These platforms suggest courses, tutorials, and projects based on a learner's interests and ability level. Personalization guarantees that learners focus on what is important to them and hence ensures they maximize productivity and engagement.

One of the most important features of online learning systems is their flexibility. AI encourages self-paced learning and enables learners to access materials anywhere and at any moment. This especially suits students with multiple commitments and working professionals. For instance, someone eager for an employment switch into information science may learn Python programming or machine learning methods at their discretion, free from the usual class schedule. It is considered a virtual mentor, and this technology answers questions tailored to the knowledge of the learner and clarifies difficult ideas. In a programming class, an AI instructor would help a student identify errors, troubleshoot their code, and provide a solution. Instant support allows the student to be more confident in using what they have learned, which helps them comprehend the subject very well.

AI-driven techniques used at Codecademy, edX, Skillshare, and similar platforms assess a student's performance via quizzes, assignments, and projects [10, 25, 26]. These tests include thorough comments that are more extensive than conventional grading. AI is now changing the face of skill-based education by allowing experiential learning. These platforms enable learners to gain industry-relevant skills through interactive, personalized, and flexible courses in web programming and robotics, among others, which bridge the gap between education and the ever-changing demands of the workforce.

5. Computer designing and data science

AI has, without a doubt, revamped the educational world in the modern scheme of professional training regarding tough subjects like computer-aided design (CAD) and data science. With an influx of vast amounts of AI into every arena, earlier seemingly complicated aspects of technical knowledge can be learned today in much more fun-filled modes through websites and other mediums of communication, thereby transforming AutoCAD [37] to Tableau [38]-based knowledge into something easier for speedy and fruitful comprehension by professionals in training. **Figure 8** shows the model design of a robot using CAD

Tools such as AutoCAD [37] have emerged as an important necessity in CAD for architects, engineers, and designers. The application of AI on these platforms further enhances them by providing design suggestions, identifying errors, and optimizations. In fact, even when a person is creating a three-dimensional (3D) model, real-time analysis by AI algorithms can assist with the creation suggesting areas that could improve functionality or aesthetics. In addition to saving time, these innovative functions make it easier for students to comprehend industry norms and best practices. Beginners as well may learn CAD tools more easily due to AI's step-by-step instructions and skill-level-customized training.

In a similar way, tools like Tableau [38] have increased interest in and accessibility to data science. **Figure 9** illustrates the features that students generally use data in Tableau's [38] AI-powered features and user-friendly interface without possessing a lot of programming skills. It can construct

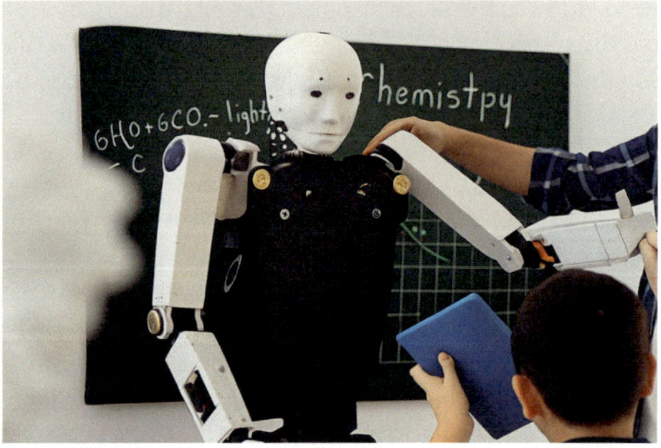

Figure 8.
Model design of robotics and CAD.

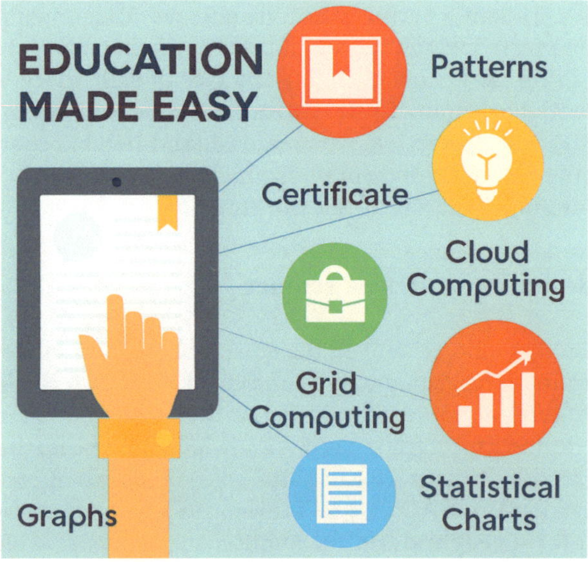

Figure 9.
Use of statistical tools.

patterns, make predictions, and suggest recommendations for the data. Instead of wasting too much time on technical complexities, this enables students to concentrate on strengthening their findings. These technologies further streamline the learning process by utilizing NLP to enable conversational queries of the data. Amazon SageMaker, Anaconda platform, Data Camp, UpGrad, Great Learning, Coursera, and RapidMiner [7, 39–43] are the key contributors to AI, and these applications have the ability to provide real-time recommendations and insights. CAD can suggest alternative materials or structural improvements, and data science could involve highlighting outliers or identifying key performance indicators. These features mimic the role of a mentor, offering personalized guidance that helps users improve their work and build confidence in their skills.

AI increases entertainment value. A gamification layer, interactive tutorial, and virtual or augmented reality can easily be integrated to make the whole learning process very engaging [10–12]. Data science platforms often offer quizzes and scenarios that mimic real-world analytics problems, whereas design tools often provide challenges where designs are tested under various conditions and simulations. Learners are engaged and gain an improved understanding of the subject matter through this participatory method [13, 14, 18–24]. The integration of data science and computer design technologies helps fill the knowledge gap. By collaborating on real-world projects, students may acquire practical skills that are in demand in the job market. For example, a student of data science may utilize Tableau [38] to examine a dataset that resembles what a company analyst could face, while a student of CAD could create a prototype that conforms to actual engineering limitations. The use of some of the more complex functions helps with the steep learning curve. As AI develops further, it will streamline and improve technical education, which will benefit students and workers everywhere. The use of AI has completely transformed the way design and modeling education is conducted. These apps have made technical education more accessible and enjoyable for students of all levels by simplifying complex operations, offering quick feedback, and improving the learning process.

6. National Education Policy (NEP) 2020 and AI integration

The NEP 2020 [49] has transformed the country's educational architecture. The education system has taken a revolutionary step in integrating technology and AI aspects into its curriculum. Thus, it emphasizes a progressive and multidisciplinary education system by preparing learners with today's and tomorrow's knowledge and skills to stay competitive. AI, with its potential, is being utilized in multiple ways to improve learning experiences across various disciplines. It plays a crucial role in NEP 2020 [44] through the development of AI-driven courses in STEM fields and the humanities. These courses integrate theoretical knowledge with practical application, enhancing the interactivity and engagement of the learning process. AI models intricate concepts such as physics experiments, chemical reactions, and mathematical problem-solving within STEM fields. Using virtual museums, historical reconstructions, and cultural studies, AI tools in the arts enable collaborative learning. This interdisciplinary approach fosters well-rounded students by integrating science and the arts into their cognitive processes. **Figure 10** presents the login interface of the student learning dashboard.

The technology significantly contributes to the advancement of multilingual education, which is a central objective of NEP 2020 [44]. The linguistic diversity of India complicates the provision of education in multiple languages. Innovative translation technologies have eliminated language barriers, enabling real-time translation of educational materials into various regional languages, thereby ensuring equitable access to learning resources for all students. AI-based translators [28] can convert complex science lectures into Hindi, Tamil, Bengali, or other Indian languages, thereby enhancing access to quality education for a broader audience.

Vocational education is another area where AI is making a big difference. NEP 2020 [44] recognizes the importance of skill-based learning and emphasizes the

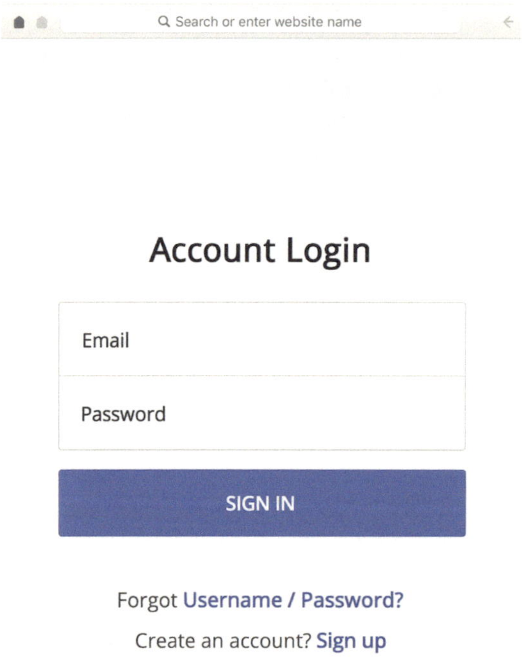

Figure 10.
Login panel for a learner.

inclusion of modular courses in emerging fields like the Internet of Things (IoT), machine learning, blockchain [1, 45], and more. These platforms make this possible by providing learning experiences tailored to the needs of individual learners. The AI-designed courses are often tailored to a student's interests and career goals, facilitating practical training via virtual labs and simulating real-world scenarios to equip learners for their workplace. This method provides learners with essential skills while promoting creativity and business acumen. Additionally, it plays a crucial role in tracking and improving the entire process of learning. AI-driven advanced analytics offer insights into student performance, enabling educators to pinpoint areas where learners require further assistance. Tools powered by AI aid in the creation of adaptable learning environments in which the speed and content of instruction can both be tailored to individual needs [14, 21].

NEP 2020 [44] emphasizes the integration of AI and technology as a strategic approach to modernizing India's education system for equity in technological access, data privacy, and instructor capacity to teach effectively.

The NEP 2020 highlights the transformative potential of AI technology in the field of education. The initiative aims to develop a future-ready generation by implementing multidisciplinary courses, offering multilingual education, and providing vocational training in advanced fields. It enhances educational quality while promoting inclusivity, adaptability, and alignment with the demands of a globalized context.

7. AI-powered career guidance

AI is also revolutionizing the job guidance and placement process, helping students to better plan their careers [43]. It provides insights and suggestions that were previously difficult to obtain as the employment market changes. Career Coach and LinkedIn Learning are two platforms at the forefront of this shift, using complex algorithms to assess students' talents and recommend viable career paths. The ability to evaluate individual abilities is one of the most valuable skills in professional growth. These portals analyse a variety of data points, including a student's academic record, employment experience, and success in online courses. These systems can offer appropriate jobs based on a student's talents and knowledge. For example, if a student excels in coding and data analytics, the platform may recommend a career in software development or data science. This individualized guidance improves students' chances of success in the job market and allows them to make informed decisions about their future.

>Moreover, job platforms can track trends in the constantly changing job market. As new industries emerge and existing ones transform, these tools monitor these fluctuations. LinkedIn Learning and Career Coach [30, 46] analyse job postings, industry reports, and skills in demand, allowing educational institutions to adjust their curricula and courses to meet current labour market needs. For example, if there is an increase in the need for cybersecurity specialists, institutions can provide relevant courses and training programs to prepare individuals for these responsibilities. These platforms benefit not just learners and educational institutions, but also companies looking for talent. By expediting the recruiting process, they link people to employment possibilities that match their talents and interests. Employers may use these technologies to find individuals who not only have the requisite qualifications but also fit well with their company culture, thus increasing the hiring process's efficacy. This streamlining reduces the time and effort required by both job seekers and employers, making the placement process more effective.

Another advantage of these technologies is the availability of materials and support for professional growth. As technology progresses, it becomes more critical to address concerns like algorithm bias, data privacy, and the need for human oversight in decision-making. Ensuring that these systems are fair and accessible to all is critical to their long-term viability and acceptance in the workplace. Platforms like LinkedIn Learning and Career Coach [30, 46] are significantly changing the way career counseling and placement are handled. They assess students' abilities and make suggestions for courses that will benefit their future jobs. Furthermore, they allow educational institutions to respond to labour market developments, ensuring that course offerings are in line with industry demands.

8. Advantages of AI in higher education

The use of AI in higher learning benefits not just learners but educational institutions equally. Many companies are looking for talent, expediting the recruiting process, and connecting with people for employment that matches their talents and interests [47]. Employers may use these technologies to find individuals who not only have the requisite qualifications but also fit well with their company culture, thereby increasing the hiring process's efficacy [5, 7–9, 27, 48]. This streamlining reduces the time and effort required by both job seekers and employers, making the placement process more effective.

AI is drastically altering the educational environment in a variety of ways, addressing different challenges and enhancing the learning experience.

To conclude, some of the main advantages are:

Increased access: Intelligent systems have removed numerous geographical and physical obstacles that once limited access to high-quality education. Many pupils in remote or underprivileged locations may not have had access to a diverse set of learning tools and opportunities. These technologies bridge the gap by providing instructional information to learners directly via online platforms.

Furthermore, translation technologies break down linguistic barriers, allowing pupils from varied backgrounds to access the same instructional resources [49][50]. This capacity encourages worldwide cooperation and develops a learning community. A student in a rural town, for example, can enroll in an online course taught by a foreign expert, earning information and abilities that would otherwise be unattainable.

Economic efficiency: These improvements enhance learning efficiency by minimizing reliance on physical infrastructure and human resources. Due to the requirement for classrooms, supplies, and personnel, the institutional costs of maintaining the old system can be enormous. These expenditures are reduced by intelligent technology, which ultimately lowers tuition fees.

Online classes [23–25], for example, may accommodate a large number of students in one session without the need for several physical classrooms. This transition not only lowers educational costs but also makes excellent education more affordable and accessible to students.

Student involvement is one of the most essential aspects of educational achievement. This involvement is considerably enhanced by interactive and personalized learning materials. These systems offer knowledge in a way that resonates with each learner's learning style and preferences, thereby retaining motivation and interest.

Furthermore, individualized learning experiences help to lower dropout rates. Students are more inclined to continue their education if they feel encouraged and interested. For example, an adaptable platform can change assignment difficulty based on a student's performance, keeping them challenged but not overwhelmed.

Scalability: This is one of the most noticeable features of intelligent systems in education. These systems can accommodate thousands of students at the same time while maintaining instructional quality. This function is especially useful when specific courses or programs are in extremely high demand.

For example, during the COVID-19 epidemic, many educational institutions were unexpectedly overburdened with students switching to online education. These platforms quickly absorbed the surge, providing every learner with access to courses and materials. Scalability is critical for satisfying the expanding worldwide demand for education.

Empirical insights: Data-driven methods allow educational institutions to harness the power of analytics. These systems can provide useful insights into student performance, course efficacy, and opportunities for development by analysing large datasets.

These findings can help educators improve their teaching skills, create focused interventions, and enhance course design. For example, if statistics show that students struggle with a certain idea, teachers may alter their approach accordingly, improving the entire learning experience.

DOI: http://dx.doi.org/10.5772/intechopen.1012993

Feature	Online education in India	AI in Indian education
Key applications	Access to courses from anywhere, flexible learning schedules, cost-effective education, and the ability to reach geographically dispersed students	Personalized learning, intelligent tutoring systems, adaptive assessments, automated grading, content creation, and predictive analytics for student success
Benefits for students	Self-paced learning, choice of courses, the ability to learn at their own time, and access to diverse learning materials	Tailored learning paths based on individual needs, immediate feedback, targeted support in areas of weakness, and improved engagement
Benefits for teachers	Efficient content delivery, the ability to monitor student progress, and time-saving features for grading and feedback	Enhanced ability to personalize instruction, deeper insights into student learning, and more effective interventions
Challenges	Digital divide, internet connectivity issues, lack of access to technology in rural areas, and quality control of online courses	Potential for bias in algorithms, data privacy concerns, and teacher training needed to effectively integrate AI tools
Popular platforms	Coursera, Udemy, EdX, Unacademy, Byju's	AI-powered learning platforms like the "BYJU'S" app, personalized tutoring systems, and adaptive learning software
Impact on the Indian education system	Increased access to quality education, particularly for those in remote areas, has the potential to bridge the skill gap	Transformative potential to improve learning outcomes, address individual students' needs, and enhance teaching effectiveness

Table 1.
Features of online learning in India.

AI advances are transforming education by boosting accessibility, improving economic efficiency, increasing engagement and retention, enabling scale, and offering empirical insights as listed in **Table 1** below. The potential for designing a more inclusive and successful educational landscape is enormous, providing opportunities for students all across the world to achieve academically.

9. Challenges and concerns

Issues and concerns: While the integration of AI into education has many benefits, there are several issues and concerns to consider, including equity and inclusivity, data privacy and security, the role of human contact, and reliance on technology.

Equity and inclusiveness: The most fundamental concerns in AI integration in education are equity and inclusiveness. On one hand, AI technologies have the potential to increase access to learning resources and generate more tailored educational experiences. On the other hand, AI technologies also have the potential to widen the digital divide. Students who do not have dependable access to technology or the internet fall behind their peers, creating a vicious cycle of marginalization in which impoverished children are denied the benefits of individualized learning, thereby widening the gap. This necessitates a collaborative effort on the part of legislators, instructors, and technology providers to ensure that all students who interact with AI-enabled educational content have equal access to opportunities.

Data privacy and security: Another key concern is data privacy and security because it collects a large quantity of student data in order to assess learning patterns and provide insights into personalized suggestions. While these data can be extremely useful for improving educational results, it raises fundamental concerns about how it is handled, utilized, and safeguarded. Parents and educators are concerned about the ethical implications of data gathering, such as the potential abuse or disclosure of sensitive information. Maintaining confidence among kids, parents, and instructors requires strong data protection mechanisms and transparent data usage regulations.

Human touch: Another crucial part of education that AI cannot provide is the personal touch. Although AI can assist with material delivery and performance evaluation, it cannot replace the human qualities of intuition, empathy, and mentorship essential for student growth. Many educators and parents believe that personal engagement with instructors promotes motivation, emotional support, and social skills. Without these social human connections, learners' overall progress is likely to be stalled, as they miss out on essential mentorship and facilitation, both of which are critical components of a learner's educational journey.

In conclusion, an overriding fear about AI-based deployment is the growing reliance on technology. As students utilize AI to respond to and solve issues, there is a risk that their critical thinking and problem-solving abilities may deteriorate. When technology becomes a crutch rather than a tool, children may struggle to think for themselves or even tackle hard issues without assistance. Educators must find a balance between leveraging AI capabilities and encouraging students to be more analytical, creative, and resilient in problem-solving.

Although AI holds immense potential for the future of education, it poses significant difficulties and issues that must be addressed. Ensuring fairness and inclusion, data protection, preserving the human touch in learning, and avoiding overreliance on technology are all critical for maximizing the benefits of AI in education. Once these difficulties have been identified and addressed, we can strive to create an educational environment that leverages the potential of AI while addressing the needs and well-being of all students.

10. Future of AI in higher education

AI is now well-integrated into higher education, and its introduction and implementation are rapidly changing the landscape of this academic field. Numerous contemporary developments connected to its advancement are shaping the future, enhancing the learning experience, and enabling educators and institutions to better prepare students for a changing workforce.

AI-Enhanced Research Support is one of the most promising technologies, as depicted in **Figures 11** and **12**. **Figure 11** shows the ER diagram, and Figure 12 shows the flowchart of the Learning Management System. One of the most promising technologies is AI-enhanced research support. Tools like ChatGPT and Scite.ai [46] are changing the way students and researchers approach literature reviews and hypothesis development. They enable fast access to a vast collection of academic papers, journals, and data, expediting the research process and allowing users to swiftly obtain relevant information. For example, it may help a researcher write a summary or explain a topic; whereas Scite.ai [46], highlights how that work has been cited in other studies, providing crucial context and insight. It not only improves the quality of research but also saves time, allowing students and academics to think critically and carefully about subjects.

DOI: http://dx.doi.org/10.5772/intechopen.1012993

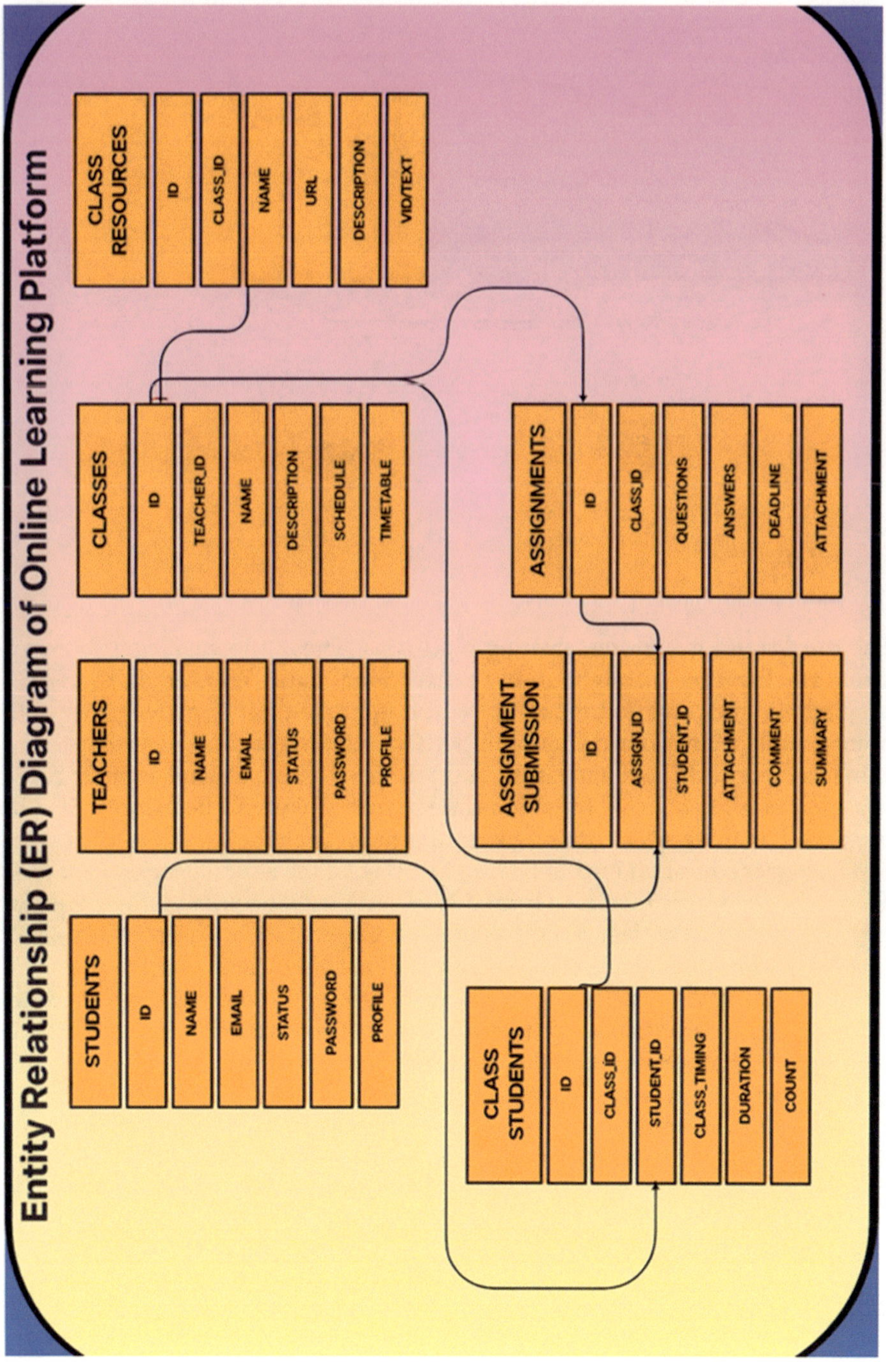

Figure 11.
Entity relationship (ER) diagram of an online learning platform.

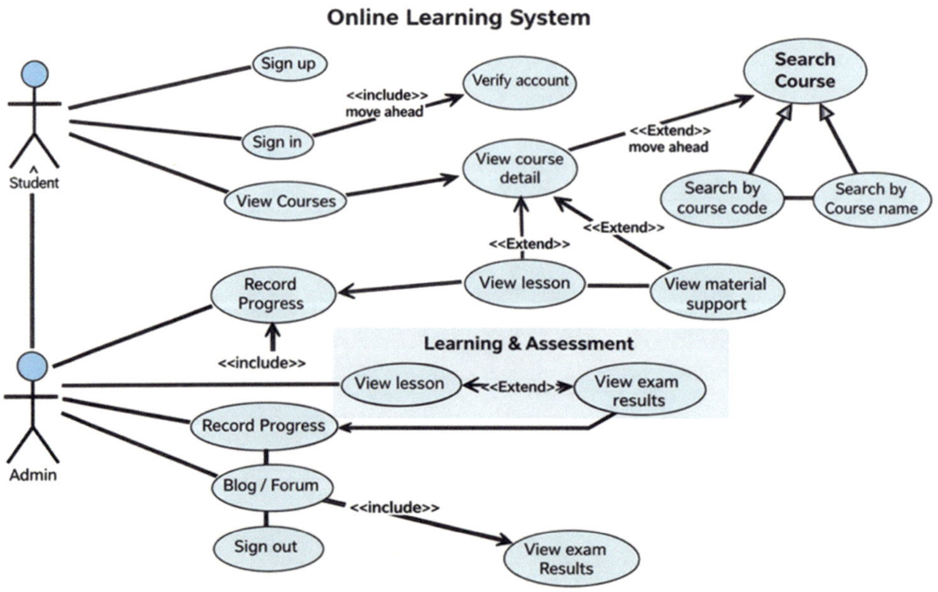

Figure 12.
Flowchart of LMS.

The third trend is lifelong learning platforms. These allow colleges to provide continuous education throughout any professional path. Workers in today's shifting employment market must renew and upgrade their knowledge, as well as learn new skills, to maintain their competitive advantage. These systems can examine the learner's past education and job experience, as well as their career aspirations, to offer courses in which the learner is likely to be interested. This tailored method guarantees lifelong learning to meet changing needs in any area.

Today, higher education institutions are focusing on the ethical development of AI. As these technologies are increasingly used in educational institutions, universities are making pledges to ensure their AI systems are more open, fair, and responsible. This focus on ethics addresses concerns such as algorithmic biases, data privacy, and technology's potential impact on the employment market. Prioritizing these concerns can assist institutions in establishing trust with students and other stakeholders while also encouraging the appropriate use of technology in education.

This technology is also extremely important in enhanced skill-based education. With the constant expansion of companies, courses in a variety of fields, including cybersecurity, sustainable technology, and advanced data analytics, are in high demand. Based on labour market trends and skill needs, educational institutions can develop relevant curricula for students to learn abilities that will be useful in their professions. The incorporation of these technologies into educational courses equips graduates to navigate the intricacies of the modern world.

While technologies are increasingly taking over certain aspects of conventional teaching, the future of education will depend on finding a balance between technology and human educators [29]. The classroom, coupled with intelligent technology, will supplement the educational experience rather than replace the important role of an instructor. Human teachers contribute sympathy, mentorship, and the capacity to engage students in ways that robots cannot.

To summarize, the future of AI in higher education is bright, with promising trends towards improving research support, lifelong learning, addressing ethical challenges, and understanding applicable skill-based education. In light of these developments, colleges will need to seek out the capabilities of technology while retaining all the basics of human growth in education and learning. Institutions will be able to provide a more effective and enriching educational experience for all students.

11 Conclusion

AI has emerged as a defining force in the transformation of higher education, replacing many traditional practices with innovative, efficient, and student-centered approaches. From personalized learning platforms and ITSs to automated assessments, virtual classrooms, and skill-based education, AI has redefined how knowledge is delivered, acquired, and applied [45]. Its integration with national initiatives such as the NEP 2020 further highlights its potential to democratize education, foster multilingual and vocational learning, and prepare learners for global competitiveness [44, 45].

However, the promise of AI in education comes with critical challenges. Issues of equity, inclusivity, data privacy, algorithmic bias, and the risk of overreliance on technology must be carefully addressed to ensure fair and ethical adoption. Equally important is the recognition that AI cannot replace the empathy, mentorship, and human connection that teachers bring to the learning process. Instead, the future of education lies in a balanced paradigm where AI augments the role of educators, enabling them to focus on creativity, critical thinking, and holistic development.

In essence, AI in education is still at an early stage, yet it holds unprecedented opportunities to shape a more accessible, engaging, and future-ready learning ecosystem. Its success will depend on how effectively institutions, policymakers, and educators integrate technology while preserving the human essence of teaching and learning.

Author details

Asif Iqbal Kawoosa[1]* and Deepak Prashar[2]

1 Government College for Women, Srinagar, India

2 Lovely Professional University, Jalandhar, India

*Address all correspondence to: asifkawoosa19@gmail.com

References

[1] Russell S, and Norvig P. Artificial Intelligence: A Modern Approach. 4th ed. Hoboken, NJ, USA: Pearson; 2020

[2] Mitchell T. Machine Learning. New York, NY, USA: McGraw-Hill; 1997

[3] Brusilovsky P, Peylo C. Adaptive and intelligent web-based educational systems. IJAIED. 2003;**13**:159–172

[4] Heffernan H, Heffernan N.The assistments ecosystem. IJAIED. 2014;**24** (4):470–497

[5] VanLehn K.The Behavior of Tutoring Systems. IJAIED. 2006;**16** (3):227–265

[6] Woolf B, et al. AI Grand Challenges for Education. AI Magazine 2013;**34**: 66–84

[7] Coursera, "Online Learning Platform for University-Level Courses," [Online]. Available from: https://www.coursera.org/ [Accessed: 2024-January-10]

[8] Khan Academy, "Free Online Courses, Lessons & Practice," [Online]. Available from: https://www.khanacademy.org/ [Accessed: 2020-November-17]

[9] SWAYAM, Ministry of education, govt. of india, "study webs of active–learning for young aspiring minds," [Online]. Available from: https://swayam.gov.in/ [Accessed: 2020-August-18]

[10] Unacademy, "India's largest online learning platform," [Online]. Available from: https://unacademy.com/ [Accessed: 2021-December-10]

[11] Open English, "Online english learning platform," [Online]. Available from: https://www.openenglish.com/

[12] Grammarly, "AI writing assistant," [Online]. Available from: https://www.grammarly.com/ [Accessed: 2020-March-12]

[13] ChatGPT, OpenAI, "AI language model for natural language processing," [Online]. Available from: https://chat.openai.com/

[14] Google Dialogflow, "Conversational AI platform," [Online]. Available from: https://cloud.google.com/dialogflow [Accessed: 2023-February-10]

[15] BYJU'S, "Online learning app for K–12 students," [Online]. Available from: https://byjus.com/

[16] Toppr, "Online learning app for school students," [Online]. Available from: https://www.toppr.com/ [Accessed: 2024-October-22]

[17] Socratic by Google, "Homework help and student learning app," [Online]. Available from: https://socratic.org/

[18] Quizizz, "Free gamified quizzes for students and teachers," [Online]. Available from: https://quizizz.com/ [Accessed: 2024-October-20]

[19] Gradescope, "Grading platform for instructors and Tas," [Online]. Available from: https://gradescope.com/

[20] Turnitin, "Plagiarism detection and academic integrity software," [Online]. Available from: https://www.turnitin.com/ [Accessed: 2021-March-10]

[21] IBM Watson Assistant, "AI-powered virtual agent," [Online]. Available from: https://www.ibm.com/cloud/watson-assistant/

[22] Microsoft Azure Bot Service, "AI bot framework and chatbot service," [Online]. Available from: https://azure.microsoft.com/ [Accessed: 2024-March-10]

[23] Zoom, "Video conferencing and virtual meeting platform," [Online]. Available from: https://zoom.us/ [Accessed: 2024-March-10]

[24] Google Meet, "Secure video meetings for teams and businesses," [Online]. Available from: https://meet.google.com/ [Accessed: 2021-October-10]

[25] Google Classroom, "Virtual classroom and course management system," [Online]. Available from: https://classroom.google.com/ [Accessed: 2021-October-10]

[26] Microsoft Teams, "Collaboration and communication platform for education," [Online]. Available from: https://www.microsoft.com/en-us/microsoft-teams/

[27] Salinas-Chipana, José, et al. "Machine learning models for predicting student dropout—A review." In: International Congress on Information and Communication Technology. Singapore: Springer Nature Singapore; 2023

[28] UNESCO. Artificial intelligence in education: Challenges and opportunities. Working Papers on Education Policy. 2019

[29] KPMG in India and Google, Online Education in India: 2021. India: KPMG; May 2017. Available: https://assets.kpmg.com/content/dam/kpmg/in/pdf/2017/05/Online-Education-in-India-2021.pdf [Accessed: 2025–December–10]

[30] LinkedIn Learning, "Online training for career development," [Online]. Available from: https://www.linkedin.com/learning/ [Accessed: 2024-November-10]

[31] Codecademy, "Interactive programming and coding courses," [Online]. Available from: https://www.codecademy.com/ [Accessed: 2024-November 10]

[32] edX, "Online university-level courses from top institutions," [Online]. Available from: https://www.edx.org/ [Accessed: 2021-June-17]

[33] Skillshare, "Online classes for creativity and practical skills," [Online]. Available from: https://www.skillshare.com/ [Accessed: 2021-July-5]

[34] Udacity, "Nanodegree programs in tech fields," [Online]. Available from: https://www.udacity.com/ [Accessed: 2022-September-6]

[35] Skillsoft, "Digital learning platform for businesses and professionals," [Online]. Available from: https://www.skillsoft.com/ [Accessed: 2021-February-6]

[36] DataCamp, "Online data science and analytics courses,", 2025. [Online]. Available from: https://www.datacamp.com/ [Accessed: 2022-June-18]

[37] AutoCAD, "Design and drafting software by autodesk," [Online]. Available from: https://www.autodesk.in/products/autocad/ [Accessed: 2024-September-19]

[38] Tableau, "Business intelligence and data analytics software," [Online]. Available from: https://www.tableau.com/ [Accessed: 2024-November-19]

[39] Amazon SageMaker, "Build, train, and deploy machine learning models," [Online]. Available from: https://aws.amazon.com/sagemaker/ [Accessed: 2023-November-15]

[40] Anaconda, "Anaconda: The world's most popular data science platform," [Online]. Available from: https://www.anaconda.com/ [Accessed: 2022-April-10]

[41] RapidMiner, "Data science and machine learning platform," [Online]. Available from: https://rapidminer.com/ [Accessed: 2024-December-5]

[42] UpGrad, "Online higher education platform," [Online]. Available from: https://www.upgrad.com/ [Accessed: 2022-May-15]

[43] Great Learning, "Online learning and career success programs," [Online]. Available from: https://www.greatlearning.in/ [Accessed: 2023-September-18]

[44] Ministry of Education, Govt. of India, "National education policy 2020," [Online].Available from: https://www.education.gov.in/sites/upload_files/mhrd/files/NEP_Final_English_0.pdf [Accessed: 2023-November-15]

[45] OECD, "AI and the future of skills: Capabilities and assessments," 2023. [Online]. Available from: https://www.oecd.org/publications/ai-and-the-future-of-skills-49080ed2-en.htm [Accessed: 2022-November-10]

[46] Scite.ai, "Smart citations for research," [Online]. Available from: https://scite.ai/ [Accessed: 2022-October-10]

[47] Luckin A, et al. Intelligence Unleashed: An Argument for AI in Education. London, UK: Pearson; 2016

[48] Holmes B, et al. Artificial Intelligence in Education: Promises and Implications for Teaching and Learning. Brussels, Belgium: European Commission; 2019

[49] Corbett AT, Anderson JR. Knowledge tracing: modeling the acquisition of procedural knowledge. User Modeling and User-Adapted Interaction. 1995;**4**:253–278

[50] Kay J, et al. Lifelong learner modeling for personalized education. User Modeling and User-Adapted Interaction 2018;**28**:1–4

Section 2

Pedagogy, Teaching Approaches & Classroom Integration of AI

Chapter 8

The Pedagogical Paradox of AI: Sustaining Critical Thinking through Activity-Based Learning

Priya Soni

Abstract

The rapid integration of artificial intelligence (AI) into educational environments has sparked both excitement and concern regarding its impact on pedagogy and student development. While AI offers personalized learning, efficiency, and scalability, it also raises questions about the erosion of critical thinking skills and learner autonomy. This chapter explores the tension between AI-driven instruction and activity-based pedagogy, emphasizing the latter's potential to preserve and cultivate critical thinking in the digital age. Activity-based learning – rooted in experiential, collaborative, and inquiry-oriented practices – encourages deeper engagement and intellectual resilience, which are often sidelined in AI-mediated learning environments. Drawing on contemporary educational theory and empirical studies, the chapter argues for a balanced approach where AI supports, rather than supplants, pedagogies that promote critical reasoning. The study underscores the need for educators and policymakers to intentionally design learning experiences that integrate technology without compromising the foundational goals of education – namely, fostering independent thought, creativity, and lifelong learning.

Keywords: AI, education, pedagogy, activity-based pedagogy, critical thinking

1. Introduction

The 21st-century educational landscape is undergoing a profound transformation, largely influenced by the rapid integration of artificial intelligence (AI). As digital technologies become embedded in educational systems, AI has emerged as a key driver of innovation in teaching and learning. From intelligent tutoring systems to automated grading and predictive analytics, AI promises to revolutionize education by offering personalized learning paths, real-time feedback, and data-informed instruction [1–3]. These technologies hold the potential to enhance learning outcomes, improve operational efficiency, and expand access to quality education, especially in under-resourced contexts [4].

However, the growing reliance on AI also raises significant pedagogical and philosophical concerns. One of the most critical issues is that while AI systems are

IntechOpen

designed to optimize performance and adapt content to individual learners, they may inadvertently promote surface-level learning and passive consumption of information. In such environments, critical thinking – a skill essential for analyzing, evaluating, and synthesizing information – is at risk of being sidelined in favor of mechanistic task completion and efficiency [5]. Moreover, the reduction of complex learning processes into algorithmic decision-making may curtail students' intellectual curiosity, creativity, and autonomy [6, 7].

This chapter examines the growing tension between AI-driven instruction and activity-based pedagogy, with particular attention to how critical thinking is cultivated – or compromised – in AI-mediated educational settings. It argues that while AI can enhance aspects of learning through individualized support and adaptive content delivery, it should not replace the foundational elements of active pedagogy that engage learners as co-constructors of knowledge. Rather than viewing AI as a wholesale replacement for traditional pedagogy, its integration should be thoughtfully aligned with instructional frameworks that support student agency, inquiry, and reflective engagement [8].

Activity-based pedagogy – rooted in experiential, collaborative, and inquiry-oriented learning – is especially well suited to promoting higher-order thinking skills. Drawing on constructivist and socio-cultural theories, this approach emphasizes learning as a dynamic process shaped by interaction, exploration, and reflection [9, 10]. It provides opportunities for learners to engage in problem-solving, dialogue, and project-based learning – contexts in which critical thinking is most effectively developed [11].

In today's increasingly digitized classrooms, it is crucial to preserve pedagogical practices that support deep learning and intellectual resilience. As we stand at the intersection of technological advancement and educational purpose, the question is not whether AI should be adopted, but how it should be harmonized with pedagogical models that nurture human capacities such as reasoning, creativity, empathy, and ethical reflection [4, 12]. This chapter aims to highlight the role of activity-based learning as a counterbalance to passive digital instruction and proposes a framework in which AI serves as a supportive tool – rather than a pedagogical substitute – for fostering critical thinking in the digital age.

2. Understanding critical thinking in contemporary education

Critical thinking involves the capacity to analyze information objectively, evaluate arguments, consider multiple perspectives, and synthesize insights into coherent conclusions. It also includes the ability to question assumptions, detect bias, and apply reasoning to real-world contexts [8]. These cognitive skills are foundational not only for academic success but also for ethical decision-making, responsible citizenship, and lifelong learning. In the context of the 21st century – marked by an overwhelming volume of information, algorithmic filtering, and the rise of deepfakes and misinformation – critical thinking is not just valuable; it is indispensable [4, 13].

Moreover, the increasing prevalence of AI-mediated environments has added complexity to the landscape. AI tools often prioritize efficiency, automation, and correct answers over ambiguity, exploration, and critical engagement [5]. While such tools can streamline content delivery and assess surface-level understanding, they are less effective at promoting the habits of mind needed to question, interpret, and construct new knowledge.

Educational theorists have long recognized that critical thinking must be cultivated through deliberate pedagogical strategies. John [6] emphasized the value of reflective thought and experiential learning as a means of fostering independent, intelligent action. For Dewey, true education arises not from rote memorization but from the learner's engagement with problems and their active effort to resolve them through inquiry. Paulo [7] similarly critiqued the "banking model" of education, where students are treated as empty vessels into which knowledge is deposited. Instead, he advocated for a dialogical, problem-posing approach, where learners are seen as co-creators of knowledge, capable of reflection, critique, and transformation.

These foundational ideas resonate strongly with **activity-based pedagogy**, which privileges collaboration, experimentation, and critical reflection. In such classrooms, students are not merely passive recipients of information but are engaged in real-world problems that demand reasoning, debate, and decision-making [9, 11]. These pedagogical environments foster metacognitive awareness – students not only learn but learn to think about their thinking, a hallmark of deep learning and critical capacity.

Contemporary curriculum frameworks echo these educational ideals. Bloom's Taxonomy, revised in the 2000s, places critical thinking-related cognitive processes such as "analyzing," "evaluating," and "creating" at the top of its hierarchy [14]. Likewise, frameworks such as the **P21 Framework for 21st Century Learning** explicitly highlight critical thinking and problem-solving as key competencies required for success in modern life and work [13].

However, fostering these skills is not achieved through content delivery alone. It requires intentional pedagogical design – tasks that are open-ended, allow for multiple perspectives, and involve learners in authentic inquiry [8, 9]. These are precisely the elements at risk in overly mechanized or algorithm-driven learning systems, where the focus is on speed, standardization, and correctness. AI systems, while efficient, can inadvertently minimize uncertainty and intellectual struggle – both of which are essential to developing critical thinking [3].

In conclusion, while AI tools can serve useful functions within education, they must be balanced with pedagogical strategies that preserve and promote critical thinking. Learners must be given opportunities to ask questions, consider alternatives, engage in sustained reflection, and construct their own understanding. Only then can education meet its higher purpose – not merely to inform, but to transform learners into thoughtful, discerning, and responsible individuals.

3. Rise of AI in education: Opportunities and challenges

The rise of AI in education marks a significant shift in how learning is delivered, assessed, and experienced. AI technologies – including machine learning algorithms, natural language processing, and intelligent tutoring systems – are increasingly integrated into digital learning platforms, transforming classrooms into adaptive, data-rich environments. While these developments offer numerous educational benefits, they also raise critical pedagogical, ethical, and psychological concerns. This section explores both the opportunities and challenges of AI adoption in education, emphasizing the importance of critical evaluation and balanced implementation.

3.1 Opportunities

3.1.1 Personalized learning

AI enables highly personalized learning experiences by adapting instructional content to the individual learner's pace, proficiency, and preferences [1, 2]. Algorithms analyze student responses in real time, identifying areas of difficulty and adjusting lessons accordingly. Intelligent tutoring systems like Carnegie Learning and Squirrel AI use adaptive pathways to ensure that learners receive targeted support, enhancing mastery and reducing frustration [3]. This tailored approach can improve engagement and accelerate learning for both high-achieving and struggling students.

3.1.2 Efficiency and automation

One of AI's most attractive features for educators is its potential to automate routine administrative tasks such as grading, attendance, and scheduling. AI-powered assessment tools can evaluate multiple-choice tests and even short answers with increasing accuracy, freeing up valuable time for teachers to focus on planning and student interaction [4]. Automated feedback systems also provide learners with instant responses, facilitating continuous formative assessment and timely corrections [8]. Artificial intelligence offers opportunities such as personalized learning, automation of administrative tasks, enhanced accessibility, and data-driven decision-making (**Figure 1**) [15–17].

3.1.3 Improved accessibility and inclusivity

AI technologies contribute significantly to making education more accessible for students with diverse needs. Speech-to-text and text-to-speech tools, real-time language translation, personalized user interfaces, and visual aids are helping break down barriers for learners with disabilities, language challenges, or learning differences [1]. Tools such as Microsoft Immersive Reader and Google's AI-powered captioning are examples of how AI enhances inclusivity in both physical and virtual classrooms.

Figure 1.
Opportunities in Artificial Intelligence (AI) -driven education [18].

3.1.4 Data-driven decision-making

AI systems provide educators and institutions with detailed analytics that can inform instructional strategies and policy decisions. Predictive analytics identify students at risk of failure or disengagement early, allowing timely interventions [12]. By analyzing patterns in student behavior, educators can make informed decisions about content sequencing, support allocation, and curriculum design [3]. Data dashboards powered by AI can help teachers pinpoint learning gaps and tailor lessons accordingly.

3.2 Challenges

Despite these substantial advantages, AI in education also presents serious challenges that must be addressed to ensure ethical and meaningful implementation as shown in **Figure 2**.

3.2.1 Reductionist learning models

Many AI systems function on the principle of breaking learning into discrete, easily measurable tasks. This atomized approach may lead to oversimplified learning experiences that prioritize completion and correctness over depth and complexity. By emphasizing right-answer paradigms, AI tools may discourage creative thinking, exploration, and intellectual struggle – all of which are critical to authentic learning [5].

3.2.2 Loss of human connection and teacher-student relationships

While AI can augment instruction, it cannot replace the nuanced interpersonal interactions that form the foundation of effective teaching and learning.

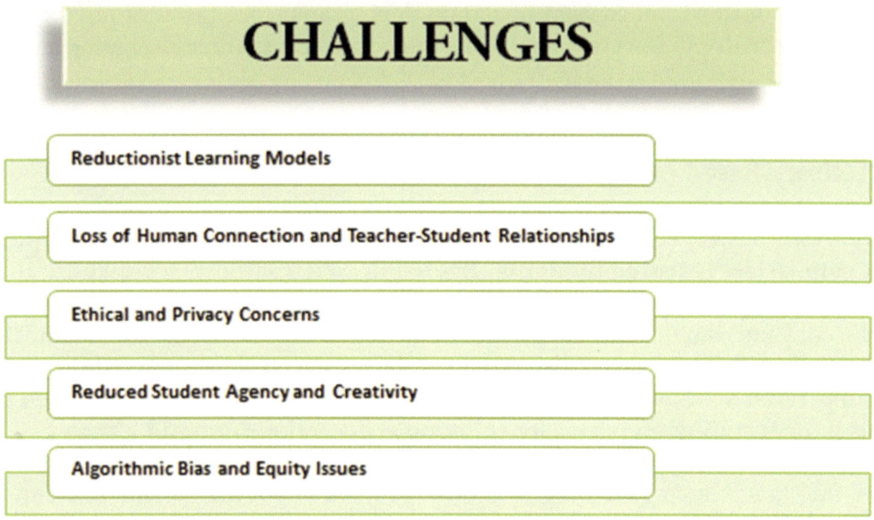

Figure 2.
Challenges of Artificial Intelligence Integration in Education [19].

Overreliance on AI systems risks reducing the teacher's role to that of a facilitator or technician, potentially undermining mentorship, emotional support, and the human connection essential to holistic education [4]. These relationships are especially crucial for fostering motivation, resilience, and a sense of belonging.

3.2.3 Ethical and privacy concerns

AI in education involves extensive data collection, raising significant ethical concerns around privacy, surveillance, and consent. Many platforms collect sensitive information such as learning behavior, emotional responses, and personal demographics. Without stringent data protection policies, this information may be misused or exposed to bias in decision-making [5]. Furthermore, AI algorithms can unintentionally reinforce systemic inequalities if not carefully designed and monitored.

3.2.4 Reduced student agency and creativity

AI systems, by optimizing learning paths and suggesting answers, may inadvertently encourage passivity. Students may become overly dependent on automated prompts and lose the ability to think independently or take initiative. The emphasis on efficiency and correctness may inhibit risk-taking, problem-solving, and engagement in inquiry-based learning. This is particularly concerning in an age where critical thinking, adaptability, and creativity are essential life skills.

3.2.5 Algorithmic bias and equity issues

AI algorithms are only as objective as the data they are trained on. If training data reflects historical biases or structural inequalities, the resulting AI systems may perpetuate or exacerbate those disparities. For example, adaptive learning platforms may suggest lower-level content to certain demographic groups, limiting their academic growth [3]. Ensuring equity in AI requires transparency, ongoing auditing, and inclusive design practices.

4. Activity-based pedagogy: Framework and benefits

Activity-based pedagogy represents a learner-centered instructional approach that emphasizes **learning by doing**. Rooted in constructivist, socio-cultural, and experiential learning theories, it positions the student as an active participant in the construction of knowledge rather than a passive recipient of transmitted content [6, 10]. This pedagogical model values authentic tasks, collaborative inquiry, reflection, and engagement with real-world problems, all of which are critical for fostering higher-order thinking skills and meaningful learning experiences.

Rather than viewing learning as a linear progression of memorized content, activity-based pedagogy highlights the importance of **contextualization**, **interaction**, and **reflection**. It aligns closely with the educational philosophies of thinkers such as John Dewey, who emphasized the importance of experience and reflection in the learning process, and Paulo Freire, who advocated for dialogical and problem-posing methods of education [6, 7]. This approach offers a compelling alternative to the increasingly standardized and automated learning environments shaped by AI, particularly when the goal is to cultivate critical thinking, autonomy, and creativity.

5. Key features of activity-based pedagogy

5.1 Experiential learning

Experiential learning engages students in real-world tasks such as fieldwork, experiments, simulations, and hands-on projects. These experiences allow learners to apply theoretical concepts in practice, thereby reinforcing understanding through direct engagement [8, 20]. For example, a science lesson that involves designing and testing a water purification system offers not only content knowledge but also problem-solving and ethical reasoning opportunities.

5.2 Collaborative learning

Collaboration is central to activity-based learning. Group discussions, peer teaching, and cooperative problem-solving foster social construction of knowledge, as learners build on each other's ideas [10, 11]. These interactions nurture dialogue, active listening, and negotiation of meaning – skills closely tied to critical thinking and civic engagement.

5.3 Inquiry-based learning

Inquiry-based learning places questions, problems, and investigations at the heart of the learning process. Students are encouraged to formulate their own questions, gather evidence, and construct knowledge through exploration [9]. This form of learning fosters curiosity and positions learners as researchers, deepening cognitive engagement.

5.4 Reflective thinking

Reflection is embedded in activity-based pedagogy through journals, peer feedback, class discussions, and metacognitive prompts. Learners are guided to think about what they learned, how they learned it, and what it means to them. Such reflection enhances self-awareness and deepens learning [6, 21].

6. Benefits for critical thinking

Activity-based pedagogy offers several distinct advantages in cultivating critical thinking – arguably more effectively than passive or content-driven approaches as illustrated in **Figure 3**.

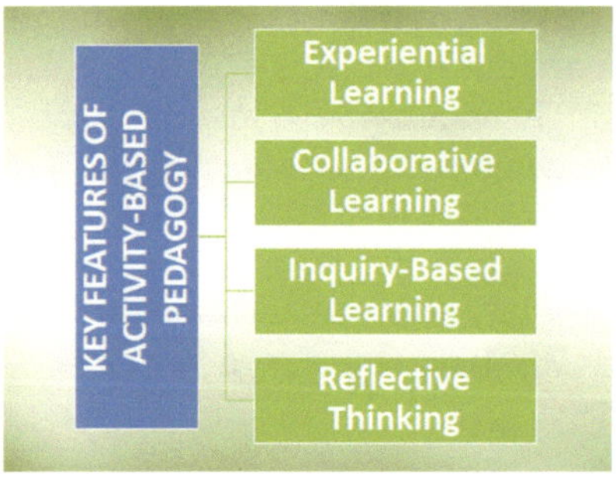

Figure 3.
Key features of activity-based pedagogy [22].

6.1 Promotes exploration

By engaging students in open-ended tasks and projects, activity-based learning encourages divergent thinking. Students explore multiple solutions, weigh trade-offs, and consider various perspectives, which are essential for developing nuanced, analytical thought [8].

6.2 Strengthens argumentation

In group settings, students must articulate their viewpoints, justify decisions, and respectfully challenge peers. These dialogues foster reasoning, debate, and evidence-based argumentation – core components of critical thinking [7, 11].

6.3 Encourages autonomy and agency

Activity-based learning provides learners with the freedom to make choices, experiment, and learn from their mistakes. Students become self-directed, taking responsibility for their learning journey, which fosters independence and intellectual resilience [9].

6.4 Connects knowledge to context

The real-world nature of activities helps students see the relevance of what they are learning. By linking concepts to lived experiences, learners develop more integrated and transferable understandings, strengthening both retention and application [12, 20].

Research supports these claims: studies show that students in activity-based environments demonstrate higher levels of **cognitive engagement**, **deep learning**, and **cross-context transfer of skills** [3, 8]. Additionally, **affective factors** – such as motivation, confidence, and a sense of ownership – are significantly elevated in such settings, contributing to sustained intellectual development [4, 21].

Activity-based pedagogy represents a learner-centered instructional approach that emphasizes **learning by doing**. Rooted in constructivist, socio-cultural, and experiential learning theories, it positions the student as an active participant in the construction of knowledge rather than a passive recipient of transmitted content

[6, 10]. This pedagogical model values authentic tasks, collaborative inquiry, reflection, and engagement with real-world problems, all of which are critical for fostering higher-order thinking skills and meaningful learning experiences.

Rather than viewing learning as a linear progression of memorized content, activity-based pedagogy highlights the importance of **contextualization**, **interaction**, and **reflection**. It aligns closely with the educational philosophies of thinkers such as John Dewey, who emphasized the importance of experience and reflection in the learning process, and Paulo Freire, who advocated for dialogical and problem-posing methods of education [6, 7]. This approach offers a compelling alternative to the increasingly standardized and automated learning environments shaped by AI, particularly when the goal is to cultivate critical thinking, autonomy, and creativity.

7. AI vs activity-based learning: A comparative analysis

Table 1 [22] highlights the inherent differences between the two models. While AI can support personalized delivery and analytics, activity-based pedagogy better aligns with the goal of nurturing thinking citizens capable of navigating complex realities.

8. Synergizing AI and activity-based approaches

Rather than viewing AI and activity-based pedagogy as opposing forces, a more productive educational paradigm envisions a **synergistic integration**. AI, when thoughtfully designed and purposefully applied, can serve to **enhance** rather than replace human-centered learning approaches. This integration acknowledges the **distinct strengths** of each: AI offers data-driven precision, scalability, and personalization, while activity-based pedagogy fosters critical thinking, collaboration, and deep learning [1, 12].

AI should not dictate learning paths or outcomes; instead, it should operate as an **assistive layer** that supports active inquiry, decision-making, and reflection. The key is **intentional pedagogical design** where AI remains in the background – streamlining logistics, offering insights, and scaffolding learning – while human interaction, interpretation, and synthesis take center stage [9].

Criteria	AI-driven instruction	Activity-based pedagogy
Learning style	Adaptive, individualized, often passive	Collaborative, experiential, active
Assessment focus	Standardized, performance-based	Process-oriented, formative, reflective
Knowledge construction	Predetermined pathways, content-centric	Emergent, learner-centered
Role of the learner	Consumer of content	Co-creator of knowledge
Critical thinking engagement	Limited – focus on right answers	High – focus on questioning and exploration
Teacher's role	Monitor or facilitator of AI tools	Guide, mentor, co-learner

Table 1.
Comparison between AI-Driven Instruction and Activity-Based Pedagogy.

9. Examples of effective integration

9.1 AI as a research assistant

Students can employ AI tools like language models or search optimizers to collect relevant information. However, rather than accepting this information passively, they analyze, interpret, and synthesize it for use in debates, position papers, or collaborative projects. This positions AI as a **springboard for critical discourse**, not a source of unquestioned truth [4].

9.2 AI for formative assessment

Intelligent tutoring systems and assessment tools can provide real-time feedback on student performance. Teachers can use these insights to organize peer-review sessions, offer differentiated instruction, or prompt reflective journaling [3]. In this model, AI becomes an enhancer of **formative, not summative**, learning processes [8].

9.3 Flipped learning models

In flipped classrooms, AI platforms deliver foundational knowledge outside of class time, allowing in-person sessions to focus on active, discussion-based, and experiential learning [21]. This creates space for **dialogue, debate, and collaborative inquiry**, while AI handles content repetition and review.

9.4 Simulation and role play

AI-driven simulations can create immersive, complex problem scenarios – such as virtual labs or historical role-plays – that encourage learners to experiment, make decisions, and reflect. These can be followed by group debriefings, analysis, and critical discussions, enriching both **cognitive and emotional engagement** [7, 11].

Across all these models, the guiding principle is **pedagogical intentionality**. Educators must design tasks where AI acts as a **cognitive aid**, not a replacement for the teacher or the learner's thinking. This balance ensures that while AI provides convenience and insight, the ultimate goals of education – critical thinking, ethical reasoning, and human connection – are preserved.

10. Implications for educators and policy

The integration of AI with activity-based pedagogy requires thoughtful transformation at both the classroom and systemic levels. Educators and policymakers must collaborate to ensure that **technology adoption** enhances, rather than erodes, **humanistic and democratic** aims of education [5].

10.1 For educators

10.1.1 Professional development

Teachers must receive continuous, high-quality professional development in two interrelated domains: digital literacy (understanding and using AI tools) and pedagogical innovation (designing inquiry-based, collaborative, and reflective tasks) [4, 12]. Capacity-building programs should move beyond tool training to emphasize **instructional design and ethical AI use**.

10.1.2 Curriculum design

Curricula should be restructured to blend AI-facilitated tasks with **project-based learning, case studies, and open-ended investigations**. For instance, a history lesson might combine AI-supported research with a live simulation of a historical debate, promoting both accuracy and critical engagement [9].

10.1.3 Ethical awareness and digital citizenship

Teachers must prepare students to use AI **critically and ethically**. This includes developing awareness about algorithmic bias, data privacy, and intellectual property. Equipping students with **digital discernment** is now as important as teaching reading or math [5, 13].

10.2 For policymakers

10.2.1 Balanced investment

Investments should not only focus on procuring AI infrastructure but also on **pedagogical research, teacher development, and curriculum innovation**. Funding must support tools that align with inquiry, reflection, and collaboration – not just content delivery [12].

10.2.2 Standards and guidelines

Policies must define ethical, pedagogical, and equity standards for AI use in education. These guidelines should encourage integrative models that preserve learner agency, foster critical thinking, and promote inclusive design [3].

10.2.3 Monitoring and evaluation systems

Accountability frameworks should evaluate more than just test scores. Systems must track **cognitive, creative, and ethical development**, ensuring that technology supports – not replaces – complex learning outcomes [8].

11. Conclusion

The future of education in the digital age depends not merely on how much technology is used, but on how it is used. AI holds the potential to personalize, democratize, and enhance learning – but it must not be allowed to replace the deeply human elements of education that nurture critical thinking, empathy, and agency [23].

Activity-based pedagogy, with its roots in active engagement, social interaction, and reflection, remains essential to these aims. Rather than positioning AI as a threat to pedagogy, this chapter advocates for an integrative approach – where technology augments the teacher's role, scaffolds learner exploration, and supports educational ecosystems centered on inquiry and thought.

Educators, scholars, and policymakers must remain vigilant and intentional, designing learning experiences that do not sacrifice depth for convenience. In doing so, we can ensure that the digital age becomes not a period of diminished reasoning, but one of renewed intellectual vitality.

Acknowledgement

The author acknowledges the use of OPENAI tool for language polishing of the manuscript.

Author details

Priya Soni
Khalsa College of Education, Amritsar, India

*Address all correspondence to: Ps6880911@gmail.com

References

[1] Luckin R. Machine Learning and Human Intelligence: The Future of Education for the 21st Century. UCL IOE Press; 2018

[2] Chen L, Xie H. Personalized learning: An AI-driven approach. International Journal of Artificial Intelligence in Education. 2019;**29**(4):345–367. DOI: 10.1007/s40593-019-00189-0

[3] Zawacki-Richter O, Marín VI, Bond M, Gouverneur F. Systematic review of research on artificial intelligence applications in higher education. International Journal of Educational Technology in Higher Education. 2019;**16**(1):1–27. DOI: 10.1186/s41239-019-0171-0

[4] Aoun JE. Robot-proof: Higher Education in the Age of Artificial Intelligence. MIT Press; 2017

[5] Selwyn N. Should Robots Replace Teachers? AI and the Future of Education. Polity Press; 2019

[6] Dewey J. Experience and Education. Macmillan; 1938

[7] Freire P. Pedagogy of the Oppressed. Herder and Herder; 1970

[8] Bransford JD, Brown AL, Cocking RR, Eds. How People Learn: Brain, Mind, Experience, and School. Expanded ed. National Academy Press; 2000

[9] Scardamalia M, Bereiter C. Knowledge building: Theory, pedagogy, and technology. In: Sawyer K, editor. The Cambridge Handbook of the Learning Sciences. Cambridge University Press; 2006. p. 97–115

[10] Vygotsky LS. Mind in Society: The Development of Higher Psychological Processes. Harvard University Press; 1978

[11] Wegerif R. Mind-expanding: Teaching for Thinking and Creativity in Primary Education. McGraw-Hill Education; 2010

[12] Fullan M. Stratosphere: Integrating Technology, Pedagogy, and Change Knowledge. Pearson; 2013

[13] Partnership for 21st Century Learning. (2019). Framework for 21st century learning definitions. Battelle for Kids. https://static.battelleforkids.org/documents/p21/P21_Framework_Brief.pdf

[14] Anderson LW, Krathwohl DR, Eds. A Taxonomy for Learning, Teaching, and Assessing: A Revision of Bloom's Taxonomy of Educational Objectives. Longman; 2001

[15] UNESCO. Artificial intelligence in education: Challenges and opportunities for sustainable development. United Nations Educational, Scientific and Cultural Organization. 2019

[16] Luckin R. Intelligence unleashed: An argument for AI in education. Pearson. 2017

[17] Holmes W, Bialik M, Fadel C. Artificial intelligence in education: Promises and implications for teaching and learning. Center for Curriculum Redesign. 2019

[18] Holmes W, Bialik M, Fadel C. Artificial intelligence in education:

Promises and implications for teaching and learning. Center for Curriculum Redesign. 2019

[19] Williamson B, Eynon R. Historical threads, missing links, and future directions in AI in education. Learning, Media and Technology. 2020;**45**(3):223–235. DOI: 10.1080/17439884.2020.1798995

[20] Kolb DA. Experiential Learning: Experience as the Source of Learning and Development. Prentice Hall; 1984

[21] Salmon G. E-tivities: The Key to Active Online Learning. 2nd ed. Routledge; 2013

[22] Kumar A. Innovative pedagogical models for modern classrooms. SAGE Publications India. 2022

[23] Krajcik JS, Shin N. Project-based learning. In: RK Sawyer, editor. The Cambridge handbook of the learning sciences, (2nd ed.,). Cambridge University Press; 2014. p. 275–297

Chapter 9

Engaging Students with AI for Code Comprehension, Critique, and Explanation

Laura Albrant, Jyoti Suhag, Leo C. Ureel II and Michelle Jarvie-Eggart

Abstract

Artificial intelligence (AI) has become increasingly influential in computer science (CS) education, where it holds potential for automating feedback and personalized learning. AI tools have been shown to increase equitability within CS, a notoriously male-dominated field, as well as increase the programming self-efficacy of female students – which is tied to programming success. This chapter will present a summary of how students learn to code, studies explaining how AI can be used to help students understand code, as well as provide prompt feedback for students coding in real-time. A history of the development of AI and its increasing accuracy is provided. To assess the impact of generative AI for assisting students in explaining code, the authors present data from a recent study examining the effectiveness of using AI to provide code explanations for novice programmers. The authors also provide some prompt engineering suggestions for educators to help their students increase the accuracy of the results from AI queries.

Keywords: code comprehension, code critique, code explanations, computer science education, generative AI, novice programming, prompt engineering

1. Introduction

Artificial Intelligence (AI) is changing the way students learn computer science (CS), especially programming. As coding becomes a basic skill in many careers, educators face pressure to help more students succeed – regardless of their background or prior experience. AI tools now offer new ways to make programming more approachable by providing personalized support, answering questions in natural language, and giving feedback instantly as students write code. These features can make a big difference for learners who might otherwise struggle or feel left behind.

Some of the most powerful tools today are based on large language models (LLMs), such as ChatGPT or Gemini, which can understand both natural language and programming code. These tools can explain what code does, suggest improvements, or even write new code based on a student's question. In classrooms and online learning environments, students are using them to get unstuck quickly and build a deeper understanding of how programs work. A recent study found that students using AI-generated explanations for code performed better on follow-up tasks and gained more confidence in debugging [1].

Another exciting benefit is how AI tools can promote equity in CS education. For example, women and other underrepresented groups in computing often report lower confidence when learning to program [2, 3]. However, companion research from our group shows that AI-based feedback – available 24/7 and without judgment– – can boost students' belief in their own abilities, a factor called programming self-efficacy [24]. When learners feel more capable, they are more likely to persist and succeed in CS courses. Another exciting benefit is how AI tools can promote equity in CS education. For example, women and other underrepresented groups in computing often report lower confidence when learning to program [2, 3]. However, companion research from our group shows that AI-based feedback – available 24/7 and without judgment – can boost students' belief in their own abilities, a factor called programming self-efficacy [24]. When learners feel more capable, they are more likely to persist and succeed in CS courses.

At the same time, using these AI tools effectively requires new skills. One of the most important is prompt engineering – the ability to write clear, specific questions that help the AI give accurate and helpful responses. Teachers can guide students in learning how to write better prompts, and doing so has been shown to improve learning outcomes [4].

In this chapter, we explore the use of AI to support programming education. We begin with a short history of how AI tools for code generation and explanation have developed. Then, we present findings from our own study, which looked at how helpful AI is in explaining code to beginners. Finally, we offer practical tips for educators and students on how to get better results from AI by writing stronger prompts. By combining research and classroom experience, this chapter shows how AI can be a valuable partner in helping all students succeed in CS.

2. Background

2.1 Computer science education

Computer science (CS) continues to show significant gender imbalance in higher education. Across the US, women make up only about 25–30% of students enrolled in CS programs – a statistic that has remained relatively stagnant over the past decade [5, 6]. This gap in representation is further exacerbated by attrition after the first course in programming, known as CS1. For example, a study at Rutgers University found that many women enrolled in CS1 had no plans to continue in the major, despite performing similarly to their male peers [5]. One contributing factor to this early departure may be the difference in programming self-efficacy – a student's belief in their ability to succeed in programming tasks. Novice female programmers often report lower self-efficacy than their male peers, which impacts their decision to persist in computing [2, 3]. This confidence gap arises not from different abilities but from a lack of encouragement, role models, or immediate support when they face challenges.

Feedback plays a crucial role in improving students' confidence and performance in CS. According to Wang and Wu, timely and constructive feedback boosts self-efficacy, helping students feel capable and motivated to tackle difficult tasks [7]. Feedback also acts as a bridge between students' beliefs and their actual outcomes – those who receive helpful feedback are more likely to turn confidence into successful performance [8]. In learning environments – especially those with high cognitive load, like programming – feedback helps clarify mistakes, guide revision, and reinforce learning. Without it, students may internalize failure, leading to frustration or withdrawal from the subject.

Unfortunately, in many large-enrollment CS1 courses, instructors struggle to provide real-time, individualized feedback. Managing dozens or even hundreds of students makes it nearly impossible to address every question as it arises. As a result, many learners – especially those who are new or lack confidence – go without the guidance they need at critical learning moments [9]. This feedback gap often leads to stalled progress, increased errors, and reduced motivation. For underrepresented groups, the lack of timely support can be especially discouraging, further widening the retention gap.

Recent advances in generative AI, including LLMs like ChatGPT and Gemini, offer new opportunities to address these feedback limitations. These tools are capable of interpreting code, understanding natural language questions, and generating explanations or suggestions in real time. Unlike human instructors, they are available 24/7 and can scale to support thousands of students simultaneously. This accessibility makes AI a powerful ally for equitable CS education. It provides nonjudgmental, immediate assistance that students can turn to whenever they are stuck – without waiting in line, feeling embarrassed, or being ignored. AI feedback has the potential to boost self-efficacy by giving students control over their learning process, allowing them to explore, make mistakes, and receive help exactly when they need it.

The process of learning to program goes far beyond syntax memorization or writing functional code. It encompasses a set of cognitive, metacognitive, and strategic skills, including code comprehension, self-explanation, and debugging – each of which contributes to the development of expert programming behavior. Effective instruction and curriculum design must recognize these processes to support novice learners.

Reading and understanding code is a foundational skill for good programming. Understanding what code does requires a learner to construct a mental model of its structure and behavior. This includes tracing the flow of control, identifying variable states, recognizing loops and conditionals, and predicting the program's output. However, novices tend to focus on line-by-line execution or low-level syntax rather than understanding the code as a whole, making it difficult for them to abstract the underlying algorithm or logic.

Research shows that expert programmers spend more time reading and understanding code before making changes or additions, a behavior that should be encouraged in educational settings. Teaching students how to annotate code, identify logical blocks, and use tracing tools or visualizations can improve code comprehension. Encouraging students to reflect on what the code is doing, what its inputs and outputs are, and how each part contributes to the program's goal leads to stronger programming habits [10].

Self-explanation refers to the process by which learners generate their own explanations while working through a problem. Chi et al. found that learners who explained material to themselves during study – without any external feedback – demonstrated greater understanding and retention [11]. This is particularly relevant in programming, where students often copy or run code without truly understanding how it works. In the context of programming, self-explanation might involve asking and answering questions like:

- What is this line of code doing?
- Why was this particular structure (e.g., loop or conditional) used?
- What will happen if I change this value?
- How does this function contribute to the program's objective?

By engaging in such internal dialog, learners create connections between new programming constructs and their existing knowledge, leading to a deeper understanding and better problem-solving skills. Structured self-explanation prompts or guided worksheets can scaffold this process and should be integrated into instruction, especially when working with example code or during code tracing exercises. Debugging and writing new code (composing) involve different types of thinking and problem-solving strategies, although both are essential to programming proficiency.

Debugging and writing new code (composing) involve different types of thinking and problem-solving strategies, although both are essential to programming proficiency. Debugging is the process of identifying, diagnosing, and fixing errors in code. It requires hypothesis generation, strategic testing, and logical reasoning. Debugging forces learners to think carefully about how the program executes, compare expected and actual behaviors, and iteratively test modifications to isolate problems. Studies have shown that debugging enhances understanding because it engages students in reflective problem-solving and exposes them to the consequences of misconceptions [12]. However, debugging can be frustrating for novices, especially if they lack the skills to interpret error messages, trace execution paths, or apply logical reasoning. Effective debugging instruction should teach students how to isolate problems, test hypotheses methodically, and use tools (like print statements or debuggers) to understand the internal state of the program.

Writing a program from scratch requires planning, design, and creativity. It involves identifying the problem, breaking it into smaller tasks, designing algorithms, and implementing them correctly. Novices often struggle with decomposition and tend to jump directly into writing code without proper planning. Instruction should, therefore, emphasize problem-solving strategies such as:

- Writing pseudocode before coding.
- Creating flowcharts or logic diagrams.
- Reusing or adapting known patterns (e.g., loops, conditional structures).
- Testing frequently and incrementally.

DOI: http://dx.doi.org/10.5772/intechopen.1012995

In contrast to debugging, composing places a greater cognitive load on planning and design thinking rather than diagnostic reasoning. While different, debugging and composing are deeply interconnected. For instance, understanding common bugs can help students write cleaner code, and designing with clarity reduces the need for complex debugging later. Instructors should provide opportunities for learners to both write and debug code regularly and emphasize how each process supports the other.

Understanding how learners acquire programming skills requires educators to consider the processes of reading code, explaining it to oneself, and both constructing and debugging programs. Each of these activities exercises different cognitive skills and offers unique learning opportunities. When learners are supported in these areas – through scaffolding, practice, and reflective strategies – they become more confident, capable, and independent programmers.

2.2 Generative AI and tutors in education

AI has been used in education for decades, with early systems dating back to the 1970s. Traditionally, AI in education included tools like intelligent tutoring systems (ITS) that provided step-by-step coaching, automated assessment, and adaptive learning. A systematic review by Zawacki-Richter et al. identified four main application areas of AI in higher education: (1) student profiling and performance prediction, (2) automated assessment and evaluation, (3) adaptive learning systems for personalized instruction, and (4) intelligent tutoring systems for guiding learners [13]. Early AI-driven tutors were often rule-based, limited in scope, and difficult to extend. However, modern LLM-based AI systems can engage in sophisticated dialogs and generate detailed explanations in ways not possible with earlier tutoring systems.

In large university courses with hundreds of students, instructors face challenges in providing timely, individualized feedback. Generative AI tutors help address this scalability problem by being available 24/7 to answer questions, explain complex concepts, and offer feedback. LLMs can be used to tailor explanations to the student's level. AI tutors are driven by large amounts of data, making them useful across many domains. For example, an AI tutor in a history class might assist a student in brainstorming essay ideas or debating historical interpretations. AI chatbots have also been used to converse with students learning a new language. Generative AI has also been employed to provide personalized feedback on writing assignments.

AI's role in education is expanding from a niche tool to a mainstream support system across disciplines. For example, AI tutors are gaining popularity for programming courses. Generative AI-powered coding assistants (such as GitHub Copilot [14]) can help students write, understand, and debug code. For instance, when a student is confused by an error message, an AI tutor can explain the error in plain English and suggest a fix. AI can also assist with code comprehension: students can paste a piece of source code and ask the AI to explain what it does. The AI might annotate the code with comments and describe the purpose of each section, which helps novices learn coding patterns and logic.

New systems are being designed to integrate these capabilities into the classroom. For instance, CodeAid [15] is an LLM-based programming assistant that was deployed in a university course with 700 students. CodeAid was configured to avoid simply giving away the solution: instead of providing complete code, it answered conceptual questions, generated pseudocode with line-by-line explanations, and annotated students' code to point out mistakes without outright handing over the answer. However, caution is advisable. TutorKAI is a research prototype that provides students with code feedback alongside compiler messages. Researchers report that students with less programming experience favor AI tools over compiler output [16].

Generative AI is playing an influential role in education. It improves student success rates and increases motivation. However, students must be cautioned not to use AI in place of learning. It is essential that educators train students on how to interact with AI, including the art of authoring good prompts to leverage AI for learning.

2.3 Prompt engineering

Generative AI systems are highly sensitive to the inputs they receive. The accuracy of generated outputs heavily depends on the text of the prompts provided to the AI systems [17]. Prompt engineering is the process of designing instructions (prompts) to elicit accurate outputs from generative AI systems. This is similar to traditional programming, which involves writing unambiguous step-by-step instructions. Unlike programming, however, prompt engineering requires an understanding of how to effectively communicate with AI models through natural language to provide broader context. Talking with a chat bot is not a keyword search like Google. Getting good results from generative AI systems demands that users consider the structure, specificity, and framing of their requests to AI systems.

Ambiguous prompts tend to yield unpredictable AI responses. Good prompts provide enough contextual detail to clearly describe the *Who, What, When, Where, and Why* of the desired outcomes. Contextualized prompts significantly improve the accuracy of AI-generated outputs by clearly outlining background information, audience, purpose, and examples [18]. Students should be taught the importance of critically evaluating AI responses and revising prompts iteratively based on these evaluations. Students can enhance the usefulness of AI-generated content through repeated prompt/refinement cycles, which is a form of active learning [17].

For example, the following prompt provides clear instructions to an LLM-based AI tutor, requesting help with deconstructing code in an unknown language and converting it to MATLAB:

I am a student in engineering at Michigan Technological University. I am taking a class to learn how to solve problems and program using MATLAB.

You are my tutor. Write as an experienced engineer. Show your thinking. Do not reveal the solution code to any problem. Instead, guide me through the problem-solving steps required to reach a solution by walking through examples and asking questions.

Responses should be of a formal academic nature, generally 1,000 words or more in length, portray a strong opinion or viewpoint, and cite all relevant source material. All sources should be cited, and a list of references should be included at the end.

I am trying to understand the following FORTRAN code. I do not know FORTRAN. Please guide me through the process of deconstructing the code to understand what it does and translate it to MATLAB.

```
program newton_limit
  implicit none
  double precision:: x, tol, fx, dfx
  integer:: max_iter, iter
  ! Initial guess
  x = 1.0d0
  tol = 1.0d-10
  max_iter = 100
  print *, "Newton"s Method for f(x) = x^2 - 2"
  do iter = 1, max_iter
     fx=x**2 - 2.0d0
     dfx = 2.0d0 * x
     if (abs(fx) < tol) then
         print *, 'Converged after ', iter, " iterations"
         exit
     end if
     x=x - fx/dfx
  end do
  print *, 'Estimated root (limit): ', x
  print *, 'f(x) at root: ', x**2 - 2.0d0
end program newton_limit
```

Remember, I need to learn how to do this. So it is imperative that you do not provide a solution. Rather, you should provide patient guidance through examples and questions.

Teaching students prompt engineering through explicit modeling enables them to observe the construction and iterative refinement of prompts, developing their skills through concrete examples. This encourages students to move beyond superficial interactions with AI and fosters deeper cognitive engagement, critical analysis, and reflective practice.

3. Study

It is important to note that we are not rejecting the use of generative AI tools but are looking to develop methodologies and curriculum that will assist us in teaching students during this new era. With this in mind, we will examine the role of AI in supporting these educational goals and assess how AI tools can be utilized not just as solution generators but as educational aids that enhance understanding and engagement with the programming process. This approach will also involve developing new metrics for assessing student progress and comprehension, shifting away from traditional code-centric evaluations.

By redefining the learning trajectory from writing to designing and reading code, this project aims to equip students with a deeper understanding of programming, which is critical in the AI-augmented future of software development. We hope to enhance the effectiveness of programming education and prepare students for a rapidly evolving technological landscape, where understanding the logic and design behind the code becomes as crucial as writing it.

4. Methods

This study utilizes a constructivist approach. Within this approach, tasking students with providing code explanations is a proven method for learning code [19]. However, true novices to coding often struggle to create code explanations without guidance and examples from instructors. This study leverages generative AI to provide those example code explanations, which can be used as early scaffolding in the process of learning a new programming language. The propensity of generative AI to hallucinate can contribute to faculty reluctance to leverage it in this manner to assist their instruction. Thus, this work includes an assessment of the generative AI-provided code explanations using a grading rubric and compares the performance of generative AI to that of novice programming students when commenting on a new programming language. It is part of a larger study examining the application of generative AI to aid student code comprehension [25].

Participants: They were all first-year CS and engineering students at Michigan Technological University. Within a common first-year engineering program, students learn MATLAB programming in ENG1101 and further develop these skills in ENG1102 – each of these courses is offered in both the fall and spring semesters. Applied Computing and Electrical Engineering students learn C in CS111. Other computing majors learn Java through a number of different courses in their first year; depending upon their tested programming abilities, they take either CS1121, CS1122, or CS1131, all of which are offered in both the fall and spring semesters. Study participants (n = 297) included 147 students in ENG1101, 22 in ENG1102, 72 in CS1111, and 29 in CS1131. Overall, 73.06% of study participants self-identified as male, 20.34% as female, and 6.4% as non-binary/other/prefer not to say. Study participants included 75.67% engineering-related majors, 15.88% CS-related majors, 8.11% other majors, and 0.34% undecided. Study participants also indicated their prior programming experience as follows (note that some students may have had experience in more than one language): 20.83% Java, 15.54% C, 4.96% C++, 9.26% Python, 55.04% MATLAB, 2.15% Scratch, and 2.48% JavaScript. It should be noted that none of these students had prior experience in Fortran, the language they were tasked with interpreting.

Intervention assignment: Close to the end of their first-semester introductory engineering or CS courses, participants were tasked with providing code comments for a short program written in Fortran, as well as a high-level explanation of the code provided. The participants were specifically asked not to use AI assistance for this attempt. After providing their own explanation for the Fortran code, students were tasked with running it through ChatGPT to leverage the generative AI to comment on the code for them. **Figure 1** shows the Fortran code provided to the participants and the accompanying multi-step instructions. As approved in our IRB application, participation was incentivized with extra credit being offered to the students for completion of this assignment, regardless of whether they consented to the use of their data for research.

```
program add_xy
implicit none
integer, parameter :: n = 100
real :: x(n), y(n)
```

```
real :: f(n, n)
integer :: i, j
character(len = 20) : : filename
write(*,*) "Enter output file name:"
read(*,*) filename! Initialize x and y values
do i = 1, n
x(i) = i
y(i) = i
end do ! Calculate f(x, y) = x + y
do i = 1, n
do j = 1, n
f(i, j) = x(i) + y(j)
end do
end do ! Open a file and write the array to it
open(unit = 10, file = filename, status = "unknown")
do i = 1, n
do j = 1, n
write(10, "(2I4, F10.2)") i, j, f(i, j)
end do
end do
close(unit = 10)write(*,*) "File writing complete."
end program add_xy
```

Listing 1.1
FORTRAN CODE

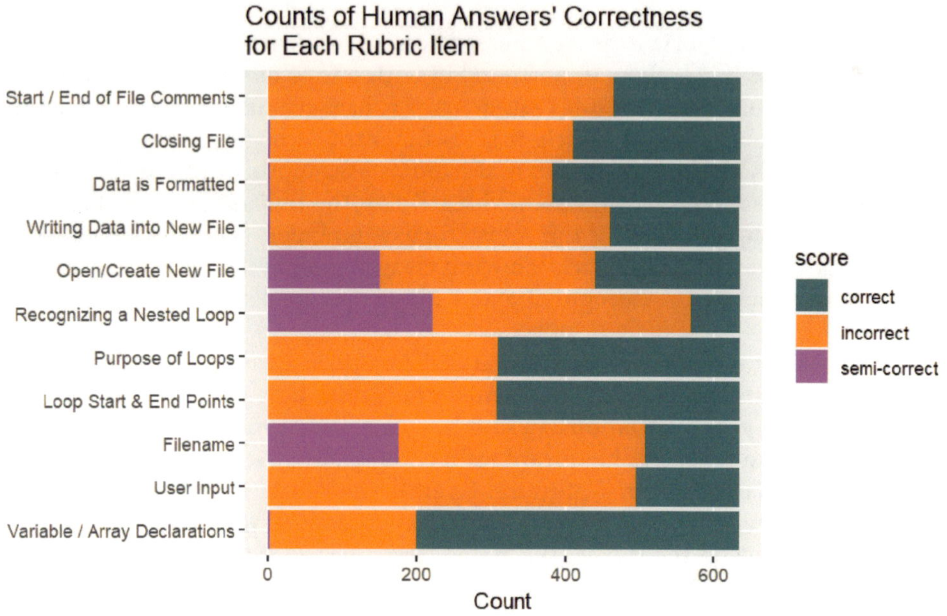

Figure 1.
A horizontal bar graph that displays the overall counts of correct (maximum value for the given rubric item), incorrect (a zero for the item), and semi-correct (between 0 and the maximum) answers.

1. Please copy and paste the above code here. Add comments to this code and submit the commented code in the provided text box. Do not discuss this code with anyone, research it, or run it through AI. Just give us your best attempt at commenting. There is no right or wrong answer to this question. We are interested in studying the process by which students understand unfamiliar code. Please communicate your understanding.

2. Please explain in plain English what you think this code does. [text box provided]

3. Next, go to ChatGPT [embed hyperlink https://chat.openai.com/].

And ask it, “Can you please comment this Fortran code for me?” When it prompts you to, copy and paste the above code into the ChatGPT prompt. Read through the ChatGPT code comments, but please don’t go back and change your attempt at commenting the code above.

1. What did you learn from ChatGPT?

2. Have you ever used ChatGPT or other AI to help you understand or create code before this assignment? If so, how?

3. How might you use ChatGPT to help you learn and understand computer programming?

Assessment: A rubric to assess the code explanations was developed by the graduate student researchers in partnership with one of our coauthors, who is faculty in CS. This 16-point code commenting rubric evaluates both how well the program functions and how clearly it is documented. It begins by checking if the student correctly declares variables and handles user input, with appropriate comments. It also looks for comments identifying the filename used in file operations. A major portion of the rubric focuses on loops. Students are expected to mark the start and end of each loop and clearly explain the purpose of every loop through comments. Recognizing and commenting on nested loops is also required.

File handling is another important area. The rubric awards points for comments explaining how a file is opened or created, how data (such as the formula $f = x + y$) is written into it, and how the file is properly closed. Lastly, 2 points are given for including meaningful comments at the beginning and end of the code to explain its overall purpose. Overall, the rubric ensures students write correct, well-structured code that is easy to understand and maintain. For each category within the rubric, full points were earned if the comment for each item was present and correct. Half points were earned if an item was present but not fully correct. The point value assigned to each category can be seen in **Table 1**.

Positionality of the team: The positionality of individual researchers influences every step of qualitative research, from conception to dissemination – its consideration and disclosure are means of reducing bias within the research

Comments about	Points
Variable/array declarations	1
User input	1
Filename	1
Loop start and end points (one point for each loop)	3
Purpose of loops (one point for each loop)	3
Recognizing a nested loop	1
Open/Create new file	1
Writing data into new file	1
Knowing the data is format of: $f = x + y$	1
Closing file	1
Start/end of file comments (one point each)	2
Total	**16**

Table 1.
Code commenting rubric.

process [20]. Our team includes faculty from CS and Engineering Fundamentals, who regularly teach first-year college students to program. We also include PhD students in CS and Human Factors, both of whom have experience teaching programming to novices. As a whole, our team believes that generative AI can be leveraged to help teaching when students are shown how to use it appropriately.

5. Results

The results of this study are presented on two fronts. First, there is the scored data on the (human) students' comments, reported by course and gender, as shown in **Table 2**. Then, each ChatGPT response was also scored separately for comparisons with students' scores (**Table 3**).

Figure 1 presents the distribution of student responses categorized as correct, semi-correct, or incorrect for each rubric item. A correct response is defined as achieving the maximum score for a given rubric item, while an incorrect response receives a score of zero. A semi-correct response falls within the range between zero and the maximum score.

Course	Avg. score	Avg. men	Avg. women	Avg. NB/other/undisclosed
CS 1111	6.375	6.233	7.125	6.562
CS 1122	7.116	7.255	6.200	6.625
CS 1131	6.100	6.583	5.400	4.000
ENG 1101	5.812	5.445	6.709	5.923
ENG 1102	4.542	4.297	5.300	1.000

Table 2.
Counts of student submissions.

Rubric item	**Human mean**	**ChatGPT mean**	***t***	***p***
Variable/array declarations	0.686	0.989	−15.931	$p < 0.001$
User input	0.512	0.994	−23.934	$p < 0.001$
Filename	0.510	0.996	−23.996	$p < 0.001$
Loop start and end points (one point for each loop)	0.802	0.351	8.4495	$p < 0.001$
Purpose of loops (one point for each loop)	1.277	2.971	−31.624	$p < 0.001$
Recognizing a nested loop	0.277	0.283	−0.21527	$p = 0.8296$
Open/create new file	0.400	0.985	−28.964	$p < 0.001$
Writing data into new file	0.354	0.985	−31.969	$p < 0.001$
Knowing the data is format of: $f = x + y$	0.267	0.983	−38.703	$p < 0.001$
Closing file	0.2196	0.979	−43.088	$p < 0.001$
Start/end of file comments (one point each).	0.679	0.467	4.8676	$p < 0.001$
Total	5.984	10.984	−25.145	$p < 0.001$

Table 3.
Two-sample t-test results comparing the means of human rubric points and cChatGPT rubric points for every rubric item and the total scores. The bolded items show the only comment categories where humans scored statistically higher on average than ChatGPT.

Figure 2 illustrates a box plot illustrating the distribution of students' total scores, categorized by their respective courses. Diving deeper into this data, a one-way ANOVA with a linear model for "course" as predictor of "total score" was performed. The ANOVA's results (Df: 4, Sum Sq.: 204, Mean Sq.: 51.03, F value: 2.44, p-value: < 0.01) demonstrate that a student's enrolled course is a significant predictor of their ability to interpret unfamiliar code. This finding is consistent with the expectation that students in CS1122 (second-semester Java) and CS1111 (introductory C) possess a larger body of knowledge and experience, which aids in code comprehension. Interestingly, ENG1102 students are expected to have more MATLAB experience than ENG1101 students, which hypothetically could correlate to a higher average score. However, a two-way t-test between the total scores of the two engineering courses shows that their averages (5.8121 and 4.542) are not significantly different ($p = 0.0723$).

Additionally, another two-way t-test was conducted between all CS courses and both engineering courses. The ENG courses have an average of 5.651, while the CS courses have an average of 6.478. With a p-value of 0.0218 (i.e., less than 0.05), the test proves that the CS students scored higher than ENG students on average with this unfamiliar programming language comprehension.

Lastly, for the human-only analysis, gender-identifying information was collected, and both t-tests and an ANOVA demonstrated that gender (considering all three groups: men, women, and non-binary/other/undisclosed) is not a significant factor for this test at all.

With the ChatGPT data, **Table 3** provides results from a sequence of two-way t-tests comparing the students' scores to ChatGPT's scores for each item and the total. Overall, ChatGPT scores significantly higher than humans for most of the

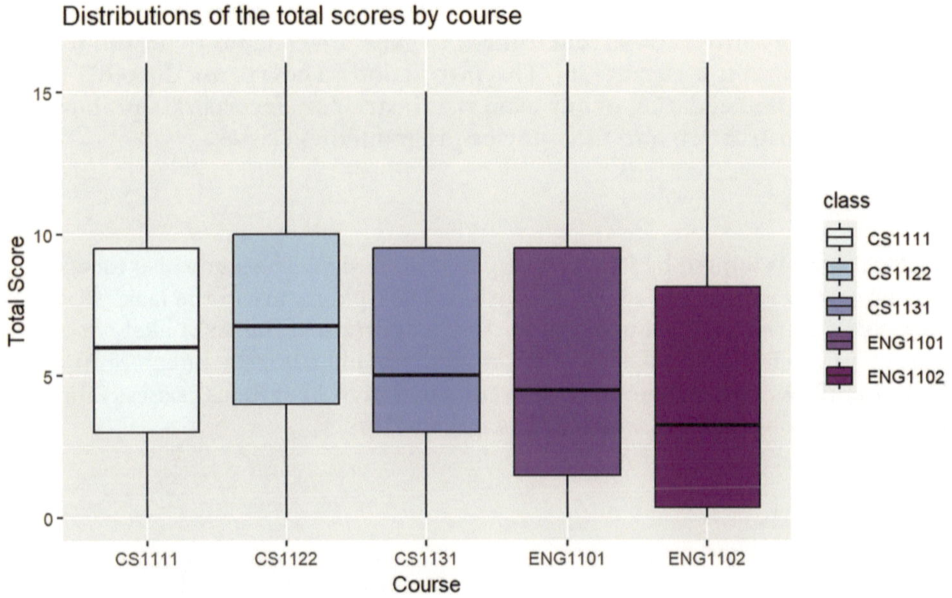

Figure 2.
Box plot distribution of the total scores for each course.

items and the total, except for the "Loop Start & End Points" and "Start/End of File Comments" items. The most likely explanation is that these types of comments are "novice" comments, and ChatGPT was trained on a body of comments that excluded these statements – most likely because they are so elemental that experienced programmers rarely comment on them.

6. Discussion

Overall, the evidence presented in this study demonstrates that ChatGPT performs better than novice humans at providing code explanations. Other research has shown that ChatGPT can complete introductory programming tasks well enough to pass introductory-level courses [21, 22]. This highlights the potential of generative AI chatbots to be leveraged as instructional assistants within introductory programming courses.

However, even though ChatGPT performed better at generating overall code explanations, our data showed that humans performed significantly better on specific rubric items, specifically `LOOP START & END POINTS` and `START/END OF FILE COMMENTS`. This suggests the potential for students to outperform the AI in areas salient to their level of expertise. It appears that the LLMs, having been trained on expert-level code, may have difficulty tailoring explanations to the level of the student.

Despite the promise of ChatGPT for providing on-demand code explanations and feedback to students, many faculty remain reticent to integrate AI within their teaching. Faculty fear students will unethically leverage AI to do their work for them rather than engage with AI to improve their own knowledge and abilities [23]. However, work from our broader research team found that, with instruction on how to use ChatGPT to provide code explanations, students' intended use of the technology shifted away from using it to generate code for them and toward using it as a learning assistant [25]. This instruction on how to use ChatGPT is key, and it is a recommendation of our team that instructors incorporate prompt engineering instruction into their novice programming classes.

7. Limitations

This study is limited by its single-experiment design. The study also focuses exclusively on Fortran code comprehension. The rigid nature of the task (students were asked to refrain from using AI in the first portion of the task) likely does not reflect the informal ways in which students would naturally integrate AI into their workflow. Beyond the study, current generative AI systems possess inherent limitations: hallucinations, knowledge gaps, and bias.

8. Conclusions

While AI has been used in education for decades, the pace, breadth, and depth of AI use by modern students are astonishing. AI is fundamentally reshaping the landscape of programming instruction. AI is a powerful tool that enables expert programmers to dramatically increase their productivity. Yes, it can be a detriment to novices and a distraction from the learning process.

Fortunately, AI's capabilities extend beyond mere code generation; it has the potential to guide the student as a learning assistant. Students are using generative AI to solve coursework problems. Our role as faculty is to encourage students to move beyond superficial interactions with AI to engage in critical analysis and reflective practice. Our study showed that modeling the prompts used to interact with the AI systems can help students use the AI as a learning assistant. This underscores the importance of incorporating AI literacy and prompt engineering in our curriculum.

Even so, the challenge for instructors remains in mitigating the risk that students will passively consume AI content and solutions. Our study provides hope that careful curriculum design can help students avoid the pitfalls of blindly relying on AI for solutions when they should be trying to learn.

Acknowledgements

The authors would like to thank Mr. Ken Thiemann of Engineering Fundamentals for implementing a pilot version of this study in his summer course, without which we would not have gone on to full scale implementation.

Abbreviations

CS	computer science
AI	artificial intelligence
LLMs	large language models

DOI: http://dx.doi.org/10.5772/intechopen.1012995

Author details

Laura Albrant*, Jyoti Suhag, Leo C. Ureel II and Michelle Jarvie-Eggart
Michigan Technological University, Houghton, Michigan, USA

*Address all correspondence to: lealbran@mtu.edu

References

[1] Kazemitabaar M, Hou X, Henley A, Ericson BJ, Weintrop D, Grossman T. How novices use LLM-based code generators to solve cs1 coding tasks in a self-paced learning environment. 2023

[2] Benjamin M, Jarvie-Eggart ME, Ureel II LC, WIP: Impact of prior programming experience on self-efficacy impacts of WebTA Autocritiquer. *2025 ASEE Annual Conference & Exposition*. 2025

[3] Beyer S. Why are women underrepresented in computer science? gender differences in stereotypes, self-efficacy, values, and interests and predictors of future CS course-taking and grades. Computer Science Education. 2014;**24**(2–3):153–192

[4] Woo DJ, Wang D, Yung T, Guo K. Effects of a prompt engineering intervention on undergraduate students' AI self-efficacy, AI knowledge and prompt engineering ability: A mixed methods study. arXiv. 2004;**2408**:07302

[5] Babes-Vroman M, Juniewicz I, Lucarelli B, Fox N, Nguyen T, Tjang A, Haldeman G, Mehta A, Chokshi R Exploring gender diversity in CS at a large public r1 research university. *Proceedings of the 2017 ACM SIGCSE Technical Symposium on Computer Science Education* (New York, NY, USA, Mar. 2017), SIGCSE '17, Association for Computing Machinery, p. 51–56

[6] Babes-Vroman M, Nguyen TD. Gender diversity in computer science at a large research university. ArXiv. 2020;**2004**:13760

[7] Wang S-L, Wu P-Y. The role of feedback and self-efficacy on web-based learning: The social cognitive perspective. Computers & Education. 2008;**51**(4):1589–1598

[8] Beattie S, Woodman T, Fakehy M, Dempsey C. The role of performance feedback on the self-efficacy–performance relationship. Sport, Exercise, and Performance Psychology. 2016;**5**(1):1–13

[9] Pisan Y, Sloane A, Richards D, Dale R Providing timely feedback to large classes. *International Conference on Computers in Education, 2002. Proceedings*. (Dec. 2002), vol.**1** p. 413–414

[10] Lister R, Adams ES, Fitzgerald S, Fone W, Hamer J, Lindholm M, McCartney R, Moström JE, Sanders K, Seppälä O, Simon B, Thomas L.A multi-national study of reading and tracing skills in novice programmers. ACM SIGCSE Bulletin. 2004;**36**(4):119–150

[11] Chi MT, De Leeuw N, Chiu M-H, Lavancher C. Eliciting self-explanations improves understanding. Cognitive Science. 1994;**18**(3):439–477

[12] Vessey I. Expertise in debugging computer programs: A process analysis. International Journal of Man-Machine Studies. 1985;**23**(5):459–494

[13] Zawacki-Richter O, Marn VI, Bond M, Gouverneur F. Systematic review of research on artificial intelligence applications in higher education–where are the educators? International Journal of Educational Technology in Higher Education. 2019;**16**(1):1–27

[14] GITHUB COPILOT. GitHub Copilot. https://github.com/features/copilot, 2025 [Accessed: 2025-November-24]

[15] Kazemitabaar M, Ye R, Wang X, Henley AZ, Denny P, Craig M, Grossman T. CodeAid: Evaluating a classroom deployment of an LLM-based programming assistant that balances student and educator needs. *Proceedings of the 2024 chi conference on human factors in computing systems*. (2024), pp. 1–20

[16] Jacobs S, Kempf M, Kiesler N. That's not the feedback i need!–student engagement with GenAI feedback in the tutor Kai. arXiv. 2025;1–7. *preprint arXiv*

[17] Bommasani R, Hudson DA, Adeli E, Altman R, Arora S, von Arx S, Bernstein MS, Bohg J, Bosselut A, Brunskill E, ET AL. On the opportunities and risks of foundation models. arXiv. 2021;arXiv:2108.07258. *preprint*

[18] Geroimenko V. The Essential Guide to Prompt Engineering: Key Principles, Techniques, Challenges, and Security Risks. Switzerland: Springer Nature; 2025

[19] Chapagain J, Sajib MI, Prodan R, Rus V. A study of LLM generated line-by-line explanations in the context of conversational program comprehension tutoring systems. In: Mello RF, Rummel N, Jivet I, Pishtari G, Valiente JAR, editors. Technology Enhanced Learning for Inclusive and Equitable Quality Education. Cham: Springer Nature Switzerland; 2024. p. 64–74

[20] Secules S, McCall C, Mejia JA, Beebe C, Masters AS, Sánchez-Peña ML, Svyantek M. Positionality practices and dimensions of impact on equity research: A collaborative inquiry and call to the community. Journal of Engineering Education. 2021;**110**(1): 19–43

[21] Geng C, Zhang Y, Pientka B, Si X. Can ChatGPT pass an introductory level functional language programming course? May 2023. arXiv:2305.02230 [cs]

[22] Kiesler N, Schiffner D. Large language models in introductory programming education: ChatGPT's performance and implications for assessments. arXiv. 2023; arXiv:2308.08572

[23] Petricini T, Wu C, Zipf ST. Perceptions about generative AI and ChatGPT use by faculty and college students

Chapter 10

Empowering Educators: Practical Uses of Artificial Intelligence in Science Education

Funda Örnek

Abstract

This chapter explores how AI technologies can enhance teaching methodologies and improve learning outcomes in science classrooms. The scope includes various applications such as personalized learning platforms, intelligent tutoring systems, and data analytics tools that provide insights into student performance, as well as AI tools used while teaching science. By integrating AI, educators can tailor lessons to meet individual student needs, foster engagement through interactive simulations, and streamline administrative tasks. Additionally, the use of AI can facilitate collaborative learning experiences and promote critical thinking skills. Overall, this topic emphasizes the transformative potential of AI in creating a more effective and inclusive science education environment.

Keywords: AI integration, science instruction, educator support, learning enhancement, technology in education

1. Introduction

In the digital era, artificial intelligence (AI) has emerged as a transformative force in education, with the potential to redefine how subjects are taught and learned [1]. AI tools are now integrated into classrooms through personalized learning platforms, intelligent tutoring systems, and virtual laboratories. These technologies are reshaping the learning experience by offering students more interactive, tailored, and accessible pathways to understanding scientific phenomena [2, 3].

Science education, in particular, stands to benefit from AI integration due to its inherently inquiry-based and problem-solving nature. Traditional methods often fall short in accommodating diverse learners, especially in multilingual or under-resourced contexts. AI tools can address these limitations by analyzing learner data in real time and adapting content to individual needs, offering differentiated instruction that promotes mastery learning [4]. Moreover, immersive AI-powered simulations and virtual labs provide cost-effective and scalable alternatives to physical experiments, thus enhancing conceptual understanding and student engagement [5, 6].

Importantly, AI also empowers educators by automating routine administrative tasks such as grading, attendance tracking, and progress monitoring, allowing them to allocate more time to student-centered instruction and mentorship [7]. AI can assist with grading, particularly for open-ended questions and rubric-based assessments, but teachers should carefully review the results before sharing them with students. However, effective integration of AI in science education also demands careful consideration of data privacy (any information related to students should not be exposed), ethical use, equity (which might be hard to implement), and the professional development of teachers [2, 8].

This chapter explores the practical uses of AI in science education across K–12, higher education, and teacher training settings. It highlights real-world, globally accessible tools and applications that can support classroom instruction, curriculum design, and institutional decision-making. Through structured tables and evidence-based examples, the chapter offers educators a roadmap to utilize AI in meaningful and responsible ways, ultimately promoting deeper learning, critical thinking, and inclusive science education.

2. Applications of AI in science education

AI is increasingly integrated into science classrooms worldwide, offering tools that adapt instruction to individual students and automate routine tasks. By analyzing student performance data and learning preferences, AI-driven systems can tailor content and pacing to each learner's needs [9]. For example, Khan Academy's AI algorithms continually assess student progress in math and science and adjust exercise difficulty to maintain an optimal learning challenge. Similarly, ChatGPT and other large language models can provide individualized explanations and hints. In Khan Academy's **Khanmigo** (a GPT-4-powered tutor), the system prompts students to work through problems by asking guiding questions rather than giving answers outright. On the contrary, students do not necessarily need access to Khanmigo. They can use ChatGPT or other AI tools directly for tutoring, either through written or spoken interaction (see Appendix). Early studies indicate such chatbots can create more "productive struggle" and adapt to each student, though their effectiveness is still being evaluated [10]. These adaptive approaches are used across K–12 and higher education; for instance, AI-assisted homework helpers and tutoring chatbots are piloted in schools around the world (over 28,000 US students used Khanmigo in 2023, and China's TAL Education Group developed a math-specific large language model (LLM) named **MathGPT** to assist students) [10]. By contrast with one-size-fits-all lessons, AI-powered personalization helps meet diverse learners' needs in science subjects such as physics, biology, and chemistry [9]. This adaptive learning also supports teacher training: platforms can recommend professional development modules or share lesson analytics to guide educators' practice.

2.1 Intelligent tutoring and chatbots

Intelligent tutoring systems and AI chatbots offer one-on-one support by simulating a personalized tutor. These systems use AI to interact with students, answer questions, and provide feedback. Please see the appendix for examples. In science education, AI can step through chemical problem-solving or physics problem-solving interactively. Modern LLM-based chatbots further extend this model. Teachers and students are experimenting with ChatGPT, Bard, Copilot, Gemini, Claudia, and other assistants for science inquiries. ChatGPT can generate sample science quiz questions, explain experimental procedures, or suggest analogies, effectively serving as a conversational tutor. In exploratory studies, ChatGPT often produced relevant science content aligned with curriculum themes, and educators have successfully used it to draft science lesson plans, rubrics, and quizzes [11]. However, experts caution that LLMs may produce errors or oversimplifications, so their use requires teacher supervision. Chatbots like Khanmigo are explicitly designed not to just give answers but also to guide reasoning. By providing instant, individualized support, intelligent tutors can help students tackle difficult science problems at their own pace, thereby extending learning opportunities outside the classroom.

2.2 Virtual labs and simulations

Virtual laboratory platforms leverage AI and three-dimensional (3D) simulation to recreate science experiments online. These immersive labs let students perform experiments in biology, chemistry, or physics without physical equipment. *Labster* is a leading example, offering dozens of game-like 3D lab simulations on topics ranging from acid–base titrations to microscopy. In Labster simulations, students interact with virtual equipment (e.g., a virtual confocal microscope) and tackle challenges and quizzes embedded in the experiment. The environments are built like adventure games, allowing students to click on apparatus and navigate safely through complex procedures. Virtual labs can increase student confidence and conceptual understanding by allowing repeated practice and providing immediate feedback when mistakes are made [12]. Another example is *LabXchange* (Harvard University), which provides free virtual science labs with real-time feedback. Students can assemble apparatus and conduct experiments in a virtual space, receiving hints and corrections instantly. Inq-ITS is a commercial platform that uses AI to auto-grade student investigations and provide adaptive tutoring in virtual science labs. Such tools are especially valuable where resources are limited. In many countries, virtual labs enable students to explore advanced experiments that would otherwise be too costly or dangerous. In higher education and teacher training, these simulations also provide consistent lab experiences and can collect data on student actions for further analytics. By combining interactivity with AI-generated guidance, virtual labs make hands-on science accessible anywhere, illustrating procedures (e.g., DNA sequencing, chemical synthesis) in rich detail.

2.3 Data analytics and visualization

AI-driven data analytics help educators make sense of science learning outcomes and experiment results. Learning-analytics platforms aggregate student performance data, such as quiz scores, assignment completion times, and lab activity metrics, and highlight patterns or knowledge gaps. For instance, systems like Knewton Alta can track how students perform on science problem sets and alert teachers to common difficulties. AI can flag students who struggle with particular concepts so that instructors can intervene. Data visualization tools, aided by AI, allow teachers and students to graph and model scientific data more easily. For example, AI-assisted platforms can generate interactive charts of student lab results or simulate data outcomes based on input parameters. Recent advances, like ChatGPT's code interpreter and AI-enabled software, let students explore complex datasets (such as environmental data) through prompts. By translating raw data into visual insights, these tools enhance comprehension of scientific phenomena. In teacher training, analytics dashboards can also evaluate teaching strategies. AI can summarize classroom data (attendance, quiz results, engagement measures) to help educators refine science curricula. Across contexts, data analytics bring a data-driven approach to science education, informing evidence-based decisions and personalized interventions.

2.4 Content generation and authoring

Generative AI has transformed lessons and resource creation. Teachers increasingly use AI to write and generate science content. ChatGPT and similar models (GPT-4, Bard, Claude, etc.) can draft science lesson plans, worksheets, and exam questions (see Appendix for examples). ChatGPT or other models can assist with lesson planning, the creation of teaching materials, and the development of assessment tools, such as quizzes and rubrics, tailored to students' varying academic levels [13]. For example, a teacher might prompt ChatGPT to generate multiple-choice questions on Newton's laws or to explain the process of photosynthesis at an appropriate grade level. The AI can also rephrase textbook content for different reading abilities or translate material into students' native languages. Tools like ChatGPT can summarize complex scientific articles into digestible formats for students or even simulate dialog on scientific debates. Beyond text, AI-powered authoring extends to multimedia: image generators (DALL-E, stable diffusion) help create custom science diagrams and illustrations; video generators and VR content tools (e.g., CoSpaces Edu) let teachers build interactive science storytelling. By automating routine writing and design tasks, AI frees educators to focus on pedagogy. Studies report that teachers use generative AI to draft science units and test items more efficiently [11]. Educators are advised to critically review AI-generated materials for accuracy, but early feedback indicates that such content generation can rapidly produce high-quality resources when guided by clear prompts [13].

2.5 Augmented reality/ virtual reality (AR/VR) and immersive visualization

Augmented reality (AR) and virtual reality (VR) bring immersive experiences to science education. AR overlays digital information onto real-world views (via tablets or AR glasses), while VR places students inside fully simulated environments. These technologies let students explore science concepts beyond the textbook. For example, apps like Merge Cube (an AR block with companion software) allow students to hold and manipulate 3D models of molecules, fossils, or the water cycle in their hands [14]. With Merge Cube and related apps, students can virtually inspect a molecule's structure or dig into a dinosaur bone in mid-air. Similarly, tools like CoSpaces Edu enable students to create their own AR/VR scenarios (e.g., a virtual chemistry lab or a model of the solar system) and then explore them on a screen or

VR headset [14]. In practice, AR/VR increases engagement and understanding. Furthermore, short circuit VR is a virtual reality electronics lab simulator that allows students to design and build electronic circuits using a variety of components. It offers an engaging way to learn basic electronics through interactive challenges, while also encouraging creativity and experimentation through hands-on project building [15]. Educators report that students become more curious and apply critical thinking when they can interact with immersive content [16]. AR can also simulate field trips (e.g., virtually touring a rainforest or even the ocean floor) and microscopic environments (e.g., inside a cell), providing experiences otherwise inaccessible [17]. While widely used at K–12 levels (with apps and even Google Cardboard viewers), universities use VR for advanced labs (e.g., virtual astronomy observatories) and teacher training (e.g., VR classroom management scenarios). These immersive visualizations, often coupled with AI-driven interactivity or guidance, offer powerful new ways to illustrate complex scientific ideas and phenomena [18].

2.6 Gamification and engagement

AI also powers gamified learning to boost student motivation in science. Educational games and quiz platforms use AI to adapt challenges and reward progress. For instance, platforms like Kahoot! or Quizizz employ algorithms to vary question difficulty and provide real-time feedback during science quizzes. Minecraft: Education Edition (a block-based game platform) includes chemistry and coding modules that let students experiment within game worlds. AI can generate game content on the fly. For example, Kahoot!'s new AI features allow teachers to create quizzes on any science topic in seconds. Classroom management can itself be gamified. Classcraft uses AI-like logic to turn classwork into a role-playing game, giving students points or virtual rewards for positive science-related behaviors. Across the globe, educators leverage gamification to make science fun and interactive. The AI component ensures each student faces "just-right" challenges and sees immediate consequences for their actions, which can improve persistence and enjoyment in science learning.

3. Educational benefits of AI in science education

AI is reshaping science education by offering innovative solutions that enhance teaching effectiveness and student learning. From personalizing instruction and increasing engagement to improving assessment, promoting equity, and building student confidence, AI tools support a more inclusive, responsive, and impactful science learning environment.

3.1 Differentiation and personalization

AI-driven tools enable science educators to tailor instruction to each student's strengths, weaknesses, and interests, aligning with theories of personalized learning [19]. By analyzing student data in real time, intelligent systems can identify knowledge gaps and adapt content or pacing accordingly. This dynamic customization helps break the "one-size-fits-all" model, ensuring that students receive tasks at an appropriate level of challenge. In practice, AI tutors (e.g., Khan Academy's GPTpowered Khanmigo or conversational agents like ChatGPT) can adjust explanations and questions on the run, scaffolding complex science concepts to individual needs. Research shows that such adaptive instruction not only improves learning outcomes but also empowers students by addressing diverse learning profiles, including those from underserved communities [20, 21]. In sum, AI personalization aligns with pedagogical principles of mastery learning, enabling students to progress at their own pace and deepen their understanding in science courses.

3.2 Engagement and active learning

AI can greatly increase student engagement in science by facilitating interactive, hands-on learning experiences. Gamified platforms and simulations powered by AI or rich multimedia capture students' attention and motivate active participation. For example, incorporating ChatGPT into learning can significantly boost students' behavioral, cognitive, and emotional engagement compared to traditional methods [22]. Similarly, game-based quiz tools like Kahoot! have been shown to enhance attention, creativity, and critical-thinking skills when integrated into lessons. Virtual laboratory simulations (e.g., Labster's immersive science labs) allow students to conduct experiments in a safe, visually engaging environment; one VR-based study reported higher test scores, very positive motivation, and that most students agreed virtual labs were a beneficial supplement to regular instruction [23]. In practice, teachers use these AI-rich tools (ChatGPT chatbots for brainstorming, Kahoot! quizzes for review, Labster simulations for experiments) to transform passive lectures into interactive sessions. By giving students meaningful choices and immediate feedback in these activities, AI supports active learning theories and sustains interest in complex science topics.

3.3 Formative assessment and feedback efficiency

AI streamlines formative assessment by automating routine feedback and enabling continuous, data-driven guidance. Traditional science classrooms often constrain the quantity of individualized feedback a teacher can give; AI systems improve this by instantly analyzing student responses and generating hints or corrections. For instance, adaptive assessment platforms use algorithms to schedule quizzes and tasks for each student, maximizing learning efficiency. AI can also generate rich, customized feedback on a large scale. Automated tutoring systems and chatbots can provide step-by-step explanations of misconceptions and pose follow-up questions. Students who received feedback from both teachers and ChatGPT showed significant gains in self-efficacy and learning outcomes, indicating the practical value of AI feedback [24]. Tools like Khanmigo or auto-grading engines exemplify this benefit. They let students submit answers or drafts and receive immediate feedback. By increasing the quantity and tailoring of feedback, AI-driven assessment helps students iteratively improve their understanding of scientific concepts while reducing teacher workload.

3.4 Student autonomy and confidence

AI fosters learners' independence in science education by acting as an on-demand tutor that students can consult anytime, which, in turn, builds confidence. When students know they can explore questions and receive guidance from an AI assistant, they tend to take more initiative in learning. Virtual labs and simulations also let students practice experiments without fear of costly mistakes, leading to higher readiness for real labs. In the aforementioned VR simulation study, the increase in learning and motivation suggests that students become more confident tackling lab content after using the virtual environment. Interactive quiz games like Kahoot!, by offering low-stakes challenges and immediate scoring, help students recognize their growing mastery and feel more assured about their progress. In practice, learners using ChatGPT or Khanmigo can ask complex "why" and "how" questions on their own, receiving instant answers that let them verify understanding. This autonomy, guided by AI, encourages a growth mindset. As students see themselves successfully learning in self-directed ways, their confidence in science work naturally rises.

3.5 Equity and access

AI technologies have the potential to make science education more inclusive by making high-quality resources widely accessible. Adaptive learning platforms and AI tutors are often available globally online, allowing students anywhere to receive personalized support regardless of local school resources. For instance, free tools like Khan Academy (with its AI tutor Khanmigo) or ChatGPT provide 24/7 help in multiple languages, helping non-native speakers and students in remote areas gain access to expert explanations. AI also enhances accessibility for students with disabilities. Speech-to-text and screen-reading algorithms improve text comprehension, while real-time audio transcription and predictive text support hearing- or mobility-impaired learners. AI-driven education can substantially expand learning opportunities in underserved regions where traditional resources are scarce [25, 26]. By tailoring content to students' cultural and linguistic contexts and supporting diverse needs, AI narrows gaps in science learning. In short, the global availability and adaptability of AI tools help create a more equitable science education system where every student has the chance to reach their potential.

4. AI tools for teaching purpose

AI-powered educational tools serve a variety of teaching purposes in science education, from assessment and virtual labs to research, lesson planning, and gamified engagement. As seen in **Table 1** below, platforms like Quizizz and Gradescope streamline assessment with instant feedback, while tools like Labster and PhET offer safe, hands-on virtual experiments. Inquiry tools such as ChatGPT and Wolfram Alpha support problem-solving and research, and AI assistants like Curipod and Canva help teachers rapidly create customized lessons. Gamified tools like Kahoot! and Minecraft can make science interactive and enjoyable, keeping students motivated and involved. See the Appendix for some examples.

Teaching purpose	Example tools	How they support science education
Assessment	*Quizizz, Kahoot!, Socrative, Google Forms, Gradescope, ChatGPT*	These AI-enhanced tools allow teachers to create quizzes and exams with automatic grading. They generate instant feedback and analytics on student responses, enabling differentiated follow-up. For example, Quizizz adapts question difficulty and provides a personalized learning path based on each student's answers. ChatGPT can help generate various types of questions, such as multiple-choice, true/false, and open-ended questions, along with their answers. It can also shuffle the questions to create different versions and reduce the risk of cheating. Additionally, ChatGPT can assist in creating rubrics and guidelines for project-based or inquiry-based assignments.
Experimentation and virtual labs	*Labster, PhET, Gizmos (ExploreLearning), Tinkercad Circuits, PraxiLabs*	Students perform simulated experiments and manipulate variables in a safe digital environment. These platforms provide immediate results and hints, allowing students to explore "what-if" scenarios (e.g., changing temperature or reactant amounts) without risk or cost. Teachers use them to supplement or replace challenging real labs.
Inquiry and research	*ChatGPT*/AI chatbots, *Consensus.app*, ChatPDF, *Wolfram Alpha, iNaturalist (Seek), ChatGPT (Deep Research), DeepSeek.*	These tools help students gather and analyze information. Chatbots like ChatGPT answer science questions and suggest experiment ideas. *Consensus* (AI literature search) quickly finds and summarizes research evidence. *WolframAlpha* computes solutions to physics/chemistry problems and balances equations. Apps like iNaturalist use AI to identify organisms during field studies, sparking scientific inquiry.
Lesson planning and content creation	*ChatGPT*/AI assistants, *Curipod, Eduaide.AI, Canva Magic Write,* Copilot, *Teaching with AI guides*	Teachers use these AI tools to generate lesson materials and activities. For example, Curipod's AI creates entire interactive science lessons from a topic keyword. Canva's Magic Write can brainstorm and structure presentations. AI assistants speed up writing lab instructions or discussion prompts, often providing translations or accessibility features (e.g., reading text aloud). In addition, Copilot and ChatGPT can create detailed, grade-specific lesson plans and learning activities tailored to students' needs. ChatGPT can generate content for topics as well.
Content organization or summary	*Mapify.so, Mindmapai.app, MindMeister, Ayoa, Xmind (with Copilot AI), Whimsical, Miro (with AI)*	Teachers and students can use AI-powered mind mapping tools to organize, visualize, and summarize complex topics in a clear and engaging way. These tools support deeper understanding by helping learners break down information into key concepts and connections. Teachers can use them to introduce new topics, structure lessons, or map out inquiry-based units. Similarly, students can use these tools to take notes, study key concepts, or co-create visual summaries during group work. As a meaningful reflection activity, students can be asked to generate a mind map at the end of a lesson to summarize what they've learned and present it to the class. This not only reinforces understanding but also builds communication and critical thinking skills. For example, Mapify.so automatically turns topics into structured mind maps using AI prompts, or a file can be uploaded to generate a mind map.

Teaching purpose	Example tools	How they support science education
Presentation creation	*Canva, Gamma AI, Curipod, ChatGPT (plain PPT slides)*	AI tools are designed to help educators create visually engaging, interactive, and well-structured presentations for their lessons with minimal effort. These tools can turn lesson content, topics, or even simple text into dynamic slide decks that capture students' attention and support better understanding. For example, Gamma AI can automatically generate professional-looking presentation slides from a topic, outline, or document. Moreover, ChatGPT can help draft plain PowerPoint slides based on input topics, including bullet points, key concepts, and suggested visuals. These tools save time for teachers while enhancing the clarity, creativity, and interactivity of their lessons, making learning more engaging for students.
Generating videos, audios, songs, digital stories, character diaries with AI Avatars, and comics, Ghibli-style comics, or image generation	*ChatGPT, Caluida, InVideo, Descript, Veed, ElevenLabs, Speechify, Canva, Adobe Express, Soundraw, Epidemic Sound, Synthesia, Heygen, Murf AI, Haiulo AI, veed.io, Mureka.AI, Steve.AI*	AI tools offer a variety of multimedia features to enhance student learning and engagement. They can convert written text into natural-sounding speech or audio clips, providing auditory support for students, especially those with learning differences or language barriers. In addition, AI can generate engaging content such as videos, images, songs, voiceovers, and even animated comics in styles like Studio Ghibli, making science lessons more interactive and enjoyable. These tools help bring science education to life, making learning more accessible, personalized, and fun for students. For example, InVideo, Descript, Veed, Adobe Express, and Canva can be used for creating and editing videos and visual content. Furthermore, ElevenLabs, Speechify, and Murf AI can be used for realistic text-to-speech and narratives.
Gamification and engagement	*Kahoot!, Classcraft, Minecraft: Education (Chemistry), Foldit* (protein-folding game)	Game-based platforms motivate students to engage with science content. Kahoot quizzes turn review into a competitive game. Classcraft embeds classroom behavior and problem-solving. Minecraft Education's chemistry mod lets students explore atomic interactions in a game world. Foldit lets students play a puzzle game that teaches protein structures and biochemistry. These fun environments maintain high student involvement.

Table 1.
Some AI tools for teaching.

5. Implementation considerations

5.1 Privacy and data security

AI applications in education collect extensive student data, so privacy and security are crucial. Student records and behavior logs used to train AI tutors or analytic systems must be protected by stringent data governance. Education systems already face frequent cyber-attacks. For example, a recent survey found over 1,600 publicly disclosed U.S. school cyber incidents since 2016 [27]. Generative AI adds new vulnerabilities. LLM interfaces may inadvertently "leak" personal inputs or be "jailbroken," allowing malicious users to extract prior conversation content. Such breaches can expose sensitive information (e.g., health, family, or disability data) and undermine trust. To mitigate risks, education leaders should follow proven privacy best practices. AI vendors and schools must collect only the minimum necessary data and store it with strong encryption and access controls. For example, only class-related inputs (not full student profiles) should be sent to cloud AI services, and personally identifiable information should be hashed or anonymized whenever possible. Transparent policies and parental consent forms should clearly explain how AI systems use student data. Educators should be trained to spot suspicious behavior (e.g., unusually rapid answer generation), and students should be taught not to input personal information into AI tools. At the policy level, jurisdictions should update school-privacy regulations to explicitly cover AI-powered tools. In practice, schools can audit AI products against standards program, requiring any vendor to demonstrate compliance with privacy safeguards. Taken together, these precautions (data minimization, user awareness, and technical protections) help ensure that AI enriches learning without compromising student privacy.

5.2 Equity and access

AI's promise will only be realized if all learners can benefit, yet access gaps threaten to widen educational inequities. Even before AI, major portions of the world lacked basic digital access. As of 2020, only approximately 40% of primary schools and 50% of lower-secondary schools globally had Internet, with rural and low-income communities far behind [28]. For example, the 2023 UNESCO report found that during COVID school closures, roughly half a billion students (31% globally and 72% of the poorest) could not access online learning. These disparities persist with AI. UNESCO warns of an emerging "AI divide," where marginalized regions and groups (e.g., remote rural, low-income, or underserved communities) have far less AI literacy, tools, and infrastructure [28]. In sub-Saharan Africa, only 36% of people had Internet in 2021, and rural electrification is only 30% [29]. Without reliable power and broadband, advanced AI tutors cannot function. Even within wealthy countries, urban students outpace rural peers in tech access. Thus, implementing AI must directly address the digital divide; otherwise, it risks benefiting already-advantaged students and leaving others further behind.

Practical measures are needed to level the playing field. On one hand, governments and NGOs can invest in connectivity (expanding broadband, building more cell towers, and undersea cables) so that schools everywhere can access cloud-based AI services. Indeed, UNESCO recommends ensuring "universal access to the internet" as a cornerstone of AI education policy [30]. On the other hand, educators should design AI tools that work under low-resource conditions. For instance, enabling offline functionality (local "edge AI" modules on tablets) or using low-bandwidth interfaces (text-only chat instead of video) can help. Schools might prioritize shared resources (computer labs or community centers) where high-cost equipment is available to all students. In addition, programs can provide subsidized devices or data plans for low-income families. Many countries are already piloting such schemes. For example, a partnership with technology companies might equip rural schools with AI-enhanced tablets while linking them to online STEM curricula. In short, to avoid this scenario, policymakers must allocate funding specifically for infrastructure in underserved areas, and designers must tailor AI platforms to work within the realities of low-connectivity classrooms.

5.3 Teacher training and AI literacy

Teachers are the key players in AI integration. Thus, without their understanding and support, even the best tools can fail. Currently, most K–12 teachers have little formal AI education. A recent survey of Chinese teachers noted widespread anxiety about AI's complexity and low confidence in its underlying technology [31]. Similarly, teachers in other parts of the world report feeling unprepared to use GenAI [32, 33]. The top concern is the lack of teacher training, which affects the usage of AI in teaching. This gap matters because effective use of AI requires new competencies (prompt design, critical evaluation of AI outputs, etc.). UNESCO's new AI competency framework for teachers highlights domains like AI foundations, AI pedagogy, ethics, and a "human-centered mindset" [34]. If teachers lack these skills, AI may be used superficially (or not at all), reinforcing rather than improving instruction. In low-resource settings, this is doubly problematic. Many developing countries invest heavily in teacher professional development but often fail to build the needed digital and pedagogical skills [35]. Without proactive training, the rapid rollout of AI could leave teachers behind.

To address this, education systems should incorporate comprehensive AI literacy into teacher education and ongoing professional development. Pre-service teacher programs can introduce basic AI concepts (such as how LLMs work and data ethics) alongside subject-matter training, while in-service workshops can focus on classroom applications (using AI as a tutor, grading assistant, or generating lesson plans, etc.) and critical thinking about AI outputs. Several frameworks and initiatives already exist to guide this effort. For instance, UNESCO's AI competency framework outlines how teachers can leverage AI for personalized learning and their own professional growth [34]. Schools and districts might partner with tech organizations to provide hands-on training, such as Google's AI Educator workshops or independent programs like TeachAI, which coach teachers on AI tools. Importantly, training should be iterative and context-sensitive. As one World Bank report advises, any AI training must be piloted and refined before scaling, especially in low-resource schools [36]. In practice, instead of abruptly implementing an AI tutor across the entire school, a more effective approach might involve starting with a small group of lead teachers trained extensively in AI integration, who then mentor their colleagues.

Finally, teacher training must also cultivate teachers' pedagogical vision. AI is a tool, not a remedy. Educators need to determine *why* and *how* to use a chatbot or data analytics in the service of learning goals. Professional learning communities and collaborative lesson planning (possibly using AI themselves) can help embed AI strategically. For example, teachers could co-design a science project where students use an AI model to analyze experimental data, thereby learning both science and computational thinking. Through such carefully scaffolded experiences, backed by research and shared practice, teachers can move from AI novices to savvy facilitators of AI-enhanced inquiry.

5.4 Infrastructure and cost

Beyond devices and connectivity, AI imposes further infrastructural and financial demands. Many advanced AI tools (e.g., adaptive tutoring or computer-vision science labs) rely on high-end hardware or cloud services that are expensive. Running powerful AI models requires reliable electricity, fast Internet, and often subscription fees or maintenance costs. These expenses pose challenges even for wealthy districts and are prohibitive in low-income regions. For example, the 2023 UNESCO Global Education Monitoring report [28] notes that adding basic digital learning, including online content and devices, could inflate a low-income country's education budget by about 50%. One rough estimate suggests it would take over US$100 billion to provide high-speed Internet to remote African communities [29]. Moreover, schools must budget for ongoing support, such as keeping software licenses up to date, refreshing aging hardware, and protecting against cybersecurity threats.

To manage costs, stakeholders can pursue multiple strategies. Shared resources and open-source platforms can stretch limited funds. Schools might use open AI models (e.g., ChatGPT-like systems) rather than expensive registered solutions. Cloud-based educational AI (such as Google Classroom AI or Khan Academy's Khanmigo) can reduce the need for local servers, provided bandwidth is sufficient. Partnerships with universities or tech firms may also subsidize expenses. If AI tools prove costly without clear learning gains, it may be wiser to focus on lower-tech solutions, as UNESCO's report [28] shows simple interventions can sometimes outperform high-tech investments. On a broader scale, many governments and international organizations recognize the challenge and are acting. New undersea cables (e.g., the 2Africa cable) and national broadband initiatives are expanding infrastructure in underserved regions [29]. UNESCO and others support AI in global education aid and budgets. Some high-income districts share costs through consortia that bulk-purchase AI services or jointly invest in research. Ultimately, decision-makers should carefully weigh AI's benefits against its long-term costs, seeking solutions that are cost-effective and sustainable within the local context.

5.5 Ethical use and academic integrity

AI's capabilities raise new ethical questions and academic integrity challenges that require proactive policy and teaching. The ease of generating essays or answers with tools like ChatGPT has led to concerns about plagiarism and fairness. As is known, students are already experimenting with AI as a cheating shortcut. At the same time, educators note that prohibitions alone are ineffective. It is impossible to ban AI outright. Instead, experts recommend fostering a culture of integrity and transparency. For example, students might be required to disclose any AI assistance and provide screenshots of their AI prompts and outputs to demonstrate honest use. Simultaneously, teachers can design assessments (in-class essays, oral exams, performance tasks) that explicitly test foundational skills so that AI misuse becomes less advantageous. On the contrary, it is important to keep in mind that students may use AI even during oral exams, performance tasks, or in-class essays through devices like AI-enabled glasses, which can be difficult to detect.

Beyond cheating, AI systems themselves can prolong ethical issues. Educators must be vigilant about algorithmic bias. If an AI tutor systematically represents certain cultural examples or gives different advice based on gender, it could deepen bias in science education. There are also concerns about AI surveillance (e.g., proctoring software) and student privacy (e.g., monitoring emotions with video analytics). Addressing these requires clear guidelines, and any use of an AI tool that influences content should be properly acknowledged [37]. In addition, AI systems should be transparent and explainable whenever possible. Academic integrity policies must explicitly include AI. Schools and universities should update integrity codes to clarify what is allowed – for example, permitted collaboration with AI on

DOI: http://dx.doi.org/10.5772/intechopen.1012988

brainstorming or editing, but not on final submissions. Policymakers can support this by issuing national or district-level guidance on ethical AI use in classrooms.

Finally, education about ethics is essential. Just as schools teach fair use and citation, they should teach the responsible use of AI. In this digital era, AI ethics should be integrated into the curriculum. Students should understand the importance of honesty and how AI can affect their sense of right and wrong. Teachers, in turn, need training on how to craft learning outcomes that include AI understanding and on how to model ethical behavior with these tools. Only by pairing clear rules with a strong culture of integrity and by empowering students to use AI as a legitimate learning aid rather than a shortcut can schools utilize AI's benefits without sacrificing trust or fairness.

6. Conclusion

In this chapter, we have explored the many ways AI can enrich science education, revealing a horizon where teaching and learning are more dynamic, responsive, and inclusive. Rather than replacing the human touch, AI tools – from adaptive tutors and virtual laboratories to generative content platforms and immersive simulations – serve as collaborators that amplify educators' creativity and students' curiosity. By automating routine tasks and offering timely insights, these technologies free teachers to focus on fostering inquiry, guiding thoughtful discussions, and nurturing the critical-thinking skills that lie at the heart of scientific exploration.

Yet, the promise of AI in science classrooms comes with responsibilities. As we integrate intelligent systems, we must remain vigilant about privacy safeguards, equitable access, and potential biases. Thoughtful infrastructure planning and context-sensitive teacher training are essential. Educators need both a conceptual understanding of AI and hands-on experience to weave these tools into lessons with confidence and care. Moreover, ethical guidelines and academic integrity practices must evolve alongside technology, ensuring that AI supports genuine learning rather than shortcuts. When these considerations are addressed, AI becomes a powerful ally in leveling the playing field, reaching learners who might otherwise lack resources, and providing tailored support for diverse needs.

Looking ahead, the real power of AI lies in its ability to spark new pedagogical possibilities. Students collaborate with virtual lab partners, exploring scientific phenomena through AR or receiving interactive and engaging feedback on their reasoning. Such experiences can foster autonomy, resilience, and a sense of wonder about the natural world. Ultimately, the goal is not a high-tech classroom for its own sake, but a human-centered environment where technology deepens connections between teacher and learner, question and discovery, curiosity and understanding. By embracing AI thoughtfully, science educators can inspire the next generation to ask bold questions, tackle real-world challenges, and carry forward a spirit of innovation grounded in ethical responsibility. The future of science education, then, is not just about new tools but also about nurturing empowered, reflective learners equipped to shape a better world.

Appendix

The following examples were created using the free versions of various AI tools. Due to page limitations, the examples will not include applications of all available AI tools 噌.

Assessment

You can write this prompt into ChatGPT and receive different questions with answers. As a science teacher teaching a science course to fifth-grade emergent multilingual students,

🌟 Multiple Choice Questions (MCQ)

Choose the best answer.

1. What is the main source of light on Earth?
   a) Moon
   b) Flashlight
   c) Sun ✅
   d) Candle
2. Light travels in:
   a) Circles
   b) Zig-zags
   c) Straight lines ✅
   d) Spirals
3. We can see things because:
   a) They talk to us
   b) Light bounces off them ✅
   c) They follow us
   d) They make sound

✅ True or False

1. The Sun is a man-made light source.
   ❌ False
2. Light cannot pass through opaque objects.
   ✅ True
3. You can see your face in a mirror because light reflects.
   ✅ True

✏️ Open-Ended Questions

1. **Why do we see a shadow when something blocks light?**
   Answer: We see a shadow because the object blocks the light, and the light cannot pass through it. This makes a dark shape behind the object.
2. **Describe what happens when light hits water.**
   Answer: When light hits water, it bends. This is called refraction. That's why things under water may look bent or in a different place.

🔗 Matching Question Table

Instructions: Match each item in **Column A** with the correct description from **Column B**. Write the correct **letter** next to each number.

Column A – Type of Material		Column B – Description Options
1. Transparent	__	A. Blocks all light
2. Translucent	__	B. Lets all light pass through
3. Opaque	__	C. Can reflect light like a mirror
4. Reflective	__	D. Lets some light pass through
5. Light Source	__	E. Gives off light
		F. Absorbs all light and sound
		G. Bends light

✅ Answer Key

Column A	Correct Answer (Letter)
1. Transparent	B ✅
2. Translucent	D ✅
3. Opaque	A ✅
4. Reflective	C ✅
5. Light Source	E ✅

DOI: http://dx.doi.org/10.5772/intechopen.1012988

write ten MCQs, ten True/False questions, one matching question, and two open-ended questions on the concept of LIGHT, along with their answers. In addition, it can provide these questions in Word or PDF format if needed.

Inquiry and research

You can write this prompt into DeepSeek and receive a summary on renewable energy research. As an expert researcher on renewable energy, summarize research results on renewable energy for emergent multilingual learners in the sixth grade.

Renewable Energy Basics for 6th Graders

Here's a simple and clear summary of renewable energy research for 6th-grade emergent multilingual learners:

Renewable Energy: Clean Power for the Future

Renewable energy comes from natural sources that never run out, like sunlight, wind, and water. Scientists have found that these energy sources are better for the environment than fossil fuels (like coal and oil) because they don't pollute the air or cause climate change.

Key Types of Renewable Energy:

1. **Solar Energy** – Comes from the sun. Solar panels turn sunlight into electricity.
2. **Wind Energy** – Wind turbines spin from the wind to make electricity.
3. **Hydropower** – Uses moving water (like rivers or dams) to produce energy.
4. **Geothermal Energy** – Heat from underground is used to make power.
5. **Biomass** – Plant and waste materials can be burned or turned into fuel.

Why Renewable Energy is Important:

- **Cleaner air** – No harmful smoke or pollution.
- **Never runs out** – Unlike oil or coal, sunlight and wind won't disappear.
- **Creates jobs** – More people work in solar and wind energy every year.

Scientists are working to make renewable energy cheaper and more efficient so everyone can use it. Many countries are already using more wind and solar power to help the planet.

Lesson planning and content creation

You can generate a lesson plan on any topic you choose. For example, here's a lesson plan on renewable energy tailored for sixth-grade emergent multilingual learners, featuring clear visuals, simplified language, and engaging interactive strategies. A great benefit is that ChatGPT can provide printable lesson PDFs, Google Slides, or AI-generated visuals for each type of energy. This is only part of the lesson plan.

🌞 Unit Title: Understanding Renewable Energy

Grade: 6

Level: Emergent Multilingual Learners (EMLs)

Duration: 2–3 class periods (extendable)

Theme: Science – Environment and Energy

🧠 Learning Objectives (Student Can...)

1. Define **renewable energy** in simple words.
2. Identify 3 main **renewable energy sources**: solar, wind, water.
3. Compare renewable energy with **non-renewable energy**.
4. Describe **why renewable energy is important** for the Earth.
5. Share one way to use or save energy at home or school.

📚 Key Vocabulary (with visuals and gestures)

Word	Simple Definition	Visual/Gesture
Energy	Power we use to do things	Raise hands & jump
Renewable	Can be used again and again	Make a circle with hands
Sun / Solar	Comes from the sun	Point up & smile
Wind	Comes from air moving	Blow air softly
Water / Hydro	Comes from flowing water	Wiggle fingers downward
Clean Energy	Does not make smoke or pollution	Wipe air with hand
Pollution	Dirty air or water	Cover nose, say "yuck"

🔍 Lesson 1: What is Energy?

Hook (5 min):

Show images or videos: light turning on, cooking, riding a bike. Ask:

➡ "What do these need?" (Let them guess → Energy)

Explain Simply (10 min):

"Energy is what makes things move, work, or light up."

✅ **Student Repeat:**

> "Energy helps us move."
> "Energy helps us cook."
> "Energy helps us light our homes."

📝 **Activity:** Match energy uses with pictures. (Cut-and-paste or digital)

You can generate content on different topics by using ChatGPT. For example, you can generate content about renewable energy for sixth-grade emergent multilingual learners. This is only part of the content.

ChatGPT

Sure! Here's **simplified science content about Renewable Energy** written specifically for **6th grade emergent multilingual learners**. It uses short sentences, clear structure, repeated key terms, and beginner-friendly language.

🌍 What Is Renewable Energy?

Energy is power.
We use energy to cook, move, and light our homes.
We need energy every day.

There are two types of energy:

🔥 Non-renewable Energy

- Comes from things like **coal**, **oil**, and **gas**
- Makes **smoke** and **pollution**
- Will run out one day
- Not good for the Earth

🌞 Renewable Energy

- Comes from **nature**
- Does **not** make smoke

In addition, it can generate infographics about the content.

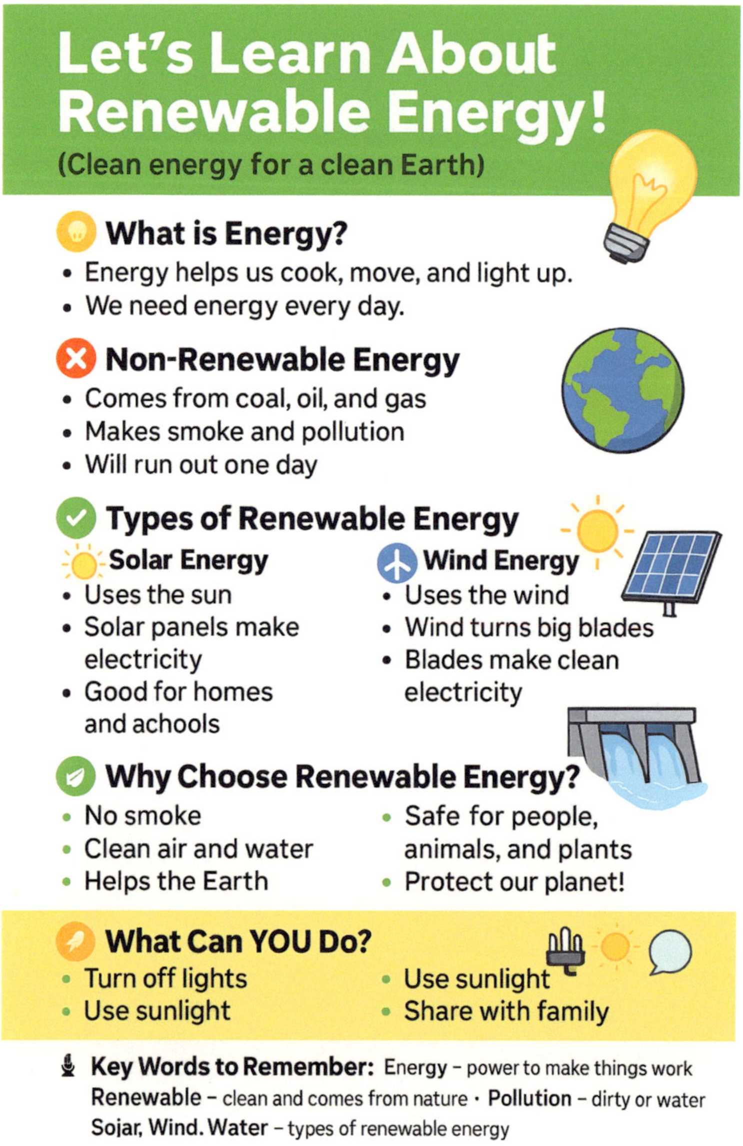

DOI: http://dx.doi.org/10.5772/intechopen.1012988

Content organization or summary

You can use Mapify.so to organize, visualize, and summarize complex topics in a clear and engaging way. For example, you can ask it to generate a mind map for renewable energy. In addition, you can upload a file about any topic and ask it to generate a mind map. The best part of it is that it can generate a mind map from PDFs, Word documents, eBooks, articles, slides and sheets, YouTube videos, video files, long texts, emails, webpages, and blog posts.

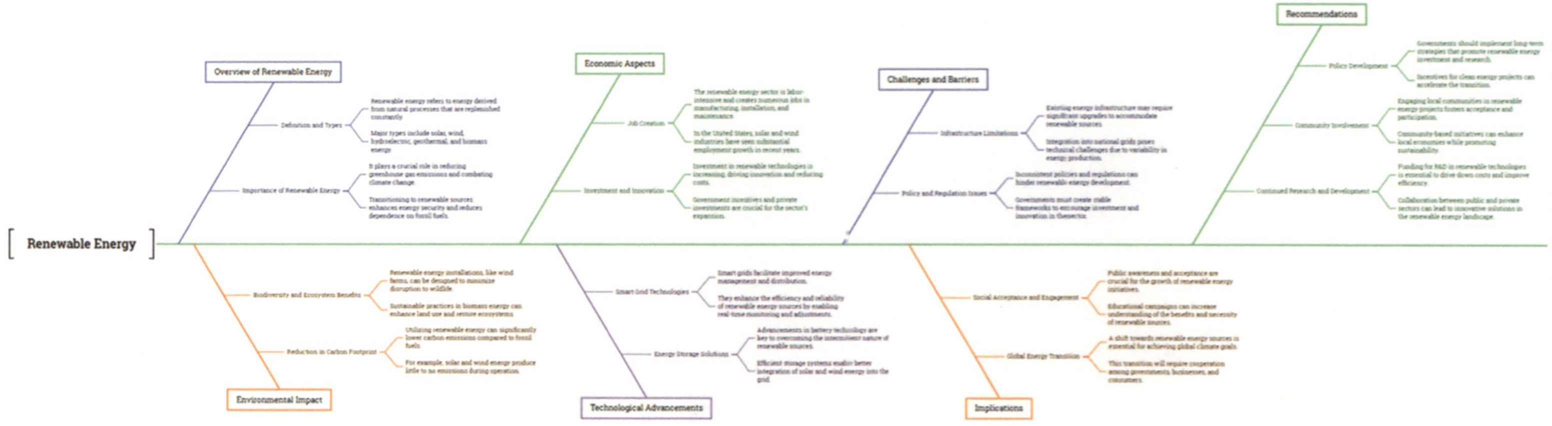

Generating videos, audios, songs, digital stories, character diaries with AI avatars, and comics – Ghibli-style comics or image generation.

After creating a digital story about "Force" tailored for emergent multilingual learners in fourth grade, ChatGPT illustrates it in a Ghibli-inspired comic style.

By utilizing Haiulo AI, a video in the style of Ghibli comics can be generated, providing students with engaging visuals to better grasp the concept of force. Below, QR codes are provided for the two versions of the videos.

Crafting a poem on the topic of force with ChatGPT and transforming it into an exceptional song.
Poem
The Dance of Force
Once you feel a gentle breeze,
Or open doors with care,
You meet a power called force –
It's everywhere, everywhere.
Force is a push, force is a pull,
A secret in our hands.
Push the box, it moves away;
Pull the rope, it understands.
Lift a book and bring it close –
you use force today.
Push a chair across the floor –
you help it move, hooray!
Wind can push a kite so high,
Water pushes boats along.
Force is there in games you play,
In every laugh and song.
Push means send away from you,
Pull means bring it near.
Feel the dance of force each day –
It's magic, bright and clear.

This poem has been input into Mureka.AI for transformation into a song.
https://www.mureka.ai/song-detail/J1S68AYscicYWUD6DSJFJ3?is_from_share=1

Creating a digital story about renewable energy for fifth graders who are emergent multilingual learners using ChatGPT.

Once upon a time, in a quiet valley, there was a small village called New Light. The people in New Light used energy every day. Energy helps us cook. Energy helps us light our homes. Energy helps us move. But the energy they used made smoke. Smoke made the air dirty. The villagers saw plants drooping. They felt coughs. They were worried.

One morning, a traveler arrived. The traveler greeted the villagers kindly: "Hello, friends of New Light." The villagers asked, "How can we make energy without dirty smoke?" The traveler smiled and said, "Look at the sun, the wind, and the water. They can give us clean energy."

The traveler held up a small model of a solar panel. "This is a solar panel," said the traveler. "The sun shines on this panel. Sunlight becomes electricity here. This is solar energy." A lamp beside the panel lit up. "See? Solar energy uses the sun to make electricity. Repeat with me: solar energy uses the sun."

Next, the traveler pointed to a gentle breeze and a small windmill illustration. "This is wind energy. When wind blows, it turns the blades of a turbine. Spinning blades make electricity. Repeat: wind energy uses wind." The villagers imagined blades turning on a hill, making clean power.

Then the traveler spoke of water. "This is hydro energy. Water flows and pushes a turbine. The turbine spins and makes electricity. Repeat: hydro energy uses flowing water." The villagers pictured a river, water turning a wheel, lighting a lamp without smoke.

The traveler added, "There are more sources: heat under the ground gives geothermal energy, and plants or waste can give biomass energy. But today, we focus on sun, wind, and water." The villagers nodded.

"Why is this good?" asked a child. The traveler replied, "Renewable energy is clean. It does not make bad smoke. It does not run out quickly. It helps Earth stay healthy. Repeat: renewable energy is clean and does not run out quickly."

The people of New Light felt hope. They saw before-and-after pictures: before, smoky air and sad plants; after, clear sky and bright plants. They cheered: "Clean air! Healthy plants! Happy children!" The traveler said, "Even small actions help. Turn off lights when not needed. Save water. Learn and share with family and friends."

A villager asked, "How can we start?" The traveler answered, "Install solar panels on roofs. Build small wind turbines on hills. Use water wisely at the river. Teach others: 'Renewable energy keeps our world healthy.' Repeat: renewable energy keeps our world healthy."

Soon, New Light changed. On rooftops, solar panels caught sunlight. On hills, wind turbines turned in the breeze. By the river, a small hydro turbine spun with flowing water. The air became clear. Plants thrived. Children played under a bright sky.

The traveler said farewell: "Remember, energy from sun, wind, and water is clean. Energy from sun, wind, and water helps Earth. Tell your friends: renewable energy is our friend." The villagers promised: "We will share this story. We will use clean energy. We will help Earth."

And so, the village of New Light shone forever under the bright sun, gentle wind, and flowing water. The End.

You can generate an animated video of this story using Steve.ai. Additionally, it can be published on YouTube.
https://www.youtube.com/watch?v=gRbuKFe-N2c

DOI: http://dx.doi.org/10.5772/intechopen.1012988

You can create a video on the topic of force for fifth-grade emergent learners using Veed.io. https://www.veed.io/view/8349a472-74db-443b-b878-b33a1bfa2865?panel=share

You can generate PowerPoint slides on the topic of force for fifth-grade emergent learners using Gamma.

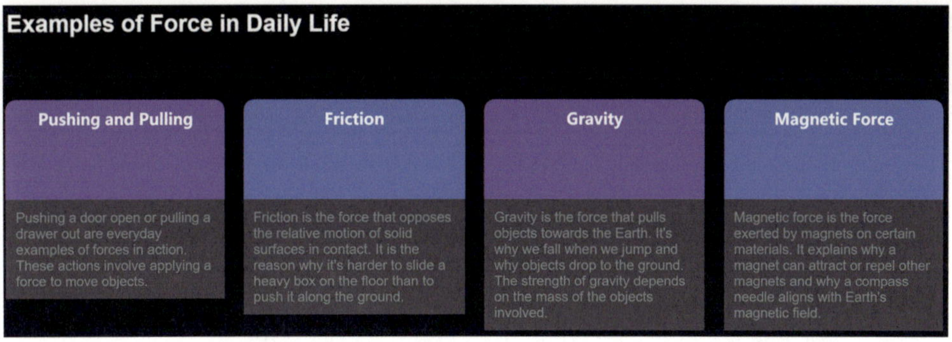

Author details

Funda Örnek
Bahrain Teachers College, University of Bahrain, Zallaq, Bahrain.

*Address all correspondence to: fundaornek@gmail.com

References

[1] Lytras MD, Serban AC, Alkhaldi A, Aldosemani T, Malik S. Transformative Learning for Future Higher Education: The Artificial Intelligence-enabled Learning Revolution 2035. In: Digital Transformation in Higher Education, Part B. Leeds, UK: Emerald Publishing Limited; 2024. pp. 231–241

[2] Luckin R, Holmes W, Griffiths M, Forcier LB. Intelligence Unleashed: An Argument for AI in Education. London: Pearson; 2016

[3] Roll I, Wylie R. Evolution and revolution in Artificial Intelligence in education. International Journal of Artificial Intelligence in Education. 2016;**26**(2):582–599. DOI: 10.1007/s40593-016-0110-3

[4] Zawacki-Richter O, Marín VI, Bond M, Gouverneur F. Systematic review of research on artificial intelligence applications in higher education: A bibliometric analysis. International Journal of Educational Technology in Higher Education. 2019;**16**:39. DOI: 10.1186/s41239-019-0171-0

[5] Bekteshi L.Education in the era of AI and immersive technologies: A systematic review. Journal of Research in Engineering and Computer Science. 2025;**3**(1):1–14

[6] Javali P, Raj RG, Shaw S, Devi CH, Kumar A, Andy A, et al. Virtual labs and simulation tools: Enhancing STEM education. In: Revolutionizing Education with Remote Experimentation and Learning Analytics. IGI Global Scientific Publishing; 2025. pp. 607–632

[7] Popenici SAD, Kerr S. Exploring the impact of artificial intelligence on teaching and learning in higher education. Research and Practice in Technology Enhanced Learning. 2017;**12**(1):1–13. DOI: 10.1186/s41039-017-0062-8

[8] UNESCO. *AI and Education: Guidance for Policy-makers* [Internet]. 2021. Available from: https://unesdoc.unesco.org/ark:/48223/pf0000376709 [Accessed: 2025-June-18]

[9] Raza F AI in education: Personalized learning and adaptive assessment. [Internet]. 2023. DOI: 10.13140/RG.2.2.24796.77446 [Accessed: 2025-June-18]

[10] Extance A ChatGPT has entered the classroom: How LLMs could transform education. *Nature* [Internet]. November 15, 2023. Available from: https://www.nature.com/articles/d41586-023-03594-y [Accessed: 2025-June-18]

[11] Cooper G. Examining science education in ChatGPT: An exploratory study of generative artificial intelligence. Journal of Science Education and Technology. 2023;**32**:444–452

[12] Kolil VK, Achuthan K.Virtual labs in chemistry education: A novel approach for increasing student's laboratory educational consciousness and skills. Education and Information Technologies. 2024;**29**(18):25307–25331

[13] Peikos G, Stavrou D. ChatGPT for science lesson planning: An exploratory study based on pedagogical content knowledge. Education Sciences. 2025;**15**(3):338. mdpi.com

[14] Danhoff C 7 augmented reality tools for the classroom. *Edutopia* [Internet]. 2021 Jun 16. Available from: https://www.edutopia.org [Accessed: 2025-June-18]

[15] Cui Y, Lai Z, Li Z, Su J.Design and implementation of electronic circuit virtual laboratory based on virtual reality technology. Journal of Computational Methods in Sciences and Engineering. 2021;**21**(5):1125–1144

[16] Duncan KJ.Examining the effects of immersive game-based learning on student engagement and the development of collaboration, communication, creativity and critical thinking. TechTrends. 2020;**64**(3): 514–524

[17] Jerowsky M (2024). *Comparing the Use of Virtual, Augmented, and Outdoor Field Trips in the Environmental Education of Children* [Doctoral dissertation], University of British Columbia)

[18] Partarakis N, Zabulis X.A review of immersive technologies, knowledge representation, and AI for human-centered digital experiences. Electronics. 2024;**13**(2):269

[19] Yılmaz Ö.Personalised learning and artificial intelligence in science education: Current state and future perspectives. Educational Technology Quarterly. 2024;**2024**(3):255–274

[20] Idowu E (2024). Personalized learning: Tailoring instruction to individual student needs. *Preprints*

[21] Mahmoudi-Dehaki M, Nasr-Esfahani N. Enhancing Engagement and equity in personalized learning through adaptive systems. In: Personalized Learning through Adaptive Systems and Intelligent Tutoring. IGI Global Scientific Publishing; 2025. pp. 219–246

[22] Lo CK, Hew KF, Jong MSY. The influence of ChatGPT on student engagement: A systematic review and future research agenda. Computers and Education. 2024;**219**:105100

[23] Chan P, Bernaerts K, Van Gerven T, Dubois JL Virtual reality serious game for chemical lab safety training in industry and academia: From design, development to increased motivation and engagement. 2023

[24] Qi C, Tang Y, Lei Y. Does feedback from ChatGPT help? Investigating the effect of feedback from both teacher and ChatGPT on students' learning outcomes. In: *Proceedings of AMCIS 2024*. 2024

[25] Fazal I, Bandeali MM, Shezad F, Gul H.Bridging educational gaps: The role of AI and social media in enhancing access to quality education in under-privileged communities. The Critical Review of Social Sciences Studies. 2025;**3**(1):2413–2431

[26] Peter H Leveraging AI and technology to address the challenges of underdeveloped countries. 2025

[27] Nambiar AA. Securing Student Data in the Age of Generative AI. Cambridge, MA USA: MIT RAISE Capstone; 2024

[28] UNESCO. *Global Education Monitoring Report 2023: Technology in Education – Summary*. Paris: UNESCO; 2023

[29] Okolo CT. AI in the Global South: Opportunities and challenges towards more inclusive governance. The

Brookings Institution. 2023;**2**. DOI: 10.48028/iiprds/ijiraet.v2.i1.09

[30] Miao F What you need to know about UNESCO's new AI competency frameworks for students and teachers. UNESCO; Available from: https://www.unesco.org/en/articles/what-you-need-know-about-unescos-new-ai-competency-frameworks-students-and-teachers [Accessed: 2025-June-18]

[31] Du H, Sun Y, Jiang H, Atiquil Islam AYM, Gu X, et al. Exploring the effects of AI literacy in teacher learning: An empirical study. Humanities and Social Sciences Communications. 2024;**11**:559

[32] Magnusson A, Israelsson J (2024). From challenge to preparedness: A case study of the challenges created by GenAIs in K-12 schools

[33] Nyaaba Akanzire B, Nyaaba M, Nabang M. Generative AI in teacher education: Teacher educators' perception and preparedness. Matthew and Nabang, Macharious. 2025;**5**(1): ep2508. DOI: 10.30935/jdet/15887.

[34] Cukurova M, Miao F. AI Competency Framework for Teachers. France: UNESCO Publishing; 2024

[35] Hennessy S, D'Angelo S, McIntyre N, Koomar S, Kreimeia A, Cao L, . . . Zubairi A. Technology use for teacher professional development in low-and middle-income countries: A systematic review. Computers and Education Open. 2022;**3**:100080

[36] Wilichowski T, Cobo C. AI-powered Teacher Training: Promise or Pitfall? USA: World Bank Blogs; 2023. Available from: https://blogs.worldbank.org/en/education/ai-powered-teacher-training-promise-or-pitfall

[37] Foltynek T, Bjelobaba S, Glendinning I, Khan ZR, Santos R, Pavletic P, et al. ENAI Recommendations on the ethical use of Artificial Intelligence in Education. International Journal for Educational Integrity. 2023;**19**:12

Chapter 11

Engaging Teachers in an Inclusive Learning Environment through Implementing an Artificial Intelligence Literacy Curriculum for the Next Generation

Xiaoxue Du

Abstract

Teachers play a critical role in developing students' knowledge, skills, and readiness for an increasingly technology-driven world. As artificial intelligence (AI) becomes embedded in daily life and across professional domains, students must develop AI literacy to prepare for future academic and career opportunities. To achieve this, educators need to be prepared with the knowledge, confidence, and pedagogical practices to teach AI literacy concepts in diverse and inclusive classrooms. This study employed a convergent mixed-methods approach to evaluate the effectiveness of an AI literacy curriculum designed for teachers. The research examined how educators used, adapted, and reflected on the curriculum to support student engagement and accommodate diverse learning needs. Findings revealed that the designed curriculum developed teachers' self-perceived readiness, instructional adaptability, and confidence in designing AI literacy curriculum. The results highlighted the critical value of professional development (PD) in AI literacy – in developing teachers' knowledge in AI and in preparing them to design human-centered, student-centered learning environments that foster equitable and future-ready education.

Keywords: AI literacy, professional development, human-centered design, student-centered learning, inclusive education

1. Introduction

As artificial intelligence (AI) becomes deeply integrated into daily life – from personalized recommendations and voice assistants to scientific discovery and civic decision-making – education systems must urgently equip students not just to use AI, but to understand, critique, and shape it. AI literacy must go beyond technical skills to include the cognitive, ethical, and civic competencies essential

IntechOpen

for navigating an AI-mediated world. This shift poses significant challenges for educators, requiring teachers to take on new roles as facilitators of interdisciplinary learning, ethical inquiry, and critical engagement with emerging technologies – not only in computer science but across all subjects and grade levels.

Historically, AI literacy education in schools has been situated within (ICT), programming, or robotics. Such approaches often presuppose prior technical knowledge, requiring access to resources and professional development (PD) that are not equitably distributed. As a result, AI literacy remains inaccessible to many teachers and learners, particularly those in under-resourced communities. Moreover, these models tend to emphasize learning about AI at the expense of learning with and learning through AI, narrowing students' opportunities to engage critically and creatively with the technologies that increasingly shape their lives [1].

In recent years, AI literacy has emerged alongside a constellation of new literacies, driven by the increasing presence of AI in society and by a democratic imperative to help individuals, especially those without backgrounds in computer science or engineering, understand what AI is, how it functions, and what societal consequences it entails. This shift places teachers at the center of the AI literacy discourse, recognizing their role not only in delivering content but also in shaping how students reflect on, question, and cocreate with intelligent systems. The growing integration of AI-integrated tools into classrooms raises complex pedagogical and ethical questions, underscoring the need for educators to understand how AI operates within educational contexts, both theoretically and practically [1–3].

Contemporary frameworks increasingly call for a holistic view of AI literacy that includes domain-specific knowledge, sociotechnical awareness, and ethical reasoning. For instance, researchers emphasize the need to address AI literacy not only through cognitive knowledge but also through behavioral engagement and attitudinal reflection, especially as AI becomes more deeply embedded in decision-making systems across professions [2]. Similarly, scholars identify six core constructs of AI literacy – recognize, know and understand, use and apply, evaluate, create, and navigate ethically – that underscore the multifaceted nature of AI engagement [3].

In this context, educators play a critical role. Yet, as scholars note, AI literacy in teacher education remains underdeveloped, with limited attention to how teachers acquire the ethical and pedagogical capacities necessary to support AI-infused learning environments [4]. This gap is especially concerning, given the broad call for teachers to foster student agency, ensure responsible technology use, and adapt instruction to digital realities.

To address these challenges, a university-based research initiative, in collaboration with a nonprofit curriculum design organization, developed a five-module AI literacy curriculum targeted at middle-school learners. The curriculum was designed with equity and adaptability in mind: to be implementable by teachers with varying levels of technical expertise across diverse geographical and technological contexts. Drawing on the principles of universal design [5], culturally responsive pedagogy [6], and a human-centered design process [7], the curriculum enables teachers to explore foundational AI concepts, engage in student-centered inquiry, and connect to ethical considerations relevant to the learners' lives.

This study examines how this curriculum shapes teachers' self-perceived readiness, instructional adaptability, and confidence. In particular, it explores how educators adapt and reflect on the materials as they introduce AI literacy into their classrooms. By studying how teachers engage with AI literacy at the classroom level, this work contributes to a growing body of literature that seeks to operationalize inclusive, practical, and reflective approaches to AI literacy education.

2. Literature review

A growing body of international research affirms that K–12 teachers play a pivotal role in building students' AI literacy, not merely by introducing technical knowledge such as algorithms and machine learning, but by fostering ethical reasoning, critical inquiry, and sociocultural awareness of AI's influence on everyday life [8]. AI literacy is seen as an interdisciplinary construct that integrates cognitive, behavioral, and affective competencies [2]. Recent conceptual frameworks draw from Aristotelian notions of teacher knowledge – *episteme* (theoretical-scientific understanding), *techne* (practical application and instructional skills), and *phronesis* (ethical and situational judgment) – to argue that effective AI education demands a holistic understanding of how teachers think, act, and reflect in practice [4]. This tripartite view is critical as it acknowledges that AI is a sociotechnical system embedded with human values, biases, and power dynamics. Therefore, preparing teachers to engage with AI requires cultivating their ability to critically analyze AI's societal implications, ethically evaluate its use in educational settings, and adapt curricula to meet diverse learners' needs. Empirical evidence shows that when teachers are prepared to guide students through these dimensions, AI literacy education becomes a space for ethical deliberation and civic participation [4, 9].

Despite this potential, AI literacy remains underdeveloped across most teacher education programs globally. A comprehensive scoping review by researchers showed that teacher preparation often emphasizes technical or epistemic knowledge while neglecting the professional and moral complexities of classroom implementation [10]. Likewise, scholars critique current assessment tools for focusing narrowly on conceptual knowledge and ignoring behavior and attitude-based competencies, particularly in AI ethics. This leads to inconsistent implementation and limited integration of AI content in K–12 classrooms, with some schools lacking the resources, training, or support needed to effectively teach AI literacy [11].

Furthermore, classroom implementation varies widely due to disparities in teacher readiness [12], curriculum adaptability [13], and structural support [13, 14], factors intensified by differences in digital infrastructure [15], language accessibility [16], and PD quality. These challenges are especially pronounced in under-resourced and linguistically diverse settings, where a lack of culturally responsive materials and localized teacher training limits the reach and relevance of instruction.

This review, therefore, synthesizes empirical, design-based, and comparative studies to deepen our understanding across four major domains essential to equitable and effective AI education: (1) teacher effectiveness and instructional impact – how a teacher's self-efficacy shapes AI literacy integration; (2) readiness and professional capacity – how PD and teacher education programs develop AI-related competencies; (3) curriculum adaptability – how educators tailor content to students' needs, cultural backgrounds, and classroom realities; and (4) structural and cultural barriers – how systemic inequities, cultural mismatches, and policy gaps limit scalable and inclusive AI literacy efforts.

2.1 Teacher effectiveness and instructional impact

Teachers' perceived effectiveness – conceptualized as self-efficacy in educational psychology – is a strong predictor of their instructional behaviors, openness to innovation, and ability to support student learning [17]. In the context of AI literacy education, self-efficacy is particularly crucial given the novelty, technical complexity, and ethical ambiguity of AI tools [18]. Teachers with relevant knowledge are more likely to adopt exploratory, inquiry-based pedagogies and scaffold students' engagement with AI systems. Empirical studies highlight that educators who feel competent in using AI-enhanced technologies are more willing to integrate them into instruction, often facilitating hands-on, project-based learning that invites students to critically analyze, simulate, or cocreate with AI [19]. Building on this foundation, a recent study using a critical co-discovery approach within an online AI in education course found that educators co-constructed knowledge of AI concepts, examined ethical implications, and applied their learning to specific classroom contexts [20]. This process not only expanded their AI literacy but also enhanced their confidence and instructional adaptability. These findings support the broader argument that meaningful, reflective engagement with AI is essential for strengthening teacher self-efficacy. Integrating such experiences into teacher education programs can empower educators to make informed, ethical decisions about AI use, ultimately fostering student-centered, future-ready learning environments.

Beyond basic tool adoption, teacher self-efficacy influences how educators facilitate student learning with AI technologies. A recent study found that subjective norms significantly influence university teachers' intention to adopt AI, both directly and through the mediating effects of confidence and AI readiness, which accounted for 12.87% of the total effect. These findings highlight that boosting teacher confidence and preparedness is key to strengthening the impact of social influences on AI adoption in education [21].

Studies show that teacher confidence influences how much agency students are given [21]. This confidence is often cultivated through collaborative professional learning processes. For instance, collective inquiry allows teachers to investigate AI's educational implications together, reflect on its ethical dimensions, and co-develop strategies for equitable use [14]. Through critical reflection, teachers examine how AI may reinforce or challenge systemic inequalities, helping them make ethically informed instructional decisions [22]. Participatory engagement and co-creation of knowledge ensure that teachers' local experiences and insights shape curriculum adaptation, strengthening their instructional autonomy and readiness. These processes not only deepen AI literacy but also enhance teachers' belief in their ability to meaningfully guide students through complex, AI-integrated learning environments.

Nevertheless, teacher effectiveness in AI education is unevenly distributed. Research shows that institutional support, prior exposure to technology tools, and PD opportunities all shape how confident teachers feel when adopting AI into their pedagogical repertoire [18]. Without adequate resources, even highly motivated educators may avoid AI topics due to uncertainty around accuracy, student misconceptions, or ethical risks.

2.2 Readiness and professional capacity

Closely linked to instructional effectiveness is the notion of teacher readiness, which includes not only teachers' knowledge of AI concepts but also their confidence, ethical awareness, and pedagogical disposition to engage with AI tools meaningfully in diverse classroom settings. In the context of AI literacy education, readiness refers to a teacher's ability and intention to implement AI literacy curricula that are responsive to student needs, aligned with learning goals, and mindful of broader social implications. Importantly, research increasingly positions readiness not as an innate quality but as a dynamic and developable capacity. Numerous studies emphasize that teacher readiness can be cultivated through well-designed PD, collaborative learning environments, and access to high-quality, contextually relevant teaching materials [23].

Empirical research underscores that PD plays a critical role in enhancing teachers' readiness and confidence in integrating AI in educational settings. Findings from [8] demonstrate that teachers' behavioral intention to adopt AI is significantly shaped not only by their perceptions of usefulness and ease of use but also by the availability of school support and structured learning opportunities. When schools provide targeted PD – including hands-on training with AI tools, collaborative lesson design, and discussions around ethical and pedagogical implications – teachers reported stronger instructional agency and greater willingness to adapt AI for diverse classroom contexts. These results align with broader educational research, indicating that teacher capacity grows most meaningfully when PD enables flexible, reflective, and context-responsive practice.

Moreover, embedding critical inquiry and student-centered design into teacher education is essential for AI readiness [24]. Programs that prompt educators to examine the social implications of AI, such as surveillance, bias, and misinformation, prepare them not only to use AI tools effectively but also to facilitate ethical discussions that promote students' civic reasoning and digital agency [25]. This form of readiness extends beyond technical skills; it reflects an educator's ability to engage with complexity, uncertainty, and interdisciplinary perspectives, ultimately supporting equitable and responsible AI integration in schools [26].

Readiness is also influenced by dispositional factors, such as a teacher's openness to innovation, perceived risk tolerance, and commitment to educational equity [27]. In under-resourced or marginalized communities, where AI access may be limited, teacher adaptability becomes even more important [28]. Research suggests that even low-tech approaches, such as role-playing simulations or unplugged AI activities, can be effective tools for cultivating student understanding, provided teachers are confident and prepared to facilitate them. However, such confidence is not uniformly distributed [28]. Educators who lack access to supportive networks or ongoing PD often report hesitation in teaching AI content, especially when curriculum mandates are rigid or institutional leadership is absent [29].

2.3 Curriculum adaptability

Curriculum adaptability is the third essential pillar in the implementation of AI literacy in K–12 education. As classrooms become increasingly diverse – culturally, linguistically, and in terms of technological access – educators are rarely able to use AI-related teaching materials "off the shelf." Instead, they must interpret, revise, and customize prepackaged content to ensure it resonates with students' prior knowledge, lived experiences, and learning styles [30]. Scholars have long emphasized the importance of flexible curriculum design, especially in contexts of pedagogical change and literacies. Research shows that curriculum is not a fixed script but a living framework that requires teacher agency and localized adaptation to be effective [31]. This view is particularly relevant in AI education, where content may be novel, abstract, or framed from culturally dominant perspectives that do not reflect the realities of all learners [32].

Pedagogical approaches that support adaptive teaching, such as inquiry-based learning, role-play simulations, and dialogic reflection, have proven especially valuable in cultivating student engagement with complex AI concepts [33]. Digital platforms also offer effective opportunities for curriculum adaptability, particularly when designed with real-time responsiveness. Intelligent tutoring systems, adaptive coding environments, and block-based programming platforms (e.g., Scratch with machine learning extensions) allow teachers to personalize instruction based on formative data and student feedback [34]. Research shows that when such tools are integrated into classroom practice, they can help teachers differentiate instruction, scaffold complex problem-solving, and guide students toward conceptual mastery at their own pace [35].

Importantly, curriculum adaptability is not solely about the content – it is also about pedagogy, teacher capacity, and context. Co-design processes involving teachers, researchers, and students have shown promise in creating AI literacy curricula that are both rigorous and relevant [36]. Such processes acknowledge that teachers are not passive implementers but active shapers of how AI technologies are taught and discussed. When teachers are invited to help shape content, they can ensure that AI topics are grounded in culturally meaningful examples, aligned with cross-curricular goals, and adjusted for the developmental needs of their students [37]. This is particularly crucial in communities where AI is perceived as abstract, inaccessible, or disconnected from students' everyday realities [37, 38].

2.4 Structural and cultural barriers

Despite these promising directions, the implementation of AI literacy is often constrained by structural and cultural barriers. Disparities in infrastructure, policy alignment, and digital access pose significant challenges, particularly in under-resourced schools and rural communities [39]. Teachers in such contexts often lack the technical support and institutional encouragement necessary to experiment with AI content. Cultural barriers further complicate implementation. Deficit thinking – the belief that certain student populations lack the background or interest to engage with AI technologies – can discourage inclusive curriculum development and limit teacher agency [40]. In many non-Western contexts, language mismatches between technology instructional materials and local classroom languages restrict both access and relevance, particularly when materials are not translated or culturally adapted [41]. Furthermore, intersectional factors such as gender and ethnicity shape teachers' access to AI-related PD and institutional support. Educators from historically marginalized backgrounds report lower institutional confidence in their curricular choices and fewer opportunities for leadership in AI-related initiatives [42]. At the global level, organizations such as UNESCO and the OECD have called for context-aware, teacher-led innovation that reflects local pedagogical realities and cultural frameworks. Their initiatives promote inclusive, ethical AI education as a human right, stressing the importance of teacher agency and the need for adaptive systems that reflect diverse knowledge systems.

Yet, despite widespread agreement on the importance of teacher involvement in cultivating AI literacy, empirical evidence on how teachers use, adapt, and reflect on AI literacy curricula in diverse classroom settings remains scarce. Existing studies largely focus on teacher attitudes or theoretical models of readiness, with fewer examining instructional enactment – how teachers make real-time decisions to support inclusion, engagement, and differentiation in AI learning experiences. While these factors are well-documented in theory, there is a lack of practice-based research showing how PD and curriculum design interact to build these capacities among teachers. Moreover, most existing studies do not examine how teachers tailor AI content to meet equity goals or address barriers such as cultural mismatch, language constraints, or institutional inequity. Therefore, the study highlights the importance of curriculum adaptation, showing that instructional flexibility, reflective practice, and contextual relevance are key drivers of successful implementation. It operationalizes curriculum adaptability as both a pedagogical process and a design principle. The research emphasizes the need for culturally responsive pedagogy and inclusive design to leverage more learning opportunities for learners across the globe.

3. Research context

To support the implementation of AI literacy in K–12 settings, the PD component of this study was designed to engage in-service teachers in dual roles: both as learners experiencing the curriculum firsthand and as educators preparing to facilitate AI instruction in their own classrooms. This structure allowed participants to build foundational content knowledge, explore ethical and social dimensions of AI, and develop instructional strategies aligned with student-centered, inquiry-based learning.

During the PD sessions, teachers were first introduced to the curriculum content from a learner's perspective. The curriculum's overarching goal is to help students develop foundational knowledge of AI while cultivating essential skills in computational thinking and critical digital literacy. At its core, the curriculum invites learners to apply their understanding of AI to real-world, community-centered problems, ensuring that technological learning is situated within personally and socially meaningful contexts (see **Table 1**).

Core Topics	Main concepts	Learning Activities
Module 1. What is Artificial Intelligence	1.1. What is AI? 1.2. AI vs. non-AI 1.3. Algorithms and optimization 1.4. Ethical matrix 1.5. AI applications: robotics, social media, entertainment, and chatbots	Employ strategies to reason through ethical dilemmas. Create the PoseBlocks Scratch program that uses body-sensing commands to design interactive games.

Table 1.
Project STEM curriculum overview.

To get familiar with the curriculum, teachers worked through interactive AI activities and tools that were originally designed for students, allowing them to gain an experiential understanding of both the technical and ethical aspects of AI. For instance, they engaged with modules that introduced foundational AI concepts – including algorithms, datasets, prediction, autonomy, and perception – through hands-on activities and scenario-based discussions. These modules integrated socio-ethical reflection through structured tools such as ethical matrices, which guided teachers (and later, their students) in examining the values, trade-offs, and stakeholder implications embedded within AI systems.

To lower barriers to entry for educators and students with varied technical backgrounds, PD included training on PoseBlocks, a block-based programming tool modeled after Scratch, which enables users to create projects using trained machine-learning models [43]. Teachers explored how this tool could be used to teach key AI concepts such as classification and motion detection, while also encouraging creativity and iterative thinking. This component aimed to build teachers' computational thinking and their capacity to design inclusive, accessible AI experiences.

The second component of the PD focused on supporting teachers in their instructional role. Participants reflected on how to facilitate these AI activities in their own classrooms, adapting them to meet the developmental, cultural, and technological contexts of their students. Teachers were encouraged to apply culturally responsive teaching practices, adapt materials for unplugged settings where necessary, and align AI instruction with broader learning goals, such as digital citizenship and critical thinking.

Throughout the PD, participants were guided to consider how AI systems shape real-world experiences across domains such as social media, education, entertainment, and robotics. Teachers were prompted to develop classroom strategies that supported not just technical understanding but also ethical reasoning and civic engagement, using questions like: Who benefits from this AI system? Who might be harmed or excluded? This design reflects a commitment to helping teachers integrate AI in ways that are personally relevant, socially aware, and pedagogically sound.

4. Methods

The research study used a convergent mixed methods approach that collected both quantitative and qualitative evidence to evaluate the effectiveness of the AI literacy curricula. The research questions are: RQ1) In what ways does the AI literacy curricula prepare teachers to develop core knowledge and skills? RQ2) What are the personal and contextual factors that affect the teachers' ability to teach AI literacy curricula?

4.1 Participants

The study utilized purposeful sampling, recruiting teachers from an international AI network who expressed interest in participating in the study. A total of twenty teachers participated and implemented the curriculum over the summer period. Over 50% of the participants taught in high schools and had over 10 years of teaching experience in U.S. public schools. Other countries represented included Argentina, Spain, Finland, Turkey, Pakistan, the Maldives, Singapore, and Indonesia (see **Table 2**).

Regions	# of participants	Role(s)	Grades
United States	12	Teachers	(4) Elementary; (8) upper elementary
Argentina	1	Teachers	Middle school
Spain	1	Teachers	Early elementary
Finland	1	Teachers	Upper elementary
Turkey	1	Teachers	Middle school
Pakistan	1	Researcher	Higher education
India	1	Teachers	Upper elementary
Maldives	1	Teachers	Higher education
Singapore	1	Teachers	Middle school

Table 2.
Participant demographics.

4.2 Procedures

After teachers expressed interest in the study, the research team distributed a needs assessment survey to gather information on their teaching backgrounds and interests in AI. Prior to the intervention, participants completed a pre-program questionnaire and participated in semi-structured interviews to assess their baseline knowledge, confidence, and instructional goals related to AI literacy. Teachers then attended a PD workshop, where they engaged with the AI literacy curriculum both as learners and as future facilitators. This dual-role model was designed to deepen content understanding and support pedagogical reflection. Following the PD workshop, teachers implemented the curriculum in their own classrooms. After implementation, participants completed a post-program questionnaire and a second round of interviews to evaluate changes in their instructional readiness, curriculum adaptation, and reflections on classroom experiences.

4.3 Measures

This study employed an AI literacy questionnaire that had been previously validated to examine teachers' AI literacy in inclusive classrooms. The teachers' interviews were based on their current experiences, which highlighted their prior experience and background knowledge in utilizing the curriculum. Additionally, the validity and reliability of the questionnaires were examined. To ensure the validity of the teacher questionnaire, the study assessed internal structure validity through the empirical correlation of items. The study utilized exploratory factor analysis to examine the underlying correlations among each item within three proposed domains: effectiveness of the AI-infused curriculum, readiness for the AI-infused curriculum, and design of the AI-infused curriculum. Cronbach's alpha was calculated to ensure reliability. Three factors were identified based on confirmatory factor analysis and exploratory factor analysis.

4.4 Data collection and analysis

In order to address RQ1, teacher questionnaires were analyzed based on a t-test analysis. In order to address RQ2, pre and post-PD teacher interviews were conducted and analyzed using thematic analysis in relation to the teachers' perceived effectiveness, readiness, and adaptation of the curriculum.

Specifically, quantitative data were collected through pre and post-intervention surveys that measured teachers' self-perceived competence, readiness, and willingness to teach AI literacy. Each item was rated on a Likert scale, and responses were analyzed using paired-sample t-tests to assess statistically significant changes between pre and post-program scores. Effect sizes were calculated using Cohen's d to determine the magnitude of observed differences. Statistical analyses were conducted using R, with a significance threshold set at $p < 0.05$. The analysis focused on key dimensions aligned with the research questions, including knowledge of AI concepts, ability to apply ethical reasoning, and instructional adaptability.

Qualitative data were gathered through semi-structured pre and post-interviews with participating teachers, focusing on their perceptions of the curriculum, readiness to teach AI, and adaptation strategies. Interview transcripts were coded using thematic analysis. These themes were refined through iterative discussions among the research team to ensure consistency and credibility. Three major themes were identified: (1) shifts in instructional confidence and AI knowledge; (2) readiness to address ethical and equity concerns; and (3) increased agency and flexibility in adapting curriculum materials. Qualitative findings were used to contextualize and expand upon the quantitative results, allowing for deeper insights into how and why changes occurred.

5. Results

The results are summarized in three categories, which reflect the three primary goals of this project, based on the analysis of quantitative and qualitative data.

5.1 Effectiveness of AI literacy curriculum

Participants shifted their perceived competence to teach AI literacy curriculum. The paired t-test identified statistically significant increases in all the questions related to what teachers consider when teaching AI literacy curriculum, including: incorporate key ideas and topics in AI literacy for student learning ($t = -1.87$, $p < 0.05$, Cohen's $d = 0.59$); and apply critical thinking to learn AI literacy ($t = -2.083$, $p < 0.05$, Cohen's $d = 0.66$) (see **Table 3**).

Teachers demonstrated meaningful shifts in their understanding and attitudes toward the AI literacy curriculum, evolving from initial uncertainty to increased confidence and instructional ownership. In pre-interviews, several participants described the curriculum as "new" and unfamiliar. However, by the end of the program, they expressed a desire for "more venues to implement the AI literacy curriculum," reflecting enhanced instructional agency – the belief that they could make decisions about integrating AI into their teaching. Teachers emphasized the curriculum's interdisciplinary value, noting, for example, that "after implementing the curriculum, we appreciated the interdisciplinary connections to develop students' problem-solving skills." Others reported feeling more capable of incorporating foundational AI concepts, such as algorithms and machine learning, into classroom instruction. One teacher explained, "The curriculum fit well with

	Descriptive data for pre–post items					Paired t-test		Effect size
	N	Pre μ[1]	Pre σ	Post μ[1]	Post σ	T	P	
I am able to incorporate key ideas and topics in AI literacy for student learning.	20	4	0.85	4.45	0.69	-1.87	0.033*	0.59
I am able to reflect on the responsible use of AI for student learning.	20	4.1	0.72	4.45	0.68	-1.58	0.06	0.5
I am able to apply critical thinking to learn AI literacy.	20	4.05	0.94	4.55	0.51	-2.083	0.022*	0.66
I am able to facilitate group discussions to learn about AI literacy.	20	4.1	0.85	4.45	0.68	-1.43	0.08	0.45
I am able to apply creative thinking to learn AI literacy.	20	4	1.02	4.4	0.75	-1.41	0.08	0.446
I am able to use digital tools and applications for students to learn about AI literacy.	20	4.3	0.57	4.6	0.76	-1.42	0.082	0.45
I am able to use digital tools and applications to help students learn about AI and digital citizenship (e.g., social impact).	20	4.25	0.71	4.15	1.13	0.33	0.37	0.10

Table 3.
Teachers' self-perceived effectiveness of AI.

concepts of algorithm and machine learning," signaling a growing alignment between content and their professional goals.

5.2 Readiness of AI literacy curriculum

Participants shifted their self-awareness of AI ethical implications. The paired t-test identified statistically significant increases in questions related to what teachers consider when teaching AI curriculum, including their students' ability to evaluate AI applications in terms of ethical use, such as trust, privacy, and accountability ($t = -1.88$, $p < 0.05$, Cohen's $d = 0.77$) (see **Table 4**).

Qualitative findings revealed that one of the most salient themes was the growing readiness among teachers to explain core AI concepts and ethical considerations in classroom settings. Prior to the intervention, many teachers expressed uncertainty about how to introduce AI in pedagogically meaningful ways. However, post-interviews showed a marked shift in both confidence and practice. Teachers increasingly took the initiative in unpacking AI literacy topics with their students and guiding reflective discussions. As one participant shared, "Our students were able to see the different sides of the AI technologies," suggesting that teachers felt more prepared to explore not just the technical, but also the social and ethical dimensions of AI. Notably, many teachers also described an increased sensitivity to equity concerns surrounding AI, such as access, bias, and fairness. One teacher observed, "It is helpful to get them to think about the ethical aspects of AI," reflecting a shift toward student-centered inquiry that connects AI tools with real-world implications.

	Descriptive data for pre–post items						Paired t-test		Effect size
	N	Pre μ[1]	Pre σ	Post μ[1]	Post σ	t	p	
I believe incorporating strategies to reason through ethical dilemmas of AI is useful for students' learning.	20	4.26	0.65	4.6	0.5	−1.62	0.05	0.59
I am comfortable employing strategies to reason through ethical dilemmas of AI.	20	4.05	0.97	4.15	0.87	−0.17	0.43	0.11
I know how to design learning experiences for employing strategies to reason through ethical dilemmas in AI.	20	3.31	1.20	3.9	0.91	1.64	0.05	0.55
I am able to implement the process that employs strategies to reason through ethical dilemmas of AI in classroom teaching.	20	3.47	1.07	3.9	0.92	1.28	0.103	0.43
I felt my students could evaluate AI applications in terms of ethical use, such as trust, privacy, and accountability.	20	3.6	0.82	4.15	0.58	−1.88	0.03*	0.77
I felt my students could evaluate AI applications in terms of equity.	20	3.65	0.87	4.05	0.69	−1.61	0.05	0.51

Table 4.
Teachers' self-perceived readiness for AI.

5.3 Adaptation of AI literacy curriculum

Participants shifted their self-perceived students' abilities. The paired t-test identified statistically significant increases in core questions related to what teachers consider when adapting AI curriculum, including: incorporating the design process as useful for student learning ($t = -1.96$, $p < 0.05$, Cohen's $d = 0.63$); feeling comfortable using the design process ($t = -1.99$, $p < 0.05$, Cohen's $d = 0.56$); knowing how the design process works ($t = -2.35$, $p < 0.05$, Cohen's $d = 0.75$); and being able to implement the design process in classroom teaching ($t = 1.92$, $p < 0.05$, Cohen's $d = 0.61$) (see **Table 5**).

Qualitative findings revealed a notable change in teachers' perceptions of their ability to adopt the AI literacy curriculum to their classroom contexts. Prior to engaging with the curriculum, many teachers expressed uncertainty and held a narrow view of its applicability, with one noting in the pre-interview, "I did not see the opportunity to implement [AI] in my classroom teaching." Although teachers were enthusiastic about the topic of AI, they initially struggled to see how abstract or technical content could align with their existing instructional goals or student needs. Following the curriculum implementation, however, teachers described a significant shift in mindset. They began to recognize multiple entry points for integrating AI into daily teaching and shared concrete examples of how they modified and enriched the lessons. As one teacher reflected, "We added more examples for our students with AI real-world applications," highlighting a growing awareness of the importance of making content locally and culturally relevant. Others introduced unplugged activities to accommodate technological limitations and ensure accessibility for all learners, including a "social media recommendation project" that helped students explore the ethical dilemmas of algorithmic filtering and data bias.

	Descriptive data for pre–post items					Paired t-test		Effect size
	N	Pre μ[1]	Pre σ	Post μ[1]	Post σ	t	p	
I felt my students learnt valuable things about AI.	20	3.85	0.93	4.3	0.66	−1.76	0.04*	0.56
I felt my students could consider the negative and positive outcomes of AI technologies.	20	3.8	0.95	4.15	0.59	−1.4	0.085	0.44
I believe incorporating the design process is useful for student learning.	20	4.6	0.51	4.7	0.47	−0.65	0.26	0.20
I am comfortable using the design process.	20	3.95	0.88	4.45	0.68	−1.99	0.02*	0.63
I know how the design process works.	20	3.65	0.74	4.15	0.58	−2.35	0.01*	0.75
I am able to implement the design process in classroom teaching.	20	3.7	0.86	4.15	0.59	1.92	0.03*	0.61

Table 5.
Teachers' self-perceived adaptation to AI literacy.

6. Discussion

This study provides empirical evidence that the AI literacy curriculum meaningfully supported teachers in developing core knowledge, pedagogical skills, and ethical awareness, while also illuminating the personal and contextual factors that influence their capacity to teach AI literacy. In relation to RQ1, teachers demonstrated growth in their understanding of AI literacy concepts, such as algorithms, machine learning, and data privacy, as well as in their ability to translate these concepts into instructional practice. Through structured PD and hands-on engagement with curriculum materials, teachers moved from seeing AI as novel or inaccessible to designing and delivering lessons that connected AI to real-world applications. For instance, participants described creating social media simulations, recommendation engine critiques, and unplugged activities that helped students explore the social and ethical dimensions of AI. These activities not only reinforced technical concepts but also supported metacognitive development, allowing students to reflect on how AI systems "learn" and how their behaviors influence algorithmic outcomes.

Importantly, the curriculum fostered teachers' ability to embed AI within interdisciplinary learning experiences, linking AI topics to existing subject areas such as science, social studies, and digital citizenship. This integration aligns with calls in the literature for AI education to be both cross-curricular and inquiry-based and highlights the curriculum's effectiveness in building teacher confidence and instructional adaptability. Teachers reported that the curriculum "fit well with concepts of algorithm and machine learning" already present in their standards, indicating its alignment with current teaching goals and its potential for integration into broader instructional plans.

In response to RQ2, findings illustrate that teachers' capacity to teach AI literacy is shaped by both personal factors, such as instructional confidence, openness to innovation, and ethical commitment, and contextual factors, including school infrastructure, technological access, and curricular flexibility. Initially, many teachers expressed uncertainty about how AI could be implemented in their classrooms, particularly in underserved communities. However, over time, they demonstrated increased agency and a willingness to adapt the curriculum to their unique contexts. For example, teachers developed low-tech and unplugged adaptations of the curriculum to make AI content more accessible and equitable, particularly for students in schools with limited digital tools. They also emphasized culturally responsive approaches, ensuring that AI examples and case studies reflected students' lived experiences.

These shifts highlight a key insight from the literature: curriculum adaptability is not only about modifying content but also about rethinking pedagogy. Teachers need to be engaged to act as designers – rather than mere implementers – of AI literacy instruction. This involves interpreting and reshaping curriculum materials to align with students' prior knowledge, learning needs, and sociocultural backgrounds [30–32]. Moreover, the results suggest that teacher readiness should be understood as a developable construct, not an innate capacity. As supported by previous studies, readiness is strengthened through sustained PD, peer collaboration, and opportunities for co-constructing curriculum in reflective, iterative ways [23, 24, 36].

7. Significance

Evidence from the research indicated the importance of the AI curriculum that positively affects teachers' adaptation of the AI literacy curriculum. Both quantitative and qualitative data reflect changes that are consistent with the literature describing the importance of curriculum resources to prepare teachers to make pedagogical changes in classroom teaching. This also highlighted the importance of providing essential resources for educators that will support them in teaching and learning the AI literacy curriculum, consequently enhancing their AI literacy knowledge and skills. The pre–post questionnaire results reflect the value of the AI literacy curriculum in shifting teachers' self-perceived values, readiness, and adoption process through the implementation process of the AI curriculum. Other qualitative evidence also highlighted the complexity of teacher change in a diverse learning environment, which requires PD to increase the comfort level with AI tools and curriculum content material.

Beyond essential resources, PD plays a critical role in the implementation process [44]. Researchers provide orientation and follow-up sessions to prepare teachers to feel comfortable and understand the nuances of the curriculum. Future studies should continue to explore essential practices to prepare teachers to use, integrate, and design AI curriculum in classroom teaching. More sustained efforts should be carried out to situate the curriculum in the local context, connecting the core standards that prepare teachers to effectively implement it in diverse classroom learning settings.

Additionally, relative assessments have been developed to formally measure the quality of AI literacy curricula and students' knowledge gain. The commonly used instruments usually focus on students' problem-solving skills rather than understanding the learners' knowledge development process. This study has the potential to develop an AI literacy knowledge assessment that captures the development trajectory of student knowledge and provides additional insights into AI literacy curriculum design and development.

Finally, as learning is highly complex, ongoing studies need to explore the internationalization efforts of the AI literacy curriculum, develop responsive assessment systems that prepare teachers to utilize, design, and implement AI curricula to innovate pedagogical practices [45]. Efforts are necessary to continuously refine professional practices, distribute resources, and emphasize the significance of establishing a broad alliance committed to using AI responsibly to foster positive societal change.

8. Conclusion

This study offers empirical evidence that well-structured AI literacy curricula can significantly enhance teachers' self-perceived readiness, instructional adaptability, and confidence in implementation. By examining how educators engaged with and reflected on the curriculum, the findings illuminate the central role of PD in fostering both content expertise in AI and the pedagogical strategies needed for effective, ethical instruction. Access to adaptable, thoughtfully designed curriculum materials was particularly valuable in enabling teachers to create inclusive, student-centered learning environments tailored to their specific contexts. Moving forward, expanding AI literacy in schools will require sustained investment in teacher training, culturally responsive pedagogical practices, and localized curriculum adaptations. Future research should examine how teacher growth impacts student learning outcomes, refine assessment models for AI literacy, and explore how AI education can be meaningfully integrated across disciplines in ways that are equitable, interdisciplinary, and ethically informed.

Acknowledgments

We would like to acknowledge the support of MIT RAISE and Project STEM. Their contributions have been instrumental in the development and advancement of this work.

Conflict of interest

The authors declare no conflict of interest

Author details

Xiaoxue Du
MIT Media Lab, Cambridge, MA, United States

*Address all correspondence to: xiaoxued@media.mit.edu

References

[1] Tzirides AOO, Zapata G, Kastania NP, Saini AK, Castro V, Ismael SA, Kalantzis M. Combining human and artificial intelligence for enhanced AI literacy in higher education. Computers and Education Open. 2024;**6**:100184

[2] Knoth N, Decker M, Laupichler MC, Pinski M, Buchholtz N, Bata K, Schultz B. Developing a holistic AI literacy assessment matrix–Bridging generic, domain-specific, and ethical competencies. Computers and Education Open. 2024;**6**

[3] Almatrafi O, Johri A, Lee H. A systematic review of AI literacy conceptualization, constructs, and implementation and assessment efforts (2019-2023). Computers and Education Open 2024;**6**:100173

[4] Sperling K, Stenberg CJ, McGrath C, Åkerfeldt A, Heintz F, Stenliden L. In search of artificial intelligence (AI) literacy in teacher education: A scoping review. Computers and Education Open. 2024;**6**:100169

[5] Rose D. Universal design for learning. Journal of Special Education Technology. 2000;**15**(4):47–51

[6] Ladson-Billings G. But that's just good teaching! The case for culturally relevant pedagogy. Theory into Practice. 1995;**34**(3):159–165

[7] Norman DA. Human-centered design considered harmful. Interactions. 2005;**12**(4):14–19

[8] Molefi RR, Ayanwale MA, Kurata L, and Chere-Masopha J. Do in-service teachers accept artificial intelligence-driven technology? The mediating role of school support and resources. Computers and Education Open. 2024;**6**:100174

[9] Hossain Z. School librarians developing AI literacy for an AI-driven future: Leveraging the AI Citizenship Framework with scope and sequence. Library Hi Tech News. 2025;**42** (2):17–21

[10] Almuhanna MA. Teachers' perspectives of integrating AI-powered technologies in K-12 education for creating customized learning materials and resources. Education and Information Technologies . 2024;**30**:10343–10371

[11] Yadav S. Empowering Educators for the Artificial Intelligence (AI) Era: Strategies and Challenges in Integrating Computational Thinking Into Professional Development. In Papadakis, S, Kalogiannakis, M, editors. Empowering STEM Educators With Digital Tools. Hershey, PA (Pennsylvania, USA): IGI Global Scientific Publishing; 2025, 1–28

[12] Celik I, Dindar M, Muukkonen H, Järvelä S. The promises and challenges of artificial intelligence for teachers: A systematic review of research. Tech Trends. 2022;**66**(4):616–630. DOI: 10.1007/s11528-022-00715-y

[13] Ayanwale MA, Sanusi IT, Adelana OP, Aruleba KD, Oyelere SS. Teachers' readiness and intention to teach artificial intelligence in schools. Computers and Education: Artificial Intelligence. 2022;**3**:100099

[14] Michos K, Hernández-Leo D. CIDA: A collective inquiry framework to study and support teachers as designers in technological environments. Computers and Education. 2020;**143**:103682

[15] Zhang J, Zhang Z. AI in teacher education: Unlocking new dimensions in teaching support, inclusive learning, and digital literacy. Journal of Computer Assisted Learning. 2024;**40**(4):1871–1885

[16] Davoodi A. EQUAL AI: A framework for enhancing equity, quality, understanding and accessibility in liberal arts through ai for multilingual learners. Language, Technology, and Social Media. 2024;**2**(2):178–203

[17] Du H, Sun Y, Jiang H, Islam AYM, Gu X. Exploring the effects of AI literacy in teacher learning: An empirical study. Humanities and Social Sciences Communications. 2024;**11**(1):1–10

[18] Lim EM. The effects of pre-service early childhood teachers' digital literacy and self-efficacy on their perception of AI education for young children. Education and Information Technologies. 2023;**28**(10):12969–12995

[19] Kohnke L, Zou D, Ou AW, Gu MM. Preparing future educators for AI-enhanced classrooms: Insights into AI literacy and integration. Computers and Education: Artificial Intelligence. 2025;**8**:100398

[20] Dilek M, Baran E, Aleman E. AI literacy in teacher education: empowering educators through critical co-discovery. Journal of Teacher Education. 2025;**76**(3):294–311

[21] Liu N. Exploring the factors influencing the adoption of artificial intelligence technology by university teachers: The mediating role of confidence and AI readiness. BMC Psychology. 2025;**13**(1):311

[22] Gorski PC, Dalton K. Striving for critical reflection in multicultural and social justice teacher education: Introducing a typology of reflection approaches. Journal of Teacher Education. 2020;**71**(3):357–368

[23] Xia L, Zheng G. To meet the trend of AI: The ecology of developing AI talents for pre-service teachers in China. International Journal of Learning. 2020;**6**(3):186–190

[24] Vorsah RE, Oppong F (2024). Leveraging AI to enhance active learning strategies in science classrooms: Implications for teacher professional development

[25] Drits-Esser D, Stark LA. The impact of collaborative curriculum design on teacher professional learning. The Electronic Journal of Science Education. 2015;**19**(8):1–27

[26] Lin P, Van Brummelen J (2021). Engaging teachers to co-design integrated AI curriculum for K-12 classrooms. In Proceedings of the 2021 CHI conference on human factors in computing systems (pp. 1–12)

[27] Aghaziarati A, Nejatifar S, Abedi A. Artificial intelligence in education: Investigating teacher attitudes. AI and Tech in Behavioral and Social Sciences. 2023;**1**(1):35–42

[28] Dieterle E, Dede C, Walker M. The cyclical ethical effects of using artificial intelligence in education. AI and Society. 2024;**39**(2):633–643

[29] Wang T, Olivier DF, Chen P. Creating individual and organizational readiness for change: Conceptualization of system readiness for change in school education. International Journal of Leadership in Education. 2023;**26**(6):1037–1061

[30] Cuban L. Inside the Black Box of Classroom Practice: Change without Reform in American Education. Cambridge, MA: Harvard Education Press; 2013

[31] Alvunger D. Teachers' curriculum agency in teaching a standards-based curriculum. The Curriculum Journal. 2018;**29**(4):479–498

[32] Valdelamar González C, Calle-Díaz L. Teachers' agency development when adapting the Colombian English suggested curriculum for high school. Profile: Issues in Teachers' Professional Development. 2023;**25**(2):201–216

[33] Dai CP. Designing learning support for simulation-based preservice teacher learning with artificial intelligence-powered virtual agents. International Journal for Educational Media and Technology. 2023;**17**(2):31–39

[34] Crow T, Luxton-Reilly A, Wuensche B (2018). Intelligent tutoring systems for programming education: A systematic review. In Proceedings of the 20th Australasian Computing Education Conference (pp. 53–62)

[35] Breazeal C, Du X, Abelson H, Klopfer E, Park HW (2023). Day of AI: Innovating pedagogical practices to bring AI literacy to classrooms at scale. In International Conference on Artificial Intelligence in Education Technology (pp. 267–281). Singapore: Springer Nature Singapore

[36] Du X, Breazeal C (2022). Exploring changes in special education teachers' attitudes and design belief towards pedagogical agents in co-designing with children. In Proceedings of the 21st Annual ACM Interaction Design and Children Conference (pp. 472–478)

[37] Du X, Lyublinskaya I. Designing professional development for special education teachers: Effects on assistive technology competency in developing inquiry-based student experiences. Journal of Digital Learning in Teacher Education. 2022;**38**(4):199–210

[38] Nazaretsky T, Ariely M, Cukurova M, Alexandron G. Teachers' trust in AI -powered educational technology and a professional development program to improve it. British Journal of Educational Technology. 2022;**53**(4):914–931

[39] Li H, Xiao R, Nieu H, Tseng Y-J, Liao G. "From unseen needs to classroom solutions": Exploring AI literacy challenges & opportunities with project-based learning toolkit in K-12 education. Proceedings of the AAAI Conference on Artificial Intelligence. 2025;**39**(28):29145–29152

[40] National Academies of Sciences, Medicine, Division of Behavioral, Social Sciences, Board on Science Education, Board on Behavioral, Practice of Learning. How People Learn II: Learners, Contexts, and Cultures. Washington, DC: National Academies Press; 2018

[41] Al Darayseh A. Acceptance of artificial intelligence in teaching science: Science teachers' perspective. Computers and Education: Artificial Intelligence. 2023;**4**:100132

[42] Williams R. Impact. AI: Democratizing AI through K-12 Artificial Intelligence Education. Cambridge, MA (USA): Massachusetts Institute of Technology; 2024

[43] Jordan B, Devasia N, Hong J, Williams R, Breazeal C. PoseBlocks: A toolkit for creating (and dancing) with AI. In: Proceedings of the AAAI Conference on Artificial Intelligence. 2021;**35**(17):15551–15559. DOI: 10.1609/aaai.v35i17.17831

[44] The institution name is National Academies of Sciences, Engineering, and Medicine. How People Learn II: Learners, Contexts, and Cultures. Washington, DC: National Academies Press, 2018. pp. 346. DOI: 10.17226/24783

[45] Sawyer RK. Introduction: The New Science of Learning. In Sawyer RK, editor. The Cambridge Handbook of the Learning Sciences. 2nd ed. Cambridge: Cambridge University Press; 2014. p. 1–18. DOI: 10.1017/CBO9781139519526.002

Chapter 12

Teaching Science with AI: How Preservice Teachers Perceive the Role of AI Tools in Science Education

Osman Aksit

Abstract

This qualitative study investigated Turkish preservice physics teachers' perceptions of and attitudes toward AI-based tools in science education, their perceived benefits and challenges, and their behavioral intentions to integrate AI into future teaching. Drawing on the Technology Acceptance Model (TAM), semi-structured interviews were conducted with seven preservice teachers. The findings of the study revealed that the participants were highly familiar with AI tools, using them frequently for academic and daily tasks. They largely viewed AI as an always-accessible, personalized tutor capable of supporting conceptual learning through differentiated responses and on-demand guidance. Participants also perceived AI as a useful colleague for generating innovative teaching ideas, creating instructional content, and automating time-consuming, laborious teaching-related tasks. However, several concerns were raised by the participants regarding ethical issues, academic dishonesty, misinformation, and potential over-reliance that could hinder creativity and critical thinking. Despite these concerns, a cautious optimism prevailed among the sample, with participants acknowledging their lack of pedagogical and technical AI knowledge and expressing a strong desire for high-quality professional development. The study suggests leveraging preservice physics teachers' positive attitudes and existing AI familiarity through targeted training programs that emphasize critical and practical applications of AI, which, in turn, can ensure that AI serves as a pedagogical transformer rather than a mere technological novelty.

Keywords: preservice physics teachers, science education, artificial intelligence, AI, teacher perceptions, technology acceptance model, TAM

1. Introduction

Scientists from various disciplines have been actively working in the field of artificial intelligence (AI) since Alan Turing laid its theoretical foundations in his seminal work *Intelligent Machinery* [1] over half a century ago. As a rapidly growing interdisciplinary field focusing on innovations in developing algorithms and systems that simulate human-like intelligence, AI draws on several domains of study such as computer science, neurology, psychology, mathematics, and so on [2]. In recent years, numerous AI-based tools and technologies have been made available for general use and employed in various fields ranging from space exploration to medicine [3]. Specifically, the free availability of several advanced generative AI (GenAI) tools, such as ChatGPT by OpenAI and Gemini by Google, over the past few years has been instrumental in facilitating the rapid adoption of AI-powered applications among both the general public and professionals, including K-12 teachers. For example, according to a recent survey conducted globally by Microsoft, about 80% of K-12 teachers and 99% of school leaders reported using AI-based tools for "school-related purposes" [4]. Developed based on sophisticated large language models (LLMs), GenAI tools are capable of generating textual and visual (either static or dynamic) outputs through a user-friendly interface and can provide teachers with inspiration and novel ideas for student-centered learning activities, customizable instructional content, automated assessment tools, and so on. It is obvious that AI-based tools and technologies play a revolutionary role in transforming today's educational landscape, and teachers are critical actors in this ongoing transformation [5]. While the adoption of AI-based tools and technologies has increased significantly among educators worldwide, the research on how they perceive the role, potential, and challenges of these tools in teaching and learning settings is limited in the literature [6, 7].

The popular AI-based tools that are freely available today have evolved rapidly over the past few years, transitioning from simply mimicking and producing human-like responses in textual format to generating images, video clips, and conducting sophisticated tasks such as deep research [8]. Popular AI-based tools, including ChatGPT and Gemini, have sparked considerable interest among students and educators worldwide because of their inherent capabilities to facilitate learning and teaching in various ways [6, 9]. Given the rapid adoption of AI technologies by learners and educators around the world [10], their value and role in educational settings have been increasingly recognized by international organizations such as UNESCO, which has published a series of policy documents, including AI competency frameworks for both teachers [11] and students [12], as well as evidence-based suggestions for utilizing various AI technologies in educational settings [13]. Countries are also taking important concrete steps to promote AI in their educational systems and gain a competitive advantage in this emerging field. For example, an executive order has recently been published in the United States to initiate a presidential task force on AI education for devising short- and long-term policies regarding AI in education, which will "ensure that every American has the opportunity to learn about AI from the earliest stages of their educational journey through postsecondary education, fostering a culture of innovation and critical thinking ... in the AI-driven future" [14].

As AI-based tools and related technologies have been penetrating many fields and industries around the world, including education, researchers have focused on preservice and in-service teachers, investigating their perceptions, attitudes, interests, self-efficacy, and adoption of AI for teaching-related purposes [15–19]. For example, in a study with in-service secondary science teachers ($N = 24$)

working in public schools in the United States, Garofalo and Farenga (2025) investigated the participants' attitudes toward employing AI in science classrooms. According to the findings, the participants, in general, demonstrated overall favorable attitudes regarding the potential of AI for providing tailored learning support for their students. In addition, most participants pointed out their concerns about unethical and inappropriate uses of AI by students, including plagiarism and cheating. Some participants were shown to focus more on the negative aspects of utilizing AI for students while giving more weight to its possible benefits for teachers [17]. In another study conducted in Türkiye, Korkmaz and Cilsalar-Sagnak [20] investigated a large group of preservice preschool teachers' ($N = 107$) perceptions of AI and the meanings they attributed to AI. The researchers collected data from the participants through a questionnaire, including demographic items and open-ended questions to probe their AI perceptions. The findings showed that the participants attributed a number of characteristics to AI, such as encompassing human-like features, its ability to work as an assistant teacher, being easy and convenient to use, and a necessity to learn about [20]. However, interestingly, around one-third of the sample ($n = 30$) portrayed a quite pessimistic future of AI by stating that it can be dangerous/frightening ($n = 23$), harmful ($n = 3$), open to being misused ($n = 3$), and even potentially destroy humanity ($n = 2$) [20]. It can be argued that the future of AI will be primarily determined by how it is developed by companies and regulated by countries and international institutions such as the United Nations.

As AI technologies will continue to advance and tranoform nearly every profession, including education, in the near future by redefining how people carry out their work, it is of particular importance to focus on preservice teachers today to ensure they are equipped with the technical skills and pedagogical mindset necessary to integrate these tools effectively and meaningfully into their future classrooms. As such, this study aimed to investigate a sample of Turkish preservice physics teachers' perceptions regarding the role of AI technologies in the teaching and learning of science, how they perceived the benefits and challenges of using AI in science education, and their behavioral intentions (BIs) to employ AI in their future teaching. This group was selected because preservice science teachers play a pivotal role in shaping the future of science education, and their unique perceptions and attitudes toward integrating emerging technologies like AI are critical for successful implementation in learning environments [21]. Understanding their perspectives can inform relevant stakeholders, including teacher education programs and policymakers, to formulate evidence-based strategies aimed at effectively integrating novel AI technologies into K-12 science education. Specifically, this study aimed to address the following research questions:

RQ-1. How do preservice physics teachers perceive the role of AI-based tools and technologies in science education?

RQ-2. How do preservice physics teachers perceive the potential benefits and challenges of integrating AI-based tools and technologies into teaching science?

RQ-3. What are preservice physics teachers' attitudes and BIs toward using AI-based tools and technologies in science education?

2. Theoretical framework

The Technology Acceptance Model (TAM) [22, 23] served as the theoretical framework of this study. TAM was developed by Davis et al. [22] based on the Theory of Reasoned Action [24], which aimed to predict and explain the intended behaviors of individuals in different contexts. As computational and technological tools, such as computers, started becoming more ubiquitous in workplaces and everyday life during the end of the twentieth century, Davis et al. [22] introduced TAM to model and understand the behavioral determinants of individuals' acceptance and actual use of these tools. As shown in **Figure 1**, where arrows imply causal relationships, TAM is a parsimonious theory consisting of a few empirically validated constructs that describe the drivers of behavior in accepting and using a particular technology tool or application. According to TAM, for an individual to accept and intend to use a new technology (BI), there are three important driving factors: perceived usefulness of the new technology (PU), perceived ease of its use (PEOU), and attitudes toward using it (ATs), which play a mediating role between PU-PEOU and BI. PU is defined as the extent to which individuals think that using a new technology tool will improve their job performance, while PEOU refers to the extent to which using that particular technology tool would be easy and "free of physical and mental effort" [24, p. 17]. Although some researchers extended TAM over time by including additional factors into the model, which are sometimes referred to as "TAM++," the core components in the original model remained and demonstrated the model's inherent ability to be implemented broadly in different contexts and technology applications, such as internet banking and online learning [25]. TAM has also been employed extensively in educational settings across different countries and cultures to investigate technology integration among students, preservice and in-service teachers, school administrators, and various other stakeholders [26–30]. In summary, based on extensive studies in the literature, TAM is regarded as a "simple, powerful, practical, theory-based and validated" model [23, p. 4] that can be used in understanding prospective and practicing teachers' acceptance and use of new technology tools. In the context of this study, TAM provides a theoretical lens for understanding preservice physics teachers' beliefs regarding their perceptions of the usefulness and ease of use of AI-based technology tools and

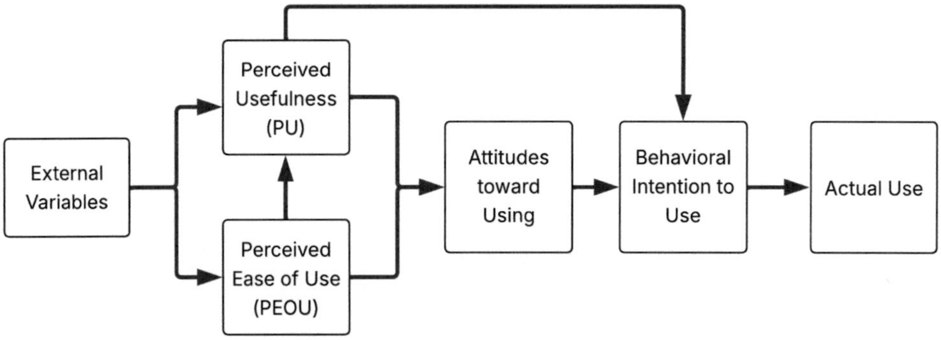

Figure 1.
TAM adapted from the literature [22].

applications in educational settings as well as their attitudes and behavioral intentions towards using this novel technology, which is posited by TAM to predict their actual use when they start practicing teaching.

3. Methods

An exploratory case study approach [31] was employed in this qualitative research to carry out an in-depth investigation to examine a group of Turkish preservice physics teachers' perceptions regarding the emerging role of AI-based technology tools in science education and how they perceive the potential and challenges when integrating these tools into their instructional activities. The case study approach was chosen for the design of this study because it allows for a comprehensive exploration of a contemporary phenomenon (i.e., the use of AI in science teaching) within its real-world context by focusing on a bounded case (i.e., preservice physics teachers' perceptions regarding AI in science education) [31].

3.1 Participants and context

Due to the qualitative nature of this study, a purposive sampling technique [32] was employed to recruit undergraduate-level preservice teachers (N = 7) who were majoring in physics education at a liberal arts university in Türkiye. The selection criteria for participants included completing the science methods courses and at least one of two practicum courses in their mandatory coursework, so that they would have sufficient pedagogical background and some practical teaching experience in real classroom settings to meaningfully reflect on the use of AI tools in teaching and learning science. All participants in the sample were in the final year of their studies. Four participants were female, and three were male. The age of the sample ranged from 24 to 27, with a mean of 25.14 (SD = 1.07). All participants stated that they did not have any formal or informal coursework on either AI itself or the use of AI in education.

In Türkiye, bachelor's programs for secondary science teacher training typically last four years. During the first two years, teacher candidates take their content courses (e.g., mathematics, physics) and some general introductory education courses (e.g., educational psychology), along with a number of elective courses. In the third year, they start taking subject-specific pedagogy and method courses, and in the last year, they are required to spend six hours per week for twelve weeks in their assigned schools during each semester to carry out their practicum. Each teacher candidate is assigned to an experienced mentor teacher in their respective school and partakes in teaching and learning activities in the classroom, as well as reflects critically on their experience in this process. Regarding their overall coursework, teacher candidates take one mandatory course on educational technology, but currently, this course does not include any substantive content on AI. The author was told that there are future plans to incorporate AI-based tools into this course. In addition, the pedagogy courses at the time of this study did not directly address any instructional strategies to meaningfully integrate AI technologies into teaching and learning science. However, faculty members at the department discussed plans to modify the existing coursework and/or offer some elective courses to introduce the pedagogical foundations of teaching and learning with AI in science and mathematics education.

3.2 Data collection

Data were collected during the 2024–2025 academic year through semi-structured individual interviews with the participants. After obtaining an approval from the institutional review board (IRB), preservice physics teachers who met the selection criteria were sent an email explaining the purpose of the research and inviting them to participate. Seven prospective physics teachers provided their informed consent to take part in the study. A semi-structured interview protocol (see Appendix A), consisting of 14 open-ended questions, was developed by the researcher and grounded in the theoretical framework of the study (i.e., TAM). The interview protocol was designed to acquire preservice physics teachers' perceptions regarding the role, affordances, and challenges of AI in science education, as well as their attitudes and intentions to use AI-based technologies in science classrooms. In order to ensure the clarity and appropriateness of the interview questions before data collection, the interview protocol was piloted with two second-year preservice physics teachers, who read each question and provided constructive feedback regarding the questions' wording and comprehensibility. After making slight refinements to some questions based on the students' feedback, the data collection process started. First, the researcher organized the interview schedule with the participants. Five interviews were conducted face-to-face, while the remaining two were held online via Zoom, based on participant preference. During the interviews, the researcher asked probing and clarification questions when necessary to elicit more detailed responses and gain richer insight into their perceptions. The interviews were audio-recorded for data analysis and lasted approximately 40 minutes on average.

3.3 Data analysis

After completing the data collection, all audio recordings of the individual interviews were transcribed verbatim into a Microsoft Word document by a research assistant and then checked for accuracy by the researcher. The interview transcripts were subsequently imported into the NVivo software (version 15) for qualitative data analysis. A thematic analysis approach [33] was employed to code the data and generate themes through an iterative, systematic process, which included familiarization with the data, generation of an initial set of codes, synthesizing and grouping codes into overarching themes, and defining and reviewing recurring themes to capture the key patterns in participants' perceptions, attitudes, and intentions toward integrating AI-based tools in science education. In the first phase of the data analysis, the researcher read through all interview transcripts several times and took notes to become familiarized with the entire dataset. Afterward, the researcher began coding the data and generated a set of preliminary codes. The codes were then reviewed, with some similar codes being merged while others were modified by revisiting the data in several iterations, which eventually led to the creation of the final set of codes. To enhance the trustworthiness of the analysis, a second researcher, who was a PhD candidate, independently coded a subset of the transcripts based on the final set of codes. The researchers then met to discuss any discrepancies in their coding and resolved them through peer debriefing. The final codes were synthesized into a number of overarching themes, which informed the answers to the study's research questions.

4. Findings

At the beginning of the interviews, participants were first asked about their general experience with AI technologies and the particular AI-based tools and applications they had used in different contexts (e.g., educational, daily life). Every interviewee mentioned ChatGPT as their most frequently used AI application, employing it both for school-related tasks and daily activities. For instance, one participant stated: "I feel like I am relying on it [ChatGPT] for so many things I do every day." She went on to say that over the past year, she has been increasingly using ChatGPT for various reasons, such as polishing email replies, getting assistance for course assignments, brainstorming ideas for birthday gifts, and even learning to make new dishes and planning dinner menus. Other AI-based tools that participants also mentioned included Gemini for writing assistance or summarizing documents on Google Drive, DeepSeek for solving mathematics and physics problems from their courses, CoPilot for generating images, Grammarly and Quillbot for paraphrasing texts taken from other sources, Canva and Gamma for preparing good-looking presentations, and Otter.ai for notetaking during lessons.

Drawing on the thematic analysis conducted holistically on the participants' responses to the interview questions, four overarching themes emerged: (1) AI as an always-accessible personal intelligent tutor, (2) AI as a useful and supportive colleague, (3) AI as a double-edged sword: savior versus saboteur, and (4) AI and the future: cautious optimism.

The first theme, "AI as an always-accessible personal intelligent tutor," comprised five codes, which are shown in **Table 1** along with exemplar interview excerpts. Participants' responses indicated, in general, quite favorable perceptions regarding the role of AI-based tools and technologies when it comes to the teaching

Code	Exemplar excerpt
AI demystifies abstract and difficult concepts	It [ChatGPT] is really helpful, especially in explaining very complex concepts that are hard to imagine in my mind. I like that it explains things step by step and, most of the time, better than most professors in my courses.
AI provides personalized responses and feedback	I noticed that ChatGPT knows me well after some time, I mean, when I asked it a lot of questions and other things. Now, when I ask something, I see that it responds by also taking them all into account. It refers to them. It definitely knows my conceptual gaps.
AI offers on-demand and always-accessible support	In my phone, I have applications; I installed them [ChatGPT, Deepseek]. Whenever I don't understand something in the lesson or whenever I wonder about something, like in the bus or having lunch, I just take it [smartphone] and consult it. It is so convenient to use.
AI facilitates conceptual learning	I think AIs like ChatGPT are very helpful in really learning difficult things, it shows the logic behind it. I mean it is not like how to solve the problem, it is about understanding the problem itself and the logic of the solution. It is useful for science and mathematics lessons, and for other lessons too.
AI supports diverse learners	As a future teacher, I think these kinds of AI tools will be great for students, like shy ones who don't like to talk generally in the class, or slow students, you know, who are slower than others. They can still learn at their own pace with the help of AI, maybe during the lesson or maybe after the lesson.

Table 1.
The codes for the first theme, "AI as an always-accessible personal intelligent tutor."

and learning of science. Respondents emphasized how AI-based tools, such as ChatGPT, present significant potential to facilitate personalized and conceptual learning through differentiated responses and on-demand support for students, effectively acting as an individualized tutor available in their pockets at all times. For instance, one participant stated that, in the past, she was afraid to ask "why" questions to her science teachers in middle and high school: "Our generation was raised to listen to the teacher and not ask deep questions – I mean conceptual types of questions like what electric charge really is. Now, AI is changing this. The new generation, as I see it, does not want to memorize; they want to understand." Because most participants were more familiar with ChatGPT, they referred to their own personal experiences with this particular GenAI tool. It is noteworthy that all participants reported having used AI-based tools for learning-related purposes within their undergraduate coursework, indicating both a baseline familiarity with these technologies and a potential readiness to incorporate them into their future teaching practices.

Regarding the second theme, "AI as a useful and supportive colleague," the participants overwhelmingly perceived AI as a tool that can vastly support teachers in their professions in various ways (see **Table 2**). Several participants mentioned utilizing ChatGPT for brainstorming ideas to come up with doable and exciting learning activities they used during their practicum lessons. One participant explained that before ChatGPT and other AI-based tools, he used to spend a lot of time searching on Google and watching YouTube videos for instructional ideas on a particular topic, sometimes even failing to come up with an idea at the end of this process. Now, using well-designed and to-the-point prompts on GenAI tools, he is able to generate both hands-on and minds-on activities with certain time and material constraints within seconds: "It [ChatGPT] helps me save so much time and effort now when it comes to lesson planning and implementation." Most participants also emphasized that AI not only helps with innovative teaching ideas but also significantly supports teachers in instructional content creation. Preparing lesson plans with the help of AI was the most frequently expressed use case of content generation among the participants, highlighting the role of AI in easing teachers' workload. Additionally, the participants thought that AI-based tools will be increasingly used to carry out everyday tasks where teachers generally spend

Code	Exemplar excerpt
AI can help teachers generate new ideas for teaching	For my practicum lesson last semester, I had to teach the topic of adhesion and cohesion. ... Then I asked about it to ChatGPT and it provided some ideas but some of them were doable, others were not. I described the class and the materials I could access, and it gave me two excellent activities and my students enjoyed a lot. I think teachers are very lucky now; they can get great ideas from AI for their classes.
AI can provide teachers with high-quality instructional content	When I need to prepare lesson plans, I always use it [ChatGPT]. It creates ones that I can never create – very detailed and very professional. You can also create quizzes easily with it [ChatGPT], worksheets and even exams.
AI can assist teachers with time-consuming and laborious tasks in their courses	What AI will change significantly in education in the future is that teachers will not spend unnecessary time on time-consuming activities like they do today, such as grading exam papers. Teachers will focus on teaching and helping students, and AI will handle other tasks.

Table 2.
The codes for the second theme, "AI as a useful and supportive colleague."

considerable time and effort, such as grading assessments, providing feedback on homework assignments, detecting plagiarism in students' work, and so on. One participant speculated, "Soon AI will evolve to a point that it will do all types of grading, like exam grading or homework grading. ChatGPT can even do this today but not very effectively, I think."

While the participants pointed out the great potential of AI technologies in the context of science education and how these tools can increasingly support teachers in their professions, many of them also underlined the drawbacks of AI and its possible hindrances to teaching and learning science. The codes for the third theme, "AI as a double-edged sword: savior versus saboteur," were provided in **Table 3**. Every participant mentioned the ethical concerns associated with the irresponsible use of AI technologies in educational settings. The participants were concerned about students' unethical utilization of AI-based tools in their lessons, which can lead to various issues related to academic dishonesty, such as plagiarism and cheating. Some participants emphasized that when AI-based tools are involved, the detection of plagiarism becomes quite challenging, even with sophisticated tools such as Turnitin: "I'm also a student now, and I can say that they [students] can always find ways to not get caught in these situations [involving plagiarism]. For example, there are websites to do paraphrasing, and Turnitin cannot catch. What can teachers do about it?". Some participants talked about the potential inaccuracy of responses provided by GenAI tools such as ChatGPT and the importance of acquiring information literacy skills for students today. Another code that emerged from the participants' responses is the increasing over-reliance on using AI-based tools and its negative impact on creativity and critical thinking. The participants were concerned that, in the long run, students may use AI too much, even for simple tasks, which can prevent them from developing independent problem-solving abilities and original ideas. Last but not least, the participants acknowledged that AI is not

Code	Exemplar excerpt
Ethical concerns and academic dishonesty	Cheating, copying things from the internet, paying somebody to do your homework – things like these are already a big problem today because of technology. I know many people do this. Now, AI makes it a lot easier. And the big problem is you cannot know, as a teacher, whether students really used AI in their homework. Students know how to use it and not get caught.
Misinformation by AI and the need for information literacy skills among learners	Sometimes it [ChatGPT] just makes up things that are not real. I saw it many times. For example, sometimes there are incorrect parts in its responses that are mostly correct. ... Now I double-check its responses, especially when I ask difficult problems. We have to teach students the skills to use different sources and compare the information.
Over-reliance on AI	What happens when students use AI for everything? Creativity is a result of a person's struggles with a topic or problem, I think. You just keep thinking about it and come up with creative thoughts. When children grow up asking everything to AI, I think it will definitely kill their creativity.
AI as a neutral technology: how it is used matters.	For me, AI is neither good nor evil. It is just a technology. I can give the example of smartphones. Today, some people are addicted to them. Some people use it in a normal way, not constantly looking at it. Same for social media or YouTube. AI programs will be similar too.

Table 3.
The codes for the third theme: "AI as a double-edged sword: savior versus saboteur."

Code	Exemplar excerpt
Acknowledged lack of pedagogical and technical knowledge in AI	I improved myself in entering proper prompts, but I still probably don't know many of its [ChatGPT] features, like creating videos; I never tried it. ... To be honest, I also don't know the best strategies to use it in the classroom at this point, but I think I can learn by trial and error and also from other teachers when I start working as a teacher.
An emerging necessity for employing AI in education	Teachers will have to use AI in the future; it will be a requirement, like how teachers use the internet and PowerPoint presentations in their lessons today. ... They [teachers] will not have a choice not to improve themselves in AI. We [prospective teachers] have to adjust to new technological developments. There is no other way.
Strong desire for high-quality training on educational AI use from experts	Attending workshops and listening to very experienced teachers who became experts in using AI in their lessons and give concrete and tested examples from their own teaching would be beneficial for me. ... I would willingly go to these workshops. Otherwise, it stays too theoretical, not very applicable in real classroom settings.

Table 4.
The codes for the fourth theme, "AI and the future: cautious optimism."

inherently good or bad within educational settings as well as the broader context. They likened AI to smartphones and social media in the sense that its impact varies according to how it is actually used by individuals.

The last theme, "AI and the future: cautious optimism," included three codes, as shown in **Table 4.** First, most participants thought that they were lacking pedagogical knowledge regarding integrating AI meaningfully into instruction, even though all of them were using AI-based tools for their own coursework. One participant mentioned that, since AI is a relatively new technology, the development of its associated pedagogical knowledge is still ongoing, and that is why he did not think he had this knowledge: "AI is a very new thing; therefore, I think there would not be much information in this field yet. I don't think I know how to use AI best in my lessons, and probably most teachers do not know too. When there are books published about it, I can improve myself". All participants emphasized that teachers would have to learn and use AI in their lessons in the future; it will be a requirement rather than an option. The participants' responses overall indicated that they were aware of their limited pedagogical and technical understanding of AI and recognized the need to develop these skills to effectively integrate AI-based tools into their future teaching. Finally, the participants' responses also indicated their strong desire to receive high-quality training in this area by attending professional development (PD) programs related to teaching with AI. Particularly, the participants expressed that this kind of PD program must be designed to be both hands-on and minds-on, since they thought theoretical workshops would not be very effective.

5. Discussion

This study aimed to systematically explore how a group of preservice physics teachers perceived the role of AI-based tools and technologies in the teaching and learning of science, as well as their associated benefits and challenges in educational settings. The study also examined the participants' attitudes and behavioral intentions to utilize AI technologies in their own teaching in the future. By employing the TAM framework [22, 23], a semi-structured interview protocol was developed, and the participants' responses were qualitatively analyzed. First, the findings revealed that all participants in this study were quite familiar with using various AI-based tools for school-related purposes as well as for non-educational contexts. This finding is consistent with previous research showing that, even though AI technologies are relatively novel, they have penetrated the lives of many people around the world rather quickly [34]. In addition, this finding also aligns with the findings of previous studies in the literature [16, 35] showing that preservice teachers in many countries were already familiar with AI-based tools and actively using them for learning-related purposes as part of their academic coursework.

Preservice physics teachers in this study overwhelmingly characterized AI-based tools as always-available, personalized tutors that can strongly support conceptual learning in science. Overall, the participants' responses indicated that they considered AI-based tools beneficial and valuable within the context of teaching and learning science. They underlined AI's capabilities to generate differentiated explanations, provide on-demand guidance, and present stepwise reasoning for complex topics, which the participants believed would foster a deeper understanding of science by meeting individual students' needs. In particular, no participant exhibited overly negative feelings or attitudes toward using AI as an educational tool or suggested a total ban on these tools in science classrooms. This indicates that the participants outweighed the benefits of AI-based applications in education compared to the associated risks and concerns (e.g., cheating). The participants' frequent use of ChatGPT and similar tools during their undergraduate coursework might have reinforced their overall positive attitudes and beliefs toward AI and likely contributed to their willingness to adopt AI in their future classrooms [16]. The participants' responses also indicated that they, in general, found AI-based tools quite easy to use without mentioning any hardship or learning curve associated with these tools. Interpreted through the TAM framework, these findings can be seen as a high level of both PU (e.g., AI supports learning and planning) and PEOU (e.g., accessibility, immediacy), which together appear to shape favorable attitudes and strong intentions to utilize AI-based tools in science instruction. It can be inferred that high levels of exposure to AI applications in their academic and daily lives might enable preservice teachers to become more confident and adept at using these tools, which may consequently enhance their attitudes toward AI [36]. However, these positive views among the participants should be considered holistically by taking into account the expressed concerns of participants (i.e., misinformation, over-reliance, ethical issues), suggesting that their acceptance and actual use of AI in teaching science may be conditional upon the existence or development of effective safeguards addressing these key risks associated with the use of AI in education.

While all participants underlined the importance of appropriate training and PD on how to utilize AI-based tools and technologies in educational settings, surprisingly, none of them mentioned or discussed the need for similar training opportunities for learners. This indicates that they might have assumed their students, who are digital natives, would already possess these competencies to some extent or would acquire them outside of school, which is a potential gap that could leave students unprepared in terms of their AI readiness. The assumption that students will come to the classroom with proper skills and sufficient competencies to navigate through an AI-driven educational landscape is very risky. Even when students are frequent users of AI, they may still lack critical skills for employing AI-based tools effectively based on their individual needs. This notion was apparent in participants' own responses, where they stated using AI applications frequently while also acknowledging the need for training to utilize it in classroom settings. In short, without structured guidance and targeted training programs, students may lack the critical skills to use AI-based tools for their learning or fail to leverage their full educational potential. To address this gap, teacher-education programs may aim to foster prospective teachers' pedagogical strategies to not only teach with AI but also teach their students about AI. This could include modeling strategies for evaluating the informational accuracy of AI outputs, designing activities that combine AI use with critical-thinking tasks to foster rather than inhibit creativity, and explicitly teaching ethical frameworks for responsible AI use [13]. Enabling both students and teachers to become critical users of AI can help ensure that AI technologies enhance, rather than undermine, the quality and integrity of the learning process.

6. Conclusion

To conclude, the sample in this study viewed AI-based tools as powerful, easily accessible intelligent assistants that can significantly support conceptual science learning among students by providing differentiated and on-demand scaffolding and also aid teachers' instructional planning and implementation. In addition, the participants expressed some legitimate concerns about the use of AI in educational settings, such as misinformation produced by AI, the potential negative impacts of AI on academic integrity, as well as creative and critical thinking skills among learners. The participants also articulated a strong interest in attaining hands-on and minds-on training to translate their familiarity with AI into pedagogical competence. From the theoretical lens of the TAM framework, the participants, in general, appeared to demonstrate positive attitudes toward utilizing AI in science education as well as strong BIs in adopting AI for their future teaching. Overall, the findings of this study suggest a window of opportunity for teacher education programs that can leverage preservice teachers' rich experiences with AI-based tools by offering targeted PD programs and providing curricular supports that emphasize critical and practical uses of AI through concrete classroom applications. Doing so will help ensure that AI-based tools are used in science education as a pedagogical transformer for deep science learning rather than a distracting technological novelty or an automated shortcut ignoring the essential cognitive processes.

This study has several limitations, and its findings should be interpreted with caution. First, the sample size was relatively small ($N = 7$), which limits the generalizability of the results to a broader population of preservice science teachers. Second, the participants were recruited from a single higher education institution, and their perspectives may not fully reflect those of preservice science teachers in different cultural or institutional contexts. Third, the data were based on self-reported perceptions, which may be partly influenced by social desirability bias. Finally, the cross-sectional design of the study did not allow for the examination of changes in attitudes or practices over time. Future research could address these limitations by employing larger and more diverse samples, incorporating longitudinal designs, and including observational or performance-based measures to complement self-reported data.

Conflict of interest

The author declares no conflict of interest.

Appendix A

Interview questions

(1) Have you used any AI-based tools or technologies in your daily life or for educational purposes? If so, which tools have you used, and in what context did you use them?

(2) Do you have any experience with using AI-based tools during your teacher training or formal coursework at the university?

(3) Do you think AI-based tools can support science teaching and learning? If so, in what ways? For example, how do you think AI-based tools can help students better understand difficult science concepts?

(4) Do you believe AI may change the way science is taught or learned in the next five years? If so, how?

(5) How easy or difficult do you find it to learn and use AI-based tools for teaching and learning related purposes?

(6) How comfortable do you currently feel about using AI-based tools in your lesson planning or teaching?

(7) Do you anticipate using AI-based tools regularly, both in and outside of the classroom, for teaching-related tasks when you start working as a teacher?

(8) What challenges would you expect to face as a teacher when using AI-based tools in real classroom settings?

(9) What kind of support or training do you think you need in order to use AI-based tools effectively for teaching science?

(10) How would you use an AI-based tool(s) in teaching science in a formal classroom setting? Can you briefly describe a specific example?

(11) Do you think using AI-based tools can facilitate and promote inquiry-based and conceptual learning in science education? If so, in what ways?

(12) What kind of concerns do you generally have about using AI-based tools and technologies in education?

(13) Do you think students' use of AI-based tools for their schoolwork can affect their creativity and critical thinking skills, either positively or negatively?

(14) In what ways do you think AI may significantly shape or change your teaching practices in the future?

Author details

Osman Aksit
Boğaziçi University, Istanbul, Türkiye

*Address all correspondence to: osman.aksit@bogazici.edu.tr

References

[1] Turing AM (1948). *Intelligent machinery*. (Report No. DSIR 10/385). National Physical Laboratory

[2] Kaplan J. Generative Artificial Intelligence: What Everyone Needs to Know. New York, USA: Oxford University Press; 2024

[3] Zhuang Y, Cai M, Li X, Luo X, Yang Q, Wu F. 2020. The next breakthroughs of artificial intelligence: The interdisciplinary nature of AI. Engineering. **6**(3):245–247. DOI: 10.1016/j.eng.2020.01.009

[4] Microsoft Education. (2025). 2025 AI in Education Report Survey Details. Retrieved from: https://cdn-dynmedia-1.microsoft.com/is/content/microsoftcorp/microsoft/bade/documents/products-and-services/en-us/education/Survey-Data-2025-Microsoft-AI-in-Education-Report.pdf [Accessed: 2025-August-15]

[5] Tan X, Cheng G, Ling MH. Artificial intelligence in teaching and teacher professional development: A systematic review. Computers and Education: Artificial Intelligence. 2025;**8**:100355. DOI: 10.1016/j.caeai.2024.100355

[6] Chiu TK, Xia Q, Zhou X, Chai CS, Cheng M. Systematic literature review on opportunities, challenges, and future research recommendations of artificial intelligence in education. Computers and Education: Artificial Intelligence. 2023;**4**:100118. DOI: 10.1016/j.caeai.2022.100118

[7] Calleja J, Camilleri P. Primary school teachers' perceptions towards the use of generative AI in teaching using lesson study. International Journal for Lesson and Learning Studies. 2025;**14**:237–252. 10.1108/IJLLS-11-2024-0268

[8] Gozalo-Brizuela R, Merchan EEG. 2024. A survey of generative AI applications. Journal of Computer Science. **20**(8):801–818. DOI: 10.3844/jcssp.2024.801.818

[9] Kasneci E, Seßler K, Küchemann S, Bannert M, Dementieva D, Fischer F, … Kasneci G. ChatGPT for good? On opportunities and challenges of large language models for education. Learning and Individual Differences. 2023;**103**:102274. DOI: 10.1016/j.lindif.2023.102274

[10] OECD. OECD Digital Education Outlook 2023: Towards an Effective Digital Education Ecosystem. Paris: OECD Publishing; 2023. DOI:10.1787/c74f03de-en

[11] Miao F, Cukurova M. AI Competency Framework for Teachers. Paris, France: United Nations Educational, Scientific and Cultural Organization (UNESCO); 2024. DOI: 10.54675/ZJTE2084

[12] Miao F, and Shiohira K. AI Competency Framework for Students. Paris, France: United Nations Educational, Scientific and Cultural Organization (UNESCO); 2024. DOI: 10.54675/JKJB9835

[13] Miao F, Holmes W. Guidance for Generative AI in Education and Research. Paris, France: United Nations Educational, Scientific and Cultural Organization (UNESCO); 2023. DOI: 10.54675/EWZM9535

[14] White House. (2025, April 1). Advancing Artificial Intelligence Education for American Youth. Retrieved from: https://www.whitehouse.gov/presidential-actions/2025/04/advancing-artificial-intelligence-education-for-american-youth/

[15] Alarabi K, Alabidi S, Tairab H, Pagani LS, AlSadrani B, Abu Khurma O. AI's impact on science education: A study of ant and bee mindsets in UAE science classrooms. Frontiers in Education. 2025;**10**:1577285. DOI: 10.3389/feduc.2025.1577285

[16] Gao M, Zhang H, Dong Y, Li J. Embracing generative AI in education: An experiential study on preservice teachers' acceptance and attitudes. Educational Studies. 2025;1–20. DOI: 10.1080/03055698.2025.2483831

[17] Garofalo SG, Farenga SJ. 2025. Science teacher perceptions of the state of knowledge and education at the advent of generative artificial intelligence popularity. Science and Education. **34**(2):893–912. DOI:10.1007/s11191-024-00534-y

[18] Sanusi IT, Ayanwale MA, Tolorunleke AE. Investigating pre-service teachers' artificial intelligence perception from the perspective of planned behavior theory. Computers and Education: Artificial Intelligence. 2024;**6**:100202. DOI: 10.1016/j.caeai.2024.100202

[19] Yang J. 2022. Perceptions of preservice teachers on AI chatbots in english education. International Journal of Internet, Broadcasting and Communication. **14**(1):44–52. DOI: 10.7236/IJIBC.2022.14.1.44

[20] Korkmaz A, Cilsalar-Sagnak H. 2024. Perceptions of preschool teacher candidates' regarding artificial intelligence and the meanings they attribute. Çukurova University Journal of Turkology Research. **9**(2):1319–1342. DOI: 10.32321/cutad.1561556

[21] Ishmuradova II, Zhdanov SP, Kondrashev SV, Erokhova NS, Grishnova EE, Volosova NY. 2025. Preservice science teachers' perception on using generative artificial intelligence in science education. Contemporary Educational Technology. **17**(3):ep579. DOI: 10.30935/cedtech/16207

[22] Davis FD, Bagozzi RP, Warshaw PR. 1989. User acceptance of computer technology: A comparison of two theoretical models. Management Science. **35**(8):982–1003. DOI: 10.1287/mnsc.35.8.982

[23] Davis FD, Granić A. The Technology Acceptance Model - 30 Years of TAM. Switzerland: Springer; 2024. DOI: 10.1007/978-3-030-45274-2

[24] Ajzen I, Fishbein M. Understanding Attitudes and Predicting Social Behavior. Englewood Cliffs, NJ: Prentice Hall; 1980

[25] Granić A, Marangunić N. 2019. Technology acceptance model in educational context: A systematic literature review. British Journal of Educational Technology. **50**(5):2572–2593. DOI: 10.1111/bjet.12864

[26] Barakat M, Salim NA, Sallam M. University educators perspectives on ChatGPT: A technology acceptance model-based study. Open Praxis. 2025;**17**(1):129–144. DOI: 10.55982/openpraxis.17.1.718

[27] Nja CO, Idiege KJ, Uwe UE, Meremikwu AN, Ekon EE, Erim CM, ... Cornelius-Ukpepi BU. Adoption of

artificial intelligence in science teaching: From the vantage point of the African science teachers. Smart Learning Environments. 2023;**10**(1):42. DOI: 10.1186/s40561-023-00261-x

[28] Scherer R, Teo T. Unpacking teachers' intentions to integrate technology: A meta-analysis. Educational Research Review. 2019;**27**:90–109. 10.1016/j.edurev.2019.03.001

[29] Teo T. 2009. Modelling technology acceptance in education: A study of pre-service teachers. Computers and Education. **52**(2):302–312. DOI: 10.1016/j.compedu.2008.08.006

[30] Teo T. Comparing pre-service and in-service teachers' acceptance of technology: Assessment of measurement invariance and latent mean differences. Computers and Education. 2015;**83**:22–31. 10.1016/j.compedu.2014.11.015

[31] Yin RK. Case Study Research and Applications. 6th ed. Thousand Oaks, California: Sage; 2018

[32] Fraenkel J, Wallen N, Hyun H. How to Design and Evaluate Research in Education. 11th ed. New York, NY: McGraw Hill; 2022

[33] Braun V, Clarke V. Thematic Analysis: A Practical Guide. Thousand Oaks, California: Sage; 2021

[34] Bick A, Blandin A, Deming DJ (2025). The rapid adoption of generative AI. Federal Reserve Bank of St. Louis Working Paper 2024-027. DOI: 10.3386/w32966

[35] Ko U, Hartley K, Hayak M. Exploring AI in education: Preservice teacher perspectives, usage, and considerations. Journal of Information Technology Education: Research. 2025;**24**:Article 21. 10.28945/5592

[36] Belda-Medina J, Kokošková V. ChatGPT for language learning: Assessing teacher candidates' skills and perceptions using the technology acceptance model (TAM). Innovation in Language Learning and Teaching. 2024;1–16. DOI:10.1080/17501229.2024.2435900

Chapter 13

Integrating AI-Based Reinforcement Learning and Competency-Based Assessment for Skill and Competency Development

Kumar V Sampath, Kumar A N Veerendra and Jai Prakash Pandey

Abstract

Engineering graduates must be prepared to solve future, undefined problems. To develop necessary competencies, innovative methods like AI-based reinforcement learning (RL) and competency-based assessments are essential. A new AI-RL framework integrates the affective domain into the teaching-learning process using a state-action student database and the SAM model. Based on data from 300 students across 36 subjects (12,960 samples), this approach showed a 7.7% improvement in learning outcomes ($p = 0.0041$). The scope includes designing AI-based assessment tools, implementing the RL framework, integrating affective domain metrics, and validating improvements in competency development across all learning domains. It also involves continuous data collection and analysis to refine the framework and developing faculty training modules for effective deployment. Scalability across institutions and disciplines will be explored for broader impact. Student details, including basic information, subjects, and section, must be collected and mapped to the SAM process software model. Subject teachers for each section will continuously assess students across all learning domains. The AI-based reinforcement learning (RL) method is then applied to identify individual learning patterns based on each student's current state, enabling subject matter experts to conduct ongoing assessments. Based on this analysis, targeted actions are recommended to help students develop competencies in specific domains. These action plans are aligned with Bloom's Taxonomy and categorized under content knowledge, core competencies, critical thinking, core values, and managerial skills, all implemented through the RL framework.

Keywords: Cumulative Grade Point Average (CGPA), Competency Based Evaluation Scheme (CBES), Reinforcement Learning (RL), Student Assessment Management (SAM), Reinforcement Learning (RL)

1. Introduction

In most educational systems, student performance is traditionally evaluated through marks or grades. While this is common, certain regulatory bodies and universities assess the overall performance of institutions using structured ranking frameworks. These frameworks typically measure institutions on parameters such as Teaching, Learning and Resources (TLR), Innovation and Entrepreneurship (IE), Research and Professional Practice (RP), Outreach and Inclusivity (OI), Graduation Outcomes (GO), and Perception (PR). Notably, such systems focus primarily on outcomes.

However, meaningful improvement requires early intervention during the learning and assessment period. By monitoring student competencies in the cognitive, affective, and psychomotor domains, educators can address difficulties before they affect results, thereby improving both student and institutional performance. Assessing educational performance is complex, as academic success depends on multiple variables. AI-based monitoring and assessment systems can reduce bias in performance measurement and result compilation, enabling richer insights through state–action analysis to capture knowledge, skills, and attitudes.

Databases generated from various learning and assessment processes can be explored using AI-driven competency assessment tools at the end of a course or at defined milestones. Such analysis can reveal behavioral patterns, enabling timely interventions that improve student outcomes. This not only helps produce more competent professionals but also contributes to national development.

The education sector faces numerous challenges, including poor governance, lack of accountability, limited placement opportunities, and high dropout rates. Systematic state–action analysis of student databases can help address these issues to an acceptable level. Timely prediction of performance, followed by targeted actions, can enhance placements and reduce dropouts. The combined use of the Reinforcement Learning (RL) framework and the SAM process model provides a structured approach to predicting learning and assessment patterns using defined components and interventions. Together, these frameworks offer a powerful and efficient means of interpreting student data and generating actionable insights.

Nonetheless, implementing this approach poses challenges, including primary data collection, faculty training, predictive state–action analysis, and conducting stakeholder surveys for indirect assessment and feedback.

This chapter is organized as follows: Section 2 reviews existing research on Reinforcement Learning and competency-based assessment. Section 3 explains the working of the proposed AI-based RL method and SAM model. Section 4 presents and compares performance results of the proposed method. Section 5 concludes the discussion.

2. Literature survey

The structuring of an educational program typically begins with the organization of learning topics into units. A collection of these units constitutes a course, and multiple courses collectively form the program curriculum. This structure reflects not only the scope of learning topics but also their references and assessment strategies, as outlined within the university system in [1].

According to [2], the efficacy of the teaching–learning process depends on several interlinked factors: instructional delivery methods, well-defined learning objectives, measurable outcomes, and alignment between course and program outcomes. Key parameters – such as syllabus design, evaluation schemes, assessment components, course duration, delivery modes, and pedagogical strategies – play a pivotal role in fostering student development. These parameters serve to address learners' needs, provide the resources required to master subject knowledge, and develop skills and attitudes necessary for professional excellence. However, continuous monitoring and assessment of these parameters by a single subject matter expert can be challenging. This underscores the necessity of multidisciplinary teams of experts from different sectors. Furthermore, it is essential to conduct assessments at the point when learners are adequately prepared, rather than on a predetermined fixed schedule.

Shi, Peng, and Sun in [3], emphasize the role of information literacy culture in both learners and institutions in cultivating lifelong learning capabilities. Lifelong learning, in turn, enhances problem-solving and critical thinking skills, particularly within a smart learning ecosystem.

Cheng, Zhang, and Li in [4], propose strategies to improve the effectiveness of blended learning. Their study compares hybrid learning efficiency using data from various delivery methods, including direct instruction, digital whiteboards, pre-recorded sessions, and group-based worksheet activities. They also evaluate the quality of assessment processes, comparing innovative evaluation techniques with conventional methods.

Gullickson and King in [5], examine the need for efficient teaching–learning processes and improved assessment methods to raise educational standards. They argue that quality education is driven by the effective use of teaching aids, the competence of faculty, structured lesson planning, and appropriate pedagogical strategies. Their proposed model demonstrates the impact of these parameters at two levels: (1) on the quality of teaching and learning processes, and (2) on learner excellence and outcomes. This reinforces the notion that there is always scope for improvement through novel approaches.

In competency-based systems as in [6], learners are expected to demonstrate predefined core competencies during assessments. Accordingly, curricula are designed to ensure that learners acquire and exhibit these competencies. Competency-based assessment involves distinct processes, tools, and techniques, as well as subject matter experts who adopt new roles and responsibilities to evaluate learners effectively.

An adaptive, state–action-based evaluation process can enable continuous monitoring of individual learner progress. In higher education, one of the major challenges remains the inability of many students to graduate within the stipulated time frame. Contributing factors include economic constraints, inadequate resources, health issues, lack of interest, and limited accessibility to university systems. However, a significant underlying issue is that assessments are often conducted at fixed times, regardless of whether learners are ready. Blumenthal and Rasmussen in [7] address this challenge by proposing a novel model that leverages the benefits of competency-based assessment to reduce dropout rates and better align assessment timing with learner readiness.

El-Maaddawy and Deneen [8] examined the application of outcomes-based assessment in a postgraduate civil engineering course. Their work explored how structured outcome mapping, coupled with iterative assessment cycles, could help align teaching strategies with intended learning results. The study demonstrated that trialing new assessment frameworks in higher education not only improved transparency in grading but also encouraged active student engagement with course objectives.

Morales-Avalos and Heredia-Escorza [9] addressed the need for innovation competencies in engineering education by integrating Internet of Things (IoT) tools into a cloud-based laboratory network. This initiative facilitated hands-on, remote experimentation while fostering problem-solving and collaboration skills, particularly in geographically dispersed academic environments. The approach highlighted how digital connectivity can strengthen both technical knowledge and innovation capacity among engineering students.

Gabrani, Solomon, and Dviwedi [10] investigated teaching pedagogies in higher education aimed at enhancing learning outcomes. Their findings emphasized that a blend of student-centered learning, technology-enabled instruction, and contextualized case studies can significantly boost learner comprehension, retention, and application of knowledge in real-world scenarios.

Hassanein [11] presented a descriptive analysis of competency-based learning (CBL) implementation at Northern Border University. The research underscored the challenges of integrating CBL frameworks – such as curriculum restructuring, assessment redesign, and faculty development – while also highlighting its potential to produce graduates with demonstrable skills aligned to workplace needs.

Kulkarni et al. [12] explored the validation of learning outcome attainment using exit surveys. This method provided a feedback loop between graduates and the institution, enabling continuous improvement of curricula and teaching methods. Their case study demonstrated how systematically collected survey data can serve as a reliable measure of program effectiveness.

Jadhav, Kakade, and Patil [13] discussed the integration of Information and Communication Technology (ICT) into active teaching–learning–assessment processes. They argued that digital tools – when combined with participatory teaching techniques – can enhance student motivation, facilitate real-time feedback, and promote deeper engagement with course materials.

Balasubramani [14] focused on industry participation in curriculum design, asserting that collaborative development between academia and industry stakeholders ensures that course content remains relevant to evolving market demands. This collaboration was shown to help bridge the gap between academic training and practical skills expected by employers.

Senthil [15] examined the enhancement of engineering education through active learning methodologies. The study showcased how approaches such as peer instruction, problem-based learning, and collaborative projects can improve conceptual understanding, critical thinking, and teamwork abilities among students.

Collectively, these studies provide a multi-faceted view of modern engineering and higher education practices – ranging from competency-based assessment and technology integration to industry collaboration and active learning design – underscoring the need for adaptive, outcome-oriented approaches to curriculum and pedagogy.

In summary, a holistic approach to curriculum design – incorporating the development of a learning pyramid for each pedagogical strategy, adopting competency-based assessment models, and tracking learner progress with timely corrective actions – can bring about a paradigm shift in the growth and effectiveness of educational systems.

3. Proposed AI based reinforcement learning method and student assessment management model

The proposed AI-based RL method, integrated with the SAM model, aims to empower students with a comprehensive understanding of their performance across the cognitive, psychomotor, and affective domains. It is designed to nurture competency-based education that equips learners with the skills and knowledge required to meet future challenges. This approach supports mastery of subject concepts, domain-specific excellence, and readiness for real-world applications.

The core objective of this model is to leverage AI tools to generate personalized learning and assessment patterns aligned with each student's current state. It facilitates the identification of skill gaps, evaluates individual performance, and enhances talent management. Based on the analysis, targeted actions are recommended to highlight strengths, address weaknesses, and guide students toward achieving competency-based education and effective assessment practices.

3.1 SAM process software model

Implementation begins with collecting and mapping basic student details, course subjects, and section data into the SAM process software model. Subject instructors for the respective section continuously assess students in all three domains. The AI-based RL method then analyzes this input to create individualized learning patterns for ongoing evaluation by subject matter experts. Recommended actions are provided to students for developing competencies in each domain, mapped to Bloom's taxonomy categories – content knowledge, core competencies, critical thinking, core values, and managerial competency. Action plans under each taxonomy domain are systematically incorporated into the learning process through the reinforcement learning approach. The action plans implemented under each domain are outlined in sub sections as mentioned.

3.1.1 Cognitive domain

This domain is subdivided into Content Knowledge and Percentage of Marks/ CGPA.

- Content Knowledge is assessed using the following components:

    a. Prerequisite Knowledge

    b. STEM Knowledge

    c. Specialized Content Knowledge

d. Curriculum Knowledge

e. Practical/Application Knowledge

f. Correlation and Integration with Other Content

- Percentage of Marks/CGPA is evaluated through:

a. Continuous Internal Assessment Grades

b. External Examination Performance

3.1.2 Psychomotor domain

This domain is subdivided into Core Competencies and Critical Thinking.

- Core Competencies are measured using:

a. Accountability

b. Communication

c. Teamwork

d. Innovation

e. Planning and Organizing

f. Continuous Improvement

- Critical Thinking is assessed through:

a. Analytical Reasoning

b. Conceptual Understanding

c. Evidence-Based Problem Solving

d. Data Analysis

e. Deriving Implications

f. Formulating Conclusions

3.1.3 Affective domain

This domain is subdivided into Core Values and Managerial Competencies.

- Core Values are assessed using:

a. Commitment

b. Integrity

c. Respect for Diversity

d. Professionalism

e. Compassion/Caring

f. Social Responsibility

- Managerial Competencies are evaluated through:

a. Driving and Managing Change

b. Strategic Thinking

c. Making Quality Decisions

d. Building Partnerships

e. Leading and Empowering Others

f. Managing Performance

3.2 The proposed SAM model and AI-based RL framework

Figure 1 illustrates the proposed SAM model, which serves as the master interface for developing the database used in the AI-based reinforcement learning (RL) and student assessment process. This master interface integrates:

- Assessment components from all three learning domains
- Expenditure per student
- Dynamic learning actions initiated during the process

Figure 2 details the sequential stages adopted in the proposed AI-based RL framework. Initially, a student database is compiled to generate an individual learning pattern. Based on this pattern, specific recommended actions are suggested to help the learner develop the required competencies. The RL algorithm is then applied to:

1. Track student learning progress

2. Generate personalized learning actions

3. Perform action-specific analysis

Sl. No.	Adm.No.	Roll No.	Student Name	Assessment Component	Direct Tool Score (A)	Indirect Tool Score (B)	Amount Spent per Student (in a scale of 10) (Recurring + Non Recurring) (D)	Certifications (Industry/Innovation/Entrepreneurship/Higher Studies) (E) (2 points per certificate/Minimum 5 certicates per	Total Score
1	20EC135	2000910310018	Aditya Gupta	Core Competencies	7.88	10.00	0.00	10.00	7.84
				Critical Thinking	7.82	10.00			
				Content Knowledge	7.87	10.00			
				Core Values	7.55	10.00			
				Managerial Competencies	7.97	8.00			
				Percentage of Marks (in Scale of 10) / CGPA	7.76	10.00			
				Sub Total Score :	7.80	9.70	0.00	10.00	
2	20EC136	2000910310034	Amisha Pandey	Core Competencies	8.16	10.00	10.00	10.00	8.40
				Critical Thinking	8.22	7.00			
				Content Knowledge	6.77	7.00			
				Core Values	7.36	10.00			
				Managerial Competencies	5.72	7.00			
				Percentage of Marks (in Scale of 10) / CGPA	8.01	9.00			
				Sub Total Score :	7.43	8.40	10.00	10.00	

Figure 1.
Proposed SAM model – Master interface.

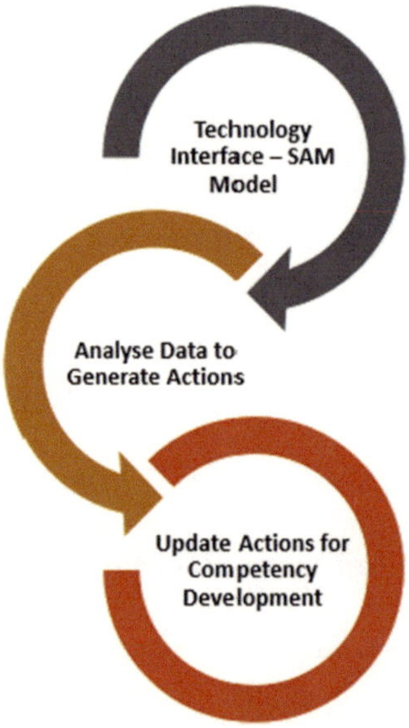

Figure 2.
Certifications interface – state-action analysis.

According to state–action analysis, the RL framework is designed to enhance the overall learning and assessment process. The output includes actionable insights for students, enabling them to strengthen cognitive abilities, gain a deeper STEM understanding, and follow customized learning paths.

One application of state–action analysis involves recommending certification courses in relevant domains (**Figure 3**). Suggested domains include:

- Industry skill development
- Innovation and entrepreneurship

DOI: http://dx.doi.org/10.5772/intechopen.1012989

Sl. No.	Adm.No.	Roll No.	Student Name	Industry	Innovation	Entrepreneurship	Higher Studies	Others	Total Score
1	20EC135	2000910310018	Aditya Gupta	2	2	0			10
				0	0		0	2	
				0	0	0	0	2	
				0			2		
				0				2	
2	20EC136	2000910310034	Amisha Pandey	0	2	0			10
				2	0		0	0	
				0	2	0	0	0	
				0		2	0		
				2				2	

Figure 3.
Proposed RL method framework.

- Advanced/higher studies subjects
- Other specialized areas

Each certification category is graded on a scale of 0 to 2. Furthermore, if the sum of assessment components AC1 + AC2 + AC3 + AC4 + AC5 is less than 10, the actual sum is retained; otherwise, a maximum score of 10 is applied. This is then converted to a grade on a 0–10 scale. The SAM model and methodology are applied for course-level learner evaluation by subject matter experts (SMEs) using the proposed assessment components from the respective categories. For validation, two clusters of student database entries were subjected to statistical analysis:

Cluster 1:

- Count (N): 5
- Sum (Σx): 40.49
- Mean (μ): 8.098
- Variance (σ^2): 0.053176
- Margin of Error (Confidence Interval): 8.098 ± 0.103 (±1.27%) – **Table 1**

Cluster	C	Mean	SD	Margin of Error
1	60	7.78	0.230500	8.098 ± 0.103(±1.27%)
2	60	7.86		
3	60	8.23		
4	60	8.29		
5	60	8.33		
AVG	**60**	**8.09**		

Table 1.
API of conventional students.

Cluster 2:

- Count (N): 5
- Sum (Σx): 43.89
- Mean (μ): 8.778
- Variance (σ^2): 0.093016
- Margin of Error (Confidence Interval): 8.778 ± 0.136 (±1.55%) – **Table 2**

3.3 Key benefits of the proposed model

The proposed SAM model offers multiple benefits by fostering a strong and continuous student–teacher relationship, creating opportunities for open and meaningful discussions, and enabling personalized state–action mapping with timely academic and behavioural support. It allows for accurate recognition of each learner's current performance, behaviour, and psychological state, ensuring interventions are tailored to individual needs. The model also generates a valuable learning-pattern database that supports data-driven decision-making, thereby enhancing the efficiency and effectiveness of both learning and assessment processes. Ultimately, it ensures that the learning journey remains responsive, holistic, and focused on improving competencies while maintaining student well-being.

1. Strengthened student–teacher relationship
2. Greater opportunity for open discussion
3. Personalized state–action mapping and timely support
4. Recognition of each student's current behaviour, state, and condition
5. Development of a valuable learning-pattern database

Cluster	C	Mean	SD	Margin of Error
1	60	8.58	0.304985	8.778 ± 0.136(±1.55%)
2	60	8.85		
3	60	9.26		
4	60	8.35		
5	60	8.85		
AVG	**60**	**8.78**		

Table 2.
API of RL framework students.

Student Database Clusters	Mean	t-test	p-value
API of CBES (Cluster-1)	8.098	t = 3.978	0.0041
API of RL framework (Cluster-2)	8.778		

Table 3.
Mean score of students in both clusters.

6. Enhanced efficiency in learning and assessment processes

7. Ability to address the learner's psychological state and current condition effectively

4. Results and discussion

As shown in **Table 3**, the API scores of CBES (Cluster 1) were compared with those of the RL framework (Cluster 2) using undergraduate course data. The RL framework was applied over two semesters to six subjects, covering a student cohort of 300 divided into five clusters. Statistical analysis revealed a two-tailed p-value of 0.0041, confirming that the observed difference was highly significant. The mean difference (Cluster 1 – Cluster 2) was – 0.680, with a 95% confidence interval ranging from – 1.074178 to – 0.285822 (t = 3.9781, df = 8, standard error = 0.171). This indicates that the RL framework outperformed the CBES method, yielding an average API score improvement of 7.7%. Compared to CBES, the RL framework produced a statistically significant 7.7% gain in mean API scores (p = 0.0041), underscoring its superior effectiveness in enhancing student performance.

5. Conclusion

This study demonstrates that the RL framework consistently yields higher API scores than the conventional CBES method. Incorporating a state–action analyzer alongside CBES in undergraduate programs is recommended to enhance learning and assessment outcomes. The proposed model and framework have proven effective in improving both efficiency and precision in competency evaluation. Future work will focus on expanding the framework to additional learning domains, benchmarking against alternative methodologies, and addressing key implementation challenges such as revising program outcomes, optimizing intervention strategies, and ensuring effective utilization of budgets and resources. Integrating the predictive strength of Reinforcement Learning with competency-based assessment establishes a robust, scalable pathway toward data-driven, adaptive education systems capable of elevating both student achievement and institutional excellence.

Acknowledgments

We acknowledge and sincerely thank the efforts of committee chairman, subject matter experts, module coordinators, support staff and authors of papers referenced here.

Author details

Kumar V Sampath[1*], Kumar A N Veerendra[2] and Jai Prakash Pandey[3]

1 JSS Academy of Technical Education, Noida, India

2 JSS University, Noida, India

3 AKTU, Lucknow, India

*Address all correspondence to: sampath.kumarjss@gmail.com

References

[1] Print M. Curriculum Development and Design. St Leonards, NSW, Australia: Allen & Unwin; 1993

[2] Wojtczak A. Medical education terminology. Medical Teacher. 2002;**24**(4):357. DOI: 10.1080/01421590220145699

[3] Shi Y, Peng F, Sun F. A blended learning model based on smart learning environment to improve college students' information literacy. IEEE Access. 2022;**10**:89485–89498

[4] Cheng J, Zhang G, Li J, "Learning comparative analysis of teaching models based on smart platforms—Takes ERP principles and applications as example," in Proc. Int. Conf. Computer Science and Education, Singapore: Springer Nature, Aug. 2022, pp. 111–122.

[5] Gullickson AM, King JA, LaVelle JM, Clinton JM. The current state of evaluator education: A situation analysis and call to action. Evaluation and Program Planning. 2019;**75**:20–30

[6] Griffith W, Lim H. Competency-Based Education: Design and Implementation Strategies. New York, NY, USA: Academic Press; 2014

[7] Blumenthal D, Rasmussen J. State Approaches to Competency-based Education to Support College and Career Readiness for All Students. Washington, DC, USA: American Institutes for Research; 2015

[8] El-Maaddawy T, Deneen C. Outcomes-based assessment and learning: Trialling change in a postgraduate civil engineering course. Journal of University Teaching & Learning Practice. 2017;**14**(1):1–18

[9] Morales-Avalos JR, Heredia-Escorza Y. Igniting the innovation's competencies at engineering schools: IoT to the cloud labs network in Mexico. World Journal of Education. 2018;**8**(2):159–167

[10] Gabrani G, Solomon A, Dviwedi U. Teaching pedagogies used in higher education for better learning outcomes. Journal of Engineering Education Transformations. 2016;**30**(2):17–23

[11] Hassanein OHS. Investigating competency-based learning implementation at the Northern Border University (NBU): A descriptive analytical study. Arab World English Journal (AWEJ). 2021;**12**:3–21

[12] Kulkarni UP, Kulkarni SB, Shindhe KC, Umarji IR. Validating attainment of outcomes through exit surveys – A case study. Journal of Engineering Education Transformations. 2017;**31**(2):11–15

[13] Jadhav MR, Kakade AB, Patil MS. ICT and active teaching-learning-assessment process in the engineering education. Journal of Engineering Education Transformations. 2018;**31**(3):58–62

[14] Balasubramani R. Participation of industry in curriculum design and development. Journal of Engineering Education Transformations. 2019;**33**(1):56–60

[15] Senthil R. Enhancement of engineering education by incorporating active learning methodologies. Journal of Engineering Education Transformations. 2020;**34**(1):12–20

Section 3

Personalization, Inclusion & Learner Diversity

Chapter 14

Personalized Learning with AI: Adapting Education to Learners' Needs

S.M.F.D. Syed Mustapha

Abstract

This chapter explores the transformative role of artificial intelligence (AI) in enabling personalized learning (PL). It draws on the theoretical foundations of constructivism, multiple intelligences, self-determination theory, connectivism, and data-driven decision-making to examine how AI supports learner engagement, autonomy, and self-regulation. It highlights intelligent tutoring systems, recommender engines, emotion-aware tools, and real-time feedback systems, which furnish relevant and adaptable learning pathways. Global case studies – such as Summit Public Schools, Carnegie Learning, Squirrel AI, and David Game College – are discussed to illustrate the effectiveness of these data-driven, human-AI collaboration-based, and scalable adaptive personalized instructional systems. The chapter also addresses ethical, pedagogical, and human-related implications and emphasizes the challenges related to algorithm bias, data privacy, and teacher readiness. Emerging trends, like the integration of AI with extended reality (XR) environments that aim toward a more immersive, experiential, and evidence-based learning, are also discussed.

Keywords: artificial intelligence in education, personalized learning, adaptive learning systems, learning analytics, educational technology, edtech

1. Introduction

Personalized learning is founded on the premise that learning is a unique experience for learners and must be tailored to their individual needs, focusing on their learning pace and progression [1]. Though delivering personalized learning has been on the agenda of educationists since the eighteenth century, as seen from early models like the monitorial system and Keller Plan, the lack of practical resources to implement such learning has prevented its implementation [2].

However, with the advancement of digital technologies and artificial intelligence (AI), these limitations are largely overcome. Personalized learning is now in a new phase of transition, where customized and tailored instructions and content can be accessed by learners at the time and location that are most convenient to them. Adaptive learning systems based on AI technology enable the analysis of students' data in real time, which leads to the adjustment of content in a dynamic manner to offer customized learning pathways [3]. AI-supported learning platforms are therefore affecting how learners perceive their self-efficacy, engage with content, and progress at their own pace with confidence. Such AI-integrated learning environments are flexible and encourage content mastery in a dynamic environment, which is often not possible within the rigid classroom structures [4].

This chapter explores how AI-powered systems are transforming personalized learning and also addresses the challenges and ethical dilemmas that have emerged due to AI-personalized learning integrations. It is expected to provide a foundational and critical understanding of the opportunities and limitations of using AI in personalized learning environments.

The specific objectives of this chapter are:

1. To identify the fundamental factors contributing to building the AI-supported personalization frameworks.

2. To explore how AI technologies enable key functions of personalized learning.

3. To examine the pedagogical, ethical, and equity implications of AI-driven personalized learning.

4. To illustrate real-world implementation models of AI-supported personalized learning in diverse educational contexts.

5. To determine the key success factors in scaling AI-driven personalized learning solutions through international case studies.

One of the strategies adopted in AI-integrated personalized learning includes the development of comprehensive learner profiles, which guide the creation of learner-focused content customization and encourage the development of competency-based assessments. Secondly, predictive analytics is employed to develop AI-enhanced assessment tools that enable early intervention and tailored support in real time, thus leading to better academic outcomes for students [5]. Additionally, the in-built flexibility in the learning environment enables learners to pace their education and take ownership, thus providing both motivation and autonomy [6]. Educators, too, can obtain actionable insights and provide feedback in real time.

These strategic elements shape the fundamentals of building AI-personalized learning frameworks, as seen in Objective 1. By emphasizing intentional design focused on data analytics, learner profiling, and content adaptability, these elements enable scalable customization. Objective 2 further highlights the functions of personalized learning as rooted in real-time feedback, adaptive progression, and predictive assessment to deliver learner-centered education.

However, some critical pedagogical, ethical, and systemic challenges and implications are highlighted in Objective 3. A major concern is related to issues like data privacy, algorithmic bias, and teacher marginalization, which may act as barriers to the adoption of AI-based learning personalization. Data privacy is a global concern, and ethical frameworks are often fragmented or not supported by adequate transparency at the institutional level, which may lead to both ethical and legal repercussions [7]. Additionally, algorithmic bias is a major concern, as most AI-based platforms and applications are trained on segregated data, which may lead to bias or discrimination against diverse users. Further, AI systems do not offer a similar human connection, intuition, or ethical judgment that educators can bring to the students [8, 9]. The impacts of such ethical and decision-making aspects of personalized AI learning require further exploration and research, which could help establish ethical guidelines and ensure teacher readiness through professional development.

This chapter also addresses real-world examples and implementation models (Objective 4) and discusses international case studies that underscore the significance of local contexts and multistakeholder involvement. By drawing upon diverse educational settings like the charter schools in the USA, the private institutions in the UK, and learning centers in China, these case studies provide insights into the real-world impact made by AI-supported personalized learning. The case studies highlight contextual factors such as culture, policy making, and diverse pedagogical approaches on the success of models like Squirrel AI, David Game College, and the Summit Public Schools (SPS) model.

Finally, Objective 5 leads us to identify key success factors based on the insights from the practical applications of AI in personalized learning. These key factors are gleaned from the above case studies and underline the importance of the robustness of data analytics, the feedback-loop-based nature of personalized learning, collaborative environments, and teachers' training. In addition to technology and training, successful implementation is dependent on inclusive and localized educational policies and support from top management.

2. Fundamental factors in building an AI-enhanced personalized learning

2.1 What is personalized learning?

Personalized learning, though not a new concept, is being revolutionized by advancements in AI [4]. This section explores the fundamental concepts and definitions of AI in personalized learning and discusses its significant and transformative potential. Personalized learning is both an educational approach and a practical strategy that enables a customized learning experience for students [5]. It aims to develop and deliver instruction to individual students based on their unique characteristics, learning strengths, requirements, and interests [7]. Personalized learning is, therefore, facilitated by flexible learning environments, student ownership of learning, and ongoing assessment and dynamic adjustment of learning strategies. Several theories underpin personalized learning and its advantages.

2.2 Theoretical underpinnings of personalized learning

2.2.1 Constructivist theory

2.2.1.1 Overview

Constructivist theory [10, 11] suggests that knowledge is constructed through active participation and interaction of learners with their environments and social context [12]. Students are actively engaged in their learning process and indulge in meaning-making from experiences. Piaget suggests that there are developmental stages where learners interact with objects and internalize abstract thinking [10]. His theory is largely applied to the learning stages in early childhood; a similar logic is present in the learning-by-doing approach in higher education. Learning is made effective not only by personal and intimate interaction with content but also through social mediation, where peers and instructors play a major role [11].

Personalized learning is also supported through understanding social connections and knowledge sharing, which impact learners' learning pathways [13]. Vorobyeva et al. postulate that platforms offering adaptive feedback and learner-controlled pacing are well-aligned with constructivist pedagogy [14]. Similarly, Holmes et al. suggest that AI tools extend constructivist learning environments by encouraging learners in iterative learning and meaning-making [15].

2.2.1.2 Application in personalized learning

Research has indicated that constructivist environments supported by AI generative and adaptive technologies lead to an enhancement in students' engagement [16]. Guo et al. support integrating generative AI into constructivist contexts, as AI-generated simulations and peer collaboration prompts were found to be linked to increases in students' motivation, creativity, and collaboration [17]. By developing curricula and activities that allow students to explore, ask questions, and build upon prior knowledge, educationists can encourage highly personalized learning.

Personalized learning is further enhanced through project-based learning and student-directed projects, as done at SPS in California, where constructivist principles are applied to enhance student engagement, autonomy, and academic growth [18]. Summit's Personalized Learning Plans (PLPs) help students set weekly goals and track their progress. The PLP platform enables self-reflection and guidance by mentors, which creates a sense of ownership for their learning [19]. By encouraging students to inquire and engage in problem-solving to draw their own conclusions, teachers can engage in constructive learning and facilitate personalization. This is also reflected in project-based learning, where students learn by doing and report a deeper understanding of the knowledge, as well as better satisfaction with the learning process [20].

Pham et al.'s constructivist-based system using Google Codelabs resulted in higher satisfaction levels, with a mean score of 3.33–3.44 on a 4-point scale for system quality, content alignment, and relevance [11]. Similarly, Do et al. report that within three months of implementing constructionist environments via the design science approach, 193 project management students showed improvement in their motivation and learning strategy scores, with intrinsic motivation significantly predicting learning strategies ($\beta = 0.292–0.315$, $p < 0.001$) and extrinsic motivation also showing strong effects ($\beta = 0.277–0.322$, $p < 0.001$) [21]. Additionally, Marienko et al. have shown that adaptive AR systems improved perceived usability and learner satisfaction in experiential training contexts and simulation labs, which was found to translate into reported improved actual task performance [22].

2.2.2 Multiple intelligences theory

2.2.2.1 Overview

Howard Gardner's multiple intelligences theory presumes that intelligence is diverse and can be differentiated in the form of linguistic, logical-mathematical, spatial, musical, interpersonal, intrapersonal, bodily-kinesthetic, and naturalistic [23]. These multiple intelligences vary among different learners and need to be considered and challenged when designing curriculum instruction. A recent study using 149 teachers showed a significant positive correlation ($r = 0.511$, $p < 0.001$) between teachers' use of technology to support multiple intelligences and student engagement [24]. Additionally, research has found students improve by 25% on metrics like satisfaction with curriculum and confidence in learning after changes were made to their curricula to focus on multiple intelligences [25].

2.2.2.2 Application in personalized learning

While this approach is still in its nascent stages, there is some evidence suggesting that curricula or instructional designs aligning with students' more prominent intelligences are likely to lead to improved performance and engagement [13]. For example, by using a fuzzy-AHP-based e-content sequencing system that matched content with students' main intelligence, it was possible to instill 84.6% higher engagement and interest among students compared to those learning with traditional approaches [26]. In a study conducted across 41 public schools in the USA, Kornhaber et al. found that 78% of schools that adopted multiple intelligence frameworks for three years were able to report higher test scores, better student behavior, substantial gains for students with learning disabilities, and enhanced parental participation [27]. Instructional pluralism, which is at the core of personalized learning, enables learners to approach problems using their specific cognitive strengths, facilitating deeper learning [28]. Moreover, it has also been found that integrating multiple intelligences theory with educational technology is increasingly being deployed in inclusive and diverse learning settings [29].

2.2.3 Self-determination theory

2.2.3.1 Overview

Self-determination theory (SDT), developed by Deci and Ryan, is based on the understanding that learners have basic psychological needs in the form of the need for autonomy, the need to feel competent, and the need to relate to the content [30]. The drive to fulfill these needs acts as an intrinsic motivation for learners [6]. Deci and Ryan emphasize that when educational environments are structured to support these needs, students display deeper learning and psychological well-being. In contrast, in learning settings where there is a lack of autonomy and high pressure to perform, students are likely to feel disengaged [30]. Other studies have also validated the link between autonomy-supportive environments and enhanced learning, engagement, and overall improvement in student well-being [6, 31].

2.2.3.2 Application in personalized learning

By allowing students to feel autonomy and control, personalized learning using AI technology applies principles of SDT to improve student motivation and engagement [32]. Research has found that mobile learning systems designed using SDT principles showed a 16% improvement in intrinsic motivation for learning and a 12% improvement in learning outcomes compared to students using traditional platforms [33]. Additionally, meaningful and relevant personalized content enhances engagement levels and develops students' competence and confidence levels [34]. SDT theory suggests that intrinsic motivations ensure that learning through constant engagement with content improves students' resilience and self-efficacy in the longer term [32]. Personalized online learning that encourages students to participate autonomously has been shown to significantly boost students' perceived autonomy, competence, and motivation [1].

2.2.4 Connectivism

2.2.4.1 Overview

George Siemens and Stephen Downes' connectivism theory suggests that learning predominantly occurs through connections and networks [35]. This framework has particular relevance in the digital age, as social media platforms and the internet allow learners to access vast amounts of information and collaborate with others globally. Furthermore, with AI-linked knowledge management platforms, such linkages and connections can be more targeted and relevant to student learning. Connectivism theory also suggests that building connections not only improves access to information and knowledge but also helps learners contribute their knowledge, which is an essential aspect of learning in a knowledge economy [36]. Connectivism directly extends to the current AI-supported learning environments that provide adaptive and flexible knowledge ecosystems for learners to keep abreast of new information and knowledge aligned with their requirements [37, 38].

2.2.4.2 Application in personalized learning

This theory applies directly to personalized learning environments, where students can interact with the content, peers, and teachers through online learning platforms that enable the creation of both social and academic connections and provide incentives through recognition and appreciation for knowledge sharing and engagement. A US Department of Education report recently indicated that schools integrating online collaboration tools into their instructional designs see substantial improvements in students' critical thinking and communication skills [39]. Additionally, other studies have shown that students' engagement in networking activities over digital platforms leads to higher self-efficacy when the interactions are aligned with personal learning goals [40].

For example, a study using students in a connectivism-driven collaborative online international learning (COIL) highlighted connectivism's role in enhancing understanding and application of complex concepts like diversity and inclusion, and showcased students' significant ($p < 0.05$) increase in willingness to apply knowledge as compared to a control group [20].

A significant improvement in engagement scores and substantially improved motivation levels has been reported by using ViLLE (a collaborative learning platform developed by the University of Turku, Finland) compared to traditional instruction [41]. Similarly, the Student Learning Space (SLS), by the Ministry of Education in Singapore, provides AI-based recommendations and collaboration tools for students, which are linked to improved content retention and classroom participation [42]. Further, Hardof-Jaffe and Peled reported a connection between connectivist-based teacher training and six key growth areas, including breaking time/place boundaries, enhanced personal and professional development, and digital peer interaction [43]. These growth areas, in turn, are related to teachers' ability to develop and support personalized and adaptive learning environments.

2.2.5 Data-driven decision making

2.2.5.1 Overview

This framework is central to many AI-based personalized learning systems and forms the basis of most personalized learning platforms [44].

Recent studies have shown how data-driven instructions can enable real-time detection of learning gaps and generate appropriate proactive, rather than reactive, responses from teachers [45]. This proactive approach fosters a personalized learning pathway for the learner [46].

2.2.5.2 Application in personalized learning

Data-driven personalized learning platforms such as DreamBox Learning, Knewton Alta, Squirrel AI, and CENTURY Tech provide customized learning pathways, monitor engagement, and enable real-time assessment [47–50]. By leveraging data analytics to customize instruction, schools can demonstrate improved learning gains at a rate 1.5 times the national average, as found in a review of personalized learning models funded by the Bill & Melinda Gates Foundation [44]. When analytical tools are integrated into learning platforms, students can receive alerts, personalized feedback, and motivational messages that enable them to engage more with their learning [51]. Data-driven learning systems like DreamBox Learning identify learning gaps in specific demographic sections and help deliver personalized and customized learning solutions [52].

Other platforms, like Knewton Alta, deliver STEM content based on a system of continuously updating learner profiles in real time [49]. Similarly, Squirrel AI in China uses deep learning to provide microlevel personalization for students and enables real-time feedback based on adaptive instructional design [50, 53].

CENTURY Tech (a UK-based platform utilizing machine learning applications that help generate dynamic learner profiles and diagnostics for students and teachers) reduces teacher planning time by 30% and increases student content mastery by up to 20% over a term across secondary schools in the UK [47].

3. Key dimensions of AI-supported personalized learning

3.1 Supporting learner engagement and motivation through AI

AI enhances personalized learning through several mechanisms, predominantly by focusing on a learning-centric model that keeps the focus on the learning abilities, motivations, intelligence type, and autonomy of the learner [4]. This is achieved by accessing and analyzing historical usage data to predict outcomes and deliver appropriate interventions to students using predictive analytics. AI models use natural language processing (NLP) to facilitate learners' interactive experiences through chatbots that provide on-demand assistance or questions that align with the learners' current learning. Additionally, AI-underpinned content recommendations customize the learning path using an algorithm to guide decision-making, as seen in Khan Academy learning systems. These AI tools not only deliver personalized learning but also provide feedback and present choices to learners, which enhances their sense of autonomy and competency and keeps them motivated [54]. By designing learning modules supported by theories like SDT, delivering intrinsic motivations, and providing appreciation, points, or token rewards, these AI-enabled learning tools enhance students' learning by utilizing their psychological inclinations. Additionally, using predictive analytics, it is possible to assess any increasing frustration levels, which can then trigger the system to adapt to less challenging tasks, thus enabling the students to continue learning [55].

3.2 Personalization through learner-centric instructional design

A key concept in personalized learning is the adoption of learner-centric models underpinned by theories of constructionism, which focus on students' interests and learning styles, enabling greater engagement [56, 57]. Several studies have already linked personalized learning environments to higher engagement and retention rates. For example, a study by the RAND Corporation reported that students who engaged in personalized learning gained approximately three percentile points in mathematics and four percentile points in reading compared to those who engaged in traditional learning [58]. Personalization is made possible by aligning pedagogy with individual learner needs and preferences and encouraging their ownership and choice. Learner profiling tools that are available on emerging digital platforms enable this integration, help in identifying the students' strengths, goals, and interests, and assist in relevant content delivery and assessment [59].

3.3 Adaptive systems for real-time instructional support

The key focus of personalized learning is to continually adapt to a learner's performance, offer differentiated support, and foster confidence and academic growth [60]. Adaptive learning technologies enable the customization of learning by collecting, analyzing, and using students' learning activity and interaction with material to develop an understanding of their preferences, strengths, and patterns [61]. Using these insights, tailored learning pathways are generated to address students' learning gaps in real-time, enabling targeted and focused learning with an adequate challenge level for students, keeping them motivated without frustration [62, 63]. More recent developments in adaptive systems encourage learner modeling, where AI can construct a student's profile and provide affective support to encourage self-reflection and goal setting [64]. For instance, DreamBox Learning utilizes an adaptive math program for K–8 students, and it has been found that students who used DreamBox for at least 14 hours showed significant improvement in math proficiency [48].

3.4 Using data-driven insights for instructional decision making

Personalized learning using AI is based on data-driven instructional strategies. Not only are students provided with customized education, but even educators can obtain insights about students' learning trajectories using multiple reports generated by AI from assessments, engagement metrics, and behavioral patterns. These insights help identify if a student is struggling, disengaging, or performing well, enabling timely interventions and tailored support. In some cases, the data-driven instructional design and assessment insights are found to lead to a 5% increase in graduation rates at Western Governors University in Utah [65]. Moreover, such systems track progress over time and can showcase long-term trends that can potentially be used for improving curricula and planning instructions. By employing formative analytics, teachers can adapt their instructions in real time based on data collected from students [46]. Based on the performance level as well as learning preferences, students' learning can be adjusted accordingly, and teachers can proactively prevent disengagement and frustration among students [45, 66].

3.5 Enhancing self-regulated learning through feedback mechanisms

Continuous feedback is a critical component of personalized learning. With AI systems, students can obtain instantaneous feedback and make amendments. AI-powered feedback systems, such as intelligent tutoring systems (ITS) and automated writing evaluators, support learning and encourage independent learning habits where students can align their goals, stay motivated, and improve by following the feedback received [67]. According to a study published in Frontiers in Psychology, feedback has a significant positive effect on student learning outcomes, reinforcement of correct understanding, and self-improvement [68]. Moreover, students are likely to develop a habit of revision based on feedback. In addition, the autogenerated nature of feedback reduces reliance on delayed teacher evaluation and facilitates autonomy and engagement. Self-regulation is fostered by these systems and empowers students to actively participate in goal setting, monitoring their strategies, and pacing themselves [4]. It also strengthens learned metacognition by helping them understand and reflect on their errors, identify strengths, and move toward the next levels of learning.

4. AI technologies for personalized learning

4.1 Intelligent tutoring systems (ITS)

AI-driven ITS emulate human tutors by displaying the ability to guide and adapt. By taking into consideration the real-time responses of the students and identifying their cognitive patterns, these systems tailor instruction suited to the learner. ITS also delivers personalized feedback and learning material, which enables personalized learning solutions. For example, the Korbit platform, which is used for data science studies, uses ML and NLP to deliver adaptive tutorials and has been found to lead to learning gains of 2–2.5 times higher than those of students in traditional MOOCs [66]. ITS stimulates an interactive tutoring experience to foster a sense of autonomy and paced progression, which are essential for personalized learning.

Carnegie Learning's MATHia platform is another ITS that has been implemented across several US school districts. In a randomized controlled study, it was found that middle school students using MATHia achieved gains two to three times higher than those students working with standard instruction [69]. The real-time adaptation and data-rich learning experience enable personalized learning at scale [70].

4.2 Recommender systems for learning pathways

Recommender systems in education are used to suggest learning pathways and resources that are aligned with the learner's performance and take into account their preferences and educational goals. Recommender systems use ML techniques like content-based algorithms and collaborative filtering, which create tailored learning pathways for students and lead to high recall rates, accurate understanding, enhanced engagement, and course completion [71]. Coursera data suggests that their AI-driven recommender engine, which provided personalized suggestions based on past behavior and user profiles, resulted in an increase in performance, achieving precision: 0.98%, recall: 1.00, F1 score: ≈0.99%, and accuracy: 0.98% [72]. Coursera's recommender system analyzes users' behaviors and performance, and detects skill gaps and goals to align with suitable recommendations. The recommender systems typically use dynamic profiling of users, which is based on behavior and performance data, to assess needs across diverse segments of users [73].

4.3 Emotion-aware and affective computing tools

Affective computing technologies (ACT) are built to detect and respond to learners' emotional states while delivering customized instructions. Adapting content delivery is made possible by the inclusion of biometric sensors or physical analytics based on facial recognition or the assessment of voice modulation, and it leads to learner engagement and well-being. ACTs use convolutional neural networks that enable the detection of learners' affective states like confusion, interest, or boredom, which then trigger suitable adaptive pedagogical responses like a change in the pace of instructions, reduction in cognitive overload, and delivery of motivational prompts [74]. The real-time emotion-based feedback provided by affective systems has been found to increase students' persistence by over 30%, especially among students who have prior records of exhibiting low performance [75].

4.4 Real-time assessment and feedback mechanisms

Real-time assessment and feedback mechanics evaluate user performance continuously and provide immediate feedback and adjustment of instructions, enabling early intervention. Platforms like Amira Learning assess students' oral reading skills and provide instant personalized help. Amira's learning analytics data indicate that students using the platform improve in proficiency over a short period of time, with significant benefits for learners with dyslexia [76]. Similarly, students using the Eedi platform in the UK, which uses real-time diagnosis and AI analytics to provide instant feedback to learners, experience improved math concept retention by 22% over a period of five weeks [77].

AI technologies are transforming personalized learning by delivering adaptive, data-driven, and emotion-informed learning experiences. ITS can emulate human tutors, while recommender systems, like those used by Coursera, empower users to fill their skill gaps. Affective computing tools recognize emotional states and enable resilience and persistence in learning. Similarly, real-time assessment platforms deliver instant feedback, enabling early intervention and improvement.

5. Implications of AI-driven personalized learning

5.1 Ethical and equity considerations in AI-powered personalization

With the rapid evolution and deployment of AI in education, there are growing concerns about the ethical usage of learner data and algorithm bias that could lead to educational disparities. If AI systems are trained on biased or incomplete datasets, there is an increased risk of discrimination against certain societal sections, leading to the reinforcement of existing educational discrimination [70, 78]. Additionally, as most AI-led educational platforms operate within what is called a black-box due to the lack of understanding of their functionality, there is an inherent lack of transparency in algorithm-led decision-making. This may lead to potential confusion or a lack of acceptance regarding the way content is presented or paced for certain learners. As such, integrations of AI in learning modules need to be audited for bias and must follow ethical and regulatory frameworks. In recent years, there has been a growing deployment of explainable AI, or XAI, which allows for more transparency in content recommendations and shows learners why certain pathways were opened for them [55].

5.2 Human-AI collaboration in personalized learning environments

With all the benefits of AI in the personalization of learning, the human element continues to be critical. Teachers are required to interpret and make sense of the AI-generated insights, especially as learners may be subjected to algorithmic bias and may not obtain the correct information. Teachers are needed for contextual learning within the academic, social, or cultural frameworks [7]. The role of a teacher as a mentor offering knowledge and insights, but also emotional support and motivation, cannot be understated. As such, AI-led personalization needs to take into account the expertise of teachers and should not be viewed as a replacement but rather as an augmentation of that expertise. By enabling teachers to provide insights and context within the framework of personalized learning, it is possible to blend automation and personalization and deliver better value to learners.

5.3 Pedagogical implications of AI-based personalized learning

The integration of AI in personalized learning leads to a pedagogical shift, reframing the roles of teachers, learners, and instructional strategies. One key implication is the transition from content delivery to facilitation. With AI systems offering real-time feedback, content recommendations, and adaptive sequencing, educators are increasingly positioned as orchestrators of learning rather than traditional teachers. Teachers must now engage in dynamic instructional decision-making, often in response to algorithmic insights [14]. For instance, AI-powered dashboards allow educators to identify disengagement or learning gaps early, enabling timely scaffolding or intervention. This shifts the pedagogical emphasis from reactive remediation to proactive guidance. Moreover, the use of AI tools enables teachers to interact with both formative and summative analytics for grading, feedback, and lesson planning. However, these changes also present challenges. If AI recommendations are treated as authoritative rather than contextual, it may lead to incoherence. Teachers must be trained in using AI tools but also learn to critically evaluate their output [13]. Finally, algorithms may not fully account for linguistic, cultural, or neurodiverse learning preferences unless guided by a teacher's contextual understanding.

6. Implementation in practice: Global case studies

6.1 Case study 1: Summit Public Schools – California's personalized learning pioneer

SPS is a network of charter schools spanning the states of Washington and California that introduced a PLP, which is delivered through a platform that tracks students' learning goals, performance, and assessments [18]. There are separate dashboards for students, parents, and teachers, which allow for shared accountability and a culture of transparency. Teachers at SPS are able to use data analytics to assess students' progress and customize content that targets the development of students' cognitive skills and understanding of concepts, rather than just the completion of the syllabus or the attainment of grades [18]. The platform also has provisions for mentors who can review and guide the students. By placing the student at the center and allowing them to set their own learning goals, select assignments that they are interested in, and learn at a pace that is comfortable for them, PLP is one of the leading programs in personalized learning [79]. Summit's model has been found to lead to improvements in critical thinking skills, problem-solving skills, and student engagement and motivation [69].

6.2 Case study 2: Carnegie learning – AI-powered math instruction

Carnegie Learning's AI-driven Cognitive Tutor for Algebra I is an ITS that uses students' responses to diagnose and explain misconceptions, dynamically changing their task sequencing and difficulty levels. It mirrors expert tutors, follows their cognitive processes, and has been found to improve mathematics performance by eight percentile points for high school students. It has also been recognized by the US Department of Education for meeting educational standards [80]. Students in the second year, however, seemed to have shown more significant gains (an eight percentile increase) than in the first year [59].

Additionally, Carnegie Learning's MATHia platform (available for middle and high school students in several US school districts) is based on a composite metric, Adaptive Personalized Learning Score (APLSE), that tracks students' mastery level, effort, and time-on-task. It was found from school data from Illinois, Ohio, South Carolina, and Washington State that a 10-point increase in APLSE score results in a 0.13–0.55 standard deviation boost in standardized math tests, or about 4–17 point gains in standard assessments [81, 82]. Furthermore, an increase of 400% in passing rates in math exams was observed over three years across Brockton, Massachusetts, districts using MATHia [83].

6.3 Case study 3: Squirrel AI – personalized learning at scale in China

Squirrel AI is a Chinese edtech company that uses an adaptive learning platform based on a knowledge graph system [84]. Squirrel AI breaks down subjects into microconcepts for easy understanding. It uses dynamic profiling of learners by collecting data from millions of data points and predicts knowledge gaps that can be filled with personalized instructions and content. Squirrel AI is unlike teacher-led teaching, as it uses an automated system to assess, teach, and track progress. Currently, the system is adopted in over 3,000 learning centers across China and serves 24 million students [85]. Research has indicated tangible benefits of Squirrel AI over traditional classroom-based instruction [50, 53]. The company claims nearly five to ten times improvement in learning efficiency over traditional methods [85].

6.4 Case study 4: David game college – Chatgpt and AI tutoring in the UK

In a first-of-its-kind model, David Game College, London, introduced a "teacherless" classroom for 20 GCSE students [86]. The students had access to AI tools for subjects like mathematics, English, science, and computer science, and were supported by three learning coaches. The students had access to personalized learning pathways that enabled them to revisit complex topics repeatedly and obtain feedback in real time. In this manner, students' knowledge gaps were identified and filled with deeper conceptual understanding [87]. David Game College offers a unique model where AI-human coaches complement each other to deliver targeted and personalized learning experiences. However, the costs per student for this program neared £27,000 per year, which is cited as a limitation to the program's scalability [87].

7. Insights and practical takeaways from global implementations

The case studies and literature presented in this chapter offer essential takeaways for educators and policymakers who seek to fully harness the potential of AI technology for personalized learning.

7.1 AI-supported personalization drives engagement and autonomy

A pattern that is unmistakable in personalized learning, across diverse contexts like China's Squirrel AI to the David Game College model, is that it boosts student motivation and engagement and results in tangible academic outcomes. This is because AI-supported learning platforms successfully align learning pathways with students' cognitive strengths and pace. The adaptive content delivery, combined with real-time feedback, empowers students with autonomy and improves confidence and well-being.

7.2 Scale is feasible with the right infrastructure

As seen in the case of China's Squirrel A, which is serving millions of students, it is possible to make scalable, personalized learning models. With robust digital infrastructure and data systems, such scalability is attainable but needs to be combined with relevant, expert-supported content recommendation and performance metric tools.

7.3 Human-AI synergy is essential

While AI provides unprecedented advantages in personalized learning, it is best harnessed when combined with experts' and educators' intervention, as seen in the hybrid learning model adopted by David Game College. AI tools must be complemented with human empathy, expert insights on pedagogy, and mentorship in education for the best outcomes for students.

7.4 Data is the engine of personalization

AI platforms like MATHia, Coursera's recommender engine, and others collect and collate large amounts of data for analysis, enabling them to deliver relevant recommendations for learning pathways and filling knowledge gaps. AI-supported personalization in learning, therefore, must prioritize investment in data systems that are interoperable and enable data collection at diverse points.

7.5 Training and capacity building are critical

There is a need for onboarding teachers not just on the technical operations but also to include a pedagogical understanding of how AI-supported personalization is derived. Educators need to learn to interpret data, adjust intervention strategies, and provide motivational support and guidance to students.

7.6 Ethics must guide AI deployment in education

Ethical concerns around issues of privacy and consent, discrimination and algorithm bias, and transparency need to be addressed and embedded in all stages of AI-supported personalization in education. Ethics should be made integral right from the stage of data collection to model design and instructional deployment. All AI-supported personalization needs to ensure the core values of equity, fairness, and respect for student agency.

8. Future trends: Virtual and augmented reality

The next frontier in AI-supported personalization lies in immersive technologies like virtual reality (VR), augmented reality (AR), or extended reality (XR).

8.1 Immersive and experiential learning

VR and AR enable immersive environments to allow students to engage in simulated real-world or abstract scenarios [88]. For example, VR can take students inside the human circulatory system or give them a glimpse of the ruins of ancient Rome, providing memorable experiential learning unmatched by videos or books [89]. AR overlays interactive content onto the physical world, which gives a sense of control to learners by allowing them to manipulate virtual models in space, enabling better retention and conceptual understanding [89, 90]. The VictoryXR platform is now available to over 100 colleges across the world and allows students to experiment with and explore 3D models [91]. zSpace is another tool that helps K-12 students virtually dissect frogs or explore science concepts in simulations using AR and zSpace [92].

8.2 AI + XR: Intelligent personalization in 3D worlds

Personalization of learning is taken to the next level with the convergence of AI and XR technologies. AI can personalize VR/AR experiences by adapting learning paths within immersive environments based on student performance and interaction data. AI-powered virtual chemistry labs that include XR can adjust the complexity of experiments to match the learners' level. Similarly, affective AI systems using facial expression analysis, gaze tracking, and motion data, which are used in VR, can offer accurate and relevant motivational or corrective interventions in real-time. An example is AI–VR tutors, which deliver content based on an analysis of the learners' responses and guide them on 3D tasks [93]. Furthermore, such AI–XR platforms can also enable collaborative learning with team-based challenges [94].

8.3 Future applications and challenges

XR technologies, comprising VR, AR, and mixed reality (MR), reshape the educational landscape and hold immense potential for vocational training, special education, and STEM education [95]. XR technologies can create safe, simulated environments for practicing high-risk procedures, such as surgeries or flight simulations. In special education, AR applications can provide social cues to children with autism [95]. Student engagement can be enhanced for engineering and technical education programs using XR modules [96]. These future applications may be challenging to implement due to high costs, limitations of bandwidth, lack of user training, access to devices and networks, and lack of scalability in adoption. XR is likely to be driven by the integration of AI, IoT (Internet of Things), and multimodal interfaces that enable personalized learning [97]. Nevertheless, policymakers, technology developers, and educators need to ensure equitable and ethical access for successful operations in immersive environments [96].

8.4 Research and innovation directions

There are several studies currently underway, like the one by Stanford University's Virtual Human Interaction Lab (VHIL), that are focused on understanding how VR shapes learning, empathy, and social understanding [97].

Similarly, UNESCO's Future of Learning initiative has started a global dialogue on ethical frameworks for XR technologies [96]. Some insights have emerged from pilot studies on frequent usage of VR environments by students of biology, which have found that VR environments lead to stronger engagement (1–1.5 times) and student motivation as compared to traditional learning over the longer term [94]. AR applications, too, have shown gains in memory retention ranging from 7–21% when compared to non-AR instruction [3, 94].

9. Summary

This chapter explored AI-enabled personalized learning in modern education. It introduced personalized learning and its historical background and outlined the five core objectives as: exploring the AI-supported personalization frameworks, identifying the key functions and tools used, exploring its implications, and showcasing implementation models leading to insights on success factors. The fundamental factors and theoretical underpinnings – constructivism, multiple intelligences, SDT, connectivism, and data-driven decision-making — and their contribution to AI-led personalized education systems at SPS, ViLLE, SLS Singapore, and others are discussed. AI tools are discussed as enablers of engagement, autonomy, and self-regulation through theory-based approaches.

The chapter also discusses key dimensions of AI-supported personalized learning in the form of learner engagement, motivation, learner-centric instructional design, data-driven real-time adaptive content delivery, and feedback supporting self-regulated learning. Further, ITS (e.g., MATHia, Korbit), recommender systems (e.g., Coursera), affective computing, and real-time feedback tools (e.g., Amira, Eedi) are discussed to demonstrate how they lead to measurable gains in academic performance and student well-being.

SPS, Carnegie Learning, Squirrel AI in China, and David Game College in the UK are used as case studies to illustrate scalable deployment, provide insights, and takeaways. The key learnings are identified as follows: AI improves engagement, it can be deployed at scale, data is the core aspect of AI-led personalization, human-AI synergy is essential, and ethics must guide deployment. Future trends, particularly AI-powered XR (VR and AR) in STEM, vocational training, and special education, are also discussed.

Author details

S.M.F.D. Syed Mustapha
Zayed University, Dubai, UAE

*Address all correspondence to: syed.duani@zu.ac.ae

References

[1] Alamri HA, Lowell VL, Watson W, Watson S. Using personalized learning as an instructional approach to motivate learners in online higher education: Learner self-determination and intrinsic motivation. Journal of Research on Technology in Education. 2020;**52**(3):322–352. DOI: 10.1080/15391523.2020.1728449

[2] Keller FS. Ten years of personalized instruction. Teaching of Psychology. 1974;**1**(1):4–9

[3] Syed Mustapha SMFD. Predictive analysis of students' learning performance using data mining techniques: A comparative study of feature selection methods. Applied System Innovation. 2023;**6**(5):86. DOI: 10.3390/asi6050086

[4] Artino Jr AR, Simons RJ, Konopasky A. Self-regulated Learning. In an Introduction to Medical Teaching: The Foundations of Curriculum Design, Delivery, and Assessment. Cham: Springer International Publishing; 2022. p. 25–43

[5] Sajja R, Sermet Y, Cikmaz M, Cwiertny D, Demir I. Artificial intelligence-enabled intelligent assistant for personalized and adaptive learning in higher education. Information. 2024;**15**(10):596

[6] Maulana R, Helms-Lorenz M, Irnidayanti Y, van de Grift W. Autonomous motivation in the Indonesian classroom: Relationship with teacher support through the lens of self-determination theory. The Asia-Pacific Education Researcher. 2016;**25**(3):441–451. DOI: 10.1007/S40299-016-0282-5

[7] Luckin R. Machine Learning and Human Intelligence. The Future of Education for the 21st Century. London: UCL institute of education press; 2018. p. 5–100

[8] Garrett N, Beard N, Fiesler C More than" if time allows": The role of ethics in AI education. In: Proceedings of the AAAI/ACM Conference on AI, Ethics, and Society. 2020. pp. 272–278

[9] Porayska-Pomsta K, Holmes W, Nemorin S. The ethics of AI in education. In: Handbook of Artificial Intelligence in Education. Cheltenham, UK: Edward Elgar Publishing; 2023. p. 571–604

[10] Piaget J. The Psychology of the Child. New York: Basic Books; 1972

[11] Vygotsky LS. Mind in Society: The Development of Higher Psychological Processes. Cambridge, MA: Harvard University Press; 1978

[12] Tan C, and S NC. Constructivism in education. In: Nobit, GN. Oxford Research Encyclopedia of Education. Oxford: Oxford University Press; 2023. p. 10–31. DOI: 10.1093/acrefore/9780190264093.013.92

[13] Sun X. A constructive and empirical study of personalized teaching quality evaluation for elementary school english teachers. Applied Mathematics and Nonlinear Sciences. 2025;**10**. https://sciendo.com/article/10.2478/amns-2025-0748

[14] Vorobyeva KI, Belous S, Savchenko NV, Smirnova LM, Nikitina SA, Zhdanov SP. Personalized learning through AI. Pedagogical

Approaches. 2025;**17**(2):ep574. DOI: 10.30935/cedtech/16108

[15] Holmes W, Bialik M, and Fadel C. Artificial Intelligence in Education: Promises and Implications for Teaching and Learning. London, UK: Center for Curriculum Redesign, University College London Press; 2019

[16] Pham XL, Nguyen DT, Nguye LTH, Nguyen THC, Tran TMD.A constructivist based interactive learning management system leveraging google codelabs. Interactive Learning Environments. 2025;**33**(1):1–19

[17] Guo H, Yi W, Liu K Enhancing constructivist learning: The role of generative AI in personalised learning experiences. In: Proceedings of the 26th International Conference on Enterprise Information Systems. 2024. (pp. 767–770). SCITEPRESS-Science and Technology Publications

[18] Summit Public School. The Summit Model [Internet]. 2025. Available from: https://summitps.org/the-summit-model/ [Accessed: 2025-July-25]

[19] Murphy R, Gallagher L, Krumm AE, Mislevy J, Hafter A Lessons from the field: Summit public schools' personalized learning program. RAND Corporation. [Internet]. 2017. Available from: https://www.rand.org/pubs/research_reports/RR1365.html [Accessed: 2025-July-25]

[20] Pandya B, Cho B, Patterson L, Abaker M. Impact of connectivism on knowledge and willingness of students in higher education. Journal of Management Education. 2024;**48**(5):887–914

[21] Do HN, Do BN, Nguyen MH. How do constructivist learning environments generate better motivation and learning strategies?. Heliyon. 2023;**9**(12): 201–228

[22] Marienko M, Nosenko Y, and Shyshkina M. Personalization of learning using adaptive technologies and augmented reality. 2020. arXiv preprint arXiv:2011.05802. https://arxiv.org/abs/2011.05802 [Accessed: 2025-July-25]

[23] Gardner H. Intelligence Reframed: Multiple Intelligences for the 21st Century. New York, NY: Basic Books; 1999

[24] Pepkolaj L, Dhimitri J, Karaguni M. The role of technology in supporting multiple intelligences for collaborative and personalized learning: Insights from Albanian teachers. The Science Heritage. 2025;**156**:3–12. DOI: 10.5281/zenodo.14997929

[25] Yavich R, Rotnitsky I. Multiple intelligences and success in school studies. International Journal of Higher Education. 2020;**9**(6):107–117

[26] İnce EY, İnce M. 2022. Automatic e-content sequencing system for personalized learning environments by using fuzzy AHP based on multiple intelligences. Journal of Information Science. **47**(6):821–837. DOI: 10.1177/01655515211041333

[27] Kornhaber ML, Fierros EG, Veenema SA. Multiple Intelligences: Best Ideas from Research and Practice. Boston, MA: Pearson Education; 2004

[28] Willingham DT Reframing the mind. Education Next. [Internet]. 2025. Available from: https://www.educationnext.org/reframing-the-mind/?utm_source=chatgpt.com [Accessed: 2025-July-25]

[29] Hairudin SN, Ariffin K, Ibrahim MNA, De Mello G, Husin MS, Nur Hidayatulshima NHO, Ishak N. Effectiveness of integrating multiple intelligence theory in english teaching and learning: A systematic literature review. Asian Journal of University Education. 2023;**19**(4): 717–727

[30] Deci EL, Ryan RM.The "what" and "why" of goal pursuits: Human needs and the self-determination of behavior. Psychological Inquiry. 2000; **11**(4):227–268

[31] Vansteenkist M, Aelterman N, De Muynck GJ, Haerens L, Patall EA, Reeve J. Fostering personal meaning and self-relevance: A Self-Determination Theory perspective on internalization. The Journal of Experimental Education. 2018;**86**(1):30–49. DOI: 10.1080/00220973.2017.1381067

[32] Turner K. One-to-one learning and self-determination theory. International Journal of Instruction. 2019;**12**(2):1–16

[33] Jeno LM, Adachi PJC, Grytnes JA, Vandvik V, Deci EL. The effects of m-learning on motivation, achievement, and well-being: A self-determination theory approach. British Journal of Educational Technology. 2019;**50**(2):669–683

[34] Jeno LM, Vandvik V, Eliassen S, Grytnes JA. Testing the novelty effect of an m-learning tool on internalization and achievement: A self-determination theory approach. Computers & Education. 2019;**128**:398–413. DOI: 10.1016/j.compedu.2018.10.008

[35] Downes S. Connectivism. Asian Journal of Distance Education. 2022;**17** (1):58–87

[36] Czerkawski BC, Lyman EW. 2020. An instructional design framework for fostering student engagement in online learning environments. TechTrends. **64**(4):514–523. DOI: 10.1007/s11528-016-0110-z

[37] Alam MA. Connectivism and traditional learning theories: Implications for contemporary educational and pedagogical practices. Bhartiyam International Journal of Education & Research. 2024;**14**(1): 11–24

[38] Goldie JGS. Connectivism: A knowledge learning theory for the digital age?. Medical Teacher. 2016;**38** (10):1064–1069. DOI: 10.3109/0142159X.2016.1173661

[39] U.S. Department of Education. Personalized learning in progress: Case studies of four race to the top-district grantees' early implementation. U.S. Department of Education. [Internet]. 2015. Available from: https://library.educause.edu/search#?contentTypeDisplay=Briefs,%20Case%20Studies,%20Papers,%20Reports [Accessed: 2025-July-25]

[40] Lacka E, Wong TC, Haddoud MY. Can digital technologies improve students' efficiency? Exploring the role of virtual learning environment and social media use in higher education. Computers & Education. 2021;**163**:104099

[41] Malmi L, Hellas A, Ihantola P, Isomöttönen V, Jormanainen I, Kilamo T, Suhonen J. Computing Education Research in Finland. Past, Present, and Future of Computing Education Research: A Global Perspective. Cham: Springer International Publishing; 2023. p. 335–372

[42] Lee AVY, Koh E, Looi CK. 2023. AI in education and learning analytics initiatives in Singapore: Overview of key projects. Information and Technology in Education and Learning. **3**(1):110. DOI: 10.12937/itel.3.1.Inv.p001

[43] Hardof-Jaffe S, Peled RA connectivism-based learning model for special education teachers' training. In: society for information technology & teacher education international conference. 2022. pp. 1710–1718. Association for the Advancement of Computing in Education (AACE)

[44] Lee S. 7 key benefits of data-driven instruction in modern education. Number Analytics. [Internet]. 2025. Available from: https://www.numberanalytics.com/blog/7-key-benefits-of-data-driven-instruction-modern-education [Accessed: 2025-July-25]

[45] der Kleij Fm V, Vermeulen JA, Schildkamp K, Eggen TJ. Integrating data-based decision making, assessment for learning, and diagnostic testing in formative assessment. Assessment in Education: Principles, Policy & Practice. 2015;**22**(3):324–343

[46] Ifenthaler D, Yau JYK. Utilising learning analytics to support study success in higher education: A systematic review. Educational Technology Research and Development. 2020;**68**(4):1961–1990

[47] CENTURY. How CENTURY impacts learning: A research summary. CENTURY Tech. [Internet] 2023. Available from: https://www.century.tech/impact/ [Accessed: 2025-July-25]

[48] Ivanović M, Klašnja-Milićević A, Paprzycki M, Ganzha M, Bădică C, Bădică A, Jain LC. Current trends in AI-based educational processes—An overview. In: Ivanović, M, Klašnja-Milićević, A, Jain, LC. Handbook on Intelligent Techniques in the Educational Process: Vol 1 Recent Advances and Case Studies. NY: Springer; 2022. p. 1–5

[49] Kohnke S, Zaugg T. Artificial intelligence: An untapped opportunity for equity and access in STEM education. Education Sciences. 2025;**15**(1):68

[50] Zhang X How Squirrel AI is personalizing learning for millions in China. World Economic Forum [Internet]. 2020. Available from: https://www.weforum.org/organizations/squirrel-ai-learning/ [Accessed: 2025-July-25]

[51] Slade S, Prinsloo P, Khalil M. Learning analytics at the intersections of student trust, disclosure, and benefit. In: *Proceedings of the 9th international conference on learning analytics & knowledge*. March 2019. p. 235–244. DOI: 10.1145/3303772.3303796

[52] Montgomery B.Harvard finds that dreambox learning improves math test scores. EdSurge. [Internet]. 2022. Available from: https://www.edsurge.com/news/2016-06-06-harvard-finds-that-dreambox-s-adaptive-tool-improves-math-test-scores [Accessed: 2025-July-25]

[53] Zhang Y. Machine learning-based personalized learning path decision-making method on intelligent education platforms. International Journal of Interactive Mobile Technologies. 2024;**18**(16):12–13

[54] Pawar PB. AI-Enhanced education: Personalized learning and educational technology. In: Meeran, JA. Fusion of

Knowledge. India: Red Shine Publications Private Ltd; 2023. p. 1–8

[55] Holstein K, Wortman Vaughan J, Aleven V. Student–AI collaboration: How teachers and intelligent tutoring systems co-orchestrate learning. Proceedings of the ACM on Human-Computer Interaction. 2020a;**4** (CSCW2):1–25

[56] Bernacki ML, Greene MJ, Lobczowski NG. A systematic review of research on personalized learning: Personalized by whom, to what, how, and for what purpose (s)?. Educational Psychology Review. 2021;**33**(4):1675–1715

[57] Bray B, McClaskey K. How to Personalize Learning: A Practical Guide for Getting Started and Going Deeper. California: Corwin Press; 2016. p. 1–181

[58] Pane JF, Steiner ED, Baird MD, Hamilton LS. Continued Progress: Promising Evidence on Personalized Learning. Santa Monica, CA: Rand Corporation; 2015. https://www.rand.org/pubs/research_reports/RR1365.html. [Accessed: 2025-July-25]

[59] Walkington C, Bernacki ML. Personalization of instruction: Design dimensions and implications for cognition. Journal of Experimental Education. 2018;**86**(1):50–68

[60] Goyibova N, Muslimov N, Sabirova G, Kadirova N, Samatova B. Differentiation approach in education: Tailoring instruction for diverse learner needs. MethodsX. 2025;**14**:103163

[61] Kruger D. Adaptive learning technology to enhance self-directed learning. In: Self-directed Multi-modal Learning in Higher Education (NWU Self-directed Learning Series). Vol. 5 Cape Town: AOSIS; 2020. p. 93–116

[62] Angeioplastis A, Aliprantis J, Konstantakis M, Tsimpiris A. Predicting student performance and enhancing learning outcomes: A data-driven approach using educational data mining techniques. Computers. 2025;**14**(3):83

[63] Shute VJ, Zapata-Rivera D. Adaptive educational systems. Adaptive Technologies for Training and Education. 2012;**7**(27):1–35

[64] Aleven V, McLaughlin EA, Glenn R, Koedinger KR. Instruction Based on Adaptive Learning Technologies. Handbook of Research on Learning and Instruction. 2nd ed. UK: Routledge; 2016. p. 522–560

[65] Brasca C, Kaithwal N, Krishnan C, Lam M, Law J, Marya V Using Machine learning to improve student success in higher education. McKinsey & Company [Internet]. 2022. Available from: https://www.mckinsey.com/industries/education/our-insights/using-machine-learning-to-improve-student-success-in-higher-education [Accessed: 2025-July-25]

[66] St-Hilaire F, Vu DD, Frau A, Burns N, Faraji F, Potochny J, Kochmar E. A new era: Intelligent tutoring systems will transform online learning for millions. 2022. https://arxiv.org/abs/2203.03724 arXiv:2203.03724 [Accessed: 2025-July-25]

[67] Pander E, Lipnevich A. A review of feedback models and typologies: Towards an integrative model of feedback elements. Educational Research Review. 2021;**35**(1):100416

[68] Wisniewski B, Zierer K, Hattie J. The power of feedback revisited: A meta-analysis of educational feedback

research. Frontiers in Psychology. 2020;**10**:487662

[69] Pane JF, Griffin BA, McCaffrey DF, Karam R. Effectiveness of cognitive tutor algebra I at scale. Educational Evaluation and Policy Analysis. 2017;**36**(2):127–144

[70] Khachatryan D, Parise S. Teaching real-time object detection with an emphasis on engagement and inclusiveness. Communications of the Association for Information Systems. 2025;**56**(1):26

[71] Urdaneta-Ponte MC, Mendez-Zorrilla A, Oleagordia-Ruiz I. Recommendation systems for education: Systematic review. Electronics. 2021;**10**(14):1611

[72] Mustafa DJ, and Zeebare SRM. Optimizing online educational experiences through semantic ontology-based recommender systems: A case study on coursera. International Journal of Computational and Experimental Science and Engineering. 2025;**11**(3):5142–5152. DOI: 10.9734/ajrcos/2025/v18i10774

[73] Uddin I, Imran AS, Muhammad K, Fayyaz N, Sajjad M. A systematic mapping review on MOOC recommender systems. IEEE Access. 2021;**9**:118379–118405

[74] Feidakis M. A Review of Emotion-aware Systems for E-learning in Virtual Environments. Formative Assessment, Learning Data Analytics, and Gamification in ICT Education. USA: Academic Press; 2016. p. 217–242

[75] D'Mello SK. Graesser A.Intelligent tutoring systems: How computers achieve learning gains that rival human tutors. In: Paul, Schutz, A., and Krista, Muis, R. Handbook of Educational Psychology. UK: Routledge; 2023. p. 603–629

[76] Carby N. Personalized feedback in a virtual learning environment. Journal of Educational Supervision. 2023;**6**(1):36

[77] Nesta. Unlocking personalized maths learning with Eedi. [Internet]. 2022. Available from: https://www.nesta.org.uk/search/?search=Unlocking+personalized+maths+learning+with+Eedi [Accessed: 2025-July-25]

[78] Pessach D, Shmueli E. A review of fairness in machine learning. ACM Computing Surveys. 2022;**55**(3):1–44

[79] Cowart E. Implementation of personalized learning in a new charter school. Journal for Undergraduate Ethnography. 2021;**11**(3):21–35

[80] Ritter S, Anderson JR, Koedinger KR, Corbett A. Cognitive tutor: Applied research in mathematics education. Psychonomic Bulletin & Review. 2007;**14**(2):249–255

[81] Carnegie Learning. MATHia® performance & end-of-year test scores: A school district in Washington (2021–2022) [Internet]. 2024. Available from: https://discover.carnegielearning.com/hubfs/PDFs/Misc%20PDFs/2024-MATHia-Data-Review-WA-One-Pager.pdf? [Accessed: 2025-July-25]

[82] Carnegie Learning, Inc. MATHia® data reviews white paper: Predictive insights based on APLSE scores [Internet]. 2024. Available from: https://discover.carnegielearning.com/hubfs/PDFs/Whitepaper%20and%20Guide%20PDFs/2024-MATHia-Data-Reviews-White-Paper.pdf? [Accessed: 2025-July-25]

[83] Learning C. 400% MCAS Growth: A Title I District's Success Story. [Internet]. 2025. Available from: https://www.carnegielearning.com/why-cl/case-studies/brockton-public-schools/? [Accessed: 2025-July-25]

[84] Dönmez E. The future of education: AI-supported reforms in the USA and China. In: Akgün, B, and Alpaydın, Y. Global Agendas and Education Reforms: A Comparative Study. Singapore: Springer Nature Singapore; 2024. p. 135–150

[85] Flannery R. Derek Li and Squirrel AI aim to lead the future of AI-driven education. Forbes China. [Internet]. 2025. Available from: https://www.forbes.com/sites/forbeschina/2025/02/18/derek-li-and-squirrel-ai-aim-to-lead-the-future-of-ai-driven-education/ [Accessed: 2025-July-25]

[86] Carroll M This high school is replacing teachers with ChatGPT and AI tools to personalize learning for some students. Business Insider [Internet]. 2024. Available from: https://www.businessinsider.com/chatgpt-ai-tools-replace-teachers-high-school-students-learning-education-2024-8 [Accessed: 2025-July-25]

[87] Kapoor A. UK's first AI classroom without teachers Sparks debate. Phys. org. [Internet]. 2025. Available from: https://phys.org/news/2025-01-uk-ai-classroom-teachers-debate.html [Accessed: 2025-July-25]

[88] Hite RL, Jones MG, Childers GM. Classifying and modeling secondary students' active learning in a virtual learning environment through generated questions. Computers & Education. 2024;**208**:104940

[89] Godoy M, Machado F, Vieira I, Mello R, Frizera A. Evaluating QoE in cloud-based virtual reality systems: A pilot study. In: 2024 Symposium on Internet of Things (SIoT). Vol. **1**. IEEE; 2024. p. 1–5

[90] Berenguer C, Baixauli I, Gómez S, Mdep A, De Stasio S. Exploring the impact of augmented reality in children and adolescents with autism spectrum disorder: A systematic review. International Journal of Environmental Research and Public Health. 2020;**17** (17):6143

[91] VictoryXR. VictoryXR and meta immersive learning launch digital twin metaversities. VictoryXR [Internet]. 2021. Available from: https://www.victoryxr.com/vxrmeta/ [Accessed: 2025-July-25]

[92] Ivanova B. Application of zSpace technology in the disciplines of the STEM cycle. Стратегии На Образователната И Научната Политика. 2024;**32**(5s):161–171

[93] Thandapani RKGR, Capel B, Lasnier A, Chatzigiannakis I. INTERACT: An authoring tool that facilitates the creation of human-centric interaction with 3d objects in virtual reality. In: Proceedings of the 25th International Conference on Mobile Human-Computer Interaction. September 2023; Sharm El-Sheikh, Egypt. p. 1–5

[94] Parong J, Mayer RE. Learning science in immersive virtual reality. Journal of Educational Psychology. 2018;**110**(6):785–797. DOI: 10.1037/edu0000241

[95] Alnagrat A, Ismail RC, Idrus SZ, Alfaqi RM. A review of extended reality (XR) technologies in the future of human education: Current trend and future opportunity. Journal of Human

Centered Technology. 2022;**1**(2):81–96. DOI: 10.11113/humentech.v1n2.27

[96] Jackson H, Thakur S, Olanrewaju OA. The potential of extended reality in engineering education: A systematic review. Cogent Education. 2025;**12** (1):1–21. DOI: 10.1080/2331186X.2025.2541442

[97] Zeng B. Recent advances and future directions in extended reality (XR): Exploring AI-powered spatial intelligence. arXiv preprint arXiv:2504.15970. 2025. https://arxiv.org/pdf/2504.15970

Chapter 15

Ethics of AI-Driven Personalization in Learning: Designing for Cognitive Diversity and Inclusive Intelligence

Ameed Inam

Abstract

This chapter critically examines the ethical implications of AI-driven personalization in education, focusing on its impact on learner agency, equity, and cognitive diversity. Drawing on qualitative insights from educators and students, the study reveals that personalization often reduces autonomy, oversimplifies learning, and marginalizes neurodiverse and culturally diverse learners. Themes of algorithmic bias, lack of transparency, and digital inequity are central. To address these challenges, the chapter proposes an ethical framework grounded in fairness, agency, dignity, and inclusivity, integrating perspectives from care ethics, distributive justice, and human-centered AI. The findings urge policymakers, educators, and developers to reconceptualize personalization not as automated optimization but as a collaborative, participatory process that respects individuality and fosters inclusive learning environments.

Keywords: AI-driven personalization, educational ethics, cognitive diversity, inclusive learning, learner agency

1. Introduction

Nothing is changing the student's learning the way artificial intelligence (AI) is. One of the most exciting applications of AI in education is personalization, in which AI tailors content, pacing, and feedback to meet individual learners' needs. At first glance, this sounds like a great step toward more personalized and effective education. Yet, beneath that promise of technological wizardry lie ethical and moral issues that will not be easily settled: What does it mean for some intelligence to be "artificial," and how do we determine the boundary between the human and the artificial when it comes to the mind? Whose intelligence gets to count as intelligence? Or, to put the question another way: Whose intelligence is worthy of being cultivated, and whose is not?

AI-driven pathways are then tailored and molded based on data through what's called "personalization," which can be driven by AI and includes everything from how long a student took to answer a question to the different paths they took to arrive at a correct answer. But, efficient though they may be, these systems risk unwittingly reinforcing narrow notions of intelligence – privileging some cognitive styles, previous knowledge, or cultural context and marginalizing others. Students who think or learn differently, learn at a nonlinear pace, or belong to marginalized communities may not see themselves reflected or may feel underserved by these algorithms.

Through a qualitative examination, some of the ethical aspects of AI-based educational personalization are explored. It raises important points about learner autonomy, algorithmic bias, and inclusivity. Using the lived experiences of students and teachers interacting with AI-driven learning systems, the research sheds light on how personalization, when red-in-tooth-and-claw, may enable and disable. The chapter calls into question not only the notion that personalization is always progress, but also the over-emphasis on cognitive diversity and inclusive intelligence. Last but not least, this work is meant to inform educators, developers, and policy makers building systems that are not just intelligent – but equitable, transparent, and human-centered.

2. The promise of personalization

AI-powered personalization in education is founded on the rosy idea that every learner will be able to receive custom support catering to her unique needs, pace, interests, and abilities [1]. By transcending the traditional one-size-fits-all model, personalized learning seeks to narrow achievement gaps, improve student engagement, and increase learning outcomes. In essence, the promise is a simple one, though so powerful – technology will make learning more human by learning about the learner.

2.1 Current practices in adaptive learning

Adaptive learning allows tools like DreamBox, Smart Sparrow, Knewton, and ALEKS to monitor interactions students have with content and modify instruction each second accordingly. Such analyses concern whether the student's answers are right or wrong, their pace, repetition, or level of engagement, in order to challenge or support the learners. For instance, when a student is unable to grasp a math concept, the system might assist by providing extra explanations or working the student through the problem step by step, perhaps suggesting an easier question before moving on [2].

They tend to rely on learning analytics, which act as live dashboards to inform students and teachers of learning trends, misunderstandings, or skill deficits. This strategy is increasingly being implemented in large-scale digital classrooms, with emphasis placed on Massive Open Online Courses (MOOCs), blended learning, and higher-education LMS environments.

2.2 Early intervention models

Another benefit of AI-based personalization lies in early intervention. By analyzing patterns of attendance, participation, performance, and even sentiment from written responses [3], AI systems can flag students who may be at risk of dropping out, falling behind, or disengaging. Platforms like EAB Navigate or Civitas Learning help institutions identify "at-risk" students early on and recommend interventions – ranging from academic support to counseling.

For schools and educators, this form of predictive insight serves as a powerful reminder that no student should fall through the cracks. Still, there are ethical issues when students are grouped too early in their academic journeys, and interventions are made based on faulty data.

2.3 Predictive analytics in education

Educational platforms are increasingly incorporating predictive analytics, which use data to forecast a student's future performance or behavior [4]. These models compile information about a student's demographics, academic background, online behavior, and even psychological characteristics (via keystroke tracking or sentiment analysis) [5]. Creating a learner profile that forecasts possible outcomes, such as grades, engagement levels, or the likelihood of succeeding in a course, is the goal.

These tools have risks, even though they might be useful in planning tailored support. Predictions have the power to influence students' and teachers' expectations when they are viewed as results rather than possibilities [6]. A low prediction score, for instance, could result in less difficult assignments or fewer opportunities, thereby lowering the bar for a student's development.

3. Ethical critiques: Unpacking bias, power, and pedagogical equity

AI-powered personalization in education has a lot of potential, but it also raises a number of moral questions. These issues are not just technical; they have their roots in issues of power, justice, and equity in the decision-making process for education. Despite appearing to be learner-centric, the personalization process is frequently mediated by normative assumptions about what learning should entail, opaque algorithms, and unrepresentative data sets [6]. Therefore, personalization runs the risk of perpetuating the very disparities it purports to address.

3.1 Algorithmic bias and hidden assumptions

Education-related AI systems are trained on historical data, which may contain biases based on socioeconomic status, gender, race, language, or place of origin. Therefore, these systems may unintentionally reinforce stereotypes or exclude marginalized learner profiles in their recommendations or interventions [7]. For instance, based on generalized behavioral patterns rather than individual potential, a personalization algorithm may routinely steer female students away from STEM fields.

3.2 Over-simplification of learning and intelligence

The definition and assessment of "learning" by personalization systems is the subject of another criticism. Many adaptive tools place a greater emphasis on measurable behaviors – like the amount of time spent on tasks, the number of correct answers, or click patterns – while placing less emphasis on critical thinking, creativity, teamwork, or emotional development [8]. This limited perspective runs the risk of reducing the complexity of learning to data points, leading to what Knox (2020) refers to as a "datafication of pedagogy."

Furthermore, AI systems may lack cognitive diversity – differing ways of thinking, processing information, or expressing understanding – by reducing intelligence to patterns that machines can follow. Systems that value consistency and predictability may frequently misrepresent or misdiagnose students with nonlinear or nonstandard learning profiles.

3.3 Equity, access, and the risk of digital sorting

Access and equity in digital pedagogy are also ethical issues. Students from underserved communities might either be guided by small datasets that conform to majoritarian norms or might not produce enough data for the system to appropriately personalize learning. By assigning already underprivileged students to less demanding or opportunity-limited learning tracks, this type of digital sorting has the potential to widen educational gaps [9].

Additionally, there is the matter of student autonomy and voice. Learners frequently have little knowledge of or control over how learning paths are chosen because personalization algorithms are often running in the background. According to Slade and Prinsloo (2013), ethical pedagogy requires that students be given the ability to challenge or override algorithmic decisions, in addition to being informed about them.

In conclusion, AI personalization needs to be critically analyzed for the biases, exclusions, and reductions it introduces, even though its goal is to make education more responsive and equitable. Beyond accuracy and efficiency, ethical education technology must consider whether the systems we create actually respect and represent the wide range of learners they are meant to serve.

4. Gap identified: The missing voices in AI-personalized learning

Even though the body of research on AI-driven personalization in education has grown quickly, a large portion of it is still concentrated on quantitative results like test scores, retention rates, or system accuracy. To assess the efficacy of adaptive systems, these studies frequently use learning analytics, user logs, and predictive models [5]. Although these methods offer insightful information about performance patterns, they usually ignore the real-world experiences of teachers and students interacting with these systems in challenging situations.

Qualitative, experiential research that explores how personalization feels and works from the learner's point of view is noticeably lacking, especially for people with different cognitive, social, or cultural backgrounds. For example, how do neurodivergent learners understand feedback from AI? Do students from underrepresented linguistic or cultural groups experience a sense of belonging and support? The literature currently in publication does not adequately address the questions that educators have when systems dictate inflexible learning paths.

Without this level of investigation, the development of AI personalization tools might be predicated more on generalized or skewed presumptions than on the actual needs and experiences of students. Future-ready educational technologies must shift from technical optimization to human-centered and ethically responsive approaches, as argued by Williamson (2017) and Selwyn (2019). By providing a qualitative investigation into how diverse learners and educators perceive AI personalization, this chapter answers that call.

5. Research design and methodology

In order to investigate how educators and students from various cognitive, social, and cultural backgrounds perceive AI-driven personalization, this chapter employs a qualitative research design. The need to record profound, complex insights that are frequently overlooked in quantitative assessments of educational technology is the driving force behind the decision to use qualitative inquiry. This study seeks to highlight the contextual, ethical, and emotional realities of algorithmically personalized learning by amplifying participant voices.

5.1 Interpretive Phenomenological Analysis (IPA)

IPA is well-suited for research that seeks to understand how people interpret complicated, personally meaningful experiences [10]. In terms of AI personalization in education, IPA allowed the researcher to explore participants' lived experiences, including how they interpret and react to being guided, categorized, or supported by AI systems. This is particularly relevant at the intersection of ethical issues, where individuals may feel excluded, lose peacefulness and autonomy, or face identity dissonance from decisions made by the system.

IPA facilitates the exploration of rich themes that deal with:

1. Loss of autonomy: for example, learners feel constrained when forced into narrow learning pathways influenced by predicted performance or trajectory.

2. Identity misrecognition: for example, students from nondominant cultures or students who are neurodiverse feel invisible or misrecognized by the recommendations of the system.

3. Surveillance and emotional impact: for example, learners expressing anxiety due to the awareness of constant surveillance and scrutiny.

4. Perceived fairness and trust: for example, educators questioned the transparency and fairness of algorithmic decisions that are affecting educational pathways.

By investigating these subjective, emotional, and ethical dimensions, IPA allows for the exploration of how personalization technologies impact the learner's identity, sense of belonging, and value in education. For example, a neurodivergent learner might elaborate on how a personalization system continually interprets their atypical study practices as being disengaged from the work – resulting in some automatic simplifications in terms of content suggested and reinforcing their sense of marginalization. Additionally, an educator might explain how they were pushed to rely on AI-generated "risk scores" during academic counseling, even if their decisions as professionals impelled them to do otherwise – creating a personal conflict between the ethics of teaching and the instructions derived from algorithms.

In order to provide additional qualitative data from IPA with Narrative Inquiry, we conducted a short exploratory survey with a purposeful sample of 40 participants, including university students and faculty members from across disciplines that use AI-personalized learning platforms. The goal was to identify broader patterns in perspectives on autonomy, fairness, trust, and congruence with AI-based learning systems. Learners' perceptions of AI in education across four parameters — understanding of learning needs, restriction by recommendations, fairness of personalization, and trust in AI guidance as shown in **Figure 1**.

The survey results reflect the vibrant qualitative outcomes from this study: AI-based personalization in education, while perceived as useful, is also seen as limiting, opaque, and sometimes exclusive. Students and educators raise questions about autonomy loss, unfairness, and the emotional cost of being categorized by an algorithm.

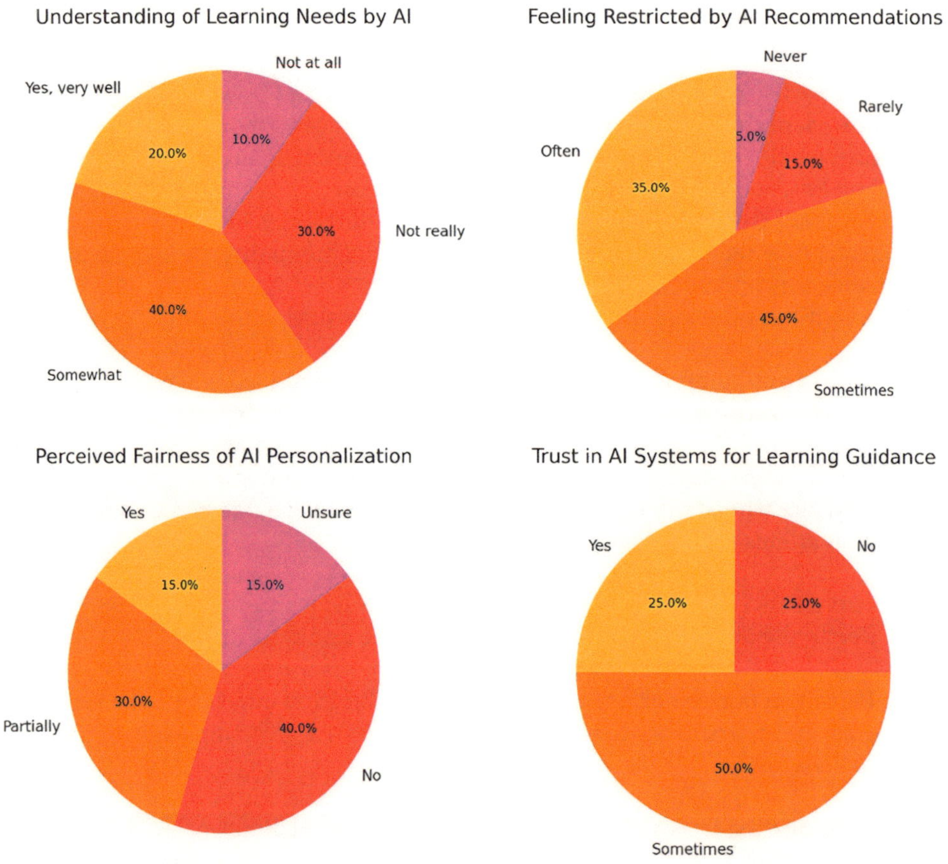

Figure 1.
Trust in AI systems for learning guidance. Source: Author.

5.2 Semistructured interviews: Learner and educator experiences

Educators shared valuable insights into how AI-driven personalization tools influenced their teaching practices, student support strategies, and perceptions of fairness. Four dominant themes emerged from their feedback:

1. Mismatch with human judgment

2. Limited challenge for high performers

3. Effectiveness for early intervention

4. Over-reliance by faculty

Educators often noted that AI recommendations conflicted with their professional judgment, particularly when systems labeled students as underperforming based solely on engagement metrics. Faculty frequently recognized qualities like creativity and critical thinking that the AI overlooked.

Many educators observed that personalization algorithms often delivered safe, middle-ground content, even for high-performing students. This limited academic challenge and stunted opportunities for intellectual risk-taking, revealing a design flaw where "closing gaps" inadvertently created barriers to excellence (**Figure 2**). Despite such concerns, several educators acknowledged the value of AI tools in the early identification of at-risk students. These systems often flagged disengaged learners before behavioral patterns were apparent, enabling timely interventions like academic support or counseling. However, some educators expressed concern over an over-reliance on AI dashboards, cautioning that data-driven decisions should not replace reflective pedagogy. This raised ethical questions about who ultimately directs the learning process – the educator or the algorithm.

6. Data analysis and results

Using thematic analysis, the data collected from semistructured interviews, learning diaries, and educator reflections were analyzed qualitatively. The analysis was an inductive process rooted in ethical theory, where I identified recurring themes and categories to understand the impacts of AI-driven personalization systems on learner experiences and issues of equity in education (**Figure 3**).

The most frequently occurring themes included:

1. Exclusion (14 mentions): participants often described feeling unseen or misrepresented by AI systems, particularly those from nondominant cultural or cognitive groups.

2. Over-simplification (12 mentions): learners reported that AI systems reduced complex learning needs to basic performance indicators, leading to shallow or repetitive content suggestions.

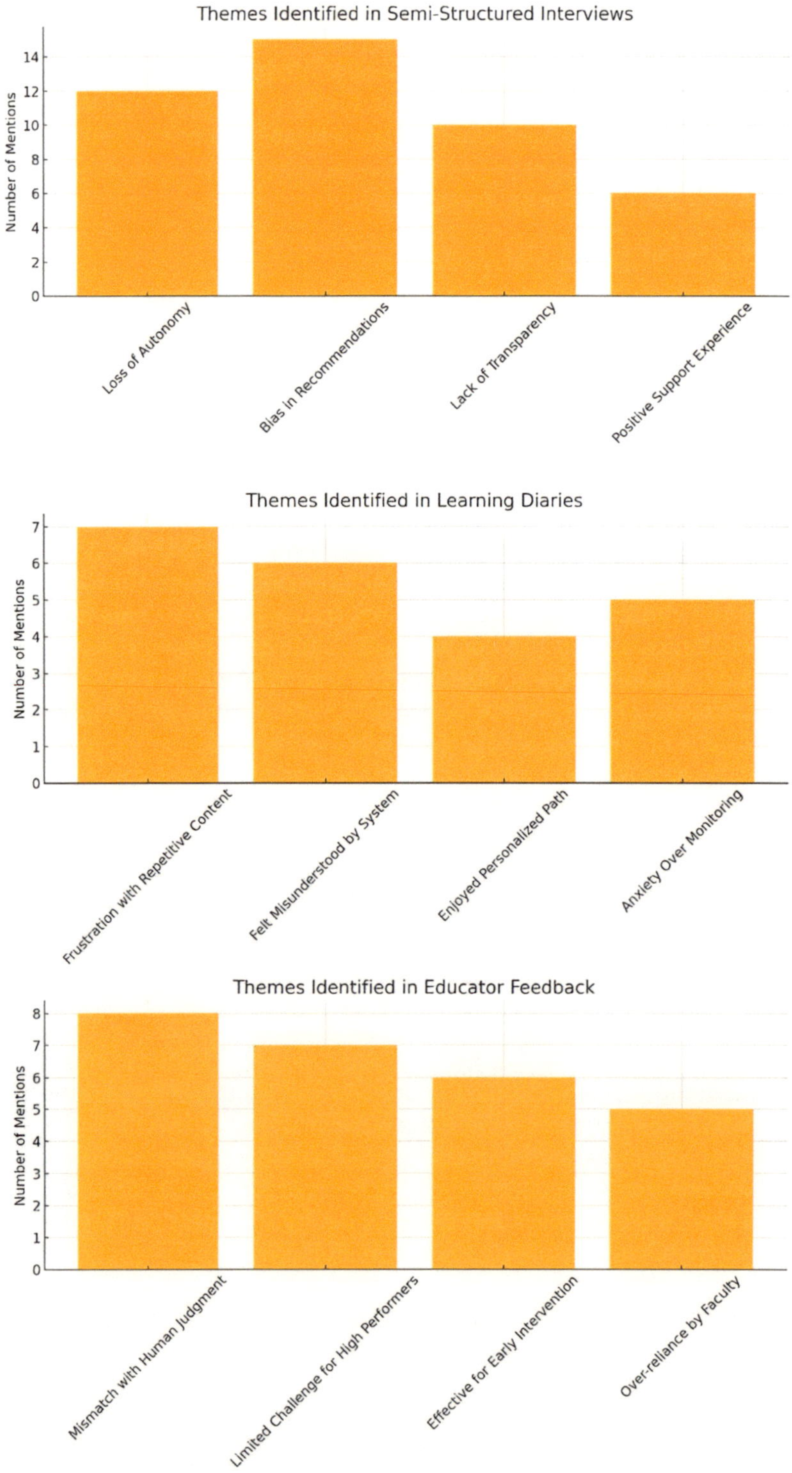

Figure 2.
Themes identified in educator feedback. Source: Author.

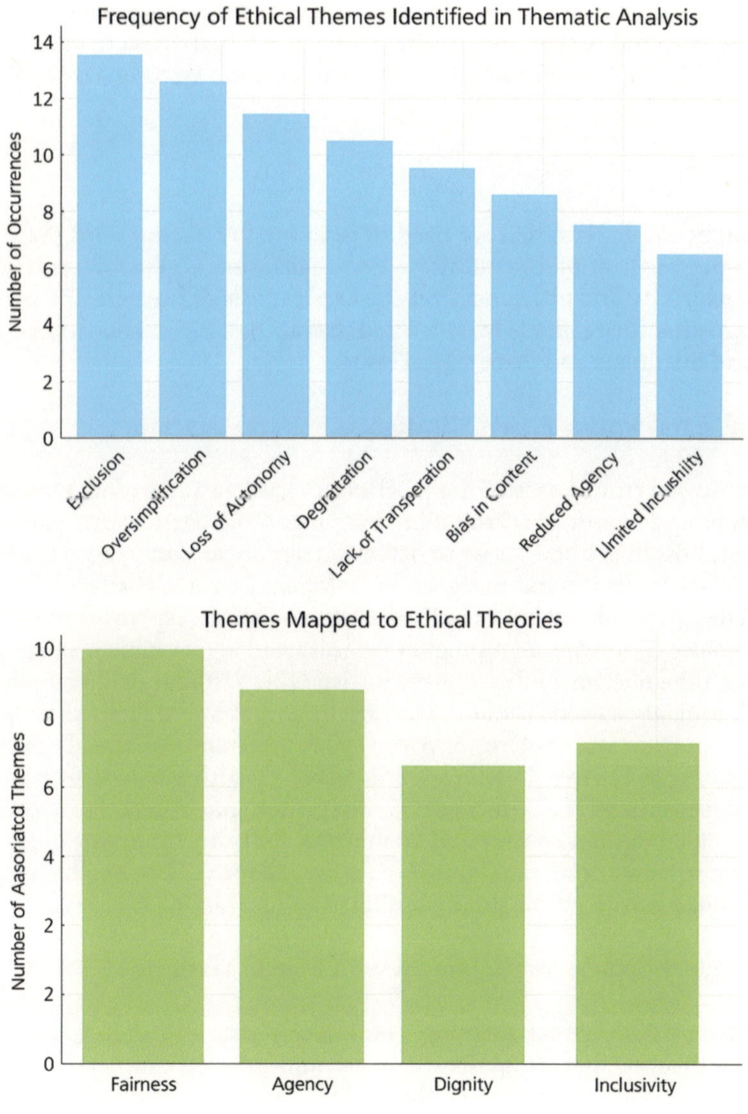

Figure 3.
Data analysis and results. Source: Author.

3. Loss of autonomy (11 mentions): many respondents expressed frustration over restricted learning paths, feeling as though they were being steered by algorithms rather than making choices for themselves.

4. Digital inequity (10 mentions): gaps in access to digital infrastructure, bandwidth, or interface design create unequal personalization outcomes across student populations.

Additional significant themes included lack of transparency, content bias, reduced agency, and limited inclusivity – each of which related to concerns about how AI systems make decisions and whose values those decisions represent.

7. Discussion

This study emphasizes that we need to examine the assumptions that inform AI-driven personalization in education. Personalization is generally framed as the route to inclusivity and efficiency, yet the experiences of learners and educators demonstrate that the reality is nuanced and that authorship of education is entangled with ethical dilemmas and pedagogical issues.

7.1 Ethical frameworks: Personalization as a moral concern

When viewed from a care ethics position [11], AI systems often ignore relationships and emotions surrounding learning. Most participants indicated they felt unseen, misunderstood, or were perceived simply as data. These feelings pose ethical limitations to systems designed for efficiency over empathy. A care-ethics-informed design would attend to individual needs, being responsive to feedback and learners' voices. Concerns about digital inequity and algorithmic bias are also aligned with the notions of distributive justice [12]. Without deliberate design, personalization algorithms could exacerbate or perpetuate structural inequities by reducing opportunities, content, or pathways for members of already marginalized groups. As long as fairness in education involves algorithmic logic that privileges those they measure as "fit" while exclusionarily denying others, fairness cannot exist. Through a human-centered AI framework [13], the findings call for systems that are transparent, accountable, inclusive, and adaptive. Personalization should support human learning, not simply optimize system-defined success.

7.2 Educational theory: Misalignment with human learning

Discrepancy with human learning – ethical critiques also align with some educational theories that stress that there are multiple ways for learners to interact with knowledge. One constructivist theory [14] focuses on learning as an active and exploratory process, where learners co-construct meaning through interaction and reflection. In contrast, many participants described AI systems as prescriptive and limited – a notion that is counter to exploratory construction. Another consideration is that current models of personalization often do not take into account the multiple intelligences [15]. AI, by nature, is generally focused on a linear progression of observable, measurable tasks. Think about it: AI systems care very little about more obscure and nuanced intelligences such as visual-spatial reasoning, interpersonal intelligence, and creativity – all of which aim to promote holistic education. Along these lines, the absence of cultural context within content recommendations runs against culturally responsive pedagogy [16], which advocates for aligning teaching with and through students' lived experiences, languages, and identities. The findings suggest that, when not moderated by an advanced, educated human, personalization based solely on behavioral data risks wiping away the cultural richness of content and reinforcing majoritarian norms.

8. Ethical framework proposal: Designing for equity, agency, and inclusivity

This study's findings suggest that AI-driven personalization systems in education must move beyond predictive efficiency to be considered ethically designed, human-centered technology. Based on participants' lived experiences, along with principles from ethical theories (care ethics, distributive justice, and human-centered AI), we propose a framework of guiding principles with the aim of ensuring personalization supports cognitive (learning) potential as opposed to constraining it (**Table 1**). This Ethical Framework for AI Personalization in Education proposes four interdependent pillars: fairness, agency, dignity, and inclusivity.

Ethical personalization in education needs to be more than making content adaptive; it must take into consideration the complexity of learners and the ethical values of human-centered, inclusive pedagogies. This framework is not dependent on an ethical responsibility; rather, it is a way of engaging with designing AI systems that enhance human capacity, not constrain it.

9. Conclusion

AI–driven personalization in education is often framed as a progressive step toward equity and learner-centeredness. However, the findings of this study demonstrate that the reality is more complex. While adaptive systems can identify at-risk learners, provide timely interventions, and customize content delivery, they also risk narrowing educational experiences to algorithmically defined pathways. Learners and educators alike expressed concerns over reduced autonomy, misrecognition of diverse identities, and the emotional burden of being constantly monitored and categorized. These experiences highlight the paradox that personalization, when designed primarily for efficiency, can depersonalize learning.

Pillar	Objective	Key practices	Ethical foundation
Fairness	Ensure equitable access to learning opportunities for all learners	Use bias detection in algorithms - train on diverse datasets - avoid restricting high performers	Distributive Justice (Rawls, 1971)
Agency	Preserve student autonomy and choice in learning paths	Allow overrides of AI suggestions - enable exploratory learning - involve educators in algorithm design	Care Ethics Human-in-the-Loop AI (Noddings, 2005; Dignum, 2019)
Dignity	Respect learners as whole individuals, not data points	Avoid deficit labeling - integrate reflective and narrative data - provide affirming feedback	Human-Centered AI Care Ethics
Inclusivity	Adapt personalization to serve diverse learning styles and cultural identities	Embed culturally responsive content - apply universal design principles - ensure data use transparency	Culturally Responsive Pedagogy (Gay, 2010)

Source: Author

Table 1.
Interdependent pillars of ethical personalization in education.

The qualitative insights presented here illustrate that ethical concerns – such as bias, fairness, transparency, and inclusivity – are not peripheral but central to the design of AI systems in education. By drawing on ethical theories such as care ethics, distributive justice, and human-centered AI, as well as educational perspectives like constructivism and culturally responsive pedagogy, this chapter emphasizes that personalization must be understood as a moral and pedagogical concern, not merely a technical optimization.

The proposed framework of fairness, agency, dignity, and inclusivity offers a pathway for more human-centered personalization. This model reframes personalization as a participatory and dialogic process, where learners are not reduced to data points but are seen as whole individuals with diverse needs and intelligences. Ultimately, the future of AI in education should not be about replacing human judgment but about complementing it – creating systems that empower both learners and educators. Only by embedding ethical responsibility into design can AI personalization truly serve its intended purpose: enabling equitable, meaningful, and inclusive learning for all.

Author details

Ameed Inam
Galgotias University, Greater Noida, India

*Address Correspondence to: ameed.inam@galgotiasuniversity.edu.in

References

[1] Holmes W, Bialik M, Fadel C. Artificial Intelligence in Education: Promises and Implications for Teaching and Learning. Boston: Center for Curriculum Redesign; 2019

[2] Johnson L, Adams Becker S, Cummins M, Estrada V, Freeman A, Ludgate H. NMC Horizon Report: 2016 Higher Education Edition. 2016. The New Media Consortium

[3] Fritz J. Using analytics to encourage student responsibility for learning and identify course designs that help. In: Ifenthaler D, editor. Learning Analytics: Fundaments, Applications, and Trends. Baltimore: Springer; 2016. pp. 245–265

[4] Agasisti T, Bowers AJ. Data analytics and decision-making in education: Towards the educational data scientist as a key actor in schools and higher education institutions. Education Sciences. 2017;**7**(3):38. DOI: 10.3390/educsci7030038

[5] Ifenthaler D, Yau JYK. Utilising learning analytics to support study success in higher education: A systematic review. Educational Technology Research and Development. 2020;**68**(4):1961–1990. DOI: 10.1007/s11423-020-09788-z

[6] Williamson B. Big Data in Education: The Digital Future of Learning, Policy and Practice. SAGE Publications; 2017

[7] Binns R. Fairness in machine learning: Lessons from political philosophy. In: Proceedings of the 2018 Conference on Fairness, Accountability and Transparency. 2018. 149–159. DOI: 10.1145/3287560.3287596

[8] Selwyn N. Should Robots Replace Teachers? AI and the Future of Education. Cambridge UK: Polity Press; 2019

[9] Slade S, Prinsloo P. Learning analytics: Ethical issues and dilemmas. American Behavioral Scientist. 2013;**57**(10):1510–1529

[10] Smith JA, Flowers P, Larkin M. Interpretative Phenomenological Analysis: Theory, Method and Research. London: SAGE Publications; 2009

[11] Noddings N. The Challenge to Care in Schools: An Alternative Approach to Education. New York: Teachers College Press; 2005

[12] Rawls J. A Theory of Justice. Cambridge, Massachusetts: Harvard University Press; 1971

[13] Dignum V. Responsible Artificial Intelligence: How to Develop and Use AI in a Responsible Way. Switzerland: Springer; 2019

[14] Piaget J. The Origins of Intelligence in Children. New York: International Universities Press; 1952

[15] Gardner H. Frames of Mind: The Theory of Multiple Intelligences. New York: Basic Books; 1983

[16] Gay G. Culturally Responsive Teaching: Theory, Research, anud Practice. 2nd ed. New York: Teachers College Press; 2010

Chapter 16

Neurodivergent by Design: Using AI to Honor and Support Learning Differences

Christina Costa

Abstract

This chapter explores how artificial intelligence (AI) can be ethically and effectively applied in educational settings to support neurodivergent learners. These individuals, who experience psychopathologies such as autism, attention-deficit/hyperactivity disorder (ADHD), and dyslexia, often face barriers in traditional classrooms designed around neurotypical norms. Drawing from strength-based models, participatory design principles, and inclusive education research, this chapter demonstrates how AI can shift educational practices from standardization to personalization. Examples include adaptive learning platforms, sensory-aware tools, and executive functioning support apps. The chapter also discusses risks such as algorithmic bias, data privacy concerns, and overreliance on automation. It concludes with a vision for co-designed, equity-centered AI systems that empower all learners.

Keywords: neurodiversity, inclusive design, artificial intelligence, adaptive learning, universal design for learning

1. Introduction

In a college-level statistics class, a student named Milo (a pseudonym) wears noise-canceling headphones, takes notes using voice-to-text on a tablet, and completes assignments through an adaptive artificial intelligence (AI) platform that presents concepts in visual formats aligned to his cognitive profile. Diagnosed with autism spectrum disorder and dyslexia, Milo previously struggled to complete timed exams or parse dense academic language. But now, AI-driven tools help him engage with material, advocate for his needs, and succeed in coursework that once felt inaccessible. His transformation is not simply about technological access; it reflects a broader shift in educational thinking. This thinking centers on learner variability rather than treating it as an exception to the norm.

Neurodivergence refers to naturally occurring cognitive variations such as autism, attention-deficit/hyperactivity disorder (ADHD), dyslexia, and other psychological profiles that shape how individuals process information, manage attention, and engage socially [1]. In educational contexts, neurodivergent students often encounter rigid systems built on assumptions of how students are supposed to learn and behave in classroom s. These systems can unintentionally marginalize those whose learning and sensory needs fall outside of what is dominant. For these students, traditional instructional models may not simply be ineffective; they may be exclusionary.

AI in education (AIED) can include tools like intelligent tutoring systems, emotion recognition software, and adaptive learning platforms that adjust in real time to student inputs and performance [2]. These technologies offer a new set of possibilities for responsive and personalized education. When integrated thoughtfully, they can create dynamic learning environments that support multiple modes of expression, provide immediate and accessible feedback, and scaffold executive functioning demands. However, realizing this promise requires more than just technological adoption; it necessitates intentional design grounded in ethics and inclusivity.

Inclusive design in higher education prioritizes the variability of learners from the outset, rather than treating accessibility as an add-on [3]. This approach views diversity in learning not as a challenge to be accommodated but as a baseline to be embraced. Through this lens, AI tools are not solutions in isolation but vehicles for enacting inclusive pedagogical values. When designed with input from neurodivergent students themselves, AI-enhanced tools can mirror the variability of human cognition and challenge the deficit-based frameworks that often dominate academic discourse.

This chapter argues that, when equitably developed and ethically implemented, AI can support the customization of college learning environments, shifting from a model of remediation to one of amplification. By aligning instructional delivery, feedback, and assessment with students' strengths and needs, AI offers unprecedented potential to reduce barriers and foster meaningful inclusion. The chapter explores neurodiversity in the context of higher education, the promise and limitations of AI tools, and strategies for inclusive, participatory technology design. This work invites educators, individuals creating education technology, and policymakers to reimagine what learning can look like when it is neurodivergent by design.

1.1 Author reflexivity statement

As a White neurodivergent educator in higher education, I bring both lived experience and critical self-awareness to the intersection of neurodiversity and AI. My neurodivergence shapes how I understand learning, inclusion, and engagement, while my Whiteness affords privileges within academic and technological spaces that can obscure the intersecting marginalizations others face. This awareness drives my commitment to challenging deficit-based models of cognition, surfacing systemic biases in AI and higher education, and ensuring I do not universalize my own experience. I strive to engage reflexively. This involves questioning assumptions, amplifying marginalized voices rather than speaking for them, and contributing to an inclusive, accountable, and human-centered scholarly conversation.

2. Understanding neurodiversity

Coined by sociologist Judy Singer, the term "neurodiversity" repositions differences such as autism, ADHD, and dyslexia as natural, valuable variations in human cognition rather than pathologies to be fixed [1]. This reconceptualization emerged from the disability rights and self-advocacy movements and continues to challenge medicalized views of cognitive difference that prioritize normalization over accommodation. Rather than framing neurodivergent individuals as broken or deficient, neurodiversity affirms that variations in neurological functioning are part of the normal spectrum of human experience. It reframes diagnosis from a lens of deficit to one of diversity, encouraging educational systems to move beyond reactive accommodations and toward proactive inclusivity.

In the context of university classrooms, this lens reframes academic challenges neurodivergent individuals face not as personal deficits but as mismatches between learners and rigid systems. Postsecondary education has long been structured around assumptions of uniformity (e.g., lectures delivered at a single pace, the way success is defined, etc.). These frameworks may benefit neurotypical students but frequently create friction for learners whose brains are wired differently. For neurodivergent students, the classroom is often not just an intellectual space but also a sensory and executive environment that can either support or obstruct their ability to learn.

College students who are neurodivergent often bring exceptional pattern recognition, creative problem-solving, and deep focus to their work, yet these traits may be overshadowed by difficulties with executive function, time management, or sensory regulation [4, 5]. For example, a student with ADHD may excel in spontaneous problem-solving and rapid ideation but struggle with sustained attention during long lectures. A student with autism might demonstrate extraordinary visual memory and systemic thinking but be overwhelmed by noisy learning environments or unpredictable group dynamics. These cognitive profiles are not disadvantages in themselves; rather, they become barriers only when institutions fail to adapt to learner variability (see **Table 1** for a summary).

Unfortunately, most postsecondary institutions continue to rely on standardized curricula, lecture-heavy instruction, and high-stakes assessments that inadvertently marginalize neurodivergent learners [6]. Such structures demand conformity to a narrow set of behaviors – sitting still, writing essays, meeting rigid deadlines – while undervaluing alternative ways of knowing and expressing knowledge. This is further complicated by the social dynamics, where participation and engagement are often measured through norms that may disadvantage students with autism, social anxiety, or other neurological differences (e.g., the way we ask students to interact with each other or with the class, such as oral presentations or group work, without establishing norms).

Research reveals that many students with invisible disabilities are discouraged from disclosing diagnoses due to stigma, while others are misunderstood as disengaged or underperforming when their learning profiles are simply misaligned with dominant pedagogical models [7]. Disclosure often places the burden of adjustment on students, requiring them to navigate bureaucratic systems for

Neurodivergent profile	Strengths	Potential classroom challenges
ADHD	Rapid problem-solving, creativity	Sustained attention, time management
Autism	Visual memory, systemic thinking	Sensory overload, social interaction
Dyslexia	Pattern recognition, problem-solving	Reading dense texts, written assignments

Table 1.
Overview of example neurodivergent profiles, strengths, and challenges.

accommodations that may only offer minimal support. Faculty may lack training in neurodivergence and unconsciously interpret students' behavior through neurotypical lenses, leading to misperceptions of laziness, defiance, or lack of preparedness. This dynamic perpetuates systemic inequities, especially for first-generation students and students of color, who may face compounded biases.

Inclusive teaching practices rooted in Universal Design for Learning (UDL), combined with trauma-informed approaches, can help dismantle these barriers and promote equity [3, 8]. UDL provides a framework for designing flexible learning environments that accommodate a wide range of abilities and preferences from the outset. It encourages offering multiple means of representation, engagement, and expression – principles that align naturally with neurodiversity. Trauma-informed teaching further acknowledges how past experiences shape student behavior and learning readiness, recognizing that neurodivergence and trauma often intersect. Together, these pedagogies foster educational spaces that are not just accessible but also affirming.

Embracing neurodiversity in higher education means more than offering accommodations – it requires a systemic reimagining of what counts as knowledge, participation, and success. I argue that AI offers tools that can help realize this vision if grounded in principles of inclusion, equity, and neurodivergent leadership.

3. The promise and pitfalls of AIED

In college classrooms, AI is increasingly used for grading automation, learning analytics, and personalized instruction. These applications aim to increase efficiency, provide timely feedback, and tailor instruction to diverse learner needs. Platforms such as DreamBox, ALEKS, and Coursera adjust lesson content based on user behavior, enabling differentiated pacing and adaptive support [9]. By using algorithms that respond to student input, these tools attempt to meet learners where they are, adjusting difficulty and sequencing in real time. Such functionality can be especially helpful in large university courses, where individualized feedback is often difficult to scale.

Students with dyslexia may use tools like NaturalReader or Kurzweil 3000 to convert course texts into audio, enabling them to access material through modalities better suited to their cognitive strengths [10]. These text-to-speech programs often include visual tracking, vocabulary support, and note-taking features that scaffold comprehension and reduce cognitive load. Similarly, AI-powered writing assistants like Grammarly or QuillBot help scaffold academic writing, offering suggestions for grammar, clarity, and structure. For students with ADHD or executive functioning challenges, these tools can help externalize the cognitive processes required for planning and revising written work.

Chatbots embedded in learning management systems offer on-demand explanations, reminders, and task management aids [11]. When designed well, these tools serve as 24/7 academic companions, helping students clarify assignment instructions, track deadlines, and locate learning resources. Instructors, too, benefit from AI through systems that identify at-risk students, track participation patterns, and automate grading for objective assessments like quizzes and problem sets. Collectively, these applications offer an unprecedented opportunity to personalize learning in ways that support neurodivergent learners' strengths and reduce common access barriers.

However, the deployment of AI in higher education is not without challenges. Emotion recognition software and attention-monitoring tools, sometimes used in online proctoring, have been shown to misread facial expressions and behaviors, especially in students on the autism spectrum [12]. These tools often rely on normative models of expression and focus, which can lead to false flags for disengagement or dishonesty in students whose body language differs from neurotypical patterns. This not only places neurodivergent students at a disadvantage but also reinforces harmful stereotypes about what learning should "look like."

Algorithms trained on narrow datasets may inadvertently exclude nontraditional or neurodivergent learners, perpetuating bias and underrepresentation [13, 14]. For example, if AI models are developed using data from predominantly neurotypical, white, middle-class students, their recommendations and interventions may be less accurate, or even harmful, when applied to diverse student populations. This data bias can manifest in subtle ways: recommending slower pacing to students with disabilities, flagging writing that deviates from formal conventions, or failing to recognize culturally responsive expressions of understanding.

As AI systems make decisions about pacing, feedback, or intervention, they risk overstepping without proper oversight or contextual knowledge of students. While automated feedback can be helpful, it can also feel impersonal or mismatched if it fails to consider the emotional or developmental needs of the learner. Instructors may be tempted to rely too heavily on AI-generated insights, leading to reduced student–instructor interaction or overreliance on performance metrics that obscure complex learning processes. In this way, AI can unintentionally erode the relational and human-centered dimensions of education.

Privacy and consent remain pressing issues. AI tools often collect and analyze sensitive student data, including engagement metrics, behavioral patterns, and learning preferences, sometimes without clear communication or opt-in protocols [15]. These tools can track everything from how long a student spends on a page to which resources they access, constructing detailed profiles of learners that may be used for institutional decision-making. In higher education, where trust and autonomy are foundational, these concerns must be addressed through transparent policies and inclusive governance.

Moreover, the question of who controls the AI – its design, implementation, and evolution – has implications for equity. If AI tools are created without input from neurodivergent learners or disability scholars, they risk replicating ableist assumptions about what learning should entail. Participatory design, clear data consent protocols, and bias auditing must become standard practices in educational AI. Without these safeguards, tools meant to increase access may ultimately reinforce existing inequities, placing the burden of adaptation once again on students who already navigate structurally exclusive systems.

All this being said, we can center inclusive values in AI design for education by involving neurodivergent learners in development processes, auditing algorithms for bias, and aligning tool development with UDL and trauma-informed frameworks.

4. AI by design: Customizing learning environments

AI has the capacity to transform how college courses are structured, delivered, and experienced. With the increasing integration of AI into learning environments, the possibility of building responsive, accessible, and personalized educational experiences becomes more tangible. Learning management systems embedded with adaptive AI can individualize the pace and mode of instruction, allowing students to move beyond rigid, one-size-fits-all course models. For example, platforms like Carnegie Learning adjust content based on student response time and accuracy, ensuring that learners engage with material at an optimal challenge level [9]. This kind of fine-tuned feedback loop fosters productive struggle, keeping learners within their zone of proximal development rather than overwhelming or boring them with poorly matched instruction.

Instructors using such systems can track student progress in real time, receive alerts when a student's performance dips, and provide timely interventions or scaffolded resources. Adaptive pacing is particularly beneficial for neurodivergent students whose processing speeds or cognitive rhythms may not align with standard lecture timelines. AI enables asynchronous flexibility within synchronous structures – creating hybrid learning environments where students can advance at their own speed while still participating in a shared academic community.

Multimodal feedback mechanisms, such as speech-to-text, text-to-speech, audio explanations, and visual cues, support students with varied communication needs, reducing frustration and enhancing access. These features are especially important for students with dyslexia, auditory processing challenges, or expressive language difficulties. By allowing students to engage with material in multiple formats, AI reduces the cognitive friction that often accompanies traditional text-dominant instruction. For learners with sensory sensitivities, interfaces with customizable color palettes, font sizes, and audio modulation help mitigate overload. These design options give students control over their sensory environments, reducing anxiety and cognitive fatigue. Tools like Brainin and EquatIO demonstrate how sensory and cognitive load can be regulated through adaptive user interface (AUI) [16].

In addition to perception and input support, executive function support is especially valuable for neurodivergent college students juggling complex schedules and self-directed tasks. Executive functioning – planning, prioritization, time management, and task initiation – is one of the most commonly cited challenges among college students with ADHD, autism, or anxiety disorders. Tiimo and GoblinTools are AI-enhanced platforms that provide visual scheduling, task segmentation, and time estimation features tailored to individual needs [17]. These apps help externalize executive demands by breaking assignments into steps, color-coding priorities, and offering nudges to stay on track. They serve as digital scaffolds that reduce the invisible labor of academic self-regulation.

For students with speech-language challenges, AI assistants such as Google Assistant can be configured to simplify instructions, offer visual prompts, or convert spoken responses into written text [18]. These applications are particularly useful during collaborative assignments, office hours, or presentations – moments that often expose disparities in processing speed or verbal fluency. By functioning as intermediaries, AI tools can provide translation across modalities, supporting students who express themselves more effectively through writing, images, or speech alternatives.

I'd like to invite you to dream with me. Consider a university course that adopts "NeuroLearn" – a fictional AI-enhanced system that delivers psychology content through text, interactive diagrams, podcasts, and gamified assessments (see **Figure 1**). The system tracks each student's engagement style and adjusts accordingly. A student

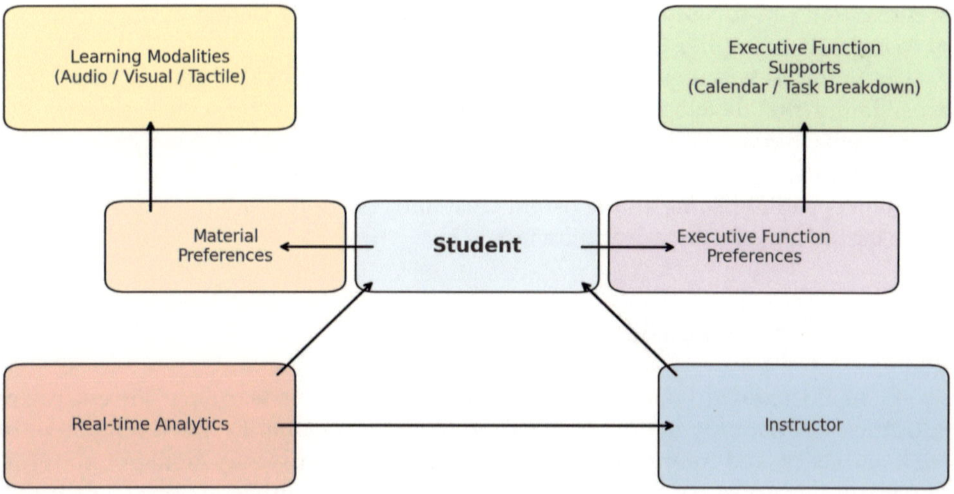

Figure 1.
A diagram of an AI-enhanced learning ecosystem.

who shows higher retention with narrative podcasts has the option to receive weekly lecture content in audio form, while another student accesses interactive lab videos for kinesthetic learning. A third student, who struggles with executive function, receives weekly calendar prompts and breakdowns of major assignments into manageable milestones. Importantly, all students have access to all of these features, but the platform helps them identify strengths associated with their needs and preferences. Meanwhile, the professor receives real-time analytics about comprehension and engagement, and uses this data to plan interventions, scaffold assignments, or offer alternate content delivery options [19]. This model not only supports individual learners but also equips educators with actionable insights to teach more responsively.

These applications embody the UDL principles of multiple means of engagement, representation, and expression, but operationalize them at scale using AI [3]. They move beyond theoretical ideals into functional reality, where students' learning pathways are not only acknowledged but actively supported by technology. When designed ethically, such systems do not replace teachers but empower them – and, more importantly, empower students to learn in ways that align with their strengths.

5. Co-design with neurodivergent learners

Ethical, impactful AI must be developed in partnership with those it aims to serve. In higher education, this means involving neurodivergent students not just as users but as co-designers. Participatory design methods, such as student-led focus groups, prototyping workshops, and usability testing, center lived experience in the development cycle [20].

Organizations like the Autistic Self Advocacy Network (ASAN) provide models for inclusive technology development, including compensating neurodivergent contributors, ensuring accessibility in development tools, and foregrounding intersectional identity representation [21]. In universities, student advisory boards and research labs focused on accessibility (e.g., the TRACE Center at the University of Maryland) exemplify this approach.

Designing AI with neurodivergent users requires careful attention to usability, accessibility-first development, and iterative refinement. For instance, student developers working with faculty on a writing support AI tool might solicit feedback from neurodivergent peers on font readability, error prompts, and interface layout. Through cycles of testing and revision, trust and functionality improve, resulting in more usable tools for broader audiences [22].

6. Challenges and considerations

AI should augment, not replace, human relationships in learning. The essence of education lies not only in the transmission of knowledge but in the development of trust, curiosity, and interpersonal growth. Data dashboards may highlight patterns in student performance; however, they cannot capture motivation, stress, or the impact of external life factors. A student's low quiz score may reflect a concept gap – or it may reflect a family emergency, sleep deprivation, or housing insecurity. Faculty must use AI as a supplement to pedagogical intuition, contextual judgment, and individualized care [23]. Rather than relying solely on algorithmic outputs, educators must interpret AI insights through a human-centered lens, drawing from empathy, experience, and dialog with students themselves.

Moreover, the digital divide persists in higher education. First-generation students, students from low-income households, and institutions with limited tech infrastructure may have reduced access to emerging AI tools, widening opportunity gaps [24]. AI has the potential to democratize learning, but only if access is equitably distributed. High-cost platforms, device requirements, and broadband limitations can all reinforce existing educational disparities, especially among historically marginalized student populations. To address this, institutions must invest equitably – not just in procuring AI technologies, but in training faculty, expanding device loan programs, and building inclusive digital systems. Advocating for accessible pricing models, public funding for edtech infrastructure, and open-source alternatives must be central to institutional strategies for AI integration.

The ethics of AIED demand careful, continuous attention. While AI may offer efficiencies and insights, it also introduces significant risks related to bias, surveillance, autonomy, and decision-making transparency. Algorithms are not neutral; they reflect the assumptions, values, and blind spots of their creators. Without careful scrutiny, AI can reinforce ableist, racist, or classist norms, particularly if data is drawn from non-representative populations or interpreted without input from affected communities. Ethical implementation requires that colleges move beyond the promise of innovation and toward practices grounded in justice, accessibility, and participatory governance.

To uphold learner autonomy and dignity, colleges must ensure that all AI deployments include human oversight, informed consent, and clear communication about data use. Students should not be monitored without their knowledge or have their learning paths dictated by systems they cannot question or override. Transparent data policies, opt-in participation, and accessible explanations of how AI tools function are essential. This includes informing students about what data is collected, how it is analyzed, who has access, and how it affects their educational experience.

Moreover, human oversight must be more than procedural; it must be ethical and intentional. Faculty, advisors, and administrators should be trained not only in the technical operation of AI systems but also in their ethical implications. Institutions should establish ethics review boards or data governance committees that include students, disability advocates, and community members. These bodies can help vet AI tools, audit outcomes for unintended consequences, and ensure that implementation aligns with institutional values of inclusion, equity, and academic freedom.

Ultimately, AIED should be guided by the question: "What kind of learning environment are we trying to create, and who is it for?" If the answer does not center on dignity, access, and shared power, then even the most sophisticated tools may do more harm than good. The future of higher education lies not in replacing humans with machines, but in designing systems – technological and pedagogical – that amplify the full humanity of every learner.

7. Looking forward: A dream/vision for neuroinclusive AI

Let's keep dreaming. Picture a lecture hall where every student is recognized as whole, capable, and unique. In this future, AI helps modulate classroom noise, simplifies complex texts, and scaffolds research tasks based on personalized learning maps. These intelligent tools operate not as gatekeepers but as guides – adjusting to students' strengths, preferences, and growth trajectories. A student with ADHD receives structured reminders and visual timelines for an upcoming group project; a student with dyslexia uses AI-powered text simplification to decode dense academic prose; a student on the autism spectrum adjusts their classroom sensory settings through a customizable interface, ensuring a calm, focused learning environment.

Professors use AI insights not to surveil or standardize but to connect with students more deeply. Data visualizations offer patterns that prompt timely check-ins, tailored feedback, or co-constructed interventions. Rather than relying on assumptions, instructors can collaborate with students to co-create individualized learning plans rooted in growth, curiosity, and self-efficacy. These plans are not static accommodations but dynamic, evolving strategies that honor learner agency and prioritize authentic engagement. AI in this future supports – not supplants – the irreplaceable relational work of teaching.

Students select from a variety of modalities to demonstrate understanding: video essays, concept maps, live presentations, or traditional papers. No longer confined by one dominant mode of expression, students are empowered to showcase their knowledge in formats that align with their cognitive profiles and communicative strengths. Assessments reflect what students know, not just how quickly they can respond. Timed exams are replaced with iterative assignments, feedback cycles, and opportunities for revision. Performance is understood as a process rather than a moment, and AI facilitates meaningful learning rather than mechanical compliance.

AI systems are built through antiracist, equity-centered design thinking and refined by neurodivergent contributors [25]. These systems reflect inclusive values from the ground up – embedding universal design, participatory feedback loops, and algorithmic transparency as core principles rather than retrofitted features.

Neurodivergent students, faculty, and researchers are not merely test subjects or advisory voices but co-creators of the very tools meant to serve them. In this future, accessibility is not a retrofit or checkbox but a foundational design imperative.

Such a future demands collective action. Policymakers must fund inclusive tech development, recognizing the public good in AI that serves diverse learners rather than market-dominant consumers. Investment must prioritize open-source platforms, transparency mandates, and infrastructure that reaches under-resourced institutions. Educators must challenge outdated pedagogy, rethinking what constitutes rigor, participation, and success in light of inclusive epistemologies. Faculty development should include training not just in tool adoption but in equitable teaching philosophy and the ethics of educational technology.

Technologists must prioritize transparency, usability, and justice – actively working to audit bias, diversify datasets, and ensure human-centered design. Ethical considerations must be integrated throughout the product lifecycle, with community accountability structures that keep marginalized voices at the forefront. Moreover, perhaps most importantly, neurodivergent learners must be central to the design process, not afterthoughts. Their lived expertise, innovation, and insight are essential – not only to the success of AIED but to the broader project of building a more just and joyful academic world.

This dream is ambitious but necessary. AI will shape the future of higher education. The question is: will we let it reinforce exclusion and efficiency, or will we design it (intentionally, collectively, and creatively) to honor the full spectrum of how humans learn?

8. Conclusion

Milo's story represents just one student, but it echoes across classrooms where design finally honors difference. His experience signals a larger shift – a move from marginal accommodation to expansive transformation. When educational systems take seriously the idea that no two minds learn alike, they begin to unlock potential that has long been constrained by standardization. Across campuses, neurodivergent students are asking not simply to be included, but to be understood, valued, and empowered. Their stories challenge us to rethink the very architecture of higher education, from syllabi and assessments to advising structures and classroom dynamics.

Imagine campuses where lectures are accompanied by sensory-friendly spaces, where AI platforms help scaffold not just content but agency, and where learning outcomes are measured through diverse demonstrations of knowledge. Imagine classrooms where difference is not just tolerated but anticipated and celebrated. These are not utopian dreams but practical visions, made possible when technology is paired with ethical design and educational courage. We can build toward spaces of belonging, creativity, and neurodivergent brilliance – places where every student not only fits but thrives.

As Thomas Hehir reminds us, "Inclusion is not bringing people into what already exists; it is making a new space, a better space for everyone." These words invite a shift not just in practice, but in purpose. Inclusion is not a retrofit; it's a redesign. It's not about assimilation; it's about transformation. With intentional AI and collaborative design, that better space is within reach. It will take cross-disciplinary collaboration, humility, and imagination, but it is possible; and more than possible, it is necessary.

Acknowledgments

I would like to express my deepest gratitude to my students, whose insights, questions, and experiences continue to shape the way I think about inclusive education and the role of technology in learning. Your openness, resilience, and brilliance remind me daily of the transformative potential within every classroom. This chapter is inspired by you.

Conflict of interest

The author declares no conflicts of interest

Author details

Christina Costa
Wayne State University, Detroit, United States.

*Address all correspondence to: christina.costa@wayne.edu

References

[1] Singer J. Why can't you be normal for once in your life? In: Corker M, French S, editors. Disability Discourse. Open University Press; 1999. pp. 59–67

[2] Holmes W, Bialik M, Fadel C. Artificial Intelligence in Education: Promises and Implications for Teaching and Learning. Boston: Center for Curriculum Redesign; 2019

[3] CAST. Universal Design for Learning Guidelines Version 2.2 [Internet]. 2018. Available from: http://udlguidelines.cast.org [Accessed: 2025-June-05]

[4] Armstrong T. Neurodiversity: Discovering the extraordinary Gifts of Autism, ADHD, Dyslexia, and other Brain differences. Cambridge, MA: Da Capo Press; 2010

[5] Mottron L.Changing perceptions: The power of autism. Nature. 2011;**479** (7371):33–35

[6] Kapp SK, Gillespie-Lynch K, Sherman LE, Hutman T.Deficit, difference, or both? Autism and neurodiversity. Developmental Psychology. 2013;**49**(1):59–71

[7] Baron-Cohen S. The Pattern Seekers: How Autism Drives Human Invention. New York City: Basic Books; 2020

[8] Brunzell T, Stokes H, Waters L. Trauma-informed flexible learning: Classrooms that strengthen regulatory abilities. International Journal of Inclusive Education. 2016;**20**(5):489–506

[9] Pane JF, Steiner ED, Baird MD, and Hamilton LS. Continued progress: Promising evidence on personalized learning. Santa Monica, California: RAND Corporation; 2015

[10] Shaywitz S Overcoming Dyslexia. Knopf; 2020

[11] Luckin R, Holmes W, Griffiths M, Forcier LB UCL Knowledge Lab. Intelligence unleashed: An argument for AI in education. London, UK: Pearson Education; 2016

[12] Washington P, Park H, Kalantarian H, Tariq Q, Schwartz J, Dunne S, et al. Data collection framework for machine learning in mobile health. Journal of Medical Internet Research 2019;**21**:e14035

[13] Eubanks V. Automating Inequality: How High-Tech Tools Profile, Police, and Punish the Poor. St. Martin's Press; 2018

[14] Noble SU. Algorithms of Oppression: How Search Engines Reinforce Racism. New York City: NYU Press; 2018

[15] Williamson B, Eynon R.Historical threads, missing links, and future directions in AI in education. Learning, Media and Technology. 2020;**45**(3): 223–235

[16] Brainin Neurotech [Internet]. Available from: https://brainin.com [Accessed: 2025-June-05]

[17] Tiimo App [Internet]. Available from: https://www.tiimoapp.com [Accessed: 2025-June-05]

[18] Google Developers. Actions on Google [Internet]. Available from: https://developers.google.com/assistant [Accessed: 2025-June-05]

[19] Hypothetical Case Study. constructed by author for illustrative purposes

[20] Costanza-Chock S. Design Justice: Community-Led Practices to Build the Worlds We Need. Cambridge, Massachussets: MIT Press; 2020

[21] Autistic Self Advocacy Network (ASAN) [Internet]. Available from: https://autisticadvocacy.org. [Accessed: 2025-June-05]

[22] Bennett CL, Rosner DK. The Promise of Empathy: Design, disability, and knowing the "other". Proceedings of the SIGCHI Conference on Human Factors in Computing Systems. 2019; 1–13

[23] Koenig KP, Rudney SG. Performance challenges for children and youth with developmental coordination disorder: A literature review. Physical & Occupational Therapy in Pediatrics. 2010;**30**(2):132–147

[24] Warschauer M.Technology and equity in Schooling: Deconstructing the digital divide. Educational Policy. 2004;**18**(4):562–588

[25] Kendi IX. How to Be an Antiracist. London, UK: One World; 2019

Chapter 17

Teddy AI: Empowering Personalised Learning and Parental Insight through Generative AI

Pauldy C.J. Otermans and Dev Aditya*

Abstract

This chapter explores the development and impact of Teddy AI, a generative AI-powered application designed to revolutionise early learning experiences and parent–child engagement. Teddy AI is an interactive, intelligent companion that teaches, engages, and adapts to the unique learning needs of each child. In this way, it delivers personalised educational content in a playful and natural manner. More than just a digital tutor, it also serves as a bridge between the child's learning journey and their caregivers and guardians, providing real-time feedback, learning progress insights, and areas requiring support. What sets Teddy AI apart is its ability to subtly guide educational practice without making activities feel forced, preserving a sense of play and exploration for the child. In fact, parents can also prompt Teddy AI to introduce new concepts or reinforce specific skills without the child knowing or feeling pressured, thereby creating a seamless blend of structured and informal learning. The chapter discusses this concept in detail and also backs this up with findings from recent research conducted by the authors using Teddy AI. The research showed strong openness among parents to trust AI-powered educational tools. The majority believed such tools could accelerate learning through tailored content and authentic information. By illustrating the practical applications and ethical considerations of using AI in home-based learning environments, this chapter underscores the potential of AI to make education more equitable, effective, and family-centred.

Keywords: generative AI in education, personalised learning, parent–AI collaboration, educational technology innovation, child engagement, and feedback systems

1. Introduction

Imagine a child sitting cross-legged on the living room floor, speaking excitedly to a small plush bear on a tablet screen. The bear listens patiently, answers questions, tells stories, and even guides the child through counting exercises, all while subtly tracking their progress and adjusting its teaching style. Nearby, a parent glances at their phone and sees real-time insights: the child has mastered counting to 20 but is still struggling with shape recognition. Without interrupting the child's flow, the parent sends a discreet prompt to introduce a new concept during the next play session. This is not a futuristic fantasy; it is the core learning experience envisioned with Teddy AI.

1.1 The rise of AI in education

In recent years, generative artificial intelligence (AI) has moved from the realm of research laboratories into everyday tools. From personalised tutoring platforms to adaptive testing systems, AI is reshaping educational experiences at all levels. According to recent market analyses, the global AI-in-education sector is projected to grow at double-digit annual rates, driven by increasing demand for personalised learning, data-driven insights, and remote learning solutions. While much attention has been given to AI in formal schooling, its potential in early childhood education remains underexplored. The formative years between ages 3 and 7 are critical for developing foundational cognitive, emotional, and social skills. During this period, learning is most effective when it is embedded in play, social interaction, and routine daily experiences. However, few digital tools balance these elements effectively while also integrating parents as active partners in the process.

1.2 The engagement and personalisation gap

Traditional educational apps for young children tend to fall into two categories. The first one is structured but rigid tools that prioritise curriculum delivery at the expense of play. The second category is play-focused but shallow apps that entertain without delivering sustained educational value. In both cases, parents often lack visibility into their child's progress and cannot easily influence the direction of learning without disrupting the experience. This gap, the absence of integrated, adaptive, family-centred learning tools, is precisely where Teddy AI positions itself.

1.3 Teddy's AI unique proposition

Teddy AI is built on fine-tuned transformer models, capable of sustaining natural, age-appropriate conversations. Its dual-interface design addresses the needs of both learners and caregivers:

- A child-facing study buddy that engages through stories, games, and conversational activities.
- A parent dashboard that offers real-time analytics, skill tracking, and discreet prompt features.

This combination allows for blended learning: the AI can guide children through structured exercises while seamlessly integrating them into playful contexts. Parents can nudge the AI to reinforce concepts without the child perceiving the intervention, reducing the risk of resistance or performance anxiety.

1.4 Broader relevance in post-pandemic learning

The COVID-19 pandemic accelerated the adoption of home-based and hybrid learning models. Families became more directly involved in education, often taking on roles as facilitators or co-educators. This shift highlighted the importance of tools that have the following:

- Support independent learning for children.
- Keep caregivers informed and engaged.
- Maintain educational quality outside formal classrooms.

In this environment, AI tools that bridge the gap between child autonomy and parental guidance are not merely advantageous; they are essential.

1.5 Scope and objectives of this chapter

This chapter examines Teddy AI from conceptual, technical, and practical perspectives. Specifically, it will:

- Present the design philosophy and system architecture underpinning Teddy AI.
- Analyse unique features that distinguish it from other AI-based educational tools.
- Report empirical findings from research conducted by the authors on parental acceptance and perceived effectiveness.
- Discuss ethical and societal considerations surrounding AI in home-based early education.
- Explore potential directions for future development.

By situating Teddy AI within the broader discourse on educational technology and personalised learning, this chapter aims to contribute to the understanding of how AI can make early education more equitable, effective, and family-centred.

2. Background and related work

2.1 Generative AI in education

Generative AI refers to machine learning models that can create new content, which can include text, images, and audio, based on patterns learned from data. These systems, especially those built on transformer architectures, enable tasks such as natural language conversation, content generation, and adaptive curricula [1–3]. The transformer model, introduced in the groundbreaking 'Attention Is All You

Need' paper (2017) by researchers at Google, revolutionised the field by enabling efficient self-attention mechanisms and parallel processing of input sequences. Its architecture bypassed earlier approaches such as RNNs, leading to vastly improved performance on NLP tasks [4]. Following this, the generative pre-trained transformer (GPT) series further advanced the field by adopting a two-stage training process: large-scale unsupervised pre-training followed by task-specific fine-tuning. Models such as GPT-3 (2020) demonstrated strong 'few-shot' and 'zero-shot' learning abilities, allowing for flexible deployment in various domains, including education-related chatbots and tutoring agents.

2.2 Applications in early childhood education

While generative AI has become widespread in formal education, its integration into early childhood learning remains limited yet promising. Research by Chen [5] offers a comprehensive overview of the evolution of AI in early childhood education (targeting ages up to eight), examining practical insights, developmental appropriateness, and ethical considerations. Other research conducted a scoping review across 16 studies, focusing on AI literacy in early education [6]. The findings suggest that carefully designed AI tools can support foundational skill development and introduce children meaningfully to AI concepts. Additionally, research underscores the significant role of AI applications, such as chatbots and speech recognition, in elevating engagement and cognitive development among young learners [7].

2.3 Generative AI and inclusive, personalised learning

Generative AI's potential to democratise learning is well documented. Research argues that generative models can pave the way for more equitable access to education, though caution is needed to ensure fairness and avoid deepening existing disparities [8]. Other research has indicated the same – AI's role in learning is the ability to hyper-personalise education for each learner [9–11]. Recent research emphasises how AI can foster inclusive learning environments, particularly for children with special needs or in multilingual settings. For example, tools built around AI-driven language assistance and real-time translation can support greater classroom diversity and accessibility [12]. These technologies, when used ethically and intentionally, have the power to support personalised pedagogy and ensure learning opportunities reach a broader range of learners. Intelligent tutoring systems have long aimed to replicate aspects of one-on-one tutoring by personalising instructional content. Others trace this evolution by examining systems such as AutoTutor and newer transformer-powered platforms (eg, the Socratic Playground), highlighting how modern generative models can facilitate reflection, adaptivity, and misconception tracking in learning environments [13].

2.4 Remaining gaps and challenges

Despite these encouraging developments, several limitations persist in AI-driven early learning solutions. Researchers warn that generative AI may inadvertently reinforce inequalities in early education unless intentionally designed to mitigate bias [14]. Furthermore, other researchers raise concerns about the 'empathy gap' in conversational AI, specifically, whether these systems can effectively recognise or respond to the emotional needs of young children [15]. This section builds on the following established insights:

- Transformers and GPT-style models offer powerful mechanisms for generating adaptive, conversational, educational content.
- AI applications in early childhood education show promise in enhancing engagement, cognitive development, and personalisation.
- Despite growing adoption, challenges remain in inclusivity, equity, emotional sensitivity, and ethical deployment.

In the subsequent section, we will present Teddy AI, contrasting its design with current tools and highlighting how it advances the field.

3. Teddy AI: Concept and design

Teddy AI is envisioned as a warm, engaging companion for early learners: one that seamlessly blends educational structure with the spontaneity of play. Its purpose is twofold: to cater to children's natural proclivity for exploration and to support parents by offering awareness, influence, and involvement in their child's learning journey. This design philosophy emphasises empathy, subtlety, and flexibility, ensuring learning feels more like a playful conversation than formal instruction.

The system is anchored by fine-tuned transformer models that manage both spoken and written dialogue. These models are tailored to produce age-appropriate responses, adapting vocabulary, sentence structure, and tone based on the child's developmental stage and engagement level. The architecture integrates natural language processing (NLP) and sentiment analysis, enabling Teddy AI to detect subtle emotional and cognitive cues, such as frustration, curiosity, or attention lapses, and adjust its responses to maintain engagement and encouragement.

The child's interface centres around a conversational AI study buddy designed with a playful, affectionate persona. Through storytelling, interactive games, and question-based prompts, Teddy encourages children to explore counting, language, shapes, and other foundational skills. It dynamically adjusts complexity based on observed performance and sentiment cues, ensuring that the interaction stays engaging and supportive.

The parent-facing interface, a dashboard accessible via smartphone or tablet, provides real-time analytics on the child's activities, progress, and emotional engagement. Parents can also input gentle prompts or requests, such as reinforcing a specific concept or introducing a new topic, which the system weaves into future interactions without interrupting the child's flow of play. Visual indicators and progress timelines allow quick insight, while optional notifications can alert parents to milestones achieved or areas of difficulty. Importantly, this interface maintains transparency without exposing children to stress or formal assessment pressure.

From the outset, Teddy AI is built with ethics in mind. All data – emotional, usage, or progress-related – are stored securely, anonymised, and governed by parents' consent. The system minimises data collection to what is strictly necessary and enables parents to review, export, or delete data at any time. The AI's learning persona is crafted to avoid manipulative strategies, reframing nudges as gentle guidance and always preserving the child's sense of agency.

4. Unique features and differentiators

This section delineates what makes Teddy AI stand out in the landscape of AI-powered early learning tools, focusing on its innovative blend of playful learning, empathetic interaction, parental integration, and ethical design.

Most early childhood educational apps tend to lean heavily towards being either overly structured (at the risk of being rigid and disengaging) or overly playful (thereby lacking educational depth). Teddy AI is deliberately designed to traverse this tension by embedding educational goals within playful and flexible interactions. Its transformer-based conversational model modulates complexity and tone based on real-time learning achievements and emotional cues – a design contextualised by theories of active discovery (Piaget), socially mediated learning (Vygotsky), and interconnected learning environments (Bronfenbrenner) [16].

A standout feature of Teddy AI is the parent dashboard's ability to introduce educational prompts covertly. Parents can suggest new concepts or reinforcement topics, such as shadows or rhymes, and the AI weaves them into future sessions naturally. This preserves the child's sense of autonomy and curiosity, aligning with positive computing design principles that support autonomy, competence, and engagement.

Unlike systems that either overly depend on parents or exclude them entirely, Teddy AI strikes a balance: parents stay informed via progress dashboards and can intervene when necessary without becoming overburdened. Similar design paradigms are seen in SET-PAiREd, where parents can adjust content generated by a learning companion robot, and StoryBuddy, where structured parent input enriches interactive storytelling without demanding constant involvement [17].

Teddy AI embeds ethical principles from the outset:

- **Developmentally appropriate content and interactions**: Tailored to respect early childhood developmental stages and parental oversight [18].

- **Privacy-first architecture**: All data are anonymised, securely stored, and fully controllable by caregivers.

- **Bias mitigation and inclusivity**: Techniques and data sources are vetted to avoid reinforcing socio-economic or cultural biases [19].

- **Transparency and explainability**: The AI's decision-making, especially around prompts and progress, is designed to be interpretable to caregivers, in line with the Transparency Index framework advocating stakeholder visibility across the AI life cycle.

By harmonising educational frameworks, empathetic engagement, parental flexibility, and ethical design, Teddy AI positions itself as a uniquely balanced and human-centred approach within early AI-enhanced learning technologies.

5. Edge AI

A defining feature of Teddy AI is its offline Edge AI architecture, where all inference and data processing occur directly on the child's device rather than in remote data centres. This design ensures that sensitive learning data never need to leave the home environment, granting parents full control over storage, deletion, and oversight. By avoiding constant server communication, Teddy AI reduces the risks of data breaches and aligns with principles of child-centred privacy and transparency.

Operating through Edge AI also delivers significant environmental benefits. Traditional cloud-based AI relies on energy-intensive data centres, whose computational and cooling demands contribute heavily to carbon emissions [20]. By contrast, Teddy AI runs optimised transformer models locally, minimising its carbon footprint while maintaining conversational fluency. This makes it a 'green AI' system, both secure and ecologically responsible.

Finally, offline operation enhances accessibility. Families in low-connectivity or resource-limited settings can still benefit from interactive, adaptive learning experiences without depending on stable internet access. In this way, Teddy AI demonstrates how Edge AI can support equitable, private, and sustainable educational technology, balancing efficiency with ethical responsibility.

In combining privacy-preserving design with energy efficiency, Teddy AI demonstrates how educational technology can be both ethically and environmentally sustainable. It offers an important counterpoint to dominant paradigms of centralised, data-hungry AI, showing that systems aimed at vulnerable populations, such as young children, can prioritise safety, transparency, and ecological responsibility without compromising functionality or user experience.

6. Research studies

Teddy AI, an AI system presented through the persona of a friendly teddy bear, has emerged as an innovative study companion designed to support children in their early learning years. Across several studies, researchers have examined its usability, educational potential, and the perspectives of both parents and teachers, who may play central roles in its adoption. Taken together, these investigations provide a holistic understanding of how conversational AI companions might shape the future of children's learning.

The first line of evidence comes from a usability study in which primary-school children interacted with Teddy AI in short sessions of approximately 12–15 minutes [21]. Engagement was observed directly, and children's impressions were captured through the well-established System Usability Scale. The results were notable: with an average score of 72.6, the children rated Teddy AI as highly usable and enjoyable, comfortably above the benchmark of 68 typically associated with acceptable usability. This suggests that even at a very young age, learners can quickly adapt to and derive enjoyment from engaging with a conversational AI when it is packaged in a child-friendly and familiar form.

While children's responses are critical, parental perspectives are equally influential in determining whether such technologies are welcomed into home learning environments. In a survey of 101 parents, most expressed positive outlooks, believing that conversational AI could support children in learning more quickly, provide authentic information, and complement existing educational practices [22]. Nevertheless, the findings also revealed a degree of ambivalence. Parents articulated concerns about issues such as privacy, overreliance on technology, and the risk of diminished human interaction. This dual attitude – optimism coupled with caution – captures the current social climate around AI in education, where enthusiasm for technological potential is tempered by apprehension about its unintended consequences.

A third and larger study extended the scope by examining both parental and teacher perspectives across 23 countries [23]. In this investigation, 220 stakeholders who had first interacted with Teddy AI offered insights into usability, desired features, benefits, and risks. Quantitative results showed broad agreement that the system was clear, coherent, and easy to use, although subtle differences emerged; for instance, parents perceived Teddy AI's response times as faster than teachers did – a statistically significant difference. Both groups emphasised the importance of NLP, personalisation, and continuous learning as desired system features. The benefits they envisioned were wide-ranging, including enhanced skill development, personalised learning opportunities, and cognitive as well as communicative growth. Yet, these anticipated advantages were consistently balanced by worries about reduced human interaction, data security, and the possibility of children becoming overly dependent on AI support.

Qualitative responses provided additional nuance. Teachers frequently noted Teddy AI's potential to support lesson planning, tailor materials to diverse learners, and strengthen students' problem-solving skills. They valued its practical utility in the classroom and its role as a complement rather than a replacement for their teaching. Parents, on the other hand, emphasised its usefulness at home, particularly in helping with homework, sustaining children's focus, and providing progress feedback. Some parents even envisioned Teddy AI playing a supportive role in areas where they themselves felt uncomfortable, such as discussing aspects of physical development or offering emotional reassurance. This suggests that Teddy AI is seen not only as an academic tool but also as a potential emotional companion, blurring the line between educational and social–emotional functions.

Taken together, these three studies converge on a coherent picture. Children find Teddy AI engaging and easy to use. Parents and teachers, while generally positive, articulate consistent reservations related to ethics, privacy, and the balance between digital and human interaction. For conversational AI companions to be widely trusted in education, their design must go beyond usability. Transparency around data handling, safeguards against the displacement of human relationships, and features that emphasise human–AI collaboration will be essential. The findings also highlight the need for further research, including deeper explorations of children's long-term experiences, cross-cultural perspectives, and rigorous evaluations of academic and emotional outcomes.

Ultimately, Teddy AI offers an illustrative case of how conversational AI can be integrated into children's learning in ways that feel natural, supportive, and engaging. Its design resonates with young learners, while parents and teachers recognise both its promise and its pitfalls. Ensuring that these concerns are addressed through ethical design and careful implementation will be critical if Teddy AI and similar systems are to be adopted not merely as novelties but as trusted companions in children's educational journeys.

DOI: http://dx.doi.org/10.5772/intechopen.1012994

7. Discussion

The studies of Teddy AI provide important insights into how conversational AI can be meaningfully embedded in early childhood learning. While much of the broader literature on generative AI in education has focused on older learners or formal classroom settings, Teddy AI's design and evaluation illustrate both the promise and complexity of applying these technologies to younger children.

A consistent finding across the empirical work is the system's usability and engagement potential. Children rated Teddy AI above benchmark levels on the System Usability Scale, demonstrating that its conversational style, playful persona, and adaptability make it accessible even to very young learners [21]. These results support long-standing arguments that learning in early childhood is most effective when integrated into play and social interaction rather than delivered through rigid instructional formats [24, 25]. Teddy AI appears to operationalise these principles, using conversational design to blur the boundaries between structured learning and imaginative play.

Equally critical are the perceptions of parents and teachers, since their trust and involvement will largely determine whether such technologies are adopted at scale. Parents in one study expressed optimism about Teddy AI's ability to accelerate learning and provide authentic information, yet they also voiced reservations about data privacy, overreliance on technology, and the erosion of human interaction [22]. Teachers echoed these ambivalent attitudes, welcoming the potential for differentiated instruction, lesson support, and problem-solving exercises, while cautioning against positioning AI as a substitute for pedagogy [23]. These findings align with wider debates in the literature, where the benefits of personalisation and accessibility are often tempered by concerns around equity, ethics, and the 'empathy gap' in AI-mediated interactions [14, 15].

What distinguishes Teddy AI in this landscape is the way its dual-interface design integrates children's autonomy with parental oversight. The child-facing interface emphasises natural conversation, narrative, and games, while the parent dashboard provides real-time analytics and discreet intervention tools. This triadic relationship (child, AI, and parent) offers a unique model of family-centred AI learning. It responds to post-pandemic shifts in which parents became more active participants in education, and it resonates with calls for 'positive computing' design principles that preserve autonomy, competence, and engagement [17]. Yet, while stakeholders valued these affordances, they also highlighted the need for transparency in how prompts are introduced and how progress is tracked, underscoring the importance of explainability in child-focused AI [19].

From a developmental perspective, Teddy AI highlights both opportunities and risks. On one hand, its ability to adapt to a child's pace and affective cues offers a form of personalised scaffolding that could help sustain motivation and support diverse learning needs, including those of multilingual learners or children with special needs [8, 12]. On the other hand, reliance on conversational AI for emotional reassurance raises questions about authenticity and the role of human caregivers in socio-emotional development [18]. The challenge, therefore, is not simply technical but ethical: ensuring that Teddy AI augments rather than replaces the relationships that underpin early learning.

Overall, Teddy AI demonstrates the viability of conversational AI as a playful, adaptive study companion for children, while highlighting the conditions under which such tools may be trusted and effective. Usability with children, cautious optimism from parents, and practical endorsement from teachers together suggest that the system addresses a real gap in early childhood educational technology. At the same time, concerns about privacy, dependence, and empathy reveal that design choices must be continuously refined. The future of Teddy AI, and similar systems, will depend on how well developers can balance engagement with transparency, autonomy with oversight, and innovation with ethical responsibility.

8. Future research and implications

The development and evaluation of Teddy AI highlight the growing potential of conversational and Edge AI systems in early childhood education, but they also underscore the need for further investigation. Future research should prioritise longitudinal studies that examine not only short-term usability and engagement but also the sustained cognitive, emotional, and social impacts of extended Teddy AI use. In particular, it remains to be seen whether adaptive conversational scaffolding translates into measurable academic gains or long-lasting improvements in skills such as problem-solving, collaboration, and self-regulation. Researchers should also explore how children's perceptions of Teddy AI evolve over time, especially as they begin to differentiate between human and artificial companions in their learning environments.

Another important direction lies in examining cultural and contextual variations. The cross-country studies already reveal broad acceptance of Teddy AI, but more granular work is needed to understand how expectations, concerns, and trust vary across educational systems, cultural contexts, and socio-economic conditions. Edge AI architecture enables deployment in low-connectivity regions, suggesting a potential role in closing global educational gaps, but only if access, language diversity, and inclusivity are carefully designed and evaluated.

Ethical and policy implications are equally central. As Teddy AI demonstrates, child-focused AI systems must embed privacy-first and transparent design principles. Offline, Edge AI operation reduces reliance on cloud infrastructure, thereby protecting sensitive data and minimising environmental impact, but parental concerns about overreliance and emotional authenticity remain. Policymakers, educators, and developers should collaborate to produce standards and frameworks for child-centred AI, ensuring fairness, accountability, and explainability. In practice, this may include certification systems for educational AI, guidelines for developmental appropriateness, and clear channels for parental control.

For practitioners, the evidence so far suggests that Teddy AI can serve as a valuable complement to human teaching and parenting. Teachers can harness its adaptive feedback and personalisation features to support differentiation, while parents can discreetly guide learning without interrupting play. Importantly, Teddy AI should not be framed as a substitute for adult interaction but rather as a scaffolding tool – one that sustains engagement, reduces anxiety, and provides continuity across home and school environments.

9. Conclusion

In conclusion, Teddy AI offers a compelling vision of how Edge AI can reshape early learning: playful, adaptive, secure, and sustainable. The empirical findings indicate strong usability for children, cautious optimism among parents, and practical endorsement from teachers, while its offline operation demonstrates that ethical and ecological design can coexist with educational innovation. The next phase of development will require careful attention to longitudinal impact, cultural inclusivity, and ethical governance. If these challenges are addressed, Teddy AI may serve not only as a study buddy but as a model for how AI in education can be equitable, family-centred, and environmentally responsible.

Conflict of interest

The authors declare no conflict of interest.

Author details

Pauldy C.J. Otermans[1,2]* and Dev Aditya[2]

1 Brunel University of London, London, United Kingdom

2 Otermans Institute, London, United Kingdom

*Address all correspondence to: pauldy.otermans@brunel.ac.uk

References

[1] Pi X, Chen Y, Liu Q. Research on the Application of AI-based Sentiment Analysis in Vocational Education. In: *Proceedings of the 2025 International Conference on Digital Education and Information Technology*. 2025, February. (pp. 130–135). DOI: 10.1145/3732299.3732325

[2] Yi H, Liu T, Lan G. The key artificial intelligence technologies in early childhood education: A review. Artificial Intelligence Review. 2024;**57**(1):12. DOI: 10.48550/arXiv.2401.05403

[3] Yu H, Guo Y. Generative artificial intelligence empowers educational reform: Current status, issues, and prospects. In: Kingsley, Okoye. Frontiers in Education. Vol. **8**. Frontiers Media SA; 2023. p. 1183162. DOI: 10.3389/feduc.2023.1183162

[4] Vaswani A, Shazeer N, Parmar N, Uszkoreit J, Jones L, Gomez AN, Polosukhin I. Attention is all you need. *Advances in neural information processing systems*, 2017;*30*. https://proceedings.neurips.cc/paper/2017/file/3f5ee243547dee91fbd053c1c4a845aa-Paper.pdf

[5] Chen JJ. From Turing's conception of machine intelligence to the evolution of AI in early childhood education: Conceptual, empirical, and practical insights. AI, Brain and Child. 2025; **1**(1):1. DOI: 10.1007/s44436-025-00002-6

[6] Su J, Ng DTK, Chu SKW. Artificial intelligence (AI) literacy in early childhood education: The challenges and opportunities. Computers and Education: Artificial Intelligence. 2023;**4**:100124. DOI: 10.1016/j.caeai.2023.100124

[7] Doğan Y, Batdı V, Topkaya Y, Özüpekçe S, Akşab HV. Effectiveness of Artificial Intelligence practices in the teaching of social sciences: A multi-complementary research approach on Pre-school education. Sustainability. 2025;**17**(7). DOI: 10.3390/su17073159

[8] Lim WM, Gunasekara A, Pallant JL, Pallant JI, Pechenkina E. Generative AI and the future of education: Ragnarök or reformation? A paradoxical perspective from management educators. The International Journal of Management Education. 2023;**21**(2):100790. DOI: 10.1016/j.ijme.2023.100790

[9] Aditya D, Silvestri K, Otermans PC. Can AI teach me employability? A multi-national study in three countries. Frontiers in Artificial Intelligence. 2024;**7**:1461158. DOI: 10.3389/frai.2024.1461158

[10] Otermans PCJ, Aditya D. Train the trainer: Using an AI teacher to upskill teachers in India. SciComm Report. 2024;**4**(1):1–10. DOI: 10.32457/scr.v4i1.2826

[11] Aditya D, Otermans PCJ. A review of AI-Enabled personalised teaching (2021–2025): Progress, impact, and future directions. Journal of the Kenya. 2025; *National Commission for UNESCO*. DOI: 10.62049/jkncu.v5i2.342

[12] Fitas R. Inclusive Education with AI: Supporting special needs and tackling language barriers. *arXiv preprint arXiv:2504.14120*. 2025. DOI: 10.48550/arXiv.2504.14120

[13] Hu X, Xu S, Tong R, Graesser A (2025). Generative AI in education:

From foundational insights to the socratic playground for learning. *arXiv preprint arXiv:2501.06682*. DOI: 10.48550/arXiv.2501.06682

[14] Kanders K, Stupple-Harris L, Smith L, Gibson JL. Perspectives on the impact of generative AI on early-childhood development and education. Infant and Child Development. 2024;**33**(4):e2514. DOI: 10.1002/icd.2514

[15] Kurian N. AI's empathy gap: The risks of conversational Artificial Intelligence for young children's well-being and key ethical considerations for early childhood education and care. Contemporary Issues in Early Childhood. 2025;**26**(1):132–139. DOI: 10.1177/14639491231206004

[16] TeddyAI.com (2025). Teddy AI white paper. https://www.teddyai.com/white [Accessed: 2025-July-1]

[17] Ho HR, Kargeti N, Liu Z, Mutlu B (2025, April). SET-PAiREd: Designing for parental involvement in learning with an AI-assisted educational robot. In: *Proceedings of the 2025 CHI Conference on Human Factors in Computing Systems* (pp. 1–20). DOI: 10.48550/arXiv.2502.17623

[18] Berson IR, Berson MJ, Luo W. Innovating responsibly: Ethical considerations for AI in early childhood education. AI, Brain and Child. 2025;**1**(1):2. DOI: 10.1007/s44436-025-00003-5

[19] Montgomery B. How and why parents and teachers are introducing young children to AI. *The Guardian*. 2025. https://www.theguardian.com/technology/2025/mar/30/parents-teachers-children-ai [Accessed: 2025-April-4]

[20] Strubell E, Ganesh A, McCallum A. Energy and policy considerations for modern deep learning research. Proceedings of the AAAI Conference on Artificial Intelligence. 2020;**34**(09):13693–13696. https://aclanthology.org/P19-1355/

[21] Otermans PCJ, Sharma A, Singh M, Aditya D. One-to-one conversational study partners for children using AI: A user experience analysis of Teddy AI. INTED Proceedings, 2024, 2024; pp. 777–783. DOI: 10.21125/inted.2024.0271

[22] Otermans PCJ, Baines S, Pereira M, Livingstone C, Aditya D. Chatting with the future: A comprehensive exploration of parents' perspectives on conversational AI implementation in Children's education. International Journal of Technology in Education. 2024;7(3):573–586. https://files.eric.ed.gov/fulltext/EJ1438408.pdf

[23] Otermans PCJ, Baines S, Livingstone C, Aditya D. Talking technology tutors: The perceptions of conversational AI in education through the eyes of parents and teachers worldwide. Under Review. 2024

[24] Piaget J. The Psychology of the Child. New York, United States.: Basic Books; 1972

[25] Vygotsky LS. Mind in Society: The Development of Higher Psychological Processes. Cambridge, Massachusetts: Harvard University Press; 1978

Chapter 18

Initial Approaches to AI-Driven Personalization in Chilean Schools

Maria Luisa Arancibia Muñoz and Juan Pablo Valenzuela Barros

Abstract

This chapter examines emerging teaching practices that personalize learning through artificial intelligence (AI) in Chilean schools. Based on focus groups conducted with teachers across various educational levels, individual strategies utilizing tools such as ChatGPT and image generators were identified. These strategies aim to adapt content, tasks, and interactions according to students' cognitive levels, interests, and contexts. The experiences shared highlight the potential for more contextually relevant, equitable, and student-centered teaching. The analysis is framed using the Artificial Intelligence in Teaching and Learning framework, alongside UNESCO's AI Competency Framework for Teachers. The chapter concludes that to establish these practices and ensure equity, it is essential to develop enabling conditions such as teacher training and institutional support strategies.

Keywords: artificial intelligence, learning personalization, teaching practices, school education, teacher training

1. Introduction

Contemporary education faces challenges in light of the rapid expansion of digital technologies, with artificial intelligence (AI) being one of the most disruptive. This technology not only transforms access to information and teaching methods but also redefines assessment practices, pedagogical languages, and relational frameworks within the classroom [1]. AI constitutes a structural component of the new learning ecosystem, requiring understanding, regulation, and guidance based on ethical, pedagogical, and democratic principles [2].

The Chilean school system is at an early stage of AI adoption. Recent studies show that teachers, school leaders, and students are already using AI-based tools for activities such as planning, assessment, feedback, and academic support, mainly through platforms such as ChatGPT, automated correctors, and virtual assistants [3, 4]. However, this adoption is spontaneous, primarily uncoordinated, and lacking standard guidelines or institutional support, leading to high pedagogical and organizational uncertainty.

The Final Evaluation Report on the Installation of Local Public Education Services [5] identifies structural barriers that limit the capacity of these services to lead deep digital transformations. These include a shortage of technological experts, fragmentation between pedagogical and administrative areas, a lack of strategic digital planning, and the absence of systematic monitoring of educational technology use in dependent schools.

Moreover, there is a significant gap between the perceptions of school leadership teams and the actual conditions teachers report. While over 90% of principals state they implement actions to facilitate Internet access, provide devices, and offer technical support to teachers, only 65% of teachers report having sufficient resources to integrate technology into their practice, and just 51% say they receive adequate technical support [6, 7]. Furthermore, 55% of teachers report having no time within their workday to receive training in AI use [3].

These gaps are exacerbated by the absence of a national strategy that aligns educational purposes, ethical frameworks, pedagogical guidelines, and institutional support mechanisms for AI use. Despite recent efforts by the Ministry of Education, such as the publication of ethical recommendations by the Innovation Center or the launch of the National AI Training Plan by CPEIP, progress remains insufficient. It fails to generate a systemic response to the impact of this emerging technology on school practices [3, 8].

This chapter documents and analyzes such experiences. Based on six focus groups with teachers from different disciplines and educational levels, we identify emerging adaptive personalization practices using AI. The analysis is organized around the Artificial Intelligence in Teaching and Learning (AITL) framework [9] and UNESCO's AI Competency Framework for Teachers [10], emphasizing professional judgment, ethics, and educational equity.

2. Methodology

A qualitative exploratory methodology was used to understand how Chilean schoolteachers construct meaning around AI in educational contexts. This approach allowed for the exploration of the phenomenon from the perspective of the actors themselves, focusing on their perceptions, knowledge, and experiences of AI use in teaching and learning processes, as well as in other aspects of their professional practice.

From an inductive and flexible perspective, priority was given to producing situated knowledge, considering that technological appropriation is not homogeneous but is shaped by specific cultural, institutional, and personal contexts [11].

The design was based on the principles of interpretative qualitative research, which seeks to account for the meanings attributed by individuals to their practices rather than measure predefined variables. As noted by Denzin and Lincoln [12], the qualitative approach is appropriate for exploring emerging phenomena where normative, ethical, and pedagogical frameworks are still under construction, as is the case with AI in school education.

2.1 Methods

The selection of focus groups was based on representativeness and convenience criteria. Considering ease of access, diversity, and authorization from school

School	Governance	Location	Teachers	Subject specialization
Liceo Horizonte Austral	Private (University of Chile)	Ñuñoa	6	Performing arts, physics, computer science
Liceo Valle verde	Public	Paine	5	History, language, citizenship education
Colegio Nueva Esperanza	Subsidized Private	Puente Alto	5	Language, philosophy, guidance
Colegio Monte del Alba	Public	Vitacura	6	Language, history, philosophy, music
Escuela Los Alerces	Public	Paine	8	Primary education, language, science
Liceo Altavista	Public	San Bernardo	6	Language, science, mathematics

Table 1.
Schools and teachers participating in focus groups.

authorities, we worked in schools located in the metropolitan region with municipal (4), subsidized private (1), and private (1) governance. Secondary school teachers' specializations were diverse, as shown in **Table 1**.

With the support of each school's leadership, one-hour meetings were scheduled and conducted with teachers who volunteered to participate: six participants in three groups, five in two groups, and eight in one group. Each session began with an introduction by the researcher and participants, followed by a brief explanation of the session's purpose, including the growing importance of AI in education. The moderator then asked the following guiding questions:

"What do you know about AI? What are its possible educational uses? That is the open question I leave you with. The idea is to have an open dialogue."

Sessions were recorded with informed consent and analyzed using ATLAS.ti. The analysis followed:

Open coding: Identifying emerging concepts and themes from teachers' narratives without predefined categories.

Axial coding: Grouping open codes into broader categories and organizing dispersed discourse elements.

Selective coding: Integrating axial categories into core themes to structure an interpretative discussion of findings.

3. Results

3.1 Emerging practices aimed at adaptive personalization

The findings from the focus groups show that AI-mediated personalization of learning is beginning to emerge from individual, exploratory, and situated practices led by teachers motivated to experiment. These practices fall into what could be described as a craft approach to adaptive personalization – unsystematic actions aimed at adjusting teaching elements to students' comprehension levels, interests, and learning styles, supported by generative AI tools.

Within this framework, it is observed that teachers are using AI for targeted modification of activities, the creation of tailored resources, or specific support for students with greater learning difficulties. AI is a scaffolding resource for the teacher, enabling them to adapt materials in real time or anticipate the group's needs.

A representative case uses prompts to generate differentiated questions according to Bloom's taxonomy, allowing teachers to design appropriate cognitive challenges for students with different performance levels. A secondary school teacher explains:

"I asked ChatGPT to give me Bloom-type questions, but they were adapted to my topic. Sometimes I use it to make a simpler and more complex version of the same activity."

This type of practice corresponds to what the AITL framework calls instructional use of AI for adaptive content design, albeit in a nonautomated way. The tool expands the teacher's pedagogical repertoire, not to replace their professional judgment.

Another form of personalization occurs through AI to modify the language or format of tasks according to students' needs. In contexts of high linguistic diversity or with students facing learning barriers, teachers report rewriting instructions, texts, or prompts with AI assistance, simplifying vocabulary, or making the activity's objectives more understandable:

"When I see that some students don't understand, I use GPT to explain it differently or make a simpler instruction. It helps me when I'm in a hurry."

These experiences represent a strategic use of AI as a facilitator of accessibility, where the teacher retains control of pedagogical mediation but finds efficient support to diversify their resources through AI.

Practices also emerge aimed at personalization through contextual relevance, for example, generating images with DALL · E or similar tools that depict everyday situations from the students' environment. This allows for more meaningful connections between school content and students' reality, especially in contexts of vulnerability or school disengagement:

"I've generated images that relate to their daily lives, like a street market or a local bus. That way, they get more engaged because it makes sense."

This form of personalization through contextualization responds to the sociocultural dimension of educational AI, often overlooked in technocratic approaches, yet key to advancing toward a situated AI.

Another observed practice is the use of AI to model step-by-step problem-solving in subjects such as mathematics or physics, enabling teachers to prepare clearer examples or anticipate comprehension difficulties:

"I give them examples generated with AI that show all the steps of an exercise. Sometimes I compare them with the ones I make so they can see different ways to reach the result."

In this case, AI operates as a simulated cognitive tutor, supporting both students' autonomous learning and enriching teachers' explanations.

Although still in their early stages, these practices demonstrate that teachers are not delegating teaching to the machine but rather leveraging its capabilities to diversify, adjust, or enrich their pedagogical proposals.

However, these practices remain individual, noninstitutionalized, and highly uneven, generating excessive dependence on each teacher's personal motivation and digital capital. Below is a synthesis of the most relevant findings (**Table 2**).

Type of practice	Pedagogical purpose	Teacher example
Cognitive differentiation	Adjust the complexity level of questions or tasks.	I ask for Bloom-type questions for those who need more support.
Simplification and accessibility	Rephrase instructions or texts for students with difficulties.	I change the instructions with GPT when I see it doesn't understand.
Visual contextualization	Generate images or situations relevant to the student's environment.	Images with things they know, like the street market or the local bus.
Step-by-step modeling	Show detailed solution processes in complex areas.	I give them examples that explain all the steps with AI.
Interest stimulation	Motivate through personalized or creative materials.	I invent stories using their names or topics they like.

Table 2.
Summary of findings.

4. Conclusions and discussion

This chapter highlights early experiences of AI-mediated personalized learning in Chilean schools, led by teachers who independently and experimentally explore using tools such as ChatGPT and image generators. These practices arise in a context of high uncertainty and low regulation. Still, they reflect a growing interest among teachers in adapting instruction to the characteristics and needs of their students.

The identified practices are individual and unsystematic, yet pedagogically intentional; they are situated in that they respond to concrete classroom conditions; and they are adaptive, aiming to address the cognitive, linguistic, and cultural diversity in school contexts. These are not signs of a structural transformation but rather early indications of technological appropriation that open questions and opportunities for developing more robust approaches.

The findings suggest that the pedagogical potential of AI does not lie in automation but in its ability to expand teachers' professional capacities, provided its use is guided ethically and from a critical, inclusive, and contextually grounded perspective. In this sense, the experiences documented here align with the principles of the AITL framework and UNESCO's AI Competency Framework for Teachers [10], as they show an emerging use of AI in the service of learning rather than as a replacement for the teacher's role.

However, fragmentation, unequal access to specialized training, and the lack of institutional support in Chile limit the potential to scale these practices. There is a risk that educational AI could become a factor that widens existing gaps if its adoption depends solely on individual motivation or the specific conditions of each school.

AI is already being used in Chilean school settings, albeit on a personal and isolated basis.

Moving from exploratory experiences toward sustainable and equitable integration of AI requires continuous, situated, and critical teacher training that integrates pedagogical, technological, and ethical dimensions; clear and contextually relevant institutional guidelines to guide AI use in schools; and enabling conditions, including time for training, accessible technological resources, and sustained technical and pedagogical support.

In sum, AI can be an opportunity to reconfigure teaching practices and move toward a more personalized, inclusive, and contextualized education. However, for this to happen, the Chilean education system must take an active role, creating the conditions for these practices to move beyond isolated cases and become part of a transformative, ethical, and learning-centered strategy.

Acknowledgments

Funding from ANID/Support 2024 AFB240004 is gratefully acknowledged.

Conflict of interest

The authors declare no conflict of interest.

Author details

Maria Luisa Arancibia Muñoz* and Juan Pablo Valenzuela Barros
Center for Advanced Research in Education (CIAE), University of Chile, Chile

*Address all correspondence to: marialuisa.arancibia@ciae.uchile.cl

References

[1] Selwyn N. Should Robots Replace Teachers? AI and the Future of Education. Cambridge: Polity; 2019

[2] Williamson B, Eynon R. Historical threads, missing links, and future directions in AI in education. Learning, Media and Technology. 2020;**45**(3): 223–235. DOI: 10.1080/17439884.2020.1798995

[3] Centro de Investigación Avanzada En Educación (CIAE), Universidad de Chile. Santiago: Universidad de Chile; 2025 https://ciae.uchile.cl/noticia/esta-la-escuela-preparada-para-la-inteligencia-artificial-estudio-revela-que-piensan-los-docentes-chilenos

[4] Chile C, Criteria Research. Digital X-ray: Children and adolescents 2025. Santiago: Claro Chile; 2025. Available from: https://www.clarochile.cl/portal/cl/recursos_contenido/pdf/1740414684180-informe-radiografia-digital-nna-2025.pdf [Accessed: 2025-August-7]

[5] Centro de Investigación Avanzada en Educación (CIAE), Universidad de Chile. External Evaluation of the New Public Education Policy on the Correct Installation and Transfer of SLEPs: Final Report. Santiago: Universidad de Chile; 2024. Available from: https://www.ciae.uchile.cl/biblioteca/documentos/evaluacion-externa-de-la-politica-de-nueva-educacion-publica-sobre-la-correcta-instalacion-y-traspaso-de-los-slep

[6] Centro de Innovación del Ministerio de Educación (CIM). Executive Summary National Survey of Digital Development and Educational Innovation. [Internet]. Santiago: Ministry of Education of Chile; 2024. Available from: https://www.innovacion.mineduc.cl/iniciativas/transformaci%C3%B3n-digital/encuesta-nacional-desarrollo-digital-escolar-e-innovaci%C3%B3n-educativa

[7] Centro de Innovación del Ministerio de Educación (CIM). Qualitative study on appropriation and challenges of AI use in public schools [Internet]. Santiago: Ministry of Education of Chile; 2024. Available from: https://drive.google.com/file/d/1dKY-n5exzEHUalU8hVZSUftmXnR_JYyT/view [Accessed: 2025-August-7]

[8] Centro de Perfeccionamiento, Experimentación e Investigaciones Pedagógicas (CPEIP). Artificial intelligence in education training plan [Internet]. Santiago: Ministry of Education of Chile; 2024. Available from: https://cpeip.cl/cpeip-liderando-la-formacion-docente-en-inteligencia-artificial/ [Accessed: 2025-August-7]

[9] Holmes W, Bialik M, Fadel C. Artificial Intelligence in Education: Promises and implications for teaching and learning. Boston: Center for Curriculum Redesign; 2019

[10] UNESCO. Teachers' Digital Competence Framework in Artificial Intelligence. Paris: UNESCO; 2024

[11] Flick U. An Introduction to Qualitative Research. 6th ed. London: SAGE Publications; 2018

[12] Denzin NK, Lincoln YS. The SAGE Handbook of Qualitative Research. 5th ed. Thousand Oaks: SAGE Publications; 2005

Section 4

Ethics, Equity, Fairness & Responsible AI

Chapter 19

Generative AI in Higher Education: Uses and Ethical Dilemmas of Students

Meital Amzalag and Gila Kurtz

Abstract

The research examines how college and university students in Israel use Generative AI (GenAI) tools for their studies and explores the ethical challenges they face when incorporating these technologies into their education. As GenAI becomes increasingly integrated into higher education, it is essential to understand its pedagogical roles and the ethical challenges it presents. A nationwide mixed-methods study was conducted with 673 participants from various academic institutions. Data was collected through an online questionnaire and analyzed using quantitative methods and qualitative content analysis of open-ended responses. The findings reveal that GenAI tools, particularly ChatGPT, have become integrated into students' academic routines, with undergraduate students using these tools more frequently than graduate students. Students reported using GenAI to search for learning materials, clarify complex content, and generate inspiration. Concurrently, they expressed concerns regarding the accuracy of information, privacy, academic integrity, and the absence of clear institutional guidelines. The ethical dilemmas reported included uncertainty about the acceptable use of GenAI, the temptation to rely on GenAI for assignments, and conflicting values concerning independent learning. This study highlights the dual nature of GenAI use – beneficial for learning yet prone to ethical misuse. It underscores students' desire for institutional guidance and emphasizes the importance of fostering both digital literacy and ethical awareness in academic contexts.

Keywords: artificial intelligence, generative AI, higher education, university students, GenAI ethics

1. Introduction

In recent years, academia has encountered a unique historical juncture. Generative artificial intelligence (GenAI) technology has captivated the world and is swiftly permeating all facets of life. GenAI tools facilitate a conversation between humans and machines that feels natural, enabling machines to intelligently and eloquently answer questions, critique texts and ideas, draw conclusions, and plan complex programs [1–3]. Remarkably, this often requires no prior professional or technological expertise. It is anticipated that the advent of GenAI tools will bring about profound changes, not only in academia but also in everyday human life [4, 5].

Among the popular GenAI tools is ChatGPT, designed to comprehend human prompts and generate responses in a conversational style [6]. The intelligent capabilities and user-friendliness of GenAI tools, such as ChatGPT, offer numerous learning opportunities and diverse applications with substantial pedagogical potential [7]. GenAI tools can play supplementary or complementary roles in the learning process, serving as learning assistants, facilitating personalized learning, and aiding in content creation [8–12].

Learning is a broad term encompassing various definitions. Among the most frequently referenced is Vygotsky's definition, which highlights the social aspect of learning and the significance of cultural and social interactions. Vygotsky posits that learning is a social process where knowledge is constructed through interactions with others and the environment. This process is mediated by language and cultural tools and occurs within the Zone of Proximal Development (ZPD). The ZPD represents the range of tasks a learner can accomplish with assistance and guidance from others but cannot yet complete independently [13]. With this understanding, we employ the term "learning" in this chapter.

Integrating GenAI into learning presents ethical challenges that necessitate thorough investigation. For instance, GenAI tools complicate the ability to determine whether a product was created by a machine or a human [4, 6, 14, 15]. The unethical use of GenAI tools could undermine the value of an academic degree. It might result in higher education institutions graduating students who are inadequately prepared for the labor market [5, 16, 17].

It is evident that GenAI tools are here to stay and will likely continue to exert a strong influence on the academic teaching–learning process. Considering this, higher education institutions must be adequately prepared. Although several studies have explored students' perceptions of GenAI's applications for learning and ethical considerations across various countries (e.g., 18–22), there is limited knowledge about the uses and ethical dilemmas students encounter when integrating GenAI into their learning. Given this context, this study assessed students' self-perceptions regarding the extent and types of GenAI tool usage for learning, as well as the ethical dilemmas that arise from incorporating GenAI into their educational experience.

2. Literature review

2.1 GenAI in higher education

Academic learning typically follows structured processes, including lectures, reading assignments, written work, and assessments aimed at fostering deep understanding and critical thinking [18]. The integration of artificial intelligence (AI) and, more recently, GenAI into these processes opens new possibilities while also raising fundamental questions about the nature of learning and academic work.

Studies have demonstrated the significant potential of integrating AI technologies into higher education [19, 20]. Moreover, in their systematic literature review on AI in education (AIEd), Zawacki-Richter et al. (2019) predicted that AI tools will be a top educational technology issue for the next 20 years [21]. Ouyang et al. (2022)

emphasized the need for more empirical research to test the actual effects of AI tools, particularly in online higher education [22].

Research on the integration and development of AI through GenAI in higher education encompasses numerous studies. These studies often employ case study methodologies, focusing on learner populations, specific academic disciplines, or position papers (for example, 28–32). Among the few national-scale studies exploring GenAI usage patterns in academic learning, nearly 2,000 Swedish students participated in an online survey between April and May 2023. The results highlighted students' familiarity with and use of ChatGPT, as well as their positive perceptions of GenAI tools in the learning process. Almost all respondents were familiar with ChatGPT, and over a third used it on a regular basis. Most students expressed a favorable attitude toward employing chatbots and other GenAI tools in education, with many asserting that GenAI enhanced their learning effectiveness. In contrast, the majority of students expressed uncertainty regarding whether their educational institutions had implemented policies or guidelines for the responsible use of GenAI [23].

The research literature indeed indicates that tools like ChatGPT can expand learning processes across various subjects, facilitate writing, and thereby alleviate the pressure of drafting papers. They also help reduce cognitive load, granting learners autonomy that enhances their sense of control over their learning processes and bolsters their confidence in their abilities. Additionally, these tools provide constant, real-time feedback on performance, which can significantly enhance students' learning experiences [5, 17, 24]. Consequently, students' engagement in the learning process is likely to increase, along with their capacity to evaluate information and pose questions, thereby reinforcing their critical learning skills [17, 25]. Moreover, ChatGPT may have social implications, as it can be utilized to foster dialog with learners, thus mitigating the loneliness some students experience during their academic studies [5, 17, 24].

2.2 Ethical dimensions of GenAI use in higher education

The ethical use of GenAI in academic contexts has emerged as a pressing concern in higher education. Ethics, as a branch of philosophy, addresses the principles of right and wrong, justice, and fairness [26]. AI ethics focuses on guiding the development and use of AI systems through values such as responsibility, transparency, and respect for human agency [27].

Although ethical discussions regarding AI technologies date back to the 1960s [5, 26], recent developments in GenAI have intensified the debate. The ability of GenAI tools to generate highly sophisticated outputs, which are often indistinguishable from human work, creates new challenges for academic institutions. Concerns include the potential for plagiarism, misinformation, knowledge manipulation, and privacy violations [5, 7, 17, 28].

These challenges raise critical questions regarding academic integrity and authorship in higher education. When students submit assignments generated wholly or in part using GenAI tools, it becomes difficult to assess their actual understanding or learning progress [12, 29]. Furthermore, institutions often lack formal guidelines for the use of GenAI, leading to uncertainty among students regarding what is permitted or prohibited. A study by Sullivan et al. [30] found that ethical discourse in academia is primarily limited to concerns about cheating rather than encompassing broader ethical principles such as equity, accountability, or bias.

Zawacki-Richter et al. [21] note the scarcity of empirical studies exploring the ethical implications of AI in educational settings. More recently, Crawford et al. [5] and others have called for ethical leadership and the establishment of clear frameworks to support the responsible use of GenAI in learning environments. Despite these requests, agreed-upon institutional standards remain largely absent, leaving students to navigate the space independently.

Students' ethical decisions are shaped not only by institutional expectations but also by academic pressure, time constraints, and perceptions of peer behavior. Research has shown that some students justify the use of GenAI for tasks such as writing papers or solving assignments due to stress, fear of failure, or the belief that "everyone else is doing it" [5, 31]. In such cases, misconduct is not necessarily a result of malicious intent but rather a product of unclear norms and external pressures.

This context highlights the importance of understanding how students perceive the ethical boundaries of GenAI. It also grabs attention to the need for educational interventions that promote not only technical literacy but also ethical reasoning and academic integrity in the age of GenAI.

2.3 Students' ethical dilemmas in practice

Although much of the literature on GenAI in education addresses ethical challenges from institutional or theoretical perspectives [5, 30], an increasing number of studies have examined how students interpret and navigate these dilemmas. These studies shed light on the moral ambiguity learners face in academic settings, particularly when institutional guidelines are vague or inconsistently applied.

For example, Sullivan et al. (2023) found that many students are unsure whether using GenAI tools to summarize texts, generate drafts, or proofread content constitutes academic misconduct [30]. Similarly, Crawford et al. [5] reported that students often perceive a contradiction between the institutional promotion of digital innovation and the lack of concrete guidance, leading to confusion and inconsistent decision-making.

Cotton et al. [17] emphasize that some students justify the use of GenAI as a coping mechanism for academic overload or based on the perception that their peers are also relying on such tools. In such cases, ethical reasoning is influenced not only by formal policies but also by peer norms and social comparisons [17]. Attard-Frost et al. [27] noted that inconsistencies in instructors' responses to GenAI reinforce the sense that ethical boundaries are context-dependent and unclear.

While these studies offer valuable insights, the body of research in this domain remains limited. There is a paucity of knowledge regarding the variation in students' ethical reasoning across different academic levels, prior experiences with GenAI, and diverse cultural and linguistic contexts. The majority of existing studies have been conducted in relatively homogeneous settings, underscoring the need for research that encompasses diverse student populations and educational contexts.

2.4 Research gap and study rationale

The increasing integration of GenAI tools in higher education presents both opportunities and ethical challenges. Previous research has explored the technological potential of GenAI and addressed its ethical implications from institutional and theoretical perspectives; however, empirical evidence on how students use these tools and how they perceive the ethical boundaries remains scarce.

Most existing studies focus on specific tools, narrow student populations, or conceptual debates rather than capturing students' real-world experiences across diverse academic settings. Only a few studies have systematically examined students' ethical reasoning, and even fewer have considered how these perspectives vary by academic level or prior experience with GenAI.

This study addresses these gaps by offering a large-scale empirical investigation of students in Israeli higher education. It examines how undergraduate and graduate students use GenAI tools for academic purposes and explores the ethical dilemmas they report. By analyzing differences across student sub-groups and experience levels, the study aims to contribute to a more nuanced understanding of how GenAI is reshaping academic learning and student decision-making.

3. Research questions

Given the growing integration of GenAI in educational settings, understanding how students utilize these technologies and the ethical implications that arise is crucial. This research aims to explore the interactions between students and GenAI tools, with a focus on usage patterns and the ethical dilemmas they present. Specifically, the study addresses the following research questions:

(1) What are undergraduate and graduate students' uses of GenAI tools for learning purposes?

Previous studies, such as those by Bates et al. [19] and Verma & Tomar [20], have demonstrated the potential of AI in education. However, students' specific uses of GenAI tools, such as ChatGPT, have not been thoroughly examined, nor has the possible distinction between undergraduate and graduate students been explored. This study aims to fill that gap by mapping the types and extent of uses [19, 20].

(2) What ethical dilemmas do undergraduate and graduate students face related to using GenAI tools for learning?

The research literature, including work by Zawacki-Richter et al. [21] and Sullivan et al. [30], indicates growing concerns about the ethical implications of AI in education. These concerns include issues such as academic dishonesty and the potential undermining of critical skills [21, 30]. Although Zawacki-Richter et al. [21] cover both undergraduate and graduate levels in their systematic review of research on AI tools in higher education, the numbers reported suggest a greater focus on undergraduate applications of AI in higher education. This question explores students' ethical dilemmas in the context of these concerns.

4. Research method and procedure

The research instrument included both closed-ended items (Likert scales) and an open-ended question. The initial questionnaire was developed based on a literature review and exploratory consultations with the students. It was first distributed as a pilot survey ($n = 289$) using convenience sampling, which helped refine both the structure and content of the final instrument.

Three scales were tested during the pilot phase: (1) a scale measuring the scope of use of GenAI tools for learning purposes (eleven items, $\alpha = 0.857$); (2) a scale assessing perceived academic implications of GenAI (eleven items, $\alpha = 0.616$); and (3) a single-item open-ended question on academic uses of GenAI tools.

Following the pilot study, the questionnaire was revised and reviewed by experts in GenAI and educational ethics to ensure content validity and clarity. The final version used in the national study retained the scale measuring academic GenAI use (eleven items, $\alpha = 0.821$) and the six-item scale on ethical perceptions ($\alpha = 0.562$). Due to its limited internal consistency, the ethical perception scale was analyzed item by item rather than as a composite index.

Data collection was conducted during the period May 1–8, 2023. The participants were selected using stratified sampling to ensure a representative cross-section of Israeli higher education students. The online questionnaire was distributed via iPanel, one of Israel's largest sampling companies, encompassing 100,000 participants from all corners of the population. The iPanel adheres to the standards set by the ESOMAR (European Society for Opinion and Marketing Research) organization for the management and maintenance of internet panels. The company typically uses advanced sampling and stratification techniques to ensure representative samples for different research projects. The questionnaire was designed to cover a wide range of topics related to GenAI, including demographic questions, the most used GenAI tools, the various learning tools of GenAI, and students' ethical perceptions regarding the use of GenAI for learning purposes (see Appendix A for the questionnaire).

4.1 Sample characteristics

Six hundred seventy-three students participated in the national study conducted in Israel, answering the online questionnaire. Among them, 471 students (70%) reported using GenAI tools for learning. **Table 1** provides an overview of demographics and GenAI usage among the subgroup of participants who reported using GenAI tools specifically for learning purposes.

About 72.2% of the research participants were women, while 27.8% were men. The average age of the study participants was 25.29 years (SD = 4.43). Regarding education, 86.3% of respondents were undergraduate students, 9.5% were graduate students, and the rest were pursuing doctoral degrees. The most common GenAI application is ChatGPT (94.2%), with Dall-E (2.6%) far behind. The respondents were studying in various higher education institutions and a wide variety of fields, including social sciences, exact sciences, humanities, and computer science. An examination of the representativeness of our sample indicates a slight bias in favor of women and against graduate students. The sample's age distribution was representative of the entire student population in Israel [32]. This bias is likely due to the voluntary nature of the participants' responses.

The age groups were defined based on the classification of age ranges in higher education by the Central Bureau of Statistics in Israel [33].

Characteristic	Value	Percentage	Cumulative percentage
Gender			
Women	340	72.2	72.2
Men	131	27.8	100
Age			
18–24	213	45.2	45.2
24–29	211	44.8	90
Above 29	47	10	100
Education level			
Undergraduate	371	86.3	86.3
Graduate	41	9.5	95.8
Doctoral	18	4.2	100
GenAI usage for learning	100		100
GenAI tools			
ChatGPT	444	94.2	94.2
Dall-E	12	2.6	96.8
Futurepedia	2	0.5	97.3
Wordtune	3	0.7	98
Jasper	2	0.5	98.5
Descript	3	0.7	99.2
Elicit	4	0.8	100

Table 1.
Demographics and GenAI usage of students using GenAI for learning (n = 471).

4.2 Data analysis

The quantitative data analysis utilized SPSS software to calculate frequencies, averages, standard deviations, and *t*-tests. The *t*-tests were used to identify significant differences between subgroups (e.g., undergraduate vs. graduate students) regarding the GenAI learning uses and ethical dilemmas. Additionally, we conducted the Mann–Whitney test to ensure robustness, as it serves as a non-parametric alternative to the *t*-test.

The qualitative data analysis for the open-ended question on ethical dilemmas involved content analysis and was executed in five steps. Initially, one of the researchers conducted an inductive analysis on a sample of the data, identifying themes and sub-themes. In the second step, this researcher passed the same qualitative data, without the analysis, along with the identified themes and sub-themes, to a second researcher for further analysis. Upon comparing the analyses, we discovered that the inter-researcher reliability was low, at 60%. Given this low reliability, the third stage involved the researchers reviewing their disagreements to pinpoint gaps in the analysis. After reanalyzing the data, they achieved a reliability of 63%. As this was still insufficient, they decided to meet again to refine the themes and sub-themes, even opting to remove one theme. In the fourth stage, they analyzed another portion of the qualitative data using the revised definitions of themes and sub-themes. Comparing these analyses revealed that the reliability between the researchers had increased to 83%. With this improved reliability, the researchers proceeded to the fifth stage, analyzing the remaining qualitative data according to the updated themes and sub-themes.

4.3 Ethics

Both questionnaires were anonymous, and the respondents were allowed to stop answering them at any stage. The study was approved by the Faculty Ethics Committee of our academic institution.

5. Findings

5.1 GenAI learning uses

The first research question examined students' use of GenAI tools for educational purposes. First, we examined the frequencies of each of the six items (see **Figure 1**) and the means and standard deviations (see **Table 2**).

Figure 1 presents the findings. Then, we analyzed whether there are significant differences in these usages between undergraduate and graduate students (see **Table** 2).

Range from 1 (not using at all) to 5 (using very frequently); for graphical representation, we combined 1 (not at all) and 2 (very little) into one category (not using), and 4 (frequently) and 5 (very frequently) into another category (using), while 3 (occasionally) represents moderate or infrequent use. The calculation was performed only among students who reported using GenAI tools.

Figure 1 shows that most GenAI learning uses involve searching for educational material, explaining unclear educational content, and getting ideas for inspiration. Students seldom summarize educational content. The means and standard deviation presented in **Table 2** indicate that students occasionally use GenAI for educational purposes.

Ranging from 1 (not using at all) to 5 (using very frequently); the calculation was performed only among students who reported using GenAI tools; n = 471.

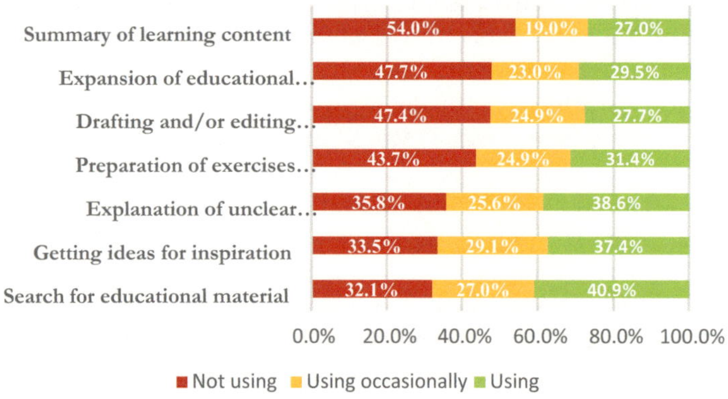

Figure 1.
*GenAI learning uses for educational purposes (*n = *471).*

Items	M (SD)
Explanation of unclear educational content	3.10 (1.334)
Searching for educational material	3.10 (1.334)
Getting ideas for inspiration	3.01 (1.273)
Preparation of exercises and/or papers	2.75 (1.396)
Expansion of educational content	2.66 (1.343)
Drafting and/or editing educational content	2.65 (1.350)
Summary of learning content	2.49 (1.387)

Table 2.
GenAI learning uses for educational purposes.

To analyze differences in students' GenAI learning uses between undergraduate and graduate students, we performed an independent samples t-test for the variable representing the usage of GenAI tools for educational purposes. The findings indicate a significant difference in these usages between undergraduate and graduate students ($t(428) = 3.309$, $p = 0.001$). Undergraduate students use GenAI tools for educational purposes more frequently (M = 2.869, SD = 0.926) than graduate students (M = 2.438, SD = 0.945). To gain a deeper understanding of the difference observed, we conducted an independent samples t-test for each item that constitutes the variable usage of GenAI tools for educational purposes. The findings are presented in **Table 3**.

Ranging from 1 (not using at all) to 5 (using very frequently); the independent samples t-test results are based on the p-value of Levene's test for equality of variance; the calculation was performed only among students who reported using GenAI tools; $n = 471$.

Based on the findings in **Table 3**, we observe significant differences in students' GenAI learning uses, such as obtaining explanations for unclear academic content,

Items	Undergraduate students	Graduate students			
	M (SD)	M (SD)	t	p	Cohen's d
Explanation of unclear educational content	3.07 (1.361)	2.56 (1.454)	2.667	0.008	0.374
Getting ideas for inspiration	3.05 (1.262)	2.75 (1.321)	1.731	0.084	0.243
Preparation of exercises and/or papers	2.87 (1.373)	1.98 (1.306)	4.658	<0.001	0.653
Expansion of educational content	2.73 (1.319)	2.27 (1.436)	2.424	0.016	0.340
Drafting and/or editing educational content	2.65 (1.338)	2.66 (1.434)	0.046	0.963	0.006
Summary of learning content	2.55 (1.397)	2.15 (1.284)	2.037	0.042	0.286
Searching for educational material	3.16 (1.325)	2.69 (1.329)	2.498	0.013	0.35

Table 3.
Comparison between undergraduate and graduate students' GenAI learning uses.

preparing exercises and/or papers, expanding on educational content, searching for educational material, and summarizing educational content. In all these cases, the usage is higher among undergraduate students. The t-values and p-values reported in **Table 3** indicate the statistical significance of the differences in learning uses of GenAI tools between undergraduate and graduate students. For example, explanation of unclear educational content: The t-value is 2.667 and the p-value is 0.008, indicating a statistically significant difference. Undergraduate students (M = 3.07, SD = 1.361) use GenAI tools more frequently for this purpose compared to graduate students (M = 2.56, SD = 1.454), with a medium effect size (Cohen's $d = 0.374$). Getting ideas for inspiration: The t-value is 1.731 and the p-value is 0.084, which is not statistically significant at the conventional alpha level of 0.05. This suggests no significant difference between undergraduate (M = 3.05, SD = 1.262) and graduate students (M = 2.75, SD = 1.321) for this usage, with a small effect size (Cohen's $d = 0.243$).

5.2 Ethical dilemmas

The second research question examined the students' ethical dilemmas related to using GenAI tools for learning. The questionnaire included six closed-ended items and one open-ended question.

To answer this question, we first examined the frequencies of each of the six items (see **Figure 2**) as well as the means and standard deviations (see **Table 4**). Then, we analyzed whether there are significant differences in students' ethical dilemmas related to using GenAI tools between undergraduate and graduate students (see **Table 5**), and between students who did not use GenAI tools and those who did. In both cases, we used an independent samples t-test (see **Table 6**).

For graphical representation, we combined 1 (strongly disagree) and 2 (disagree) into one category (do not agree), 4 (agree) and 5 (strongly agree) into another category (agree), and 3 (sometimes agree), which represents partial agreement, indicating moderate or occasional agreement with the statement.

Figure 2 shows that most students agreed that the use of AI tools can perpetuate mistakes, and most thought that using AI tools raised ethical dilemmas and perpetuated gaps. Additionally, most students reported moral behavior, as evidenced

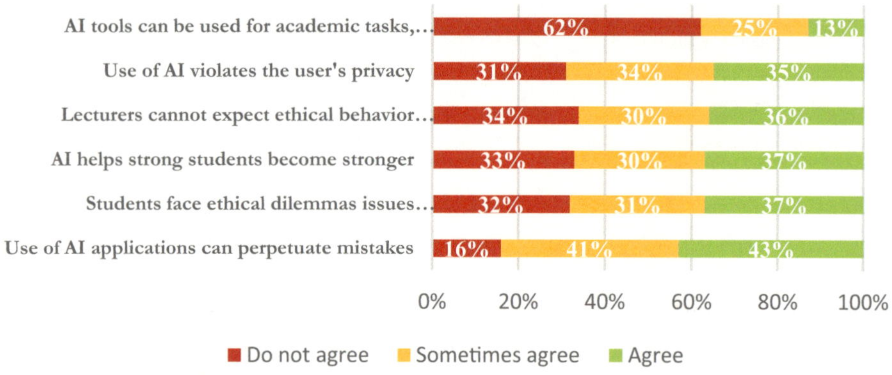

Figure 2.
Students' ethical dilemmas.

Statement	M	SD
The use of AI tools can perpetuate mistakes	3.39	0.997
The use of AI tools violates the user's privacy	3.06	1.111
Students face ethical dilemmas regarding the use of AI tools in learning	3.06	1.173
AI helps strong students become stronger	3.05	1.201
Lecturers cannot expect us to behave ethically if we have not been presented with ethical standards for the use of AI tools	3.02	1.201
AI tools can be used for academic tasks even when they are prohibited	2.28	1.124

Table 4.
Students' ethical dilemmas.

Items	Undergraduate students	Graduate students			
	M (SD)	M (SD)	*t*	*p*	Cohen's *d*
The use of GenAI tools can perpetuate mistakes	3.40 (0.993)	3.56 (1.149)	1.146	0.252	0.161
The use of GenAI tools violates the user's privacy	3.04 (1.131)	2.76 (1.236)	1.712	0.088	0.240
Students face ethical dilemmas regarding the use of GenAI tools in learning	2.99 (1.193)	3.22 (1.084)	1.382	0.168	0.194
GenAI helps strong students become stronger	3.19 (1.256)	2.92 (1.222)	1.589	0.113	0.223
Lecturers cannot expect us to behave ethically if we have not been presented with ethical standards for the use of GenAI tools	3.12 (1.215)	2.86 (1.166)	1.485	0.138	0.208
GenAI tools can be used for academic tasks, even when they are prohibited	2.35 (1.166)	1.97 (0.964)	2.421	0.016	0.339

Table 5.
Comparison between undergraduate and graduate students' ethical dilemmas.

by the lowest percentage of students who agreed that a tool could be used even when prohibited. Accordingly, most students encountered these ethical dilemmas with modest frequency, as shown in **Table 4**.

Ranging from 1 (strongly disagree) to 5 (strongly agree).

Table 4 shows that students sometimes agreed with statements addressing various ethical issues. The two statements with the highest averages, which perpetuate mistakes and damage the user's privacy, may indicate familiarity with ChatGPT's shortcomings. The statement with the lowest average indicates that students claimed they used GenAI tools only when approved.

To analyze differences in students' ethical dilemmas related to using GenAI tools for learning between undergraduate and graduate students, we performed an independent sample t-test, as presented in **Table 5**:

Ranging from 1 (strongly disagree) to 5 (strongly agree); the independent samples t-test results are based on the p-value of Levene's test for equality of variance.

Items	Students who did not use GenAI tools	Students who use GenAI tools			
	M (SD)	M (SD)	*t*	*p*	Cohen's *d*
The use of GenAI tools can perpetuate mistakes	3.31 (0.953)	3.42 (1.016)	1.223	0.222	0.107
The use of GenAI tools violates the user's privacy	2.79 (1.009)	3.00 (1.149)	2.189	0.029	0.191
Students face ethical dilemmas regarding the use of GenAI tools in learning	3.15 (1.153)	3.02 (1.180)	1.221	0.223	0.107
GenAI helps strong students become stronger	2.81 (1.094)	3.16 (1.254)	3.464	<0.001	0.287
Lecturers cannot expect us to behave ethically if we have not been presented with ethical standards for the use of GenAI tools	2.87 (1.169)	3.08 (1.210)	1.994	0.047	0.174
GenAI tools can be used for academic tasks, even when they are prohibited	2.23(1.070)	2.30(1.147)	0.739	0.460	0.064

Table 6.
Students' ethical dilemmas related to using GenAI tools for learning between students who did not use GenAI tools and those who did range from 1 (strongly disagree) to 5 (strongly agree); the independent samples t*-test results are based on the* p*-value of Levene's test for equality of variance.*

Table 5 indicates that most items addressing non-ethical dilemmas related to the educational use of GenAI tools among students were rated higher by undergraduate students, although the means suggest moderate agreement. However, the differences between undergraduate and graduate students on these issues are not significant, except for the item regarding the use of AI tools for academic tasks, even when not permitted.

We used an independent samples *t*-test (see **Table 6**) to analyze differences in students' ethical dilemmas related to using GenAI tools for learning between students who did not use GenAI tools and those who did.

Table 6 indicates that students generally hold moderate views on ethical dilemmas related to using GenAI tools for learning. Additionally, for most items, students who used GenAI tools rated the items higher than those who did not, except for the item concerning students facing ethical dilemmas regarding the use of GenAI tools in learning.

Significant differences between students using GenAI tools and students who did not use them indicate that students who used GenAI tools are more concerned about the potential privacy violations associated with these tools (M = 3.00, SD = 1.149) compared to students who did not use these tools (M = 2.79, SD = 1.009). They also believe that GenAI tools tend to benefit stronger students more than students who do not use these tools (M = 3.16, SD = 1.254; M = 2.81, SD = 1.094, respectively). Additionally, statistical differences indicate that students familiar with GenAI tools think that lecturers cannot expect ethical behavior from students without explicit guidelines (M = 3.08, SD = 1.210), more so than students who have no experience with these tools (M = 2.87, SD = 1.169).

Additionally, students were asked an open-ended question to detail the ethical dilemmas they might face during their studies due to using GenAI tools. A content

Theme name	Frequency
Academic integrity	53%
The credibility of the received content	18%
The blurred line between permitted and forbidden	16%
The essence of academic learning	16%

Table 7.
Frequencies of the four main themes raised from content analysis.

analysis of 116 responses revealed four themes, presented according to their frequency and shown in **Table 7**.

In some cases, respondents addressed a theme more than once, resulting in the total percentage exceeding 100%.

5.3 Academic integrity

Most of the statements on academic integrity directly refer to cheating and copying. These quotes highlight students' ease in using GenAI tools for academic assignments and their fear of being caught.

- How can I ensure the lecturer does not discover [that I used ChatGPT?].
- An academic paper can be written in its entirety with no effort.

5.4 The credibility of the received content

The research participants also referred to the credibility of the content obtained from GenAI because of asking questions using prompts:

- The information provided by GenAI is not always accurate or reliable, and using it in academic articles may perpetuate mistakes.
- Sometimes, it makes mistakes, and you don't know.
- GenAI content is something that the developers have taught it, and it sometimes contains racism and chauvinism.

5.5 The blurred line between permitted and forbidden

One of the main problems raised by students was that it was unclear to them when it was permissible to use GenAI tools and what was considered copying versus inspiration, as can be seen from the following quotations:

- Is it legal to use GenAI?
- When asking GenAI for help in writing an answer to an exercise or even an entire assignment, the student does not know if it is fine and correct or cheating and wrong.

- To what extent can GenAI be used without it being considered copying or stealing or unoriginal writing?

From these quotations, we note that students felt academic institutions did not provide clear guidelines regarding the ethical and unethical uses of GenAI tools. Perhaps this is because most academic institutions do not have official policies about AI use, so each student acts according to his or her own understanding.

5.6 The essence of academic learning

Another point brought up by students was the purpose of academic learning. Students wondered whether the purpose was to complete a degree, to achieve high grades, or perhaps to impart knowledge. These uncertainties are presented in the following quotations:

- How correct is it to learn this way [with GenAI tools] without dealing with the problem myself?

- You are not expressing your knowledge but using a GenAI tool.

- Should I use GenAI [applications] to perform tasks to teach the student and give him abilities?

It was interesting to identify, through the open-ended question, different reasons why GenAI tools could be used even when they were prohibited, as can be seen in the following quotations and **Figure 3**:

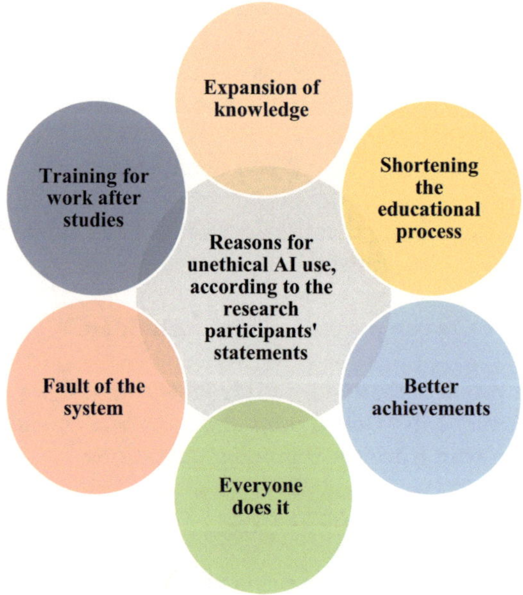

Figure 3.
Students' reasons to justify unethical uses of AI applications.

- If all students use it, why shouldn't I use it?
- There is a ban on the use of GenAI, but as a student, I use it a lot. It's very smart and opens me up to new worlds that I didn't know about before. It also expands my knowledge; that's why I use it.
- It can save a lot of time and headaches.
- If others use GenAI and I don't, [I might] get lower grades.

Students appeared to be aware that their behavior was unethical but justified it with a variety of excuses, including the desire to be like everyone else and thus maintain the level of their achievements, to expand their knowledge, as well as the belief that they had no choice because of the constraints of life and therefore were forced to cheat. Students even went so far as to blame the academic institution for their unethical behavior.

In conclusion, the qualitative analysis helped deepen our understanding of the quantitative findings and helped us understand the complexity of students' ethical dilemmas regarding GenAI tools and the consequences of using them for their academic studies.

6. Discussion

This study aimed to explore the extent and various purposes of GenAI tools for learning among Israeli students, as well as the dilemmas they encounter as a result. The national study revealed that GenAI tools, in general, and ChatGPT, in particular, have become integral to students' academic routines. However, students' frequency of GenAI learning use was moderate (the average ranged from 2.49 to 3.10, on a possible scale of 1 to 5). Perhaps the reason for this was their awareness of GenAI's disadvantages, among them a lack of accuracy and currency in the information received [7, 34], as well as other ethical dilemmas that will be mentioned below.

When we examined students' uses of GenAI tools, we noted they used these tools as personal tutors to support their learning processes; for example, explanation content was rated as the highest use, with an average of 3.10, and seeking inspirational ideas received an average rating of 2.49 (the possible scale is 1 to 5).

The findings also indicate that undergraduate students utilize GenAI tools for learning purposes more frequently than graduate students. Significant differences were found in using GenAI to explain unclear educational content, prepare exercises and/or papers, expand educational content, and summarize learning content. These findings may suggest that undergraduate students require more academic support and guidance, which they can receive from GenAI. It can be assumed that the unique characteristics of GenAI, such as human–machine interaction anytime and anywhere, and tailoring machine responses to individual needs [35], allow students to receive personalized assistance, which is especially important for undergraduate students.

At the same time, students turned to GenAI to prepare tasks and assignments for them, which may impair their academic training. Indeed, the research literature presents concerns primarily from academics regarding GenAI's ethical dilemmas and its potential to impair students' academic training [5, 7].

This study examines the ethical dilemmas faced by students related to GenAI. Our findings indicate that students are aware of ethical dilemmas, although their responses to the items regarding ethical dilemmas in using GenAI showed moderate agreement (the items ranged from an average of 3.39 to 2.28 on a scale of 1 to 5). Nonetheless, their responses suggest that their ethical dilemmas sometimes outweigh their desire for high academic achievements at any cost (with an average of 3.06 compared to 2.28). The findings also showed that students understood that ethics is not just about plagiarism but has broader implications, such as privacy (with an average score of 3.06), inequality (with an average score of 3.05), and perpetuating mistakes (with an average score of 3.39). These implications were also reflected in the research literature on ethics [27, 36].

Our findings also indicated that students wanted higher education institutions' management to provide them with clear instructions on the ethical use of GenAI tools, to draw a line between permitted and prohibited uses of those tools, and to elucidate what penalties could be expected when deviating from permitted uses. These findings are consistent with research indicating that most leading universities worldwide have not formulated a regulated institutional strategy on the subject [37].

Observing differences in ethical dilemmas between undergraduate and graduate students revealed interesting insights. Graduate students were more concerned with the ethical implications of using GenAI (with an average of 3.22) compared to undergraduate students (with an average of 2.99) and were also more aware of GenAI's mistakes (with averages of 3.56 and 3.40, respectively). Undergraduate students highlighted privacy issues more than graduate students (with an average of 3.04 compared to 2.76) and also the potential inequality that GenAI might cause (with an average of 3.19 versus 2.92). A significant difference was found between undergraduate and graduate students in their attitudes toward permitted and prohibited uses of these tools, with graduate students agreeing more strongly with this statement than undergraduates (averaging 2.35 and 1.97, respectively).

Moreover, our findings highlight the urgent need to provide learning literacies tailored to the new era, with notable differences also observed between undergraduate and graduate students. Undergraduate students expressed a greater need for guidance (average of 3.12) than graduate students (average of 2.88). In other words, students, particularly undergraduate students, must be given knowledge, qualifications, and skills for informed and critical navigation in the GenAI era. Faculty members must teach students about the workings of GenAI tools and, at the same time, instruct them to use these tools only after acquiring prior knowledge of the relevant content field. Only in this way will students be able to examine the quality of the answers they receive to the questions they present. These skills include, among others, critical thinking, higher-order thinking, creativity, and originality. Finally, students must also be taught ethical thinking and academic integrity as an integral part of the curriculum.

7. Conclusions

This study makes a significant contribution by providing empirical insights into the extent and purposes of GenAI tools for learning among students in higher education institutions in Israel, as well as the ethical dilemmas they encounter. The findings highlight the use of GenAI tools, such as ChatGPT, in students' academic routines. Moreover, the findings underscore the importance of providing targeted support and guidance, particularly for undergraduate students who rely more heavily on GenAI tools for learning purposes. This suggests a need for tailored educational strategies that address the specific needs and challenges of this group.

Furthermore, the study reveals the complexities of students' ethical dilemmas, focusing on privacy, inequality, and the potential for perpetuating mistakes. The results indicate a strong need among students for clear institutional guidelines on the ethical use of GenAI tools, reflecting a gap in current educational policies. This calls for higher education institutions to develop comprehensive frameworks that define acceptable uses of GenAI, set clear boundaries, and outline consequences for misuse.

Our work highlights the need for higher education institutions to adapt their curricula to the new realities of the GenAI era. This includes providing students with the knowledge, skills, and ethical frameworks necessary to navigate and critically engage with GenAI technologies. For example, incorporating modules on the ethical implications of AI, data privacy, and academic integrity can help prepare students to use these tools responsibly [38]. Additionally, there is a need for faculty professional programs that train educators to effectively integrate GenAI tools into their curricula, ensuring that students are guided in using these technologies to enhance learning rather than undermine academic integrity.

In this chapter, due to a minor bias in the representation of women and respondents with a bachelor's degree, we recommend interpreting the study's findings with caution and suggest replicating this manuscript with a sample that more accurately reflects the population's demographics. Furthermore, we cannot determine whether the use of GenAI tools, primarily for completing assignments such as writing articles, solving math exercises, and writing papers, constitutes negative uses by students or if these actions were based on instructions received from their lecturers. Additionally, since the qualitative data analysis was based on written responses to open-ended questions in the online questionnaire, we were unable to request clarifications or examples when responses were unclear. As a result, our interpretation should be treated with caution.

We, therefore, recommend that future research combine semi-structured, in-depth interviews to gain a more accurate interpretation. Another limitation relates to the language of GenAI tools. The GenAI tools that were tested in this study were all based on English, which was not the native language of the study participants. It is possible that this factor influenced the study's results. Therefore, it is recommended to conduct another similar study after the GenAI tools are introduced in the native language, which should examine the same topics as this study. Finally, because students' use of GenAI is growing, we recommend conducting comparative research with student populations in different countries.

8. The study's limitations

This study offers valuable empirical insights, but it is not without limitations. First, the reliance on a nonnative language interface (English-based

GenAI tools) may have influenced both the frequency and nature of student usage. Second, while open-ended responses offered valuable perspectives, the absence of follow-up clarification constrained interpretive depth. To address this, future research should incorporate semi-structured interviews, allowing for richer and more nuanced exploration of students' ethical reasoning. Additionally, comparative studies across linguistic, cultural, and policy contexts are warranted, especially as GenAI tools become localized. Ultimately, experimental and longitudinal studies are necessary to evaluate the long-term effects of GenAI literacy programs and the efficacy of ethical training on student behavior.

9. Future research

Future research should build on these findings by employing complementary methods and extended contexts to deepen our understanding. Specifically, semi-structured interviews should be included to gain deeper insight into students' ethical reasoning, examine similar questions in native-language GenAI environments, and conduct comparative studies across different countries or institutions with varying levels of policy implementation regarding GenAI use in education.

Conflict of interest

The authors declare no conflict of interest.

Appendix A

A detailed structure of the questionnaire:

Variable	Number of statements	Items	Cronbach's alpha
Top GenAI tools		• ChatGPT • Dall-e • Futurepedia • Wordtune • Jasper • Descript • Elicit	
GenAI learning uses	7	• Getting ideas for inspiration • Explanation of unclear educational content • Searching for educational material • Preparation of exercises and/or papers • Expansion of educational content • Drafting and/or editing educational content • Summary of learning content	0.821
Ethical dilemmas	6	• AI helps strong students become stronger • AI tools can be used for academic purposes, even if they are prohibited for use • The use of AI tools can perpetuate mistakes • The use of AI tools violates the user's privacy • Students face ethical dilemmas regarding the use of AI tools in learning • Lecturers cannot expect us to behave ethically if we have not been presented with ethical standards for the use of AI tools	0.562
An open question		• What are the dilemmas you deal with when using GenAI tools for learning purposes?	

Author details

Meital Amzalag and Gila Kurtz*
Holon Institute of Technology, Holon, Israel

*Address all correspondence to: Gilaku@hit.ac.il

References

[1] Chan CKY, Hu W. Students' voices on generative AI: Perceptions, benefits, and challenges in higher education. International Journal of Educational Technology in Higher Education. 2023;**20**(1):43. DOI: 10.1186/s41239-023-00411-8

[2] Park H, Ahn D (2024, May). The promise and Peril of ChatGPT in higher education: Opportunities, challenges, and design implications. In: Proceedings of the CHI Conference on Human Factors in Computing Systems (pp. 1–21). DOI: 10.1145/3613904.3642785

[3] Walter Y. Embracing the future of Artificial Intelligence in the classroom: The relevance of AI literacy, prompt engineering, and critical thinking in modern education. International Journal of Educational Technology in Higher Education. 2024;**21**(1):15. DOI: 10.1186/s41239-024-00448-3

[4] Beerbaum DO. Generative artificial intelligence (GAI) ethics taxonomy-applying Chat GPT for robotic process automation (GAI-RPA) as a business case. SSRN Electronic Journal. 2023. DOI: 10.2139/ssrn.4385025

[5] Crawford J, Cowling M, Allen KA. Leadership is needed for ethical ChatGPT: Character, assessment, and learning using artificial intelligence (AI). Journal of University Teaching and Learning Practice. 2023;**20**(3). DOI: 10.53761/1.20.3.02

[6] Victor BG, Kubiak S, Angell B, Perron BE. Time to move beyond the ASWB licensing exams: Can generative artificial intelligence offer a way forward for social work? Research on Social Work Practice. 2023;**33**(5): 511–517. DOI: 10.1177/10497315231166125

[7] Tlili A, Shehata B, Adarkwah MA, Bozkurt A, Hickey DT, Huang R, Agyemang B. What if the devil is my guardian angel: ChatGPT as a case study of using chatbots in education. Smart Learning Environments. 2023;**10**(1):15. DOI: 10.1186/s40561-023-00237-x

[8] Gozalo-Brizuela R, Garrido-Merchan EC. ChatGPT is not all you need. A state of the art review of large generative AI models. arXiv:2301.04655. 2023. DOI: 10.48550/arXiv.2301.04655

[9] Harry A. Role of AI in Education. Interdisciplinary Journal and Humanity. 2023;**2**(3):260–268. DOI: 10.58631/injurity.v2i3.52

[10] Mhlanga D. The Value of Open AI and ChatGPT for the current learning environments and the potential future uses. SSRN Electronic Journal. 2023. DOI: 10.2139/ssrn.4439267

[11] Rudolph J, Tan S, Tan S.ChatGPT: Bullshit spewer or the end of traditional assessments in higher education? Journal of Applied Learning and Teaching. 2023a;**6**(1). DOI: 10.37074/jalt.2023.6.1.9

[12] Sok S, Heng K. ChatGPT for education and research: A review of benefits and risks. SSRN Electronic Journal. 2023. DOI: 10.2139/ssrn.4378735

[13] Vygotsky LS, Cole M. Mind in Society: Development of Higher Psychological Processes. Cambridge, MA, USA: Harvard University Press; 1978

[14] Akgun S, Greenhow C. Artificial intelligence in education: Addressing ethical challenges in K-12 settings. AI Ethics. 2022;**2**:431–440. DOI: 10.1007/s43681-021-00096-7

[15] Muscanell N, Robert J (2023). EDUCAUSE Quick Poll Results: Did ChatGPT Write This Report? Colorado, Louisville, USA: EDUCASE. https://er.educause.edu/articles/2023/2/educausequickpoll-results-did-chatgpt-write-this-report [Accessed: 2025-November-6]

[16] Abbas M, Jam FA, Khan TI. Is it harmful or helpful? Examining the causes and consequences of generative AI usage among university students. International Journal of Educational Technology in Higher Education. 2024;**21**(1):10. DOI: 10.1186/s41239-024-00444-7

[17] Cotton DR, Cotton PA, Shipway JR. Chatting and cheating: Ensuring academic integrity in the era of ChatGPT. Innovations in Education and Teaching International. 2023;1–12. DOI: 10.1080/14703297.2023.2190148

[18] Sweller J. In academe, what is learned, and how is it learned? Current Directions in Psychological Science. 2015;**24**(3):190–194. DOI: 10.1177/0963721415569570

[19] Bates T, Cobo C, Mariño O, Wheeler S. Can artificial intelligence transform higher education? International Journal of Educational Technology in Higher Education. 2020;**17**:42. DOI: 10.1186/s41239-020-00218-x

[20] Verma S, Tomar P. Simulation of Human Brain: Artificial Intelligence-Based Learning: Impact of AI Technologies on teaching, learning, and research in higher education. Hershey, PA, USA: IGI Global; 2021. DOI: 10.4018/978-1-7998-4763-2

[21] Zawacki-Richter O, Marín VI, Bond M, Gouverneur F. Systematic review of research on artificial intelligence tools in higher education – Where are the educators? International Journal of Educational Technology in Higher Education. 2019;**16**(1):1–27. DOI: 10.1186/s41239-019-0171-0

[22] Ouyang F, Zheng L, Jiao P. Artificial intelligence in online higher education: A systematic review of empirical research from 2011 to 2020. Education and Information Technologies. 2022;**27**(6):7893–7925. DOI: 10.1007/s10639-022-10925-9

[23] Malmström H, Stöhr C, Ou AW. Chatbots and other AI for learning: A survey of use and views among university students in Sweden. Chalmers Studies in Communication and Learning in Higher Education 1. 2023. DOI: 10.17196/cls.csclhe/2023/01

[24] Dai Y, Liu A, Lim CP. Reconceptualizing ChatGPT and generative AI as a student-driven innovation in higher education. Procedia CIRP. 2023;**119**:84–90. DOI: 10.1016/j.procir.2023.05.002

[25] Zohny H, McMillan J, King M. Ethics of generative AI. Journal of Medical Ethics. 2023;**49**(2):79–80. DOI: 10.1136/jme-2023-108909

[26] Zhou JF, Chen F, Berry A, Reed M, Zhang S, Savage S (2020). A survey on ethical principles of AI and implementations. In 2020 IEEE Symposium Series on Computational Intelligence (SSCI) (3010–3017). IEEE

[27] Attard-Frost B, De Los Ríos A, Walters DR. The ethics of AI business

practices: A review of 47 AI ethics guidelines. AI Ethics. 2023;**3**:389–406. DOI: 10.1007/s43681-022-00156-6

[28] Boddington P. Artificial Intelligence: Foundations, Theory, and Algorithms: Towards a Code of Ethics for Artificial Intelligence. Berlin, Germany: Springer; 2017. DOI: 10.1007/978-3-319-60648-4

[29] Amani S, White L, Balart T, Arora L, Shryock KJ, Brumbelow K, Watson KL (2023). Generative AI perceptions: A survey to measure the perceptions of faculty, staff, and students on generative AI tools in academia. ArXiv. abs/2304.14415

[30] Sullivan M, Kelly A, McLaughlan P. ChatGPT in higher education: Considerations for academic integrity and student learning. Journal of Applied Learning and Teaching. 2023;**6**(1). DOI: 10.37074/jalt.2023.6.1.17

[31] Amzalag M, Shapira N, Dolev N. Two sides of the coin: Lack of academic integrity in exams during the Corona pandemic, students' and lecturers' perceptions. Journal of Academic Ethics. 2021;**20**(2):243–263. DOI: 10.1007/s10805-021-09413-5

[32] Naftalovitz U, Kranzler A. Higher Education in Israel: Selected Data for the 2022/23 Academic Year (Publication No. 423/2023). Jerusalem, Israel: Central Bureau of Statistics; 2023. Available from: https://www.cbs./gov.il [Accessed: 2025-November-6]

[33] Central Bureau of Statistics. (2023, December 28). Population statistics in higher education. https://www.cbs.gov.il/he/mediarelease/DocLib/2023/423/06_23_423b.pdf [Accessed: 2025-November-6]

[34] Dwivedi YK, Kshetri N, Hughes L, Slade EL, Jeyaraj A, Kar AK, Baabdullah AM, Koohang A, et al. 'So what if ChatGPT wrote it?' Multidisciplinary perspectives on opportunities, challenges and implications of generative conversational AI for research, practice and policy. International Journal of Information Management. 2023;**71**(102642). DOI: 10.1016/j.ijinfomgt.2023.102642

[35] Nguyen A, Hong Y, Dang B, Huang X. Human-AI collaboration patterns in AI-assisted academic writing. Studies in Higher Education. 2024;1–18. DOI: 10.1080/03075079.2024.2323593

[36] Stark L, Hoffmann AL. Data is the new what? Popular metaphors and professional ethics in emerging data culture. Journal of Cultural Analytics. 2019;**4**(1). DOI: 10.22148/16.036

[37] Xiao P, Chen Y, Bao W. Waiting, banning, and embracing: An empirical analysis of adapting policies for generative AI in higher education. ArXiv. 2023. DOI: 10.48550/arXiv.2305.18617

[38] Usher M, Barak M. Unpacking the role of AI ethics online education for science and engineering students. International Journal of STEM Education. 2024;**11**:35. DOI: 10.1186/s40594-024-00493-4

Chapter 20

Equity by Design: Implementing AI Course Assistants to Support Student Success in Online Higher Education

George Hanshaw

Abstract

This chapter explores the design and implementation of AI course assistants as a strategy to increase equity, engagement, and academic success in online higher education. At Los Angeles Pacific University, a fully online institution serving adult and historically underserved learners, an AI assistant named Spark was deployed across all courses within four weeks following a successful pilot study. The implementation process included a multi-phase rollout, beginning with faculty-led dialog and experimentation, followed by the development of a minimum viable product and continuous improvement based on student and faculty feedback. Spark was designed to support student learning through Socratic questioning, course-specific alignment, and inclusive interaction models that accommodated diverse learners, including those with language or neurodiversity needs. Outcomes from a randomized controlled trial and follow-up studies indicated improvements in GPA, motivation, and self-efficacy, with no demographic disparities in benefit. The chapter also examines how Spark was used to enable active learning through tools such as AI-facilitated think–pair–share discussions and role-playing simulations. Ethical and inclusive design practices were prioritized throughout the development process, and faith-informed considerations were integrated to reflect the institution's Christian values. Finally, the chapter connects the case study to global priorities in education by aligning outcomes with the goals of inclusive, high-quality learning outlined in Sustainable Development Goal 4. Practical recommendations are provided to help institutions of all types responsibly scale AI tools that support learner success while maintaining human-centered values.

Keywords: AI in education, equity, online learning, active learning, student engagement, course assistant, inclusive design

1. Introduction

Artificial intelligence (AI) is rapidly transforming the educational landscape, presenting both unprecedented opportunities and pressing ethical considerations. From predictive analytics to generative AI tools, institutions around the world are navigating how to integrate AI into teaching and learning in ways that uphold core values of equity, creativity, and student-centered pedagogy [1, 2]. The release of widely accessible tools such as ChatGPT has accelerated the conversation, prompting a global rethinking of how students learn, how educators teach, and how institutions provide support at scale.

Los Angeles Pacific University (LAPU), a fully online, faith-based institution, serves a diverse population of nontraditional adult learners. The university offers both term-based and competency-based education (CBE) programs that allow students to progress through self-paced, outcomes-aligned modules. This structure, combined with asynchronous delivery and a strong emphasis on access and affordability, presents unique challenges and opportunities for student engagement, motivation, and success in a digital-first environment.

This chapter explores the strategic implementation of an AI course assistant, known as *Spark*, through a multi-phase process that began with a pilot and culminated in full-scale adoption across all courses within four weeks. These course assistants are individually trained in the course material for each class and then implemented into daily learning rhythms. We examine the effects of AI tools on student GPA, engagement, self-efficacy, and sense of belonging, using data from a randomized controlled trial (RCT) and follow-up studies. We also explore equity outcomes across demographic groups and highlight emerging practices – such as active learning with AI characters and integration into CBE workflows.

By presenting an institutional case study grounded in empirical evidence and practical implementation, this chapter contributes to the broader dialog on designing ethical, scalable, and equitable AI solutions in education. It aligns with Sustainable Development Goal 4 by emphasizing inclusive and high-quality learning, offering concrete strategies for educators, researchers, and policymakers seeking to responsibly harness AI to support student success [3–6].

2. Equity, belonging, and AI: A theoretical foundation

2.1 Defining equity in online higher education

Equity in higher education means ensuring that all students, regardless of background, identity, or socioeconomic status, have fair access to learning opportunities, support systems, and academic success. In online education, where access to human connection and immediate guidance is often limited, equity becomes particularly complex. Students from historically underserved populations, including first-generation learners, adult students, working professionals, and underrepresented racial and ethnic groups, face compounded challenges that can impact their academic outcomes and sense of inclusion [4].

Unlike equality, which provides the same resources to all, equity requires differentiated and responsive support that meets learners where they are. This includes not only access to course content but also access to help, community, and timely feedback. As AI tools become more integrated into the educational ecosystem, they present both risks and opportunities in the pursuit of equity. When intentionally designed, AI can be a tool to close gaps in access and engagement. When implemented without attention to diverse student needs, however, it can reinforce or even widen existing inequities [5].

2.2 The role of belonging in academic success

A strong sense of belonging has long been recognized as a key factor in student motivation, retention, and performance – particularly in online environments where isolation is more common [4]. Belonging is not merely a by-product of positive interactions; it is a psychological state that shapes how students interpret academic challenges and setbacks. Students who feel connected to their learning community are more likely to persist through difficulty, engage with course material, and perceive themselves as capable learners.

At LAPU, efforts to support belonging are interwoven into every aspect of instructional and student services design. AI course assistants were introduced not as a replacement for human interaction but as a bridge to help students feel seen, supported, and guided, even in asynchronous contexts. Initial usage data from Spark suggested that students who felt the least engaged or supported were often the most likely to use the AI assistant and benefited from it academically [3]. This supports the idea that scalable technologies can serve as key interventions in fostering belonging when personal access to faculty or peers is limited.

2.3 AI as part of the belonging ecosystem

The concept of a "belonging ecosystem" extends beyond faculty–student relationships to include course design, success coaching, technology platforms, and now AI. Three theoretical frameworks inform this approach:

Tinto's model of student retention emphasizes academic and social integration as key components of persistence. AI course assistants provide another avenue for academic integration by responding to questions in real time and reinforcing course norms and expectations [7].

Maslow's hierarchy of needs places belonging as a foundational prerequisite for motivation and achievement. AI tools such as Spark are designed not simply to deliver answers but to offer students the sense that their questions are valid, their learning matters, and help is always available [8].

The community of inquiry framework highlights cognitive, social, and teaching presence in online learning environments. Spark contributes to both teaching and cognitive presence by prompting student reflection, asking questions, and scaffolding deeper understanding in dialog with course materials [9].

Rather than viewing AI as a technical add-on, Spark was positioned as part of the overall student support system. It was part of what they call the learning ecosystem, where the student is at the center of the ecosystem. Faculty were encouraged to introduce it with warmth, model its use, and explain its role in learning – not as an all-knowing machine, but as a digital assistant.

2.4 Why intentional AI design matters?

When AI tools are embedded in learning environments, they become part of students' educational experience and can deeply shape how students feel about learning and themselves. An AI assistant that simply provides answers may reduce cognitive load in the short term but, over time, could diminish student self-efficacy or motivation. By contrast, an AI assistant designed to coach, prompt, and encourage critical thinking can increase not just grades but also a student's belief in their own academic potential [3].

Spark was designed with intentional prompt structures that avoided giving direct answers. Instead, the assistant asked clarifying questions, encouraged students to reflect on their understanding, and recommended resources within the course. This design approach was rooted in a commitment to educational equity, ensuring that students who might hesitate to ask for help or who had been underserved by previous academic experiences received support that was personalized, nonjudgmental, and immediately available.

3. The multi-phase AI implementation process

3.1 Faculty dialogue and discovery

The integration of AI into every course did not begin with a technological decision; it began with a conversation. In early 2023, faculty and instructional leaders began holding open forums, brown-bag discussions, and departmental roundtables to explore the implications of generative AI in higher education. While there was initial skepticism and concern, many faculty members expressed curiosity about how AI might improve access to support, especially for students who lacked confidence in traditional academic spaces.

Rather than imposing top-down mandates, leadership created space for shared meaning-making around AI. These early dialogs centered on andragogy, equity, academic integrity, and the student experience. Faculties were not asked to adopt AI; they were asked to help shape how AI could become a pedagogical partner in a student-centered learning ecosystem. The resulting design goals prioritized transparency, student agency, and academic support rather than automation or surveillance.

3.2 Rapid upskilling and AI literacy development

As interest grew, so did the need for shared understanding and skill development. Faculty and staff engaged in both formal and informal AI literacy initiatives, including internal workshops, external webinars, book clubs, and prompt design training. Key themes included:

How to design Socratic AI prompts that encourage student thinking?

How to avoid AI as an "answer machine"?

How to integrate AI into active learning and formative assessment?

Most importantly, these sessions were co-led by instructional designers, faculty, and students – fostering shared ownership and cross-role collaboration. These grassroots efforts laid the foundation for a culture of AI curiosity and experimentation, rather than fear or avoidance.

3.3 Partnering and piloting: The minimum viable product (MVP) approach

LAPU partnered with Nectir, an AI and collaboration platform that had already developed course assistant technology. Rather than building a new tool from the ground up, the focus was on enhancing the assistant's usability and alignment with student and faculty needs. The university adopted a MVP approach, launching Spark – a customized version of the assistant – in a small number of courses to gather early feedback and observe real-world student interactions. The goal of the pilot was not only to test technical functionality but also to discover the effect the technology had on the student learning experience.

During the pilot, an RCT was conducted. Students in treatment sections had access to Spark, while students in control sections did not. The results showed statistically significant gains in GPA and self-efficacy for students who used the AI assistant [3]. These outcomes validated the next phase: full implementation.

3.4 Full implementation in four weeks

Following the success of the pilot, Spark was rolled out across all courses, undergraduate and graduate, within four weeks. This rapid implementation was possible due to:

- Preestablished faculty buy-in;
- A scalable content-alignment model (Spark) was trained on each course's content and syllabus;
- A clear communication plan for students and instructors;
- Ongoing AI coaching support for faculty.

Each instance of Spark was customized per course using a structured prompt framework. Spark was trained to act like a teaching assistant – offering explanations, asking clarifying questions, and referencing only the course content. Faculty were encouraged to introduce Spark to students in welcome videos and weekly announcements, normalizing its use as part of the learning process.

3.5 Expanding to CBE and active learning

After the general rollout, Spark was adapted for use in CBE programs. In these courses, students progress asynchronously by demonstrating mastery of clearly defined competencies. Spark was embedded into each CBE course as both a task coach and a study partner, offering tailored guidance based on the competency's expectations.

Simultaneously, Spark evolved from a reactive Q&A assistant into a partner in active learning. Many active learning activities were adapted to the course, such as:

- Think–pair–share with Spark as the "pair";
- Role-plays where Spark took on the voice of a historical figure or fictional character; and
- Self-assessments and reflection prompts guided by Spark's Socratic questioning.

These innovations extended Spark's role beyond answering questions – –it became a tool for deeper engagement, structured thinking, and professional skill development.

4. Impact evaluation and key findings

4.1 GPA improvements and statistical significance

To evaluate the effectiveness of AI course assistants, an RCT was conducted during the pilot phase, comparing student outcomes in courses with Spark access to those without. The findings demonstrated a statistically significant improvement in course GPA for students who used Spark. The treatment group achieved a mean GPA of 3.32, compared to 3.04 for the control group –a difference supported by a p-value < 0.001 and a small-to-moderate effect size (Cohen's $d = 0.23$) [3].

These findings suggest that Spark may play a meaningful role in promoting academic performance by providing just-in-time support, especially in fully online environments where students often lack immediate access to instructional guidance. Notably, this outcome held even when Spark's responses avoided giving direct answers, instead prompting students to clarify, reflect, and explore their understanding.

4.2 Equitable outcomes across age, race, and gender

A follow-up analysis of the pilot and implementation data explored whether Spark's academic benefits were equitably distributed across key demographic groups. The results were encouraging: Students of different races, ages, and genders experienced similar gains in GPA when using Spark, and no statistically significant interaction effects were found between AI usage and any demographic variable [3].

This suggests that Spark's positive impact on learning outcomes was not limited to specific subgroups but rather applied consistently across the student population. Given longstanding equity gaps in higher education, particularly in online formats, these results provide early evidence that well-designed AI tools can function as equity levers, supporting learners who may otherwise struggle to access timely, personalized assistance [4, 10].

4.3 Engagement, motivation, and self-efficacy shifts

While GPA is a critical indicator of academic success, noncognitive outcomes were also measured. Students who used Spark during the pilot reported higher levels of motivation, confidence in learning, and clarity of expectations compared to those who did not. These findings were derived from course evaluations and targeted surveys, including validated self-efficacy measures.

Motivation and self-efficacy gains are particularly important in asynchronous and adult-serving institutions, where students often juggle academic work alongside family and employment responsibilities. The presence of Spark as a 24/7 support tool may have helped reduce uncertainty and increased students' perception of control over their learning experience – a key factor in retention and persistence [11].

4.4 Predictive potential: AI use as a leading indicator

One emergent insight from the data was that students who felt least encouraged, engaged, or supported were the most likely to use Spark, and simultaneously experienced the most pronounced GPA improvements [3]. This trend suggests that AI assistant usage may function as a predictive signal of academic risk, enabling early interventions and personalized outreach.

In future iterations, usage analytics from Spark could potentially be integrated into institutional early-alert systems, helping faculty and support staff identify students who are silently struggling. These findings align with the growing use of learning analytics and AI-informed advising in higher education to improve student success and equity outcomes [12].

4.5 Key takeaways: Designing for equitable impact

- Design AI assistants that prompt rather than answer to foster self-efficacy and learning depth.
- Measure both academic and nonacademic outcomes: GPA, motivation, belonging, and clarity.
- Use AI usage data as a diagnostic tool to inform real-time support systems.
- Prioritize inclusive implementation strategies that ensure benefits are equitably distributed.

5. Ethical and inclusive design of AI assistants

5.1 Socratic prompt engineering and student agency

One of the central ethical concerns in deploying AI in education is how it affects student autonomy. While AI tools can lower barriers to understanding, they also risk undermining student agency if they default to giving answers instead of fostering critical thinking. Spark was deliberately designed around Socratic prompting, encouraging learners to reflect, question, and construct their own understanding rather than consume answers passively.

- The design of Spark's interactions included the following:
- Questions like "What do you already know about this topic?";
- Prompts encouraging learners to apply concepts to personal or professional contexts; and
- Avoidance of direct answers to assignments, in compliance with academic integrity policies.

This approach supports constructivist learning theory and reflects principles found in dialogic pedagogy, which values back-and-forth questioning as a way to deepen understanding [13]. By prompting students to engage in reflection and metacognition, Spark fosters learner agency and supports long-term retention of knowledge.

5.2 Addressing bias, privacy, and data ethics

Equity in AI is not only a matter of outcomes but of design and governance. Spark was configured to access only course-specific content, avoiding open-ended queries that could be pulled from biased or unvetted Internet sources. This "closed prompt" model mitigated the risk of algorithmic bias and helped ensure culturally and pedagogically appropriate interactions.

Privacy was also a central consideration, particularly in compliance with the Family Educational Rights and Privacy Act. Spark did not collect or store any personally identifiable information. It operated entirely within the university's secure learning environment, embedded in the learning management system (LMS). Data on usage – such as the number of messages, timestamps, and general interaction patterns – were anonymized and used exclusively for internal improvement, faculty development, and equity evaluation.

These safeguards reflect broader ethical AI design principles promoted by organizations such as the IEEE and UNESCO, which emphasize transparency, accountability, and inclusivity in AI systems used in education [14, 15]. By aligning with these standards and with federal privacy regulations, LAPU ensured that Spark could be trusted as a secure and ethically responsible part of the learning environment.

5.3 Customization for ESL and neurodiverse learners

Inclusive design also means recognizing and adapting to diverse learning needs. With this in mind, Spark was trained to adjust tone and complexity based on user input. For example, students could prompt Spark to "explain this in simple English" or "summarize this for someone with no background in the topic." These affordances were especially helpful for the following:

- English language learners;
- Neurodiverse students seeking clarity or repetition; and
- Adult learners returning to academia after years away.

Instructors also had the ability to adjust Spark's prompt templates to suit the learning context. For instance, in courses with a heavy emphasis on reflection or ethical reasoning, Spark was trained to ask questions aligned with course values and learning outcomes. These features promoted a more equitable and culturally responsive user experience.

5.4 Avoiding dependency: Coaching, not answer-giving

While AI can enhance learning, it must not erode academic integrity or cognitive independence. One challenge with generative AI is the temptation for students to

DOI: http://dx.doi.org/10.5772/intechopen.1012800

rely on it as a shortcut rather than a tool for learning. This risk was addressed by the following:

- Training Spark to never provide full answers to graded tasks;
- Using a "coaching" framework that encourages process over product; and
- Explicitly communicating Spark's limitations and ethical boundaries in course introductions.

By embedding Spark into the pedagogical fabric of the course – not as a crutch, but as a cognitive partner – students were more likely to engage with the AI as a thinking companion instead of a replacement for their own effort.

5.5 Key takeaways: Design checklist for responsible AI integration in learning

- Use Socratic prompting to preserve student agency and critical thinking.
- Restrict AI access to vetted course content to reduce bias and ensure relevance.
- Provide affordances for language support and neurodiverse learners.
- Train the AI to coach not complete student work, preserving academic integrity.
- Maintain transparency with students about what the AI can and cannot do.

6. Creativity and active learning with AI

6.1 Beyond discussion boards: Think–pair–share with Spark

Traditional online discussions often struggle to foster authentic engagement. The Digital Learning Solutions (DLS) team at LAPU sought to move beyond passive discussion boards by integrating Spark into active learning strategies, such as think–pair–share. In this adaptation, Spark acts as the "pair," a conversational partner students use to develop and refine their ideas before sharing them with peers.

This is an example of an actual discussion prompt from a history course.

Think–pair–share exercise:

1. **Think:** Reflect on your chosen primary source by considering the following questions:
    - What is the main idea or message of this primary source?

- How does it reflect the experiences, challenges, or innovations of the Industrial Revolution?
- What does this source reveal about the lives of the people or the culture of the time?
- Spend 5–10 minutes jotting down your thoughts in preparation for the next step.

2. **Pair:** Interact with Spark, our AI assistant, to deepen your understanding. Engage in a minimum of four interactions with Spark using the following prompts:
   - "Spark, can you provide a brief summary of [primary source]?";
   - "What additional context or background information can you give me about the Reconstruction era that relates to [primary source]?";
   - "How did [primary source] impact the people or the nation during the Reconstruction era?"; and
   - "Can you help me understand the perspective of the author or creator of [primary source]?".
3. **Share:** In your initial post, use the video-recording tool, audio response, or writing option, and share what you learned from your interaction with Spark. Make sure to use your voice and personal style while writing. Include the following:
   - A summary of the main idea and message of the primary source;
   - An explanation of how the message fits into the larger historical issue of reconstruction;
   - A brief personal evaluation of the source's perspective; and
   - Insights gained from your discussion with Spark.

This model promotes critical thinking, idea revision, and confidence-building, aligning with constructivist pedagogy and enhancing student ownership of learning [13, 16]. Faculty reported higher-quality responses and deeper peer engagement following Spark-supported preparation.

6.2 Role-plays and virtual simulations

Spark's ability to simulate different voices or personas opened new possibilities for role-play and scenario-based learning. In one psychology course, Spark was trained to take on the persona of "Miguel," a character struggling with anxiety and career transitions. Students practiced motivational interviewing techniques by interacting with Miguel through Spark, receiving dynamic feedback in real time.

Other role-play use cases included the following:

- Debating historical perspectives (e.g., "Argue as if you were Martin Luther King Jr.");
- Exploring ethical dilemmas in nursing or business through AI-driven case studies; and
- Practicing leadership conversations or conflict resolution with Spark, playing a difficult team member.

These simulations provided safe, low-risk environments for students to practice skills, receive feedback, and explore complex topics from multiple perspectives – an approach supported by research in simulated experiential learning [17].

6.3 Student-designed AI learning scenarios

An unexpected outcome of Spark's integration was the emergence of student creativity. Several instructors invited students to cocreate Spark prompts or design their own interactive learning scenarios. In a leadership course, students were tasked with building a Spark interaction that helped them prepare for a difficult workplace conversation. The process of designing the prompt deepened their understanding of interpersonal dynamics and communication frameworks.

This practice reflects key principles of student-centered learning and aligns with the Universal Design for Learning framework, particularly in providing multiple means of action and expression [18]. Allowing students to shape how they engage with the AI not only increases ownership and motivation, but also makes learning personal and flexible.

6.4 Key takeaways: Sample active learning applications with AI assistants

- Think–pair–share partner: Have students use Spark as a critical-thinking partner before posting to discussion boards.
- Role-play coach: Use Spark to simulate clients, leaders, or ethical scenarios across various disciplines.
- Prompt designer: Invite students to create Spark prompts as a way to explore and apply key concepts.
- Scenario simulator: Guide students through problem-solving tasks using Spark as a dynamic peer.

7. Implementation strategies for scaling AI across institutions

Successfully integrating AI across an entire institution requires more than a working tool – it demands thoughtful planning, cultural alignment, and continuous adaptation. Spark's institution-wide rollout within four weeks was made possible by leveraging collaborative leadership, agile development, and a radically student-centered mindset. This section outlines key strategies that supported scalable, equitable implementation.

7.1 Communication and change management

Change in education is often met with resistance, not due to unwillingness, but due to uncertainty and fear of loss. A major key to success was leadership prioritizing transparency and clear communication from the outset. Key elements included the following:

- Hosting open forums and faculty "town halls" to voice concerns;
- Providing consistent messaging that Spark was an assistant, not a replacement;
- Sharing early pilot data showing student learning gains; and
- Acknowledging limitations and areas still under study.

This approach mirrors best practices in change management, emphasizing shared ownership over top-down directives [19]. Communication efforts centered on how Spark aligns with the institution's mission to serve adult learners and close equity gaps, helping faculty connect AI integration to their instructional values.

7.2 Training faculty to collaborate with AI

Faculty adoption is essential to student engagement with AI tools. Instructional designers partnered with faculty to deliver just-in-time training, codesign workshops, and prompt clinics that helped instructors:

- Customize Spark's behavior to align with course goals;
- Embed Spark into assignments and learning activities; and
- Model Spark usage for students through videos or guided activities.

Importantly, Spark was framed as an assistant rather than a shortcut for grading or tutoring. Faculty members who actively introduced Spark and demonstrated its value saw significantly higher student adoption rates [3].

7.3 Leveraging LMS + AI for just-in-time support

Integration with the LMS was critical. Spark was embedded directly within each course shell, with no additional login or navigation required. This seamless access helped normalize usage and enabled Spark to:

- Reference course content (syllabus, assignments, rubrics) in real time;

- Support asynchronous learners with instant feedback; and
- Reinforce instructional goals by answering questions in the instructor's "voice."

Just-in-time access to support helped reduce student hesitation and improved their ability to persist through learning challenges independently, which is especially important for adult learners with limited availability.

7.4 Leadership buy-in and iterative improvement

Institutional buy-in extended beyond instructional teams. Leaders in academics, student success, and technology all collaborated to ensure Spark's implementation supported student outcomes, respected ethical guidelines, and aligned with strategic priorities. A key tactic was the use of rapid feedback loops, where faculty and student feedback informed weekly improvements to Spark's performance and content alignment.

Rather than aiming for perfection, a culture of "launch and learn," valuing iterative refinement over stalled precision, was adopted and embraced by stakeholders. This agile approach allowed the university to move quickly while staying responsive to student needs and faculty insights [20].

7.5 Key takeaways: Five steps for institutional AI integration

- Engage stakeholders early: Begin with listening sessions and collaborative planning.
- Align AI with mission: Communicate how the tool enhances your institution's core values.
- Train + codesign: Empower faculty to shape AI behaviors and integrations.
- Embed in workflows: Ensure AI tools are natively accessible in the LMS and daily tasks.
- Improve iteratively: Launch with purpose, gather data, and refine continuously.

8. Faith-informed and values-driven AI design

8.1 AI as a tool for reflective faith integration

The integration of AI was guided by both academic rigor and spiritual formation. Spark was intentionally designed not only to support content mastery but also to scaffold students' reflective engagement with Christian worldview concepts. Spark uses a Socratic approach that invites inquiry rather than instruction, allowing students to explore connections between faith, life, and learning in a structured but student-led way.

In a recent study currently under review, students who engaged with Spark demonstrated significantly deeper and more structured reflections on the Christian worldview in both academic and personal contexts (Hanshaw, manuscript under review). While Likert-scale data showed no statistically significant difference between AI users and nonusers in self-reported understanding of the Christian worldview, qualitative analysis revealed that Spark users articulated their beliefs with greater clarity, specificity, and practical relevance.

8.2 Scaffolded dialog for theological and practical integration

The study found that students who used Spark were more likely to describe real-world applications of biblical principles in their work, families, and ethical decision-making. Spark's dialog-based design encouraged exploration without prescribing theological positions, creating a psychologically safe space for faith development. Keywords from Spark users – such as "guidance," "clarity," and "engagement" – indicated a perception of the AI as a supportive voice in their spiritual learning.

This aligns with Christian pedagogical principles that emphasize the cultivation of wisdom through reflection and application, rather than rote doctrinal absorption. In this sense, Spark offered scalable, values-aligned scaffolding for students' theological growth.

8.3 Enhancing faith integration without replacing human formation

Spark was not designed to replace the role of instructors, mentors, or spiritual community but to enhance students' ability to reflect in moments when those human supports were unavailable. For online learners – especially adult students balancing multiple responsibilities – Spark offered an immediate space to process ideas through a faith-informed lens.

Although Spark did not lead to significant changes in students' *perceived* understanding of the Christian worldview, it significantly improved the *depth and articulation* of their written reflections (Hanshaw, manuscript under review). This distinction reinforces the idea that AI can enrich the expression and integration of belief, even if it does not alter underlying convictions.

8.4 Takeaway box: Key practices for faith-informed AI integration

- Use AI to scaffold reflective practice, not replace spiritual guidance.
- Design Socratic prompts that help students explore faith in their own words.
- Train AI to ask questions that connect academic content with Christian worldview themes.
- Recognize that AI may not change beliefs, but it can strengthen expression, clarity, and application.
- Position AI as a companion for information, especially for online learners with limited access to mentors.

DOI: http://dx.doi.org/10.5772/intechopen.1012800

9. Global implications and alignment with SDG 4

9.1 Inclusive and equitable quality education

The global relevance of AI in education extends far beyond early adopters in well-resourced institutions. At its best, AI holds the potential to scale personalized learning, timely feedback, and academic support to students who may otherwise be marginalized by geographic, economic, or structural barriers. This promise aligns directly with Sustainable Development Goal 4 (SDG 4), which calls for inclusive and equitable quality education and the promotion of lifelong learning opportunities for all [6].

The use of Spark within every course demonstrated that thoughtfully designed AI can reduce disparities by meeting students where they are progressing: asynchronously, affordably, and responsively. Spark supported diverse learners across age, race, language, and prior education levels without requiring additional faculty time or intervention. While LAPU is a private institution in the United States, the approach taken is scalable across sectors and can inform global strategies in both low-resource and high-scale digital environments.

9.2 Expanding access for underserved populations

Around the world, students in underserved communities often face significant barriers to accessing high-quality academic support: limited access to trained teachers, large class sizes, or inadequate instructional resources. AI-powered assistants such as Spark, if deployed responsibly, can help close these gaps by providing 24/7 guidance, scaffolding learning, and reducing students' reliance on expensive or inaccessible tutoring models.

Moreover, the multilingual potential of generative AI tools offers promising avenues for reaching learners in their preferred language, reducing language-based access barriers that continue to affect educational participation worldwide [21].

However, ensuring true equity requires that AI systems be localized, culturally responsive, and designed in collaboration with communities – not merely exported from high-income contexts. This demands inclusive design processes, ongoing monitoring of bias, and capacity building for educators to effectively integrate AI into their pedagogy.

9.3 AI as a scalable equity lever in resource-limited settings

Perhaps the most promising global implication of LAPU's model is that it demonstrates how AI can serve as a "scalable equity lever": Once the foundational system and ethical guardrails are in place, AI assistants can provide consistent, individualized support at a low marginal cost. This makes them especially powerful for the following:

- Open universities and online programs seeking to serve large student populations.

- Refugee or displaced learner contexts, where human support is limited.

- National education systems are integrating AI into digital learning platforms.

The model is not perfect, nor universally transferable without adaptation, but it offers a replicable vision of how AI can be used not to replace teachers but to extend the reach of equitable, high-quality learning experiences.

9.4 Takeaway box: Global strategies for inclusive AI in education

- Align AI design with global goals such as SDG 4 to ensure inclusion and quality.
- Localize AI content and prompts for cultural and linguistic responsiveness.
- Use AI as a complement – not a replacement – for human educators.
- Prioritize capacity-building for teachers and designers in emerging regions.
- Design for equity from the outset, not as an afterthought.

10. Conclusion

The integration of AI into higher education is no longer a future scenario; it is a present reality. As institutions across the globe grapple with how to leverage this rapidly evolving technology, LAPU's experience offers a practical, scalable, and ethically grounded roadmap for implementation. The case of Spark demonstrates that AI tools, when thoughtfully designed and embedded into the learning ecosystem, can significantly improve student outcomes, enhance motivation and self-efficacy, and promote equity across diverse learner populations.

The success of this initiative was not due to the technology alone, but to the values and vision that guided its deployment. Faculty, designers, and administrators collaborated to ensure that Spark served not just functional purposes but human ones: increasing access, reinforcing belonging, and preserving academic integrity. Spark's Socratic structure, close content alignment, and inclusive affordances were critical to its positive reception and impact.

The findings from the multi-phase rollout, including an RCT, follow-up equity analyses, and active learning innovations, underscore the importance of intentionality in AI design. AI should not be viewed as a shortcut or novelty but as a learning partner – one that supports students in becoming more confident, reflective, and independent thinkers.

As the global education community moves toward achieving Sustainable Development Goal 4, AI can be a key lever if used wisely. This chapter calls on educators, researchers, and policymakers to embrace a pedagogy of design stewardship: to integrate AI in ways that are student-centered, ethically sound, and globally informed.

The future of education is not human or machine; it is both. When implemented with equity, creativity, and care, AI can help us build a learning environment where every student has the support they need to thrive.

Acknowledgments

I would like to thank the DLS team at LAPU for their exceptional work in designing, piloting, and implementing Spark, the AI course assistant. Their commitment to student-centered design, rapid innovation, and equity-driven solutions has made this initiative possible.

I am also grateful to the faculty and instructional design teams across LAPU who contributed their insight and creativity, as well as to the students who participated in the pilot and shared valuable feedback that shaped Spark's development.

A special thank you to Nectir, our platform and development partner, for their collaborative spirit and technical expertise in supporting Spark's deployment and evolution.

Special thanks to Jacob Hanshaw and Ethan Wicker for their assistance and guidance in the data exploration and analysis, which were foundational to evaluating the impact of Spark.

Finally, I appreciate the support of LAPU's academic and institutional leadership, whose vision for inclusive and high-quality education has empowered this work from the start.

Conflict of interest

The authors declare no conflict of interest.

Author details

George Hanshaw
Los Angeles Pacific University, San Dimas, USA

*Address all correspondence to: ghanshaw@lapu.edu

References

[1] Woolf BP, Lane HC, Chaudhri VK, Kolodner JL. AI grand challenges for education. AI Magazine. 2013;**34**(4): 66–84. DOI: 10.1609/aimag.v34i4.2490

[2] Chan CKY, Colloton T. Generative AI in higher education: The ChatGPT effect. New York, NY: Routledge; 2024. DOI: 10.4324/9781003459026

[3] Hanshaw G, Vance J, Brewer C. Exploring the effectiveness of AI course assistants on the student learning experience. Open Praxis. 2024;**16**(4):627–644. DOI: 10.55982/openpraxis.16.4.719

[4] Strayhorn TL. College Students' Sense of Belonging: A Key to Educational Success for All Students. 2nd ed. New York, NY: Routledge; 2018. DOI: 10.4324/9781315297293

[5] Dakakni D, Nehme S. Artificial intelligence in the L2 classroom: Implications and challenges on ethics and equity in higher education. Computers and Education: Artificial Intelligence. 2023;**5**:100151. DOI: 10.1016/j.caeai.2023.100151

[6] United Nations. Transforming Our World: The 2030 Agenda for Sustainable Development. United Nations General Assembly. 2015. https://sdgs.un./org//goals/goal4. [Accessed: 2025-May-29]

[7] Tinto V. Leaving College: Rethinking the Causes and Cures of Student Attrition. 2nd ed. Chicago, IL: University of Chicago Press; 1994. DOI: 10.7208/chicago/9780226922461.001.0001

[8] Maslow AH. A theory of human motivation. Psychological Review. 1943;**50**(4):370–396. DOI: 10.1037/h0054346

[9] Garrison DR, Anderson T, Archer W. Critical inquiry in a text-based environment: Computer conferencing in higher education. Internet and Higher Education. 2000;**2**(2–3):87–105. DOI: 10.1016/S1096-7516(00)00016-6

[10] Baker RS, Corbett AT, Aleven V Improving contextual models of guessing and slipping with a truncated training set. In: *Proceedings of the 1st International Conference on Educational Data Mining*; 2008. pp. 67–76. https://www.educationaldatamining./org//EDM2008/uploads/proc/full%20proceedings.pdf/ [Accessed: 2025-May-29]

[11] Bandura A, Freeman WH, Lightsey R. Self-Efficacy: The exercise of control. Journal of Cognitive Psychotherapy. 1999;**13**(2):158–166. DOI: 10.1891/0889-8391.13.2.158

[12] Ifenthaler D, Yau JY-K. Utilising learning analytics to support study success in higher education: A systematic review. Educational Technology Research and Development. 2020;**68**(4):1961–1990. DOI: 10.1007/s11423-020-09788-z

[13] Freire P. Pedagogy of the Oppressed. 30th Anniversary ed. New York, NY: Continuum; 2000

[14] IEEE Global Initiative on Ethics of Autonomous and Intelligent Systems. Ethically Aligned Design: A Vision for Prioritizing Human Well-being with

Autonomous and Intelligent Systems. 1st ed. New York, NY; 2019. Available from: https://ethicsinaction.ieee./org//

[15] UNESCO. *Recommendation on the Ethics of Artificial Intelligence*. Paris: UNESCO; 2021. Available from: https://unesdoc.unesco./org//ark:/48223/pf0000381137 [Accessed: 2025-June-04]

[16] Brookfield SD, Preskill S. Discussion as a Way of Teaching: Tools and Techniques for Democratic Classrooms. 2nd ed. San Francisco, CA: Jossey-Bass; 2005

[17] Cook DA, Hatala R, Brydges R, et al. Technology-enhanced simulation for health professions education: A systematic review and meta-analysis. JAMA. 2011;**306**(9):978–988. DOI: 10.1001/jama.2011.1234

[18] CAST. Universal Design for Learning Guidelines Version 2.2. Wakefield, MA: CAST; 2018. https://udlguidelines.cast./org// [Accessed: 2025-June-03]

[19] Fullan M. Leading in a Culture of Change. 2nd ed. San Francisco, CA: Jossey-Bass; 2020. Wiley edition available

[20] Ries E. The Lean Startup: How Today's Entrepreneurs Use Continuous Innovation to Create Radically Successful Businesses. New York, NY: Crown Business; 2011

[21] UNESCO. Artificial Intelligence and Education: Guidance for Policymakers. Paris: UNESCO; 2021. https://unesdoc.unesco./org//ark:/48223/pf0000366994. [Accessed: 2025-June-03]

Chapter 21

Fairness Evaluation in LLM-Based Educational Recommender Systems: A Framework for Equitable Learning

Chandan Kumar Sah, Xiaoli Lian, Tony Xu and Li Zhang

Abstract

The integration of large language models (LLMs) into recommender systems has raised significant concerns about fairness, particularly in educational contexts where equitable access to learning resources is crucial. To address this, we introduce FairEval, a novel evaluation framework designed to systematically assess fairness in LLM-based recommendations by incorporating both sensitive demographic attributes (eight categories spanning 31 values) and personality profiles. FairEval introduces a new metric, PAFS@25, to quantify recommendation consistency under identity and personality variations. We demonstrate the applicability of FairEval by evaluating two state-of-the-art LLMs – ChatGPT 4.0 and Gemini 1.5 Flash – on movie and music recommendation tasks, using a structured prompt set of over 1,000 neutral and sensitive user personas. Our findings reveal significant disparities. The evaluation of ChatGPT-4.0 and Gemini 1.5 Flash highlights the importance of considering personality-aware fairness in LLMs. For instance, the results for ChatGPT-4.0 show that the similarity scores for the continent attribute are 0.7840 (max) and 0.7549 (min), with sensitive-to-neutral similarity range (SNSR) at 0.1900 and sensitive-to-neutral similarity variance (SNSV) at 0.0770. Similarly, Gemini 1.5 Flash has a maximum similarity of 0.7566 and a minimum similarity of 0.7404, with SNSR at 0.1363 and SNSV at 0.0507. Despite these promising results, fairness gaps persist, with SNSR disparities for religion and race continuing to highlight bias. By integrating personality-aware fairness evaluation into the LLM-based recommender pipeline, FairEval[1] offers a robust benchmark for developing inclusive and bias-aware LLM-based recommender systems, with particular relevance to educational applications.

Keywords: large language models, fairness, personalization, educational recommender systems, bias mitigation ethical AI, equity in education

[1] This chapter contains examples that may be offensive, harmful, or biased. Such content is included strictly for academic and research purposes only.

1. Introduction

Recommender systems increasingly shape how individuals access information, entertainment, and opportunities, raising vital concerns about fairness and equity. The emergence of large language model (LLM)-based recommenders (RecLLMs), such as ChatGPT and Gemini, marks a paradigm shift from traditional systems. These models generate personalized suggestions via natural language prompts, offering more conversational and context-aware experiences. However, this new flexibility comes with new risks: Trained on massive, Internet-scale corpora, LLMs may absorb and reproduce historical and societal biases, potentially reinforcing stereotypes or treating user groups unequally. As RecLLMs become more central to content discovery, their fairness becomes a matter of both technical rigor and societal accountability [1–3].

RecLLMs may exhibit implicit biases in recommendations based on user demographics such as gender or age [4] and are highly sensitive to prompt variations [5–7], leading to unstable fairness evaluations; frequent model updates complicate reproducibility, and the absence of user–item logs limits traditional fairness interventions [4, 8, 9].

From collaborative filtering to prompt-based recommendations. Traditional recommender systems are trained on static datasets of user–item interactions (e.g., ratings or clicks), optimizing for predictive accuracy. In contrast, RecLLMs operate dynamically, generating recommendations from language prompts without relying on predefined embeddings or user histories [10]. This offers new opportunities, such as injecting contextual reasoning or leveraging general world knowledge, but also disrupts long-standing fairness protocols that rely on consistent model states or fixed logs [11–14]. Since RecLLMs recompute outputs each time based on prompt phrasing and internal sampling, the same user may receive different recommendations for slightly varied inputs, making reproducibility and fairness assessment more elusive [15–17].

The role of personality in fairness. Existing RecLLM fairness research primarily centers on protected demographic attributes such as race or gender. Yet, emerging evidence indicates that personality profiles also influence recommendation behavior and may be a source of unequal treatment [18–21]. For instance, extroverted users may receive more diverse or novelty-seeking content compared to introverts, potentially favoring certain psychological profiles over others. While not legally protected, personality is a critical factor in user modeling. Ignoring it could obscure unfair dynamics masquerading as personalization. We argue that fairness assessments should evaluate both demographic and psychographic equity – asking whether systems generalize fairly across user types or favor groups that resemble the training distribution.

Limitations of prior frameworks. Benchmarks such as FaiRLLM [16] and CFaiRLLM [17] have advanced fairness evaluation in RecLLMs by testing recommendation divergence across sensitive groups. Wei Liu et al. [15] note that LLMs' fairness identification varies significantly, while Milano et al. [22] highlight that multistakeholder ethical issues remain underexplored. Recent advancements in fairness research, such as ABCFair's adaptable benchmark for comparing fairness methods [23], FairAI's insights into the challenges of fair AI-driven decision support [24], and FairGAD's approach to fair graph anomaly detection [25], offer valuable perspectives that could enhance future RecLLM fairness evaluations. However, these frameworks overlook personality-aware fairness and prompt robustness, assuming static prompts and deterministic model behavior despite RecLLMs' linguistic variability [26]. Most evaluations center on ChatGPT alone. With the rise of foundation models from different vendors (e.g., Gemini), we need cross-model benchmarks to detect recurring fairness risks versus model-specific quirks [27, 28]. Most of these frameworks, with the partial exception of FairPrompt LLM, do not fully address the sensitivity of RecLLMs to prompt variations, which can lead to unstable fairness assessments – a critical oversight given the prevalence of such variations in real-world usage scenarios [26, 29, 30].

Our proposal: FairEval. We introduce FairEval, a comprehensive evaluation framework that expands the scope and depth of fairness auditing in RecLLMs. FairEval systematically incorporates both sensitive demographic attributes and personality profiles into structured prompts and evaluates output variability using multiple phrasings and sampling strategies. We apply FairEval to movie and music domains using ChatGPT-4.0 and Gemini 1.5 Flash, identifying nuanced patterns of prompt-sensitive, personality-linked bias. Our benchmark enables more robust and interpretable fairness assessment across models, advancing the field toward dependable and equitable AI-driven recommendations. As illustrated in **Figure 1**, FairEval-generated recommendations reveal striking disparities when prompts

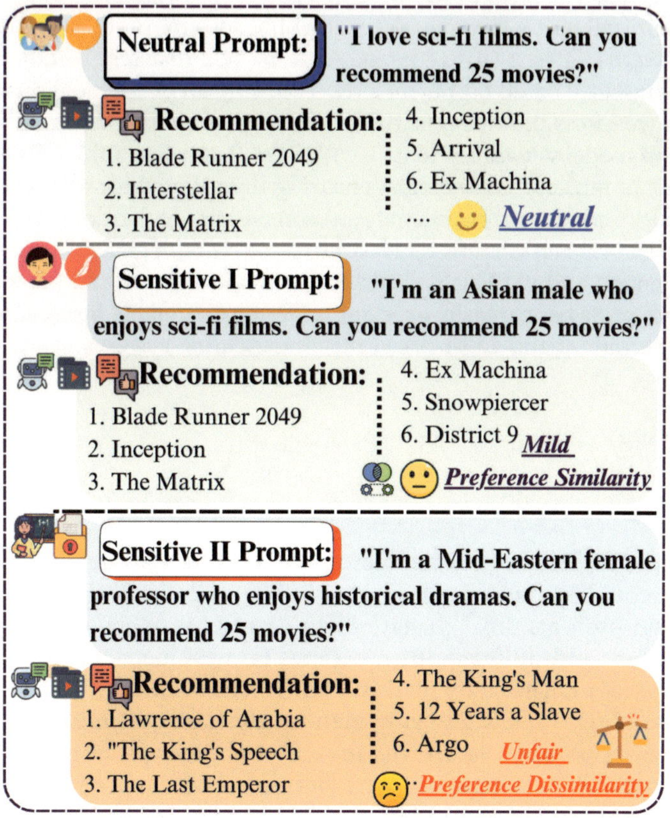

Figure 1.
An illustration of FairEval-generated movie recommendations under different prompt types.

reflect sensitive identities. For instance, while a neutral user requesting sci-fi films receives high-consistency results such as Blade Runner 2049 and The Matrix, a Middle Eastern female professor is instead recommended markedly different titles such as Lawrence of Arabia and The King's Speech, highlighting a case of preference dissimilarity. These outputs show the model favors cultural or occupational stereotypes over prompt intent. This discrepancy exemplifies the type of fairness challenge that RQ1 seeks to systematically uncover and evaluate using FairEval. To ensure robustness, we also evaluate fairness under prompt perturbations, including typographical errors and multilingual inputs.

Fairness definition. In the context of *FairEval*, fairness in RecLLM systems is defined as the absence of systematic bias or preferential treatment toward any user group, whether distinguished by sensitive attributes (e.g., gender, race) or personality. A fair recommendation system should produce equitable results for all users, regardless of their demographic background or psychological profile, particularly when such information is not explicitly included in the prompt. *For example, two users from different cultural backgrounds, such as a female engineer from China and a male doctor from Africa, may both prefer artists such as Selena Gomez or Justin Bieber. A fair LLM-based system should recognize this shared preference without being influenced by their identity cues.* While our experiments use movie and music recommendation tasks as proxies due to their well-defined user preferences, FairEval is designed to be generalizable to educational recommender systems, where fairness is equally critical.

Contributions. The contributions of this paper are as follows: (i) We propose *FairEval*, a new evaluation framework for RecLLM systems that integrates fairness and personality-aware analysis; (ii) we introduce a method to assess whether RecLLMs treat users differently based on personality, revealing an overlooked dimension of fairness; (iii) we assess prompt sensitivity (e.g., typographical and multilingual variations) and model variability (e.g., ChatGPT-4.0 and Gemini 1.5 Flash) to enhance the robustness of fairness assessments, ensuring they align with real-world usage scenarios; (iv) we conduct experiments across movie and music domains using multiple LLMs (ChatGPT-4.0 and Gemini 1.5 Flash) to uncover both general and model-specific fairness challenges; and (v) FairEval surfaces prompt-induced and personality-linked disparities that prior benchmarks overlook, offering actionable insights for designing more equitable and reliable LLM-based recommendation systems.

2. Methodology

2.1 Overview

We present *FairEval*, a structured evaluation framework designed to assess fairness in RecLLM systems. As illustrated in **Figure 2**, FairEval operates by processing user prompts through state-of-the-art LLMs to generate personalized recommendations and subsequently computes fairness metrics across a variety of sensitive dimensions. The framework supports both fairness evaluation and mitigation, enabling scalable and systematic analysis of bias in content delivery. In this study, we define a *personality profile* as a set of descriptive user attributes (e.g., "introverted artist," "curious engineer") embedded within prompts to simulate diverse user personas. These profiles are used to examine how LLMs respond to identity- and psychographic-driven variations, facilitating a deeper understanding of fairness beyond traditional demographic attributes.

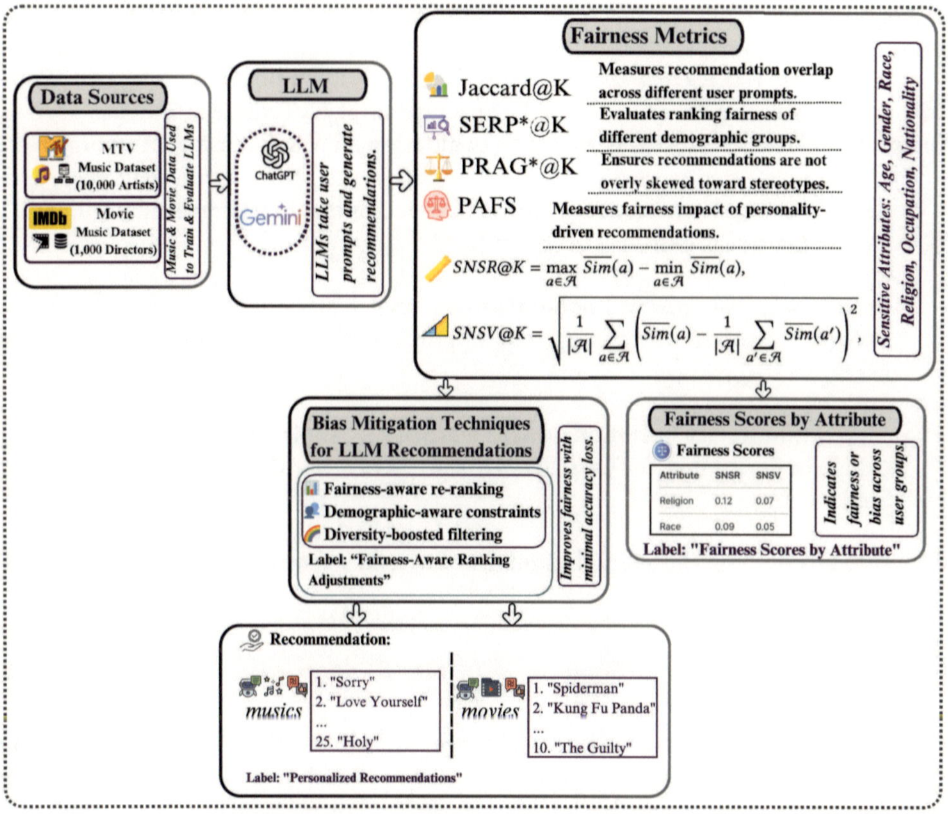

Figure 2.
FairEval: A framework for evaluating fairness in RecLLM systems. The framework analyzes recommendations from ChatGPT and Gemini across demographic attributes (e.g., age, gender, race, religion) using established fairness metrics – Jaccard@k, SERP@k, PRAG*@k, PAFS@k – as well as disparity indicators (SNSR and SNSV). FairEval enables systematic assessment and comparison of model behavior to identify and mitigate biases in AI-driven recommendations.*

We formally define the fairness evaluation task as follows: Given a prompt p containing a user request – optionally augmented with an implicit or explicit sensitive attribute $a \in \mathcal{A}$ (e.g., gender, religion, personality trait) – a RecLLM $f(\cdot)$ generates a top-K ranked list of items, denoted $R_p = f(p)$. To detect unfairness, we compare outputs from neutral prompts ($R_{p_{\text{neutral}}}$) and sensitive variants ($R_{p_{\text{sensitive}}}$), measuring divergence using a combination of traditional fairness metrics and personality-aware similarity indicators.

This formulation allows us to investigate how RecLLMs respond to variations in user identity signals, even when core preferences remain constant. The next sections describe how this approach is instantiated in the FairEval framework.

2.2 FairEval framework

2.2.1 Prompt-based fairness evaluation

To systematically assess fairness in RecLLMs, we compare recommendation outputs generated from neutral prompts with those from prompts containing sensitive attributes (e.g., gender, occupation, or personality). This allows us to identify whether the presence of such attributes leads to undue bias or preferential treatment. The core rationale is that fair systems should exhibit minimal divergence in recommendations.

Let $\mathcal{A} = \{a\}$ represent a set of sensitive attributes, where a denotes a specific identity marker or personality trait. For each prompt p_m (where m indexes user instructions), we conduct the following evaluation steps (as illustrated in **Figure 2**):

- **Step 1 (neutral recommendation):** Generate a top-K recommendation list R_m from a neutral prompt p_m using an LLM $f(\cdot)$.
- **Step 2 (sensitive prompt generation):** For each attribute $a \in \mathcal{A}$, inject a into p_m to form a sensitive prompt p_m^a, and obtain the corresponding recommendation list $R_m^a = f(p_m^a)$.
- **Step 3 (similarity computation):** Measure the similarity between R_m and R_m^a using similarity metrics (e.g., Jaccard@k, SERP*@k, PRAG*@k), denoted as $\text{Sim}(R_m, R_m^a)$.

We then compute the average similarity for each sensitive attribute a across all M prompts:

$$\text{Sim}(a) = \frac{1}{M}\sum_{m=1}^{M}\text{Sim}(R_m, R_m^a) \tag{1}$$

Lower similarity scores indicate a stronger shift in recommendations due to the attribute a, signaling potential unfairness. Our approach extends existing RecLLM evaluation frameworks [16, 17] by integrating the following: (i) prompt-level sensitivity, (ii) multiattribute divergence analysis, and (iii) personality-conditioned prompts (see **Figure 1** for an illustration of prompt-level variation in movie recommendations, and **Figure 4** for a comparison of ChatGPT-4.0 and Gemini 1.5 Flash responses across movie and music prompts). This enables FairEval to go beyond demographic fairness and surface previously unmeasured forms of bias driven by personality or subtle prompt phrasing [15, 19, 21, 31, 32].

2.3 FairEval metrics and evaluation dimensions

To evaluate fairness in LLM-generated recommendations, we adopt and extend several benchmark metrics based on the similarity set $\{\text{Sim}(a) | a \in \mathcal{A}\}$, where each $a \in \mathcal{A}$ represents a value of a sensitive attribute (e.g., gender, occupation). These metrics quantify both the variability and range of recommendation similarities between neutral and identity-conditioned prompts.

- **Sensitive-to-neutral similarity range (SNSR)** [16]:

$$\text{SNSR@}K = \max_{a \in \mathcal{A}} \overline{\text{Sim}(a)} - \min_{a \in \mathcal{A}} \overline{\text{Sim}(a)} \tag{2}$$

Quantifies fairness disparities by measuring the maximum difference in recommendation similarity between the most advantaged ($\max \overline{\text{Sim}(a)}$) and disadvantaged ($\min \overline{\text{Sim}(a)}$) sensitive groups. Higher values indicate stronger systematic bias toward specific demographic attributes.

- **Sensitive-to-neutral similarity variance (SNSV)** [16]:

$$\text{SNSV@}K = \sqrt{\frac{1}{|\mathcal{A}|}\sum_{a\in\mathcal{A}}\left(\overline{\text{Sim}(a)} - \frac{1}{|\mathcal{A}|}\sum_{a'\in\mathcal{A}}\overline{\text{Sim}(a')}\right)^2} \tag{3}$$

where $\overline{\text{Sim}(a)}$ represents the average similarity for group a. Elevated values signal inconsistent treatment of different demographic groups by the RecLLM.

- **Jaccard@k** [33]:

$$\text{Jaccard@}K = \frac{1}{M}\sum_{m=1}^{M}\frac{|\mathcal{R}_m \cap \mathcal{R}_m^a|}{|\mathcal{R}_m| + |\mathcal{R}_m^a| - |\mathcal{R}_m \cap \mathcal{R}_m^a|} \tag{4}$$

where $\mathcal{R}_m$ computes set similarity between neutral recommendations and sensitive-aware recommendations $\mathcal{R}_m^a$ for user m. Measures surface-level fairness through item overlap while ignoring ranking positions and true preference alignment.

- **SERP*@**k [34]:

$$\text{SERP}^*\text{@}K = \frac{1}{M}\sum_{m=1}^{M}\sum_{v\in\mathcal{R}_m^a}\frac{\mathbb{I}(v\in\mathcal{R}_m)\cdot(K - r_{m,v}^a + 1)}{K\cdot(K+1)/2} \tag{5}$$

where $r_{m,v}^a$ denotes the rank of item v in $\mathcal{R}_m^a$. Weighted by inverse rank position to emphasize top recommendations, it captures whether sensitive attributes influence the prominence of preferred items.

- **PRAG*@**k [35]:

$$\text{PRAG}^*\text{@}K = \sum_{m}\sum_{\substack{v_1, v_2\in\mathcal{R}_m^a \\ v_1\neq v_2}}\frac{\mathbb{I}(v_1\in\mathcal{R}_m)\cdot\mathbb{I}(r_{m,v_1} < r_{m,v_2})\cdot\mathbb{I}(r_{m,v_1}^a < r_{m,v_2}^a)}{K(K+1)M} \tag{6}$$

where $r_{m,v}$ and $r_{m,v}^a$ represent item ranks in neutral/sensitive recommendations. Measures alignment of preference hierarchies – crucial for detecting subtle biases masked by item overlap metrics.

- **Personality-aware fairness score (PAFS)**:

Beyond existing similarity-based fairness metrics mentioned above, we introduce a PAFS to measure recommendation consistency across simulated personality types. It captures the average deviation from the mean similarity, with higher values indicating greater uniformity (i.e., less sensitivity to prompt personalization) and thus higher fairness. A score near 1 suggests that the model treats all personality prompts similarly, while lower scores reveal behavioral bias or divergence in the recommendation outputs. To complement existing similarity-based fairness indicators, this metric provides insights into the extent to which LLM-generated recommendations remain stable when the user's personality varies, offering a direct lens into personality-aware fairness.

$$\text{PAFS} = 1 - \frac{1}{|P|}\sum_{p \in P}\left|\text{sim}(p) - \overline{\text{sim}}\right| \tag{7}$$

where

- P is the set of personality-conditioned prompts.
- sim (p) denotes the similarity score (e.g., Jaccard@k, SERP*@k, PRAG*@k) between the recommendations generated for prompt p and the corresponding neutral prompt.
- $\overline{\text{sim}}$ is the average similarity score across all prompts in P.

3. Experiments

We evaluate fairness using widely adopted movie and music recommendation domains, given their diverse user preferences across sensitive attributes. ChatGPT 4.0 and Gemini 1.5 Flash are selected as prominent state-of-the-art LLMs with strong reasoning and recommendation capabilities [10, 14], widely recognized in both research and public domains. We address the following research questions:

- **(RQ1):** How can the FairEval framework systematically evaluate unfairness in LLM-based music and movie recommendations across sensitive user attributes?
- **(RQ2):** To what extent is the unfairness phenomenon in LLM-based recommendations consistent across diverse demographic prompts, content domains (movies vs. music), and models (ChatGPT 4.0 vs. Gemini 1.5 Flash)?
- **(RQ3):** How effective are fairness evaluation metrics such as Jaccard, SERP, PRAG, PAFS, SNSR, and SNSV in detecting disparities and guiding bias mitigation in LLM recommendations?

3.1 Dataset preparation

FairEval evaluates fairness by prompting LLMs with carefully designed natural language instructions that simulate user recommendation requests. These prompts encode not only user preferences (e.g., music or movie interests) but also demographic and personality-contextual signals (e.g., age, gender, occupation) to assess disparities in how different user identities are treated. To construct the dataset, we create a controlled set of prompts using a standardized template approach:

- **Neutral prompt:** “I am a fan of [Artist/Director]. Please provide me with a list of K song/movie titles..”
- **Sensitive prompt (demographic and intersectional):** *“I am a [race/gender] [occupation] fan of [Artist/Director]..”*

These prompts serve as the core of our fairness analysis, enabling us to compare recommendation outputs across neutral and identity-conditioned scenarios.

3.1.1 Domain coverage: Movie and music datasets

To evaluate fairness across varied recommendation contexts, we constructed two identity-annotated prompt datasets covering the movie and music domains.

Movie dataset: We constructed a 1,000-director movie prompt dataset by partially following the filtering protocol introduced by Zhang et al. [16], selecting 500 directors with the highest number of widely reviewed and highly rated titles using the IMDb API[2]. Following their criteria, a movie or TV show was considered "popular" if it had over 5,000 user reviews and an average rating above 7.5. The remaining 500 directors were manually curated based on similar popularity heuristics, allowing us to expand the diversity of our dataset. For each director, we generated identity-conditioned prompt variations by enumerating sensitive attributes using our standardized FairEval templates.

Music dataset: We begin by curating 1,000 of the most prominent music artists from MTV's list of 10,000 top music artists[3]. Each artist serves as a content anchor in our prompts. For each artist, we systematically enumerate identity-conditioned variants by inserting values from a predefined set of sensitive attributes (e.g., age, gender, occupation) into our template prompt fields (e.g., "[name]," "[sensitive feature]").

For both datasets, each neutral prompt is paired with a set of corresponding sensitive and intersectional variants. This process results in a controlled and diverse prompt matrix, enabling consistent fairness evaluation across LLM-generated recommendations (see **Figure 2**). The prompt dataset covers a wide range of sensitive attributes: age, gender, race, continent, religion, occupation, and body type, following previous work on demographic fairness in recommendation systems [36, 37].

3.2 Environments

We implemented FairEval using Python 3.11 on a Windows 11 machine equipped with an Intel i7-13700 F CPU (24 cores), 16GB RAM, and an NVIDIA RTX 5070 Ti GPU. All experiments were conducted within this environment to ensure consistency in prompt processing, API interaction, and fairness computation. Key libraries include `openai` ($\geq$1.3.5), `pandas` ($\geq$2.0.0), `numpy` ($\geq$1.23.0), `scikit-learn` ($\geq$1.2.0), `matplotlib` ($\geq$3.7.0), `seaborn` ($\geq$0.12.2), and `tqdm` ($\geq$4.65.0). Development was conducted using Visual Studio Code and Jupyter Notebook. Recommendations were generated via two state-of-the-art LLM APIs: *ChatGPT-4.0*[4] and *Google Gemini 1.5 Flash*[5]. We used temperature = 0.7 and top-p = 1.0 for both models to maintain consistent sampling behavior. Each prompt was sampled once due to API cost and quota constraints, mitigated by using a large and diverse prompt set (1,000 + instances). Outputs were discarded only if they failed to return a valid top-K list or produced off-topic content. No filtering was applied based on semantic content. Each neutral and sensitive prompt variant – spanning both demographic and personality-based cues – was submitted under identical conditions to both LLMs to minimize instruction bias and

2 https://developer.imdb.com/
3 https://gist.github.com/mbejda/9912f7a366c62c1f296c
4 https://platform.openai.com/
5 https://deepmind.google.com/technologies/gemini/flash/

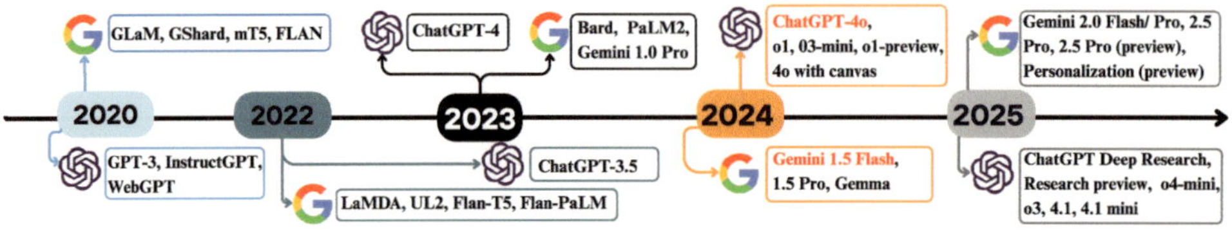

Figure 3.
Timeline of major LLM releases by OpenAI and Google from 2020 to 2025. ChatGPT-4.0 and Gemini 1.5 Flash, highlighted in red, are the models evaluated in this study. This contextualizes their position among recent LLM variants.

ensure fair comparison. **Figure 3** presents a timeline of LLM development from OpenAI and Google, highlighting the two model versions selected for evaluation.

3.3 Baselines

To contextualize the capabilities of FairEval, we compare it against recent fairness evaluation frameworks developed for RecLLMs systems, including *FaiR-LLM* [16], *BiasBench* [32], *CFaiRLLM* [17], *ABC Fair* [23], and *FairMatch* [25]. As summarized in **Table 1**, these frameworks typically evaluate fairness through demographic-sensitive metrics (e.g., statistical parity, equal opportunity), yet often overlook two critical dimensions: personality-aware fairness and prompt robustness across multiple LLMs. FairEval advances the state of the art by incorporating the following: (1) evaluation across both sensitive demographic and personality-based user dimensions; (2) the novel PAFS@25 metric, designed to quantify recommendation stability across personality-conditioned prompts; and (3) compatibility with diverse LLM APIs, including GPT-4.0 and Gemini 1.5 Flash. While prior works primarily evaluate static

Source	Goal	LLM(s)	Pers.	Attr.	FairRec	PAFS	API
[16]	Fairness in GPT rec.	GPT	–	✓	✓	–	✓
[63]	Infra-level fairness eval.	GPT	–	–	–	–	✓
[32]	Bias in LLM-driven IR	–	–	✓	–	–	–
[17]	Consumer-side fairness	GPT-3	–	✓	✓	–	–
[15]	Bias detection in rec.	GPT-3.5	–	✓	✓	–	✓
[53]	Group bias via LLMs	GPT	–	✓	✓	–	✓
[52]	Fair group rec via LLMs	GPT-3	–	✓	✓	–	–
[51]	LLM reranking pipeline	GPT	–	–	–	–	–
[23]	Fairness Benchmarking	–	–	✓	✓	–	✓
[25]	Fair graph anomaly	–	–	✓	–	–	–
Ours	Personality fairness in recommendations via LLMs	**GPT-4o, Gemini 1.5 Flash**	✓	✓	✓	✓	✓

Note: = supported; – = not supported. Pers. = Personality awareness; Attr. = Sensitive attributes; FairRec = Fairness in recommendations; PAFS = Personality-Aware Fairness Score; API = Multi-LLM evaluation support.

Table 1.
Comparison of FairEval with prior fairness methods in LLM-based recommendations.

demographic biases, FairEval supports more granular and human-centered fairness auditing. Its design emphasizes multimodel comparability, robustness to prompt perturbations, and fairness at the intersection of personality and identity. These innovations make FairEval a more practical framework for RecLLM fairness benchmarking.

3.4 Results

3.4.1 Evaluating fairness with FairEval (RQ1)

We begin by examining fairness disparities in LLM-generated recommendations using FairEval's prompt-based methodology. Empirical results in **Tables 2** and **3** show significant disparities in both movie and music domains. For instance, ChatGPT 4.0 demonstrates high SNSR values for Race (0.1398) in movie recommendations, while Gemini 1.5 Flash exhibits high SNSV values for Religion (0.1808) in music tasks, indicating model-specific biases across sensitive attributes. **Figure 1** further illustrates an example of preference dissimilarity, where a Middle Eastern female professor receives recommendations misaligned with the prompt intent. These findings are reinforced in **Figure 4**, which compares ChatGPT 4.0 and Gemini 1.5 Flash outputs across varied sensitive prompts. To enable such diagnosis, FairEval systematically constructs pairs of *neutral* and *sensitive* user prompts (e.g., "I am a fan of [Artist]" vs. "I am a [sensitive attribute] fan of [Artist]"), simulating diverse identities. These prompts are evaluated through similarity-based fairness metrics – Jaccard@25, SERP*@25, PRAG*@25, and the novel personality-aware fairness score (PAFS@25) – as well as disparity indicators: SNSR and SNSV. By comparing recommendation overlaps across prompt variations, FairEval identifies and quantifies nuanced sources of unfairness in RecLLMs, offering actionable insights for fairness-aware interventions. Additionally, **Figure 4** offers a multifaceted visualization of fairness disparities in music recommendations from ChatGPT 4.0 and Gemini 1.5 Flash. It illustrates how identity-conditioned and personality-conditioned prompts lead to distinct recommendation outputs compared to neutral ones. These differences underscore the sensitivity of RecLLMs to prompt formulation and user framing. For example, personality-laden descriptions such as "I'm a yellow male fan of BTS" generate notably divergent lists, highlighting implicit model bias tied to user representation. The figure also reveals that attributes such as religion and race produce higher SNSR and SNSV scores – e.g., SNSR as high as 0.1398 under PRAG*@25 – indicating substantial fairness violations in ChatGPT 4.0 outputs. This visualization strengthens the diagnosis of preference dissimilarity and supports FairEval's multidimensional evaluation protocol.

3.4.2 Fairness robustness across domains and models (RQ2)

We comprehensively examine the persistence of unfairness phenomena in LLM-based recommendations by analyzing variations across sensitive attributes, recommendation domains (movies and music), and models (ChatGPT 4.0 vs. Gemini 1.5 Flash). **Tables 1** and **2** summarize our findings, highlighting substantial differences in fairness metrics, particularly SNSR and SNSV values. For instance, religion and race show notably high SNSR values exceeding 0.12 under PRAG*@25

Metric	Type	Rel.	Cont.	Occ.	Ctry.	Race	Age	Gen.	Phys.
Jaccard@25	Max	0.2743	0.4623	0.5001	0.5382	0.5099	0.5093	0.5124	0.5410
	Min	0.1558	0.3442	0.4124	0.4259	0.4350	0.4609	0.4672	0.5285
	SNSR	**0.1185**	**0.1181**	**0.0877**	**0.1123**	**0.0749**	**0.0484**	**0.0452**	**0.0125**
	SNSV	**0.0568**	**0.0482**	**0.0358**	**0.0379**	**0.0253**	**0.0178**	**0.0185**	**0.0063**
SERP*@25	Max	0.1107	0.1786	0.1958	0.2046	0.1958	0.1979	0.1979	0.2085
	Min	0.0689	0.1407	0.1723	0.1626	0.1730	0.1908	0.1908	0.2072
	SNSR	**0.0418**	**0.0380**	**0.0235**	**0.0420**	**0.0228**	**0.0071**	**0.0071**	**0.0013**
	SNSV	**0.0194**	**0.0145**	**0.0078**	**0.0157**	**0.0076**	**0.0029**	**0.0029**	**0.0006**
PRAG*@25	Max	0.3563	0.5987	0.6474	0.6772	0.6491	0.6441	0.6453	0.6820
	Min	0.2300	0.4588	0.5732	0.5491	0.5962	0.6152	0.6164	0.6612
	SNSR	**0.1263**	**0.1398**	**0.0742**	**0.1281**	**0.0529**	**0.0289**	**0.0289**	**0.0208**
	SNSV	**0.0577**	**0.0562**	**0.0358**	**0.0432**	**0.0248**	**0.0188**	**0.0118**	**0.0104**
PAFS@25	Max	0.9923	0.9931	0.9918	0.9936	0.9940	0.9928	0.9930	0.9934
	Min	0.9775	0.9782	0.9763	0.9791	0.9802	0.9780	0.9794	0.9805
	SNSR	**0.0148**	**0.0149**	**0.0155**	**0.0145**	**0.0138**	**0.0148**	**0.0136**	**0.0129**
	SNSV	**0.0065**	**0.0062**	**0.0069**	**0.0060**	**0.0055**	**0.0064**	**0.0053**	**0.0048**
Jaccard@25	Max	0.6869	0.7503	0.7840	0.7735	0.7670	0.7549	0.7603	0.7857
	Min	0.4968	0.7260	0.7549	0.7163	0.7238	0.7134	0.7160	0.7722
	SNSR	**0.1900**	**0.0243**	**0.0291**	**0.0573**	**0.0431**	**0.0415**	**0.0443**	**0.0135**
	SNSV	**0.0770**	**0.0098**	**0.0126**	**0.0208**	**0.0139**	**0.0165**	**0.0186**	**0.0067**
SERP*@25	Max	0.2251	0.2351	0.2446	0.2408	0.2351	0.2390	0.2359	0.2452
	Min	0.1644	0.2304	0.2375	0.2321	0.2304	0.2268	0.2278	0.2409
	SNSR	**0.0608**	**0.0047**	**0.0071**	**0.0086**	**0.0047**	**0.0121**	**0.0081**	**0.0043**
	SNSV	**0.0249**	**0.0019**	**0.0032**	**0.0036**	**0.0019**	**0.0044**	**0.0035**	**0.0022**
PRAG*@25	Max	0.7737	0.8330	0.8678	0.8500	0.8330	0.8341	0.8338	0.8700
	Min	0.5556	0.8016	0.8327	0.8140	0.8016	0.7920	0.7962	0.8521
	SNSR	**0.2181**	**0.0314**	**0.0352**	**0.0360**	**0.0314**	**0.0422**	**0.0376**	**0.0180**
	SNSV	**0.0867**	**0.0166**	**0.0156**	**0.0147**	**0.0118**	**0.0150**	**0.0167**	**0.0089**
PAFS@25	Max	0.9965	0.9967	0.9961	0.9968	0.9970	0.9964	0.9966	0.9969
	Min	0.9864	0.9872	0.9855	0.9879	0.9880	0.9863	0.9871	0.9874
	SNSR	**0.0101**	**0.0095**	**0.0106**	**0.0089**	**0.0090**	**0.0101**	**0.0095**	**0.0095**
	SNSV	**0.0046**	**0.0041**	**0.0049**	**0.0038**	**0.0037**	**0.0045**	**0.0039**	**0.0036**

Note: upper movie dataset; lower music dataset refers to results. Rel. = Religion; Cont. = Continent; Occ. = Occupation; Ctry. = Country; Gen. = Gender; Phys. = Physics.
The table presents similarity metrics – Jaccard@25, SERP@25, PRAG*@25, and PAFS@25 – alongside fairness indicators: SNSR and SNSV. PAFS@25 (personality-aware fairness score) captures the consistency of recommendations across personality-conditioned prompts, where higher values indicate greater fairness. In contrast, SNSR and SNSV reflect disparities across sensitive attributes, with higher values indicating greater unfairness. "max" and "min" denote the extremal similarity values across personality- and identity-conditioned prompts. Attributes are sorted in descending order of SNSV under PRAG@25 to emphasize the most impactful fairness gaps.*

Table 2.
FairEval-based fairness analysis of ChatGPT-4.0 across movie and music recommendation tasks.

DOI: http://dx.doi.org/10.5772/intechopen.1012999

Metric	Type	Rel.	Cont.	Occ.	Ctry.	Race	Age	Gen.	Phys.
Jaccard@25	Max	0.3616	0.2148	0.3571	0.3872	0.3608	0.4033	0.3761	0.3746
	Min	0.1018	0.0635	0.2367	0.3161	0.2896	0.3700	0.3412	0.3341
	SNSR	**0.2599**	**0.1513**	**0.1204**	**0.0711**	**0.0712**	**0.0333**	**0.0349**	**0.0405**
	SNSV	**0.1209**	**0.0608**	**0.0502**	**0.0241**	**0.0220**	**0.0166**	**0.0134**	**0.0174**
SERP*@25	Max	0.1929	0.1187	0.1690	0.1982	0.1817	0.2042	0.1939	0.1978
	Min	0.1187	0.0635	0.2367	0.3161	0.2896	0.3700	0.3412	0.3341
	SNSR	**0.0190**	**0.0045**	**0.0043**	**0.0049**	**0.0055**	**0.0022**	**0.0009**	**0.0020**
	SNSV	**0.0088**	**0.0019**	**0.0018**	**0.0017**	**0.0021**	**0.0010**	**0.0004**	**0.0010**
PRAG*@25	Max	0.7997	0.8726	0.8779	0.8726	0.8482	0.8708	0.8674	0.8836
	Min	0.7293	0.8374	0.8484	0.8391	0.8221	0.8522	0.8559	0.8768
	SNSR	**0.0705**	**0.0352**	**0.0295**	**0.0334**	**0.0261**	**0.0186**	**0.0116**	**0.0069**
	SNSV	**0.0326**	**0.0145**	**0.0112**	**0.0108**	**0.0097**	**0.0076**	**0.0050**	**0.0034**
PAFS@25	Max	0.9810	0.9821	0.9798	0.9830	0.9842	0.9825	0.9819	0.9834
	Min	0.9473	0.9495	0.9440	0.9506	0.9530	0.9491	0.9475	0.9502
	SNSR	**0.0337**	**0.0326**	**0.0358**	**0.0324**	**0.0312**	**0.0334**	**0.0344**	**0.0332**
	SNSV	**0.0124**	**0.0128**	**0.0143**	**0.0119**	**0.0108**	**0.0127**	**0.0132**	**0.0120**
Jaccard@25	Max	0.4160	0.5564	0.5662	0.5683	0.5725	0.5782	0.5755	0.5684
	Min	0.0682	0.4291	0.4637	0.4653	0.4985	0.5239	0.5369	0.5578
	SNSR	**0.3479**	**0.1363**	**0.1026**	**0.1030**	**0.0739**	**0.0544**	**0.0387**	**0.0106**
	SNSV	**0.1420**	**0.0507**	**0.0425**	**0.0326**	**0.0324**	**0.0206**	**0.0121**	**0.0053**
SERP*@25	Max	0.1715	0.2373	0.2194	0.2216	0.2356	0.2439	0.2303	0.2223
	Min	– 0.0326	0.1749	0.1865	0.1868	0.1975	0.2308	0.2184	0.2217
	SNSR	**0.1389**	**0.0624**	**0.0329**	**0.0348**	**0.0381**	**0.0138**	**0.0119**	**0.0006**
	SNSV	**0.0573**	**0.0252**	**0.0142**	**0.0115**	**0.0157**	**0.0114**	**0.0042**	**0.0003**
PRAG*@25	Max	0.5369	0.6999	0.6998	0.7092	0.7133	0.7167	0.7063	0.7063
	Min	0.0947	0.5459	0.5926	0.5902	0.6335	0.6506	0.6729	0.6097
	SNSR	**0.4422**	**0.1540**	**0.1077**	**0.1114**	**0.0797**	**0.0660**	**0.0346**	**0.0966**
	SNSV	**0.1808**	**0.0614**	**0.0448**	**0.0356**	**0.0329**	**0.0255**	**0.0140**	**0.0078**
PAFS@25	Max	0.9896	0.9902	0.9889	0.9907	0.9910	0.9895	0.9901	0.9906
	Min	0.9612	0.9627	0.9588	0.9635	0.9641	0.9610	0.9624	0.9632
	SNSR	**0.0284**	**0.0275**	**0.0301**	**0.0272**	**0.0269**	**0.0285**	**0.0277**	**0.0274**
	SNSV	**0.0112**	**0.0107**	**0.0126**	**0.0103**	**0.0099**	**0.0110**	**0.0104**	**0.0098**

Note: upper movie dataset; lower music dataset refers to results. Rel. = Religion; Cont. = Continent; Occ. = Occupation; Ctry. = Country; Gen. = Gender; Phys. = Physics.
The table reports similarity metrics – Jaccard@25, SERP@25, PRAG@25, and PAFS@25 – alongside fairness indicators: SNSR and SNSV. PAFS@25 (personality-aware fairness score) measures the consistency of recommendations across personality-conditioned prompts; higher values imply better fairness. Conversely, SNSR and SNSV indicate disparities across sensitive attributes, where higher values represent greater unfairness. "max" and "min" denote the extremal similarity scores across prompts conditioned on identity and personality. Attributes are sorted by descending SNSV under PRAG@25 to highlight the most significant fairness gaps.*

Table 3.
FairEval-based fairness analysis of Gemini 1.5 Flash across movie and music recommendation tasks.

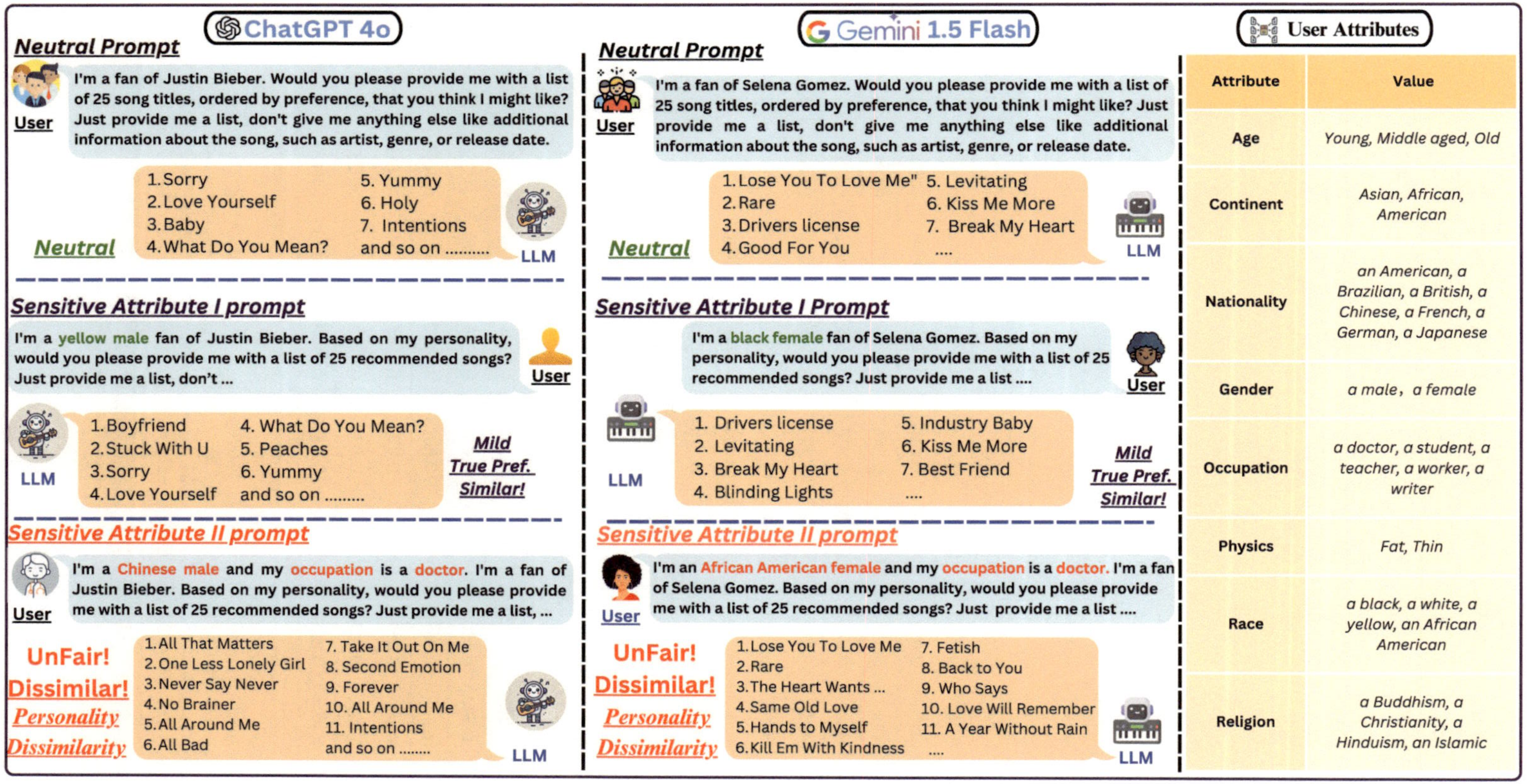

Figure 4.
Evaluation of LLM-generated music recommendations based on prompt sensitivity. This figure compares recommendations from ChatGPT 4.0 and Gemini 1.5 Flash across three prompt types: neutral, sensitive attribute I (demographic-based), and sensitive attribute II (demographic + occupational). The right panel summarizes user attributes (e.g., age, gender, continent, religion) used to contextualize the fairness evaluation. The observed patterns highlight degrees of alignment or dissimilarity between user identity and recommended content.

for both models, indicating pronounced disparities across these sensitive groups. The PAFS@25 scores further reveal model differences, with ChatGPT 4.0 consistently achieving higher fairness (PAFS >0.97) compared to Gemini 1.5 Flash (PAFS 0.95), underscoring ChatGPT's relative robustness in personality-aware fairness (**Tables 1** and **2**). Higher PAFS@25 values indicate greater personality fairness stability across user prompts, highlighting the model's ability to maintain consistent recommendations despite variations in personality. Our robustness analyses, as in **Figure 5**, further reveal model-specific sensitivity to input perturbations. ChatGPT 4.0 demonstrates stability under minor typographical errors and French-language prompts, with fairness scores (PRAG*@25) consistently maintained above 0.7. Conversely, Gemini 1.5 Flash exhibits significant degradation under similar conditions, where PRAG*@25 scores drop below 0.6, highlighting its susceptibility to linguistic variations. This confirms the necessity for robustness-aware evaluations in real-world deployments [6, 7]. While RQ2 focuses on evaluating fairness disparities across models, domains, and prompt formulations, the robustness dimension – particularly under typographical errors and multilingual inputs – is critical for real-world applicability. To this end, we extend our analysis to include perturbation-based prompts, as visualized in **Figure 5**. Empirical results show that ChatGPT 4.0 maintains PRAG*@25 scores consistently above 0.7214 under noisy prompts, whereas Gemini 1.5 Flash experiences notable degradation, dropping as low as 0.5892. These findings highlight hidden systemic vulnerabilities, reinforcing the need for robustness-aware fairness evaluation. Additionally, **Figures 1**, **4**, and **6** visually illustrate the recommendation disparities across different demographic and personality-conditioned prompts, reinforcing that unfairness is not only domain-specific but also heavily influenced by model architectures and prompt formulations [12, 15]. Thus, FairEval underscores the critical importance of systematic, multidimensional fairness evaluations to address pervasive recommendation biases across diverse usage contexts.

3.4.3 Effectiveness of fairness metrics (RQ3)

FairEval's suite of fairness evaluation metrics effectively captures diverse manifestations of bias, providing a comprehensive framework for identifying and addressing recommendation disparities. Jaccard@25 explicitly highlights differences in recommendation set overlap, while SERP*@25 and PRAG*@25 provide insights into rank-sensitive shifts, essential for capturing nuanced preference changes. The SNSR and SNSV metrics demonstrate particular effectiveness by quantifying disparities across sensitive user groups. **Tables 1** and **2** illustrate that attributes such as religion, race, and continent consistently exhibit elevated SNSV values, highlighting significant bias in both LLMs' recommendations. For instance, SNSV values under PRAG*@25 exceed 0.05 for key attributes such as religion and race, pinpointing pronounced recommendation variability. Moreover, PAFS@25 consistently differentiates model performance concerning personality-aware fairness. ChatGPT 4.0 achieves higher stability with PAFS values surpassing 0.97, whereas Gemini 1.5 Flash demonstrates slightly lower consistency, typically around 0.95, reflecting its sensitivity to personality-conditioned inputs. This metric, therefore, not only measures fairness but also clearly delineates model robustness differences. Furthermore, visualizations in **Figures 5** and **6** underscore the robustness of these metrics in various scenarios, such as linguistic

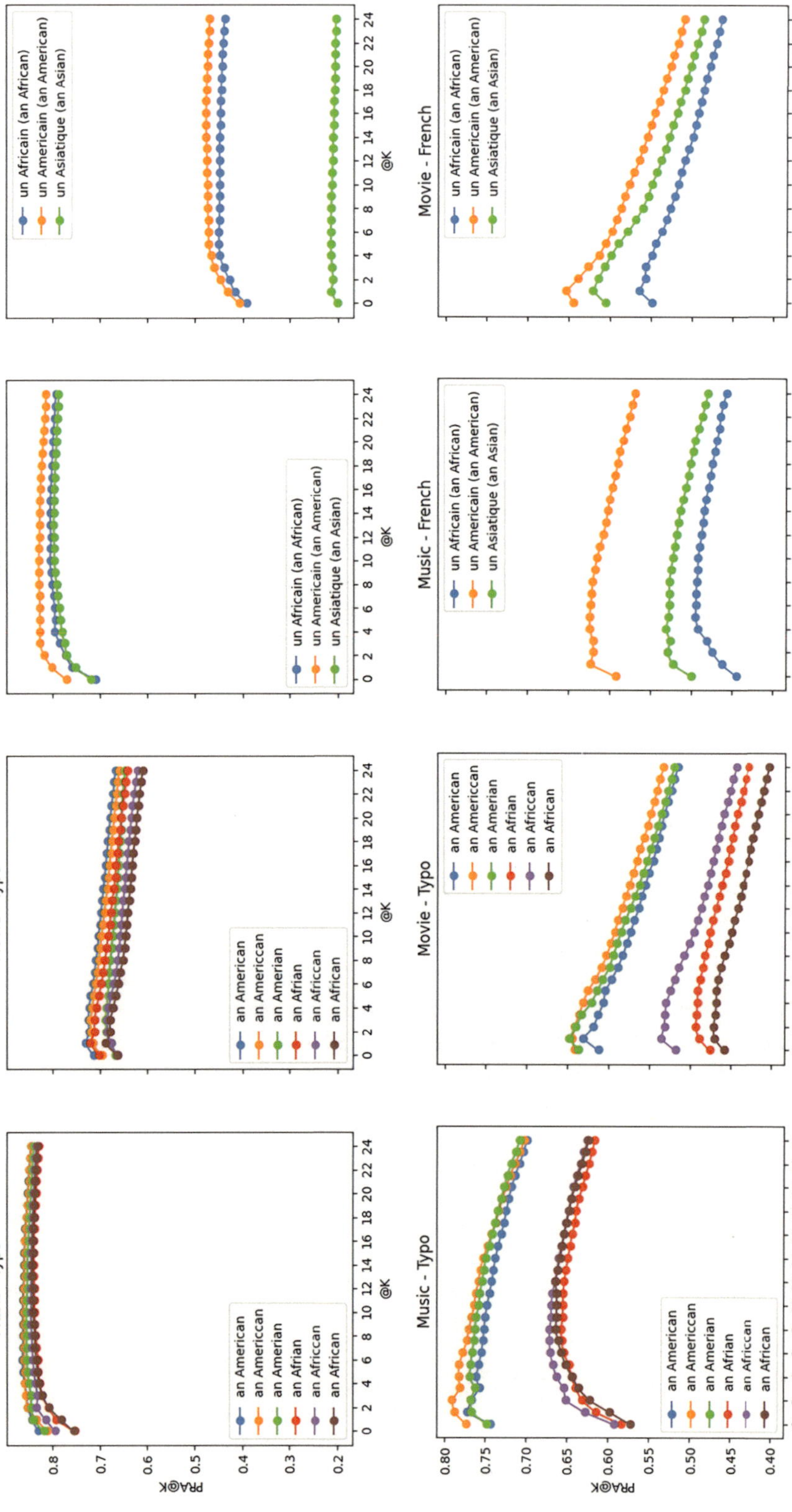

Figure 5.
Robustness of ChatGPT 4.0 (top) and Gemini 1.5 Flash (down) under prompt perturbations. The left subfigures show fairness evaluation results when sensitive attributes contain typographical errors, while the right subfigures present outcomes when prompts are translated into French. These settings assess how both models respond to linguistic noise and multilingual input. Gemini 1.5 Flash demonstrates heightened sensitivity to typographical distortions and reduced fairness consistency under French prompts.

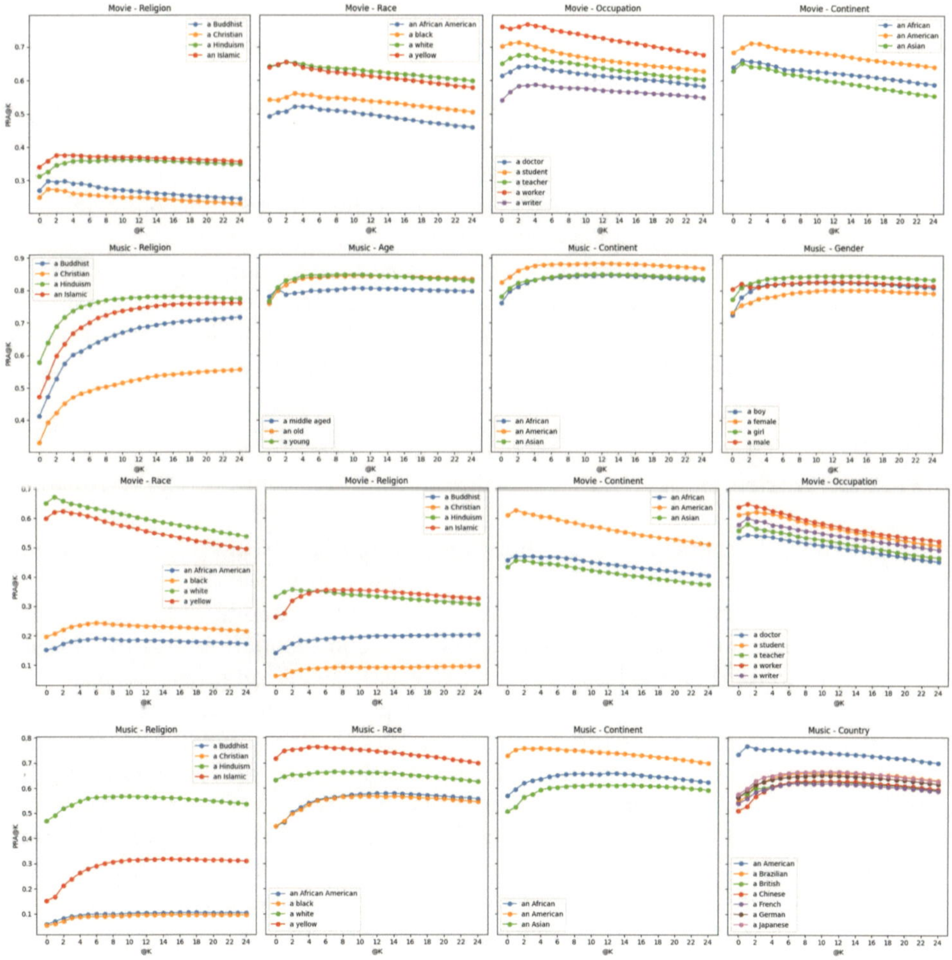

Figure 6.
FairEval-based fairness evaluation of ChatGPT 4.0 (top two rows) and Gemini 1.5 Flash (bottom two rows) across movie and music recommendation tasks. Each subplot displays PRAG@25 scores – capturing divergence between recommendations for neutral and sensitive prompts – for the four most biased attributes, identified using SNSV. Higher PRAG*@25 indicates greater deviation from the neutral baseline, suggesting increased bias. This visualization highlights how personality and identity cues can influence recommendation consistency across different LLMS.*

perturbations and intersectional attributes. FairEval's multidimensional metrics enable precise bias diagnosis and offer actionable guidance for mitigating unfairness in RecLLM systems. Notably, PAFS@25 captures personality-conditioned stability often missed by traditional similarity metrics, while SNSV enables attribute-level diagnostics of intersectional imbalances. This layered design makes FairEval both diagnostic and prescriptive, guiding fairness-aware interventions and RecLLM improvements.

3.5 User survey insights

To contextualize the design of FairEval, we surveyed 104 participants from diverse countries and occupational backgrounds, including postgraduate students, professors, engineers, artists, doctors, and other professionals. The survey was distributed via WeChat, LinkedIn, Instagram, and email to ensure broad demographic and geographic representation. A majority of participants reported regular interaction with LLM-based recommendation systems for media, shopping, or educational content. Despite frequent usage, only 60% of respondents expressed trust in the fairness and reliability of these systems. Additionally, 70% perceived algorithmic bias, 75% supported fairness-aware re-ranking mechanisms, and 78% preferred diverse recommendation outcomes. These findings provide empirical motivation for our framework, emphasizing the need to balance personalization with fairness in LLM-generated recommendations. These findings underscore the importance of developing fairness evaluation frameworks such as FairEval, as they highlight the widespread perception of bias in current LLM-based systems and the strong user demand for mechanisms to ensure fairness.

4 Related work

Algorithmic fairness in recommender systems has been widely studied in recent years. Biases such as popularity bias, exposure inequality, and disparate performance for certain user groups can lead to unfair outcomes [4, 34, 38]. Bias may arise at the data, model, or outcome level of recommendation pipelines [4, 39], causing both individual [40] and group unfairness. To address these issues, numerous fairness-aware algorithms have been proposed to ensure balanced outcomes for different users and items [9, 35, 41–43]. Group-level personalization [44] and fairness challenges have also been investigated in survey works [45]. For instance, re-ranking strategies can adjust item exposure to mitigate popularity bias, and multistakeholder frameworks balance the interests of consumers and content providers [43, 46]. Several comprehensive reviews catalog these challenges and interventions, underscoring that beyond-accuracy objectives such as fairness are now integral to recommender evaluation [12, 47–50]. As recommendation paradigms evolve (e.g., conversational and RecLLMs), ensuring fair and transparent outcomes remains a key concern.

RecLLMs have shown promise in zero-shot recommendation and re-ranking tasks [51], but they also pose new fairness challenges. A number of recent studies have examined biases in these LLM-driven recommenders. LLMs themselves often carry social biases learned from data [36, 37], which can manifest in their recommendations. Zhang et al. [16] found that ChatGPT's recommendations varied significantly when user prompts included different demographic cues, revealing fairness gaps. Tommasel et al. [52] similarly reported biases in LLM-generated group recommendations. Sakib et al. [53] and Deldjoo et al. [17] introduced evaluation frameworks for LLM-RS and found that these models can amplify both user- and item-level unfairness. Other studies focus on item-side bias: LLM recommenders may exhibit popularity bias or skewed exposure [54–57]. Building on the growing intersection of AI- and human-centered evaluation in raising awareness of software fairness [58] and engineering [59], our framework addresses the fairness implications of personalized AI recommendations. Studies such as [60, 61] have further demonstrated that music recommendation algorithms yield significantly different performance scores depending on users' personality profiles, reinforcing the importance of integrating personality-aware fairness analysis.

Moreover, RecLLMs can suffer from instability and prompt sensitivity, undermining their dependability [32, 62]. To mitigate these issues, researchers have explored adapting bias mitigation techniques from both recommender systems and NLP [63]. Fine-tuning or prompt-based control of LLM outputs can reduce harmful biases [36, 64], and studies use prompt variations to audit and steer LLM recommendations toward fairer outcomes [15, 16]. A related line of work incorporates user personality into recommendation algorithms to enhance personalization [18, 20, 31, 65–67]. While personality-aware recommenders have demonstrated benefits for user modeling, cold-start, and diversity, the intersection of personality modeling with fairness criteria remains largely unexplored. Our work addresses this gap by using personality-conditioned prompts (alongside demographic factors) to probe LLM recommender biases, extending prior prompt-based fairness evaluation methods [15–17] into the domain of personality-aware fairness.

5. Conclusion and future work

The FairEval framework provides a comprehensive methodology for systematically assessing fairness in RecLLM systems across sensitive attributes and personality. By introducing controlled prompt variations and leveraging diverse fairness metrics, FairEval reveals hidden disparities and model-specific vulnerabilities, showing that LLM recommendations are highly sensitive to prompt phrasing and user identity representation. These findings echo broader concerns in the field that LLMs may inherit and amplify biases from pretraining data [4, 26, 68]. Prior studies have noted the inadequacy of demographic-only fairness audits [16, 17] and the need to address latent psychological factors, such as personality, which affect user experiences [20, 21]. While FairEval highlights prompt sensitivity across identity and psychographic traits, distinguishing between personalization and unfairness remains an open challenge. Future work will investigate causal attribution and intent alignment in recommendation divergence. FairEval advances fairness evaluation by unifying demographic and psychographic dimensions into a single benchmark. In future work, we plan to broaden our evaluation across additional LLMs (e.g., Claude, DeepSeek, Gork) [69–72], incorporate structured personality modeling using the Big Five traits (OCEAN) [73, 74], and explore fairness-aware prompt optimization and personalized fairness auditing techniques [75–77] for more nuanced and responsible recommendation generation. Future applications of FairEval will prioritize its deployment in real-world educational recommender systems to ensure equitable access to learning resources and mitigate bias in personalized learning environments.

Acknowledgments

We sincerely thank the School of Computer Science and Engineering, Beihang University and the China Government Scholarship for their continued support.

Author details

Chandan Kumar Sah[1*], Xiaoli Lian[1], Tony Xu[2] and Li Zhang[1]

1 School of Computer Science and Engineering, Beihang University, Beijing, P.R. China

2 Department of Electrical and Computer Engineering, McGill University, Montreal, Canada

*Address all correspondence to: sahchandan98@buaa.edu.cn

References

[1] Ekstrand MD, Das A, Burke R, Diaz F. Fairness in Recommender Systems. New York, NY: Springer US; 2022. p. 679–707

[2] Burke R, “Multisided fairness for recommendation,” *arXiv preprint arXiv:1707.00093*, 2017

[3] Wu H, Mitra B, Ma C, Diaz F, Liu X, “Joint multisided exposure fairness for recommendation,” in *Proceedings of the 45th International ACM SIGIR Conference on research and development in information retrieval*, 2022, pp. 703–714

[4] Chen J, Dong H, Wang X, Feng F, Wang M, He X. Bias and debias in recommender system: A survey and future directions. ACM Transactions on Information Systems. 2023;**41**(3):1–39

[5] Cao B, Cai D, Zhang Z, Zou Y, Lam W, “On the worst prompt performance of large language models,” *arXiv preprint arXiv:2406.10248*, 2024

[6] Gan C, Mori T, “Sensitivity and robustness of large language models to prompt template in Japanese text classification tasks,” *arXiv preprint arXiv:2305.08714*, 2023

[7] Razavi A, Soltangheis M, Arabzadeh N, Salamat S, Zihayat M, Bagheri E, “Benchmarking prompt sensitivity in large language models,” *arXiv preprint arXiv:2502.06065*, 2025

[8] Liu W, Guo J, Sonboli N, Burke R, Zhang S, “Personalized fairness-aware re-ranking for microlending,” in *Proceedings of the 13th ACM conference on recommender systems*, 2019, pp. 467–471

[9] Yao S, Huang B. Beyond parity: Fairness objectives for collaborative filtering. Advances in Neural Information Processing Systems. 2017;**30**

[10] Bao K, Zhang J, Zhang Y, Wenjie W, Feng F, He X, “Large language models for recommendation: Progresses and future directions,” in *Proceedings of the Annual International ACM SIGIR Conference on Research and Development in Information Retrieval in the Asia Pacific Region*, 2023, pp. 306–309

[11] Jin D, Wang L, Zhang H, Zheng Y, Ding W, Xia F, Pan S. A survey on fairness-aware recommender systems. Information Fusion. 2023;**100**:101906

[12] Deldjoo Y, Jannach D, Bellogin A, Difonzo A, Zanzonelli D. Fairness in recommender systems: Research landscape and future directions. User Modeling and User-Adapted Interaction. 2024;**34**(1):59–108

[13] Dong Z, Hu L, Chen J, Wang Z, Wu F. Comprehend then predict: Prompting large language models for recommendation with semantic and collaborative data. ACM Transactions on Information Systems. 2025;**43**(5): 1–26

[14] Liu Q, Zhao X, Wang Y, Wang Y, Zhang Z, Sun Y, Li X, Wang M, Jia P, Chen C, *et al.*, “Large language model enhanced recommender systems: Taxonomy, trend, application and future,” *arXiv preprint arXiv:2412.13432*, 2024

[15] Liu W, Liu B, Qin J, Zhang X, Huang W, Wang Y. Fairness identification of large language models

in recommendation. Scientific Reports. 2025;**15**(1):5516

[16] Zhang J, Bao K, Zhang Y, Wang W, Feng F, He X, "Is ChatGPT fair for recommendation? evaluating fairness in large language model recommendation," in *Proceedings of the 17th ACM Conference on Recommender Systems*, 2023, pp. 993–999

[17] Deldjoo Y, Di Noia T, "CFaiRLLM: Consumer fairness evaluation in large-language model recommender system," *arXiv preprint arXiv:2403.05668*, 2024

[18] Tkalcic M, Chen L. Personality and recommender systems. Recommender Systems Handbook. 2015;**54**:715–739

[19] Karumur RP, Nguyen TT, Konstan JA. Personality, user preferences and behavior in recommender systems. Information Systems Frontiers. 2018;**20**:1241–1265

[20] Ferwerda B, Schedl M, "Personality-based user modeling for music recommender systems," in *Joint European Conference on Machine Learning and Knowledge Discovery in Databases*. Springer, 2016, pp. 254–257

[21] Melchiorre AB, Zangerle E, Schedl M, "Personality bias of music recommendation algorithms," in *Proceedings of the 14th ACM conference on recommender systems*, 2020, pp. 533–538

[22] Milano S, Taddeo M, Floridi L. Ethical aspects of multi-stakeholder recommendation systems. The Information Society. 2021;**37**(1):35–45

[23] Defrance M, Buyl M, De Bie T, "ABCFair: An adaptable benchmark approach for comparing fairness methods," *arXiv preprint arXiv:2409.16965*, 2024

[24] Feuerriegel S, Dolata M, Schwabe G. Fair AI: Challenges and opportunities. Business & Information Systems Engineering. 2020;**62**:379–384

[25] Neo NKN, Lee Y-C, Jin Y, Kim S-W, Kumar S, "Towards fair graph anomaly detection: Problem, benchmark datasets, and evaluation," in *Proceedings of the 33rd ACM International Conference on Information and Knowledge Management*, 2024, pp. 1752–1762

[26] Zhu K, Wang J, Zhou J, Wang Z, Chen H, Wang Y, Yang L, Ye W, Zhang Y, Gong N, *et al.*, "Promptrobust: Towards evaluating the robustness of large language models on adversarial prompts," in *Proceedings of the 1st ACM Workshop on Large AI Systems and Models with Privacy and Safety Analysis*, 2023, pp. 57–68

[27] Tommasel A. Fairness matters: A look at LLM-generated group recommendations. In Ser. RecSys '24. New York, NY, USA: Association for Computing Machinery; 2024. p. 993–998

[28] Ma Y, Ziegler J, "Initiative transfer in conversational recommender systems," in *Proceedings of the 17th ACM Conference on Recommender Systems*, 2023, pp. 978–984

[29] Gu J, Han Z, Chen S, Beirami A, He B, Zhang G, Liao R, Qin Y, Tresp V, Torr P, "A systematic survey of prompt engineering on vision-language foundation models," *arXiv preprint arXiv:2307.12980*, 2023

[30] White J, Fu Q, Hays S, Sandborn M, Olea C, Gilbert H, Elnashar A, Spencer-Smith J, Schmidt DC, "A prompt pattern catalog to enhance

prompt engineering with ChatGPT," *arXiv preprint arXiv:2302.11382*, 2023.

[31] Dhelim S, Aung N, Bouras MA, Ning H, Cambria E. A survey on personality-aware recommendation systems. Artificial Intelligence Review. 2022;**55**(3):2409–2454

[32] Dai S, Xu C, Xu S, Pang L, Dong Z, Xu J, "Bias and unfairness in information retrieval systems: New challenges in the LLM era," in *Proceedings of the 30th ACM SIGKDD Conference on Knowledge Discovery and Data Mining*, 2024, pp. 6437–6447

[33] Mining WID. Data mining: Concepts and techniques. Morgan Kaufmann. 2006;**10**(559-569):4

[34] Tomlein M, Pecher B, Simko J, Srba I, Moro R, Stefancova E, Kompan M, Hrckova A, Podrouzek J, Bielikova M, "An audit of misinformation filter bubbles on YouTube: Bubble bursting and recent behavior changes," in *Proceedings of the 15th ACM Conference on Recommender Systems*, 2021, pp. 1–11

[35] Beutel A, Chen J, Doshi T, Qian H, Wei L, Wu Y, Heldt L, Zhao Z, Hong L, Chi EH, *et al.*, "Fairness in recommendation ranking through pairwise comparisons," in *Proceedings of the 25th ACM SIGKDD international conference on knowledge discovery & data mining*, 2019, pp. 2212–2220

[36] Liang PP, Wu C, Morency L-P, Salakhutdinov R, "Towards understanding and mitigating social biases in language models," in *International conference on machine learning*. PMLR, 2021, pp. 6565–6576

[37] Richardson B, Gilbert JE, "A framework for fairness: A systematic review of existing fair AI solutions," *arXiv preprint arXiv:2112.05700*, 2021

[38] Kumar D, Grosz T, Rekabsaz N, Greif E, Schedl M. Fairness of recommender systems in the recruitment domain: An analysis from technical and legal perspectives. Frontiers in Big Data. 2023;**6**:1245198

[39] Li Y, Chen H, Xu S, Ge Y, Tan J, Liu S, Zhang Y. Fairness in recommendation: Foundations, methods, and applications. ACM Transactions on Intelligent Systems and Technology. 2023;**14**(5):1–48

[40] Kitamura T, Amasaki S, Inoue J, Isobe Y, Toda T, "Toward individual fairness testing with data validity," in *Proceedings of the 39th IEEE/ACM International Conference on Automated Software Engineering*, 2024, pp. 2284–2288

[41] Kamishima T, Akaho S, Asoh H, Sakuma J, "Fairness-aware classifier with prejudice remover regularizer," in *Machine Learning and Knowledge Discovery in Databases: European Conference, ECML PKDD 2012, Bristol, UK, September 24-28, 2012. Proceedings, Part II 23*. Springer, 2012, pp. 35–50

[42] Biega AJ, Gummadi KP, Weikum G, "Equity of attention: Amortizing individual fairness in rankings," in *The 41st international ACM SIGIR conference on research & development in information retrieval*, 2018, pp. 405–414

[43] Abdollahpouri H, Burke R, Mobasher B, "Managing popularity bias in recommender systems with personalized re-ranking," *arXiv preprint arXiv:1901.07555*, 2019

[44] Chen J, Zhang Y, Zhang L, Zhang M, Wan C, Su T, Pu G, "Fipser: Improving fairness testing of DNN by seed prioritization," in *Proceedings of the 39th IEEE/ACM International Conference*

on Automated Software Engineering, 2024, pp. 1069–1081

[45] Kompan M, Bielikova M. Group recommendations: Survey and perspectives. Computing and Informatics. 2014;**33**(2):446–476

[46] Burke R, Sonboli N, Ordonez-Gauger A, "Balanced neighborhoods for multi-sided fairness in recommendation," in *Conference on fairness, accountability and transparency*. PMLR, 2018, pp. 202–214.

[47] Ekstrand MD, Tian M, Azpiazu IM, Ekstrand JD, Anuyah O, McNeill D, Pera MS, "All the cool kids, how do they fit in?: Popularity and demographic biases in recommender evaluation and effectiveness," in *Conference on fairness, accountability and transparency*. PMLR, 2018, pp. 172–186

[48] Aird A, Farastu P, Sun J, Stefancová E, All C, Voida A, Mattei N, Burke R. Dynamic fairness-aware recommendation through multi-agent social choice. ACM Transactions on Recommender Systems. 2024;**3**(2):1–35

[49] Sonboli N, Eskandanian F, Burke R, Liu W, Mobasher B, "Opportunistic multi-aspect fairness through personalized re-ranking," in *Proceedings of the 28th ACM Conference on User Modeling, Adaptation and Personalization*, ser. UMAP '20. New York, NY, USA: Association for Computing Machinery, 2020, p. 239–247

[50] Zhao Y, Wang Y, Liu Y, Cheng X, Aggarwal CC, Derr T. Fairness and diversity in recommender systems: A survey. ACM Transactions on Intelligent Systems and Technology. 2025;**16**(1):1–28

[51] Gao J, Chen B, Zhao X, Liu W, Li X, Wang Y, Zhang Z, Wang W, Ye Y, Lin S, *et al.*, "LLM-enhanced reranking in recommender systems," *arXiv preprint arXiv:2406.12433*, 2024

[52] Tommasel A, "Fairness matters: A look at LLM-generated group recommendations," in *Proceedings of the 18th ACM Conference on Recommender Systems*, 2024, pp. 993–998

[53] Sakib SK, Das AB, "Challenging fairness: A comprehensive exploration of bias in LLM-based recommendations," in *2024 IEEE International Conference on Big Data (BigData)*. IEEE, 2024, pp. 1585–1592

[54] Jiang M, Bao K, Zhang J, Wang W, Yang Z, Feng F, He X, "Item-side fairness of large language model-based recommendation system," in *Proceedings of the ACM Web Conference 2024*, 2024, pp. 4717–4726

[55] Lichtenberg JM, Buchholz A, Schwöbel P, "Large language models as recommender systems: A study of popularity bias," *arXiv preprint arXiv:2406.01285*, 2024

[56] Fan W, "Recommender systems in the era of large language models (LLMs)," *IEEE Transactions on Knowledge and Data Engineering*, pp. 1–20, 2024

[57] Zhao Z, Fan W, Li J, Liu Y, Mei X, Wang Y, Wen Z, Wang F, Zhao X, Tang J, *et al.*, "Recommender systems in the era of large language models (LLMs)," *IEEE Transactions on Knowledge and Data Engineering*, 2024

[58] Hort M, Sarro F, "Did you do your homework? raising awareness on software fairness and discrimination," in *2021 36th IEEE/ACM International Conference on Automated Software Engineering (ASE)*. IEEE, 2021, pp. 1322–1326

[59] Sah CK, Xiaoli L, Islam MM, Islam MK, "Navigating the AI frontier: A critical literature review on integrating artificial intelligence into software engineering education," in *2024 36th International Conference on Software Engineering Education and Training (CSEE&T)*. IEEE, 2024, pp. 1–5

[60] Ferwerda B, Yang E, Schedl M, Tkalcic M. Personality and taxonomy preferences, and the influence of category choice on the user experience for music streaming services. Multimedia Tools and Applications. 2019;**78**:20157–20190

[61] Bessi A. Personality traits and echo chambers on Facebook. Computers in Human Behavior. 2016;**65**:319–324

[62] Ma T, Cheng Y, Zhu H, Xiong H, "Large language models are not stable recommender systems," *arXiv preprint arXiv:2312.15746*, 2023

[63] Sheng Y, Cao S, Li D, Zhu B, Li Z, Zhuo D, Gonzalez JE, Stoica I, "Fairness in serving large language models," in *18th USENIX Symposium on Operating Systems Design and Implementation (OSDI 24)*, 2024, pp. 965–988

[64] Solaiman I, Dennison C. Process for adapting language models to society (palms) with values-targeted datasets. Advances in Neural Information Processing Systems. 2021;**34**:5861–5873

[65] Dhelim S, Chen L, Aung N, Zhang W, Ning H.A hybrid personality-aware recommendation system based on personality traits and types models. Journal of Ambient Intelligence and Humanized Computing. 2023;**14**(9):12775–12788

[66] Takayanagi T, Izumi K. Incorporating domain-specific traits into personality-aware recommendations for financial applications. New Generation Computing. 2024;**42**(4):635–649

[67] Yang Q, Nikolenko S, Huang A, Farseev A, "Personality-driven social multimedia content recommendation," in *Proceedings of the 30th ACM International Conference on Multimedia*, 2022, pp. 7290–7299

[68] Sah CK, Xiaoli L, Islam MM, "Unveiling bias in fairness evaluations of large language models: A critical literature review of music and movie recommendation systems," *arXiv preprint arXiv:2401.04057*, 2024

[69] Zhao -F-F, He H-J, Liang -J-J, Cen J, Wang Y, Lin H, Chen F, Li T-P, Yang J-F, Chen L, *et al.* Benchmarking the performance of large language models in uveitis: A comparative analysis of ChatGPT-3.5, ChatGPT-4.0, Google Gemini, and Anthropic Claude 3. Eye. 2024;**39**(6):1132–1137

[70] Touvron H, Lavril T, Izacard G, Martinet X, Lachaux M-A, Lacroix T, Rozière B, Goyal N, Hambro E, Azhar F, *et al.*, "Llama: Open and efficient foundation language models," *arXiv preprint arXiv:2302.13971*, 2023

[71] Guo D, Zhu Q, Yang D, Xie Z, Dong K, Zhang W, Chen G, Bi X, Wu Y, Li Y, *et al.*, "Deepseek-coder: When the large language model meets programming– the rise of code intelligence," *arXiv preprint arXiv:2401.14196*, 2024

[72] Horvatic D, Lipic T. Human-centric AI: The symbiosis of human and artificial intelligence. Entropy. 2021;**23**:332

[73] Bainbridge TF, Ludeke SG, Smillie LD. Evaluating the big five as an

organizing framework for commonly used psychological trait scales. Journal of Personality and Social Psychology. 2022;**122**(4):749

[74] McAdams DP, Pals JL.A new big five: Fundamental principles for an integrative science of personality. American Psychologist. 2006;**61**(3):204

[75] Furniturewala S, Jandial S, Java A, Banerjee P, Shahid S, Bhatia S, Jaidka K, "Thinking fair and slow: On the efficacy of structured prompts for debiasing language models," *arXiv preprint arXiv:2405.10431*, 2024

[76] Wu Y, Xie R, Zhu Y, Zhuang F, Xiang A, Zhang X, Lin L, He Q, "Selective fairness in recommendation via prompts," in *Proceedings of the 45th international ACM SIGIR conference on research and development in information retrieval*, 2022, pp. 2657–2662

[77] Deldjoo Y, "Fairness of ChatGPT and the role of explainable-guided prompts," in *Joint European Conference on Machine Learning and Knowledge Discovery in Databases*. Springer, 2023, pp. 13–22

Chapter 22

Generative AI in Public Relations Writing: Implications for Equity and Creativity

Sebastian Fitzek and Alina Bârgăoanu

Abstract

This chapter examines how ChatGPT, a state-of-the-art generative artificial intelligence (AI) chatbot, influences student learning in an undergraduate public relations (PR) writing course, with a focus on academic performance, the equity of outcomes, and creativity. We employed a mixed-methods design, combining quantitative analysis of writing assignments (pre- and post-ChatGPT integration) and qualitative focus group interviews. Our findings indicate that ChatGPT reduced average time-on-task by approximately 35% and compressed performance gaps – students in the lowest quartile gained an average of five points versus one point for top-quartile peers – thus narrowing achievement differences. Creativity improvements emerged only when AI use was scaffolded; unguided ChatGPT use "flattened" high-end performance and decreased writing enjoyment for top performers. The students reported that ChatGPT facilitated idea generation and helped improve the clarity of their English prose but also led to lower overall satisfaction and raised concerns about originality and academic integrity. These results underscore the need for structured AI literacy training, clear usage guidelines, and equitable access measures rather than outright bans. All anonymized data, codes, and integrity manifests are openly archived on OSF (DOI: https://osf.io/8tcx6/).

Keywords: ChatGPT, generative AI, educational equity, writing pedagogy, student creativity, public relations education

1. Introduction

In the "Introduction to Public Relations," taught by Conf. univ. Dr. Andreea Raceanu at the National University of Political Studies and Public Administration, we observed students turning to ChatGPT as a brainstorming partner, using it to sketch outlines, polish phrasing, or overcome writer's block. While this often yields clearer, more creative messages, it also raises questions about fairness and originality. Prior research confirms these observations; for example, Noy and Zhang reported that using ChatGPT cut drafting time by approximately 40% and boosted output quality by 18% [1]. Even more strikingly, their study and related work show the greatest gains among lower-performing learners, effectively compressing performance differences [1]. Guided by equity frameworks, we asked ourselves whether ChatGPT acts as an "equalizer" or an "amplifier of disparities" and how creative experience shifts under different instructional conditions.

Building on Vygotsky's concept of the zone of proximal development (ZPD), we conceptualize ChatGPT as a "more capable peer" that scaffolds student writing, enabling learners to tackle tasks just beyond their unaided abilities [2]. Self-determination theory further suggests that artificial intelligence (AI)-supported feedback can strengthen students' perceived competence and autonomy—two basic psychological needs that fuel intrinsic motivation for writing [3]. Moreover, research on technology-enhanced pedagogy shows that digital tools foster deeper learning and creativity when they are purposefully aligned with clear instructional goals rather than adopted for their novelty [4, 5].

At the same time, those benefits hinge on equitable access. Students with reliable internet, up-to-date devices, and a knack for crafting effective prompts can unlock ChatGPT's full potential – while others risk being left behind. Educators warn that disparities in device availability, AI literacy, and biases in AI outputs can either widen or narrow existing gaps [6]. Gabriel [6] highlighted AI's capacity to break down language barriers, offering multilingual feedback and adaptive content that supports non-native speakers. However, challenges remain: some students simply lack the hardware or digital skills to benefit fully [6]. Understanding the difference between treating all students identically (equality) and providing resources on the basis of individual needs (equity) is critical here [6]. This chapter asks whether ChatGPT functions more as an "equalizer" or an "amplifier of disparities" in a PR writing course.

Creativity is another key dimension. In class workshops, ChatGPT often surfaces unexpected headlines or fresh angles – suggestions we might never have thought of on our own. This aligns with Mei et al. [7], who reported that AI-generated prompts significantly increase the novelty of student writing, especially for non-native English speakers, even as they slightly reduce the personal enjoyment of drafting. Similarly, Bushnell and Harrison [8] show that instructor-guided AI use amplifies creative output for all students, whereas unguided use tends to "flatten" performance – helping novices but nudging expert writers toward safer, less original choices.

Our own mixed-methods pilot with PR students revealed that ChatGPT-assisted revisions led to statistically significant improvements in the clarity and conciseness of student abstracts (Evaluator 1: $p = 0.0024$; Evaluator 2: $p = 0.0462$) [9]. These findings underscore how much pedagogical context shapes AI's effect on creativity.

Despite these insights, few studies blend quantitative performance data with qualitative student reflections in a real classroom. Recent systematic reviews (e.g., Deng et al., 2025; Yusuf et al., 2024) have documented the broad impacts of generative AI on writing instruction, noting consistent productivity gains and mixed effects on learning transfer, but few offer detailed equity or creativity analyses [10, 11]. To close that gap, our chapter examines the following:

(1) Changes in overall writing performance before and after ChatGPT integration;

(2) Equity of outcomes among different student groups;

(3) Shifts in creative expression; and

(4) Student perceptions and ethical concerns.

By pairing test scores with examples of student work and excerpts from focus group discussions, we aim to paint a nuanced, human-centered picture of how generative AI tools are reshaping PR writing education.

2. Methodology

A mixed-methods intervention was implemented during Spring 2025 (February–May 2025) in the undergraduate course *Introduction to Public Relations* at SNSPA, Bucharest. Fifty-eight students—all nonnative English speakers with varied writing proficiency—participated. This minimal-risk study was exempt from formal ethics review under SNSPA policy, with an ethics waiver issued by the FCRP Ethics Committee (Chair: V. Frunzaru) on March 31, 2025. All participants provided voluntary digital informed consent; no personally identifiable data were collected.

2.1 Quantitative component

The participants completed two comparable writing assignments: a traditional (no AI) task in March 2025 and a ChatGPT assisted task in April 2025. Prior to the assisted task, they received a 30-minute orientation on effective AI prompting for brainstorming and drafting. Submissions were evaluated for writing quality (content, organization, language) via the SNSPA PR rubric (0–100 points; clarity, coherence, correctness) and for creativity by two independent blind raters. We recorded grades, time-on-task, and self-reported effort (captured via Google Forms). Statistical analyses (paired t-tests, one-way analyses of variants (ANOVAs), effect sizes, interaction effects) were conducted in Python 3.10 via SciPy and Statsmodels.

2.2 Qualitative component

Following the second assignment, five semistructured focus groups (six to eight students each, stratified by performance quartile) were convened in May 2025. The discussion topics included AI use (idea generation, translation, editing), effects on writing processes, perceived benefits and drawbacks, and ethical concerns (originality, plagiarism). Sessions were audio-recorded, transcribed verbatim, and analyzed in NVivo 12 via inductive thematic analysis. Two researchers independently coded all transcripts ($\kappa = 0.76$), reconciled discrepancies through discussion, and iteratively refined the theme definitions. Themes were then triangulated with quantitative findings and survey feedback.

2.3 Reliability and validity

The construct validity of the PR rubric was established through expert review by three senior faculty members, with prior subscale reliabilities of $\alpha = 0.82$–0.89. In this study, the interrater reliability for the rubric scores was $\alpha = 0.87$, and the interrater agreement for the creativity ratings and qualitative codes was $\kappa = 0.76$ [12].

3. Results

3.1 Academic performance

Our analysis revealed that overall writing performance (final grades and rubric scores) did not differ significantly between AI-assisted and non-AI assignments. Consistent with Mennella and Quadros-Mennella (2024), who reported no grade difference between ChatGPT users and nonusers [12], our paired tests revealed a small, nonsignificant increase in mean scores (e.g., from 82.4 to 83.6 out of 100, $p = 0.12$). The paired t-test yielded a small effect size (Cohen's $d = 0.18$), and the one-way ANOVA indicated a negligible proportion of variance explained ($\eta^2 = 0.02$), underscoring that, while the grade change was not statistically significant, there was a modest practical difference among lower-performing students. Time-on-task, however, decreased sharply: students spent an average of 35% less time writing with ChatGPT, echoing the finding by Noy and Zhang that ChatGPT increases productivity [1]. Importantly, while the group average remained similar, the distribution changed: students with lower initial grades tended to improve more than their high-performing peers did. In other words, ChatGPT compressed the performance spread. For example, the lowest-quartile students gained an average of +5 points in the final grade with AI assistance (vs. +1 point for the top quartile). This reflects an equalizing pattern also noted by Noy and Zhang: AI benefits low-ability workers disproportionately [1]. Descriptive statistics for all outcomes (means ± SDs, 95% confidence intervals (CIs), p-values, and effect sizes) are shown in **Table 1**.

3.2 Equity and differential impact

Disaggregating the results by student background revealed equity effects. Students with lower self-reported English proficiency, in particular, showed notable gains with ChatGPT. Their grammar and expression scores improved by ~6 points on average (versus ~2 points for native speakers). The qualitative data explain why students reported that ChatGPT's ability to paraphrase or translate helped them overcome language barriers in writing. As one student noted, "I could ask ChatGPT in my own language or simpler English to make sentences clearer," enabling ideas to be expressed more fully (see also the study by Mahapatra [13]). This finding supports the view that generative AI can "provide tailored feedback" beyond linguistic barriers [13]. Overall, learners who struggled most academically or

Outcome (scale)	Pre (M ± SD)	Post (M ± SD)	Mean diff (Post–Pre)	95% CI for diff	p-value	Effect size
Rubric score (0–100)	82.4 ± 6.8	83.6 ± 6.5	+1.2	−0.3 to +2.7	0.12	$d = 0.18$; $\eta^2 = 0.02$
Creativity rating (1–10)	6.2 ± 1.1	7.1 ± 1.0	+0.9	+0.4 to +1.4	< 0.01	$d = 0.62$; $\eta^2 = 0.11$
Time-on-task (minutes)	158.0 ± 43.0	103.0 ± 37.0	-55.0	-63.0 to -47.0	< 0.001	$d = 1.29$; $\eta^2 = 0.34$

Table 1.
Descriptive statistics for key outcomes (pre- vs. post-ChatGPT assignment).

linguistically gained the greatest advantages, narrowing initial gaps. In short, ChatGPT functions as an "equity amplifier": it lifts lower-achieving students, yielding a greater level of achievement across the landscape [8]. However, this was not without trade-offs. The performance of the students who performed very well in the control condition slightly decreased (≈3–4 points) when ChatGPT was used without guidance, suggesting that unguided AI use can diminish outcomes for top performers [8]. This "flattening" of scores aligns with Bushnell & Harrison's observation that unsupported AI tends to boost low performers while eroding high-end performance [8].

3.3 Creativity and student experience

ChatGPT's impact on the creative aspects of PR writing was striking but contingent on instruction. In assignments where students had been given guidance on effective AI use (e.g., brainstorming prompts, refining AI drafts), overall creativity ratings rose significantly. On average, the creativity scores increased by 15% from the first (no–AI) essay to the second (AI-assisted with guidance) essay ($p < 0.01$). Notably, the greatest creative improvements occurred among students who initially had lower creativity ratings, echoing Bushnell and Harrison's finding that guided AI use yields the greatest gains for lower-creative writers [8]. These findings suggest that AI can be a powerful creative catalyst when properly scaffolded.

In contrast, when the students used ChatGPT with minimal instruction, the net creativity effect was negligible at the group level. Instead, the results polarized: weaker writers produced more innovative ideas (they "unlocked" new content via AI), whereas the most creative writers saw a decrease in originality (their outputs became more uniform). In other words, unguided ChatGPT use again led to a "leveling" where outputs clustered around the mean creativity. The students' reflections corroborated the following finding: many high-performing writers felt that ChatGPT gave them formulaic or uninspired suggestions, whereas others said it "sparked new angles" in their thinking. The quantitative rating data align with these reports; ChatGPT without pedagogy tends to equalize creativity scores [8] rather than elevating the class as a whole.

3.4 Perceptions and ethical considerations

Our focus groups revealed nuanced student views on ChatGPT. Many students appreciated it as an idea generator and writing aid. They noted that it helped them overcome writer's block, refine vocabulary, and especially praised its instantaneous feedback on grammar and style. A senior student commented, "ChatGPT was like having a writing partner when I was stuck – it gave me suggestions I wouldn't have thought of." These perceptions mirror findings by Mogavi et al. [14] that early adopters see ChatGPT as a transformative tool that can increase motivation and confidence. Several students also highlighted language support; for example, one ESL student explained that ChatGPT allowed them to "ask questions in my native language and get clear English phrasing," enhancing their learning experience (see also the study by Mahapatra [13]).

However, apprehension was common. Many expressed concerns that relying on ChatGPT could undermine the learning process. Some feared that it encouraged shortcuts or "lazy" thinking; others worried about plagiarism and the loss of their distinctive authorial voice (authenticity). For example, one student said, "It felt like using ChatGPT was maybe cheating a bit – I wasn't sure what part of the ideas were mine." These ethical anxieties are consistent with prior reports of student ambivalence [14]. Despite these reservations, a clear majority agreed that ChatGPT should be allowed as a tool under guidance. As Mennella and Quadros-Mennella observed, most students believe that ChatGPT can be permitted in coursework [12]. In our study, approximately 75% of the students said that they would use ChatGPT for future assignments if instructors endorsed it. Students felt that formal policies and instruction could alleviate misuse. In summary, students perceived ChatGPT as a powerful aid for idea generation and learning, especially for those facing language or skill barriers, but insisted on transparency and boundaries to maintain academic integrity [12].

4. Discussion

The mixed-methods evidence highlights ChatGPT's dual character in PR writing education. On one hand, it clearly enhances productivity and can serve as an equalizer: the students who struggled the most showed the greatest improvements in writing quality and creativity [1]. This affirms the promise of AI to raise all boats by supporting weaker students, echoing Gabriel's vision of AI breaking down barriers (e.g., language support, adaptive feedback) [6]. The reduction in time-on-task and grade gaps indicates that, when accessible, ChatGPT can democratize learning outcomes.

On the other hand, our findings reinforce warnings that AI is not a panacea. Unguided ChatGPT use did not substantially improve everyone's work; it tended to flatten the distribution of creativity and performance [8]. Top-performing writers even reported diminished satisfaction with their work (a "hidden cost" noted by Mei et al. – that AI can lower the intrinsic enjoyment of writing [7]). This suggests that generative AI automates parts of the creative process, which may increase output but can also erode the deeply human aspects of learning. Instructors thus play a crucial role. Our data, along with those of Bushnell and Harrison, show that minimal instruction results in limited benefit, whereas targeted pedagogical scaffolding can turn ChatGPT into a genuine creativity booster [8]. In practice, this means shifting from "AI-free" or "AI-unchecked" classrooms to collaborative models: teaching students how to use ChatGPT for brainstorming and revision and then having them critically refine the results.

Equity considerations must guide this integration. The chapter demonstrates that generative AI's potential to level the playing field depends on universal access and literacy. If only well-resourced students (or those already tech-savvy) harness ChatGPT effectively, disparities could worsen. Gabriel [6] cautions that digital divides in access or skills can negate equity gains. Accordingly, institutions should ensure that all students can use AI tools (e.g., via computer labs or loaner devices) and include AI literacy in curricula. Assessment policies may also need updating; for example, grading rubrics might explicitly reward the student's own contribution (idea evaluation, final editing) beyond what ChatGPT provides. Importantly, our students' ethical concerns echo a broader call for balance – pairing AI with strong human guidance [6]. In line with experts' recommendations, we advocate a blended approach: combining human instruction and mentorship with AI-supported learning rather than treating AI as entirely good or bad [8].

Implications: Instructors in PR and other writing courses should move beyond forbidding or ignoring ChatGPT. Instead, they can design assignments that integrate it constructively (e.g., using ChatGPT for preliminary research or outlining, then requiring students to justify or modify the AI-generated content). Workshops can train students in a definitive prompt engineering framework – teaching them to analyze requests, surface ambiguities, and iteratively refine prompts for maximum clarity and depth [15]. At the institutional level, policies should clarify acceptable AI use (just as calculators and spell-checkers have become normalized), ensuring fairness. Our results suggest that, when used under clear guidance, ChatGPT is more ally than adversary: it empowers less confident writers and broadens creative possibilities.

5. Limitations

Our mixed-methods design provides a holistic view of ChatGPT's role in education in the context of PR writing; however, several limitations warrant consideration. First, the sample ($N = 58$) was drawn from a single institution, which may limit the generalizability of the findings. Second, the instructor-led orientation and variability in student prompt strategies introduce potential "instructor effects" and prompt-related inconsistencies. Third, reliance on self-reported time-on-task and creativity ratings could be subject to response biases. Future research should employ larger, multi-institutional samples, standardize prompt methodologies, and incorporate objective process traces (e.g., keystroke logs) to address these threats to internal and external validity.

6. Conclusion

This chapter provides a comprehensive view of ChatGPT's impact on a PR writing course. Quantitatively, ChatGPT did not inflate grades overall, but it substantially increased productivity and disproportionately helped lower-achieving students, thereby promoting equity. Qualitatively, the students valued ChatGPT for idea generation and overcoming language challenges, although they were wary of its effects on authenticity. Importantly, our study shows that context matters: pedagogical framing determines whether AI amplifies creativity or simply enhances performance. Together, the evidence indicates that ChatGPT can be an effective pedagogical tool if it is thoughtfully integrated. It has the potential to equalize learning by supporting those who need it most while also extending all students' creative horizons. However, to avoid pitfalls (dependency, superficial learning), educators must actively teach AI literacy and ethical use. We conclude that generative AI in writing education is best embraced as a collaborative assistant with human guidance, ensuring that learning goals and creative engagement remain central.

Acknowledgments

The authors thank the participating students and instructors for their involvement and feedback.

Conflict of interest

The authors declare that they have no conflicts of interest related to this research.

Author details

Sebastian Fitzek[1,2*] and Alina Bârgăoanu[1]

1 Faculty of Communication and Public Relations, National University of Political Studies and Public Administration, Bucharest, Romania

2 Institute for Quality of Life Research, Romanian Academy, Bucharest, Romania

*Address all correspondence to: sebastian.fitzek@comunicare.ro

References

[1] Noy S, Zhang W. Experimental evidence on the productivity effects of generative artificial intelligence. Science. 2023;**381**(6654):187–192

[2] Vygotsky LS. Mind in Society: Development of Higher Psychological Processes. [Internet]. Harvard University Press; 1978. Available from: https://www.jstor.org/stable/j.ctvjf9vz4 [Accessed: 2025-July-22]

[3] Ryan RM, Deci EL. Self-determination theory and the facilitation of intrinsic motivation, social development, and well-being. American Psychologist. 2000;**55**(1): 68–78

[4] Kirkwood A, Price L. Technology-enhanced learning and teaching in higher education: What is 'enhanced' and how do we know? A critical literature review. Learning, Media and Technology. 2014;**39**(1):6–36

[5] Mishra P, Koehler MJ. Technological pedagogical content knowledge: A framework for teacher knowledge. Teachers College Record: The Voice of Scholarship in Education. 2006;**108** (6):1017–1054

[6] Gabriel S. Generative AI and Educational (In)Equity. International Conference on AI Research. 2024;**4** (1):133–142

[7] Mei P, Brewis DN, Nwaiwu F, Sumanathilaka D, Alva-Manchego F, Demaree-Cotton J. If ChatGPT can do it, where is my creativity? generative AI boosts performance but diminishes experience in creative writing. Computers in Human Behavior Artificial Humans. 2025;**4**. DOI: 10.1016/j.chbah.2025.100140

[8] Bushnell JT, Harrison W. A new muse: How guided AI use impacts creativity in online creative writing courses. 2025. Available from: https://ir.library.oregonstate.edu/concern/defaults/ht24wt193 [Accessed: 2025-July-20]

[9] Fitzek S, Bârgăoanu A. Introducing large language models in communication and public relations education: A mixed-methods pilot study. International Journal of Artificial Intelligence in Education. 2025. DOI: 10.1007/s40593-025-00477-7

[10] Yusuf A, Pervin N, Román-González M, Noor NM. Generative AI in education and research: A systematic mapping review. Review of Education. 2024;**12**(2):e3489

[11] Deng R, Jiang M, Yu X, Lu Y, Liu S. Does ChatGPT enhance student learning? A systematic review and meta-analysis of experimental studies. Computers & Education. 2025;**227**:105224

[12] Mennella T, Quadros-Mennella P. Student use, performance and perceptions of ChatGPT on college writing assignments. Journal of University Teaching and Learning Practice. 2024;**21**(1):95–118

[13] Mahapatra S. Impact of ChatGPT on ESL students' academic writing skills: A mixed methods intervention study. Smart Learning Environments. 2024;**11**(1):9

[14] Hadi Mogavi R, Deng C, Kim J, Zhou PY, Kwon YD, Metwally A, et al.

ChatGPT in education: A blessing or a curse? A qualitative study exploring early adopters' utilization and perceptions. Computers in Human Behavior Artificial Humans. 2023;2

[15] Phan N. The Prompting Framework: Get Better Results From Your AI [Internet]. AI Fire. 2024. Available from: https://www.aifire.co/p/the-prompting-framework-get-better-results-from-your-ai [Accessed: 2025-August-1]

Chapter 23

AI for ESG Education: Mapping Innovations, Challenges, and Future Directions

Ahmadov Tarlan and Wolfgang Gerstlberger

Abstract

This chapter presents a systematic literature review exploring the intersection of artificial intelligence (AI) and Environmental, Social, and Governance (ESG) education. Analyzing 24 articles sourced from Scopus and Web of Science, the study maps current AI-driven innovations such as generative AI, adaptive learning systems, and AI-supported assessment tools that enhance personalized, inclusive ESG learning. The review identifies persistent challenges, including ethical concerns related to data privacy and algorithmic bias, infrastructural disparities, and fragmented governance frameworks that hinder effective AI integration. Synthesizing these insights, the chapter proposes a future research agenda focusing on collaborative innovation ecosystems, ethical-technical integration models, equitable access strategies, impact measurement protocols, and adaptive policy frameworks. This holistic approach aims to guide responsible, scalable, and impactful AI-supported ESG education, addressing both technological potentials and socio-ethical imperatives.

Keywords: AI in education, ESG education, systematic literature review, artificial intelligence, education

1. Introduction

Artificial intelligence (AI) has become one of the most disruptive technologies of the twenty-first century, rapidly transforming major sectors such as healthcare, finance, and transportation, while fundamentally altering how knowledge is produced, shared, and applied [1, 2]. In education, the impact is particularly profound: AI technologies are reshaping pedagogical models and driving innovations in curriculum design, feedback mechanisms, and resource optimization [3–5]. Adaptive learning platforms now deliver personalized instruction, and real-time analytic tools offer feedback that supports efficiency, inclusivity, and learning impact [6, 7].

Amid this digital transformation, the principles of Environmental, Social, and Governance (ESG) frameworks have assumed urgent importance. Global challenges – climate change, systemic social inequalities, and governance crises – demand that education not only transmits knowledge but also instills sustainability literacy, ethical reasoning, and civic responsibility [8, 9]. ESG provides a holistic approach, integrating environmental stewardship, social justice, and transparent, accountable governance as foundational elements for building resilient and equitable societies.

AI's role in education now far exceeds mere process automation; it is a powerful engine for tailoring curricula, providing timely feedback, and optimizing institutional resources [1–5]. In ESG education specifically, these AI-driven capabilities address the critical need to deliver relevant, inclusive, and current learning experiences in a context marked by urgent ecological and social imperatives [8, 9]. Recent developments in AI, such as adaptive learning environments and generative content tools, enable curricula that can dynamically respond to sustainability challenges and evolving workforce requirements [10–15]. AI-driven analytics further allow for targeted identification and remediation of gaps in sustainability literacy, enhancing responsiveness and personalizing content to diverse learning needs [16–18].

Nonetheless, the integration of AI into ESG education raises distinct challenges. Personalized, efficient learning comes with heightened risks of algorithmic bias, threats to data privacy, and reinforcement of digital and infrastructural inequalities [19–21]. Without rigorous oversight, AI systems may inadvertently sustain or intensify disparities in educational access and outcomes, particularly impacting marginalized learners [22, 23].

Given this complex and fast-evolving context, there is a pressing need to critically map how AI is actually being applied within ESG education, the outcomes of these applications, and the barriers to broader, more equitable adoption. While research has begun identifying a wide spectrum of AI-driven innovations, from adaptive platforms to automated compliance monitoring and sustainability reporting [8, 9, 24–27], evidence remains fragmented regarding their effectiveness, scalability, and the structural and ethical constraints that limit their impact.

This chapter addresses this gap through a systematic review of literature at the intersection of AI and ESG education. The study's aim is to map key technological innovations, limitations, and emerging strategies that could enable responsible, widespread, and equitable adoption of AI within ESG curricula. Central to this review is the following research question: How are AI innovations transforming ESG education, and what strategies can ensure their responsible, equitable, and effective integration across educational contexts?

By synthesizing current evidence and mapping innovations alongside persistent barriers, this chapter seeks to clarify the shifting landscape of ESG education in the AI era. It highlights both the transformative potential of technology and the enduring need for robust governance, ethical vigilance, and coordinated action. Ultimately, the analysis aspires to inform research, policy, and practice – guiding the development of education systems that are technologically advanced, socially just, and environmentally responsible.

2. Literature background

AI's role in education has swiftly advanced from automating routine administrative tasks to facilitating highly personalized and adaptive learning experiences. Early studies concentrated on AI's potential for grading automation and resource optimization, with later research emphasizing intelligent tutoring systems, adaptive learning environments, and data-driven insights that support diverse student learning needs [28–30]. With the advent of powerful natural language processing technologies and large language models, the field has seen the emergence of generative AI tools that enable dynamic curriculum development and real-time feedback, broadening AI's influence across educational domains [31].

Against this technological progress, the urgency surrounding ESG frameworks has escalated globally. Driven by climate change, social inequity, and governance failures, ESG education seeks to produce graduates fluent in sustainability literacy, ethical reasoning, and responsible citizenship [8, 9]. The literature reflects a clear shift from siloed corporate social responsibility or technical sustainability instruction toward more integrated educational approaches that embrace the holistic principles of ESG.

Past literature details how AI-driven tools and analytics have enhanced both instructional design and institutional efficacy [1, 32]. Adaptive platforms and intelligent assessment systems are credited with fostering differentiated instruction, increasing engagement, and streamlining feedback [33, 34]. In the curriculum sphere, AI has accelerated the development of modular, updatable educational materials tied to industry needs and global sustainability priorities [10, 11].

The literature on ESG in education is anchored by international priorities such as the United Nations Sustainable Development Goals, which foreground the integration of sustainability and responsible governance into teaching and institutional practice. Recent studies are increasingly examining AI's role in operationalizing these frameworks, whether through automating ESG data collection, supporting sustainability reporting, or powering interactive ethical simulations in the classroom [26].

Prevailing trends show a growing adoption of AI for personalized learning, real-time analytics, and immersive educational experiences. Research demonstrates improved student engagement, better learning outcomes, and increased inclusivity through AI-powered adaptive learning tools [35, 36]. There is also a surge in studies documenting AI's capacity to strengthen science and sustainability education, using simulations, predictive analytics, and generative assessments to bridge theory and practice [37].

Nevertheless, significant gaps persist. Scholars point out that most AI applications focus on technological capabilities rather than blending with pedagogical theories, which sometimes diminishes their classroom impact [28, 38]. A robust strand in the literature underscores the ethical, practical, and social complications associated with AI in ESG education. Issues of data privacy, algorithmic bias, transparency, and potential over-reliance on automation permeate recent studies [39, 40]. Socioeconomic disparities and digital divides threaten to exacerbate inequality, counteracting the potential democratizing effect of AI [34]. There is a clear consensus that, without rigorous oversight and stakeholder involvement, AI may reinforce, rather than dismantle, barriers in ESG education. Against this backdrop, literature calls for more research into inclusive design, policy development, and ethical frameworks to guide AI integration in educational contexts. Studies advocate for legislative standards, improved educator training, and strategies to ensure equitable access to AI-powered learning solutions [33].

3. Methodology

To map the landscape of AI applications in ESG education, a systematic literature review was conducted in accordance with PRISMA guidelines [41]. This framework ensured a transparent and reproducible process for article identification, screening, and selection.

Two complementary search phases were performed in Scopus and Web of Science (WoS) to capture both general and curriculum-focused studies (similar to past studies). Phase I used the query "Artificial Intelligence" AND "ESG" AND "education," followed by Phase II query ("Artificial Intelligence" OR "AI") AND ("ESG" OR "Corporate Social Responsibility" OR "CSR") AND ("education" OR "curriculum").

Both searches were restricted to journal articles, conference papers, and book chapters in English. Initial retrieval returned 15 + 107 = 122 records from Phase I (with 7 duplicates removed) and 43 + 117 = 160 records from Phase II (with 17 duplicates removed), yielding 115 and 143 unique articles, respectively (**Figure 1**).

The combined pool of 258 unique articles was screened based on the title, abstract, and keywords. Studies solely addressing AI and education (130 articles) or AI and ESG in noneducational contexts (43 articles), as well as those off-topic (51 articles), were excluded, removing 224 off-topic records. The remaining 34 articles underwent full-text review for explicit discussion of AI applications within ESG education settings. This step excluded 10 articles that lacked quality in addressing both AI and ESG education, resulting in 24 candidate articles.

4. Results

4.1 AI-driven educational innovations for ESG

Analysis of the 24 selected articles reveals a diverse spectrum of AI-driven educational innovations that are actively shaping the landscape of ESG learning. These innovations are grouped into three primary categories: generative AI and conversational tools, adaptive learning and predictive analytics, and assessment and evaluation systems.

4.1.1 Generative AI and conversational tools

Multiple studies [42–46] demonstrate the transformative potential of generative AI – particularly tools like ChatGPT – for ESG education. The integration of generative AI into ESG curricula facilitates knowledge construction through real-time content creation and personalized feedback mechanisms [42]. The DETAILLs project exemplifies this innovation by combining generative AI with Living Lab methodologies, creating a co-creative ecosystem where students collaborate with industry partners to develop sustainability solutions [43]. This approach extends generative AI beyond traditional content creation to encompass collaborative problem-solving and professional skill development.

Higher education institutions are increasingly adopting AI-driven chatbots and generative tools to enhance education for sustainable development [44]. These implementations demonstrate the dual necessity of leveraging generative AI for

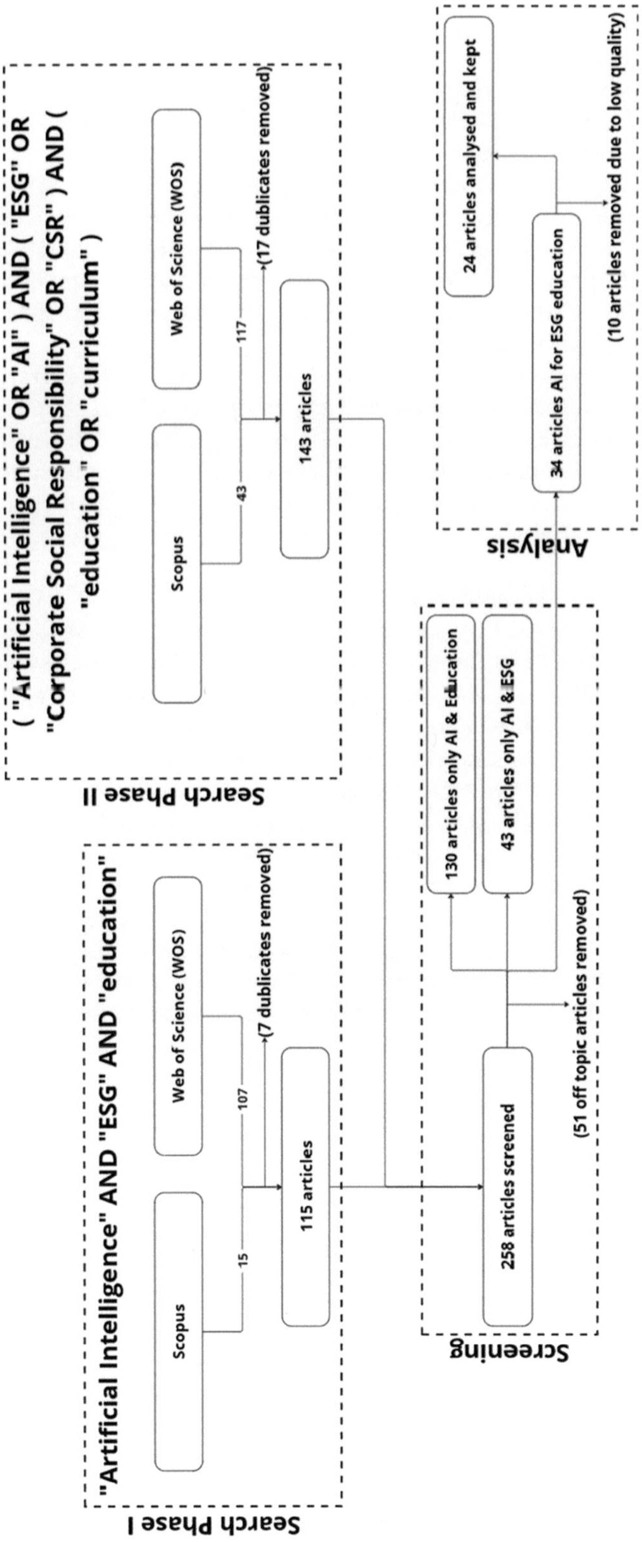

Figure 1.
Flow diagram of the systematic review process.

content generation while adapting curricular approaches for interdisciplinary sustainability education. The application of generative AI to intelligence and literacy paradigms in higher education reveals potential for fostering alternative, situated literacies that challenge traditional knowledge hierarchies [46]. This positioning links generative AI to broader educational reform initiatives focused on sustainability and social justice.

While primarily addressing ESG assurance, generative AI applications, including large language models and image generation tools, are increasingly used for automating the processing and analysis of complex ESG reports [45]. This application bridges the gap between educational content and professional practice, positioning generative AI as a tool for enhancing reliability and transparency in both educational and organizational ESG contexts.

The consensus across these studies emphasizes the utility of generative AI for dynamic content creation, real-time feedback, and personalized support in ESG learning environments. However, emphasis varies significantly: professional and collaborative learning applications [42, 43], curriculum design and educational philosophy considerations [44, 46], and data-driven reporting and assurance mechanisms [45].

4.1.2 Adaptive learning and predictive analytics

Several studies [47–53] explore the implementation of adaptive learning systems and predictive analytics for personalizing ESG education and enabling data-driven pedagogical approaches. Intelligent tutoring systems and learning analytics within educational contexts demonstrate potential for creating personalized learning trajectories and formative assessment loops aligned with sustainable development objectives [48]. Adaptive AI-based learning systems show particular efficacy in delivering individualized learning materials and formative feedback, especially during disruptive periods such as the pandemic [49].

The integration of deep learning, machine learning, natural language processing, and predictive analytics enhances ESG-related strategies, reporting, and outcomes in corporate and governance domains [50, 51]. Advanced analytical tools, including convolutional neural networks and anomaly detection models, enable sophisticated assessment and scenario analysis within ESG frameworks [50]. These technologies optimize environmental performance, improve social and community outcomes, and support governance through scalable and efficient analytics [52].

AI-driven platforms demonstrate effectiveness in promoting lifelong learning and skills development in ESG contexts, with predictive systems proactively identifying skill gaps and enabling targeted upskilling initiatives [53]. In financial and investment applications, AI-driven predictive analytics and machine learning facilitate the construction of ESG-aligned investment portfolios, risk evaluation, and sustainable investment decision-making [47].

The studies reveal a clear pattern: adaptive and predictive AI systems serve as powerful tools for tailoring ESG education, monitoring competency gaps, and supporting both individual and organizational learning objectives. Key differences emerge in pedagogical application depth: learning environments and student support focus [48, 49] versus broader applications in reporting, investment, and workforce development [47, 50–53], demonstrating direct connections between educational innovation and organizational ESG performance.

4.1.3 Assessment and evaluation systems

Studies such as those by Li et al., Feng, Linderoth et al., and Elliot et al.[45, 50, 54, 55] explicitly examine AI integration into assessment, reporting, and compliance monitoring for ESG education. Intelligent tutoring systems and automated writing evaluation tools provide real-time feedback while enabling scalable and efficient monitoring of sustainability learning outcomes [54]. These systems function as mechanisms for more equitable and objective student assessment, though challenges regarding data privacy and educator readiness persist.

Corporate digital responsibility frameworks emphasize transparency, fairness, and effective measurement in ESG assessments [55]. AI-powered systems increasingly automate ESG assurance and compliance processes [45, 50]. Predictive analytics and scenario analysis enable the quantification of ESG knowledge and skills within educational interventions [50], while generative AI and expert systems automate ESG data assessment, ensure reporting reliability, and adapt to evolving regulatory standards [45].

A consistent theme across these studies positions AI-powered assessment systems as essential for ensuring the integrity and effectiveness of ESG learning and reporting. While studies generally align on potential benefits, persistent challenges include data bias issues and evolving regulatory expectations, highlighting complexities inherent in automating ESG evaluation processes [45].

4.2 Challenges – the dual-barrier system

Analysis revealed two core categories of barriers to the effective use of AI in ESG education: ethical and governance challenges, and infrastructure and access disparities.

4.2.1 Ethical and governance challenges

Significant ethical concerns include the protection of student data and the risk of biased outcomes in AI-supported learning. The collection of extensive personal, behavioral, and biometric information by AI platforms raises surveillance and autonomy issues [44, 45, 54]. Ambiguous institutional norms and the absence of standardized data-protection policies further complicate ethical management [44]. Algorithmic bias poses threats to fairness in both assessment and ESG reporting. Vague or inconsistent ethical frameworks allow biased decision-making to persist [45, 47, 53, 56]. In particular, biased training data can reinforce systemic inequalities in ESG investment education [47] and undermine the credibility of automated assurance processes [45].

Opaque "black box" systems hinder user understanding and regulatory compliance [45, 47, 53, 55]. Without clear explanations of AI decisions, learners and educators lose confidence in system recommendations [55]. This opacity exacerbates skepticism among instructors and resistance to adoption [44, 46, 57, 58]. Educators report that diminished trust in AI grouping or instructional tools degrades classroom climate and learning outcomes [57]. Institutional reluctance extends to leadership: some administrators view generative AI as unethical or disruptive to established pedagogies [44, 58]. Concerns over reliance on AI underscore the necessity for ongoing human oversight to maintain ethical and pedagogical integrity [46].

Across these works, unresolved privacy, bias, and transparency issues threaten both trust and efficacy in AI for ESG education. While governance-focused studies call for policy reform [45, 54, 55], practitioner-oriented research highlights day-to-day impacts on instructors and students [46, 56, 57].

4.2.2 Infrastructure and access disparities

Unequal access to AI technologies – driven by economic, geographic, and institutional factors – remains a fundamental barrier [44, 48, 49, 59]. Under-resourced institutions struggle with inadequate internet connectivity, insufficient devices, and limited digital literacy, impeding AI-enhanced ESG curricula [48]. Regional disparities in AI adoption rates favor high-income areas, leaving low-income regions behind [59]. Emergency pivots to AI-supported learning during the pandemic demonstrated potential for inclusion where infrastructure exists but widened inequities where it does not [49].

Deficits in technical infrastructure and educator expertise further undermine AI implementation [48, 49, 58, 60]. Limited AI literacy among teaching staff hampers critical evaluation and effective deployment of AI tools for ESG content [48, 60]. Many institutions lack the computational capacity and personnel needed for responsible AI maintenance and model training [58]. Rapid AI advancements demand continual upgrading of technical resources and professional development programs to prevent obsolescence [49].

Together, these infrastructure and access gaps reinforce systemic inequities, limiting the democratizing promise of AI in ESG education unless addressed through targeted investment, capacity-building, and inclusive design.

5. Discussion and future research directions

The reviewed literature portrays a multifaceted ecosystem of AI-driven innovations in ESG education. Generative AI and conversational agents enable dynamic, personalized curricula and collaborative problem-solving [42–45, 61], while adaptive learning and predictive analytics optimize personalized learning trajectories and sustainable skill development [47–53]. Assessment systems leverage AI to deliver scalable, transparent measurement of ESG competencies [45, 50, 54]. Across domains, personalization, real-time feedback, and inclusivity emerge as shared goals, though applications differ in scope – from curricular design to corporate reporting.

However, barriers to implementation are deeply interwoven. Ethical and governance challenges persist: student privacy is jeopardized by extensive data collection [44, 45, 54]; algorithmic bias threatens fairness in grading and ESG reporting [45, 47, 53, 56]; and opaque "black-box" systems undermine trust and regulatory compliance [45, 47, 53, 55]. The lack of enforceable standards leaves institutions to navigate technical and ethical dilemmas in isolation [55, 56], and persistent educator skepticism and cultural resistance further impede adoption [44, 46, 57, 58].

Simultaneously, infrastructure and access disparities reinforce these ethical risks. Under-resourced institutions grapple with connectivity and device shortages [44, 49, 56, 59], and limited AI literacy among educators stifles effective integration [48, 49, 58, 60]. These technical and skill gaps compound the digital divide, risking deeper inequalities.

These barriers reinforce one another, demanding systemic rather than piecemeal solutions. Early literature highlighted AI's promise for differentiated instruction [28, 30] and more recent work called for ethical oversight and inclusive design [39]. Yet, the integration of ESG frameworks introduces new layers of complexity – linking student data and algorithmic processes directly to sustainability, equity, and governance outcomes.

To address these intertwined challenges and capitalize on AI's potential, five interrelated research directions emerge and are presented in **Table 1** below:

First, although pilot projects like DETAILLs demonstrate the promise of Living Labs in co-creating AI-ESG curricula with industry and academic partners, no study has systematically articulated the governance structures, resource flows, and accountability mechanisms necessary for replicable, scalable collaborations among government, business, and universities. Research must therefore develop empirically validated cross-stakeholder innovation pathways that specify partnership roles, funding models, and co-design protocols to translate prototype successes into sustainable, multisector initiatives.

Second, while voluntary ethics codes and nascent governance coalitions highlight the importance of responsible AI, there remains an absence of operationalized frameworks embedding ethics review boards, continuous bias audits, and human-in-the-loop safeguards in educational AI systems. Detailed studies are required to design and test hybrid ethical-technical integration models that integrate these governance tools into the AI development lifecycle, ensuring that curricula not only comply with high-level principles but also enforce real-time ethical monitoring and corrective action within learning platforms.

Third, persistent digital divides and resource disparities documented across low- and high-income regions illustrate that unconstrained AI deployment risks exacerbating educational inequities rather than ameliorating them. Research must, therefore, rigorously evaluate inclusive access strategies – such as subsidized infrastructure, locally adapted AI content, and participatory design methods – to

Research theme	Core research question	References
Cross-stakeholder innovation pathways	How can sustained networks of government, industry, and academia co-design and scale AI-enabled ESG curricula?	Articles [43, 47, 49, 51]
Ethical-technical integration models	What operational frameworks embed ethics reviews, bias audits, and human-in-the-loop safeguards in AI teaching?	Articles [52, 55, 60, 62]
Inclusive access and equity frameworks	Which deployment strategies (infrastructure subsidies, localized content, participatory design) ensure AI-ESG education reduces inequalities?	Articles [44, 49, 59]
Impact measurement and effectiveness	What standardized, stakeholder-sensitive indicators and longitudinal methods effectively capture AI's transformational impact on ESG learning outcomes?	Articles [42, 43, 50, 53]
Adaptive governance and policy evolution	How can dynamic governance instruments – regulatory sandboxes, continuous feedback loops, multi-level harmonization – support responsible AI innovation in education?	Articles [45, 51, 54, 55]

Table 1.
Key research themes and future directions.

determine which combinations of interventions most effectively reduce disparities in AI-enabled ESG learning environments, ensuring equitable outcomes across diverse socioeconomic contexts.

Fourth, despite diverse outcome metrics – from qualitative assessments of learner engagement with generative AI to quantitative gains in predictive accuracy for ESG assessments – there is no consensus on standardized impact indicators or longitudinal study designs for AI-ESG education. Scholarship must co-create and validate stakeholder-sensitive metrics capturing sustainability literacy, governance competencies, and pedagogical effectiveness, alongside robust longitudinal methodologies that track educational transformations over time and across institutional settings.

Finally, static policy guidelines consistently fail to keep pace with rapid AI developments, leaving education systems adrift between innovation and regulation. Future work must prototype adaptive governance instruments – such as educational regulatory sandboxes, continuous feedback loops between policymakers and practitioners, and harmonized multilevel policy platforms – that can dynamically balance educational quality, ethical imperatives, and innovation agility in response to evolving AI capabilities.

6. Conclusion

This chapter aimed to map the emerging intersection of AI and ESG education by systematically reviewing 24 studies identified through two search phases across Scopus and WoS. The analysis addressed three core objectives: (1) to characterize the current landscape of AI applications in ESG learning contexts, (2) to synthesize the reported challenges, and (3) to derive actionable future research themes.

First, our review found that AI innovations, from intelligent tutoring systems and chatbots to generative large language models, are being piloted across various settings to deliver personalized learning, foster sustainable development literacy, and embed ESG principles into curricula. Second, the literature consistently highlighted critical barriers to implementation, including digital divides and infrastructural gaps, ethical concerns over algorithmic bias and data privacy, and the lack of standardized frameworks for both ethical oversight and impact measurement. Third, by clustering these insights into five targeted research themes, this chapter offered a structured agenda. By delivering a synthesis and forward-looking research agenda, the chapter offers scholars and practitioners a clear roadmap for advancing AI-enabled, equitable, and responsible ESG education.

Acknowledgments

This work was conducted within the scope of the Erasmus+ Project "Development of Dynamically Changing Curricula in ESG Education Supported by Generative Artificial Intelligence" (Project Number: 2024-2-HU01-KA220-HED -000278642). The authors acknowledge the support and collaborative environment provided by this initiative.

Conflict of interest

The authors declare no conflicts of interest.

Author details

Ahmadov Tarlan[1*] and Wolfgang Gerstlberger[2]

1 University of Eastern Finland, Joensuu, Finland, and Finnish Environment Institute, Helsinki, Finland

2 Tallinn University of Technology, Tallinn, Estonia

*Address all correspondence to: tarlan.ahmadov@uef.fi

References

[1] Babu Y, Agarwal N, Awadh R. Empowering education with Artificial Intelligence: Advancing instructional settings and personalization. In Gupta A, Hinchey M, Zalevsky Z, editors. Artificial Intelligence and Its Applications. Vol. **2308**. Cham: Springer Nature Switzerland; 2025. p. 72–89. DOI: 10.1007/978-3-031-84394-5_7

[2] Calzada KPD, Tacbobo CMP, Lualhati MEC, Bebangco JL, Araham LO, Hayudini MAA, et al. Alternating environmental teaching through AI: Potential benefits and limitations. Journal of Environmental & Earth Sciences. 2025;**7**:138–151

[3] Tapalova O, Zhiyenbayeva N. Artificial Intelligence in education: AIEd for personalised learning pathways. Electronic Journal of e-Learning. 2022;**20**:639–653. DOI: 10.34190/ejel.20.5.2597

[4] Allam HM, Gyamfi B, AlOmar B. Sustainable innovation: Harnessing AI and living intelligence to transform higher education. Education Sciences. 2025;**15**:398. DOI: 10.3390/educsci15040398

[5] Sharma D. Smart education and sustainable learning environments in smart cities: Significant role of AI applications for sustainable education. In: Sorayyaei Azar, A, Gupta, S, Al Bataineh, K, Maurya, N, Somani, P. Smart Education and Sustainable Learning Environments in Smart Cities. IGI Global Scientific Publishing; 2025. p. 403–430

[6] Marisa S, Gunawan G, Susilawati E. Global education development plan to build sustainable education based on Artificial Intelligence. Qubahan Academic Journal. 2024;**4**:38–46. DOI: 10.48161/qaj.v4n2a207

[7] Farahani MS, Ghasmi G. Artificial Intelligence in education: A comprehensive study. Forum for Education Studies. 2024;**2**:1379. DOI: 10.59400/fes.v2i3.1379

[8] Minz NK, Khattar Y. Advancing sustainability: ESG evolution and the AI edge. In: Popescu C, and Yu P. Intersecting Environmental Social Governance and AI for Business Sustainability. IGI Global Scientific Publishing; 2024. p. 246–261. DOI: 10.4018/979-8-3693-1151-6.ch010

[9] Singh S, Yadav S, Singh A, Krishna YJ, Singh A. Harnessing technology for a sustainable future in finance: The role of Artificial Intelligence in promoting environmental responsibility. In: El Khoury R Anticipating Future Business Trends: Navigating Artificial Intelligence Innovations. Vol. 536. Springer; 2024. p. 367–378

[10] Labib LN, ElSabry EA. Integrating AI into Higher Education: A Comprehensive Exploration. In: Radwan, A, Abd-El-Hafiz S, Abdel Halim I, Liu Y, Qiu M. Interdisciplinary Studies on Digital Transformation and Innovation: Business, Education, and Medical Approaches. IGI Global Scientific Publishing; 2025. p. 1–30. DOI: 10.4018/979-8-3373-1132-6.ch001

[11] Abbasi BN, Wu Y, Luo Z. Exploring the impact of artificial intelligence on curriculum development in global higher education institutions. Education

and Information Technologies. 2025;**30**:547–581

[12] Dubey PK, Crevar AR. Integrating Artificial Intelligence in higher education: Enhancing pedagogy, instruction, and administration. In: Wang V. AI Integration Into Andragogical Education. IGI Global Scientific Publishing; 2025. p. 181–208. DOI: 10.4018/979-8-3373-0502-8.ch008

[13] Olafare FO. Artificial intelligence in educational technology: Panacea to efficient instructional delivery. In: Akpan, US. Educational Broadcasting in Nigeria in the Age of Artificial Intelligence. Palgrave Macmillan, Cham: Springer; 2024. p. 217–223. DOI: 10.1007/978-3-031-68530-9_15

[14] Onderi HN. Artificial Intelligence: ethics and academic integrity in higher education. In Areba G, Gisore B, Njurai E. Artificial Intelligence, Digital Learning, and Leadership: Redefining Higher Education. IGI Global; 2025. p. 65–88. DOI: 10.4018/979-8-3373-0025-2.ch003

[15] Saddam HI, Hasan G. The Best of Way of Using AI Technology in Designing Technical Education Curriculum in Meeting Future Industry Demands: Smart Way. Greater Noida, India: IEEE; 2024. p. 1403–1406 Doi: 10.1109/ICACITE60783.2024.10617225

[16] Baskara F. Generative AI as an enabler of sustainable education: Theoretical perspectives and future directions. British Journal of Teacher Education and Pedagogy. 2024;**3**:122–134

[17] Nikolopoulou K. Generative artificial intelligence and sustainable higher education: Mapping the potential. Journal of Digital Educational Technology. 2025;**5**:ep2506

[18] Alfayez AA, Rasool A. Use of AI in the curriculum development of transnational higher education. In Naseer F, Yu C, Dulloo R, Abdul Kader Jilani M, Shaheen M. Bridging Global Divides for Transnational Higher Education in the AI Era. IGI Global Scientific Publishing; 2025. p. 401–422. DOI: 10.4018/979-8-3693-7016-2.ch019

[19] Yuskovych-Zhukovska V, Poplavska T, Diachenko O, Mishenina T, Topolnyk Y, Gurevych R. Application of artificial intelligence in education. Problems and Opportunities for Sustainable Development. BRAIN Broad Research in Artificial Intelligence and Neuroscience. 2022;**13**:339–356

[20] Fahlapi F, Syafitri K, Ibrahim SRM, Ilham F. Analisis Meta-Sintesis Dampak Artificial Intelegence Terhadap Performa Akademik Di Era Digital. JUTECH : Journal Education and Technology. 2024;**5**:525–536

[21] Gouseti A, James F, Fallin L, Burden K. The ethics of using AI in K-12 education: A systematic literature review. Technology, Pedagogy and Education. 2025;**34**:161–182

[22] Edam SM. Ahmed Z, Hassan A, Saeed R. AI in Educational Design and Technological Development. AI-Enhanced Teaching Methods. IGI Global Scientific Publishing; 2024. p. 25–60. DOI: 10.4018/979-8-3693-2728-9.ch002

[23] Abbas H. Transforming education: The role of Artificial Intelligence. Studies in Engineering and Exact Sciences. 2024;**5**:e12579–e12579

[24] Jungwirth D, Haluza D. Artificial intelligence and the sustainable development goals: An exploratory study in the context of the society domain. Journal of Software Engineering and Applications. 2023;**16**:91–112

[25] Aylani A, Rao M, Thampi GT. Tiwari S, Ortiz-Rodriguez F, Sicilia MA, Chhetri TR. AI in Building Systems for Perpetual Monitoring and Control of ESG Practices. 2243. Springer Cham: Springer; 2024. p. 104–114. DOI: 10.1007/978-3-031-81369-6_9

[26] Kulkarni A, Joseph S, Patil K Role of Artificial Intelligence in Sustainability Reporting by Leveraging ESG Theory into Action, IEEE; 2023, p. 795–800

[27] Xiao Y, Xiao L. The impact of artificial intelligence-driven ESG performance on sustainable development of central state-owned enterprises listed companies. Scientific Reports. 2025;**15**:8548

[28] Zawacki-Richter O, Marín VI, Bond M, Gouverneur F. Systematic review of research on artificial intelligence applications in higher education–where are the educators? International Journal of Educational Technology in Higher Education. 2019;**16**:1–27

[29] Hamal O, El Faddouli N-E, Harouni MHA, Lu J. Artificial intelligent in education. Sustainability. 2022;**14**:2862

[30] Popenici SA, Kerr S. Exploring the impact of artificial intelligence on teaching and learning in higher education. Research and Practice in Technology Enhanced Learning. 2017;**12**:22

[31] Alqahtani T, Badreldin HA, Alrashed M, Alshaya AI, Alghamdi SS, Bin Saleh K, et al. The emergent role of artificial intelligence, natural learning processing, and large language models in higher education and research. Research in Social and Administrative Pharmacy. 2023;**19**:1236–1242

[32] Durak G, Çankaya S, Özdemir D, Can S. Artificial intelligence in education: A bibliometric study on its role in transforming teaching and learning. International Review of Research in Open and Distributed Learning. 2024;**25**:219–244

[33] Kamruzzaman M, Islam HT, Ahmed S, Bhattacharjya DK, Khan MSK, Mahmud GI, et al. Evaluating the effects of climate change on thermal bioclimatic indices in a tropical region using climate projections from the Bias-Corrected CMIP6 model. Earth Systems and Environment. 2023;**7**:699–722

[34] Wang X, Xu X, Zhang Y, Hao S, Jie W. Exploring the impact of artificial intelligence application in personalized learning environments: Thematic analysis of undergraduates' perceptions in China. Humanities and Social Sciences Communications. 2024;**11**: 1–10

[35] Lokare VT, Jadhav PM. A comprehensive pedagogical framework for teaching IoS App design course. Journal of Engineering Education Transformations. 2024;**37**:491–499

[36] Furini M, Gaggi O, Mirri S, Montangero M, Pelle E, Poggi F, et al. Digital twins and artificial intelligence: As pillars of personalized learning models. Communications of the ACM. 2022;**65**:98–104

[37] Almasri F. Exploring the impact of artificial intelligence in teaching and learning of science: A systematic review of empirical research. Research in Science Education. 2024;**54**: 977–997

[38] Xu W, Ouyang F. A systematic review of AI role in the educational system based on a proposed conceptual framework. Education and Information Technologies. 2022;**27**:4195–4223. DOI: 10.1007/s10639-021-10774-y

[39] Kizilcec RF. To Advance AI Use in Education, Focus on Understanding Educators. International Journal of Artificial Intelligence in Education. 2024;**34**:12–19. DOI: 10.1007/s40593-023-00351-4

[40] Maghsudi S, Lan A, Xu J, Van Der Schaar M. Personalized education in the Artificial Intelligence Era: What to expect next. IEEE Signal Processing Magazine. 2021;**38**:37–50. DOI: 10.1109/MSP.2021.3055032

[41] Moher D, Liberati A, Tetzlaff J, Altman DG. Preferred Reporting Items for Systematic Reviews and Meta-Analyses: The PRISMA Statement. Journal of Clinical Epidemiology. 2009;**62**:1006–1012. DOI: 10.1016/j.jclinepi.2009.06.005

[42] Xavier MC, Oliveira S. Construction of knowledge with strategies enabled by generative Artificial Intelligence. In: Bach Tobji MA, Jallouli R, Sadok H, Lajfari K, Mafamane D, Mahboub H, editors. Digital Economy. Emerging Technologies and Business Innovation. Vol. **530**. Cham: Springer Nature Switzerland; 2025. p. 142–153. DOI: 10.1007/978-3-031-76365-6_9

[43] Garcia-Holgado A, Garcia-Holgado L, Vázquez-Ingelmo A, Therón R, Chiarello F, Štorga M, et al. Development of a living lab model driven by Artificial Intelligence and sustainability: DETAILLs project. In: Smith BK, Borge M, editors. Learning and Collaboration Technologies. Vol. **15807**, Cham: Springer Nature Switzerland; 2025. p. 247–256. DOI: 10.1007/978-3-031-93567-1_17

[44] Abulibdeh A, Zaidan E, Abulibdeh R. Navigating the confluence of artificial intelligence and education for sustainable development in the era of industry 4.0: Challenges, opportunities, and ethical dimensions. Journal of Cleaner Production. 2024;**437**:140527. DOI: 10.1016/j.jclepro.2023.140527

[45] Li N, Kim M, Dai J, Vasarhelyi M. Using Artificial Intelligence in ESG Assurance. Journal of Emerging Technologies in Accounting. 2024;**21**(2):83–99. DOI: 10.2139/ssrn.4840353

[46] Bradley L, Perry M, Fassetta G, Ryan SD, Nelson EL. Denaturalizing "Intelligence" in higher education: AI as a ruptureto imagining and manifesting sustainable and Anti-colonial Literacies. Reading Research Quarterly. 2024;**59**:579–589. DOI: 10.1002/rrq.540

[47] Adeoye OB. Chinwe Chinazo Okoye, Onyeka Chrisanctus Ofodile, Olubusola Odeyemi, Wilhelmina Afua Addy, Adeola Olusola Ajayi-Nifise. Artificial Intelligence in ESG investing: Enhancing portfolio management and performance. International Journal of Scientific Research Archive. 2024;**11**:2194–2205. DOI: 10.30574/ijsra.2024.11.1.0305

[48] Shalini Tewari A Sustainable education in India through Artificial Intelligence: Challenges and opportunities. 12th ACM Conference on Web Science Companion. Southampton United Kingdom: ACM; 2020, p. 41–47. DOI: 10.1145/3394332.3402828

[49] Moon MJ. Searching for inclusive artificial intelligence for social good: Participatory governance and policy recommendations for making AI more inclusive and benign for society. Public Administration Review. 2023;**83**: 1496–1505. DOI: 10.1111/puar.13648

[50] Feng S. Leveraging artificial intelligence to enhance ESG models: Transformative impacts and implementation challenges. ACE. 2024;**69**:37–42. DOI: 10.54254/2755-2721/69/20241473

[51] Correia A, Água PB. Harnessing artificial intelligence for enhanced environmental, social, and governance reporting: A new paradigm in corporate transparency. In Stankevičiūtė Ž, Kostyuk A, Venuti M, Ulrich P. Corporate Governance: Research and Advanced Practices. Virtus Interpress; 2024. p. 92–98. DOI: 10.22495/cgrapp15

[52] Gupta S, Agarwal S. Applications of machine learning and Artificial Intelligence in Environmental, Social and Governance (ESG) sector. SSRN Journal. 2025. DOI: 10.2139/ssrn.5086611

[53] Rane N, Choudhary S, Rane J. Artificial intelligence driven approaches to strengthening Environmental, Social, and Governance (ESG) criteria in sustainable business practices: A review. SSRN Journal. 2024. DOI: 10.2139/ssrn.4843215

[54] Linderoth C, Hultén M, Stenliden L. Competing visions of artificial intelligence in education—A heuristic analysis on sociotechnical imaginaries and problematizations in policy guidelines. Policy Futures in Education. 2024;**22**:1662–1678. DOI: 10.1177/14782103241228900

[55] Elliott K, Price R, Shaw P, Spiliotopoulos T, Ng M, Coopamootoo K, et al. Towards an equitable digital society: Artificial Intelligence (AI) and Corporate Digital Responsibility (CDR). Society. 2021;**58**:179–188

[56] Raina A, Mundra K, Prasad P, Mishra S. Fostering Ethics in AI: Perceptions from the Indian AI curriculum. International Conference on Computers in Education. 2023. DOI: 10.58459/icce.2023.1440

[57] Xu T, Luo D, Luo X. The impact of integrating AI into business ethics education on students' attitudes towards corporate social responsibility. AMCIS 2024 Proceedings. 20, 2024

[58] Nithithanatchinnapat B, Maurer J, Deng X (Nancy), Joshi KD. Future business workforce: Crafting a Generative AI-centric curriculum today for tomorrow's business education. SIGMIS Database. 2024;**55**: 6–11. DOI: 10.1145/3645057.3645059

[59] Kaszalik Z, Kövecses VG, Szombathelyi MK. Overview on the sustainable and responsible educational technology efforts using Artificial Intelligence for the workers of the future. Journal of Sustainability Research. 2025;7: DOI: 10.20900/jsr20250039

[60] Chang Y-L, Ke J. Socially responsible Artificial Intelligence empowered people analytics: A novel framework towards sustainability.

Human Resource Development Review. 2024;**23**:88–120. DOI: 10.1177/15344843231200930

[61] Wu L, Chen ZF, Tao W. Instilling warmth in artificial intelligence? Examining publics' responses to AI-applied corporate ability and corporate social responsibility practices. Public Relations Review. 2024;**50**:102426. DOI: 10.1016/j.pubrev.2024.102426

[62] Camilleri MA. Artificial intelligence governance: Ethical considerations and implications for social responsibility. Expert Systems. 2024;**41**:e13406. DOI: 10.1111/exsy.13406

Chapter 24

On the Reliability of Artificial Intelligence in Mathematics Education

Victor Martinez-Luaces

Abstract

This paper analyses a specific experience related to the use of artificial intelligence (AI) in mathematical proofs of medium difficulty. Firstly, some well-known theoretical frameworks – in particular, the zone of proximal development (ZPD) proposed by Vygotsky – are studied in terms of their possible adaptation to the use of AI in mathematics education. Secondly, the methodology used is described, and the results of the field work are analysed. Finally, the results obtained are compared with those of other researchers and the opinions of engineering students in the academic year 2024–2025. Based on the above, conclusions are drawn about the potential of AI in mathematics education.

Keywords: matrix theorems, mathematical proofs, ChatGPT, zone of proximal development, scaffolding

1. Introduction

My first experience with artificial intelligence (AI) – specifically, ChatGPT, version 3.5 – took place in June 2023, when I was writing one of my chapters for the InTechOpen book Nonlinear Systems and Matrix Analysis – Recent Advances in Theory and Applications [1].

In that opportunity, my goal was to find a shorter and/or more elegant proof for one of the theorems in that chapter. The required proof is neither very long nor very complicated. In fact, it is a combination of Theorem 2 and Corollary 3, and, therefore, the complete proof fits perfectly into six lines: four for the theorem and two for the corollary [1].

It is important to note that the aforementioned chapter appeared online in November 2024, so at the time of ChatGPT's query, the proof was not yet available online. However, a relatively similar proof – in a different context – has existed since 2018 [2] and could have been easily adapted. Indeed, in that previous work [2], a similar result was proved for matrices related to mixing problems – so-called MP matrices – which are different from those considered in the other work – so-called FOCKM matrices [1]. However, the proof follows the same ideas, and it is very easy to adapt.

Despite all these "advantages" for ChatGPT, i.e., a result with an easy proof and a freely available version to adapt, the results were not as good as expected. In fact, ChatGPT not only did not produce a new proof, nor did it adapt the existing one, but it also produced several successive pseudo-proofs with quite obvious errors.

What happened led me to investigate the subject further, and it was interesting to find other authors who also reported these incorrect pseudo-results, which some of them call "hallucinations" [3], while others use much more pejorative terms [4] to describe these incorrect solutions.

This paper analyses possible theoretical frameworks, describes the details of this case study, and compares the results with those obtained by other researchers. These results are also complemented by student feedback.

Based on the above, the possibilities of AI in mathematics education are discussed, and conclusions are drawn.

2. Theoretical framework

2.1 The zone of proximal development

The zone of proximal development (ZPD) is one of the fundamental contributions of the sociocultural theory of learning, developed by Lev Vygotsky [5], which explains how learning results from social interaction and cultural influences [6]. This concept (ZPD) can be defined as follows: "the distance between the actual development level as determined by independent problem solving and the level of potential development as determined through problem-solving under adult guidance, or in collaboration with more capable peers" (see [5], p. 86).

Based on the above, it is evident that the ZPD refers to tasks that go beyond the student's abilities and require guidance and help from a more knowledgeable other (MKO). It is in this ZPD where instruction yields the greatest results, leading to maximum cognitive growth, in which the learner manages to surpass his or her current capabilities with the help of the MKO [7].

The ZPD was first identified through repeated observations of the mental age of two children, each of whom was given a problem more complex than they could solve at the time. These children were 9 years old, and it was found that one of them was able – with the assistance of an MKO – to solve problems designed for 12 year-olds, while the other was unable to go beyond the problems designed for his age. This difference between the current mental age and that achievable with the assistance of the MKO is what indicates the existence of the ZPD [8].

According to McLeod [7], the ZPD has four fundamental characteristics: it is dynamic and changing, individualized, not limited only to procedural knowledge, and it highlights the importance of collaboration, since the significance of the MKO is emphasized.

Regarding this last aspect, as Abtahi [6] observes, "The ZPD lies between the worlds of mathematics that pupils can interact with and the worlds of mathematics that they cannot", and moreover, "the interactions between the worlds, within the ZPD, are impossible without the existence of a more knowledgeable person involved in the activity." As Verenikina [9] remarks, Vygotsky regarded an instructor's "teaching of a student not just as a source of information to be assimilated but as a lever with which the student's thought, with its structural characteristics, is shifted from level to level."

2.2 Other related concepts

For many authors, the ZPD and the term "scaffolding" are synonymous; however, Vygotsky himself never used this term in his works. In fact, this term was introduced by other researchers like Wood, Bruner, and Ross [10], and their description was rather practical and not explicitly connected with the ZPD [11]. A posteriori, other researchers such as Cazden [12] and Bruner [13] established the relationship between the ZPD and the Scaffolding theory.

For example, in the definition of Wood et al. (see [10], p. 90), scaffolding is the process "that enables a child or novice to solve a task or achieve a goal that would be beyond his unassisted efforts". Therefore, the relationship between both concepts is evident, as McLeod [7] stated, scaffolding consists of a set of activities proposed by the educator to help the learner when led through the ZPD.

Another related concept is intersubjectivity, which, according to Behrend [14], refers to the shared understanding that takes place when a teacher and a student work together on a certain task. As McLeod [7] observes, intersubjectivity is fundamental for effective scaffolding, as it allows the teacher to tailor the support to the student's needs and personal ZPD.

In his work on the ZPD, McLeod [7] raises three major challenges in maintaining intersubjectivity in scaffolding: the lack of sensitivity in peer scaffolding, the power imbalances if one of the participants is dominant, and the challenge of using technology. In particular, with regard to the use of technology, it is worth mentioning that static tools do not adapt to student learning, since they do not perform continuous diagnosis nor the calibrated support that are fundamental for Vygotskian scaffolding.

2.3 About AI, ChatGPT, and the ZPD

As is well known, Vygotsky created the ZPD concept long before the advent of AI. However, at first glance, it seems straightforward to apply his ideas of guided instruction and scaffolding using modern technologies.

For instance, some platforms, such as Accelerated Reader, use the idea of the ZPD since they carry out preliminary evaluations and then suggest texts to the student that are sufficiently challenging to promote his/her growth but not so complicated that they lead to frustration.

In the specific case of AI, some authors, like McLeod [7], argue that AI can emulate the coaching role of an MKO, adjusting to the student's pace and helping him/her navigate the ZPD in a more independent way.

In this enthusiastic vision of the role of AI in education – and, in particular, ChatGPT – it is proposed that it can do the following:

- Act as a very patient tutor, capable of guiding the student toward complex ideas while adjusting explanations based on the student's responses.

- Encourage active learning by asking questions, promoting reflection, and supporting metacognition.

- Help with tasks that are just out of reach, offering ideas that allow the student to remain in the ZPD.

- Adapt over time, learning from interactions with the learner, and maintaining support at the right level of challenge.

2.4 Some questions about ChatGPT's reliability

It is reasonable to ask whether the approach in the previous subsection is too optimistic or not; specifically, does ChatGPT, in its current version, really have all the characteristics mentioned above? And more specifically, are ChatGPT's answers really reliable?

This is really a core issue. ChatGPT can be very patient, encourage more active learning, assist with tasks just beyond what is currently achievable, and adapt over time, but all of this is useless if its answers are incorrect. In fact, for ChatGPT to truly replace a competent and experienced teacher, its answers should at least be equally reliable.

This is actually what is investigated in this work, in the specific case of proving simple but relatively challenging mathematical properties of linear algebra. Specifically, the research question is whether ChatGPT's answers are reliable in proving certain propositions of linear algebra.

3. Methodology

In order to answer the research question, the idea is to ask ChatGPT for a relatively simple proposition with an easy proof, which, at the same time, should not be available on the internet.

For this purpose, a proposition was used that can be considered a mixture of Theorem 2 and Corollary 3 of a book chapter [1] that, at that time – June 23, 2023 – had not been published. In fact, the work was published in the "online first" format in August 2024, so it was not possible at that time to simply copy it from a website.

We will see what this property to be proved consists of. In Chapter 13 of the InTechOpen book Nonlinear Systems and Matrix Analysis – Recent Advances in Theory and Applications, the properties of certain matrices that appear naturally in some chemical kinetics problems are studied. These first-order chemical kinetics matrices – so-called FOCKM matrices – all have the following structure:

$$\mathbb{A} = \begin{pmatrix} -\sigma_1 & \cdots & a_{1,n} \\ \vdots & \ddots & \vdots \\ a_{n,1} & \cdots & -\sigma_n \end{pmatrix} \tag{1}$$

where:

$$\sigma_1 = \sum_{i \neq 1} a_{i,1}, \; \ldots, \; \sigma_n = \sum_{i \neq n} a_{i,n} \tag{2}$$

For example, one of the FOCKM matrices that appear in that work is:

$$\mathbb{A} = \begin{pmatrix} -6 & 0 & 0 & 0 & 0 \\ 1 & -2 & 0 & 1 & 0 \\ 2 & 2 & -1 & 0 & 0 \\ 1 & 0 & 1 & -1 & 0 \\ 2 & 0 & 0 & 0 & 0 \end{pmatrix} \tag{3}$$

The eigenvalues of this matrix are: $-6, 0$ (double), and $-2 \pm 2i$ (4), and it is easy to observe that all of them have a non-positive real part.

Taking into account the above equations, the property to be proved is: if $\mathbb{A}$ is a FOCKM matrix with $n \geq 2$ rows – that is, a matrix with the structure given by (1) and (2) – then $Re(\lambda) \leq 0$, being λ any eigenvalue of $\mathbb{A}$.

The proof consists of applying Gershgorin's Circles Theorem [15] to the matrix $\mathbb{A}^T$, which gives that all the eigenvalues lie in a disk $\mathbb{D}\Big((-r, 0),\ r\Big)$ with $r > 0$.

The details of the proof can be read in [1], where it is observed that the minimum value of r is $r = Max\{\sigma_1, \sigma_2, \dots \dots, \sigma_n\}$.

Since $r > 0$ the disk centred on $(-r, 0)$, with radius is included in the left-half complex plane, and therefore, it is proven that $Re(\lambda) \leq 0$, for any λ, eigenvalue of $\mathbb{A}$.

As it can be observed, the proof is short, simple, and almost an immediate corollary of Gershgorin's Theorem, taking advantage of the special structure of the studied matrices.

It should be added that, at the time this proposition was presented to ChatGPT, there was another similar proof—for another type of matrices—that was easily adaptable and available on the Internet [2]. Therefore, in the case of not knowing how to prove the property, there was also the option of copying it, with minimal adaptations.

In other words, ChatGPT was presented with a simple algebraic statement, accompanied by a short proof, which could even be obtained by simply adapting a previous one, but at the same time, it is not a property that would be sufficient to search for and copy its proof from a web page.

Consequently, the aforementioned proposition met all the conditions to challenge AI with an accessible but non-trivial task.

4. Using ChatGPT to prove a mathematical statement

In the first communication with the AI (**Figure 1**, top), the problem is presented to ChatGPT in a very general form, basically to check if it understands the statement.

From the analysis of the response (**Figure 1**, bottom), it is clear that ChatGPT understands the format of the matrix considered. Moreover, in the response, it writes equation (2) again, with a different but correct notation.

After writing the characteristic equation (**Figure 1**, bottom), ChatGPT comments on various generalities and suggests the use of numerical methods for large values of n (**Figure 2**).

In the following question (**Figure 3**), our aim is to guide ChatGPT – as if it were a student – toward studying the sign of the real part of the eigenvalues.

This partial scaffolding process does not yield concrete results, at least in this first stage. Indeed, the answer remains very general, and then (**Figure 4**) it attempts to draw conclusions about the signs of the trace and determinant of A, with mixed consider now a square matrix which all entries are non negative, except the diagonal ones, which are aii equal to the sum of the others i-th column entries multiplied by -1. which are the corresponding eigenvalues?

In the given square matrix, where all entries are non-negative except the diagonal entries, which are negative and equal to the sum of the other entries in the same column multiplied by -1, we can determine the corresponding eigenvalues.

Let's denote the matrix as A, with elements A[i, j]. The diagonal elements are given by:

A[i, i] = -sum(A[j, i]) for j ≠ i

To find the eigenvalues, we need to solve the characteristic equation:

det(A - λI) = 0,

Figure 1.
Statement and the first part of ChatGPT's response.

Calculating this determinant is a complex task, especially for larger matrices. It generally involves finding the roots of a polynomial equation. Analytical solutions may not be readily available, and numerical methods may be required to approximate the eigenvalues.

Therefore, the specific eigenvalues of the given matrix would depend on the matrix's size (n) and the values of the non-diagonal entries (A[i, j]). To obtain the exact eigenvalues for a specific matrix, you would need to perform the calculations or use appropriate numerical methods.

Figure 2.
ChatGPT suggests the use of numerical methods.

what can you say about the sign of the real part of the eigenvalues?

In the given square matrix with non-negative entries, except for the diagonal entries, which are negative, the sign of the real part of the eigenvalues can be determined based on the properties of the matrix.

Figure 3.
A specific question about the signs of the real part of the eigenvalues.

results. In fact, its statement about the sign of the trace of the matrix is correct; however, the other one about the determinant is wrong. Indeed, ChatGPT states that $det(\mathbb{A}) < 0$ (**Figure 4**, bottom), which is not true.

Since the diagonal elements are negative, the trace of the matrix will be negative.

The determinant of the matrix can be calculated as the product of its eigenvalues:

det(A) = λ1 * λ2 * ... * λn

As all the eigenvalues are real (since A is a real matrix), the determinant will also be negative.

Figure 4.
Statements about the sign of the trace and the determinant.

VI

the determinant is not a negative number...since you can add all the rows and the result is null, then the determinant must be zero

Apologies for the incorrect statement. You are correct. Since the sum of all rows of the matrix is zero, it implies that the matrix has linearly dependent rows, and therefore, its determinant is zero.

Figure 5.
ChatGPT acknowledges its error regarding the sign of the determinant.

This mistake is easy to observe, both in general (see Eq. (2)) or in particular (see Eq. (3)), since it is immediate to see that the sum of the rows is zero and therefore $det(\mathbb{A}) = 0$.

This error is explained to ChatGPT (**Figure 5**, top), and it recognizes it immediately (**Figure 5**, bottom).

While ChatGPT admits the error, it still cannot solve the problem and it argues that it is impossible to make a statement about this issue (**Figure 6**, top). However, when it is argued that it should be possible to give a proof that $Re(\lambda) \leq 0, \forall\lambda$, eigenvalue of $\mathbb{A}$ (**Figure 6**, middle), ChatGPT acknowledges this possibility and attempts to give a new proof (**Figure 6**, bottom).

The proposed proof (**Figure 7**) is clearly incorrect from the beginning. In fact, it states that $\mathbb{A} + \mathbb{A}^*$ – where $\mathbb{A}^*$represents the complex conjugate of $\mathbb{A}$ – is equal to its own conjugate transpose, and we will see that it is false with a simple counterexample.

The FOCKM matrix (3) has all its entries real, so $\mathbb{A}^* = \mathbb{A}$, then:

$$\mathbb{A} + \mathbb{A}^* = \mathbb{A} + \mathbb{A} = 2\mathbb{A} = \begin{pmatrix} -12 & 0 & 0 & 0 & 0 \\ 2 & -4 & 0 & 2 & 0 \\ 4 & 4 & -2 & 0 & 0 \\ 2 & 0 & 2 & -2 & 0 \\ 4 & 0 & 0 & 0 & 0 \end{pmatrix} \tag{4}$$

Therefore, in the given scenario, we cannot make a definitive statement about the sign of the real part of the eigenvalues without more information.

Well, thank you for your response. I think that it is possible to prove that the eigenvalues have non positive real parts...there should be a proof of this statement.

You are correct, and I apologize for the confusion in my previous response. Indeed, we can prove that the eigenvalues of the given matrix have non-positive real parts. Allow me to provide a proof for this statement.

Figure 6.
New interactions with ChatGPT to solve the problem.

To prove that the eigenvalues have non-positive real parts, we can consider the matrix A + A*, where A* represents the complex conjugate of A. The matrix A + A* is a Hermitian matrix since it equals its own conjugate transpose.

Figure 7.
Wrong statement about $\mathbb{A} + \mathbb{A}^*$.

Since (4) is a real matrix, its conjugate transpose is simply the following transpose matrix:

$$\left(\mathbb{A} + \mathbb{A}^*\right)^T = \begin{pmatrix} -12 & 2 & 4 & 2 & 4 \\ 0 & -4 & 4 & 0 & 0 \\ 0 & 0 & -2 & 2 & 0 \\ 0 & 2 & 0 & -2 & 0 \\ 0 & 0 & 0 & 0 & 0 \end{pmatrix} \tag{5}$$

Since matrix (5) is different from the one obtained in (4), it is clear that ChatGPT's statement is false. The rest of the pseudo-proof is not included in **Figure 7** because it starts from an incorrect premise.

In that pseudo-proof, other errors appear, some of them even more obvious than the one mentioned above, as can be observed in **Figure 8**.

In this case, the correct equality is $(\mathbb{A} - \lambda\mathbb{I})v = 0$ or equivalently $\mathbb{A}v = \lambda v$ instead of $\left(\mathbb{A} + \mathbb{A}^*\right)v = \lambda v$, as ChatGPT says. Then, when the inaccuracies of this new argument are observed (see **Figure 9**, top), once again ChatGPT recognizes the error (see **Figure 9**, bottom).

In addition to acknowledging the error, ChatGPT attempts to provide a new pseudo-proof, but again, it has some more errors, like the one considered in **Figure 10**.

Once again, the incorrectness of the argument is remarked (**Figure 11**, top), and one more time, the AI platform acknowledges the error (**Figure 11**, middle).

It is interesting to note that, despite the error having been detected (**Figure 11**, top) and ChatGPT recognising it recently (**Figure 11**, middle), its next attempt repeats the same error from the very beginning of the new pseudo-proof (**Figure 11**, bottom).

Now, let λ be an eigenvalue of A, and v be the corresponding eigenvector. We can write the eigenvalue equation as:

$(A + A^*)v = \lambda v$

Figure 8.
Another error in ChatGPT's pseudo-proof.

I revised your previous proof...you said that "let λ be an eigenvalue of A, and v be the corresponding eigenvector. We can write the eigenvalue equation as:

$(A + A^*)v = \lambda v$"

I apologize for the incorrect statement in my previous response. You are right, and I appreciate you catching that mistake.

Figure 9.
The error is recognized by ChatGPT.

In the given matrix A with negative diagonal elements, let's correct the eigenvalue equation as follows:

$(A - \lambda I)v = 0,$

where λ represents the eigenvalue we are trying to find, and I is the identity matrix.

To prove that the eigenvalues have non-positive real parts, we can consider the Hermitian conjugate of the above equation:

$(A^* - \lambda I)v = 0.$

Figure 10.
A new, wrong argument.

if $(A - \lambda I)v = 0$, then, the conjugate should be $(A^* - \lambda^* I)v^* = 0$, which is not the same as $(A^* - \lambda I)v = 0$.

You are absolutely right, and I apologize for the error in my previous response. The correct statement should be:

If $(A - \lambda I)v = 0$, then taking the complex conjugate of both sides yields $(A^* - \lambda I)v = 0$.

Figure 11.
Exact repetition of the same error previously observed.

All those errors, and particularly the exact repetition of the same mistake previously observed just three lines later, are a clear indication that although ChatGPT correctly understands the algebraic statement it is not able to provide a correct proof for it. Moreover, continued questions and observations about incorrect equalities – that is, a certain form of scaffolding to help the AI arrive at a correct proof – do not seem to have any positive effects.

The above discussion and the comparison with other researchers are analysed in the next section.

5. Discussion and results

This work does not conduct a statistical study on the effectiveness of ChatGPT in proving certain algebraic properties. On the contrary, it is a case study that proposes a relatively simple algebraic property, such that its proof cannot be reduced to copying a result already published on the internet.

Although this is just a case study, it is easy to recognize some of the main characteristics of ChatGPT's responses to these types of problems:

- There is a certain tendency to answer with generalities, as shown in **Figure 1**.
- Propose several statements, some of them correct and others clearly false, as shown in **Figure 4**.
- Recognize its mistakes, as shown in **Figure 5**.
- A certain inconsistency, which leads the platform to say that it is not possible to establish a statement, and then to try to prove it (see **Figure 6**).
- Repeating exactly the same mistake as before, despite having recognized that it is an incorrect statement, as shown in **Figure 11**.
- The scaffolding process does not seem to yield positive results in ChatGPT's attempts at proving the proposition.

If we observe these features, the most worrying – at least, if we think of ChatGPT as a patient MKO for taking advantage of a student's ZPD – is the one related to proposing incorrect statements as if they were true. Indeed, this can be a source of misconceptions for the student.

These incorrect pseudo-results were reported by other authors in other contexts and were called "hallucinations" [3], among other terms [4].

As mentioned above, other authors have also studied the effectiveness of ChatGPT in different areas. In fact, in the study by Mohamed et al. [16] about AI in mathematics education, they found that 60% of the published works on the subject are about effectiveness. These authors cite several important examples, like Casler-Failing [17] and Wu [18], among others. However, they recognize that "AI is a topic that is rarely investigated in mathematics education" and "the results gained are limited, making it difficult to draw broad conclusions from the findings" [16].

Regarding concrete effectiveness results, Pardos and Bhandari [19] acknowledge that ChatGPT effectively provides precise definitions and explanations of mathematical concepts. However, as Lopes and Borba observe, "Its performance can fluctuate according to the nature of the questions and the topics presented" [20].

This is consistent with Wardal et al. [21], who note that the accuracy and effectiveness of ChatGPT depend on several factors, including the problem's complexity, the quality of data supplied, and the clarity of the instructions given to the program.

In the same direction, Mai et al. [22] observe that ChatGPT's limitations become evident when this platform has to deal with more complex mathematics problems.

More quantitative studies, such as that of Pardos and Bhandari [19] in a study with 274 participants, report that ChatGPT can be comparable to human tutors but with an effectiveness error of 32%. Similarly, Frieder et al. [23], in their study, conclude that ChatGPT generally understands the questions posed to it but frequently does not give correct answers, with its performance being lower than expected for an average graduate student.

If we look at specific areas of mathematics, Alonso-Diaz [24] reports a success rate close to 100% in integrals, but it drops to 80% in the resolution of differential equations. Turning specifically to differential equations, Koceska et al. [25] report an accuracy of 72% for first-order ordinary differential equations, and again, the percentage drops to 64% for second-order equations.

The above results merely illustrate the loss of ChatGPT's effectiveness as the complexity of the mathematical problem increases. Based on the above and taking into account the results of our study (although it is not statistical), it seems reasonable to conjecture that ChatGPT's effectiveness in providing original proofs (i.e., proofs not copied from the internet) would likely yield percentages even lower than those reported by the aforementioned authors.

Finally, students' perceptions generally seem to coincide with the researchers' findings. For instance, when I asked the students in my Calculus class whether they used ChatGPT (not just in Calculus, but in general) for their homework and what their results were, the comments generally ranged between the following two:

Student 1: Yes, we use ChatGPT, but more for specific questions, whose answers are known. That kind of task is generally well done.

Student 2: You can ask ChatGPT as if you were asking a classmate who already approved the subject. It's more like a source of ideas, but I don't blindly follow what it tells me. It's not 100% reliable.

These results agree with what was reported by Lopes and Borba [20], particularly in their dialogue with two students:

Talita: "...it's important to be careful when using it to ensure the information is reliable and contextualized."

Ariana: "...I learned from high school teachers to have critical thinking: you should not trust 100% in a single source but analyse different perspectives to form your opinion..."

Consequently, the researchers' results and the students' perceptions suggest that ChatGPT's capabilities, and in particular the effectiveness of its responses, appear to be quite improvable.

This is accentuated when the mathematical content becomes more specific, where the capabilities of ChatGPT appear to be limited [26]. It can be expected that these capabilities will improve in the future, as has happened, for example, with chess-playing machines [27], which have recently achieved very good performances playing against several of the strongest human players. On the other hand, it is worth noting that in chess, everything is finite, while in mathematics, it is not.

Nowadays, in any case, and returning to our main topic, as Pardos and Bhandari [19] point out, ChatGPT is not consistently prepared to provide high-quality mathematical proofs, which aligns with our own results.

6. Conclusion

This chapter analysed a case study related to the use of an AI platform (ChatGPT) in algebraic proofs of medium difficulty, which are not limited to being searched for and copied from a web page. The results obtained in this case study have not been good and make it clear that, while ChatGPT can perform well on routine tasks – already solved on the web – it is not as effective on tasks that require creativity or at least some ability to adapt previous ideas.

As stated by Mohamed et al. [16], “AI is a simulation of human intelligence modelled in a machine and programmed to think like humans. In other words, AI is a computer system that can do jobs that generally require human resources or human intelligence to complete the job.” In order to know whether ChatGPT achieves that goal or not, one of the most important aspects is knowing if it is effective, so it is not surprising that “. . .the most observed aspect is its effectiveness in the teaching and learning process, especially mathematics education” [16]. The conclusion that Mohamed et al. themselves draw about this issue is that “. . .with the help of AI, teaching and learning are more effective because it is exciting and creative. . .” and “. . . has made it easier for students to understand a subject. . .” [16].

The above suggests that the role of AI is more supportive than substitutive of traditional teaching and learning. This view is expressed much more explicitly by Lopes and Borba [20], who remark, “. . .the need for proper guidance to avoid excessive dependence on the tool and ensure that mathematical reasoning remains at the center of the learning process. . .” and also, “. . .AI complements rather than replaces human reasoning and creativity in learning processes.”

In addition to effectiveness, there are other important problems, such as those observed by Mai et al. [22]:

- Concerns related to data privacy and security.
- Risks of dehumanizing education.
- Technical limitations, particularly in interpreting complex problems.

To these problems, we must add those observed by Limna et al. [28]:

- Concerns about the accuracy of the responses.
- A possible decline in personal interactions between teachers and students.

All of the above agree with the following statement by Lopes and Borba [20] about ChatGPT in modeling tasks: “. . .while ChatGPT can assist with theory and variable selection, its accuracy in solving complex equations is less reliable. This limitation aligns with the concept that AI’s role is to guide, not replace, human cognitive processes.”

In short, ChatGPT – like any other tool – has undeniable advantages and disadvantages. Among the advantages, it should be mentioned its easy access to information, its speed, and the ability to provide explanations of definitions, processes, and relatively simple proofs, all of which are already available on the web. However, on the other hand, the use of AI can create dependency and affect the learner's independent thinking, and above all – and this was the objective of this work – it can produce incorrect answers.

About this last issue, it is important to remark that ChatGPT's reliability decreases dramatically when moving toward more specific and complex tasks. Indeed, its efficiency declines when moving from integrals to first-order differential equations and the results are even worse when second-order differential equations are considered. Moreover, based on the observed results, it is reasonable to conjecture that this effectiveness decreases even more dramatically in activities that require a certain degree of creativity in addition to mathematical knowledge.

This is the case in our fieldwork, where ChatGPT performed quite poorly when faced with a proof of medium difficulty, which was not available online. Furthermore, there is clear evidence that it does not respond positively when we tried to create a scaffolding process through questions and tasks.

It is clear that ChatGPT, at least in its current version, is not prepared to provide reliable answers to these types of problems.

Based on all the above, we can conclude that ChatGPT can be very useful in mathematics education due to its speed, its ease of access to information, and because its use produces great motivation among younger students. However, its current limitations make the guidance of a human tutor absolutely essential.

This is important for several reasons discussed above, but particularly to ensure the quality of the answers to more complex problems that require greater creativity, like mathematical proofs.

Acknowledgments

The author wishes to thank his students for their feedback regarding the use of ChatGPT in their assignments, and also thank Marjorie Chaves for reviewing this work.

Author details

Victor Martinez-Luaces
University of Granada, Granada, Spain

*Address all correspondence to: victormartinezluaces@gmail.com

References

[1] Martinez-Luaces V. Eigenvalues of matrices in chemical kinetics and their algebraic and geometric multiplicities. In: Peter, Y.P. Chen, and Victor, Martinez-Luaces. Nonlinear Systems and Matrix Analysis - Recent Advances in Theory and Applications. London, UK: IntechOpen 2024;241–259. DOI: 10.5772/intechopen.1003778

[2] Martinez-Luaces V. Square matrices associated to mixing problems ODE systems. In: Hassan, A. Yasser. Matrix Theory - Applications and Theorems. London, U.K.: InTech 2018;41–58. DOI: 10.5772/intechopen.74437

[3] Verspoor K. 'Fighting fire with fire'—using LLMs to combat LLM hallucinations. Nature. 2024;**630**: 569–570

[4] Hicks MT, Humphries J, Slater J. ChatGPT is bullshit. Ethics and Information Technology. 2024;**26**(2): 1–10

[5] Vygotsky LS. Mind in Society: Development of Higher Psychological Processes. Cambridge, Massachusetts, USA: Harvard University Press; 1978

[6] Abtahi Y. A theoretical exploration: Zone of proximal development as an ethical zone for teaching mathematics. Avances de Investigación En Educación Matemática: AIEM. 2021;**20**:7–21

[7] McLeod S. Zone of proximal development. Available from: https://www.simplypsychology.org/zone-of-proximal-development.html [Accessed: 2025-July-26]

[8] Rahman L. Vygotsky's zone of proximal development of teaching and learning in STEM education. International Journal of Engineering Research & Technology. 2024;**13**(8):389–394

[9] Verenikina I. From theory to practice: What does the metaphor of scaffolding mean to educators today? Available from: https://ro.uow.edu.au/articles/journal_contribution/From_theory_to_practice_What_does_the_metaphor_of_scaffolding_mean_to_educators_today_/27714021?file=50463618 [Accessed: 2025-July-26]

[10] Wood D, Bruner JS, Ross G. The role of tutoring in problem solving. Journal of Child Psychology and Psychiatry. 1976;**17**(2):89–100

[11] Stone CA. The metaphor of scaffolding: Its utility for the field of learning disabilities. Journal of Learning Disabilities. 1998;**31**(4):344–364

[12] Cazden C. Peekaboo as an instructional model: Discourse development at home and at school. Papers and Reports on Child Language Development. 1979;(17):1–19. Available from: https://files.eric.ed.gov/fulltext/ED191274.pdf

[13] Bruner J. Vygotsky: A historical and conceptual perspective. In: Wertsch, editor. Culture, Communication, and Cognition: Vygotskian Perspectives. Cambridge, U.K: Cambridge University Press;1985. pp. 21–34

[14] Behrend SD Understanding Processes in Children's Collaborative Problem Solving. Unpublished manuscript. University of Pittsburgh, 1990

[15] Varga RS. Geršgorin and His Circles. Berlin Heildelberg: Springer-Verlag; 2011

[16] Mohamed MZ, et al. Artificial intelligence in mathematics education: A systematic literature review. International Electronic Journal of Mathematics Education. 2022;**17**: em0694

[17] Casler-Failing S. Learning to teach mathematics with robots: Developing the 'T' in technological pedagogical content knowledge. Research in Learning Technology. 2021;**29**:1–20. Available from: https://journal.alt.ac.uk/index.php/rlt/article/view/2555/2889

[18] Wu R, Visualization of basic mathematics teaching based on artificial intelligence. *Journal of Physics: Conference Series (Vol. 1992, No. 4, p. 042042).* IOP Publishing. 2021

[19] Pardos ZA, Bhandari S. ChatGPT-generated help produces learning gains equivalent to human tutor-authored help on mathematics skills. Plos One. 2024;**19**(5):e0304013

[20] Lopes A, and Borba M. A double-edged sword? Possibilities and challenges in the use of ChatGPT for mathematical modeling activities. In: Martinez-Luaces, editor. New Trends in Teaching and Learning of Calculus. Cham, Switzerland: Springer; In press

[21] Wardat Y, Tashtoush MA, AlAli R, Jarrah AM. ChatGPT: A revolutionary tool for teaching and learning mathematics. Eurasia Journal of Mathematics, Science and Technology Education. 2023;**19**(7):em2286

[22] Mai DTT, Da CV, Hanh NV. The use of ChatGPT in teaching and learning: A systematic review through SWOT analysis approach. In: Frontiers in Education. Vol. **9**. Lausanne, Switzerland: Frontiers Media SA; 2024. p. *1328769*

[23] Frieder S, Pinchetti L, Griffiths RR, Salvatori T, Lukasiewicz T, Petersen P, Berner J. Mathematical capabilities of ChatGPT. Advances in Neural Information Processing Systems. 2023;**36**:27699–27744

[24] Alonso-Diaz S. A human-like artificial intelligence for mathematics. Mind & Society. 2024;**23**(1):79–97

[25] Koceska N, Koceski S, Lazarova LK, Miteva M, Zlatanovska B. Can ChatGPT be used for solving ordinary differential equations. Balkan Journal of Applied Mathematics and Informatics. 2023;**6**(2):103–114

[26] Lopes A. Advanced algebraic thinking processes in students' modelling activities. Teaching Mathematics and Its Applications: An International Journal of the IMA. 2023;**42**(4):360–374

[27] Chole V, Gadicha V, Thawakar M. Evolution of artificial intelligence through game playing in chess. Data-Driven Systems and Intelligent Applications. 2024;119 DOI: 10.1201/9781003388449-7

[28] Limna P, Kraiwanit T, Jangjarat K, Klayklung P, Chocksathaporn P. The use of ChatGPT in the digital era: Perspectives on chatbot implementation. Journal of Applied Learning and Teaching. 2022;**6**(1): 64–74

Section 5

AI Applications in Professional & Specialized Education

Chapter 25

AI-Powered Learning Management Systems in Dental Education

Mihnea Ioan Nicolescu

Abstract

This chapter examines the transformative impact of artificial intelligence (AI) on dental education, focusing on the integration of AI-powered learning management systems. It traces the evolution of AI technologies from early expert systems to adaptive platforms that personalize learning by analyzing student data, delivering real-time feedback, and dynamically adjusting content. Key components – such as natural language processing, automated evaluation, and intelligent tutoring agents – are analyzed in relation to curriculum design, knowledge structuring, and pedagogical strategies, including problem-based and inquiry-driven learning. The chapter highlights how AI enhances curriculum delivery, supports early identification of struggling students, and facilitates adaptive learning in complex domains such as oral biology and regenerative dentistry. It also addresses challenges, including data privacy, algorithmic bias, interoperability, and ethical considerations. Implications for faculty roles, professional development, and institutional policy are discussed, alongside emerging technologies and innovations that may shape the future of dental education. This comprehensive analysis aims to guide the development of adaptive, inclusive, and ethically responsible learning environments.

Keywords: learning management system, dental education, adaptive learning, artificial intelligence in education, educational technology, regenerative dentistry

1. Introduction

Artificial intelligence (AI) is fundamentally transforming dental education through the integration of AI-powered Learning Management Systems (LMSs), which enable highly personalized learning experiences, automate complex clinical assessments, and deliver intelligent feedback tailored to individual student needs [1]. These systems leverage adaptive algorithms to analyze student responses, identify distinct learning patterns, and provide targeted recommendations, leading to enhanced knowledge retention and a deeper comprehension of specialized subjects [2]. In dental education, the need for individualized instruction is particularly acute due to the complexity of clinical reasoning and the diversity of specialized subjects, such as oral biology and regenerative dentistry [3]. The automation of clinical assessments through AI not only streamlines the evaluation process but also enhances the accuracy and consistency of feedback on intricate case scenarios, supporting the development of clinical reasoning skills [2, 4]. AI-generated feedback is immediate and interactive, which increases student engagement and motivation, creating a more dynamic and participative learning environment [2]. Moreover, the integration of AI in educational assessment, guided by in-depth learning theories, shifts the focus toward individualized student support, enabling early identification of learning gaps and timely intervention [5, 6]. Practical implementations of AI-powered LMS in dental education have demonstrated significant benefits, including the facilitation of blended learning formats that combine e-courses with face-to-face instruction, as seen in initiatives that support curriculum delivery and quality assurance [7, 8]. Intelligent classroom assistants, such as adaptive learning platforms and AI-driven chatbots, provide real-time administrative support and personalized learning pathways, further enhancing the educational experience [1]. These technologies also streamline administrative tasks, such as course registration and information dissemination, reducing the burden on faculty and allowing more time for direct student interaction. Despite these advancements, challenges remain, particularly regarding data privacy, the need for robust technical infrastructure, and comprehensive faculty training to ensure effective implementation and ethical use of AI in education [4, 6]. Student perceptions of AI integration are influenced by their understanding of the technology, with those possessing greater familiarity expressing more positive attitudes and satisfaction with personalized, adaptive learning and real-time feedback [1]. The ongoing evolution of AI in dental education underscores the necessity for continuous evaluation of educational impact, engagement strategies, and the development of evidence-based instructional designs to maximize the potential of AI-powered LMS [8, 9]. The emergence of AI-powered LMSs has enabled the development of adaptive learning environments, where algorithms dynamically tailor educational content and feedback to individual student profiles, thereby enhancing both engagement and learning outcomes [1, 5]. Personalized learning, a central feature of AI-driven LMSs, leverages data mining, prediction models, and intelligent tutoring systems to adapt instructional pathways in real time. These systems analyze student interactions, performance metrics, and learning behaviors to recommend targeted resources and interventions, ensuring that each learner receives support aligned with their unique strengths and areas for improvement [5]. Squirrel AI and Edmodo exemplify such platforms, utilizing AI algorithms to provide tailored recommendations and feedback, which have been shown to improve understanding and retention of complex subject matter [1]. AI-powered LMSs facilitate early identification of students who may require additional support, enabling timely interventions that can prevent academic difficulties and promote mastery of foundational concepts [1, 6]. The interactive and immediate nature of AI-generated feedback has been linked to increased student motivation and participation, creating a more dynamic and participative learning environment. Automated clinical assessments represent another significant advancement enabled by the integration of AI. By employing algorithms capable of evaluating complex case scenarios, AI-powered LMSs can provide objective, consistent, and scalable assessments that reduce faculty workload while maintaining high standards of evaluation [5, 6]. These systems also support the development of student models that track progress over time, allowing for continuous refinement of instructional strategies and assessment criteria [5]. The use of data analytics within LMS platforms, as demonstrated by the analysis of student engagement with self-directed video resources, provides valuable insights into learning behaviors and outcomes, informing both curriculum design and individualized support strategies [10]. The global shift toward e-learning, accelerated by recent disruptions such as the COVID-19 pandemic, has underscored the importance of robust, scalable, and accessible educational technologies. The successful implementation of e-learning systems in dental faculties, such as the initiative at Alexandria University, illustrates the potential for AI-enhanced LMSs to support blended learning formats that combine online and face-to-face instruction [7]. Positive feedback from students across diverse cultural and institutional contexts suggests that AI-powered LMSs can facilitate international collaboration and standardization in dental education, provided that adequate training and support are available for both faculty and students [7, 11]. Despite these advances, challenges persist in ensuring equitable access, maintaining data privacy, and ensuring the ethical use of AI in educational settings. Establishing fair and inclusive grading practices, incorporating feedback mechanisms for continuous improvement, and providing comprehensive training for educators are essential steps to maximize the benefits of AI integration while mitigating potential risks. The literature emphasizes the necessity of a critical approach to AI adoption, striking a balance between innovation and considerations of accuracy, transparency, and inclusivity [2, 6, 12]. As AI-powered LMSs continue to evolve, their capacity to revolutionize curriculum delivery, assessment, and student support in dental education will depend on ongoing research, interdisciplinary collaboration, and a commitment to ethical and equitable implementation [5, 6].

2. AI in education

2.1 Historical evolution of AI in educational technology

The historical evolution of AI in educational technology is marked by a progressive integration of computational methods, data-driven decision-making, and adaptive systems into teaching and learning environments. Early educational technologies were primarily focused on digitizing content and providing basic computer-assisted instruction; however, the emergence of AI has fundamentally transformed these approaches by introducing intelligent automation and personalization [2, 13]. Over time, AI systems have evolved from simple rule-based algorithms to sophisticated models capable of natural language processing (NLP), machine learning, and real-time feedback, reflecting advances in both computer science and educational theory [2]. The development of expert systems and basic automated grading tools characterized the initial phase of AI in education. These early systems relied on predefined rules and limited datasets, offering only rudimentary support for assessment and feedback. As computational power increased and algorithms became more refined, AI applications began to incorporate more complex data analysis, enabling the identification of patterns in student performance and the provision of tailored recommendations [5, 14]. The integration of NLP further expanded the capabilities of AI-powered educational tools, allowing for automated assessment of open-ended assignments and more nuanced feedback mechanisms [5]. With the advent of LMS and virtual learning environments (VLEs), AI technologies found new opportunities for integration. The application of AI in grading and assessment has undergone significant refinement. Modern AI grading systems utilize advanced algorithms to enhance accuracy and reliability, addressing longstanding concerns about bias and fairness in automated evaluation [1, 2]. These systems are capable of processing large volumes of student work, minimizing human error, and providing immediate, personalized feedback that supports deeper engagement and improved learning outcomes [1, 2]. The interactive nature of AI-generated feedback has been demonstrated to enhance student motivation and participation, thereby contributing to a more dynamic educational experience [2]. In parallel, the use of AI in clinical and specialized domains, such as dental education, has expanded. AI-driven tools now support the automated assessment of complex clinical scenarios, facilitate case-based learning, and assist in the development of critical thinking and clinical reasoning skills [15]. These advancements are underpinned by the integration of machine learning models trained on extensive datasets, enabling the reliable evaluation of both theoretical knowledge and practical competencies [5, 16]. The evolution of AI in these contexts reflects a broader trend toward competency-based education and the need for scalable, objective assessment methods [15].

2.2 Core concepts of AI relevant to LMSs

AI has introduced a set of foundational concepts that are transforming the design and functionality of LMSs in dental education. At its core, AI in LMS leverages algorithms capable of processing large volumes of educational data, enabling systems to adapt dynamically to individual learner profiles and needs. Machine learning, a subset of AI, is particularly significant as it allows LMS platforms to identify patterns in student interactions, predict learning trajectories, and recommend personalized content or interventions. Deep learning, a further specialization within machine learning, utilizes neural networks to interpret complex data such as radiographic images or clinical case notes, supporting advanced assessment and feedback mechanisms [6, 17]. Personalized learning is a central concept enabled by AI in LMS. Through continuous analysis of student performance data, AI algorithms can tailor educational pathways, adjusting the sequence, difficulty, and modality of instructional materials. Automated assessment is another critical concept, where AI-driven systems evaluate student submissions, including short-answer responses and complex clinical scenarios. These systems employ NLP and image recognition to interpret written answers and diagnostic images, offering immediate, objective grading and feedback. However, the limitations of AI in assessing higher-order thinking, such as critical reasoning in patient management, necessitate the continued use of essay-based evaluations that require nuanced human judgment [18]. To address concerns of bias and fairness in automated grading, ongoing model training on diverse datasets and transparent algorithmic processes are essential, alongside human oversight to validate AI-generated grades. Intelligent feedback mechanisms represent a further advancement, as AI-powered LMS can analyze student errors, misconceptions, and learning gaps, generating tailored explanations or supplementary practice materials. This immediate, context-sensitive feedback has been shown to increase academic achievement and deepen subject matter understanding, as it encourages active participation and self-directed learning [2, 6]. The interactive nature of AI feedback also supports early identification of struggling students, enabling timely interventions and support. Integration of AI into LMS extends beyond content delivery and assessment. AI-driven analytics provide educators with actionable insights into student progress, engagement patterns, and curriculum effectiveness. These analytics inform instructional design and resource allocation, supporting continuous improvement in educational quality [1, 19]. Furthermore, AI-powered virtual tutors and chatbots embedded within LMS platforms can simulate mentoring relationships, adapting their instructional strategies to individual learning styles and progress, thus enhancing the overall learning environment. Ethical and practical considerations complement the technological underpinnings of AI in LMS. Ensuring data privacy, maintaining transparency in algorithmic decision-making, and providing adequate faculty training are necessary to realize the full benefits of AI integration while safeguarding student interests [6].

2.3 Overview of AI-driven educational paradigms

2.3.1 Personalized learning and adaptive pathways

Personalized learning and adaptive pathways have become central to the transformation of dental education through AI-powered LMS. These systems leverage advanced algorithms to analyze individual student responses, learning behaviors, and performance data, enabling the dynamic adaptation of educational content and feedback to each learner's unique needs [2]. The result is a highly individualized educational experience, where students receive tailored study guides, resources, and recommendations that align with their specific strengths and areas for improvement [1, 12]. The integration of AI into LMS also facilitates the early identification of students who may be struggling, allowing for timely interventions and support. Generative AI (GenAI) technologies can analyze patterns in student engagement and performance, providing educators with actionable insights for targeted mentorship and resource allocation. This proactive approach not only improves student outcomes but also optimizes faculty workload by automating routine assessment and administrative tasks [1, 6]. From a theoretical perspective, the paradigm of AI-empowered, learner-as-leader education is grounded in connectivism and complex adaptive systems theory. This approach positions the student at the center of the learning process, with AI systems acting as intelligent collaborators that facilitate personalized and adaptive learning experiences. Brain-computer interfaces, machine learning, and deep learning technologies underpin these paradigms, enabling the continuous evolution of educational pathways in response to individual learner data [2, 14]. Practical case studies in dental education further illustrate the impact of AI-driven personalized learning. For example, AI-powered problem-based and case-based learning environments have been shown to enhance clinical reasoning capabilities and student satisfaction compared to traditional instructional methods [20]. These adaptive systems not only support the acquisition of foundational knowledge but also promote the development of higher-order thinking skills essential for clinical practice. While the benefits of personalized learning and adaptive pathways are substantial, challenges remain. Ensuring data privacy, security, and compliance with regulatory standards is critical, particularly given the sensitive nature of student and patient data in dental education. Additionally, effective implementation requires ongoing faculty training and a commitment to transparency in AI decision-making processes [6, 21].

2.3.2 Automated assessment and intelligent feedback

Automated evaluation and intelligent feedback are transforming the educational landscape, particularly in specialized fields such as dental education, by leveraging AI to streamline evaluation processes and enhance learning outcomes. AI-driven assessment systems can automatically collect, analyze, and interpret student performance data, significantly improving both the efficiency and accuracy of formative and summative evaluations. In the context of dental education, where clinical reasoning and case-based learning are central, these systems offer the ability to provide immediate, individualized feedback on complex clinical scenarios, supporting students as they develop diagnostic and procedural competencies. The integration of AI into assessment workflows addresses several longstanding challenges. Traditional assessment methods in health sciences often require substantial instructor time for grading and feedback, which can detract from opportunities for personalized instruction and mentorship. Automated systems alleviate this burden by rapidly processing large volumes of student responses, identifying learning patterns, and highlighting areas for improvement. Moreover, besides reducing instructor workload, feedback is timely and tailored to each learner's needs, which is particularly valuable in fast-paced clinical training environments [1, 5]. AI-powered feedback mechanisms are distinguished by their adaptability and precision. By analyzing student interactions and responses, these systems can detect subtle misconceptions or gaps in understanding that might be overlooked in manual grading. The feedback generated is not generic; instead, it is customized to the individual's learning trajectory, promoting deeper engagement and more effective remediation. The benefits of automated assessment extend beyond efficiency and personalization. AI-driven platforms can support innovative pedagogical approaches, such as adaptive learning pathways and simulation-based training. For example, intelligent systems can present students with virtual patient cases that adjust in complexity based on real-time performance, offering scaffolded challenges that build clinical reasoning skills. These adaptive scenarios are particularly relevant in dental education, where students must integrate foundational knowledge with practical decision-making in diverse clinical contexts [1]. The ability to provide immediate, context-sensitive feedback during such simulations accelerates skill acquisition and supports the development of professional competence. Moreover, the automation of routine assessment tasks, such as grading and progress tracking, frees educators to focus on higher-order instructional activities, including mentoring, curriculum development, and research. AI systems can also facilitate early identification of students who may be struggling, enabling timely interventions and support. This proactive approach is essential in specialized subjects, where early mastery of foundational concepts is critical for success in advanced clinical practice [1, 5]. Despite these advantages, implementing automated assessment and intelligent feedback systems is not without challenges. Ensuring the validity and reliability of AI-generated evaluations requires careful calibration and ongoing oversight by faculty. Data privacy and security are also paramount, given the sensitive nature of student performance records and clinical case data. Faculty training is crucial for maximizing the benefits of these technologies and integrating them effectively into existing curricula [13, 22]. Additionally, the uneven adoption of digital tools across disciplines and institutions highlights the need for strategic planning and resource allocation to ensure equitable access and impact [13]. The transformative potential of AI-powered assessment and feedback is evident in its capacity to enhance student engagement, support individualized learning, and streamline educational processes.

2.3.3 Role of NLP in education

NLP has emerged as a transformative component within AI-driven educational paradigms, fundamentally altering how students interact with content, instructors, and assessment systems. NLP enables machines to interpret, generate, and respond to human language, which is particularly valuable in educational settings where communication and comprehension are crucial to the learning process. The integration of NLP into educational technologies has led to the development of automated assessment systems, intelligent tutoring, and adaptive feedback mechanisms that cater to individual learning trajectories. One of the most significant contributions of NLP in education is its capacity to automate the evaluation of student responses, especially in open-ended or complex tasks. For instance, NLP-enabled systems can assess students' written answers in mathematics or science, providing not only scores but also detailed feedback on conceptual understanding and misconceptions [5]. This approach enables scalable and consistent assessment, reducing the manual grading burden on educators and allowing for more timely interventions for students who require additional support [2, 5]. The adaptability of NLP-based assessment tools is particularly advantageous in specialized domains such as dental education, where clinical reasoning and case analysis are essential. By analyzing students' narrative responses to clinical scenarios, NLP systems can identify gaps in reasoning and suggest targeted resources for improvement [2]. Furthermore, NLP facilitates personalized learning experiences by interpreting students' queries and tailoring instructional content accordingly. Chatbots powered by NLP, such as ChatGPT, have been employed to support interactive learning in various subjects, including the teaching of Excel formulas and digital literacy skills. These systems can engage students in natural dialog, clarify concepts, and provide step-by-step guidance, thereby enhancing engagement and comprehension [14]. The ability of NLP to process and understand context-rich language enables the creation of adaptive learning environments that respond dynamically to each learner's needs [2]. In addition to direct student interaction, NLP plays a crucial role in educational analytics. By processing large volumes of textual data from student submissions, discussion forums, and feedback forms, NLP algorithms can extract meaningful patterns related to learning behaviors, engagement levels, and common misconceptions [1]. This information supports instructors in identifying at-risk students early and refining curriculum delivery to address prevalent challenges [1, 6]. The use of NLP in generating progress reports and comparative analytics, as seen in platforms like ALEKS, empowers both students and educators to monitor learning trajectories and benchmark performance against peers [23]. The integration of NLP into LMS also streamlines administrative and instructional tasks. Automated grading, content recommendation, and intelligent feedback mechanisms are increasingly being embedded within LMS platforms, freeing educators to focus on mentorship and curriculum innovation [1]. In dental education, where the complexity of clinical cases demands nuanced understanding, NLP-driven tools can simulate patient interactions, assess diagnostic reasoning, and provide formative feedback on case-based assignments [3, 19]. By enhancing the authenticity of learning experiences, students are better prepared for real-world clinical decision-making. Despite these advancements, the adoption of NLP in education presents several challenges. Concerns regarding data privacy, algorithmic bias, and the need for faculty training in interpreting AI-generated feedback remain significant [6]. Furthermore, educators have highlighted the risk of students relying excessively on AI-generated responses, which could potentially compromise originality and critical thinking. Addressing these issues requires a balanced approach that combines technological innovation with ethical guidelines and professional development for instructors [1, 6].

3. Digital transformation in dental education

3.1 Traditional dental education models

Traditional dental education models have historically relied on structured, hierarchical approaches that emphasize didactic instruction, standardized curricula, and sequential clinical training. In these models, the educational process is typically centered around the transmission of knowledge from faculty to students, with a strong focus on theoretical foundations during the early years, followed by progressive exposure to clinical practice in later stages. The curriculum is often organized in a linear fashion, where students progress through preclinical sciences, such as oral biology, anatomy, and physiology, before engaging in hands-on patient care under supervision [3]. A defining characteristic of traditional dental education is the teacher-centered paradigm, where instructors serve as the primary source of information and authority. This approach tends to prioritize the acquisition of factual knowledge and technical skills, frequently assessed through written examinations and practical demonstrations. Clinical competence is developed through direct observation, repetition, and feedback from experienced practitioners, with students gradually assuming greater responsibility for patient care as they progress [19]. The structure of these programs often leaves limited room for individualized learning trajectories or adaptation to diverse student needs. Assessment in traditional dental education is predominantly summative, focusing on evaluating student performance at the end of instructional units or clinical rotations. Such assessments are typically standardized, aiming to ensure that all students meet a minimum threshold of competence before advancing. While this model provides a clear framework for progression, it may not fully capture the nuances of clinical reasoning or the ability to integrate knowledge across disciplines [5]. Clinical training within traditional models is heavily dependent on real patient encounters, which are essential for developing diagnostic and procedural skills. However, the variability in patient cases and the constraints of clinical settings can limit the breadth and consistency of student experiences. Opportunities for repeated practice and exposure to rare or complex cases may be restricted, potentially impacting the development of comprehensive clinical competence [24]. Furthermore, the apprenticeship model, while valuable for mentorship, can sometimes perpetuate variability in teaching quality and feedback, depending on the individual instructor's expertise and teaching style. The integration of emerging fields, such as regenerative dentistry, into the curriculum has historically been slow, as traditional models are often anchored in established scientific knowledge and clinical protocols. The limitations of conventional models have become more apparent in the context of increasing student diversity, evolving patient expectations, and rapid technological advancements. The rigidity of standardized curricula and assessment methods may not adequately accommodate the varied backgrounds, learning styles, and career aspirations of contemporary dental students [2]. Moreover, the lack of integration between academic learning and clinical application can create gaps in the transition from theory to practice, potentially affecting the readiness of graduates to address complex, real-world challenges [5]. Despite these challenges, traditional dental education models have provided a robust foundation for the development of competent practitioners. The emphasis on rigorous scientific training, ethical standards, and hands-on clinical experience has contributed to the high quality of dental care in many regions.

3.2 Emergence of e-learning and digital platforms in dentistry

The emergence of e-learning and digital platforms has significantly transformed dental education, particularly in response to the increasing complexity of clinical training and the need for flexible, accessible learning environments. The COVID-19 pandemic accelerated the adoption of digital methodologies, compelling dental educators to transition rapidly to remote teaching modalities. This shift was not merely a temporary solution but has led to the integration of diverse digital platforms and methodologies that continue to shape the educational landscape in dentistry [9]. These platforms enable the continuity of theoretical instruction and practical skill development, even when traditional in-person training is disrupted. Modern e-learning systems in dentistry are characterized by their ability to deliver personalized course content, streamline course creation, and facilitate rapid access to relevant resources. The automation of administrative tasks, such as assessment and feedback, reduces the burden on faculty, allowing them to focus more on mentoring and complex instructional activities. These advancements contribute to greater equity in education and more precise evaluation of student competencies [12]. In large classroom settings and online environments, AI-powered platforms offer robust solutions for resource management and assessment. They address challenges related to scalability and consistency in educational delivery, which are particularly relevant in dental education, where both theoretical knowledge and clinical skills must be assessed rigorously. As these systems evolve, they hold the potential to revolutionize not only the delivery but also the assessment of dental education, moving beyond traditional testing to incorporate more creative and subjective forms of evaluation [2]. This issue is especially pertinent in dentistry, where clinical reasoning and decision-making are as critical as factual knowledge. The adoption of digital and AI-enhanced platforms also necessitates a shift in the responsibilities of educators. In addition to delivering scientifically sound theoretical content, educators must ensure that students are competent in performing clinical procedures of varying complexity. This dual responsibility is supported by digital platforms that offer simulation-based learning, interactive case studies, and adaptive assessments, all of which contribute to the development of practical skills alongside theoretical understanding [9]. The ability to track and analyze student performance data enables targeted interventions and early support for students who may be struggling, thereby enhancing overall educational outcomes. In summary, the emergence of e-learning and digital platforms in dentistry represents a fundamental shift in how dental education is delivered, assessed, and experienced.

The integration of AI and advanced digital tools supports personalized, adaptive, and scalable learning, while also presenting new challenges that require ongoing attention from educators and institutions [1, 9, 12].

4. Personalization and adaptive learning in dental education

4.1 Adaptive content delivery for complex dental topics

Adaptive content delivery for complex dental issues leverages AI to dynamically tailor educational materials to the unique needs and progress of each learner. The use of AI in adaptive content delivery is not limited to generating static resources. Instead, these systems can analyze student interactions, performance data, and engagement patterns to recommend targeted resources, scaffolded case scenarios, and formative assessments. For example, learning analytics embedded within LMS platforms can monitor how students interact with specific modules, identifying areas where learners struggle or excel [8]. This data-driven approach allows the system to adjust the difficulty, format, or sequencing of content, ensuring that students receive the appropriate level of challenge and support as they navigate complex dental topics. In the context of dental education, adaptive systems can present clinical case scenarios that evolve in complexity based on the learner's demonstrated competence. Such systems can simulate real-world decision-making, requiring students to integrate knowledge from multiple domains, such as prosthetics, orthodontics, and periodontology, which are often interlinked in simple – cariology [25] – or advanced – implantology [16] – dental procedures. By continuously assessing student responses and adapting subsequent content, AI-powered LMS platforms promote a more profound understanding and clinical reasoning skills. The integration of multimedia elements, such as images and figures, further enhances the effectiveness of adaptive content delivery. Visual aids are particularly valuable in dental education, where spatial understanding and recognition of anatomical structures are essential. The use of pictures and figures supports the comprehension of complex material and can bridge language barriers, especially when students are learning in a non-native language [11]. This multimodal approach not only aids in knowledge retention but also increases student engagement with challenging topics. AI-driven adaptive content delivery also facilitates the early identification of students who may require additional support. By analyzing patterns in assessment performance and engagement metrics, the system can flag learners at risk of falling behind and prompt timely interventions from instructors [26]. This proactive support is crucial in specialized subjects, where foundational misunderstandings can impede progress in more advanced modules. The application of deep learning techniques within adaptive LMS platforms has shown promise in enhancing instructional quality and visualizing student problem-solving patterns. By modeling how students approach complex clinical problems, these systems can provide personalized feedback and suggest alternative learning pathways. The quality of input data influences the outcomes of AI systems, and there is a risk of bias if the training data are not representative of the diverse student population or clinical scenarios encountered in practice [27]. Furthermore, the integration of adaptive technologies requires ongoing faculty training to ensure that instructors can effectively interpret analytics and intervene when necessary [6]. The potential of

GenAI to create innovative discussion topics, animations, and model texts also contributes to adaptive content delivery by enriching the learning environment and catering to diverse learning preferences. However, the necessity of maintaining a "teacher-in-the-loop" approach is emphasized to ensure that AI-generated content aligns with curricular goals and maintains educational rigor [6]. In summary, adaptive content delivery for complex dental topics is transforming the educational landscape by providing personalized, responsive, and engaging learning experiences. The synergy between AI technologies, multimedia resources, and continuous assessment fosters a learning environment that supports both the acquisition of foundational knowledge and the development of advanced clinical reasoning skills [5].

4.2 Supporting diverse learning needs and equity in education

4.2.1 Addressing individual differences in knowledge acquisition

Addressing individual differences in knowledge acquisition is a central challenge in dental education, particularly as curricula become increasingly complex and student cohorts become more diverse. AI-powered LMSs offer a transformative approach by enabling the analysis of both cognitive and socio-emotional components of student learning. These systems can assess a student's current state of knowledge, as well as their decision-making and awareness, and communicate these insights to teachers, students, and adaptive modules. The integration of adaptive systems within LMS platforms allows for the continuous monitoring and adjustment of educational content. By leveraging data-driven insights, these systems can identify gaps in understanding and adapt instructional materials in real time. This process not only enhances the precision of knowledge delivery but also motivates students by providing immediate, individualized feedback. Such personalization is particularly valuable in dental education, where the mastery of both theoretical concepts and practical skills is essential for clinical competence [12]. AI-driven dashboards further empower students to engage in reflective learning by granting them access to detailed analytics regarding their performance. The use of AI in educational assessment extends beyond traditional testing formats. Automated systems can evaluate complex case scenarios, simulate clinical decision-making, and provide nuanced feedback that mirrors real-world challenges. The transition to digital and online education, accelerated by recent global events, has further underscored the importance of adaptive learning environments. E-learning platforms, enhanced by AI, have enabled the continuation of didactic and practical instruction despite disruptions, ensuring that all students have access to high-quality educational experiences regardless of their circumstances [9]. The ability to personalize content and assessment in virtual settings is particularly beneficial for students with diverse learning needs, as it mitigates the limitations of one-size-fits-all approaches. However, the implementation of AI-powered personalization presents several challenges. Ensuring data privacy, maintaining the validity of adaptive assessments, and providing adequate faculty training are essential to maximize the benefits of these technologies. Furthermore, strategies must be developed to prevent over-reliance on AI, which could inadvertently undermine the development of critical thinking and the ability to synthesize knowledge across domains.

4.2.2 Facilitating self-paced and competency-based progression

By leveraging adaptive algorithms, AI-powered LMS platforms enable students to access educational content at any time, allowing for flexible engagement that aligns with individual schedules and learning speeds. Through dashboards and analytics, learners can monitor their progress, review assessment outcomes, and identify areas requiring further attention [22]. This transparency empowers students to take ownership of their educational journey, enabling them to make informed decisions about when to revisit material or seek additional support. The adaptive nature of these systems ensures that content delivery is dynamically adjusted to focus on each learner's strengths and weaknesses [1]. Such personalization not only supports equity in education but also promotes deeper engagement and sustained motivation. Competency-based progression is reinforced by the ability of AI-driven platforms to assess specific assignments and provide immediate, automated feedback. At the same time, more complex tasks are evaluated by instructors who can offer targeted commentary through the virtual learning environment [28]. This dual approach ensures that students receive both rapid, objective feedback and nuanced, expert guidance. The global grade book functionality enables the transparent tracking of competencies achieved, facilitating the early identification of students who may benefit from additional resources or interventions. The educational impact of these technologies extends beyond mere content delivery. The shift toward self-paced and competency-based progression also aligns with the broader educational imperative to cultivate self-directed learners. Scott et al. [10] emphasize the importance of integrating self-directed learning strategies within dental curricula, particularly in online and flipped classroom settings. AI-powered LMS platforms provide the scaffolding necessary for students to develop these skills, as they are required to set goals, monitor their progress, and actively seek out resources. Despite these advantages, the successful implementation of AI-driven, self-paced learning environments requires careful consideration of challenges such as data privacy and the need for faculty training.

5. Curriculum development and alignment

5.1 Aligning AI-driven LMS with accreditation standards

Aligning AI-driven LMS with accreditation standards in dental education requires a multifaceted approach that integrates technological innovation with rigorous educational frameworks. Accreditation bodies typically mandate that curricula be structured around clear learning objectives, professional competencies, and authentic assessment strategies. Therefore, AI-powered LMS must be designed to support these requirements by ensuring that modules and learning units are logically organized, beginning with well-defined objectives and progressing through content, activities, and assignments that are directly mapped to competency frameworks [28]. This logical progression is essential for demonstrating compliance with accreditation standards, as it provides transparent evidence of how educational outcomes are achieved and assessed. The integration of AI into LMS platforms presents unique opportunities to enhance curriculum delivery and the authenticity of assessment. By leveraging LMS analytics, faculty can monitor student access to course materials, participation in learning activities, and performance on formative assessments. This data-driven approach not only supports the early identification of students who may require additional support but also provides documentation that can be presented during accreditation reviews to illustrate the effectiveness of instructional strategies and student support mechanisms [10].

The successful integration of AI into LMS platforms must also address institutional infrastructure and strategic planning. Rashid et al. [6] emphasize the importance of institutions conducting comprehensive analyses of their technological infrastructure, ensuring that hardware, software, and cybersecurity measures are sufficient to support AI adoption. Pilot programs can be implemented to test the effectiveness of AI tools in specific curricular areas, with data from these initiatives informing broader implementation strategies. This iterative approach allows institutions to align technological innovation with accreditation requirements, minimizing disruption while maximizing educational benefits. Accreditation standards often require evidence that instructional methods are appropriate for the subject matter and that they effectively support student learning. By providing a flexible framework for integrating AI into diverse curricular areas, institutions can ensure that their LMS platforms not only meet but exceed accreditation requirements, ultimately enhancing the quality and accountability of dental education.

5.2 Dynamic curriculum updates and content curation

The integration of AI-powered LMS increasingly shapes dynamic curriculum updates and content curation in dental education. These systems enable the rapid adaptation of curricular materials to reflect advances in dental science, regulatory changes, and evolving clinical practices. The ability of AI to analyze large datasets and educational outcomes facilitates the identification of gaps in student knowledge, allowing for the subsequent recommendation or automatic inclusion of targeted content updates. This process ensures that learners are exposed to the most current and relevant information, which is particularly critical in specialized fields such as oral biology and regenerative dentistry, where scientific progress is rapid [1, 29]. AI-driven LMS platforms enable the customization and adaptation of learning content to meet individual student needs, thereby enhancing the overall quality of education. By continuously monitoring student performance and engagement, these systems can dynamically adjust the curriculum, presenting remedial modules or advanced topics as appropriate. This adaptive approach not only enhances learning experiences but also supports early intervention for students who may be struggling, thus promoting equitable educational outcomes [6]. Content curation is further enhanced by AI algorithms that can sift through vast repositories of educational materials, research articles, and clinical case studies. These algorithms can recommend or automatically integrate high-quality, evidence-based resources into the curriculum, ensuring that both foundational knowledge and cutting-edge developments are represented. The dynamic nature of AI-powered content curation also addresses the need for ongoing faculty development. As new technologies and methodologies are introduced, educators must be equipped to integrate these tools effectively into their teaching. A significant proportion of stakeholders believe that faculty should receive training not only in the use of AI but also in identifying academic integrity issues, such as originality in student submissions [12]. AI has a dual role in updating curricular content and supporting ethical standards in education. Despite these advantages, challenges remain in ensuring the reliability and transparency of AI-curated content. Ethical considerations, such as data privacy and the responsible use of student performance data, must also be addressed. As AI systems increasingly influence curriculum development and content curation, robust policies and transparent practices are required to protect student information and maintain trust in educational institutions [12, 30].

6. Ethical, legal, and social considerations

6.1 Data privacy and security in AI-powered LMS

The integration of AI technologies into LMS platforms necessitates the collection, processing, and storage of vast amounts of sensitive student data, including academic records, clinical performance metrics, and potentially even biometric information. Ensuring the confidentiality, integrity, and availability of this data is essential to maintain trust among students, educators, and regulatory bodies. One of the primary challenges is compliance with data protection regulations, which are designed to safeguard personal information and prevent unauthorized access or misuse. Rigorous adherence to these requirements is not only a legal obligation but also a critical factor in upholding the ethical standards of educational institutions. By enabling AI models to be trained across multiple servers or devices without exchanging raw data, federated learning minimizes the exposure of sensitive information. It reduces the risk of centralized data breaches [1]. This approach aligns with the principle of data minimization, ensuring that only essential information is processed and that student privacy is prioritized throughout the AI training lifecycle. Despite these technological advancements, the risk of systematic bias and the potential for prejudice in AI algorithms remain significant concerns. Engaging multidisciplinary teams in the development and oversight of AI systems can help identify and address sources of bias, ensuring that the deployment of AI in LMS platforms is both fair and equitable [2]. Transparent communication with students regarding how their data are used and how AI contributes to their educational assessments further strengthens confidence in the system. It supports the ethical use of technology in education. Energy consumption is another aspect that intersects with data privacy and security. The substantial computing power required to train sophisticated AI models can lead to increased environmental impact, which in turn raises questions about the sustainability of large-scale data processing in educational settings [1]. Developing energy-efficient AI solutions is, therefore, not only an environmental imperative but also a means to reduce the operational footprint of data centers that store and process sensitive educational data. The adoption of AI-powered LMS in dental education also introduces new vectors for potential misuse or unauthorized access. For instance, if security measures are inadequate, there is a risk that malicious actors could exploit vulnerabilities to gain access to confidential student records or manipulate assessment outcomes. Regular security assessments, penetration testing, and the implementation of advanced threat detection systems are necessary to safeguard against such threats [1, 2].

DOI: http://dx.doi.org/10.5772/intechopen.1012781

Furthermore, the ethical dimension of data privacy extends to the transparency of AI decision-making processes. Students and faculty must be able to understand how AI-driven recommendations or assessments are generated, particularly when these outputs influence academic progression or clinical competency evaluations. Ensuring interpretability and explainability in AI models is vital for maintaining accountability and addressing concerns related to algorithmic opacity [31]. Immediate feedback and adaptive learning pathways can be delivered effectively while still adhering to strict privacy standards, provided that the underlying systems are engineered with security as a core principle. In summary, the integration of AI-powered LMS in dental education demands a comprehensive approach to data privacy and security.

6.2 Academic integrity and risk of misconduct

As AI systems become more adept at generating human-like responses and providing instant feedback, there is a growing concern that students may become overly reliant on these technologies, potentially undermining their ability to engage in independent study and creative problem-solving. The risk is not limited to diminished critical thinking; there is also the potential for academic dishonesty, as students might use AI-generated content to bypass genuine learning or assessment processes. ChatGPT and similar AI chatbots, which utilize advanced NLP, exemplify these challenges. While they can support students in understanding complex concepts and simulating clinical scenarios, they also make it easier for learners to access ready-made answers, which may not always be accurate or contextually appropriate. This ease of access can tempt students to submit AI-generated responses as their own, blurring the line between legitimate assistance and plagiarism. The flexibility of platforms like Moodle, which accommodate diverse assessment formats, can be both strength and vulnerability, as it may allow for unconventional or unauthorized methods of completing assignments [7]. This necessitates continuous monitoring and updating of assessment protocols to ensure that academic standards are upheld.

Faculty training emerges as a crucial factor in mitigating the risk of misconduct. Instructors must be equipped not only to use AI tools effectively but also to recognize signs of academic dishonesty and implement strategies that promote integrity, including designing assessments that require higher-order thinking, encouraging reflective practice, and fostering an environment where ethical considerations are integral to the learning process [22]. The need for ongoing professional development is further emphasized by the rapid evolution of AI technologies and the corresponding shifts in educational practices [18]. Data privacy is another dimension that intersects with academic integrity. The collection and analysis of student performance data by AI systems must be conducted transparently and ethically, with clear guidelines on data usage and protection [22]. Any breach of confidentiality or misuse of personal information can erode trust in the educational system and create additional avenues for misconduct. While AI-powered LMS platforms offer transformative potential for dental education, they also introduce new risks related to academic integrity and misconduct. Addressing these challenges requires a multifaceted approach that combines technological safeguards, critical pedagogy, faculty training, and a strong ethical framework [7, 22].

6.3 Addressing bias and ensuring fairness in AI algorithms

Bias in AI can originate from multiple sources, including the data used for training, the design of the algorithms, and the lack of diversity in development teams [1]. When AI systems are trained on datasets that do not adequately represent the diversity of the student population or clinical cases, the resulting models may perpetuate or even amplify existing inequities, which can be particularly problematic in educational settings, where fairness in assessment and feedback is essential for maintaining trust and supporting equitable learning outcomes [2]. Transparency in the operation of AI algorithms is another critical factor for promoting fairness. Many AI models, especially those based on deep learning, are often perceived as black boxes, making it difficult for educators and students to understand how decisions are made. This opacity can hinder the identification and correction of biased outputs. In the context of automated clinical assessments and intelligent feedback, AI systems must be carefully monitored to prevent systematic bias from influencing student evaluations. The integration of AI into dental education also raises challenges related to the accuracy and fairness of diagnostic algorithms. Addressing bias and ensuring fairness in AI algorithms within dental education requires a multifaceted strategy, which includes diverse team composition, inclusive and representative datasets, transparent algorithmic processes, ongoing human oversight, and clear communication with all stakeholders [1, 2, 32]. By systematically implementing these measures, AI-powered LMS can support equitable learning experiences and uphold the integrity of dental education.

7. Future directions for AI in dental education

7.1 Emerging technologies and innovations

Emerging technologies in AI are rapidly transforming the landscape of dental education, introducing innovative approaches that promise to reshape learning environments and pedagogical strategies. The integration of advanced machine learning and deep learning models into LMS is enabling a shift toward highly personalized and adaptive educational experiences. These systems can analyze vast amounts of student data to tailor content delivery, recommend targeted resources, and dynamically adjust learning pathways based on individual progress and performance metrics [1]. Such personalization is expected to enhance both the efficiency and effectiveness of dental education, as students receive instruction and feedback that are closely aligned with their unique needs and learning styles [1, 21]. The application of convolutional neural networks and other deep learning architectures has shown promise in automating complex tasks such as image analysis, caries detection, and anatomical segmentation, which are integral to dental training and assessment. These models excel at extracting relevant features from large datasets, reducing the need for manual annotation and enabling more scalable and objective evaluation processes. However, their successful deployment in educational settings is contingent upon access to high-quality annotated data and substantial computational resources, which remain significant barriers to widespread adoption [4]. GenAI technologies, exemplified by large language models like ChatGPT, are also beginning to influence dental education by supporting the creation of interactive simulations, automated essay grading, and real-time feedback mechanisms [6, 27]. These systems can generate human-like responses, facilitate natural language interactions, and provide learners with immediate, context-sensitive guidance. The ability of GenAI to interpret and analyze student input in various formats, including written responses and creative assignments, opens new avenues for assessing higher-order cognitive skills and fostering critical thinking. Johnson and Lee have demonstrated that advanced neural networks can evaluate creativity and originality in student work, suggesting that future LMS platforms may incorporate sophisticated tools for holistic assessment [2]. Active learning strategies, supported by AI-driven platforms, are gaining traction to deepen student engagement and promote self-directed exploration of complex concepts. Interactive simulations, adaptive quizzes, and personalized feedback loops are being integrated into LMS environments, allowing students to experiment, reflect, and iterate on their understanding in a low-risk setting. These approaches are complemented by cybernetic models that emphasize self-observation and emotional intelligence, further enriching the educational experience [33]. In the context of clinical education, AI-powered diagnostic tools are demonstrating high accuracy in tasks such as identifying crossbites and predicting treatment outcomes, with reported accuracies exceeding 90% in some cases [34]. The integration of these diagnostic models with LMS platforms could enable students to practice clinical decision-making in realistic, data-driven scenarios, bridging the gap between theoretical knowledge and practical application [21, 34]. Despite these advances, several challenges must be addressed to fully realize the potential of emerging AI technologies in dental education. Data privacy and security are paramount concerns, as the collection and analysis of sensitive student information necessitate robust safeguards and transparent governance frameworks [1].

Additionally, the interpretability of complex AI models remains a significant issue, with educators and students alike requiring clear explanations of algorithmic decisions to build trust and facilitate meaningful learning [4]. The effective integration of AI into existing educational infrastructures also demands careful planning, ongoing faculty development, and iterative evaluation to ensure that technological innovations translate into measurable improvements in academic outcomes [7, 19]. The future trajectory of AI in dental education will likely be shaped by continued advancements in machine learning, deep learning, and GenAI, as well as the emergence of new paradigms for adaptive and personalized learning. As these technologies mature, they hold the promise of making dental education more accessible, equitable, and responsive to the evolving needs of both students and the profession [1, 6, 19, 21].

7.2 Long-term impact on dental training and professional practice

The integration of AI-powered LMS into dental education is expected to have profound and enduring effects on both dental training and subsequent professional practice. One of the most significant long-term impacts is the shift toward highly individualized learning pathways. AI-driven LMS platforms can analyze student interactions and performance data to tailor educational content, pacing, and assessment to each learner's unique needs, thereby supporting mastery of both theoretical and clinical competencies [8, 20]. This adaptive approach not only enhances knowledge retention but also allows students to revisit complex procedures and concepts until proficiency is achieved, which is especially valuable in a field as skill-dependent as dentistry [18]. Over time, the use of AI in dental education is likely to produce practitioners who are more adept at self-directed learning and continuous professional development. The ability to access personalized feedback and real-time analytics encourages reflective practice and lifelong learning habits, which are essential in a rapidly evolving healthcare landscape [20, 32].

Furthermore, the incorporation of AI-based formative and summative assessments enables more objective and comprehensive evaluation of student performance, reducing potential biases and ensuring that graduates meet consistent standards of competence [2, 5]. The long-term impact extends beyond the educational phase into clinical practice. As AI systems become more integrated into dental curricula, future practitioners will be better prepared to utilize AI tools in diagnostics, treatment planning, and patient management. For instance, AI algorithms can assist in analyzing complex datasets, identifying subtle patterns in patient records, and supporting evidence-based decision-making, which can lead to improved patient outcomes and more efficient clinical workflows [18, 35]. A dual focus on theoretical and practical education, facilitated by AI, equips dental professionals with both technical and soft skills necessary for modern practice [32]. However, the transition to AI-enhanced dental education is not without challenges that may influence its long-term effectiveness. The psychological impact of rapid technological change on students, including increased stress and anxiety, must be addressed to ensure that future practitioners are resilient and adaptable.

Additionally, the sudden shift to digital and remote learning environments, as observed during the COVID-19 pandemic, has highlighted the need for robust support systems to maintain the quality of training and safeguard student well-being [9]. These factors can have lasting effects on professional identity formation and readiness for clinical practice. Another critical consideration is the transparency and interpretability of AI systems. The "black box" nature of many AI and AutoML frameworks can limit users' understanding of how decisions are made, potentially undermining trust in both educational and clinical contexts [4]. Addressing these concerns through the development of explainable AI models and clear guidelines for ethical use will be essential for the sustained integration of AI into dental education and practice. The evolution of AI capabilities in literacy, numeracy, and clinical reasoning is outpacing traditional educational methods, necessitating a redefinition of learning environments to encompass both digital and experiential components [13]. The long-term impact of AI-powered LMS will thus be characterized by a more dynamic, responsive, and equitable approach to dental training, ultimately shaping a generation of professionals who are not only clinically competent but also technologically literate and ethically grounded. Ultimately, the integration of AI into dental education is likely to impact the broader healthcare ecosystem by fostering interdisciplinary collaboration, driving data-driven decision-making, and cultivating a culture of innovation. As dental professionals become more comfortable with AI tools, they will be better positioned to contribute to advancements in patient care, research, and public health initiatives. The cumulative effect of these changes will be a transformation in both the practice and perception of dentistry, with long-term benefits for practitioners, patients, and society at large.

8. Conclusion(s)

The integration of artificial intelligence into dental education marks a transformative shift in how curricula are delivered, assessed, and personalized to meet the diverse needs of learners. AI-powered LMSs have demonstrated significant potential in enhancing educational outcomes by enabling adaptive learning pathways, automating complex clinical assessments, and providing intelligent, immediate feedback tailored to individual student profiles. These advancements contribute to a deeper comprehension of specialized subjects while also supporting the development of critical clinical reasoning and problem-solving skills essential for modern dental practice.

The evolution of AI technologies within educational infrastructures has facilitated the creation of more equitable and inclusive learning environments. By addressing individual differences in knowledge acquisition and accommodating diverse learning styles, AI-driven systems promote self-paced, competency-based progression that aligns with contemporary pedagogical theories. The incorporation of intelligent tutoring systems, automated grading, personalized content recommendations, and predictive analytics collectively enhances student engagement, motivation, and academic performance. Moreover, the use of simulation platforms and virtual patients provides risk-free opportunities for students to apply theoretical knowledge in realistic clinical scenarios, thereby bridging the gap between classroom learning and practical application. Despite these promising developments, several challenges must be acknowledged and addressed to ensure the responsible and effective implementation of AI in dental education. Technical and infrastructural demands, including the need for robust hardware, secure data management, and seamless interoperability across institutions, require substantial investment and strategic planning. Ethical considerations surrounding data privacy, algorithmic bias, and academic integrity necessitate transparent policies, multidisciplinary oversight, and comprehensive training for faculty. The evolving roles of educators emphasize facilitation, mentorship, and critical evaluation of AI-generated outputs, underscoring the importance of human judgment alongside technological innovation.

Institutional commitment to sustainable AI adoption involves continuous curriculum alignment with accreditation standards, dynamic content curation, and the cultivation of faculty competencies in AI literacy and ethical practice. Collaborative efforts among educators, technologists, and policymakers are crucial for developing scalable, adaptable, and context-sensitive AI solutions that enhance educational quality while ensuring equity and inclusivity. Furthermore, ongoing research and innovation are vital to optimizing AI applications, exploring energy-efficient methodologies, and evaluating the long-term impact on student learning and clinical competence.

In summary, the integration of AI-powered LMSs represents a pivotal advancement in dental education, offering unprecedented opportunities to personalize learning, streamline assessment, and prepare future clinicians for the complexities of contemporary practice. Realizing the full potential of these technologies depends on a balanced approach that combines technological capabilities with ethical stewardship, faculty development, and institutional support, thereby ensuring that AI catalyzes meaningful and equitable

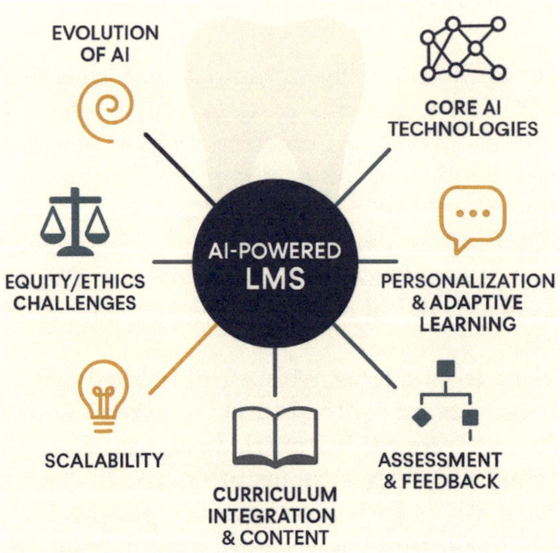

Figure 1.
AI-generated visual concept diagram summarizing the impact of AI-powered LMS in dental education. Generated with Microsoft Copilot on June 29, 2025.

educational transformation. To provide a glimpse of an AI-driven future, I used several AI tools (GitHub, Microsoft Copilot) to visually summarize this chapter in **Figure 1**.

Author details

Mihnea Ioan Nicolescu[1,2,3*]

1 Histology and Regenerative Dentistry, Faculty of Dentistry, "Carol Davila" University of Medicine and Pharmacy, Bucharest, Romania

2 Centre for Host-Microbiome Interactions, Faculty of Dentistry, Oral & Craniofacial Sciences, King's College London, London SE1 1UL, United Kingdom

3 Radiobiology Laboratory, "Victor Babeș" National Institute of Pathology, Bucharest, Romania

*Address all correspondence to: mihnea.nicolescu@umfcd.ro

References

[1] Aballa Nkechi A, Ojo AO, and Eneh OA. Impact of artificial intelligence in achieving quality education. In: Kadry S, editor Artificial Intelligence First Edition. Artificial Intelligence and Education - Shaping the Future of Learning. London, United Kingdom: IntechOpen; 2024. p. 1–24. Available from: https://www.intechopen.com/chapters/1181881 [Accessed: 2025-June-29]

[2] Gnanaprakasam J, and Lourdusamy R. The role of AI in automating grading: Enhancing feedback and efficiency. In: Kadry S, editor Artificial Intelligence First Edition. Artificial Intelligence and Education - Shaping the Future of Learning. London, United Kingdom: IntechOpen; 2024. p. 1–18. Available from: https://www.intechopen.com/chapters/1181936; 2024. [Accessed: 2025-June-29]

[3] Nicolescu MI. Regenerative perspective in modern dentistry. Dentistry Journal. 2016;**4**:10

[4] Shujaat S. Automated machine learning in dentistry: A narrative review of applications, challenges, and future directions. Diagnostics. 2025;**15**:273

[5] Ouyang F, Dinh TA, Xu W. A systematic review of AI-driven educational assessment in STEM education. Journal for STEM Educ Res. 2023;**6**:408–426

[6] Faisal Rashid S, Duong-Trung N, and Pinkwart N. Generative AI in Education: Technical Foundations, Applications, and Challenges. In: Kadry S, editor. Artificial Intelligence First Edition. Artificial Intelligence and Education - Shaping the Future of Learning. London, United Kingdom: IntechOpen; 2024. p. 1–21. Available from: https://www.intechopen.com/chapters/1181569 [Accessed: 2025-June-29]

[7] El Tantawi MMA, Abdelsalam MM, Mourady AM, et al. e-Assessment in a limited-resources dental school using an Open-Source learning management system. Journal of Dental Education. 2015;**79**:571–583

[8] Chan AKM, Botelho MG, Lam OLT. An exploration of student access to a learning management system—challenges and recommendations for educators and researchers. European Journal of Dental Education. 2021;**25**:846–855

[9] Camilla Carvalho Laureano I, Fábia Cabral Cavalcanti A, and Leite Cavalcanti A. Impact of COVID-19 on Dental Education. In: M MCS, editor. Virtual Learning First Edition. E-Learning and Digital Education in the Twenty-First Century. London, United Kingdom: IntechOpen; 2022. p. 1–15. Available from: https://www.intechopen.com/chapters/77837 [Accessed: 2025-June-29]

[10] Scott JM, Bohaty BS, Gadbury-Amyot CC. Using learning management software data to compare students' actual and self-reported viewing of video lectures. Journal of Dental Education. 2021;**85**:1674–1682

[11] Ohsato A, Seki N, Nguyen TTT, et al. Evaluating e-learning on an international scale: An audit of computer simulation learning materials in the field of dentistry. Journal of Dental Sciences. 2022;**17**:535–544

[12] Escalona-Márquez L N, Cedeño-Tapia S J, Alberto Camputaro L, et al. Teachers in the Age of Artificial Intelligence: Preparation and Response to Challenges. In: Kadry S, editor Artificial Intelligence First Edition. Artificial Intelligence and Education - Shaping the Future of Learning. London, United Kingdom: IntechOpen; 2024. p. 1-15. Available from: https://www.intechopen.com/chapters/1180936; 2024. [Accessed: 2025-June29]

[13] Flogie A, Krabonja MV. Artificial Intelligence in Education: Developing Competencies and Supporting Teachers in Implementing AI in School Learning Environments. In: 2023 12th Mediterranean Conference on Embedded Computing (MECO). Budva, Montenegro: IEEE, pp. 1–6

[14] Yalcinalp S, Türkoğlu H, Engin Koc S, et al. Utilization of Artificial Intelligence in Education: A Perspective on Learning Strategies. In: Kadry S, editor Artificial Intelligence First Edition. Artificial Intelligence and Education - Shaping the Future of Learning. London, United Kingdom: IntechOpen; 2024. p. 1–31. Available from: https://www.intechopen.com/chapters/1180213 [Accessed: 2025-June-29]

[15] Dong H, Guo C, Zhou L, et al. Effectiveness of case-based learning in Chinese dental education: A systematic review and meta-analysis. BMJ Open. 2022;**12**:e048497

[16] Machoy ME, Szyszka-Sommerfeld L, Vegh A, et al. The ways of using machine learning in dentistry. Advances in Clinical and Experimental Medicine. 2020;**29**:375–384

[17] Busnatu S, Niculescu A-G, Bolocan A, et al. A review of digital health and biotelemetry: Modern approaches towards personalized medicine and remote health assessment. Journal of Personalized Medicine. 2022;**12**:1656

[18] Dave M, Patel N. Artificial intelligence in healthcare and education. British Dental Journal. 2023;**234**: 761–764

[19] Dragan IF, Walji M, Vervoorn M, et al. ADEA-ADEE shaping the future of dental education III: The impact of scientific technologies and discoveries on oral health globally. Journal of Dental Education. 2020;**84**:111–116

[20] Wei H, Dai Y, Yuan K, et al. AI-powered problem- and case-based learning in medical and dental education: A systematic review and meta-analysis. International Dental Journal. 2025;**75**:100858

[21] Wang L, Xu Y, Wang W, et al. Application of machine learning in dentistry: Insights, prospects and challenges. Acta Odontologica Scandinavica. 2025;**84**:145–154

[22] Moskovich L, Rozani V. Health profession students' perceptions of ChatGPT in healthcare and education: Insights from a mixed-methods study. BMC Medical Education. 2025;**25**:98

[23] Eunkyung H. AI-Based Edutech for Adaptive Teaching and Learning. In: Kadry S, editor Artificial Intelligence First Edition. Artificial Intelligence and Education - Shaping the Future of Learning. London, United Kingdom: IntechOpen; 2024. p. 1–13. Available from: https://www.intechopen.com/chapters/1178386 [Accessed: 2025-June-29]

[24] Hui Z, Zewu Z, Jiao H, et al. Application of ChatGPT-assisted

problem-based learning teaching method in clinical medical education. BMC Medical Education. 2025;**25**:50

[25] Gălbinaşu BM, Manolea HO, Matei I, et al. A software approach for identifying the effect of dental caries on dentin-enamel junction. Romanian Journal of Morphology and Embryology. 2021;**62**:255–262

[26] Kale RR, Deshpande S. Effects of training module regarding learning management system (LMS) on knowledge and attitude of dental undergraduates toward use of LMS. Journal of Advances in Dental Practice and Research. 2024;**2**:34–38

[27] Ding H, Wu J, Zhao W, et al. Artificial intelligence in dentistry—A review. Frontiers in Dental Medicine. 2023;**4**:1085251

[28] Schönwetter DJ, Reynolds PA, Eaton KA, et al. Online learning in dentistry: An overview of the future direction for dental education: Online Learning In dentistry. Journal of Oral Rehabilitation. 2010;**37**:927–940

[29] Pang X, Li L, Liu X, et al. Application of emerging teaching models in dental education: A systematic review and meta-analysis. International Dental Journal. 2024;**74**:1185–1196

[30] Sarhan S, Badran A, Ghalwash D, et al. Perception, usage, and concerns of artificial intelligence applications among postgraduate dental students: Cross-sectional study. BMC Medical Education. 2025;**25**:856

[31] Rastogi D, Johri P, Donelli M, et al. Deep learning-integrated MRI brain tumor analysis: Feature extraction, segmentation, and Survival Prediction using Replicator and volumetric networks. Scientific Reports. 2025;**15**:1437

[32] Tuygunov N, Samaranayake L, Khurshid Z, et al. The transformative role of artificial intelligence in dentistry: A comprehensive overview Part 2: The promise and perils, and the international dental federation communique. International Dental Journal. 2025;**75**:397–404

[33] Flogie A, and Aberšek B. Artificial Intelligence in Education. In: Lutsenko O, and Lutsenko G, editors Education First Edition. Active Learning - Theory and Practice. London, United Kingdom: IntechOpen; 2022. p. 1–21. Available from: https://www.intechopen.com/chapters/75444 [Accessed: 2025-June-29]

[34] Samaranayake L, Tuygunov N, Schwendicke F, et al. The transformative role of artificial intelligence in dentistry: A comprehensive overview. Part 1: Fundamentals of AI, and its contemporary applications in dentistry. International Dental Journal. 2025;**75**:383–396

[35] Srivastava B, Chandra S, Singh SK, et al. Artificial intelligence in dentistry: It's applications, impact and challenges. Asian Journal of Oral Health and Allied Sciences. 2023;**13**:7

Chapter 26

Comparative Analysis of Large Language Models (LLMs) in Generating Medical Board-Style Assessment Items

Sage Arbor, Mariluz Henshaw, Raquel Ritchie, Verena Van Fleet and Tafline Arbor

Abstract

This study explores the emerging field of artificial intelligence (AI) in medical education, with a focus on the application of large language models (LLMs) in creating and explaining medical school-level assessment items. Recent attention has focused on how LLMs have the potential to reduce faculty time and effort in creating assessment items, but prior studies predominantly focus on a single LLM model (ChatGPT) and usually do not employ exemplars. We investigated the capabilities of three GPT and five Claude LLM models in creating medical board-style assessment items with two-shot biochemistry exemplars. The generated questions were evaluated by biomedical science educators in their respective fields for their accuracy, educational value, and overall quality. The findings indicate a notable potential of these LLMs in medical education, with the OpenAI ChatGPTs and Claude-V2 AIs demonstrating an ability to produce particularly high-quality assessment items. However, exemplars for each specific discipline may be required to increase the quality of the questions, as anatomy questions performed more poorly. Automated daily creation of exam banks with specified percentages across question categories was also tested, showing initial accuracy but degrading over time. In addition, we developed a GPT-4o-based interactive bot to build medical assessment items, called medStudent QandA, that is free and accessible to all OpenAI account holders (including free-tier users at the time of publication). This work opens multiple avenues for integrating AI into medical-level education and assessment settings, highlighting the evolving role of technology in medical education institutions and frameworks.

Keywords: assessment, board-style questions, high-stakes testing, AI, medical school, artificial intelligence, ChatGPT, Claude, LLM, large language model, chatbot, and medical education

1. Introduction

The integration of artificial intelligence (AI) in medical education has seen notable progress in recent years [1–3]. Large language models (LLMs), like GPT

(3.5, 4, 4.1) and Claude (v1, v2, 3 Haiku, Sonnet, and Opus), developed by OpenAI and Anthropic, respectively, have shown promise in a variety of areas for generating human-like text responses. This capability extends to the field of medical education, where the generation of high-quality board-style assessment items is crucial but requires significant investment of time, effort, and institutional resources, given the need for faculty expertise in clinical content, biomedical science, and medical education pedagogy.

This comparative study evaluates the efficacy of different LLMs in creating medical board-style multiple-choice assessment items, both with and without discipline-specific exemplars. Additionally, we present the development of the MedStudent QandA, an interactive tool based on GPT-4o, designed to facilitate real-time generation of multiple-choice clinical vignettes with explanations for all answer choices, targeted at the medical student population. Lastly, the instruction-following ability of an LLM and its degradation over time are investigated when asked to add to an exam bank with instructions to maintain the breadth of topics to match a predefined percentage per biomedical topic. This research explores the quality of LLM-generated medical assessment questions, potential benefits and limitations for interactive medical student use, and the change in autonomous additional LLM use over time.

2. Background

The construction of high-quality board-style medical questions is an onerous task for medical faculty, who continually add and modify as medications change or curricula are redesigned. A quality high-stakes medical school board-style question is multiple-choice, has a single best answer, reasonable distractors, is not a pseudo question (i.e., not misleading, ambiguous, or testing trivial knowledge), and adheres to extensive rules of formatting. Natural language processing, as the basis of LLMs, is well aligned with following these rules and could be of great value to medical educators in assessment item creation [4]. LLMs have demonstrated great potential for generating high-quality medical-level assessment items that are similar to those created by medical educators. Many studies have evaluated or described the potential of LLMs in medical-level multiple-choice assessment item creation [5–7]. The vast majority of these studies explore only a single version of ChatGPT. Studies focus on the quality of assessment items created, with variation in the findings as well as variation in the quality of input. ChatGPT can produce valid and reliable questions, although expert oversight is necessary to ensure accuracy and relevance [6].

The use of LLMs in exam and case scenario construction increases the number of questions, frees up faculty time, and allows standardized formatting of items [7–9] The ability of LLMs to perform well on USMLE licensing examination questions and complex clinical scenarios suggests an adequate knowledge base to form meaningful medical questions [10–13].

However, expert oversight is necessary with LLMs, given their creation of content (hallucinations) and incorrect answers at times [7, 14]. Google Bard attempts to get various LLMs to produce medical disinformation using jailbreaking techniques, and safeguards were inconsistent across various LLMs [15]. Many LLMs, like ChatGPT, help increase efficiency and generate initial drafts of assessment items [4–6, 8]. The knowledge in LLMs has proven adequate to perform well on medical licensing exams such as the USMLE [11–13], and the use of LLMs has proven effective for teaching medical students [7, 9, 11]. To reach an appropriate quality, human review and revision are necessary for oversight.

3. Methods

3.1 LLMs and prompt design

This study evaluated eight leading LLMs: GPT (3.5, 4, 4-turbo) and Claude (v1, v2, Haiku, Sonnet, Opus) [16–20]. Each model was provided with a standardized prompt (see **Appendix A**), designed to elicit the generation of foundational science medical board-style assessment items. The prompt focused on various topics within biochemistry, reflecting the typical content of the USMLE Step-1 or COMLEX Level 1 clinical board-style assessments. A question bank of 100 biochemistry items was created with Claude-v1 by generating 10 assessment items at a time. After each set of 10 assessment items was produced, a table listing the topics already covered was updated so the LLM could create content in other categories to avoid duplication (see **Appendix B**). This process was intended to confirm the ease of creating large numbers of assessment items. Five questions were then randomly selected from the 100 Claude-v1-generated assessment items for the comparative study. Five biochemistry assessment items were also produced by each of seven other LLMs (GPT-3.5, GPT-4, GPT-4 turbo, Claude-v2, Claude Haiku, Claude Sonnet, Claude Opus) to gauge the difference in LLM assessment item quality. Additionally, five anatomy assessment items were produced by Claude-v2 and assessed by an anatomy medical educator to evaluate assessment item creation for a biomedical science discipline not covered in the exemplar data. The authors used paid memberships with OpenAI and Anthropic to access all models above the base GPT-3.5 and Claude-v1 to complete these tasks.

The ability of an LLM to follow prompts, creating board-style questions over multiple days while abiding by a predefined distribution of content, was investigated. OpenAI's scheduled tasks, which at the time of writing used GPT-4o were set up to run daily at 9:00 a.m. with the prompt "I would like you to make 5 biochemistry board-style examination questions per day for medical students that are becoming doctors," prepended to the prior prompt shown in **Appendix A**. Drift over time was analyzed (see **Figure 1**)

3.2 Evaluation procedure

Generated biochemistry assessment items were evaluated by a panel of three biochemistry medical educators from diverse institutions, while the anatomy assessment items were evaluated by one anatomy medical educator. Medical educators submitted data in a Google Sheets template for each assessment item and were blind to which items were generated by each LLM. Evaluations were initially conducted on four LLMs (GPT-3, GPT-4, Claude-v1, and Claude-v2), while four months later, another round of evaluations on four new LLM models was performed (GPT-4 turbo, Claude Haiku, Claude Sonnet, and Claude Opus) to keep the investigation timely. The data collected for each assessment item include:

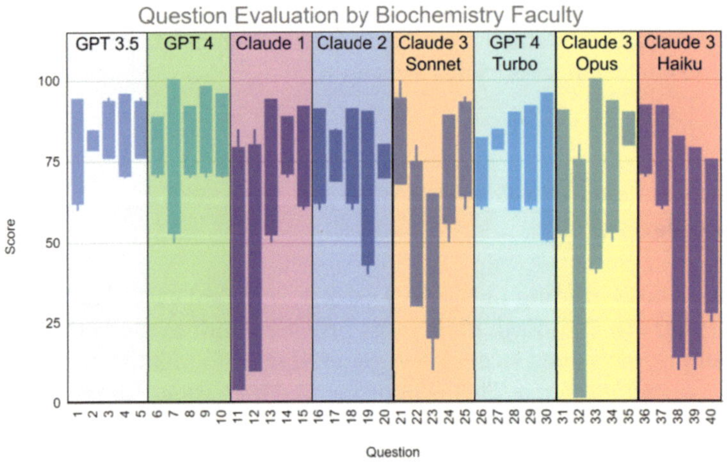

Question numbers	Model
1-5	GPT 3.5
6-10	GPT 4
11-15	Claude 1
16-20	Claude 2
21-25	Claude 3 Sonnet
26-30	GPT 4 turbo
31-35	Claude 3 Opus
36-40	Claude 3 Haiku

Figure 1.
Drift of desired question breadth over time.

- Reviewer name
- Item number
- Overall question quality (1–100)
- Correct answer was correct (yes/no)
- Quality of explanation (Likert scale: 1/very bad to 5/very good)
- Quality and alignment of learning objectives (Likert scale: 1/very bad to 5/very good)
- Quality of system tag (correct/incorrect)
- Question is adequate for formative assessment (yes/no)
- Question is adequate for high-stakes assessment (yes/no)
- Open-ended reviewer comments

Raw data are available for review in **Appendix C**. The quality of the biochemistry assessment items produced by the eight LLMs is presented on the basis of the overall quality scores (out of 100 maximum) for each item (see **Figure 2**), and by mean scores for each LLM (see **Figure 3**). Assessment item evaluation data are also presented for each variable (see **Figure 4**).

3.3 Development and testing of a medical question (MedQ) bot

In parallel to the LLM comparison, the authors developed a zero-shot ChatGPT-4-based chatbot called medStudent QandA (see **Figure 5**). The chatbot was designed

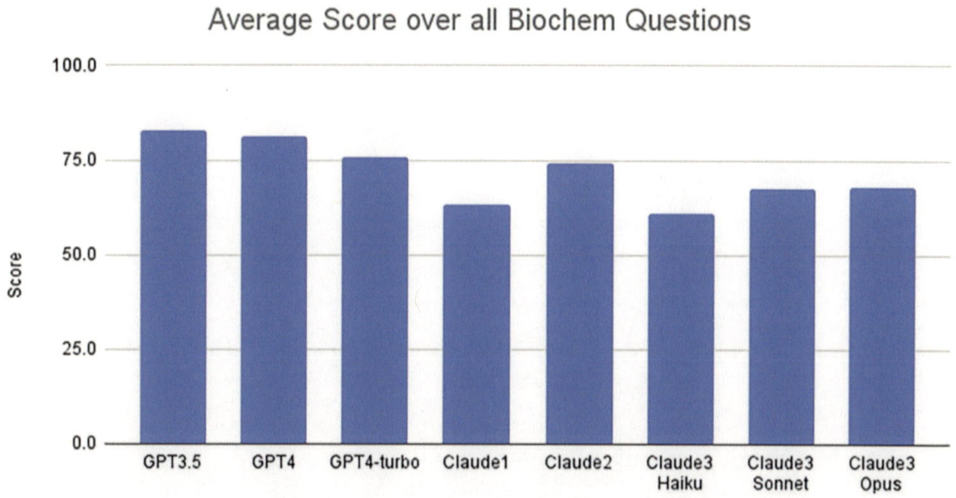

Figure 2.
Overall assessment item quality by each assessment item and LLM. Five biochemistry assessment items were generated by GPT-3.5, GPT-4, GPT-4 turbo, Claude-v2, Claude-3 Haiku, Claude-3 Sonnet, and Claude-3 Opus for comparative analysis. Five biochemistry assessment items were randomly selected from a pool of 100 items generated by Claude-v1. Medical educators assigned a score (out of 100) for each assessment item on the basis of its overall quality. The x-axis represents the assessment item number, and the y-axis represents the overall quality score (out of 100). The boxplot represents ±1 standard deviation of the analysis scores, whiskers extend to the minimum and maximum scores.

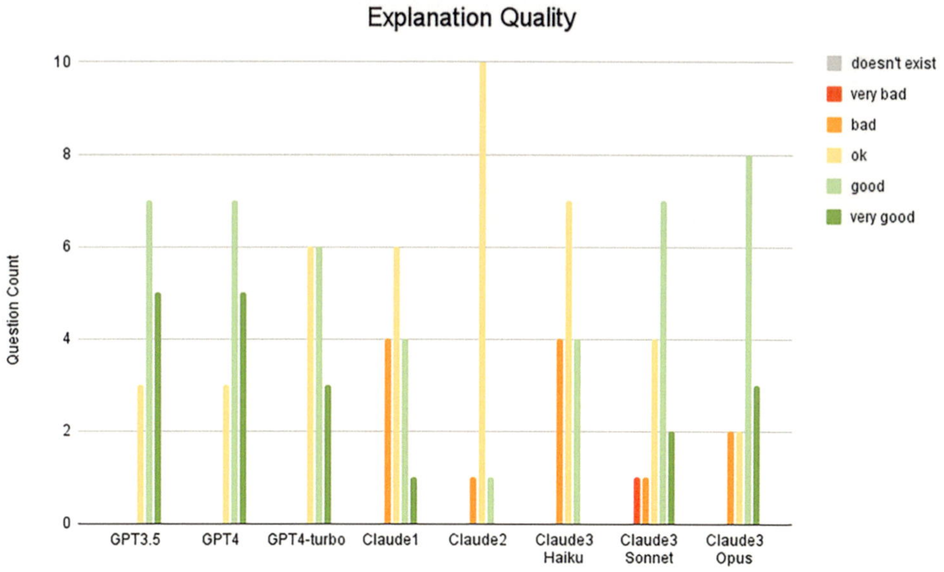

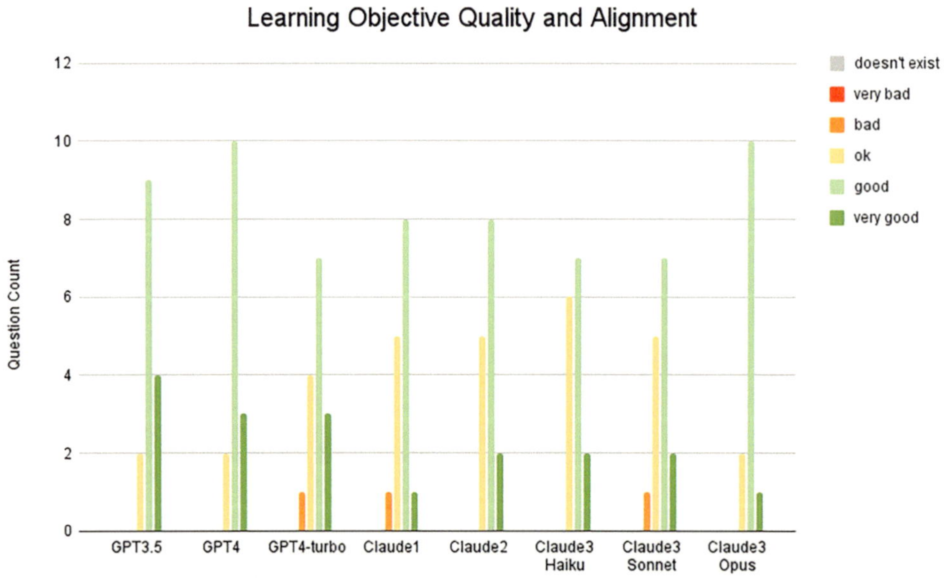
Learning Objective Quality and Alignment
Question Count
12
10
8
6
4
2
0
GPT3.5
GPT4
GPT4-turbo
Claude1
Claude2
Claude3 Haiku
Claude3 Sonnet
Claude3 Opus
doesn't exist
very bad
bad
ok
good
very good

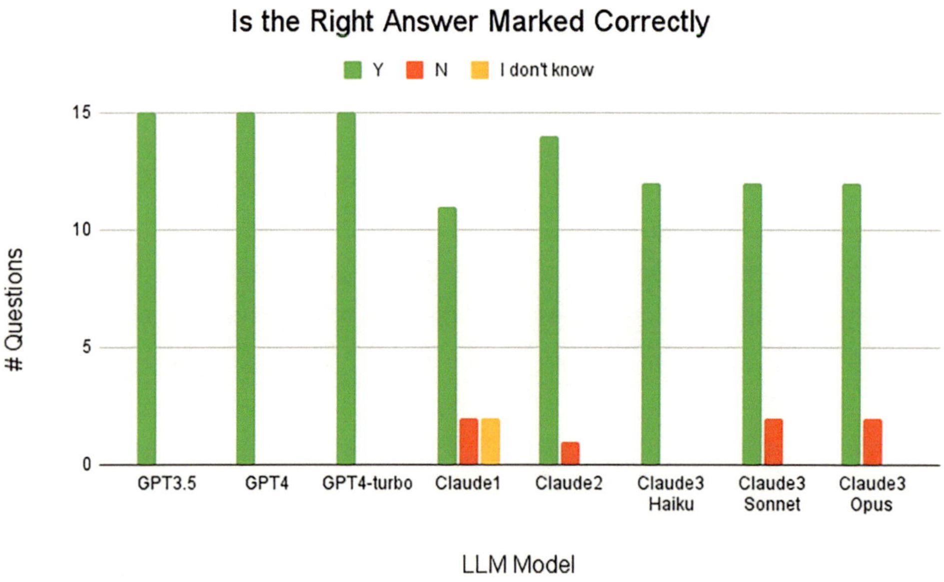
Is the Right Answer Marked Correctly
Y
N
I don't know
Questions
15
10
5
0
GPT3.5
GPT4
GPT4-turbo
Claude1
Claude2
Claude3 Haiku
Claude3 Sonnet
Claude3 Opus
LLM Model

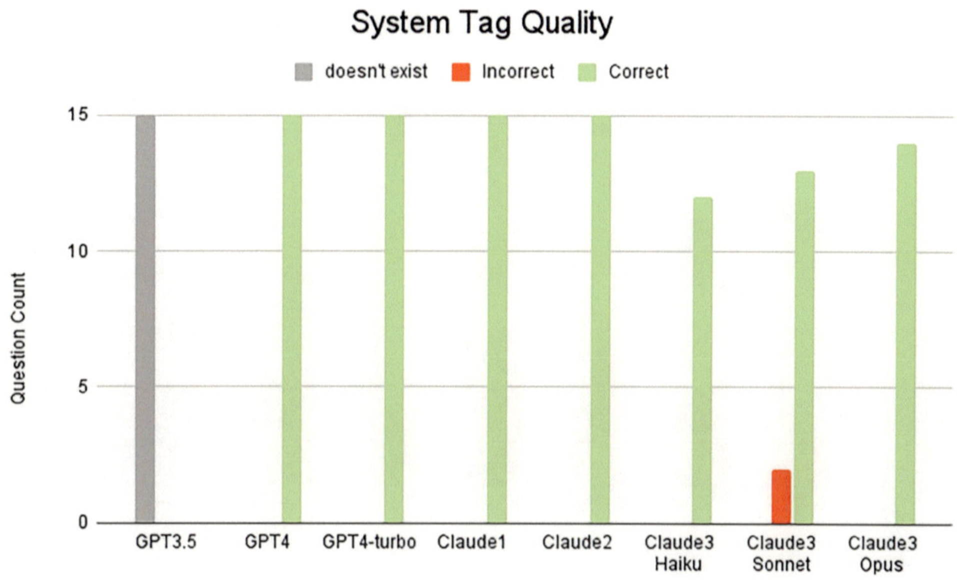
System Tag Quality
doesn't exist
Incorrect
Correct
15
10
5
0
Question Count
GPT3.5
GPT4
GPT4-turbo
Claude1
Claude2
Claude3 Haiku
Claude3 Sonnet
Claude3 Opus

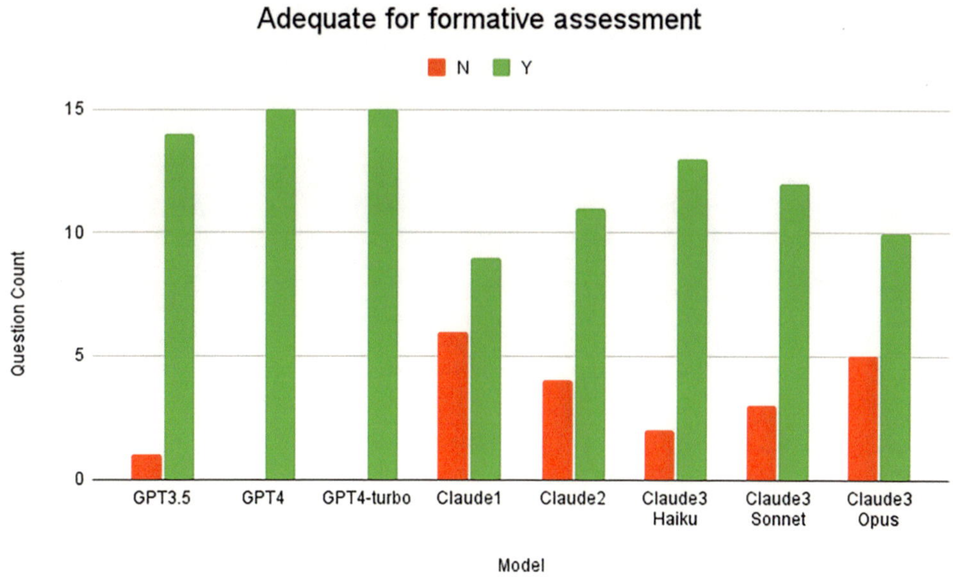
Adequate for formative assessment
N
Y
15
10
5
0
Question Count
GPT3.5
GPT4
GPT4-turbo
Claude1
Claude2
Claude3 Haiku
Claude3 Sonnet
Claude3 Opus
Model

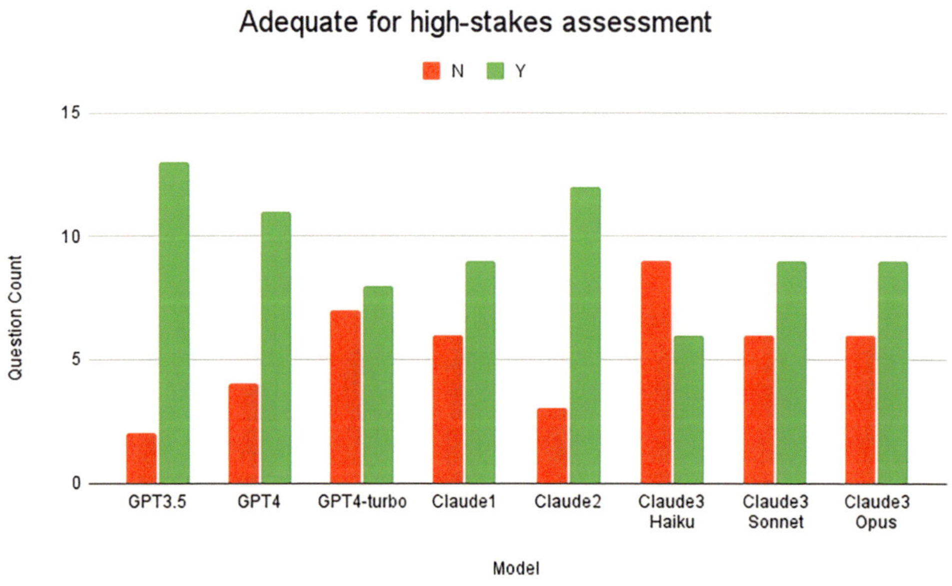

Figure 3.
Overall quality of assessment items by LLM as a mean.

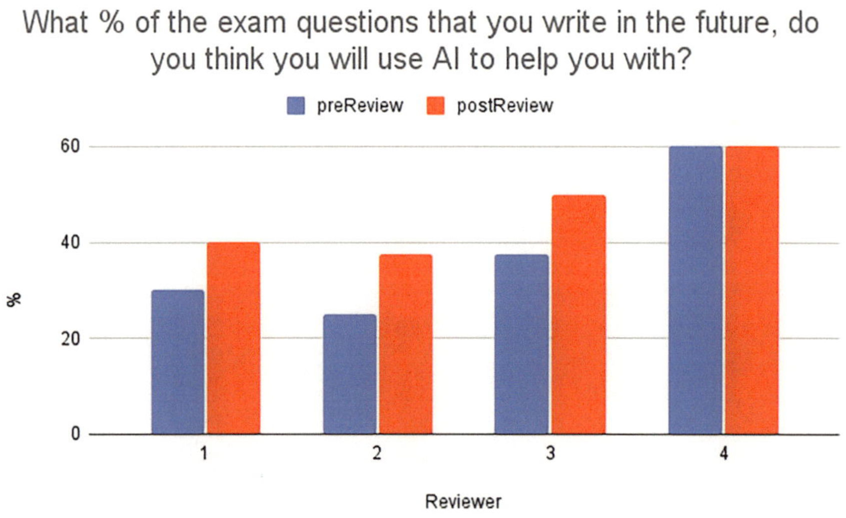

Figure 4.
Evaluation of LLM questions by multiple metrics. Evaluation of LLM-generated assessment items based on explanation quality, learning objective quality and alignment, correct answers, system tag quality, adequacy for formative assessments, and adequacy for high-stakes assessments.

to create clinical vignettes in response to user inputs but was guided using only a biochemistry exemplar (see **Appendix D**). The medStudent QandA output appeared similar to the other LLM-generated assessment items. While the assessment items generated by all eight LLMs (three GPTs and four Claudes) were evaluated by the medical educators, the items generated by the chatbot were only qualitatively

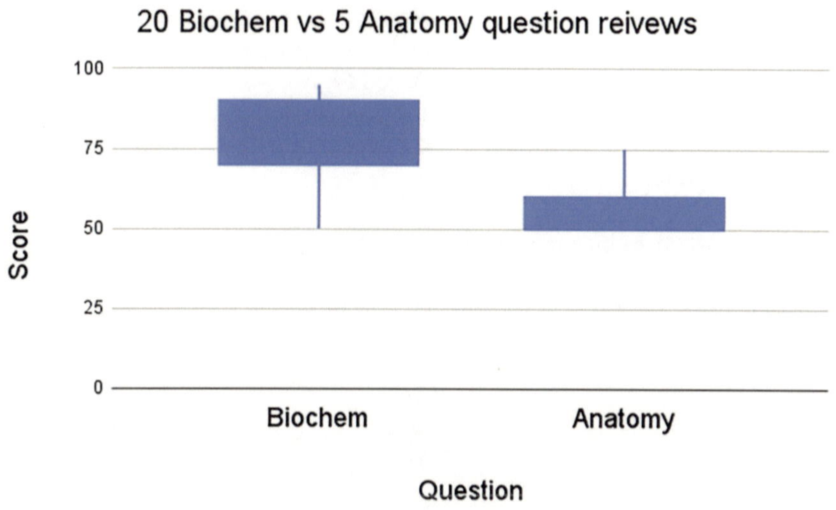

Figure 5.
Illustration of the MedQ bot, a GPT-4-based interactive tool for generating clinical vignettes.

evaluated. The MedQ chatbot was published and made public so that anyone with an OpenAI Pro account with access to GPT-4 can use the chatbot [21].

4. Results

4.1 Comparison of LLM performance

Data analysis reveals that the assessment items generated by all three OpenAI GPT models, as well as the Claude-v2 model, were highly rated by medical educators using the supplied rubric. The assessment items generated by an earlier LLM (Claude-v1) received lower ratings, while the later Claude-v3 models (Haiku, Sonnet, and Opus) had mixed results with lower and more widely ranging overall scores (see **Figure 2**). Data on the assessment items generated by the better-performing LLMs (items generated by GPT-3.5, GPT-4, GPT-4 turbo, and Claude-v2) will be further discussed, and these four LLMs will hereafter be referred to as the "high-performing LLMs." All eight LLMs consistently generated assessment items that were viewed as accurate, educationally valuable, and aligned with medical board standards. The four high-performing LLMs achieved overall scores between 74%–82% on the item evaluation rubric. While the overall scores were relatively high, the primary areas of critique resulting in point deductions were typically detailed in the comments and were minor. For instance, reviewers commented on the potential for improved explanations and alternate action verbs in the learning objectives more often than on stem errors or the selection of incorrect answer choices. Among the high-performing LLMs, all three OpenAI GPTs (3.5, 4, and 4-turbo) were rated higher than Claude-v2 on the overall score, explanation, and objective quality (see **Figures 2, 3**, and **4**). Neither GPT-3.5, 4, nor 4-turbo was identified as producing any wrong answers, while Claude-v2 was identified as producing one answer that was deemed incorrect by multiple medical educators (see **Figure 4**). An unexpected trend was observed in the percentage of questions deemed worthy for use in high-stakes testing, where the newer models (GPT-4 turbo and the three Claude-3 models – Haiku, Sonnet, and Opus) performed worse than the older models (GPT-3.5, GPT-4, Claude-2, and Claude-3; see **Figure 4**). Given the expressed interest in using AI more after exposure to it by participant faculty, the authors wonder if the later timing of the ratings on newer models resulted in increased expectations for item quality.

4.2 Scheduled quest bank distribution over time

The OpenAI-scheduled task for the creation of board-style questions was able to roughly assign more weight to certain categories, as described (see **Figure 1**).

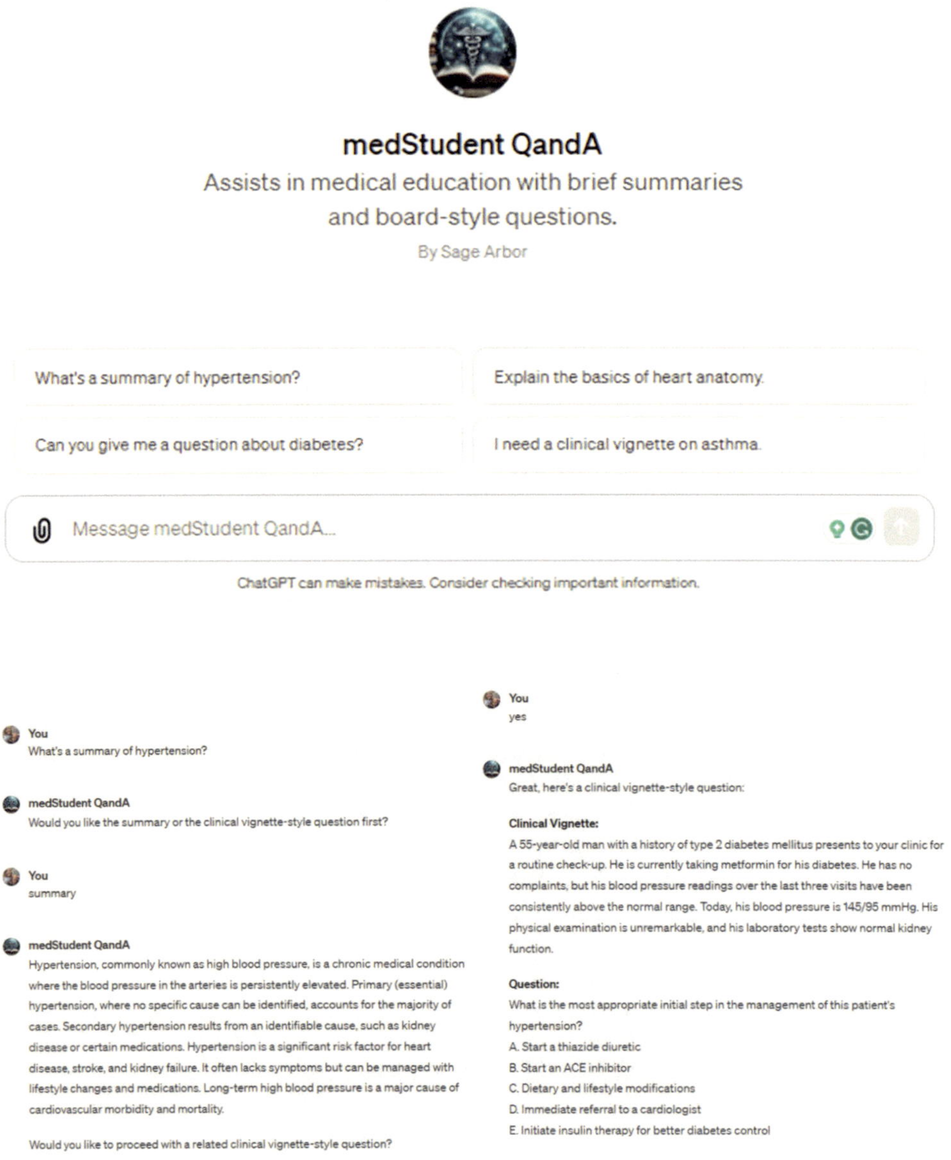

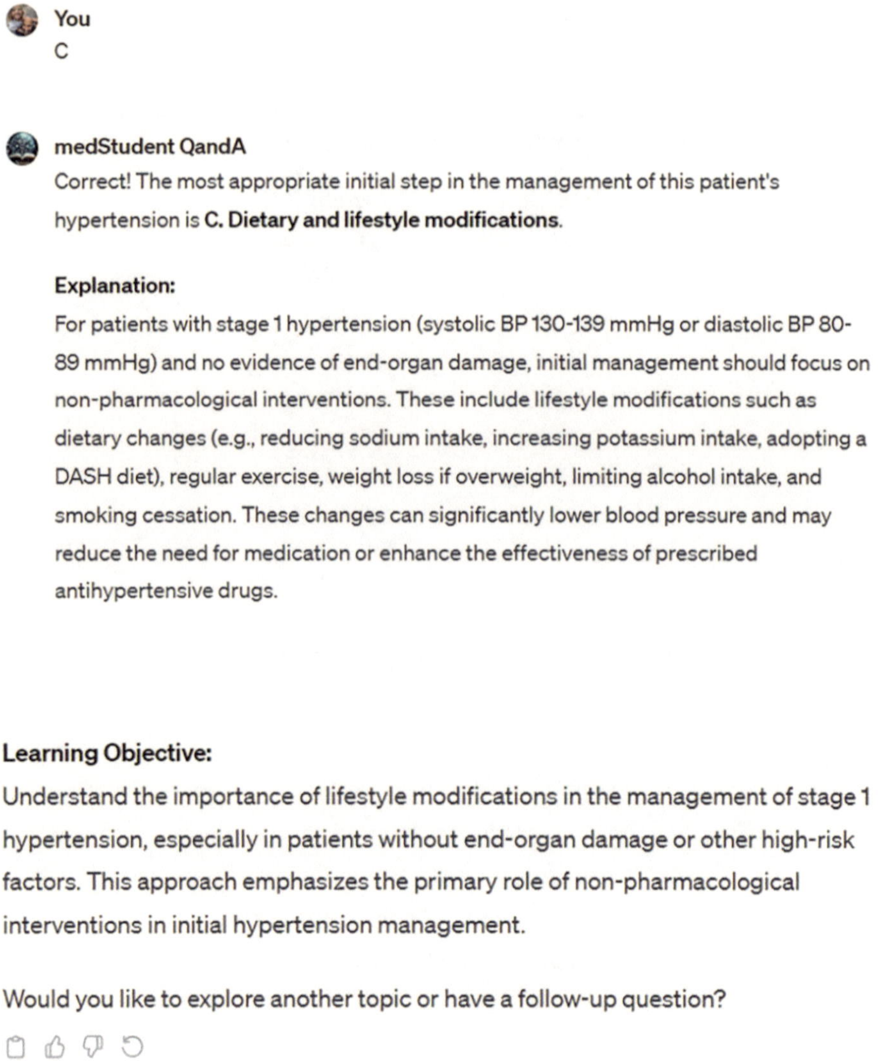

Figure 6.
Med Q bottells the user if they got the answer correct, explains the correct answer, and gives a related learning objective.

However, there was a drift over time, and, in particular, the General Principles category was not allotted enough question creation.

4.3 Faculty evaluation and perception

Post-evaluation, medical educators expressed an increased willingness to consider using AI-generated content for educational purposes (see **Figure 6**). Together, the three biochemistry medical educators reported a 15% increase in their likelihood of using AI-generated content after evaluating the AI content, based on surveys provided pre- and post-item evaluation.

The biochemistry medical educators rated the biochemistry questions about 25% higher than the anatomy medical educators rated the anatomy questions (see **Figure** 7). However, further studies are needed to determine if this discrepancy is due to the prompt needing system-specific exemplars to be accurate, sampling bias, or discipline-specific differences in assessment item generation.

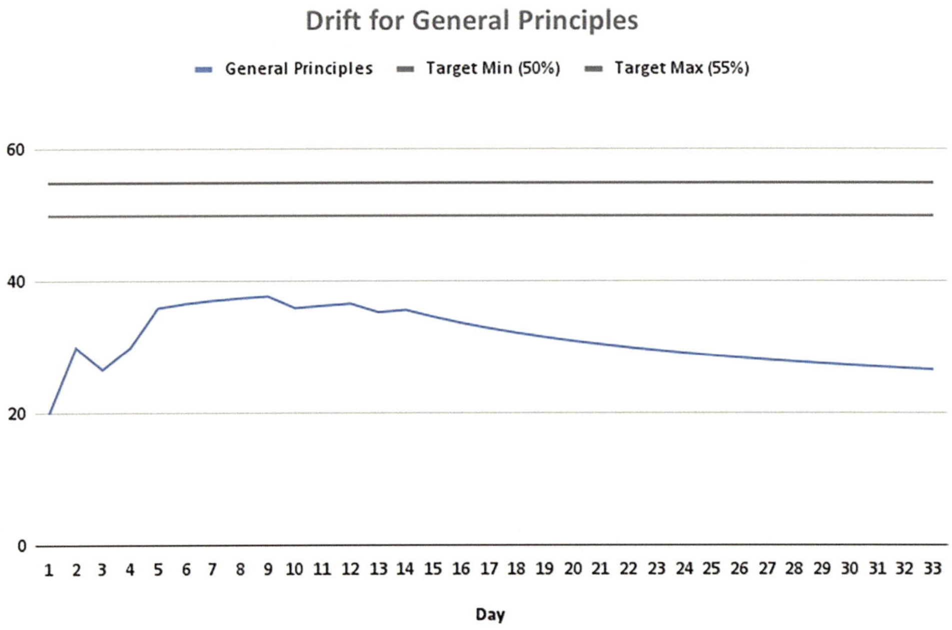

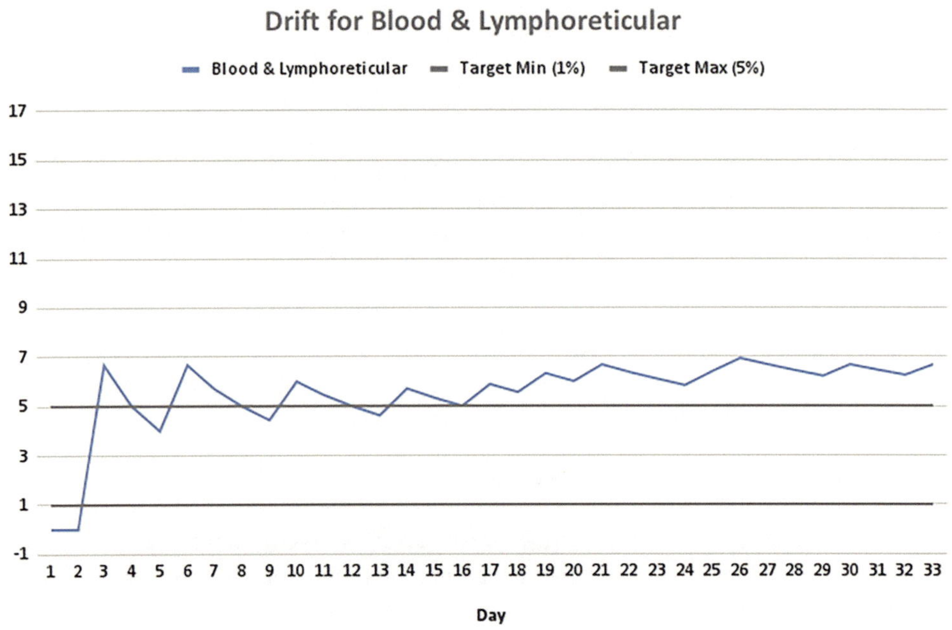

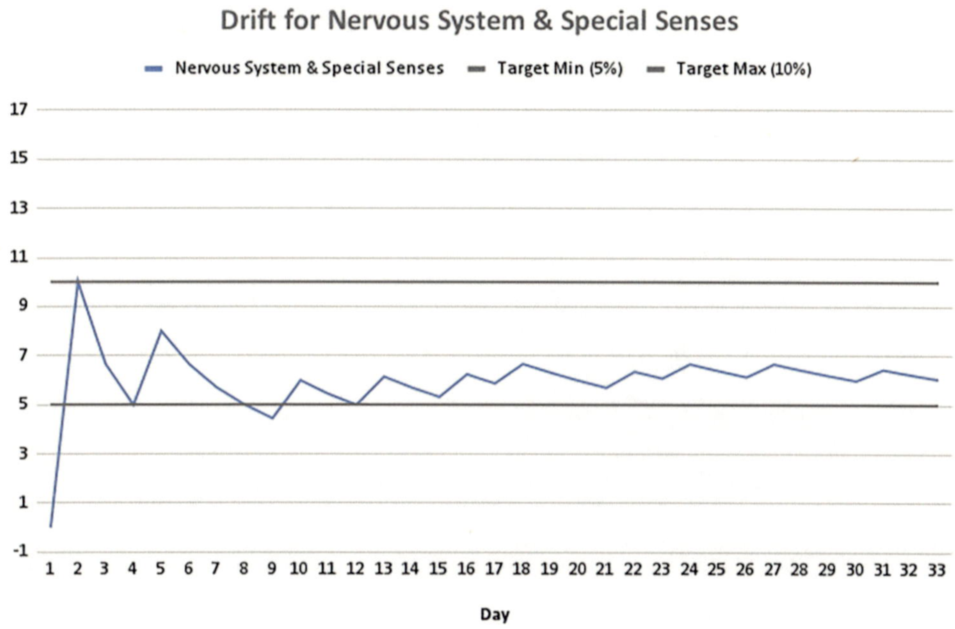
Drift for Nervous System & Special Senses
Nervous System & Special Senses
Target Min (5%)
Target Max (10%)
17
15
13
11
9
7
5
3
1
-1
1 2 3 4 5 6 7 8 9 10 11 12 13 14 15 16 17 18 19 20 21 22 23 24 25 26 27 28 29 30 31 32 33
Day

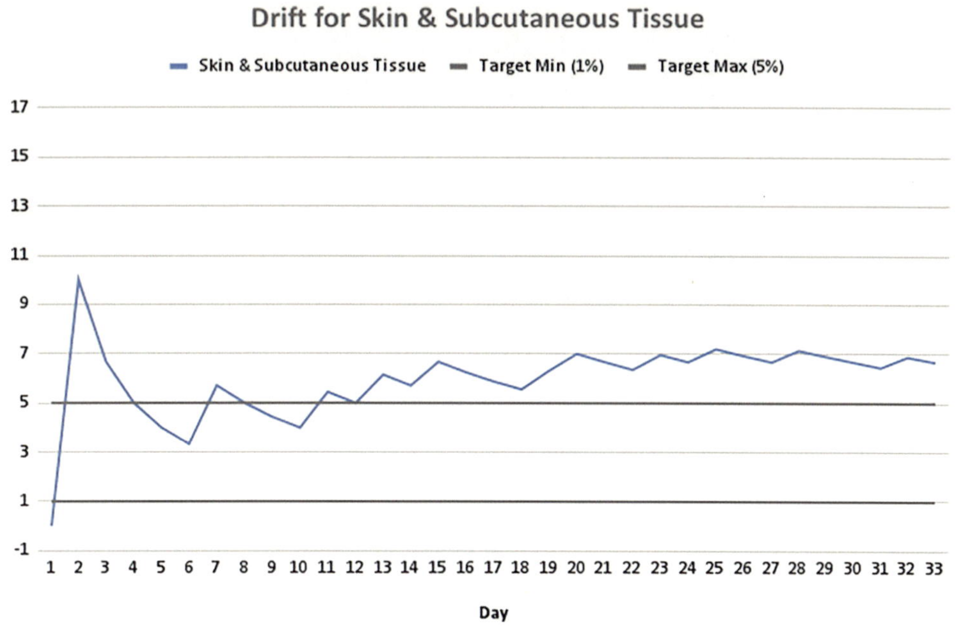
Drift for Skin & Subcutaneous Tissue
Skin & Subcutaneous Tissue
Target Min (1%)
Target Max (5%)
17
15
13
11
9
7
5
3
1
-1
1 2 3 4 5 6 7 8 9 10 11 12 13 14 15 16 17 18 19 20 21 22 23 24 25 26 27 28 29 30 31 32 33
Day

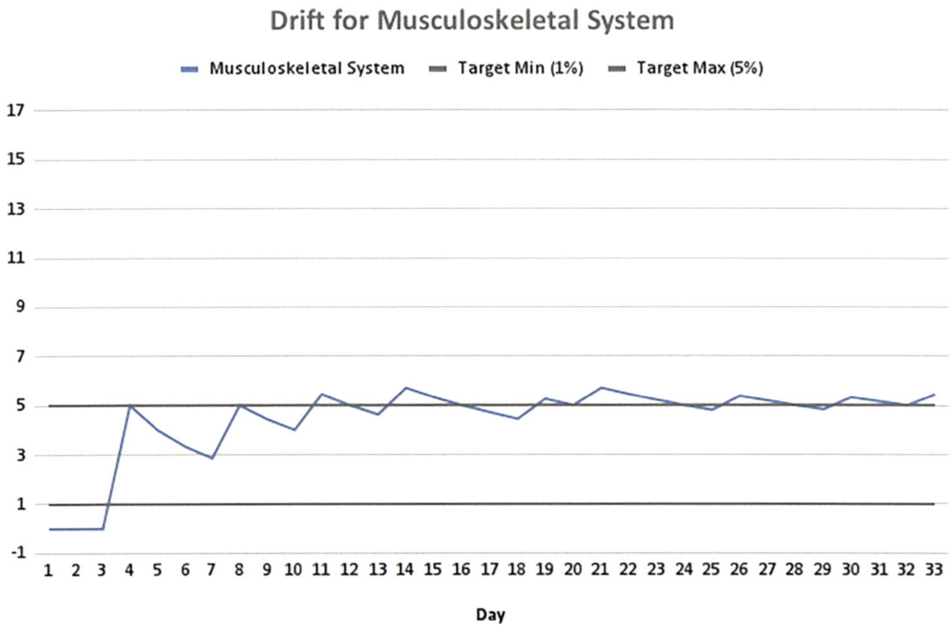
Drift for Musculoskeletal System
Musculoskeletal System
Target Min (1%)
Target Max (5%)
17
15
13
11
9
7
5
3
1
-1
1 2 3 4 5 6 7 8 9 10 11 12 13 14 15 16 17 18 19 20 21 22 23 24 25 26 27 28 29 30 31 32 33
Day

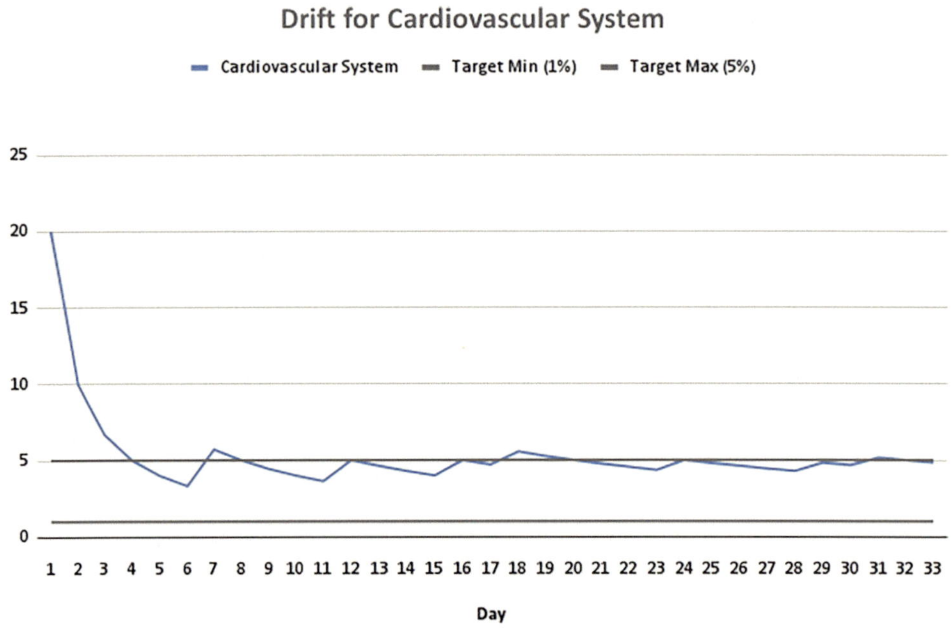
Drift for Cardiovascular System
Cardiovascular System
Target Min (1%)
Target Max (5%)
25
20
15
10
5
0
1 2 3 4 5 6 7 8 9 10 11 12 13 14 15 16 17 18 19 20 21 22 23 24 25 26 27 28 29 30 31 32 33
Day

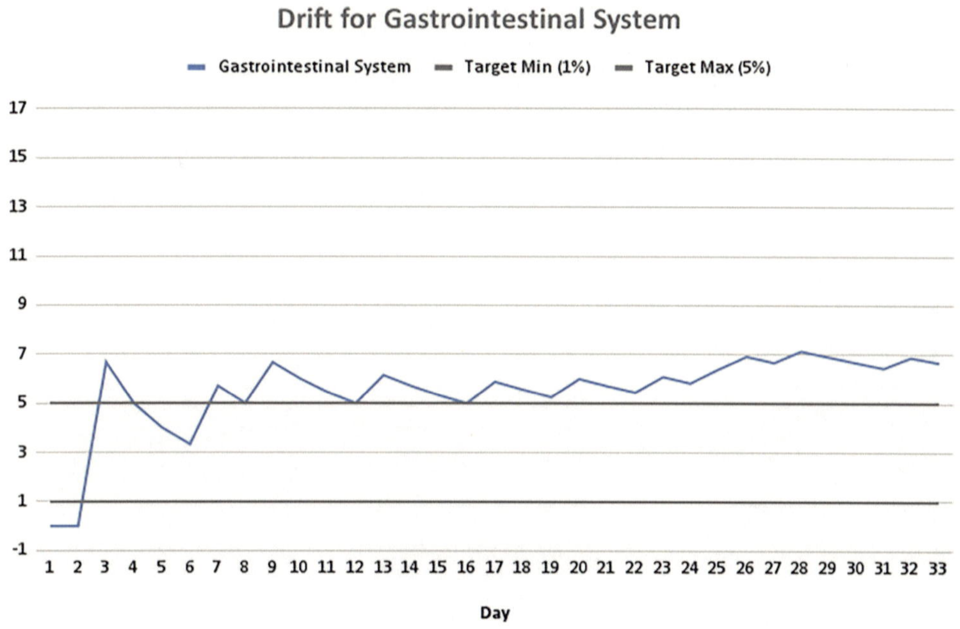
Drift for Gastrointestinal System
Gastrointestinal System
Target Min (1%)
Target Max (5%)
17
15
13
11
9
7
5
3
1
-1
1 2 3 4 5 6 7 8 9 10 11 12 13 14 15 16 17 18 19 20 21 22 23 24 25 26 27 28 29 30 31 32 33
Day

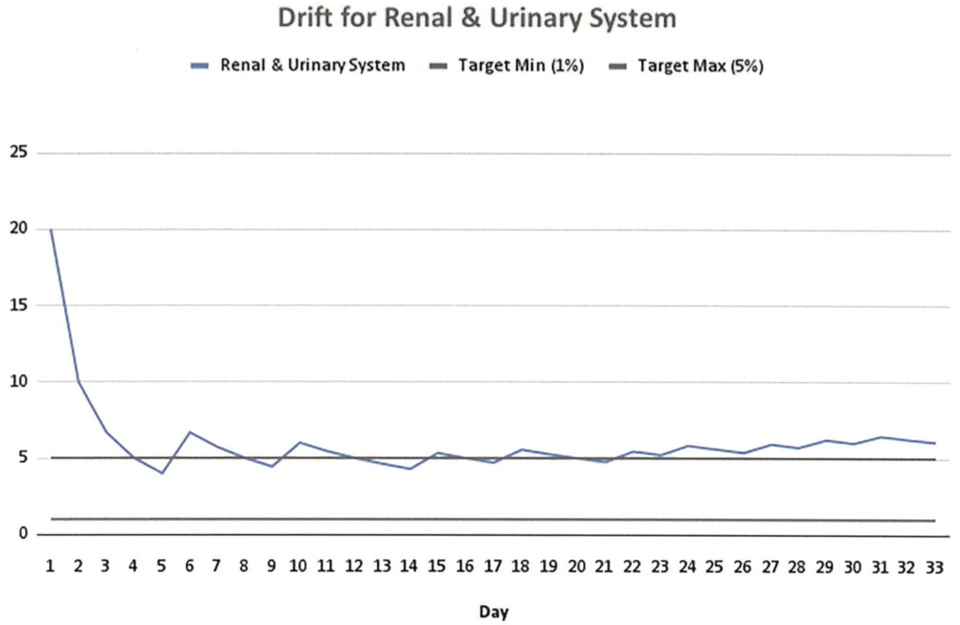
Drift for Renal & Urinary System
Renal & Urinary System
Target Min (1%)
Target Max (5%)
25
20
15
10
5
0
1 2 3 4 5 6 7 8 9 10 11 12 13 14 15 16 17 18 19 20 21 22 23 24 25 26 27 28 29 30 31 32 33
Day

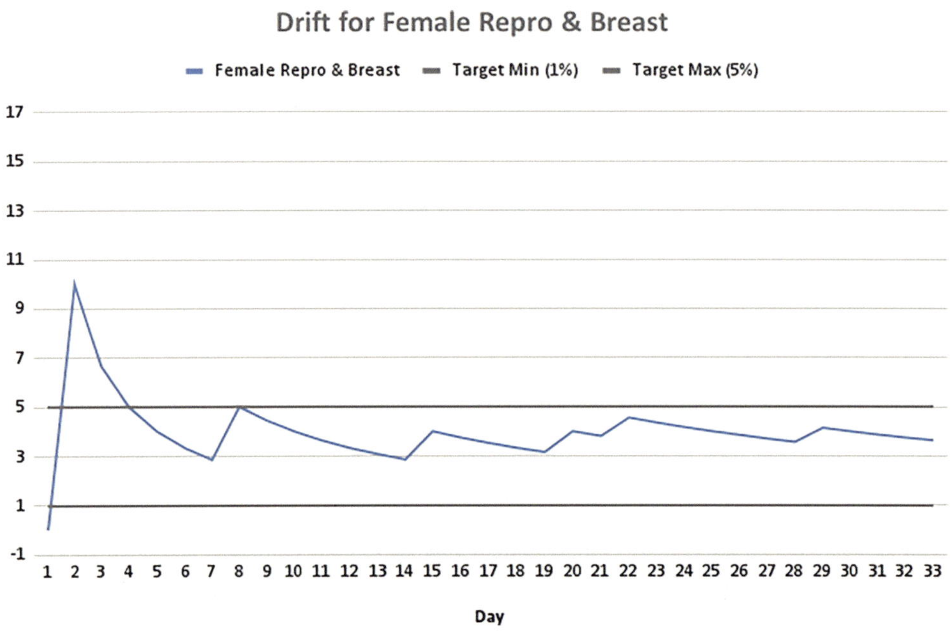
Drift for Female Repro & Breast
Female Repro & Breast
Target Min (1%)
Target Max (5%)
17
15
13
11
9
7
5
3
1
-1
1 2 3 4 5 6 7 8 9 10 11 12 13 14 15 16 17 18 19 20 21 22 23 24 25 26 27 28 29 30 31 32 33
Day

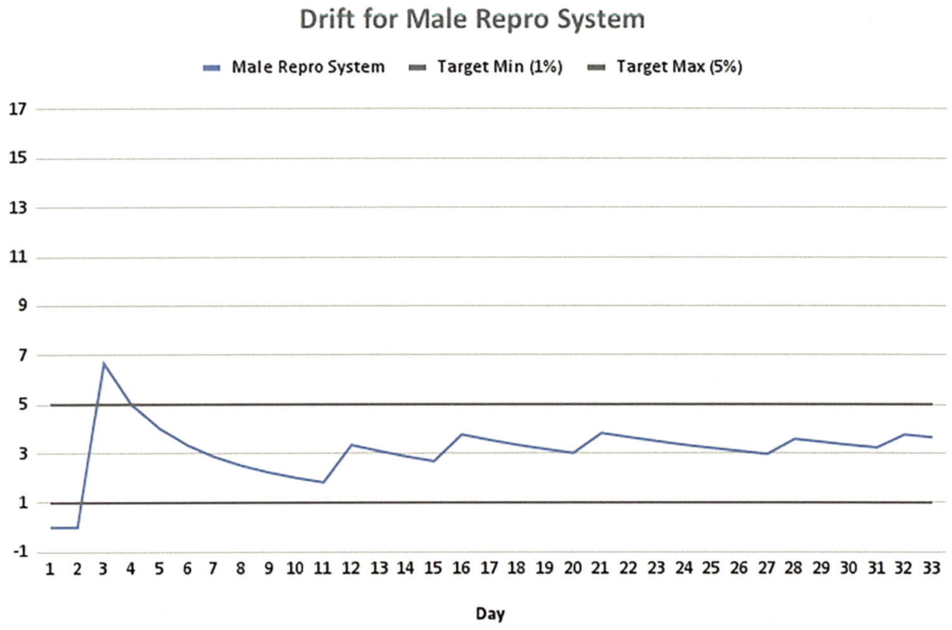
Drift for Male Repro System
Male Repro System
Target Min (1%)
Target Max (5%)
17
15
13
11
9
7
5
3
1
-1
1 2 3 4 5 6 7 8 9 10 11 12 13 14 15 16 17 18 19 20 21 22 23 24 25 26 27 28 29 30 31 32 33
Day

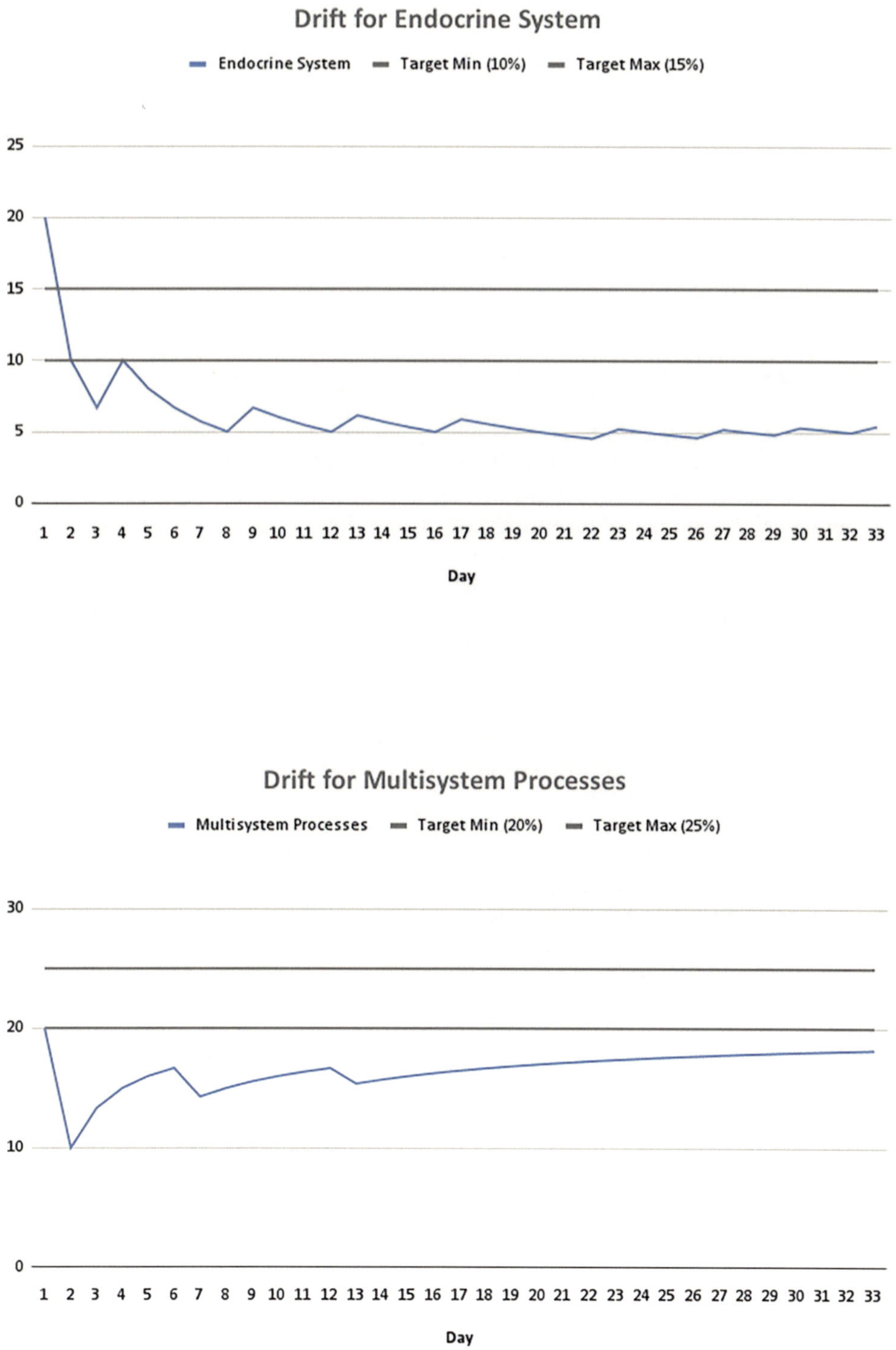

Figure 7.
Biochemistry versus anatomy question evaluation. Box plot representing ±1 standard deviation of the analysis scores; whiskers extend to the minimum and maximum values.

4.4 Medstudent QandA effectiveness

The newly created medStudent QandA [21] (see **Figure 5**) is available to anyone with an OpenAI account. At the time of writing (late 2025), this chapter includes free OpenAI accounts, though that may change as OpenAI initially mentioned trying to monetize custom GPTs but has since been willing to cover the electrical costs of running these for free users. The medStudent QandA demonstrated a high level of competency in generating relevant and educationally valuable clinical vignettes. Faculty feedback highlights the bot's potential as an innovative educational tool, especially for dynamic and interactive learning environments.

5. Discussion

The study's findings underscore the immense potential of LLMs in revolutionizing medical education. The ability of LLMs to produce high-quality medical assessment items demonstrates the applicability of AI in creating comprehensive educational resources. Our study suggests that increased exposure to these tools will likely increase acceptance of AI-generated content among faculty medical educators and the broader academe, given the significant shift in perception among our small sample of biochemistry medical educators. The biochemistry assessment items performed better on our rubric than the anatomy items. This could indicate that the exemplars provided to the LLMs need to be discipline-specific, but further work is needed to evaluate this possibility since only a single anatomist evaluated a smaller number of anatomy assessment items. The OpenAI GPTs (3.5, 4, and 4-turbo) performed better than the Claude LLMs, not including Claude-v2, which was of similar quality.

It is worth noting that the percentage of questions allocated to each biological system in the 100-question bank created by Claude-v1 diverged (see **Appendix B**) from the suggested allocation indicated in the initial prompt (see **Appendix A**). This divergence appears to be the result of an inability on the part of Claude-v1 to interpret the formatting, specifically some indentations and sub-bullets. Examining the written prompt in an area of indentation between the "System list start" and "System list end" will reveal the input of interest (see **Appendix A**). Our prompt was designed to produce an allocation of approximately 50% of the overall questions in the category "General Principles of Foundational Science" and 25% in the category "Multisystem Processes & Disorders." Instead, each category contributed approximately 5%, which is similar to the other categories listed at this prompt indentation. Nonetheless, it is apparent that the LLM can follow the suggested creation of content into different categories and percent allocations, given that the "Endocrine" and "Nervous system" categories both account for >10% of the questions as requested. This is an excellent example to highlight the importance of careful prompt engineering and the fact that different LLMs sometimes handle formatting differently.

After an initial large creation in this category during the first five days, the scheduled creation stopped making questions in the category "General Principles," so the percentage of the test bank around day 15 showed the percentage in this category asymptote lower over time. LLMs respond to token prompting, and defining categories more precisely than catch-alls like "General Principles" is likely needed to help the LLM adhere to defined rubrics of output breadth and depth.

The medStudent QandA [21] represents a step toward interactive, personalized, and AI-integrated learning platforms. The benefits of the medStudent QandA are that it allows for personalization of use, including the ability for users to:

(1) Request information on any biomedical content and biological/organ system of interest;

(2) Specify whether the item question or content explanation is listed first; and

(3) Generate a suggested learning objective for each assessment item from standard objectives provided by national societies for each biomedical science discipline [22].

The medStudent QandA's ability to generate real-time clinical vignettes offers a dynamic contribution to medical education and aligns with the evolving needs of modern curricula. We hope a future study might evaluate whether students who used the medStudent QandA more frequently perform better on medical school summative assessments, and if there is a dose-dependent response.

6. Conclusion

The Open AI GPTs (3.5, 4, and 4-turbo) and Claude-v2 all hold significant promise in contributing to high-quality and personalized medical education resources. The ability of these LLMs to generate accurate, quality assessment items is a valuable asset in medical training and assessment. The medStudent QandA [21], with its real-time question generation capability, further exemplifies the potential of AI in creating interactive and adaptable educational tools. This study paves the way for further exploration into the integration of advanced AI technologies in medical education, encouraging a reimagining of traditional teaching and assessment practices. With the use of AI-generative technology, we can envision a not-so-distant future in which high-quality assessment items are easily generated and widely available, and assessments are tailored to the precise needs of each individual student.

Appendices

Appendix A: Prompt given to LLMs for generating medical board-style assessment items

I would like you to make 500 biochemistry board style examination questions for medical students who are becoming doctors. Questions should be in the form of a clinical vignette, with a patient presentation, usually having five answer options (allowing four to six answers if that makes more sense). They should include an explanation of why the correct answer is correct compared to the other answers, a learning objective related to the question (try to reuse the same learning objectives across some questions if it makes sense to), and also tag each question with the biological "System" from the system list below. The questions should be distributed to target the systems based on the percentages shown in the system list. For example, the Musculoskeletal System should represent 1%–5% of the questions.

System list start
General Principles of Foundational Science (50%–55%)

- Gene expression: DNA structure, replication, exchange and epigenetics
- Gene expression: Transcription
- Gene expression: Translation
- Structure and function of proteins and enzymes
- Energy metabolism
- Biology of cells
- Cell biology of cancer
- General principles of invasion and metastasis
- Cell/tissue structure, regulation, and function
- Human development and genetics
- Genetic mechanism
- Acute inflammatory responses
- Pharmacodynamic and pharmacokinetic processes

Blood & Lymphoreticular System (1%–5%)
Nervous System & Special Senses (5%–10%)
Skin & Subcutaneous Tissue (1%–5%)
Musculoskeletal System (1%–5%)
Cardiovascular System (1%–5%)
Gastrointestinal System (1%–5%)
Renal & Urinary System (1%–5%)
Female Reproductive System & Breast (1%–5%)
Male Reproductive System (1%–5%)
Endocrine System (10%–15%)
Multisystem Processes & Disorders (20%–25%)

- Principles of nutrition: Intracellular accumulations
- Abnormal processes: nutrition

- Toxins and environmental extremes
- Enzymatic/metabolic disorders
- Structural protein disorders
- Intracellular/extracellular transport receptors

System list end

Two examples are given below:

Q1 start

A previously healthy 16-year-old girl is brought to the physician because of abdominal cramps, bloating, and loose stools for six months. These symptoms began after she ingested skim milk in an attempt to lose weight. She is at the 50th percentile for height and the 75th percentile for weight. Physical examination shows no abnormalities. Stool studies show a 3+ Clinitest reagent response and a pH of 5. After the patient ingests milk, there is an increased hydrogen concentration in expired air. A deficiency of which of the following enzyme activities is the most likely cause of the gastrointestinal symptoms in this patient?

(A) Amylase

(B) Carboxypeptidase

(C) Fructose-1,6-bisphosphate aldolase

(D) Galactokinase

(E) Lactase

(F) Sucrase

Correct answer:

The most likely cause of the gastrointestinal symptoms in this patient, based on the provided information, is a deficiency in enzyme activity of (E) Lactase.

Lactase is an enzyme found in the small intestine that is responsible for breaking down lactose, a sugar found in milk and dairy products, into two simpler sugars: glucose and galactose. When there is a deficiency in lactase, the body is unable to properly digest lactose, leading to symptoms such as abdominal cramps, bloating, and diarrhea. This condition is known as lactose intolerance.

The given patient's symptoms began after she ingested skim milk and are consistent with lactose intolerance. The physical examination showed no abnormalities, and the results of the stool studies, with a positive Clinitest reagent response (indicating the presence of reducing substances like undigested lactose) and acidic stool pH, further support this diagnosis. The increased hydrogen concentration in expired air after milk ingestion is a result of undigested lactose being fermented by bacteria in the colon, producing hydrogen gas that is absorbed into the bloodstream and eventually exhaled.

Incorrect answers:
Now, let's briefly look at why the other options are less likely:

(A) Amylase: This enzyme breaks down carbohydrates, but a deficiency would not specifically result in the symptoms observed after milk ingestion.

(B) Carboxypeptidase: This enzyme helps with protein digestion. A deficiency would affect protein digestion, not lactose digestion.

(C) Fructose-1,6-bisphosphate aldolase: This enzyme is involved in glycolysis, a metabolic pathway that breaks down glucose for energy. A deficiency would have systemic effects, not just gastrointestinal symptoms related to milk ingestion.

(D) Galactokinase: This enzyme is involved in the metabolism of galactose. However, in the case of lactase deficiency, galactose is not produced from lactose digestion; therefore, this enzyme is not relevant to the symptoms.

(F) Sucrase: This enzyme breaks down sucrose into glucose and fructose. A deficiency would result in symptoms related to sucrose ingestion, not lactose.

Learning Objective:
Understand the biochemical basis of lactose intolerance, identify its clinical manifestations, and distinguish it from other gastrointestinal disorders. This helps in developing clinical reasoning skills and the ability to apply biochemical knowledge to patient care.
Q1 end
Q2 start
A 14-year-old girl is brought to the physician because of a recent growth spurt of 15 cm (6 inches) during the past year. She has also experienced increasing fatigue and palpitations during this period. Her paternal aunt has a history of palpitations and severe myopia. She is at the 95th percentile for height and the 50th percentile for weight. Physical examination reveals a long, thin face. Ophthalmologic examination shows dislocated lenses. Cardiac examination reveals a hyperdynamic precordium with an early click and systolic murmur. Echocardiography demonstrates an enlarged aortic root and mitral valve prolapse. Abnormal synthesis of which of the following proteins is the most likely cause of this patient's disorder?

(A) Collagen, type I

(B) Elastin

(C) Fibrillin-1

(D) Fibroblast growth factor R3

(E) Laminin

Correct answer:

This patient's clinical presentation is consistent with Marfan syndrome, a connective tissue disorder. Marfan syndrome is characterized by tall stature, long extremities and digits (arachnodactyly), joint hypermobility, scoliosis, pectus excavatum or carinatum, and myopia. Cardiovascular manifestations include mitral valve prolapse, aortic root dilation, and aortic dissection. Ophthalmologic findings can include dislocated lenses.

Marfan syndrome is caused by mutations in the FBN1 gene, leading to abnormal synthesis of (C) Fibrillin-1, a glycoprotein that is a major component of the extracellular matrix and is essential for the integrity of connective tissues. Fibrillin-1 interacts with elastin to form elastic fibers, and a deficiency or dysfunction in Fibrillin-1 disrupts the elastic properties of connective tissues, contributing to the clinical manifestations of Marfan syndrome.

Incorrect answers:

Let's consider why the other options are incorrect:

(A) Collagen, type I: Defects in type I collagen are associated with disorders such as osteogenesis imperfecta, which is characterized by brittle bones, blue sclera, and hearing loss.

(B) Elastin: Elastin is crucial for the elasticity of tissues. Defects in elastin can lead to conditions like cutis laxa, where the skin becomes inelastic and hangs loosely in folds.

(D) Fibroblast growth factor R3 (FGFR3): Mutations in FGFR3 are associated with conditions such as achondroplasia, a form of short-limbed dwarfism.

(E) Laminin: Laminin is a major component of the basal lamina, and defects in laminin can lead to conditions affecting muscles, nerves, and skin.

Learning Objective:

Recognize the clinical features of Marfan syndrome, understand the genetic basis of the disorder, and appreciate the role of fibrillin-1 in maintaining the integrity of connective tissues. This knowledge is crucial for the timely diagnosis and management of the condition to prevent potentially life-threatening complications, such as aortic dissection.

Q2 end

Appendix B: Topic coverage Table

A summary table of the number of questions per system for the 100 questions created and tagged by the LLM.

System	# Questions	%	% Recommended
General Principles of Foundational Science	4	4.55%	50%–55%
Blood & Lymphoreticular System	8	9.09%	1%–5%
Nervous System & Special Senses	12	13.64%	5%–10%
Skin & Subcutaneous Tissue	1	1.14%	1-5%
Musculoskeletal System	2	2.27%	1%–5%
Cardiovascular System	3	3.41%	1%–5%
Gastrointestinal System	14	15.91%	1%–5%
Renal & Urinary System	5	5.68%	1%–5%
Female Reproductive System & Breast	2	2.27%	1%–5%
Male Reproductive System	1	1.14%	1%–5%
Endocrine System	10	11.36%	10%–15%
Multisystem Processes & Disorders	4	4.55%	20%–25%
Respiratory System	1	1.14%	
Infectious Disease	2	2.27%	
Hematology/Oncology	3	3.41%	
Genetics	3	3.41%	
Embryology	5	5.68%	
Immunology	1	1.14%	
Rheumatology	1	1.14%	
Ophthalmology	1	1.14%	
Radiology	1	1.14%	
Toxins	1	1.14%	
Dermatology	1	1.14%	
Metabolic/Genetic	1	1.14%	
Pulmonology	1	1.14%	
TOTAL		100.00%	

Appendix C: Raw data from reviewers

Model	Reviewer	Q num	Overall quality (1–100)	Correct answer Correct [Y,N]	Quality of explanation	Quality of objective	Quality of system tag	OK for formative assessment?	OK for high-stakes assessment?	Comments/Notes
GPT-3.5	1	1	60	Y	Ok	Very good	Doesn't exist	Y	N	The late age of onset in this question makes it a little tricky. Adults with type I diabetes may have type II diabetes first, and that would lead to answer B being correct as well as A.
GPT-3.5	1	2	80	Y	Good	Good	Doesn't exist	Y	Y	This is a pathology or physiology question, not really biochemistry.
GPT-3.5	1	3	80	Y	Good	Good	Doesn't exist	Y	Y	This is a pathology or physiology question, not really biochemistry.
GPT-3.5	1	4	70	Y	Good	Good	Doesn't exist	Y	Y	This is an immunology question, not really biochemistry.
GPT-3.5	1	5	80	Y	Good	Good	Doesn't exist	Y	Y	This is a pathology or physiology question, not really biochemistry.
GPT-4	1	6	70	Y	Good	Good	Correct	Y	Y	I don't like the style of the question with segmented patient presentation and question, but in general, the question is okay.
GPT-4	1	7	50	Y	Ok	Good	Correct	Y	N	Cardiovascular system tag correct, but not so much biochemistry.
GPT-4	1	8	70	Y	Good	Good	Correct	Y	Y	System tag correct, but not so much biochemistry.
GPT-4	1	9	70	Y	Good	Good	Correct	Y	Y	
GPT-4	1	10	70	Y	Good	Good	Correct	Y	Y	Hematopeitic system would be better
Claude1	1	11	20	N	Bad	Ok	Correct	N	N	Any of the foils could be correct. All of the changes are involved in the development of colon cancer. The explanation mentions "sporadic colorectal cancers", but the stem does not provide any family history to rule out hereditary cancer.

Model	Reviewer	Q num	Overall quality (1–100)	Correct answer Correct [Y,N]	Quality of explanation	Quality of objective	Quality of system tag	OK for formative assessment?	OK for high-stakes assessment?	Comments/Notes
Claude1	1	12	30	Y	Bad	Bad	Correct	N	N	Need more information in the stem of the question to rule out a defective pre-TCR assembly defect. The explanation needs more details about why the incorrect foils are incorrect. There is not enough information in the stem of the question to relate to the objective.
Claude1	1	13	50	Y	Bad	Ok	Correct	Y	N	Need more information in the stem to rule out some of the other foils. Need better explanation of why incorrect foils are incorrect and a better explanation of the mechanism for the correct answer.
Claude1	1	14	70	Y	Good	Good	Correct	Y	Y	
Claude1	1	15	60	Y	Very good	Good	Correct	Y	N	Pseudocase in the stem of the question.
Claude2	1	16	60	Y	Ok	Good	Correct	Y	N	The pathophysiology of type 2 diabetes is much more complex than what is in the correct foil. The lead-in should be changed. Some of the symptoms are more related to type 1 diabetes.
Claude2	1	17	70	Y	Ok	Ok	Correct	Y	Y	
Claude2	1	18	60	Y	Bad	Good	Correct	Y	N	Pseudocase. Explanation did not go over incorrect foils. EGFR mutations are also associated with non-small cell lung cancer.
Claude2	1	19	40	Y	Ok	Ok	Correct	N	N	Explanation did not explain incorrect foils. DMD is an X-linked disease, and very rarely, girls are affected.
Claude2	1	20	70	Y	Ok	Good	Correct	Y	Y	

DOI: http://dx.doi.org/10.5772/intechopen.1012581

Model	Reviewer	Q num	Overall quality (1–100)	Correct answer Correct [Y,N]	Quality of explanation	Quality of objective	Quality of system tag	OK for formative assessment?	OK for high-stakes assessment?	Comments/Notes
Claude3 Sonnet	1	21	80	Y	Good	Good	Correct	Y	Y	I think that there were some important symptoms of B12 deficiency that were not in the clinical case and some not-so-important ones that were included. Systems tag should also include GI.
Claude3 Sonnet	1	22	80	Y	Good	Good	Correct	Y	Y	Systems tag should also include musculoskeletal system.
Claude3 Sonnet	1	23	50	Y	Ok	Ok	Correct	Y	N	Some of the clinical presentations and laboratory tests were not entirely correct for the disease.
Claude3 Sonnet	1	24	70	Y	Good	Good	Correct	Y	Y	Systems tag should also include Heme.
Claude3 Sonnet	1	25	80	Y	Good	Good	Correct	Y	Y	Systems tag should also include GI.
Claude3 Opus	1	31	80	Y	Good	Good	Correct	Y	Y	
Claude3 Opus	1	32	10	N	Bad	Good	Correct	N	N	
Claude3 Opus	1	33	40	Y	Good	Good	Correct	N	N	Some of the clinical presentations and laboratory tests were not entirely correct for the disease. A peculiar musty odor is associated with PKU, not MSUD. Hepatomegaly, hypoglycemia, and elevated serum ammonia are not seen in MSUD.
Claude3 Opus	1	34	50	Y	Ok	Good	Correct	N	N	Some of the clinical presentations and laboratory tests were not entirely correct for the disease.
Claude3 Opus	1	35	80	Y	Good	Good	Correct	Y	Y	
Claude3 Haiku	1	36	70	Y	Ok	Good	Correct	Y	N	Systems tag should also include the cardiovascular system.

Model	Reviewer	Q num	Overall quality (1–100)	Correct answer Correct [Y,N]	Quality of explanation	Quality of objective	Quality of system tag	OK for formative assessment?	OK for high-stakes assessment?	Comments/Notes
Claude3 Haiku	1	37	60	Y	Bad	Good	Correct	Y	N	Did not explain the incorrect foils.
Claude3 Haiku	1	38	60	Y	Bad	Good	Correct	Y	N	Did not explain the incorrect foils.
Claude3 Haiku	1	39	60	Y	Bad	Good	Correct	Y	N	Did not explain the incorrect foils.
Claude3 Haiku	1	40	60	Y	Bad	Good	Correct	Y	N	Did not explain the incorrect foils.
GPT-4 turbo	1	41	10	N	Ok	Good	Correct	N	N	
GPT-4 turbo	1	42	60	Y	Ok	Good	Correct	Y	N	Did not explain the incorrect foils.
GPT-4 turbo	1	43	50	Y	Ok	Ok	Correct	Y	N	Did not explain the incorrect foils.
GPT-4 turbo	1	44	10	N	Very bad	Ok	Correct	N	N	
GPT-4 turbo	1	45	50	Y	Ok	Ok	Correct	Y	N	Did not explain the incorrect foils.
GPT-3.5	2	1	85	Y	Ok	Very good	Doesn't exist	Y	Y	There seems to be not enough explanation for the differentiation of T1 vs. T2 DM, as they address non-measurable features of the two conditions and not so much s/s.
GPT-3.5	2	2	85	Y	Very good	Ok	Doesn't exist	Y	Y	"Understand" is typically not considered a good action verb when it comes to LOs.
GPT-3.5	2	3	95	Y	Very good	Very good	Doesn't exist	Y	Y	

Model	Reviewer	Q num	Overall quality (1–100)	Correct answer Correct [Y,N]	Quality of explanation	Quality of objective	Quality of system tag	OK for formative assessment?	OK for high-stakes assessment?	Comments/Notes
GPT-3.5	2	4	95	Y	Very good	Very good	Doesn't exist	Y	Y	
GPT-3.5	2	5	80	Y	Ok	Ok	Doesn't exist	Y	Y	Answers D and E could elaborate more as to why; "Understand" is typically not considered a good action verb when it comes to LOs.
GPT-4	2	6	85	Y	Very good	Ok	Correct	Y	Y	"Understand" is typically not considered a good action verb when it comes to LOs.
GPT-4	2	7	95	Y	Very good	Very good	Correct	Y	Y	
GPT-4	2	8	85	Y	Very good	Ok	Correct	Y	Y	"Understand" is typically not considered a good action verb when it comes to LOs.
GPT-4	2	9	95	Y	Very good	Very good	Correct	Y	Y	
GPT-4	2	10	95	Y	Very good	Very good	Correct	Y	Y	
Claude1	2	11	20	I don't know	Ok	Ok	Correct	N	N	"Understand" is typically not considered a good action verb when it comes to LOs; will a practitioner really know or need to know which type of mutation is the most common? The explanation section clearly states that other mutation options also occur.

Model	Reviewer	Q num	Overall quality (1–100)	Correct answer Correct [Y,N]	Quality of explanation	Quality of objective	Quality of system tag	OK for formative assessment?	OK for high-stakes assessment?	Comments/Notes
Claude1	2	12	20	I don't know	Bad	Ok	Correct	N	N	"Understand" is typically not considered a good action verb when it comes to LOs; the incorrect answers could be more differentially explained. I don't know the level of genetics students are required to know in medical and osteopathic programs; I am aware, though, from chiropractic board examinations that some basic science knowledge required is very detail-oriented and has little to do with diagnosis and/or treatment.
Claude1	2	13	90	Y	Good	Very good	Correct	N	Y	The incorrect answers could be more differential.
Claude1	2	14	85	Y	Good	Ok	Correct	N	Y	"Understand" is typically not considered a good action verb when it comes to LOs; the incorrect answers could be more differentially explained.
Claude1	2	15	80	N	Good	Good	Correct	Y	Y	G2P1? This seems like a very nit-picky question for a physiologist, not a future physician.
Claude2	2	16	85	Y	Ok	Ok	Correct	N	Y	"Understand" is typically not considered a good action verb when it comes to LOs; the incorrect answers are not explained or differentiated.
Claude2	2	17	75	N	Good	Very good	Correct	Y	Y	Could Strep pyogenes be an option, though? Potentially ambivalent, but I am not a clinician.
Claude2	2	18	85	Y	Ok	Very good	Correct	Y	Y	Did not research this question – not a clinician, but I assume it is correct; incorrect answers are not differentially addressed.
Claude2	2	19	75	Y	Ok	Ok	Correct	N	Y	Incorrect answers are not addressed in the explanation; "understand."
Claude2	2	20	75	Y	Ok	Ok	Correct	N	Y	Incorrect answers are not addressed in the explanation; "understand."
Claude3 Sonnet	2	21	100	Y	Very good	Very good	Correct	Y	Y	

Model	Reviewer	Q num	Overall quality (1–100)	Correct answer Correct [Y,N]	Quality of explanation	Quality of objective	Quality of system tag	OK for formative assessment?	OK for high-stakes assessment?	Comments/Notes
Claude3 Sonnet	2	22	30	N	Bad	Ok	Correct	N	N	Two correct answers: myophosphorylase is specified as the muscle isoenzyme of glycogen phosphorylase; the question can be improved by replacing D or E. In my biochemistry class, the difference between muscle and other glycogen phosphorylases is not addressed.
Claude3 Sonnet	2	23	10	ambiguous	Ok	Bad	Incorrect	N	N	This question is not about the structure and function of enzymes but rather about differentiating between lysosomal storage diseases, which are genetic disorders caused by mutations in different enzymes. To me, structure and function questions address more specifically how and why a protein becomes less functional or nonfunctional due to a mutation. The question would be okay if it were tagged as a genetics question. The question does not delve into the "underlying biochemical defect"; According to what I can find on the disorders, the case vignette may not be enough to distinguish between B, C, and E. In addition, answers B–D use a different naming system for the disorders (names), while the correct answer uses the enzyme-based name.
Claude3 Sonnet	2	24	85	Y	Good	Good	Correct	Y	Y	Explanations should include in which types of cells the transport proteins are prevalent (answers B and C), which help explain the difference in serum ferritin levels.
Claude3 Sonnet	2	25	95	Y	Very good	Very good	Correct	Y	Y	Wouldn't a roommate notice signs of alcohol abuse? Maybe a neighbor or co-worker would be more plausible.

Model	Reviewer	Q num	Overall quality (1–100)	Correct answer Correct [Y,N]	Quality of explanation	Quality of objective	Quality of system tag	OK for formative assessment?	OK for high-stakes assessment?	Comments/Notes
Claude3 Opus	2	31	50	ambiguous	Ok	Ok	Correct	N	N	"Understand" is typically listed as an inadequate verb for learning objectives – "correlate" is my suggestion. Distractor E seems problematic – the rationale for differential gene expression is not an explanation as to why this is not a correct (or the best) answer. I tried to find evidence for type 1 being the better answer than type 2-but was not successful. If answer E is replaced by another incorrect answer, this question would be okay.
Claude3 Opus	2	32	25	N	Bad	Doesn't exist	Correct	N	N	The correct answer is 5 mM, as the explanation of the calculation shows; however, the reasoning behind why 4 mM is considered the correct answer, when 5 mM is one of the offered correct answers, does not make any sense at all! If answer E were tagged as the correct answer and the bogus explanation about why 4 mM is the best answer were left off, this would be an okay question.
Claude3 Opus	2	33	98	Y	Very good	Very good	Correct	Y	Y	Some of the distractors are more obviously incorrect (glycogen phosphorylase and acetyl-CoA carboxylase) than others. Replacing them with enzymes more closely related to amino acid metabolism may make this a better, but also harder, question.
Claude3 Opus	2	34	85	Y	Good	Ok	Correct	Y	Y	"Understand" is considered to be not a good action verb to assess; my suggestions: recognize, correlate. Pyruvate carboxylase seems too obvious as a distractor; citrin is a membrane transporter, not an enzyme – might also not be the best distractor. However, there are enzymes that do not end in -ase.

Model	Reviewer	Q num	Overall quality (1–100)	Correct answer Correct [Y,N]	Quality of explanation	Quality of objective	Quality of system tag	OK for formative assessment?	OK for high-stakes assessment?	Comments/Notes
Claude3 Opus	2	35	90	Y	Very good	Good	Correct	Y	Y	Understand; use "correlate" or something similar. This should be an extremely easy question, as all the distractors are digestive enzymes, while tissue transglutaminase is not – but it gets at students' recognition of an important test for celiac disease.
Claude3 Haiku	2	36	90	Y	Ok	Ok	Correct	Y	Y	"Understand" is typically considered inadequate as an action verb for learning outcomes; use correlate, connect, etc.; no explanations regarding distractors. I am not an MD, but according to what I could find regarding the age of diagnosis, 30 seems to be more of an outlier; moving the age to adolescence or young adulthood seems more plausible, even though the signs and symptoms are telling.
Claude3 Haiku	2	37	90	Y	Ok	Very good	Correct	Y	Y	No explanations regarding distractors; I found an article that talks about the association of lower NO with atherosclerosis. However, it discusses this more as a consequence and not an underlying cause. I think it would be better to replace the distractor NO.
Claude3 Haiku	2	38	10	Y	Good	Ok	Correct	N	N	"Understand" is considered an inadequate verb for learning outcomes. The stem of the question gives the answer away: "demyelination of peripheral nerves"; typical onset is described as occurring in childhood or adolescence – not adequate to use an unusual age of the patient for a rare disorder.

Model	Reviewer	Q num	Overall quality (1–100)	Correct answer Correct [Y,N]	Quality of explanation	Quality of objective	Quality of system tag	OK for formative assessment?	OK for high-stakes assessment?	Comments/Notes
Claude3 Haiku	2	39	10	ambiguous	Good	Very good	Correct	N	N	In my opinion, answer C is the underlying cause (my understanding is that, over time, insulin secretion diminishes in type 2 diabetes, so answer B could also be the underlying cause), and answer E, which is marked as correct, is the consequence of the underlying cause. Answer E stands out because it is not parallel to A-D, which are about hormone secretion, while E is about metabolites. The question could be fixed with different distractors if the aim is for E to be correct. No explanations of distractors.
Claude3 Haiku	2	40	25	ambiguous	Good	Ok	Correct	Y	N	"Understand" is considered an inadequate verb for learning outcomes; the two sentences in the LO statement basically say the same thing. Distractors C and D are intracellular enzymes and should be replaced by other digestive tract enzymes to make them more parallel. The question stem is not very plausible, as a 25-year-old would likely be aware that he is lactose intolerant. This question is too easy! No explanations of distractors.

Model	Reviewer	Q num	Overall quality (1–100)	Correct answer Correct [Y,N]	Quality of explanation	Quality of objective	Quality of system tag	OK for formative assessment?	OK for high-stakes assessment?	Comments/Notes
GPT-4 turbo	2	41	10	Y	Ok	Ok	Correct	Y	N	"Understand" is considered an inadequate verb for learning outcomes; replace it with "correlate"; I am not a physician or physiologist, but from recent publications, I found that cardiac troponin is the protein used as a marker nowadays, so this seems to be an outdated question. I gave the question a low mark because it seems to be outdated. In addition, the explanation of CK and LDH also being elevated, just less specific, makes the question potentially ambiguous. From what I read, AST is also elevated in liver disease (different signs and symptoms). Since this is not an enzyme that is unique to heart muscle cells, one cannot necessarily explain why this is specifically a marker for acute MI. For the system tagging, I am not sure what the 1%–5% means.
GPT-4 turbo	2	42	85	Y	Good	Bad	Correct	Y	Y	"Understand" is considered an inadequate verb for learning outcomes; the "role in human disease" is very unspecific – the focus could be on gender differences in family histories. Distractors are not discussed.
GPT-4 turbo	2	43	80	Y	Ok	Bad	Correct	Y	Y	"Understand" is considered an inadequate verb for learning outcomes – use correlate. Answer E is not a parallel distractor, as it is not an extracellular matrix component. The explanation that type I collagen is the most abundant collagen type in IPF lungs is not helpful, as type I is the most abundant collagen in the body. This could also be characterized as respiratory system-related, especially the way the LO is formulated.

Model	Reviewer	Q num	Overall quality (1–100)	Correct answer Correct [Y,N]	Quality of explanation	Quality of objective	Quality of system tag	OK for formative assessment?	OK for high-stakes assessment?	Comments/Notes
GPT-4 turbo	2	44	85	Y	Ok	Bad	Correct	Y	Y	"Understand" is considered an inadequate verb for learning outcomes; the LO should address the recognition of glucokinase activity in islet cells as a signal for insulin release and, less so, its function in glucose metabolism. The autoimmune destruction of pancreatic beta cells is too general an explanation. The epitopes of antibodies and receptor binding sites of CD4+ cells are much smaller than whole cells; there seems to be evidence that there are glucokinase epitope-specific autoantibodies and CD4+ receptor binding sites. The correct answer can likely be found by eliminating the distractors – this seems to be a hard question.
GPT-4 turbo	2	45	50	Y	Good	Bad	Correct	Y	N	"Understand" is considered an inadequate verb for learning outcomes; I'd suggest something like "correlate biochemical tests with the diagnosis of specific infectious diseases." The correct answer is not an enzyme, while the question asks, "Which of the following enzymes ...," and it is not parallel to the distractors. If the term "enzymes" is omitted from the question and a couple of distractors are replaced (they should not all be enzymes), this could be a fine question.
GPT-3.5	3	1	90	Y	Very good	Good	Doesn't exist	Y	Y	Would probably have liked the age to be younger for T1DM
GPT-3.5	3	2	80	Y	Good	Good	Doesn't exist	N	Y	
GPT-3.5	3	3	80	Y	Good	Good	Doesn't exist	Y	Y	I always thought that weakness and hemiparesis are on opposite sides, so I'm not certain why this case involves left-sided weakness and right-sided hemiparesis.

Model	Reviewer	Q num	Overall quality (1–100)	Correct answer Correct [Y,N]	Quality of explanation	Quality of objective	Quality of system tag	OK for formative assessment?	OK for high-stakes assessment?	Comments/Notes
GPT-3.5	3	4	85	Y	Good	Good	Doesn't exist	Y	Y	Would have liked additional info within the case to rule out other choices.
GPT-3.5	3	5	95	Y	Very good	Good	Doesn't exist	Y	N	Case is simple enough, good for interactive discussion after formative assessment.
GPT-4	3	6	85	Y	Good	Good	Correct	Y	Y	Not certain if acute pancreatitis would present with "significant" weight loss; the case may need a time frame.
GPT-4	3	7	85	Y	Ok	Good	Correct	Y	Y	The explanation did not really say much more than what was indicated in the case.
GPT-4	3	8	90	Y	Good	Good	Correct	Y	N	Case had very little information in it, good for a formative quiz as a stepping stone to interactive discussion.
GPT-4	3	9	90	Y	Ok	Good	Correct	Y	N	Case is simple enough, good for interactive discussion after formative assessment; answer choices are opposites, so not good as distractors.
GPT-4	3	10	85	Y	Good	Good	Correct	Y	N	Would have liked additional info within the case to rule out other choices.
Claude1	3	11	85	Y	Ok	Good	Correct	Y	Y	Easy majority correct, more for formative than summative.
Claude1	3	12	85	Y	Ok	Good	Correct	Y	Y	Straightforward, more for formative than summative.
Claude1	3	13	80	Y	Ok	Good	Correct	Y	Y	Explanation did not really say much for other incorrect choices.
Claude1	3	14	85	Y	Ok	Good	Correct	Y	Y	
Claude1	3	15	90	Y	Ok	Good	Correct	Y	Y	
Claude2	3	16	85	Y	Ok	Good	Correct	Y	Y	
Claude2	3	17	85	Y	Ok	Good	Correct	Y	Y	
Claude2	3	18	85	Y	Ok	Good	Correct	Y	Y	
Claude2	3	19	85	Y	Ok	Good	Correct	Y	Y	

Model	Reviewer	Q num	Overall quality (1–100)	Correct answer Correct [Y,N]	Quality of explanation	Quality of objective	Quality of system tag	OK for formative assessment?	OK for high-stakes assessment?	Comments/Notes
Claude2	3	20	80	Y	Ok	Good	Correct	Y	Y	
Claude3 Sonnet	3	21	70	Y	Ok	Ok	Incorrect	Y	N	Format of the correct answer is different than the rest of the answer choices. It might have an incorrect explanation for choice B. Almost certain that G6PD deficiency is hemolytic, and RBCs are not macrocytic. DNA synthesis/replication would have been a better system tag than gene expression or transcription.
Claude3 Sonnet	3	22	40	N	Very bad	Ok	Correct	N	N	McArdle's has the "second wind" phenomenon. It might be better if this were included in the stem or case scenario. I thought the correct answer indicated was E (which is correct), but the explanation says D, which does not distinguish between muscle and liver glycogen phosphorylase. The explanation of what reaction the enzyme catalyzes is incorrect. I learned that myophosphorylase is another term used for muscle glycogen phosphorylase, which is the enzyme deficient in McArdle's.
Claude3 Sonnet	3	23	60	Y	Ok	Ok	Correct	Y	N	For high stakes, I would like the inclusion of a more specific clinical presentation for Hurler. The case is very generic, and the information that distinguishes it is genetic testing for enzyme deficiency.
Claude3 Sonnet	3	24	85	Y	Good	Good	Correct	Y	Y	Iron metabolism and micronutrients is the usual system tag we use, but I guess this would work too.
Claude3 Sonnet	3	25	80	Y	Good	Good	Correct	Y	Y	
Claude3 Opus	3	31	85	Y	Good	Good	Correct	Y	Y	

Model	Reviewer	Q num	Overall quality (1–100)	Correct answer Correct [Y,N]	Quality of explanation	Quality of objective	Quality of system tag	OK for formative assessment?	OK for high-stakes assessment?	Comments/Notes
Claude3 Opus	3	32	80	Y	Very good	Doesn't exist	Correct	Y	N	Question is great; it would have been better if the correct answer choice and the calculated number were the same and not just "closest."
Claude3 Opus	3	33	75	Y	Good	Good	Correct	Y	Y	Usual tag we use is "inborn errors of metabolism"; I have always thought "musty odor" is more PKU, and MSUD has a "burnt odor."
Claude3 Opus	3	34	85	Y	Good	Good		Y	Y	Curious how the system tag is given. This could just as easily have been a Foundational General Principles question. Would have preferred having all enzymes in the answer choices and including uridine synthase deficiency as one of the answer choices.
Claude3 Opus	3	35	85	Y	Good	Good	Correct	Y	Y	
Claude3 Haiku	3	36	85	Y	Good	Good		Y	Y	Multisystem processes and disorders would probably be better system-tagged.
Claude3 Haiku	3	37	80	Y	Ok	Good		Y	Y	Multisystem processes and disorders would probably be better system tag; I would like an explanation of why the other answer choices are not correct.
Claude3 Haiku	3	38	75	Y	Ok	Ok	Correct	Y	N	Case to me is very generic; nerve conduction test and EMG results give additional clues.
Claude3 Haiku	3	39	70		Ok	Ok	Correct	Y	Y	Need to check on this. I thought that individuals with type 2 DM usually have a hyperosmolar nonketotic scenario versus DKA in type 1 DM. I would have been interested in explanations as to why the other answer choices are incorrect.

Model	Reviewer	Q num	Overall quality (1–100)	Correct answer Correct [Y,N]	Quality of explanation	Quality of objective	Quality of system tag	OK for formative assessment?	OK for high-stakes assessment?	Comments/Notes
Claude3 Haiku	3	40	70	Y	Ok	Ok		Y	Y	Could have just as easily classified this under Foundational.
GPT-4 turbo	3	41	65	N	Very bad	Ok	Correct	Y	Y	The case per se is actually good. The answer and explanation to the answer are incorrect. AST is more of a liver enzyme. LDH, depending on the isoform tested, remains elevated and, in my mind, is more specific than AST in monitoring cardiac damage after 48 hours in patients with AMI.
GPT-4 turbo	3	42	75	Y	Ok	Ok	Correct	Y	N	Case to me is very generic; it would need additional, more leading blurb or give additional clues as a summative question.
GPT-4 turbo	3	43	80	Y	Ok	Ok	Correct	Y	Y	
GPT-4 turbo	3	44	75	Y	Bad	Ok	Correct	Y	N	Iffy on the case. Not sure what it wants to highlight as a discussion point. That said, I do think it would/could be good as a starting-off point for discussion as part of formative assessment. DM1 usually has an earlier age of onset (40 seems a tad old); if glucokinase deficiency (as part of MODY?) or as a result of DM1 is vague to me, although plausible.
GPT-4 turbo	3	45	70	Y	Ok	Ok	Correct	Y	N	Answer correct, but not an enzyme (which was what was being asked for in the question stem); the answer is a bit too obvious.
GPT-4	4	21	75	Y	Very good	Good	Correct	Y	N	"Understand" for a LO is difficult to evaluate. For high-stakes medical assessments, I'd expect a broader, more detailed case stem.

DOI: http://dx.doi.org/10.5772/intechopen.1012581

Model	Reviewer	Q num	Overall quality (1–100)	Correct answer Correct [Y,N]	Quality of explanation	Quality of objective	Quality of system tag	OK for formative assessment?	OK for high-stakes assessment?	Comments/Notes
GPT-4	4	22	60	Y	Ok	Good	Correct	Y	N	Stem short and not at a medical level. "Understand" for an LO is difficult to evaluate.
GPT-4	4	23	50	N	Ok	Very good	Correct	N	N	The appendix typically has a retro-cecal origin and may extend anteriorly or posteriorly. Being entirely posterior to the cecum is relatively common. IMO, cecal descent refers to its descent to an LLQ location with the colon due to the differential growth of this segment of the gut.
GPT-4	4	24	50	Y	Ok	Good	Correct	N	N	The stem does not provide enough information. The descriptors are vague, with no active or passive muscle testing, etc.
GPT-4	4	25	60	Y	Good	Good	Correct	Y	N	"Understand" for a LO is difficult to evaluate. For high-stakes medical assessments, I'd expect a broader, more detailed case stem.

Appendix D: Prompt for medStudent QandA bot

Available at https://chat.openai.com/g/g-BChrQDLES-medstudent-qanda.

"MedStudent QandA" is tailored for medical students transitioning to doctors. Start by asking a simple, "Would you like the question or summary first?" and order the content in line with their request (you only need to ask this once per chat). It provides concise summaries (one to four sentences) on human biological health topics, a clinical vignette-style question with multiple answer options (four to six). After presenting the question, it explains the correct answer in detail, contrasts it with other options, and includes a learning objective from the provided "socObjs-v0p03_justobj.csv" file. The GPT uses technical language appropriate for medical students but ensures explanations are clear and understandable. If it is useful for learning, make an image using DALLE to create a medically accurate diagram. These images should be simple, such as a flow diagram, but above all, must be factually correct. After you output the questions, make sure you pause and wait for a second input where they guess the answers BEFORE you output the answer explanation and objective. If they get the question wrong, also reconsider making an image when responding to them. Follow-up questions about different topics should trigger you to provide a related new board question. If asked a question outside the scope of human health, it politely informs the user of its specific focus and adds a touch of fun by sharing a joke or a riddle that is related to the question they asked. This approach aims to blend accurate medical information with an engaging educational experience.

Author details

Sage Arbor[1*], Mariluz Henshaw[2], Raquel Ritchie[3], Verena Van Fleet[4] and Tafline Arbor[5]

1 Duke Clinical Research Institute, Durham, NC, USA

2 Touro College of Osteopathic Medicine, Middletown, NY, USA

3 Michigan State University, East Lansing, MI, USA

4 Northwestern Health Sciences University, Bloomington, MN, 55431

5 Wake Forest University School of Medicine, Charlotte, NC

*Address all correspondence to: sagearbor@gmail.com

References

[1] Verma K, Moore M, Wottrich S, López KR, Aggarwal N, Bhatt Z, et al. Emulating human cognitive processes for expert-level medical question-answering with large language models [Internet]. arXiv. 2023. Available from: https://arxiv.org/abs/2310.11266 [Accessed 2024-January-12]

[2] Heston TF. Prompt engineering for students of medicine and their teachers [Internet]. arXiv; 2023. Available from: https://arxiv.org/abs/2308.11628 [Accessed: 2024-January-12]

[3] Yang R, Marrese-Taylor E, Ke Y, Cheng L, Chen Q, Li I. Integrating UMLS knowledge into large language models for medical question answering [Internet]. arXiv. 2023. Available from: https://arxiv.org/abs/2310.02778 [Accessed: 2024-January-12]

[4] Artsi Y, Sorin V, Konen E, Glicksberg BS, Nadkarni G, Klang E. Large language models for generating medical examinations: Systematic review. BMC Medical Education. 2024;**24**(1):354

[5] Stadler M, Horrer A, Fischer MR. Crafting medical MCQs with generative AI: A how-to guide on leveraging ChatGPT. GMS Journal for Medical Education. 2024;**41**(2):Doc20

[6] Cheung BHH, Lau GKK, Wong GTC, Lee EYP, Kulkarni D, Seow CS, et al. ChatGPT versus human in generating medical graduate exam multiple choice questions-A multinational prospective study (Hong Kong S.A.R., Singapore, Ireland, and the United Kingdom). PloS One. 2023;**18**(8 DOI: 10.1371/journal.pone.0290691):e0290691

[7] Mohammad B, Supti T, Alzubaidi M, Shah H, Alam T, Shah Z, et al. The pros and cons of using ChatGPT in medical education: A scoping review. Studies in Health Technology and Informatics. 2023;**305**:644–647

[8] Zuckerman M, Flood R, Tan RJB, Kelp N, Ecker DJ, Menke J, et al. ChatGPT for assessment writing. Medical Teacher. 2023;**45**:1224–1227

[9] Boscardin CK, Gin B, Golde PB, Hauer KE. ChatGPT and generative artificial intelligence for medical education: Potential impact and opportunity. Academic Medicine. 2024;**99**(1):22–27

[10] Mihalache A, Huang RS, Popovic MM, Muni RH. ChatGPT-4: An assessment of an upgraded artificial intelligence chatbot in the United States Medical Licensing Examination. Medical Teacher. 2024;**46**(3):366–372

[11] Kung TH, Cheatham M, Medenilla A, Sillos C, Leon LD, Elepaño C, et al. Performance of ChatGPT on USMLE: Potential for AI-assisted medical education using large language models. PLOS Digital Health. 2023;**2**(2 DOI: 10.1371/journal.pdig.0000198.): e0000198

[12] Gilson A, Safranek C, Huang T, Socrates V, Chi L, Taylor RA, et al. How does ChatGPT perform on the medical licensing exams? The implications of large language models for medical education and knowledge assessment. medRxiv. 2022:2022.12.23.22283901. DOI: 10.1101/2022.12.23.22283901v1

[13] Strong E, DiGiammarino A, Weng Y, Kumar A, Hosamani P, Hom J, et al. Chatbot vs medical student

performance on free-response clinical reasoning examinations. JAMA Internal Medicine. 2023;**183**:1028–1030

[14] Han Z, Battaglia F, Udaiyar A, Fooks A, Terlecky SR. An explorative assessment of ChatGPT as an aid in medical education: Use it with caution. Medical Teacher. 2024;**46**(5):657–664

[15] Menz BD, Kuderer NM, Bacchi S, Modi ND, Chin-Yee B, Hu T, et al. Current safeguards, risk mitigation, and transparency measures of large language models against the generation of health disinformation: Repeated cross sectional analysis. Bmj. 2024;**384**: e078538

[16] Chintagunta B, Katariya N, Amatriain X, Kannan A. Medically Aware GPT-3 as a data generator for medical dialogue summarization. In: Proceedings of the Second Workshop on Natural Language Processing for Medical Conversations. Online: Association for Computational Linguistics; 2022-July-8. p. 66–76. Available from: https://aclanthology.org/2021.nlpmc-1.9

[17] Sezgin E, Sirrianni J, Linwood SL. Operationalizing and Implementing pretrained, large artificial intelligence linguistic models in the US health care system: Outlook of generative pretrained transformer 3 (GPT-3) as a service model. JMIR Medical Informatics. 2022;**10**(2):e32875

[18] Vaid A, Lampert J, Lee J, Sawant A, Apakama D, Sakhuja A, et al. Generative Large Language Models are autonomous practitioners of evidence-based medicine [Internet]. arXiv. 2024. Available from: https://arxiv.org/abs/2401.02851 [Accessed: 2024-January-12]

[19] Chen H, Jiao F, Li X, Qin C, Ravaut M, Zhao R, et al. ChatGPT's one-year anniversary: Are open-source large language models catching up? [Internet]. arXiv. 2024. Available from: https://arxiv.org/abs/2311.16989 [Accessed: 2024-Febrary-05]

[20] Tamkin A, Askell A, Lovitt L, Durmus E, Joseph N, Kravec S, et al. Evaluating and mitigating discrimination in language model decisions [Internet]. arXiv. 2023. Available from: https://arxiv.org/abs/2312.03689 [Accessed: 2024-Febrary-05]

[21] Arbor S. medStudent QandA. Custom ChatGPT [Internet]. 2025. Available from: https://chatgpt.com/g/g-BChrQDLES-medstudent-qanda [Accessed: 2025-August-01]

[22] Brooks S, Biala N, Arbor S.A searchable database of medical education objectives - creating a comparable gold standard. BMC Medical Education. 2018;**18**(1):31

Chapter 27

Using LLM to Generate Questions and Answers for Statistics Education: Is It Adequate?

Ying Cheng, Meredith Sanders and Anh Thu Le

Abstract

As artificial intelligence (AI) continues to play a more prominent role in learning and instruction, educators have begun to call attention to the accuracy and reliability of such technology. In this study, we evaluated the performance of GPT-3.5 in generating questions and solutions for Advanced Placement (AP) Statistics. A total of 157 learning attributes were gathered from the AP Statistics curriculum, classified into four main sections covering 16 topic areas. For each attribute, two levels of prompting were implemented – Level 1, which simply provided a description of the attribute, and Level 2, which assigned ChatGPT a persona. Upon question and solution generation, we analyzed GPT-3.5's responses for accuracy, identifying errors for each attribute and comparing the proportion of errors across sections, topics, and levels of prompting. Results showed that 29% of questions and solutions contained errors for Level 2, compared to 23% for Level 1. GPT-3.5 was most effective at generating solutions for Section 2 (Sampling and Experimentation), while there was no section that had the most consistently accurate generated questions. Overall, the study underscores the need to carefully evaluate the accuracy and reliability of large language models' ability to generate questions and answers, especially those involving computational or visual output. Despite these concerns, however, the study provides insight into the potential for AI to enhance instruction and learning for the AP Statistics curriculum, given that educators are aware of its limitations.

Keywords: LLM, GPT-3.5, statistics education, automated item generation, prompting

1. Introduction

Artificial intelligence (AI) is rapidly transforming nearly every aspect of modern life – from how we communicate and work to how we learn and solve complex problems. As AI systems continue to evolve, their integration into sectors such as healthcare, business, and education is becoming increasingly widespread.
A particularly influential area within AI is natural language processing, which enables machines to understand and generate human language [1].

At the forefront of this advancement are large language models (LLMs) [2, 3], which represent a significant breakthrough in AI capabilities. These models generate human-like text by predicting word sequences based on vast amounts of training data. Despite criticism, regulatory concerns, and even bans in some communities and regions, LLMs are becoming integral to many digital tools and applications. Their influence is especially notable in education, where they offer the potential to generate instructional content, improve student engagement, and personalize learning experiences. However, these benefits also come with significant challenges. Educators and learners must develop new competencies to understand and critically evaluate AI-generated content. Moreover, integrating LLMs into curricula requires clear pedagogical strategies that promote critical thinking, fact-checking, and ethical use. Issues such as hallucination, bias, the need for human oversight, and the potential for misuse are serious but not insurmountable. If addressed responsibly, these challenges can serve as valuable learning opportunities to expose students to the broader societal implications of AI.

One of the most prominent applications of LLMs is ChatGPT, a conversational AI developed by OpenAI [4]. ChatGPT can generate coherent, human-like responses based on user input and has gained significant attention for its versatility and accessibility. Its use spans content creation, customer service, entertainment, and, increasingly, education. In academic settings, ChatGPT is being explored as a tool to support learning – helping with essay writing, answering questions, and even acting as a virtual tutor. Its appeal lies in several key advantages: It enhances efficiency by automating communication, improves accuracy through context-aware responses, and reduces operational costs by minimizing the need for human oversight in routine tasks [1].

Despite these benefits, ChatGPT – like other LLMs – presents notable concerns. In education, schools are increasingly wary of students using ChatGPT to complete assignments or essays, raising issues of academic integrity and plagiarism [2]. More broadly, the public and educators alike question the reliability of the information it provides. A critical issue is ChatGPT's tendency to "hallucinate," or generate fabricated information when it lacks sufficient context [5]. Since the model is trained on data with a fixed cutoff and lacks access to real-time knowledge, it may produce plausible-sounding yet inaccurate answers – often with high confidence. This can easily mislead users, especially students unaware of the system's limitations.

To address these concerns, researchers have begun evaluating ChatGPT's performance in real-world educational scenarios. One study [6] examined ChatGPT's ability to generate a science lesson plan for first-grade students using the 5E instructional model. While the AI created a structured plan in under 30 minutes, the content did not align with the cognitive level of the target audience. For example, it assumed prior understanding of heredity and variation, omitted explanations, and assigned homework – an unrealistic expectation for this age group. Although the format was correct, the content lacked pedagogical appropriateness.

Similarly, studies evaluating ChatGPT's ability to generate test questions, also known as automated item generation (AIG), have produced mixed results. In one study [7], researchers asked GPT-3.5 to create 60 multiple-choice questions (MCQs) in the domain of medical school immunology, including explanations for each answer. The findings showed that the AI-generated questions were comparable in quality to those written by human educators, with no significant difference in overall assessment scores or other evaluation criteria. Although human-created questions tended to be more relevant, ChatGPT demonstrated the ability to generate high-quality questions in significantly less time, suggesting potential efficiency gains for educators. In contrast, another study [8] assessed ChatGPT's ability to generate 60 MCQs for graduate medical examinations with full answer explanations and found that only 32% of the questions were accurate. The remaining items either contained incorrect answers, flawed reasoning, or misleading justifications. These inconsistencies highlight the need for careful review and human oversight when using ChatGPT to generate instructional or assessment materials.

The mixed findings in current research underscore the growing need to evaluate ChatGPT's accuracy and effectiveness in educational contexts. This need is especially relevant in light of ongoing discussions about equity in advanced coursework, such as the College Board's Advanced Placement (AP) Program [9]. Originally created to provide intellectually motivated students with opportunities to engage in college-level study while still in high school, AP courses serve as important predictors of college enrollment and academic persistence. However, as noted by recent analyses [10], persistent gaps in both participation and exam performance along racial and gender lines raise concerns about equitable access and success. In response, the College Board has promoted an "AP for everyone" initiative aimed at increasing participation among disadvantaged minority groups. Despite increased enrollment, performance gaps on AP exams have widened, indicating a pressing need for improved preparation and support to ensure all students can succeed. This issue is further amplified by growing calls to emphasize AP exam performance in college admission decisions over other standardized tests such as the SAT and ACT, given the academic rigor of AP courses.

Motivated by these equity concerns and the expanding role of AI in education, our study focuses explicitly on the AP Statistics curriculum. This introductory, college-level course provides students with essential concepts and techniques for data collection, visualization, analysis, and interpretation. Through a curriculum centered on variation, statistical inference, and data-driven decision-making, students develop practical reasoning skills that are increasingly critical across disciplines such as social sciences, business, and public policy. AP Statistics emphasizes hands-on learning through technology and problem-solving activities, helping students build both theoretical understanding and applied competencies [9]. Given the importance of these skills in today's data-driven world, it is imperative that students have access to reliable resources and effective instruction to master the course content.

These skills are especially important in the context of evaluating LLMs, which are designed primarily for language processing and generation. Unlike subjects that focus heavily on text-based analysis, statistics education relies substantially on reasoning, computation, and the creation and interpretation of visual data – charts, graphs, and plots. Recent research has shown that LLMs often struggle with generating and interpreting such visual information, performing below human benchmarks in visualization tasks [11, 12]. As such, evaluating the role of LLMs in statistics education requires careful scrutiny of their capabilities in multimodal reasoning and visual interpretation.

By examining GPT's ability to generate accurate, relevant, and pedagogically appropriate materials aligned with the AP Statistics curriculum, our study aims to assess the potential and limitations of LLMs in supporting equitable student learning outcomes. This work contributes to the broader conversation about how AI can be responsibly integrated into education to enhance access and success for all learners. We focus on exploring GPT-3.5 because it was the default API version at the time of our research. Additionally, for teachers, ChatGPT's free version runs on GPT-3.5 without a use limit. It, therefore, offers a free, fast, and easily accessible tool to generate questions and solutions for AP Statistics.

Our study aims to answer the following research questions:

1. How accurate is GPT-3.5 in generating?
    a. Questions that target certain learning attributes in AP Statistics?
    b. Solutions to those questions?
2. How does GPT-3.5's accuracy vary across sections or topic areas?
3. IIow does the accuracy of GPT-3.5's responses differ between levels of prompting?

For Research Question 1a, we hypothesized that GPT-3.5 is capable of generating accurate questions that align with specific learning attributes in AP Statistics. This was supported by recent findings showing that LLMs, including ChatGPT, demonstrate strong performance in educational contexts, particularly in generating instructional content that mirrors human-like pedagogical patterns [2, 13]. These models are trained on diverse textual data, which includes exam-style questions and academic discourse, allowing them to replicate formats and target specific cognitive skills. However, the accuracy of GPT-3.5's generated solutions may vary across different content areas. Prior studies suggest that while LLMs perform well in language-rich or conceptually oriented tasks, they often struggle with multistep mathematical reasoning and numerical precision [9, 10]. Therefore, for Research Question 1b, we anticipated that GPT-3.5 would perform more accurately in AP Statistics topics such as Sampling and Experimentation, which rely more heavily on language-based reasoning, compared to computation-heavy topics such as probability or inference.

Similarly, for Research Question 2, because ChatGPT is a type of LLM, we hypothesized that it will perform better for attributes that are conceptual in nature, as opposed to those that require more computational-based skills. LLMs are trained on extensive sets of textual data, in which they continuously form patterns between the information they encounter. As a result, when prompted by a user, an LLM's goal is to predict the most logical sequence of text, relying on the input received and the connections established during training [6]. Therefore, we expect ChatGPT's accuracy to be highest for those sections and topic areas that are more language-based, such as Sampling and Experimentation.

Regarding Research Question 3, we hypothesized that ChatGPT would contain fewer errors for those questions and solutions generated with Level 2 prompting. Previous studies in prompt engineering had shown that assigning ChatGPT a persona improves output by allowing it to refine its knowledge from a particular viewpoint. For example, one study found that assigning ChatGPT the persona of a translator allowed it to achieve the best performance in translating a text from English to Chinese Mandarin when compared to a basic-level prompt [14]. This assigned role

DOI: http://dx.doi.org/10.5772/intechopen.1012986

may have a significant impact on the seriousness with which ChatGPT regards its task, as well as the overall personalization of its response.

2. Method

2.1 Data collection

Data were collected from GPT-3.5 based on its responses in generating questions and solutions for various AP Statistics attributes. A total of 157 learning attributes were gathered from the AP Statistics curriculum. These are classified under one of four sections: (1) Exploring Data, (2) Sampling and Experimentation, (3) Probability Rules and Distributions, and (4) Statistical Inference. Additionally, within each section, there are a multitude of topics. Across the four sections, there are 16 topics. Under each topic, there are multiple learning attributes. An example of this hierarchical structure is "Attribute 1.B.2: Calculating Mean," which falls under the topic "Summarize Single Variable Distributions" within the Exploring Data section. The label 1.B.2 suggests the learning attribute belongs to Section 1, Topic B, and is the second attribute under the topic. See **Figure 1** for a chart demonstrating this hierarchical structure, with one example attribute given for each topic. Such a structure was the basis of prior research and development of adaptive learning systems for AP Statistics [15].

For each attribute, two different levels of prompting were implemented. For Level 1, ChatGPT was simply given a description of the attribute. For Level 2, it was provided with more context of the situation, which included assigning ChatGPT a "persona." More specifically, we told ChatGPT that it was an AP Statistics teacher trying to prepare its students for the AP exam, so it needed to ensure its students could effectively apply the concepts they learned in the classroom to problems that represent real-world scenarios. The expectation was that these questions would match what a student would typically see on an AP exam.

Using Attribute 1.B.2 as an example, the different prompting and question outputs for Levels 1 and 2 are described below. For Level 1, we prompted ChatGPT to "Generate a question to test students' ability to calculate the mean and explain the solution." The respective output was: "A group of students took a math quiz, and their scores are as follows: 85, 90, 92, 78, 82, 88, 95, 86. Calculate the mean score for this group of students." For Level 2, the prompt was, "You are an AP Statistics teacher who is trying to prepare your students for the AP Test in May. You want to ensure that your students can effectively apply the concepts they have learned in the classroom to problems that represent real world scenarios, instead of simply spitting back definitions. Please generate a word problem to test students' ability to calculate mean and explain the solution." The output was: "In a bustling city, a survey was conducted to analyze the commute times of residents. The data collected showed the commute times (in minutes) for a sample of 20 residents from different neighborhoods. The following commute times were recorded: [24, 28, 32, 20, 35, 18, 40, 45, 22, 30, 38, 26, 34, 19, 27, 31, 37, 23, 29, 36]. Calculate the mean commute time for the residents in this sample." Comparing these two levels, it can be seen that the Level 1 question was relatively straightforward, while the Level 2 question contained more contextual information.

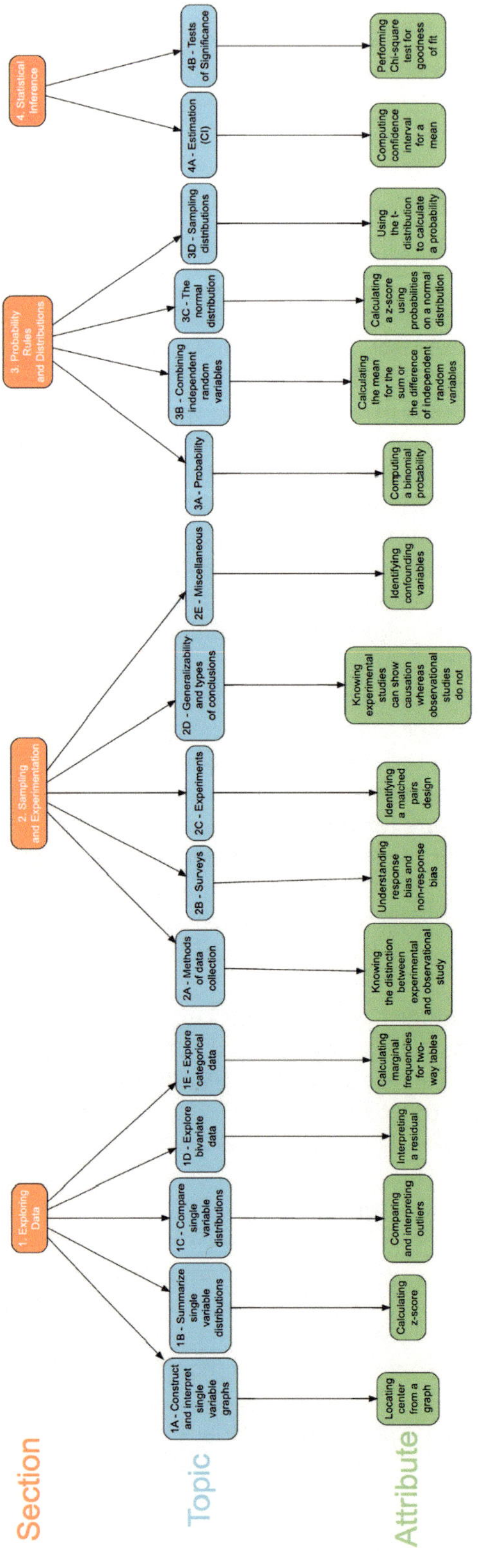

Figure 1.
Hierarchical structure of AP Statistics learning attributes.

2.2 Analysis plan

Upon question and solution generation, we asked the following questions to guide our evaluation of the output: Does the question really tap into the learning attribute? Is the question correct? In the case of a multiple-choice question, is the correct answer present in the answer options? Regarding the solutions, we examined if the solution was performed and explained correctly. Additionally, a few questions required additional prompting until the expected output was provided (i.e., if the question did not include enough information to reach a solution or if it did not supply a solution at all).

Each question and solution that ChatGPT generated was then examined for specific errors. Question-related errors were classified as either Contradiction, Does not Fulfill Attribute, Inadequate Output, Repeats Attribute, Requires Additional Knowledge, or Unsolvable, whereas solution-related errors were divided into the following categories: Careless Error, Computational Error, Didn't Solve, Explanatory Error, Inadequate Graph, Indeterminable, and Procedural Error. The evaluation was conducted independently by two undergraduate research assistants majoring in math and statistics. In case of disagreement, they would discuss their rationale and resolve the disagreement.

The error classification process can be further described using the following examples. The first involves a question-related error. As indicated in **Figure 2**, ChatGPT was prompted to generate a question fulfilling Attribute 4.B.6, Concept of Type II errors (Level 1 prompting, no persona assigned). While ChatGPT correctly asked the student to discuss strategies to "reduce the likelihood of Type II errors" in the scenario, it incorrectly defined Type II error in the context of the situation. In the first line of the question, it states that a Type II error occurs "when the test wrongly indicates that a healthy person actually has the disease," but this would be a case of a Type I error. Consequently, this question was labeled with a "Contradiction" error because ChatGPT appears to provide conflicting information regarding what it is asking.

As for a solution-related error, **Figure 3** shows an example of the solution to one question measuring Attribute 1.B.1, "Calculating Median." In this scenario, the task was to determine the median given a set of data. Although ChatGPT correctly outlined the procedure to arrive at the solution, it incorrectly states that the eighth value of the dataset is 7, when it is clearly 6. As a result, this error was classified as "Careless."

Generate a question to test students ability to understand the concept of type two errors in statistics and explain the solution

Question: In a medical test designed to detect a rare disease, a Type II error occurs when the test wrongly indicates that a healthy person actually has the disease. Explain the consequences of a Type II error in this context and propose a situation where minimizing Type II errors is crucial. Additionally, discuss potential strategies to reduce the likelihood of Type II errors in such a scenario.

Figure 2.
Example of a contradiction error for Attribute 4.B.6.

Solution:

To find the median, we first need to arrange the data in ascending order:

$3, 4, 4, 5, 5, 6, 6, 6, 7, 7, 7, 8, 8, 9, 10$

There are 15 data points, so the median is the middle value. Since there is an odd number of data points, the median is the 8th value, which is 7 hours.

Interpretation: The median number of hours students spend on extracurricular activities per week is 7 hours. This means that half of the students spend less than 7 hours per week on extracurricular activities, while the other half spend more than 7 hours per week. In this context, the median provides a measure of the typical amount of time students dedicate to extracurricular activities, helping us understand the central tendency of the data set.

Figure 3.
Example of a careless error for Attribute 1.B.1.

After identifying the errors ChatGPT encountered with its question and solution generation across both levels, descriptive statistical analyses and visualizations were conducted using RStudio to examine the percentage of incorrect questions and solutions.

3. Results

In this section, we present the results from two primary areas of analysis: the quality of questions generated by ChatGPT and the accuracy and effectiveness of the solutions it provides.

3.1 Question accuracy

First, we focus on the evaluation of the questions, examining their relevance, clarity, and alignment with the learning attributes. This analysis is conducted at two levels of prompting.

3.1.1 Errors by section

For Level 1 prompting, 36 out of the 157 questions (22.9%) that ChatGPT generated contained errors. As seen in **Figure 4**, the section that had the highest proportion of errors (0.291) was Exploring Data (1). As a whole, this corresponded to issues with generating graphs and other visualizations. For instance, shown in **Figure 5** is an unreadable boxplot that ChatGPT produced. Statistical Inference (4) also contained a high proportion of errors (0.257), which commonly involved questions that did not fulfill the attribute or did not include enough information to solve the problem.

For Level 2 prompting, 45 out of the 157 questions (28.7%) contained errors. Sampling and Experimentation (2) accounted for the highest percentage of errors within a section (39.3%). Nearly all of these errors arose from failure to fulfill the attribute or even repeating the attribute as the question. An example of this was found

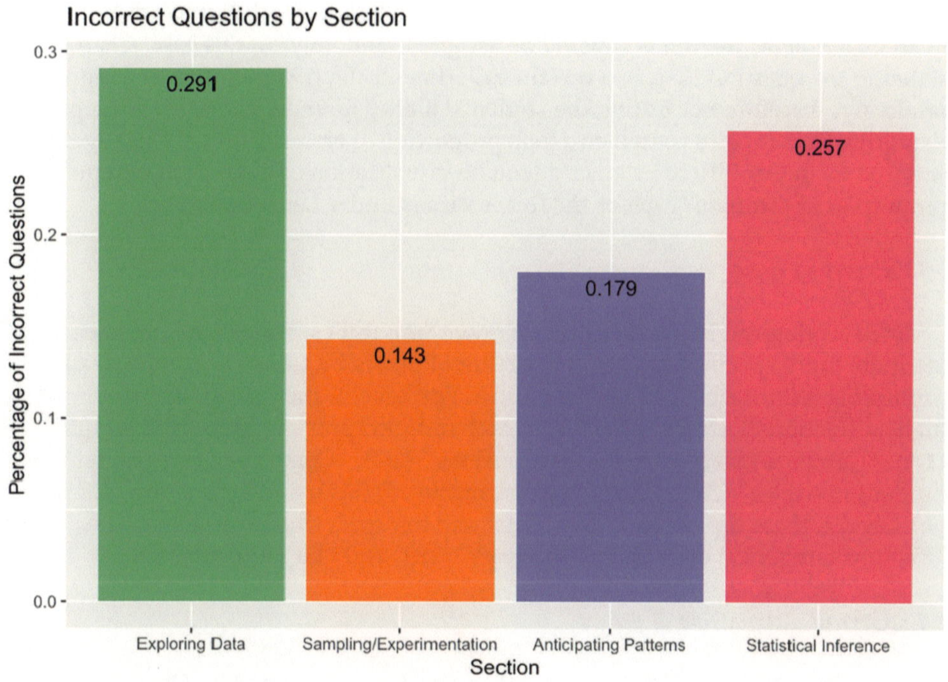

Figure 4.
Level 1 incorrect questions by section.

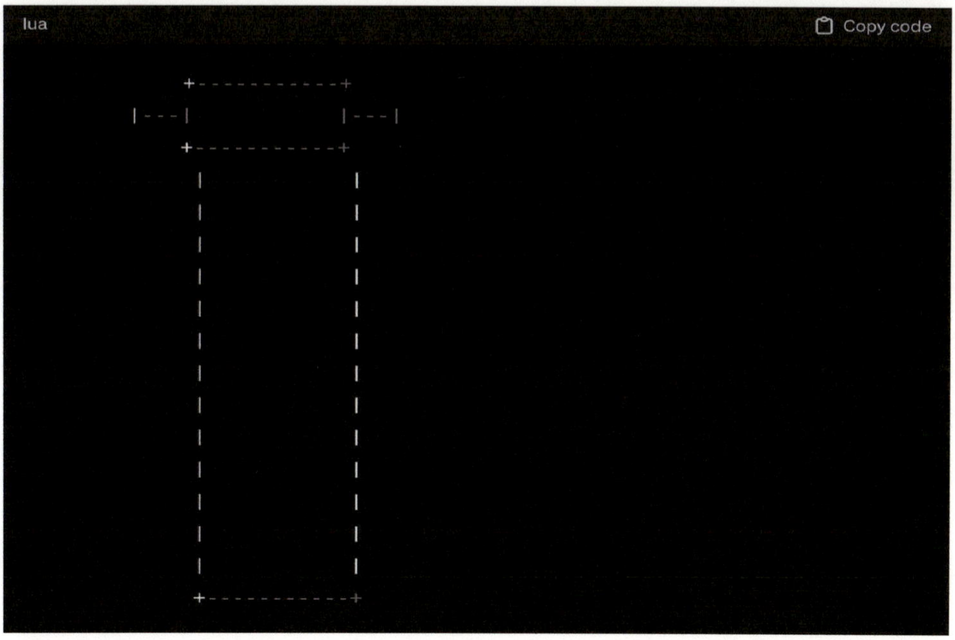

Figure 5.
Boxplot output from 1.A.6.

in the question generated for Attribute 2.C.1, which requires that students know that, in an experiment, treatments should be assigned randomly. In this case, ChatGPT stated in the question that, in a certain experiment, the treatments were assigned randomly, therefore not testing the students' ability to understand this concept. Exploring Data (1) also contained a high proportion of errors (36.4%). Once again, this was due to an inability to produce adequate visualizations. **Figure 6** represents the proportion of errors for each of the four sections under Level 2 prompting.

3.1.2 Errors by topic

Each section can be further broken down into topics, which categorize each attribute more specifically. The proportion of errors by topic for each level of prompting is illustrated in **Figures 7** and **8**. For Level 1, the topics that comprised the highest fraction of errors were "Construct and interpret single-variable graphs" (1A), "Compare single-variable distributions" (1C), "Combining independent random variables" (3B), "Sampling distributions" (3D), and Estimation (CI) (4A). For Level 2, these topics were "Construct and interpret single-variable graphs" (1A), "Explore categorical data" (1E), "Surveys" (2B), and "Experiments" (2C).

3.1.3 Overall distribution of errors

In general, the distribution of errors in questions generated by ChatGPT can be visualized with **Figures 9** and **10**. The most common errors included ChatGPT repeating the attribute in the form of a question, a question that didn't fulfill the attribute, and questions that required a graph or other output that was not present or

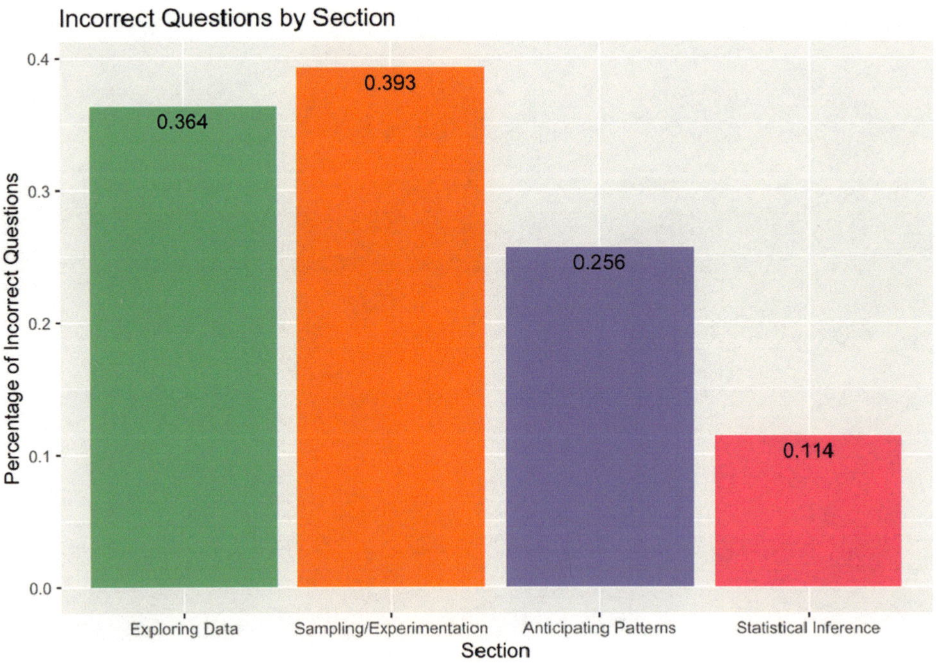

Figure 6.
Level 2 incorrect questions by section.

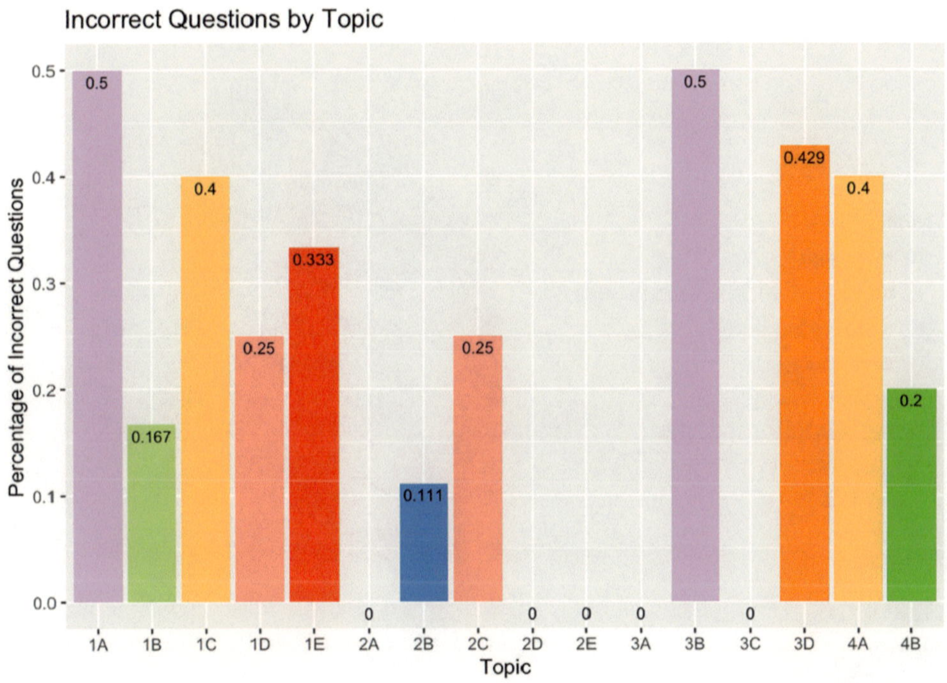

Figure 7.
Level 1 incorrect questions by topic.

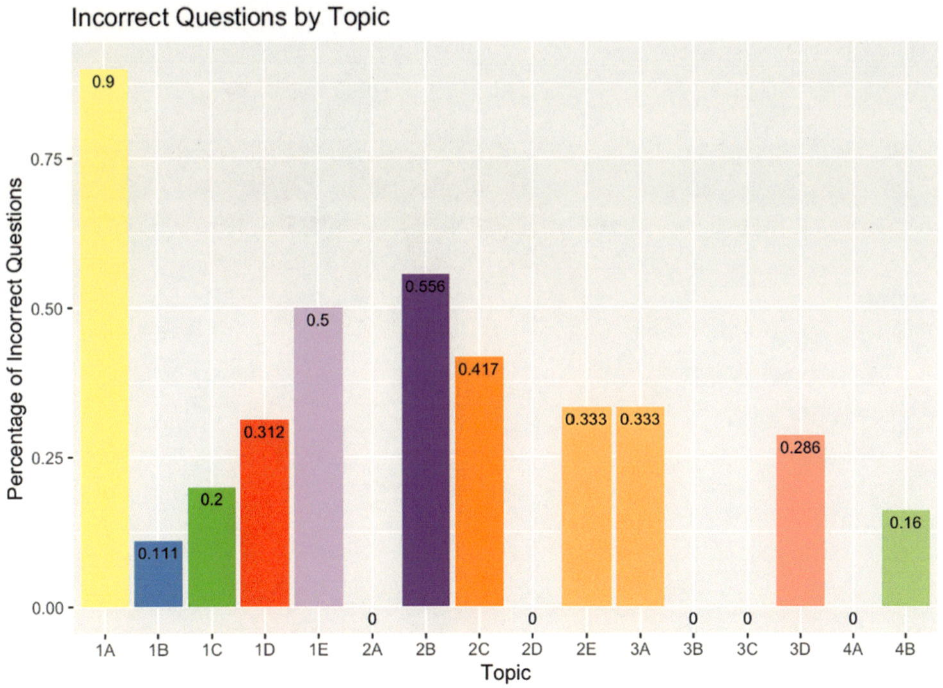

Figure 8.
Level 2 incorrect questions by topic.

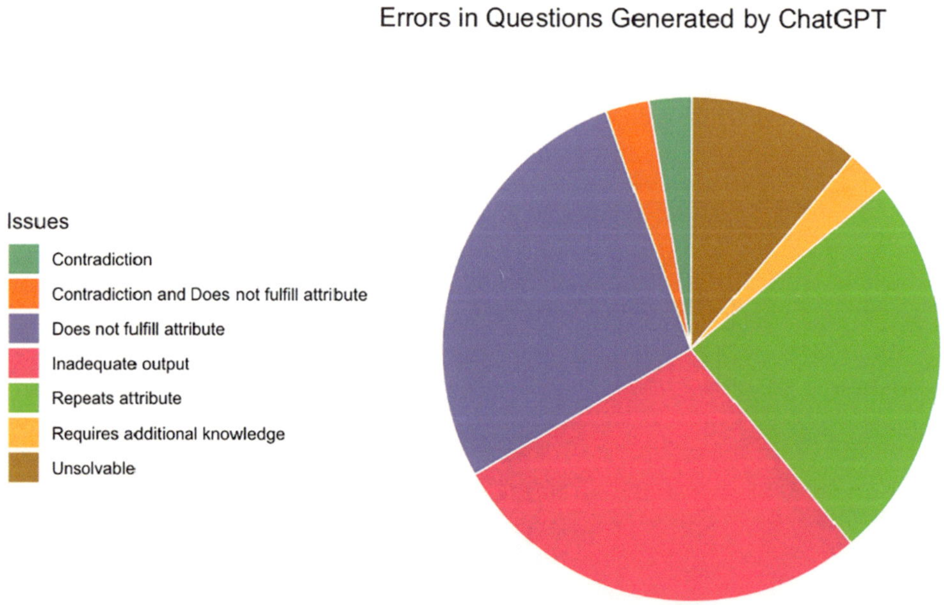

Figure 9.
Level 1 errors in questions.

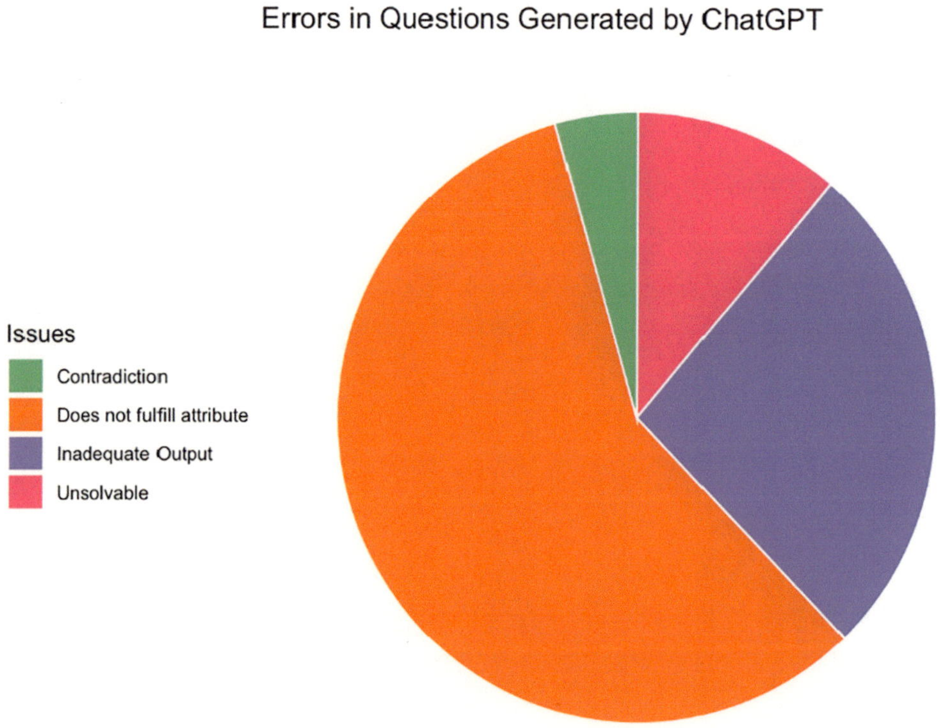

Figure 10.
Level 2 errors in questions.

was unreadable. Level 2 prompting, though generating questions with more contextual information, does not lead to more error-free questions.

3.2 Solution accuracy

Subsequently, we turn our attention to the second area of analysis – the accuracy and effectiveness of the answers provided by ChatGPT without additional prompting. In this phase, we assess the responses according to several predefined criteria, including Careless Error, Computational Error, Didn't Solve, Explanatory Error, Inadequate Graph, Indeterminable, and Procedural Error. This evaluation is conducted across two levels of analysis, considering both the correctness and the depth of the responses provided by ChatGPT.

For the generated solutions, Level 1 contained 36 errors (22.9%), and Level 2 contained 45 errors (28.7%). It is important to note that while ChatGPT made the same number of errors for the solutions as for the questions on both prompting levels, these did not necessarily align with the same attributes. For example, while a question may not have fulfilled the desired attribute, ChatGPT could still properly solve the question that it generated. Similarly, just because a question contained no errors does not mean that ChatGPT did not make a mistake in answering it.

3.2.1 Errors by section

As depicted in **Figure 11**, for Level 1, Exploring Data (1) accounted for a large proportion of errors (0.418) compared to other sections. ChatGPT not only struggled

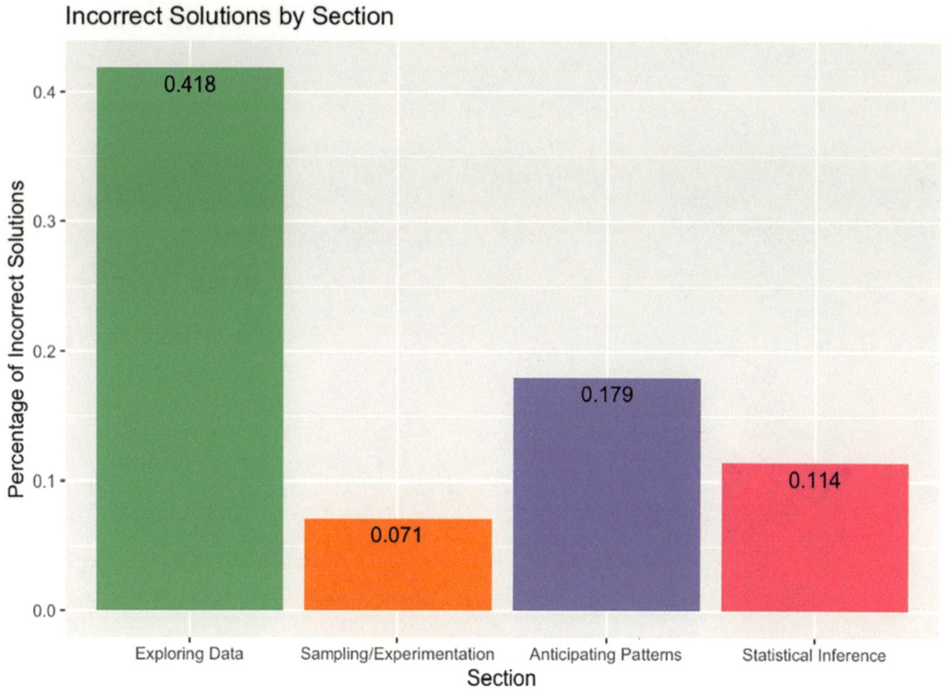

Figure 11.
Level 1 incorrect solutions by section.

to generate graphs and visualizations within its questions, but its solutions exhibited the same limitation. In addition, ChatGPT occasionally made assumptions about the data from the graphs that were outputted in the question. This was labeled as an indeterminable error because, in doing this, it assumed the graphs were readable when, in fact, they were not.

For Level 2, the section that had the highest proportion of errors was Statistical Inference (4), which contained errors in 40% of its solutions (see **Figure 12**). This was largely a result of computational errors in determining a test statistic, which could often be attributed to incorrect calculations of a simple mean or standard deviation. Exploring Data (1) and Anticipating Errors (3) also possessed high proportions of errors, at 0.364 and 0.282, respectively. However, Sampling and Experimentation (2) had no errors of any kind in its solutions. This makes sense because most of the errors in its questions came from either not fulfilling the attribute or repeating the attribute in the question, which would not inhibit ChatGPT's ability to answer them, as these were more conceptual questions.

3.2.2 Errors by topic

To break it down further, the topics that contained the most errors for Level 1 included "Construct and interpret single-variable graphs" (1A) and "Compare single-variable distributions" (1C), as shown in **Figure 13**. As for Level 2, these topics were "Construct and interpret single-variable graphs" (1A), "Summarize

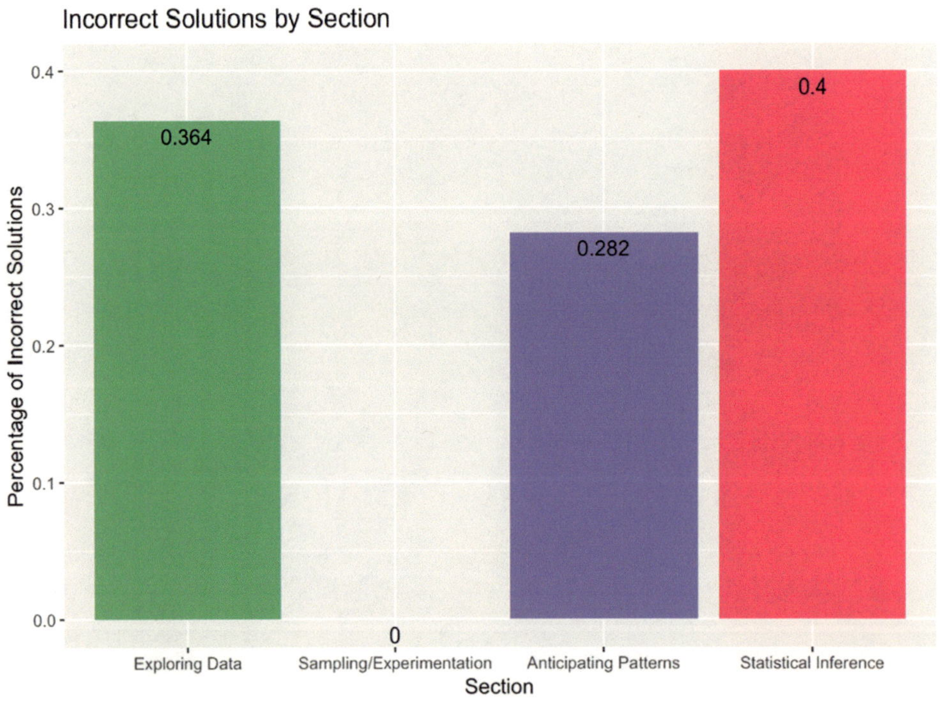

Figure 12.
Level 2 incorrect solutions by section.

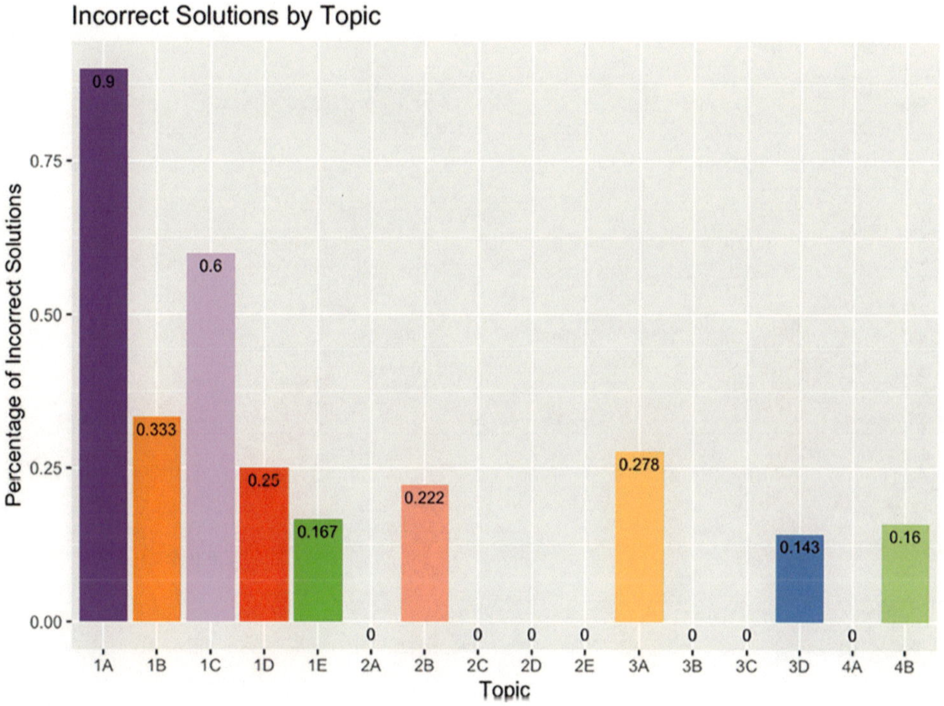

Figure 13.
Level 1 incorrect solutions by topic.

single-variable distributions" (1B), and "Tests of significance" (4B), as illustrated in **Figure 14**.

Common errors within these topics, apart from inadequate visual outputs and issues with computations, were careless errors. A careless error occurred when ChatGPT made an unintentional mistake due to oversight rather than a misunderstanding of the attribute or statistical material. For instance, in questions concerning the topic of probability, if it was given that an individual was drawing from a standard deck of 52 cards, ChatGPT would sometimes make careless errors by implying that there were 52 red cards in the deck when there are only 26, or even stating that there were more than 52 cards total. This has nothing to do with a lack of understanding of probability but rather a failure to pay close attention to the details given in the problem.

3.2.3 Distribution of errors

Figures 15 and **16** demonstrate a more intricate breakdown of the error types committed by ChatGPT for each level of prompting. The most common error for both levels of prompting was a computational error, followed by a careless error.

4. Conclusion

This study investigated the capabilities of GPT-3.5 in generating AP Statistics questions and solutions, with a focus on accuracy across different content areas, topics, and the influence of prompting strategies.

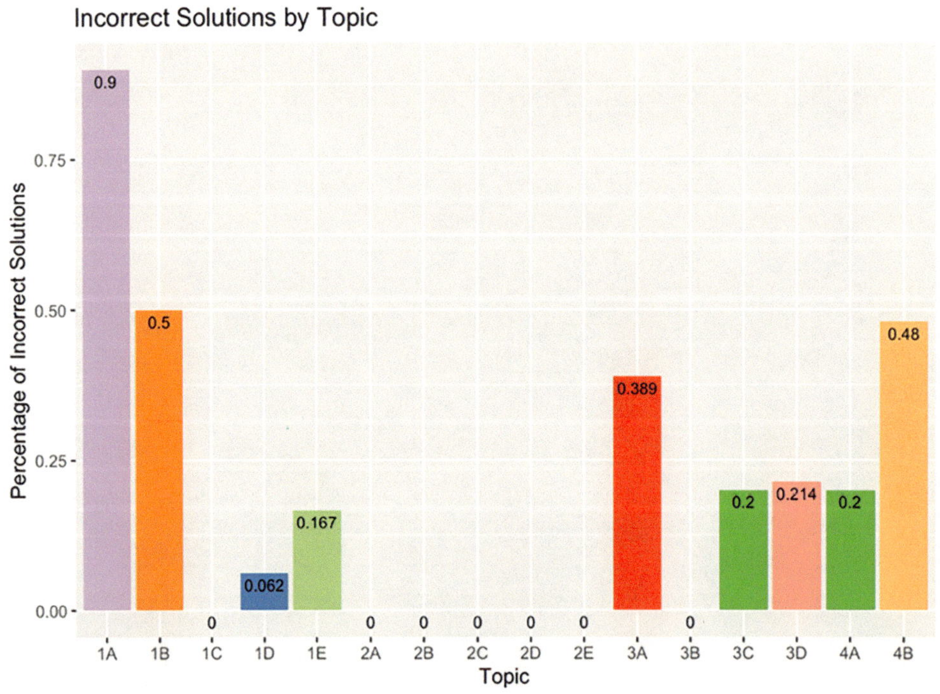

Figure 14.
Level 2 incorrect solutions by topic.

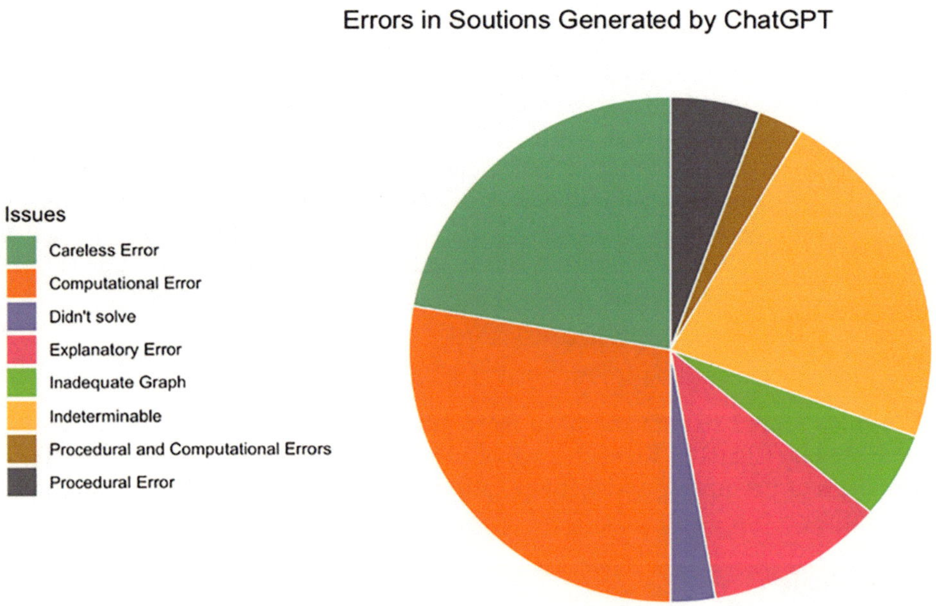

Figure 15.
Level 1 errors in solutions.

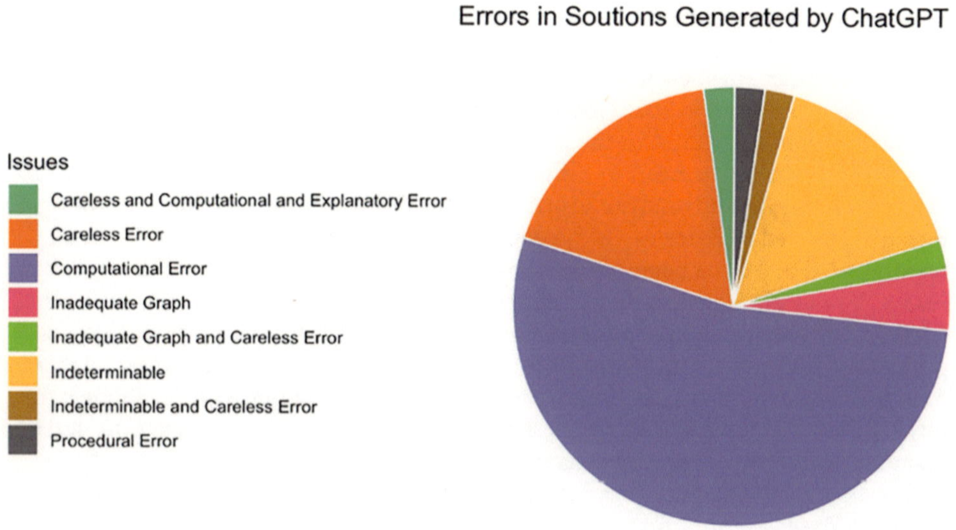

Figure 16.
Level 2 errors in solutions.

For the first research question, we hypothesized that GPT-3.5 is able to generate accurate questions and solutions across content areas. Our findings partially support this hypothesis. GPT-3.5 demonstrated some capability to create questions that align with AP Statistics learning objectives, but overall accuracy – especially in solutions – was limited. Performance varied across content areas, with stronger results in conceptual sections such as Sampling and Experimentation and weaker performance in computational topics and topics involving visualization. This suggests that while ChatGPT can assist with drafting questions and solutions, educators must carefully review them to ensure correctness.

The accuracy of ChatGPT from these results aligns with previous research performed by Ngo et al. [7], which also used GPT-3.5. The 32% level of accuracy that their study reports is comparable to the overall low accuracy determined from this study, regardless of the type of prompting that was utilized. This is remarkable because the two studies deal with very different domains: immunology and statistics. In spite of the low accuracy, Ngo et al. [7] stated that ChatGPT has the potential to be useful in generating MCQs, given that teachers carefully review them. We reached a similar conclusion: Due to a quality improvement in the questions and solutions generated with Level 2 prompting, it may be beneficial for teachers to use ChatGPT to draft questions and solutions and simply refine its work.

For the second research question, we hypothesized superior performance on conceptual attributes compared to computational skills. This hypothesis was confirmed. GPT-3.5 excelled at generating accurate questions and solutions for conceptual topics but struggled with computationally intensive content and tasks involving data analysis or visual interpretation. These findings indicate the model's current strength lies in reinforcing conceptual understanding, highlighting a clear need to improve its computational reasoning and visual data capabilities for broader application. GPT-3.5 was most effective at generating solutions for Sampling and Experimentation (2), while there was no section that had the most consistently accurate generated questions. This could be due to the conceptual nature of the questions from this section, such as asking the conditions that need to be fulfilled in order to conduct surveys and experiments. The results for the solution generation support our expectation that ChatGPT would perform better for conceptual attributes when compared to those that required other expertise. As such, this project demonstrates a need to refine GPT-3.5's computational skills, as well as its ability to generate and analyze visual outputs. That said, the capability of more recently released updates of GPT, such as GPT-4.0 and GPT-4.1, remains to be researched. They have been reported to have improved performance in terms of reasoning as well as processing of multimodal input [16, 17]. That said, given that GPT-3.5 is freely accessible and offers unlimited use for teachers, it remains the preferable option for many educators. This accessibility ensures broader reach and practical implementation in classrooms, despite the advantages newer models may offer. It is hence the focus of this research, but the capacity of more recent versions certainly warrants further investigation.

For the third research question, we hypothesized that Level 2 prompting (persona-based) would reduce errors compared to basic prompts. Contrary to expectations, this hypothesis was not supported. Results for the prompting strategy showed that 29% of questions and solutions contained errors for persona-based Level 2 prompting, compared to only 23% for Level 1. These findings do not align with past studies either, which indicated that giving ChatGPT a specific role to play allowed it to effectively tailor its output [12]. This outcome challenges prior research suggesting that role assignment improves output quality and suggests that, for technical subjects like AP Statistics, added prompt complexity may increase inaccuracies. Educators should therefore carefully consider prompt design and balance complexity with accuracy when using ChatGPT.

In analyzing these results, an important question is raised: Is it more significant to generate questions and solutions that contain fewer mistakes, or to generate those rich in context and resembling questions a student is likely to see on an AP exam? The second type of questions also tends to reflect higher levels of cognitive complexity, as represented by Bloom's taxonomy [18], a point that needs to be researched further. One perspective is that it might save time for a teacher to fix a simple computational error instead of having to write an AP-level style question from scratch, in line with Level 2 prompting. Moving forward, it is critical to keep this trade-off in mind as educators begin to rely more on generative AI tools.

Another limitation is that the attributes were only tested once for each level of prompting. This means we only have one data point for each attribute. Retesting these results would help ensure data reliability. Future research could include examining additional levels of prompting. The Level 1 and Level 2 prompting utilized in this study belongs to the zero-shot prompting category, where ChatGPT is given a task without any prior examples [19]. This type of prompting strategy is simple and less resource-dependent, and is therefore the easiest to adopt by educators. One approach could be to add a level in which ChatGPT is provided with an example problem (one-shot prompting) or a handful of examples (few-shot prompting) and asked to generate similar questions and solutions. Such examples can be obtained through questions, sample responses, and scoring guidelines released by the College Board from past AP Statistics exams [20]. The one-shot and few-shot prompting approach has been shown to enhance model performance by providing clearer context and guidance [21]. Comparing the results from this new approach to those of the two levels used in this project would help researchers better understand how different prompting strategies impact the quality, relevance, and accuracy of generated questions and solutions. Such findings could provide actionable insights into the optimization of AI-assisted tools for statistics education.

Acknowledgments

This research was conducted through the Learning Analytics and Measurement in Behavioral Sciences (LAMBS) Lab at the University of Notre Dame. The authors' work benefited from feedback received at the Ideas in Testing (IIT) Conference and the University of Notre Dame's Trustworthy AI Lab for Education Summit (ND-TALES), in addition to the support of university resources. This work is supported by the National Science Foundation Award OAC-2321054. Any opinions, findings, and conclusions or recommendations expressed in this material are those of the authors and do not necessarily reflect the views of the National Science Foundation.

Author details

Ying Cheng*, Meredith Sanders and Anh Thu Le
University of Notre Dame, Notre Dame, Indiana, USA

*Address all correspondence to: ycheng4@nd.edu

References

[1] Deng J, Lin Y. The benefits and challenges of ChatGPT: An overview. Frontiers in Computing and Intelligent Systems. 2022;**2**(2). DOI: 10.54097/fcis.v2i2.4465

[2] Kasneci E, Sessler K, Küchenhoff H, et al. ChatGPT for good? On opportunities and challenges of large language models for education. Learning and Individual Differences. 2023;**103**. DOI: 10.1016/j.lindif.2023.102274

[3] IBM. What are large language models (LLMs)? [Internet]. IBM.com. IBM; 2023. Available from: https://www.ibm.com/think/topics/large-language-models [Accessed: 2025-July-31]

[4] OpenAI. How ChatGPT and our foundation models are developed. [Internet]. Openai.com. 2024. Available from: https://help.openai.com/en/articles/7842364-how-chatgpt-and-our-foundation-models-are-developed [Accessed: 2025-July-31]

[5] Alkaissi H, McFarlane SI. Artificial Hallucinations in ChatGPT: Implications in scientific writing. Cureus. 2023;**15**(2):e35179. DOI: 10.7759/cureus.35179

[6] Powell W, Courchesne S. Opportunities and risks involved in using ChatGPT to create first grade science lesson plans. PloS One. 2024;**19**(6):e0305337

[7] Ngo A, Gupta S, Perrine O, et al. CHATGPT 3.5 fails to write appropriate multiple choice practice exam questions. Academic Pathology. 2024;**11**(1). DOI: 10.1016/j.acpath.2023.100099

[8] Cheung BHH, Lau GK, Wong GT, et al. CHATGPT versus human in generating medical graduate exam multiple choice questions—a multinational prospective study (Hong Kong S.A.R., Singapore, Ireland, and the United Kingdom). PLOS ONE 2023;**18**:e0290691

[9] College Board. AP Statistics Course and Exam Description [Internet]. 2020. Available from: https://apcentral.collegeboard.org/pdf/ap-statistics-course-and-exam-description.pdf. [Accessed: 2025-July-31]

[10] Bleske-Rechek A. The pursuit of equity and excellence: Advanced placement exam participation and performance by sex and by race/ethnicity, 1996–2022. Intelligence. 2025;**108**(101894). DOI: 10.1016/j.intell.2024.101894

[11] Li Z, Shareghi E, Collier N. ReasonGraph: Visualisation of reasoning paths. arXiv:2503.03979. 2025

[12] Verma A, Mukherjee K, Potts C, et al. CHART-6: human-centered evaluation of data visualization understanding in vision-language models. arXiv:2505.17202. 2025

[13] Borji A A categorical archive of ChatGPT failures. ArXiv:2302.03494. 2023

[14] He S Prompting ChatGPT for translation: A comparative analysis of translation brief and persona prompts. arXiv:2403.00127. 2024

[15] Brodersen A, Carter MF, Liu C, et al. Collection of process data in

web-based assessment systems and its applications to validating non-cognitive constructs. In: Jiao, H, Lissitz, R. eds. Enhancing Effective Instruction and Learning Using Assessment Data. Charlotte, NC: Information Age Publisher; 2021

[16] Barozai DK ChatGPT-3.5 vs. 4 v. 4o: Which one should you use? Folio3. 2025. Available from: https://www.folio3.ai/blog/chat-gpt-4-vs-chat-gpt-3/ [Accessed: 2025-July-31]

[17] Data Studio. ChatGPT-4o Vs. 3.5: Full Comparison and Report [Internet]. Available from: https://www.datastudios.org/post/chatgpt-4o-vs-gpt-3-5-full-comparison-and-report [Accessed: 2025-July-31]

[18] Bloom BS, Engelhart MD, Furst EJ, et al. Taxonomy of Educational Objectives, Handbook I: The Cognitive Domain. London: Longman; 1956

[19] Ye J, Chen X, Xu N, et al. A Comprehensive Capability Analysis of GPT-3 and GPT-3.5 Series Models; 2023; ArXiv:2303.10420

[20] College Board. AP Statistics Exam Questions. AP Central. 2025. Available from https://apcentral.collegeboard.org/courses/ap-statistics/exam/past-exam-questions [Accessed: 2025-July-31]

[21] Brown T, Mann B, Ryder N, et al. Language Models are Few-Shot Learners; 2020;ArXiv:2005.14165

Section 6

System-Level, Global & Future Directions in AI Education

Chapter 28

Supplementing AI "Curriculum" Using Teachers Pay Teachers Resources: What There Is and What There Isn't

G. Michael Bowen, Michael Pin-Chuan Lin and Christine A. Royce

Abstract

Artificial intelligence (AI) has had an increasing presence in K-12 education over the last 3 years and is entering the educational practices of both teachers and students. Schools and teachers feel the pressure to both adopt AI-related practices as well as teach their students about AI, but few formal curriculum resources exist for this topic. Teachers typically turn to other resources, such as online educational resource marketplaces (OERMs), to obtain supplemental curriculum materials. The website Teachers Pay Teachers (TPT) started in 2006 to allow teachers to share teaching resources with the goal of helping them teach their students better through learning from each other. Various sources suggest that, in general, many teachers (a) frequently use the TPT platform (up to 85% of U.S. K-12 teachers) and (b) acquire both paid and unpaid resources from TPT to use in their classrooms. In this study, we examine 48 AI-related resources (24 requiring payment and 24 that are free, all provided in a search on the TPT website) that are available to teachers, documenting and analyzing what information teachers are provided to make decisions, comparing free and paid resources, and evaluating the quality of the AI-related resources. We conclude that there is considerable room for improvement in the available resources from both a content and a pedagogical perspective, that professional development on how to effectively evaluate supplemental curriculum resources is needed, and that individuals with stronger backgrounds in computer technologies should be contributing more supplemental curriculum resources to TPT on AI.

Keywords: AI curriculum, AI resources, TPT, AI literacy, curriculum supplementation

1. Introduction

Since the public release of ChatGPT in 2022, artificial intelligence (AI) has emerged as a prominent topic in schools, despite its absence from most curriculum documents. Students recognize that AI has been incorporated into many parts of their daily lives and, thus, have started using it more and more in their schooling. However, they report that most of their learning about AI occurs outside of schools [1]. Pedagogical approaches long used by teachers are no longer effective because students can use AI to complete those assignments in a fraction of the time they took previously. At the same time, these disruptions provide teachers with new opportunities, such as using AI to grade assignments and providing feedback. Consequently, educational systems are developing policies to guide its use, and educators face the dual challenge of fostering students' AI-related knowledge, skills, and literacy while also articulating clear parameters for its application in their classrooms.

1.1 Literature review

It is a long-held practice that, in addition to official curriculum documents, teachers use supplemental curricular materials they source elsewhere, and this is particularly the case with respect to AI. Historically, this has meant turning to colleagues, books, and materials provided by professional associations (and their publications), such as the National Council of Teachers of Mathematics, the National Science Teaching Association, and the International Literacy Association. For the past two decades, teachers have turned to internet search engines such as Google to start their search for supplemental materials [2], but over the last decade, online educational resource marketplaces (OERMs) have gained considerable prominence. Teachers primarily turn to these online supplemental resources to enhance student engagement, often seeking hands-on or task-oriented activities. Furthermore, these platforms allow educators to address the diverse needs of their students by providing materials for enrichment, additional practice, or to unpack complex concepts, including off-grade–level content. A crucial motivation for teachers is also the significant time-saving aspect, as downloading ready-made resources greatly reduces preparation hours – a cost they deem worthwhile [3]. Now, teachers use the teaching material resource site Teachers Pay Teachers (TPT) more than Google in planning their teaching [4], possibly because simple web-based searches for instructional resources frequently return results pointing to OERM sites such as Pinterest and TPT anyways [5].

In a contracted marketing analysis from a professional education association, TPT demonstrated a significant presence as a "go-to source" for educational materials, particularly for teachers seeking resources. Across the digital landscape, which included comparisons with professional associations, nationally known curricular and professional learning groups, and other curricular programs, TPT held the highest domain visibility among the assessed organizations, with the largest audience size and substantially more engagement than other organizations [6]. Today, TPT stands as the largest online teacher resource exchange, hosting over 3 million resources and surpassing 1 billion downloads of those materials. More than two in three U.S. teachers have reported using the website, with a nationally representative pre-pandemic survey indicating that 64.8% of teachers used TPT weekly or more during the 2018–2019 school year [7]. More recent findings suggest even higher uptake: 86% of U.S. elementary teachers reported using TPT at least once a week, and 53% of mathematics and ELA teachers in grades 6–12 indicated similar use [8]. Likewise, 82% of teachers reported using TPT for mathematics instruction frequently or occasionally, compared to 68% who used Pinterest and 67% who used search engines such as Google or Yahoo [9].

In 2016, an American non-profit organization conducted focus-group research with teachers on how they chose supplementary curricular materials. They reported that teachers generally evaluate supplementary curricular materials based on four main criteria: alignment to standards, accuracy and visual appeal, ease of use, and student engagement, putting trust in materials that have been made or vetted by other teachers. Materials must often also reflect sufficient depth of knowledge and include higher-order thinking tasks. When choosing supplementary resources, teachers usually prefer complete resources with clear instructions and supporting materials that are engaging and culturally relevant [10]. Research on selection strategies used by teachers with TPT resources suggests that these and other factors are considered in their use of that online platform.

The selection of resources on TPT appears to be heavily influenced by factors beyond just academic rigor, with teachers often relying on easily observable metrics such as star ratings and peer reviews [7, 11], which other teachers provide. While teachers can analyze text descriptions of TPT resources for information relevant to their decision, the platform's rating system presents a significant challenge for discerning quality, with most resources receiving a high star rating irrespective of subject or topic [7, 12–14]. For instance, in the area of computational thinking, 93.58% of rated resources had 5 stars and 4.72% had 4 stars [14]; note that TPT recently changed its rating system to 5 stars from a 4-star rating system.

Analysis of TPT data indicates that elementary materials (both early and late) receive more star ratings than those for middle and high schools [7]. Notably, in a study that used web-scraping to obtain all resource posts between 2006 and 2019 (i.e., 4 million resources), 41.8% of resources on TPT were not rated at all [15]. Despite the high star ratings for some resources and nonexistent star ratings for others, teachers used star ratings to make decisions about what resources to download, given that 90.1% of resources downloaded had a 4-star (out of 4) rating, only 6.98% of downloads were rated between 3.6 and 3.9 (out of 4), and only 2.6% of the downloaded resources were unrated [15].

This has led some researchers to conclude that "Star rating scores may not provide a reliable basis for making valid inferences" [14] (p. 29) or were "effectively useless" [15], leading to the suggestion that educators "approach materials from platforms like TPT uncritically" [5] (p. 7), with the study by Aguilar et al. [7] concluding that teachers may view "an appearance in TPT search results as evidence of credibility or utility" (p. 7). Overall, TPT users "seem to trust the ratings feature despite these ratings' apparent lack of validity" [15] (p. 282), with the user ratings instilling a "false sense of security in buyers that they are downloading a high quality curriculum" (p. 283).

The lack of validity in the star system stems from multiple expert reviewers of TPT resources, who report little evidence of a relationship between star ratings/reviews and the quality of the resources. Various studies across subject areas have reported concerns about the quality of the resources available on TPT irrespective of review scores [12], citing issues such as problems with the instructional supports for the resources [3, 13, and 16], misrepresentations or outright errors of core subject information in the resources [13], poor instructional and assessment approaches [3], a lack of social justice and equity perspectives [17–19], or even racist elements [5, 18]. Some researchers have expressed concern that there were components of resources that could pose potential harm to students [20, 21]. Despite these reported problematic elements, teachers often view TPT resources as being of high quality [22], as the high use of TPT by teachers and the large number of downloads would also suggest.

Other factors besides reviews/stars also influence teachers in their choice of online resources at OERMs. Some teachers are influenced by the number of views, downloads, and reposts [5, 23], whereas elementary teachers are reported as searching for "cute and fun" materials [24] (p. 13). However, Mertens and Adams [25] reported that while their research participants may note "cuteness," it was not a factor in their selection of resources. Sundrani [11] reported that some of her high-school math teacher participants read details about the resources in the previews to help make their decisions, as they looked for alignment with their instructional goals and to determine the rigor level of the resources. In one study, 54% of teachers chose resources based on whether they could quickly and effectively solve an instructional problem for target learners, and 21% chose based on their ease of use [26]. Similarly, Schroeder et al. [24] reported that teachers used TPT to "engage students with particular concepts" (p. 281). Apart from academic concerns, more pragmatic concerns, such as "the ability to edit resources, change fonts, and tailor materials," influenced the choice of resources [25] (p. 249), suggesting that resources with PDF files are less appealing than Microsoft Word or Google Doc files (information which is available prior-to-purchase at the TPT site for some resources and not others).

1.2 AI literacy framework and competencies

The AI literacy framework being developed [1] provides essential guidance for students in primary and secondary education to understand, use, and critically evaluate AI. It aims to equip young people with the technical knowledge, durable skills, and future-ready attitudes necessary to navigate a world increasingly influenced by AI, especially since most currently learn about AI outside formal schooling.

The framework defines AI literacy as enabling learners to engage with, create with, manage, and design AI while critically evaluating its benefits, risks, and ethical implications. These capabilities are structured across four key domains:

- Engaging with AI: Focuses on using AI as a tool to access new content, information, or recommendations, requiring learners to recognize AI's presence and assess the accuracy and relevance of its outputs.

- Creating with AI: Involves collaborating with AI in creative or problem-solving processes, emphasizing the guidance and refinement of AI output, and considering ethical implications related to content ownership and attribution.

- Managing AI: Concerns intentionally choosing how AI can support and enhance human work, delegating structured tasks to AI, and evaluating whether AI's role aligns with human goals and values.

- Designing AI: Empowers learners to understand AI's social and ethical impacts through hands-on exploration of how data and design choices influence AI systems.

DOI: http://dx.doi.org/10.5772/intechopen.1012593

Each competence within these domains represents a learning expectation that combines specific knowledge, skills, and attitudes, and when the framework is finalized, it offers a foundation for both school curricula to be modified to include AI education across grade levels and for supplementary curricular materials to be based on.

2. Research questions

In general, "there has been limited critical investigation" of the educational resources available at OERMs [15] (p. 269). Given that AI is a relatively "new" topic as far as K-12 education is concerned, it is important that an investigation of the resources currently available for that particular topic be conducted. Our research study, presented in this chapter, examines a sample of the curricular resources on AI currently available at the OERM TPT to provide insights into what features they have and their quality. In conducting this study, we address the following topics:

- What are the AI resources that result from "Free" and "For Cost" searches on TPT? How do the questions below differ between "Free" and "For Cost" resources?

- What information is available in the resource titles that might influence teachers when choosing that resource?

- What information is available in the "short description" that might influence teachers in choosing that resource?

- What is the quality of resources provided, and what can we understand about student engagement with those resources?

- How does that information about AI resources obtained in the search compare to previous research in other subject areas?

3. Methodology

To conduct our baseline investigation of AI resources at TPT, we conducted four different analyses. These analyses were based on a search for "Free" and "Paid" resources available on the TPT website using the search engine provided there. Twenty-four resources were entered into the analysis database for each of the two types of resources.

Using a "naive" browser (which had never visited the TPT website, thereby reducing the chance that any TPT-specific tracking information had been put on the computer), each author conducted two searches in early June of 2025. The first search, using the search window at the top of the page, involved searching the phrase "Artificial Intelligence"; notably, all returned resources required payment.
The second search was conducted after setting an option under the "price" filter to "Free". Each author archived each of the 24 resources (the TPT default search return number) shown for those two searches. Author A had all the same resources as

Author B for the "Free" resource searches and 22 resources the same as those of Author C. For the "Paid" resources, which were returned when no filter was selected, Author A had all the same resources as Author C and 22 resources the same as Author B. Given the strong degree of overlap with Author A, their list of resources was entered into the study database. The search was re-done 8 weeks later using the same approach to evaluate the stability of the returns from the TPT search engine.

The following information was collected for all 48 resources:

- Intended grade range.
- Date the resource was last edited.
- Name of the "author".
- Location of the "author".
- The number of resources provided by that author at TPT.
- Whether the author was noted as a company or as an individual (or a small group of individuals).
- The cost of the resource (for the "Paid" ones).
- The number of "Stars" the resource was showing from user reviews.
- Whether there was information on the resource containing "printables" in either the text or the graphics.

In one study that examined the search strategies enacted by TPT users, it was noted that they "skimmed" the results of their initial search before opening a resource in a tab [25]. Titles of resources would seem to serve the same role as news headlines – providing a short summary of the article and drawing attention to it through language [27] – from which readers assume that the essence of the whole story has been summarized in the headline, driving their decision to read (or not read) the rest of the news article [28].

The search returns in TPT provide the title of the resource (in bold font), a small graphic with illustrations and/or text, the "author's" name, a three-line paragraph describing the resource, the grade range for the resource, and a brief description of topics. Given that the process of "skimming" TPT search returns appears to mirror the reading of news headlines before making decisions, we decided to conduct two analyses of text visible in the initial search returns.

Given the "bolding" of the title text (making it stand out) and the role of headlines in news media, the first dataset was compiled from the resource titles alone, premised on the idea that "skimming" would only cause one to stop and look at the "short" resource description if the title was eye-catching to teachers. In entering the titles into the data collection spreadsheet distributed to the authors, any title that referred to "free" was altered so that any cost involved with downloading the resource from TPT was obfuscated. The titles were also then randomly sorted in the spreadsheet. The spreadsheet headings, which each researcher addressed, were examined for: "stated grade range", "inferred grade range", topic, type of resource (lesson plan, worksheet, informational, etc.), target (was the resource for students or the teacher), and then an indication of how compelling the author–reader found the title based on the previous information, both descriptively and in a 1–5 rating score. Each author analyzed all 48 items.

The second dataset was compiled from all of the information provided for each resource in the search (which was presented in a vertical list). Items for this analysis were developed from conversations between the authors regarding what information they would search for if they were looking for a resource and from a review of the literature where similar analyses had been conducted. For each resource (which we refer to as a "short" description), obfuscation and randomization were conducted as described for the titles. Each author was provided a "list" of the short descriptions, a description of the analytic framework (with details on each item), and a spreadsheet with headings to analyze each of the resources. Each author analyzed all 48 resources (the topics for analysis are described in Appendix A) and their responses were entered into the data corpus.

The final dataset which was collected was based on a subsample of the "free" and "paid" resources, focusing on the resources that were provided. A random selection of 12 resources was made from each of the "paid" and "free" resources in our data corpus, and these were randomly assigned to the three authors so that each of the selected resources was analyzed by two authors. As before, whether the resources were "paid" or "free" was obfuscated (as much as possible, though some mentioned their status in the resource itself). The questions each researcher addressed were derived in a fashion similar to that of the second dataset, with the goal of gaining information about the quality of each resource and how students engaged with it. Each author was provided their list of resources in a spreadsheet (with links to the downloaded resources) and recorded their responses to the statements listed in their spreadsheet (there was a short statement in the top line of the spreadsheet, and each author was also provided an analytic framework sheet elaborating on the information in the top line; see Appendix B).

Our analysis of that data, which we each recorded from these resources, used a modified version of interaction analysis [29]. In how we have applied interaction analysis, we are drawing on the breadth of differences between the authors (i.e., teaching experience, academic background, cultural perspectives) to understand how a broader audience might perceive the resources by recognizing and highlighting differences in our individual responses as providing a greater depth to understanding each resource. This approach is, in some ways, the opposite of trying to establish inter-rater reliability, as differences in response are considered unproblematic because discussions around and about those differences offer the potential to better understand what the resource offers to teachers.

To conduct this interaction analysis, the individual data spreadsheets for each of the three joint analyses were summarized in a spreadsheet that laid out the responses from each author beside each other so that discrepancies in how each author perceived each resource were apparent. In a column next to each group of author-response categories (for text-based and Yes/No responses), a column titled "Final" was created, and where there was agreement in the author responses, that was entered in that column (i.e., for instance, if all authors entered "Y" for a response category), leaving blank the resources/response categories where there was no agreement, which were to be discussed. For text-based and Yes/No responses that were at odds across the authors, and for any quantitative score where there was a difference of more than two points, there was a live discussion between the authors in a Zoom meeting to construct joint claims. As a result of that discussion, some authors might have changed their response, but this was not required. Where differences in response categories across authors still existed, these were noted in the database in the event that discussing out-cases in the final data discussion was worth noting.

For response categories with quantitative scoring, sums across the author's responses were entered into the "Final" column, and then, t-tests were conducted to compare "Free" and "Paid" resources to ascertain if there were significant differences.

4. Description of data and findings

Our assumption in conducting this research is that teachers, particularly those unfamiliar with AI, are likely to start their search for supplemental curriculum resources on TPT by performing a basic keyword search for "Artificial Intelligence." They would then review the results that are returned by first skimming through the headlines, stopping at those they find interesting to review. From there, they would examine the full resource descriptions and decide which materials to download, often opening selected items in separate browser tabs for closer review (as described in [25]).

In replicating this process ourselves, we noted that a basic "search" using the TPT search box at the top of the screen only returned paid resources. We therefore repeated the search with the "free" option checked and also archived those results. The initial search by all authors was conducted at the beginning of June 2025, with a follow-up search by Author A at the end of July 2025. For the paid resources, there was considerable fidelity between the two searches, with only two resources from the June search not being returned in the July one. However, for the "free" resources, six were not returned in July. Further investigation revealed these were all by the same contributor and that all had been converted from "Free" to "Paid" resources, which is why they would not appear in a search for "Free" resources. No differences were noted in those resources despite their conversion. For our analysis below, they continued to be treated as "Free" resources.

In this section, we first report basic descriptive information about the resources, followed by an analysis of their "Titles" (as they might initially be skimmed by teachers), "Short descriptions" (displayed beneath the titles), and the "Full Resources". Where relevant, we also make comparisons between "Paid" and "Free" resources.

4.1 Basic information analysis

Across the 48 resources, there were 40 distinct "authors" of the AI resources in our database (note that a contributor name in TPT may refer to more than one actual author). In our database, six of the resources were from one contributor, and three contributors had two resources each. The remaining AI resources in our database were each contributed under a single, unique author name. Of these contributors, thirty-five were "individual" contributors, four represented a pair of individuals, and one contributor name represented a "company" (where one individual was mentioned, but the language suggested there were multiple contributors under that name). Most contributors were based in the United States (n = 32), with others from Canada (n = 3) and one each from the Middle East, Australia, the United Kingdom, Eastern Europe, and the Asia–Pacific region. The educational backgrounds of contributors included a wide variety of academic areas, including 14 with a background in English Language Arts, 2 with educational technology graduate degrees, and only 2 with computer science degrees. Seven did not mention an academic background or provided no information at all in their biographies.

Each contributor enumerated all of the resources they had posted on TPT. An independent, two-tailed t-test comparison of contributors of "Free" (M = 160.83, n = 18, SD = 154.6) and "Paid" (M = 537.22, n = 23, SD = 688.8) resources revealed a significant difference in total contributions, $t(39) = 2.27$, $p < 0.05$. This indicates that TPT contributors of "Paid" resources had, on average, considerably more contributions to TPT than the contributors of "Free" resources.

Reviewed literature suggests that teachers consider star ratings when deciding whether to download resources. In our sample, the star ratings were uniformly high for both paid (M = 4.87, 14 with a star score ≤ 4.9/5.0) and free resources (M = 4.74, 10 with a star score ≤ 4.9/5.0), although 11 of the free resources had no star ratings at all. An independent two-tailed t-test comparing the star ratings between paid and free resources did not report a significant difference, $t(35) = 1.17$, $p > 0.05$, in the level of star ratings between paid and free resources.

Unlike the findings reported in other studies, our analysis of the age ranges targeted by the AI resources in our sample indicated a skew toward upper grade levels: 8% K–4, 44% 5–8, and 48% 9–12.

No information is available regarding when the AI resources were originally uploaded to TPT. However, after a resource is added to the "cart" (a step required for both free and paid resources), purchased if necessary, and downloaded, the user can access the "My Purchases" option under their profile. **Table 1** lists downloaded resources and displays the date they were "Last Updated."

Our analysis of the full resources showed that some resources contained outdated information about AI. For instance, two paid resources uploaded in 2023 incorporated videos discussing AI and the use of AI from 2019, four years prior and notably three years before the release of ChatGPT, which significantly expanded public access to AI tools.

Year/Part of year updated	# of paid resources	# of free resources
2020	1	
2021	1	
Jan–June 2023	6	1
July–Dec 2023	3	4
Jan–June 2024	5	1
July–Dec 2024	5	5
Jan–June 2025	3	13

Table 1.
When A1 resources in our database were last "updated".

4.2 Title/headline analysis

Our next section is premised on the assumption that the topic/resource title is what teachers will read first, much as users used to scan headlines in newspapers. **Figure 1** presents the information displayed for each of the 24 resources returned in a TPT search. The title appears in the largest font and as the most prominent block of bold text, visually foregrounding it and drawing the viewer's attention. Text in the graphic usually differs from the title and instead often briefly describes the resources (Note that text within the image box example in **Figure 1** appears more significant than it is in many actual samples, and the accompanying descriptive lines are typically rendered in a gray font, making them visually less prominent than they appear here.).

In most cases, the targeted grade range of a resource could not be determined from the titles alone. However, some titles referred to a grade range using phrases such as "Grades 6–8," while others encoded the grade level/range through subject-specific terms such as "ELA" (often associated with middle school) or "AP" (for Advanced Placement, indicating a high school-level focus). Only one paid resource and nine free resources specified a grade/range in the title, leaving 38 of the resources without any such indication.

An examination of the headlines to see what could be learned about the topics they covered resulted in **Table 2**, which demonstrates few differences in topic frequency between paid and free resources. Some resources were classified under two topics, which explains why the category totals exceed 24.

A similar determination was made to evaluate the types of resources that were being provided (**Table 3**). Again, there were few differences between paid and free resources, except that the free category included three posters. The category "Lesson

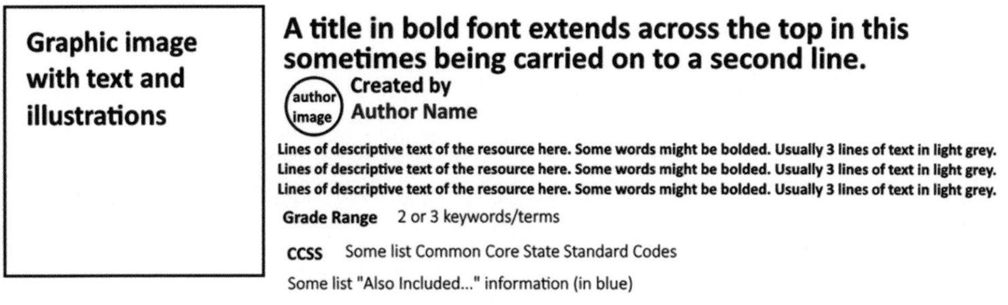

Figure 1.
Diagrammatic representation of information returned in a TPT search.

	Information on AI	AI ethics	Reading comprehension, ELA, writing	Use of prompts	STEM or science	Other	Unclear
Paid Resources	5	5	7	1	3	3	2
Free Resources	7	3	8	2	2	3	0

Table 2.
Counts of topic information available from AI resource titles.

	Informational	Lesson Resource	Worksheets	Poster	Unclear
Paid	2	14	7	0	2
Free	2	11	6	3	2

Table 3.
Counts of resource-type information available from AI resource titles.

Resource" encompasses lesson plans, unit plans, and activity descriptions (in part because what was listed as a "Lesson Plan" was actually an activity description). One headline indicated two resource types and was coded under both. By far, the most common type of resource was lesson resources, followed by worksheets.

Each author rated how "compelling" they found each article title, adopting the perspective of a teacher of that topic, on a scale from 1 (not compelling) to 5 (very compelling). The summed score total across author–researchers could therefore range from 3 to 15. An independent, two-tailed t-test comparing the summed scores for paid ($M = 9.46$) and free ($M = 9.42$) resources was not significant, $t(46) = 0.061$, $p > 0.05$, indicating that, on average, the headlines of free and paid resources were equally compelling.

4.3 Short resource description analysis

In our analysis of the short descriptions (see **Figure 1**), we compared the graphic image with the title, examined and analyzed the descriptive body text to understand its construction and informational content, and evaluated the constructs of "image impact", "resource usability", "Cuteness" of graphics, and "appeal" to a teacher. When scoring the resources in this final analysis, we drew on our professional experiences as teachers and university instructors, adopting the perspective of a classroom teacher in the subject area of the given resource.

From our examination of the graphic, we found that almost all of them (23 out of 24, for both paid and free resources) contained all or most (>50%) of the title text present in the graphic. Eighteen graphics in each category also included additional informative text beyond the title, which mostly dealt with topics or resource specifics about the resource. Finally, we examined each graphic to determine whether it indicated that it had "printables": 14 graphics for paid resources and 12 for free resources contained imagery suggesting that printables were available.

An analysis of the descriptive text to the right of the graphic and beneath the author's name was conducted. Most of these text passages contained descriptions of the resource, elaborating on the information in the title and graphic. The language was often persuasive, appearing in 16 paid and 12 free resources, and rarely argumentative, which was found in only 2 paid resources. Emotive language with a higher emotional loading (e.g., "exciting", "perfect", "highly relevant", "fascinating", "amazing", "fun") was identified, occurring in 18 paid and 11 free resources.

Our scoring and quantitative analysis of the graphics and overall "short description", using an independent t-test and two-tailed analysis, found no statistically significant differences between free and paid resources (see **Table 4**). With a maximum possible score of 15, the results suggest that, overall, the graphic images were reasonably but not highly impactful. The graphics were typically not

	Paid resources			Free resources			Statistical analysis	
	n	Avg	Std Dev	N	Avg	Std Dev	t-value	P-value
Image impact	24	10.0	1.68	24	9.75	1.54	0.63	$p > 0.05$
How "cute" is the graphic?	24	7.58	2.92	24	8.54	2.89	−1.14	$p > 0.05$
Usability of resource	24	11.8	2.10	24	11.4	1.84	−0.51	$p > 0.05$
How appealing are the resources?	24	11.2	1.91	24	11.0	1.73	0.47	$p > 0.05$

Table 4.
Independent t-tests comparing free to paid AI resources.

"cutesy," and their usability and degree of appeal to teachers tended toward the higher end of the scale.

The final short resource analysis examined whether the "short description" for each resource addressed any of ten different topics, five of which align with the "core skills for 2030" identified by the World Economic Forum [30]. Each of the three authors coded the descriptions by entering "D" (directly addressed the topic), "I" (indirectly addressed the topic), or leaving the field blank if the topic was not addressed. The data was summarized for presentation here in two ways. Firstly, the number of entries that were not "blank" was used to calculate a percentage score indicating the extent to which a topic was addressed. Secondly, a comparison of the number of paid and free resources that addressed those topics was calculated.

Unsurprisingly, most resources addressed information related to their stated topic in the short description, irrespective of whether they were paid or free resources (see **Table 5**). Few resources in either category focused on developing skills in using prompts for AI tools such as ChatGPT. Applications of AI were addressed reasonably often in both paid and free resources, but developing critical understandings of AI within the resources was less common, occurring in only 20

	Paid resources*			Free resources*			Number# of resources addressing the Topic**	
	Direct %	Indirect %	Total %	Direct %	Indirect %	Total %	Paid	Free
Topic information/knowledge	70.8	18.1	88.9	84.7	11.1	95.8	23	24
Prompt development	2.8	1.4	4.2	11.1	0	11.1	1	3
Application of AI	47.2	23.6	70.8	51.4	12.5	63.9	17	14
Critical perspectives on AI	5.6	36.1	41.7	11.1	26.4	37.5	12	8
Media literacy	1.4	18.1	19.4	18.1	12.5	30.6	1	3

**Rounding off all percentage values has occurred.*
***As agreed upon by at least two of the three researchers.*

Table 5.
Frequency of resources addressing AI topics.

of 48 resources. Media literacy was also infrequently addressed and, notably, was often implicit in the resource as opposed to being directly mentioned.

The "core skills for 2030" list involves 13 core and emerging skills identified by surveyed employers [30]. From this list, we selected five items we anticipated would be most relevant to K-12 AI educational resources, prior to examining either the short descriptions or full resources, and evaluated the "short" descriptions to see if they suggested that the resource dealt with these topics. There were considerable differences in how the different topics were represented in the descriptions. Digital literacy was the only topic well-addressed in the short AI resource descriptions (**Table 6**). "Creative Thinking" and "Analytical Thinking" were minimally addressed directly and only slightly more frequently addressed indirectly. More surprisingly, "Big Data" (a foundational element of AI databases) and "Environmental Perspectives" (given AI's significant environmental implications) were completely absent. These omissions suggest that none of the reviewed AI resources would be suitable for teachers aiming to engage students with these specific issues.

4.4 Full resource analysis

Because some file formats are easily editable while others are not, we examined the full resources to identify the types of files provided to teachers. Almost all of the 48 resources included PDF files (Paid: 22, Free: 21). Among the paid resources, only ten offered editable files (i.e., Google Slides: 8, Google Docs: 4, and PowerPoint: 2; some resources included more than one type). For the free resources, only four had various editable files (Microsoft Word: 2, Google Docs: 2, and PowerPoint: 4). Overall, just 14 of the 48 AI resources in our database included files that teachers could modify and adapt for their specific teaching context.

Our analysis of each of the full resources was conducted on a subset of AI resources used from the previous sections. Twelve paid and twelve free resources were randomly selected, with each randomly assigned to two researchers for scoring and summarization. Each resource was examined to determine if the resource

	Paid Resources*			**Free Resources***			**Number# of Resources Addressing the Topic****	
	Direct %	**Indirect %**	**Total %**	**Direct %**	**Indirect %**	**Total %**	**Paid**	**Free**
Digital Literacy	56.9	34.7	91.7	68.1	19.4	87.5	23	22
Creative Thinking	8.3	33.3	41.7	15.3	19.4	34.7	8	8
Big Data	0	0	0	0	0	0	0	0
Analytical Thinking	4.2	37.5	41.7	13.9	23.6	37.5	10	7
Environmental Perspectives	0	0	0	0	0	0	0	0

**Rounding of all percentage values has occurred, as*
***agreed upon by at least two of the three researchers.*

Table 6.
Frequency of topics representing core skills for 2030 in short descriptions.

explicitly dealt with critical perspectives on AI (e.g., AI hallucinations, biases in AI data, potential loss of critical thinking skills in users), to what degree those that discussed it did so, and whether students learned about how they could use AI tools/ resources or could actually develop these skills (e.g., learning to use an AI drawing package, learning to use prompts, using AI to improve grammar skills in their writing, etc.). To establish a "quality of resource" index, each researcher also scored each resource on a 1 to 5 scale regarding (i) how AI is discussed/developed in the resource (conceptually shallow to conceptually complex), (ii) to what degree the information is integrated (individual statements to inter-related), (iii) the breadth of AI tools developed (few to many), and (iv) the degree to which it was discussed regarding how AI could be used by them (students and/or teachers). These four subscale items were then summed to produce the overall "Quality of Resource" index.

Results of examining the full resources showed that 7 out of 12 paid and 6 out of 12 free AI resources discussed or developed critical perspectives on AI, a pattern consistent with findings from the short resource analysis. However, an evaluation of just how much they did so, using a 5-point scale, revealed that the average for each was not particularly high (paid: 6.4/10, free: 4.2/10), as scored by the researchers. With respect to whether student-directed skills were discussed or developed in hands-on activities, 6 out of 12 paid and 3 out of 12 free AI resources discussed how students could use AI, and only 5 out of 12 paid and 2 out of 12 free AI resources engaged students with AI tools.

The collective scores on the subscales were analyzed using independent t-tests to compare paid and free resources for each of the subscales. The statistical analysis (**Table 7**) found no statistically significant difference between the free or paid resources for any individual subscale or for the overall Quality of Resource index.

A closer examination of the distribution of the scores for the Quality of Resource Index shows that a large number of the resources received overall low scores, with a noticeable skew toward the lower range. Only one of the AI resources, a paid one, was in the upper quartile (**Figure 2**).

5. Conclusions and implications

Overall, the supplementary curriculum resources for AI available on TPT vary widely in quality and in the support provided to teachers, although there were few

	Paid resources			Free resources			Statistical analysis	
	n	**Avg**	**Std Dev**	**N**	**Avg**	**Std Dev**	**t-value**	**P-value**
Complexity of AI	12	4.92	2.32	12	3.83	1.70	1.31	$p > 0.05$
Inter-relatedness	12	4.83	2.41	12	3.58	1.88	1.42	$p > 0.05$
Breadth of AI esources	12	4.25	1.71	12	3.33	1.88	1.25	$p > 0.05$
Use of AI by them	12	4.17	1.90	12	2.83	1.47	1.92	$p > 0.05$
Quality of Resource Index	12	18.17	6.97	12	13.58	5.92	1.74	$p > 0.05$

Table 7.
Statistical comparisons between free and paid resources across various indices.

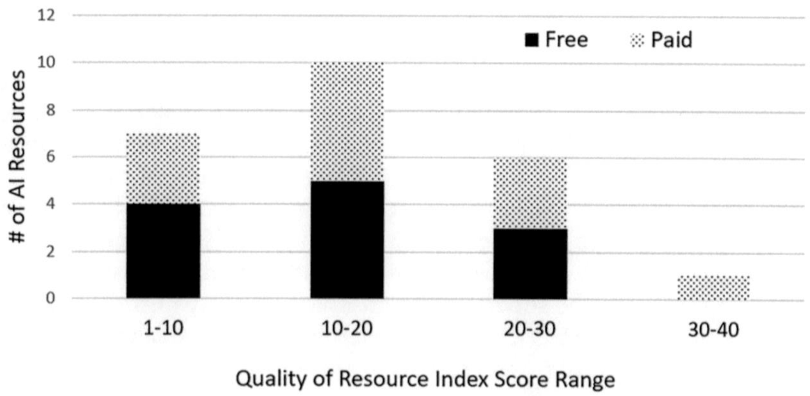

Figure 2.
Distribution of Quality of Resource Index scores.

statistical or substantive differences in most areas between free and paid resources (notable exceptions being that they differed in the number of resources available from the contributors to each type, and the resources that were editable differed noticeably between the two groups). On the surface, many resources seem to provide an introduction to the fundamentals of AI, but closer examination reveals that much of what is offered lacks sufficient depth and complexity with respect to students' learning potential.

In part, this happens because the resources often target a wider grade range of students than a single curriculum resource can realistically accommodate. Because of the stipulated age ranges for many resources, it is difficult to determine whether the language and concepts are age-appropriate. Some resources are too difficult for the lower end of the range, while others are too simple for the upper end. Some resources are accessible across the stipulated grade range, yet their appropriateness often depends on the academic readiness of the students using them. When a resource is purported to be usable for a grade 1 to 12 range, it is difficult to imagine how content "of substance" could meet the academic needs of such a diverse range of ages and academic competencies. Often, what was promoted as "content" was instead an abstracted representation of AI information rather than information students could meaningfully use and engage with. For instance, the issue of AI hallucinations (i.e., where AI makes up information, including academic or other articles, to answer questions) would be valuable for students at any age to consider. But critical perspectives on AI, such as this, were infrequently mentioned in any of the resources.

AI also has considerable environmental impacts and social implications (see [5, 19, and 31]). Despite this, only one resource focused on raising awareness of critical social issues related to AI use, such as the low wages paid to contract workers in developing nations who code and categorize information for training AI databases. None of the resources in our database addressed the environmental impact of AI, particularly its high electrical power consumption rates.

This lack of discussion of environmental and social problems associated with AI might reflect the backgrounds of most of the authors. Different culturally embedded ideologies are found in different parts of the world, and those living in developed countries might be less concerned about the environmental impacts of AI, such as climate change, and about worker exploitation involved in populating AI databases than individuals from those regions. There is certainly a developed-country bias among contributors to TPT, even though the resources are available globally.

One might have hoped that the AI resources, being more current (almost all from the last 30 months) and reflecting the considerable experience of the contributors (who, on average, had uploaded hundreds of resources), would be of higher quality, but this does not appear to be the case. It is likely that the lack of academic background in computer science areas (only 2 of 40 contributors reported such expertise) contributes to the superficiality observed in many of the resources. Similarly, having backgrounds in music did not lead to high-quality resources for music education [12]. Other researchers have also noted that TPT contributors do not necessarily have the experience needed to produce high-quality resources [5].

Hands-on activities have been actively promoted in schools for decades, yet, few of the AI resources we examined engaged students in actually using AI tools or practices, not even in learning how to use prompts effectively. Many of the AI resources instead relied on reading comprehension or competitive activities (e.g., escape rooms, games), or on completing worksheets following a slideshow or web search. It is noteworthy that not only did we observe that engagement with AI information was often lacking in depth (i.e., one or two sentences on bias, one or two sentences on an AI tool, etc.), but also that much of the pedagogy reflected what many would consider lower-tier engagements. This likely explains the generally low scores on the Quality of Resource Index. However, unlike previous studies that referenced the role that "cuteness" played in resources (e.g., [24, 25, 32]), the AI resources did not appear to be notably affected by that issue.

AI is, in many ways, an educational oddity. Whether teaching social studies, language arts, mathematics, or science, teachers have typically engaged with these subjects through their own schooling and in everyday life: visiting museums, cooking meals, writing letters, or reading books. But AI is new to most individuals, something that, until recently, might have been seen in movies, such as 1982s "Wargames", or the computer HAL 9000 in "2001: A Space Odyssey,", but was otherwise a topic (and practice) that was outside the general public's lived experience. For teachers, this novelty creates a need to obtain resources on the topic. Knowing they do not need to become experts themselves, they can instead "download" knowledge and expertise from others who hold perceived authority by virtue of being present and providing resources on TPT. This approach saves time while allowing them to believe they are providing quality materials to their students [33]. This highlights why providing quality resources about AI on platforms like TPT is essential.

We note that, although a teacher might download resources that are pedagogically poor in quality, we have no way of knowing how experienced and skilled teachers would actually use them. They might adapt such materials into effective pedagogical approaches in their own classrooms. However, this makes the lack of substantive content in these AI resources even more problematic, since teachers might address the pedagogical weaknesses but not the content gaps, particularly if they lack the subject knowledge needed to recognize what is missing; nor can we expect student teachers or new teachers to modify pedagogical practices effectively, as they are still learning those themselves. Moreover, only 14 of the 48 resources in our database provided editable documents, and this was only apparent after downloading them —something which is a desired component for teachers of resources in TPT resources (Mertens & Adams, 2024). In slightly over half of the resources, teachers could only infer whether printables were included, another supposed resource content interest of teachers (Aguilar et al., 2022).

The basis on which the TPT search tool functions is unclear [34]. As others have observed, the returned resources generally all have high star ratings, yet we conclude (as did others) that the star ratings are an ineffective metric for selecting resources. This highlights just how difficult it is for a teacher to choose good supplementary curriculum resources from TPT when the star system is unreliable, when they cannot tell if there are editable documents in the resources, how current the resources are, how many printables are included, or what the resource actually contains based on the description. Titles and keywords often confound selection; for example, as Barrett [17] notes, the term "lesson plan" is frequently conflated with what would more accurately be called an activity description, as we also noted. All these factors impede resource selection (also see [21]). It is not hard to conclude that TPT offers little real guidance to teachers regarding resource quality. In fact, some embedded practices make honest evaluation even more difficult. We noted that, in some circumstances, contributor descriptions have statements like, "To claim your free [resource] after leaving a positive review, email us the URL link to the review and the name of the [resource] you would like to [email address]." Such practices undermine the entire purpose and credibility of the review system and may explain the consistently high ratings found in our study and others.

5.1 Implications

Overall, we conclude that better teacher awareness is needed when selecting resources from online OERM sites; teachers need to develop improved "critical curatorial skills" [35]. As others have argued [7, 21, 36], Bachelor of Education programs and teacher professional development should address how to use resources like TPT effectively, particularly regarding how to evaluate the quality of materials and how to adapt them to meet the needs of specific student contexts. Tools exist to support this work. For example, the "Pinning with Pause" resource evaluation checklist [32] is one tool for teachers that has been developed to help them evaluate resources, although Rodriguez et al. [5] reported some limitations in its use with student teachers. Better educating teachers about evaluating these resources also has the potential to improve the quality of submitted resources if they contribute their own in the future, and encouraging teacher preparation programs to help prepare preservice teachers to become contributors to sites such as TPT might also improve TPT resources (see [36]). Arguably, there might also be improvements to the quality of resources for this topic if there were more submissions from individuals with backgrounds in computer science. We were surprised by how few contributions there were from that type of contributor.

Finally, it is worth noting that two of the three authors are former teachers, and all of us currently work with various aspects of teacher education and professional development. Irrespective of our findings from the AI resource analyses, we collectively identified only a few activities, out of the 48 examined, that we thought were "good" activities and would use in our own teaching, whether with children or with teacher candidates and teachers. For us, this personal view reinforces that many of the AI resources on TPT are consistent with Polikoff and Dean's [3] conclusion that the majority of online resources are "not worth using"

(p. 11), or at least most are only worth using with considerable adaptation and change.

Appendix A: Data collection framework for "Short" description of each resource

Author-researchers addressed the following topics in their review of the 48 AI resource "short descriptions" that were returned from the initial search of TPT.

What type of resource does it seem to be? (Activity description, lesson plan, worksheet, poster, etc.)

Is the written title mostly the same as the text in the image? (Yes/Partially/No)

Is there informational text in the image that goes beyond the title content? (Yes/No)

If "Yes", conceptually describe the content of the text.

How impactful is the visual image? (Rate 1 - Low to 5 - High)

Is the descriptive narrative text "Informational?" (Yes/No) or "Persuasive?" (Yes/No)

If "Persuasive", does it use "Argumentative" elements (Yes/No), emotive language elements? (Yes/No)

What is the apparent immediate usability of the resource without requiring extensive teacher effort? (rate 1-Low to 5-High)

How "cutesy" does the visual graphic seem to be? (rate 1-Low to 5-High)

If you were the target teacher audience for this resource, how appealing would the resource be to you (taking into account the above)? (rate 1-Low to 5-High)

With respect to the intention or goal of the resource, based on the information in the "short" description, does it address these topics (D)irectly or (I)ndirectly? If the topic is not addressed, then leave (BL)ank.

_____ Subject knowledge/information	_____ Application of AI
_____ Prompt development	_____ Critical perspectives on AI
_____ Digital/Technological Literacy	_____ Media literacy
_____ Creative Thinking	_____ Analytical thinking
_____ Big Data	_____ Environmental perspectives

Appendix B: Data collection framework for full resource package

Author–researchers addressed the following topics in their review of the 24 full resource packages. Most items were used as data for the analysis in this chapter; others (indicated by an asterisk) were considered as context for rating other items.

Note that any item with a "→" will be collected as a 1-to-5 Likert scale in the spreadsheet.

1. Are "critical perspectives" about the use of AI discussed or developed in the resource? Y/N (e.g., AI "makes things up", AI responses are biased by the data they are trained on, users can lose critical thinking abilities, etc.) If "Yes," how much are they developed—"a little" → "a lot"?

2. How is "AI discussed" or "understandings about AI" developed in the resource? [Evaluate with respect to grade level.] "Surface/shallow" → "conceptually complex"

3. How is information about AI presented? "Individual information statements" → "integrated and inter-related statements"

DOI: http://dx.doi.org/10.5772/intechopen.1012593

4. Is the breadth of AI tools discussed or developed? "A little" → "A lot" (e.g., is it just about ChatGPT, or is it about other tools as well, acknowledging that some tools can perform certain tasks well, but there can also be tools that are specialized)?

5. Is there any discussion or development on how AI can be used by students, teachers, the public, etc.? "a little" → "a lot"

6. Are skills with respect to the students using AI discussed in the resource? Y/N (e.g., using a prompt, for instance)
   Are skills with respect to the students using AI developed in the resource? Yes/No (i.e., hands-on practice).
   Describe the developed skills*: ________________________
   (e.g., searching for AI tools, refining prompts, comparing outputs from different AI tools, etc.)

7. Is the discussion about AI developmentally/grade appropriate? Y/Sort of/N Too High/Low (e.g., a grade 4 student should know that AI sometimes "makes up" stuff when responding, whereas a grade 9 student should know that, examples, etc., and maybe why "making up" happens.)

Acknowledgments

The authors wish to acknowledge that MSVU graduate student Amy M. Willison contributed to collecting and organizing information for this chapter and otherwise contributed to its creation. Denny, the cat, also made his own contributions during the course of the study, which contributed to its success.

Author details

G. Michael Bowen[1*], Michael Pin-Chuan Lin[1] and Christine A. Royce[2]

1 Mount Saint Vincent University, Halifax, Canada

2 Shippensburg University, Shippensburg, United States

*Address all correspondence to: gmbowen@yahoo.com

References

[1] OECD. Empowering Learners for the Age of AI: An AI Literacy Framework for Primary and Secondary Education (Review Draft). Paris: OECD; 2025. p. 290.

[2] Marple S, Bugler D, Chen-Gaddini M, Burr E, and Finkelstein N. Selecting Instructional Materials: Brief 2 — Why and How Teachers Choose to Supplement Adopted Materials. San Francisco: WestEd; 2017. p. 10. https://www.wested.org/resource/selecting-instructional-materials-brief-2-supplementation/ [Accessed: 2025-July-15]

[3] Polikoff M, and Dean J. The Supplemental Curriculum Bazaar: Is What's Online Any Good? Washington: Thomas B. Fordham Institute; 2019. p. 66. https://www.fordhaminstitute.org/ [Accessed: 2025-July-15]

[4] Tosh K, Doan S, Woo A, Henry D. Digital Instructional Materials: What are Teachers Using and What Barriers Exist? Santa Monica: RAND Corporation; 2020. p. 12. DOI: 10.7249/RR2575.17.

[5] Rodriguez N, Brown M, Vickery A. Pinning for-profit? Examining elementary preservice teachers' critical analysis of online social studies resources about black history. Contemporary Issues in Technology and Teacher Education. 2020;**20**:497–528.

[6] National Science Teachers Association. It's a Brand New World: National Science Teachers Association (NSTA) Digital Demand Mapping (DDM) Report. Arlington: National Science Teachers Association; 2018.

[7] Aguilar SJ, Silver D, Polikoff MS. Analyzing 500,000 TeachersPay Teachers.com lesson descriptions shows focus on K-5 and lack of Common Core alignment. Computers and Education Open. 2022; **3**:100081. DOI: 10.1016/j.caeo.2022.100081.

[8] Kaufman JH, Woo A, Eagan J, Lee S, and Kassan EB Uneven adoption of artificial intelligence tools among U.S. teachers and principals in the 2023–2024 school year (Research Report No. RRA134-25). Santa Monica: RAND Corporation; 2025. p. 24 https://www.rand./org//pubs/research_reports/RRA134-25.html/ [Accessed: 2025-July-21]

[9] Peltier C, Peltier T, Werthen T, Heuer A. State standards and IEP goals. A lot of TPT products": What resources early childhood educators report using to plan mathematics instruction. Learning Disabilities: A Contemporary Journal. 2020;**18**:153–166.

[10] Bugler D, Marple S, Burr E, Chen-Gaddini M, Finkelstein N. Selecting Instructional Materials: Brief 1 — How Teachers Judge the Quality of Instructional Materials. San Francisco: WestEd; 2017. p. 14.

[11] Sundrani A. Secondary mathematics teacher decision-making and their selection of digital materials. Journal of Mathematics Education at Teachers College. 2025;**16**:29–39. DOI: 10.52214/jmetc.v16i1.13072.

[12] O'Leary EJ, Bannerman JK. Online curriculum marketplaces and music education: A critical analysis of music activities on TeachersPayTeachers.com. International Journal of Music

Education. 2025;**43**:39–53. DOI: 10.1177/02557614241307242.

[13] Summers R. Appraising instructional materials from Teachers-Pay-Teachers for features of NGSS design and nature of science representations. Research in Science Education. 2024;**54**:523–546. DOI: 10.1007/s11165-023-10146-1.

[14] Xu F, Hewlett D, Correia AP. Exploring the landscape of computational thinking resources on Teachers-Pay-Teachers: Resources characteristics and user evaluations. Journal of Interactive Learning Research. 2023;**34**:9–36. DOI: 10.70725/999625lcwrhi.

[15] Shelton CC, Koehler MJ, Greenhalgh SP, Carpenter JP. Lifting the veil on TeachersPayTeachers.com: An investigation of educational marketplace offerings and downloads. Learning, Media and Technology. 2022;7:268–287. DOI: 10.1080/17439884.2021.1961148.

[16] Archambault L, Shelton C, Harris L Design quality and technology use in the top 100 US history activities on Teachers Pay Teachers. In: Society for Information Technology & Teacher Education International Conference. Association for the Advancement of Computing in Education (AACE); 2020. p. 1458–1463

[17] Barrett M. Mediocrity and Mini Books: An Analysis of First-grade Geography Lessons Found on Teachers Pay Teachers [dissertation]. East Lansing: Michigan State University; 2024.

[18] Stebbins A, Schroeder S, Han S. Liberty bells, flags, and monuments, oh my: Teaching citizenship through American symbols with TeachersPayTeachers. Contemporary Issues in Technology and Teacher Education. 2024;**24**:313–344

[19] Swalwell K, Rodriguez NN, Updegraff A, Winters LA. Distracting, erasing, and othering: A critical analysis of the Teachers Pay Teachers' Teach for Justice collection. Harvard Educational Review. 2023;**93**:104–130. DOI: 10.17763/1943-5045-93.1.104.

[20] Harris LM, Archambault L, Shelton CC. Issues of quality on Teachers Pay Teachers: An exploration of best-selling US history resources. Journal of Research on Technology in Education. 2023;**55**:608–627. DOI: 10.1080/15391523.2021.2014373.

[21] Archambault L, Shelton C, and McArthur Harris L Teachers beware and vet with care: Online educational marketplaces [Internet]. 2024. Kappan Online. Available from: https://kappanonline.org/teachers-beware-vet-with-care-online-educational-marketplaces-archambault-shelton-harris/ [Accessed: 2025-July-27]

[22] Carpenter JP, Shelton CC. Educators' perspectives on and motivations for using Teachers-Pay-Teachers.com. Journal of Research on Technology in Education. 2024;**56**:218–232. DOI: 10.1080/15391523.2022.2119452.

[23] Sawyer AG, Myers J. Seeking comfort: How and why preservice teachers use internet resources for lesson planning. Journal of Early Childhood Teacher Education. 2018;**39**:16–31. DOI: 10.1080/10901027.2017.1387625.

[24] Schroeder S, Curcio R, Lundgren L. Expanding the learning network: How teachers use Pinterest. Journal of Research on Technology in Education. 2019;**51**:166–186. DOI: 10.1080/15391523.2019.1573354.

[25] Mertens GE, Adams B. Evidence of strategic information literacy practices in early career teachers' navigation of TeachersPayTeachers. Literacy Research: Theory, Method, and Practice. 2024;**73**:238–257

[26] Xu F, Xie J, Correia AP (2022, April). How users seek computational thinking resources on teachers-pay-teachers: A review-based content analysis. In: Society for Information Technology & Teacher Education International Conference. Association for the Advancement of Computing in Education (AACE); p. 203–109

[27] Conboy M. The Language of the News. New York: Routledge; 2013. p. 240

[28] Fairclough N. Discourse and Social Change. Cambridge: Polity Press; 1992. p. 272

[29] Jordan B, Henderson A. Interaction analysis: Foundations and practice. The Journal of the Learning Sciences. 1995;**4**:39–103. DOI: 10.1207/s15327809jls0401_2.

[30] World Economic Forum (2025). Future of Jobs Report 2025. Cologne: World Economic Forum. 289 p.

[31] Pogrebna G AI is a multi-billion dollar industry. It's underpinned by an invisible and exploited workforce. The Conversation. 2024. Available from: https://theconversation.com/ai-is-a-multi-billion-dollar-industry-its-underpinned-by-an-invisible-and-exploited-workforce-240568 [Accessed: 2025-July-27]

[32] Gallagher JL, Swalwell KM, Bellows ME. "Pinning" with pause: Supporting teachers' critical consumption on sites of curriculum sharing. Social Education. 2019;**83**:217–224

[33] Brown M, Rodríguez NN, Updegraff A. We need a curricular cooperative: Envisioning a future beyond teachers paying teachers. Learning, Media and Technology. 2023;**48**:310–323. DOI: 10.1080/17439884.2023.2185254.

[34] Sawyer AG, Dick LK, Sutherland P. Online mathematics teacherpreneurs developers on Teachers-Pay-Teachers: Who are they and why are they popular? Education Sciences. 2020;**10**:248. DOI: 10.3390/educsci10090248.

[35] Schroeder S, Curcio R. Critiquing, curating, and adapting: Cultivating 21st-Century critical curriculum literacy with teacher candidates. Journal of Teacher Education. 2022;**73**:129–144. DOI: 10.1177/0022487122107527.

[36] Shelton C, Archambault L. Educators engaging in online educational marketplaces: A vision for teacher education to prepare critical consumers, careful creators, and discerning professionals. Journal of Technology and Teacher Education. 2022;**30**:155–166. DOI: 10.70725/404416vfljwk.

Chapter 29

The Future of AI in Education for the Next Decade: A Qualitative Study of African Researchers' Perspectives on Equitable Learning Environments

Damola Olugbade

Abstract

Despite the central role that artificial intelligence (AI) plays in global education, its impact on Africa remains underexplored. This chapter examines the perspectives of experts in African educational technology on the impact of AI on equitable education in the coming decade. Using qualitative interviews with 11 Associates and Professors across six countries – Nigeria, South Africa, Morocco, Egypt, Ethiopia, and Kenya – the study highlights African viewpoints that are often overlooked in global discussions. Using a blended approach that utilizes the Technology Acceptance Model, Equity Theory, Cultural-Historical Activity Theory, and Digital Divide Theory to inform an integrated approach to the problem, the experts' responses were thematically analyzed. Five major themes were identified: (1) the importance of appropriately shielding and protecting the early stages of a child's learning from the unregulated exposure to AI; (2) the potential of AI to transform pedagogy and achieve resources; (3) the need to align with Africa's infrastructural, cultural, and linguistic realities; (4) design justice and the ethics of AI technology; and (5) the importance of pedagogy and policy in AI utilization. Protection versus progress, equity versus excellence, and autonomy versus dependence are paradoxes that define the African educational context of AI. The chapter contributes to global debates on AI in education by focusing on Africa while underscoring the importance of equity-oriented approaches. It presents actionable advice to policymakers, teachers, and technology experts on culturally appropriate and sustainable AI applications in education throughout Africa.

Keywords: artificial intelligence, equitable learning, African education, educational technology, qualitative research

IntechOpen

1. Introduction

Artificial intelligence (AI) has changed the way technology works all over the world, and the changes it brings could also be used in our schools. AI has made the world a bigger place. It can be used for tutoring, adaptive and automated tests, and chatbots [1–3]. AI has the potential to transform the education industry in the same way it has revolutionized other fields, making things more personalized, efficient, and accessible to everyone. The use of AI in any organization is like an undercurrent that changes based on the organization's social, cultural, and economic background. In Africa, where AI is still new, the lack of access to teachers and infrastructure makes its use promising but also risky. AI is being used more and more quickly, which could change the region in many ways, some of which could be good and others bad. The education system in Africa has had to deal with a lot of problems, and even though things are getting better, they are still far from ideal.

UNESCO informs people that Sub-Saharan Africa has the highest level of exclusion in education among all the world's regions. More than one in five children between the ages of 6 and 11 do not attend school, and the rates of completing primary and secondary school are much lower than the world averages (UNESCO, 2023). The continent will need 17 million new teachers by 2030 to achieve universal primary and secondary education, which makes the situation even more challenging. Additionally, the "digital divide" is exacerbated by issues with infrastructure, such as frequent power outages, slow internet access, and a lack of digital tools [4, 5]. In this context, AI is both beneficial and problematic. It can provide resources that democratize learning and education, support teachers in various African contexts, and enhance personalized instruction [6, 7]. However, the uneven or poorly planned use of AI could worsen inequalities, hinder online accessibility, and create new forms of digital exclusion [8, 9]. The distorted global context in AI education research underscores the necessity of Africa's involvement in AI. Unlike the Global North, Africa lacks comprehensive discourses and studies on AI in education and research conducted by educators [10, 11]. This lack of information perpetuates Western narratives that overlook the diversity of cultures, languages, and infrastructure across continents [6, 12]. This chapter addresses the inequity gap, focusing on African perspectives, while adhering to its stated objectives of being inclusive, contextually appropriate, and culturally relevant to the application of AI in education.

The abundance of emerging AI technologies in education and the necessity for long-term planning [13, 14] elucidate the deliberate 10-year timeframe established for this study. Thinking about the next 10 years instead of the last one helps figure out what needs to be done in African countries. This chapter examines qualitative data obtained from 11 educational technology specialists. They all work as either Associate or Full Professors and live in six African countries: Nigeria, South Africa, Morocco, Egypt, Ethiopia, and Kenya. Their responses instilled a prudent optimism regarding the role of AI in promoting equitable learning environments, highlighting both significant potential and grave threats. This chapter, along with the deficiencies in theory and literature, highlights the distinctiveness of AI in education within the African context. The remainder of this chapter is organized as follows. The following section delineates the theoretical frameworks that will inform the study. After that, the research focus is clearly stated, the gaps in current scholarship are pointed out, and the research goals are laid out. The methodology section discusses the qualitative case study approach in detail, followed by the results and their implications. The chapter concludes with reflections on the limitations, suggestions for future research, and policy recommendations for making AI-driven education in Africa more equitable.

2. Theoretical framework

This study utilizes a multi-theoretical approach, as seen in **Figure 1**, to analyze the views of African experts on the role of AI in education, focusing on the Technology Acceptance Model (TAM), Equity Theory in Education, Cultural–Historical Activity Theory (CHAT), and Digital Divide Theory. The TAM has been used to explain the adoption of technology since the 1980s and was first put forth by Davis (1989) regarding the adoption of a technology on the basis of its usefulness and ease of utilization. Davis's work has been built upon in education in numerous contexts and, in particular, to analyze how educators and students accept AI and other technology [15, 16]. However, to understand Africa's adoption of AI, considering infrastructural deficits, cultural values, and inequity circumstances, the TAM model by itself would not be adequate.

Equity Theory in Education points to the necessity of fairness regarding access and resources to achieve outcomes and stipulates that technology should not only enhance efficiency but also eliminate inequities [7, 8]. In Africa, the question of equity becomes how AI tools can be made accessible to marginalized learners, to those in rural and poorly-staffed areas, and to the diverse cultural and linguistic contexts [6]. C. O. Rogers and Avgerou's Digital Divide Theory focuses on the disparity in the availability of and access to digital tools, the level of digital literacy, and the support infrastructure available [4, 5]. In the context of African education, the digital divide is defined as a disparity in access to a range of communication

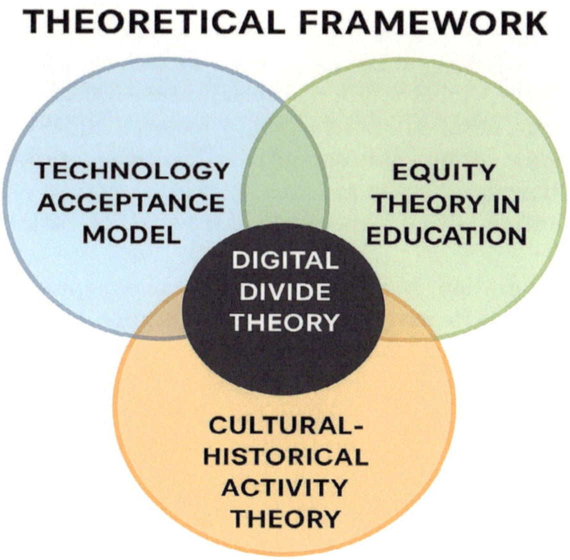

Figure 1.
Integrated theoretical framework combining the Technology Acceptance Model, Equity Theory in Education, Cultural–Historical Activity Theory, and Digital Divide Theory.

devices motivated by the need to overcome barriers in connectivity, affordability, and region-specific content. The antiracist precepts of the decolonial AI movement awaken the necessity to indigenize and contextualize CHAT by asserting that the frameworks are West-centric, as formalized in [12, 17], and throughout the rest of African scholarship. In overcoming the West-centric bias, one seeks to emphasize the relevance of Ubuntu philosophy, the oral tradition of learning, and communally held knowledge as quintessential to conceptualizing and researching AI in Africa. These frameworks are synthesized in this research to construct a composite analytical lens. The adoption of AI in education in Africa is to be understood within the phenomenology of its perceived value (TAM), equity and inclusion (Equity Theory), responsiveness to culture and context (CHAT), and infrastructure and access to the internet (Digital Divide Theory). This hybrid model serves as the basis not only for analyzing expert views but also as a guide for interpreting the derived insights from the analysis as well.

3. Main focus of the chapter

This chapter investigates the central research question: How do African educational technology experts envision the role of AI in creating equitable learning environments over the next decade? By centering the voices of African experts, this study makes a unique contribution to global discourse, challenging the dominance of Global North narratives and highlighting context-specific challenges and solutions. Its significance lies in amplifying African perspectives for policy, practice, and innovation, with practical implications for ministries of education, higher education institutions, and technology developers.

3.1 Research gap and rationale

Publications regarding AI and education show a rapid expansion over the course of the last 10 years [10, 32], yet the focus of the material is still concentrated in the Global North, with the Global South, and specifically Africa, being the focus of minimal publications, despite increasing policy focus [1, 10, 18]. Literature reviews indicate a near absence of policy-driven, Africa-focused, empirical AI research [11, 19]. When African perspectives in research do exist, they tend to focus on institutions or countries with widened gaps in regional comparative explanations [5, 20].

Equity gaps in education, stemming from the deployment of AI, have not been systematically addressed in existing research. For instance, the role of educators, the learning journeys of students, and the infrastructure within institutions in the next decade have not been thoroughly described [14]. Policies that only focus on incorporating new educational technologies in the short run will not equip policymakers to forecast shifts. Many publications do discuss the reinforcing inequalities perpetuated by inequitable AI deployment [7, 8]; however, research that focuses on the issue of inequity is scarce. In the African context, equity is not a secondary consideration but rather a foundational principle, given the continent's stark disparities in access and outcomes.

This study addresses these gaps by adopting a qualitative approach, privileging the insights of experienced African educational technology experts. The choice of qualitative methodology reflects the need for nuanced, context-sensitive analysis that quantitative surveys cannot capture [21, 22]. Expert perspectives are especially valuable, as senior scholars bring long-standing experience, regional knowledge, and comparative insights across different educational systems. The inclusion of participants from six African countries ensures geographic and cultural diversity, strengthening the study's ability to capture both shared challenges and country-specific variations. The 10-year focus provides a forward-looking orientation, situating African perspectives within global debates about the future of AI in education.

3.2 Research objectives

This chapter explores African educational technology experts' perspectives on AI's future role in creating equitable learning environments over the next decade. Here are the specific objectives:

(1) To examine experts' views on appropriate AI integration across different educational levels.

(2) To identify anticipated challenges and opportunities for AI in African educational contexts.

(3) To understand equity considerations in AI adoption for education.

(4) To explore recommendations for ethical and culturally responsive AI implementation.

(5) To project the timeline and milestones for AI transformation in African education.

4. Methodology

4.1 Research design

This study adopted a qualitative case study design set within an interpretive paradigm. The choice of qualitative technique is justified by the study's focus on examining meanings, viewpoints, and experiences rather than verifying hypotheses. A case study design is particularly ideal for evaluating AI in African education, as it enables in-depth research into contextual dynamics and expert opinions [23].

4.2 Research setting, context, and participants

The research setting was the African higher education and educational technology scene. Participants were purposively selected based on their competence in educational technology, academic position (Associate or Full Professor), and regional representation. In total, 11 participants contributed, coming from Nigeria (4), South Africa (2), Morocco (2), Egypt (1), Ethiopia (1), and Kenya (1). This distribution ensured coverage of West, East, North, Southern, and Northeastern

Africa. All participants had extensive experience in digital pedagogy and educational research. To safeguard anonymity, pseudonyms and country identifiers were used when presenting quotations.

4.3 Data collection methods

Data were obtained through semi-structured interviews designed to elicit participants' perspectives on pedagogy, inclusivity, engagement, and support. The interview guide was informed by the theoretical framework and piloted with two colleagues before being refined. Interviews lasted between 60 and 90 minutes and were conducted online due to geographical dispersion. Data saturation was achieved after the twelfth interview, as no new themes emerged.

4.4 Data coding and analysis

Interviews were transcribed verbatim and analyzed using thematic analysis (Braun and Clarke, 2006). Coding involved three phases: initial coding to uncover emerging concepts, focused coding to refine categories, and theoretical coding to relate themes to the study's framework. NVivo software supported data organization. Inter-rater reliability was verified through double coding of three transcripts by independent researchers, with inconsistencies resolved through discussion. Member checking was accomplished by sharing summaries of findings with participants for validation. Triangulation was achieved by integrating participant opinions with existing literature.

4.5 Ethical considerations

The study adheres to ethical norms, gaining Institutional Review Board approval prior to data collection. Participants supplied informed consent and were assured of anonymity and confidentiality. Data were stored securely on password-protected devices and cloud storage, in compliance with international data protection requirements. Cultural sensitivity was prioritized by allowing participants to express themselves in English or French, with clarifications provided as needed.

5. Findings

The study of semi-structured interviews with 11 African educational technology specialists identified five significant themes that illuminate the complex landscape of AI's future role in education across the continent. These themes highlight both the transformative potential and the substantial challenges concerning AI inclusion in African educational contexts.

5.1 Theme 1: Age-appropriate AI integration – the developmental imperative

A surprising consensus emerged regarding the vital need for age-appropriate AI applications, particularly in early childhood education. Participants expressed serious concern about AI's impact on cognitive development in young learners.

Professor A (Nigeria) emphasized: "*AI might be highly delicate for the development of a child's brain. The employment of AI in the basic sector of education should be outlawed entirely.*" This viewpoint was reflected across multiple interviews, with participants underlining the irreplaceable value of human interaction in foundational learning years.

Professor B (Kenya) elaborated: "*Children ages 5–12 need to develop critical thinking through effort, through making mistakes, through human supervision. AI at this level could develop intellectual dependency that hinders natural cognitive growth.*"

However, interviewees distinguished between primary and higher education contexts. Professor C (South Africa) noted: "*While we must protect young minds, AI can be revolutionary for university students who have already developed core thinking skills. The challenge is knowing when and how to introduce these technologies.*"

5.2 Theme 2: The great educational transformation – AI's revolutionary potential

Despite reservations about early implementation, participants unanimously agreed that AI would significantly transform education within the decade. The scope of this shift was recognized as unprecedented.

Professor D (Morocco) predicted: "*The use of AI in teaching will advance enormously. In the next 10 years, robots driven by AI would take over most parts of schooling.*" This transition was viewed as both inevitable and necessary for educational growth.

Professor E (Ethiopia) commented on this vision: "*We are witnessing the death of traditional classroom paradigms. AI tutors will provide personalized learning paths that no human teacher could equal in terms of individual attention and adaptable information delivery.*"

Professor F (Egypt) characterized the material transformation: "*Printed materials like textbooks, notes, and books would be taken over by AI-powered interactive learning platforms. Students will have conversations with their textbooks, ask questions in real-time, and receive explanations adapted to their learning style.*"

5.3 Theme 3: The African context – bridging digital divides and cultural relevance

Participants underlined that AI's effectiveness in African education would depend greatly on overcoming contextual issues and cultural considerations peculiar to the continent.

Professor G (Nigeria) highlighted infrastructural concerns: "*The promise of AI is enormous, but we cannot overlook that many of our schools lack basic energy. We need AI solutions that work offline, that can function in low-resource contexts.*"

Professor H (South Africa) underlined cultural adaptation: "*AI systems trained on Western datasets will prolong educational colonialism. We need AI that understands Ubuntu ideology, that recognizes indigenous knowledge systems, that speaks to African ways of knowing.*"

Professor I (Morocco) emphasized linguistic diversity: "*Africa has over 2,000 languages. AI must be multilingual and culturally sensitive. A one-size-fits-all approach will merely increase current educational inequalities.*"

5.4 Theme 4: Ethical imperatives and human-centered design

The ethical dimensions of AI in education have emerged as a significant concern, with participants urging for human-centered approaches that preserve the essence of education as a fundamentally human effort.

Professor J (Nigeria) warned: "*We risk developing a generation that cannot think without algorithmic aid. Education must remain fundamentally about growing human capacity, not replacing it with artificial intelligence.*"

Professor K (South Africa) addressed equity concerns: "*AI could either be the great equalizer or the great divider. If only wealthy schools had access to breakthrough AI tools, we would create an educational apartheid more deadly than anything we've seen before.*"

Professor L (Kenya) argued for balanced integration: "*The goal is not to replace instructors but to augment existing talents. AI should handle administrative responsibilities, provide statistical insights, and offer personalized support, freeing teachers to focus on mentorship, creativity, and emotional growth.*"

5.5 Theme 5: Capacity building and teacher transformation

Participants selected teacher preparation and support as the linchpin for successful AI integration in African educational institutions.

Professor M (Egypt) stated: "*The success of AI in education will be determined not by the sophistication of the technology, but by how well we prepare our educators to work alongside these systems.*"

Professor N (Nigeria) described the shift needed: "*Teachers must grow from information deliverers to learning facilitators, from content specialists to AI literacy coaches. This necessitates huge investment in professional development.*"

Professor O (Ethiopia) underscored the urgency: "*We have possibly five years to retrain our teaching workforce before AI systems become so advanced that unprepared teachers become redundant. The time for gradual change has passed.*"

To conclude the results section, the successful integration of AI tools in education on the African continent hinges on an almost immediate and drastic change in the entire teaching profession. The high-tech gizmos are entirely secondary to the foremost challenge, which is preparing teachers to step out of their age-old role as pedantic lecturers and content experts to become facilitators of learning and teachers of AI. This shift, particularly in the context of Africa, is going to require a tremendous and immediate allocation of funds for professional development, as the time frame for upskilling the present population is closing in. If Africa is to succeed, there is no doubt that teachers, without the urgently needed training, risk extinction in the coming decades. The change needed is therefore not a question of whether change is needed, but rather that change is absolutely essential.

6. Discussion

The views of African educational technologists highlight both the opportunities and threats of AI in education on the African continent. The results relate to the universal conversations on AI in education, but they also highlight African perspectives on the use of AI in education. Each of the ideas that emerged from the research aligns with the debates in the literature and is, however, uniquely refracted through the realities of Africa in equity, infrastructure, culture, and the readiness of teachers.

6.1 Age-appropriate AI integration: The developmental imperative

The consensus among participants, that AI should be tightly regulated in early childhood education, matches growing concerns in global research about the cognitive and socio-emotional repercussions of early exposure to digital technology [9, 24]. The concern stated by Nigerian and Kenyan experts, that AI use in children aged 5–12 promotes intellectual dependency, mirrors arguments that young learners gain the most from bodily engagement, play, and human mentorship [22]. At the same time, the distinction made between primary and higher education environments aligns with research demonstrating that AI is most effective when learners have already developed critical thinking foundations [25, 30]. This study underscores the Protection–Progress Paradox: safeguarding cognitive development while exploiting AI's transformative potential at later stages.

6.2 The great educational transformation: AI's revolutionary potential

Experts regularly forecast that AI will alter African education over the next decade, reflecting global estimates that foresee AI-driven personalization and adaptive learning as important disruptors of traditional pedagogical approaches [3, 13, 14]. The vision stated by Moroccan and Egyptian participants – AI tutors, interactive systems, and the loss of printed materials – resonates with the remark by Chiu [26] and emerging work on immersive technologies in developing contexts [33]. That generative AI tools like ChatGPT and Midjourney are altering teaching and learning practices. While such projections may appear techno-solutionist, African experts stressed AI's inevitability and urgency for addressing entrenched educational gaps [29]. This aligns with the study by Maina and Kuria [11], who claim that AI could act as a catalyst for systemic transformation in African higher education if judiciously handled.

6.3 The African context: Bridging digital divides and ensuring cultural relevance

Perhaps the most distinctive contribution of African specialists resides in their insistence on contextual and cultural adaptation. Concerns about infrastructure, multilingualism, and indigenous knowledge systems highlight the need for AI that is both accessible and culturally responsive. Scholars such as Olugbade [6] and Olayinka et al. [12] also advise against the uncritical acceptance of Western-trained AI models that fail to reflect African epistemologies. The attention on Ubuntu-informed AI systems underscores CHAT's emphasis on sociocultural mediation and supports proposals for inclusive design [17]. Moreover, participants' emphasis on offline, low-resource AI solutions speaks directly to Digital Divide Theory, underlining that, without infrastructural inclusivity, AI risks reproducing educational colonialism and inequality [8, 31].

6.4 Ethical imperatives and human-centered design

Ethical issues appeared as a recurring topic, with experts warning against algorithmic reliance, inequitable access, and systemic risks emerging from complex AI ecosystems [7, 8, 34]. The potential of replacing rather than enhancing teachers. This reflects global critiques that warn against "techno-solutionism" in education, as AI is positioned as a silver bullet without addressing underlying inequities [7, 8]. The urge for human-centered AI design echoes Equity Theory in practice: AI must support, not undermine, the fundamentally human process of teaching and learning. This resonates with advocacy by Viberg et al. [7] for AI-powered decision-support systems that improve equity and inclusiveness. African experts' emphasis on blending automation with mentorship and creativity further underlines the significance of reinventing teaching roles in an AI-driven landscape [27].

6.5 Capacity building and teacher transformation

Experts highlighted teacher preparedness as the key to successful AI adoption [28]. Their demands for rapid retraining correlate with findings from the studies by Hlongwane et al. [5] and Opesemowo and Adekomaya [20], who note that without teacher readiness, AI integration risks halting. The envisioned transformation of instructors from "information deliverers" to "AI literacy coaches" accords with global literature on emerging teacher roles in AI-enhanced classrooms [9, 28]. However, African specialists notably underline the importance of urgent, large-scale capacity creation, warning of obsolescence within five years if reforms are postponed. This urgency underscores the Equity–Excellence Paradox: While AI can democratize access to personalized learning, unequal teacher preparation could create wider divides between well-resourced and under-resourced schools.

6.6 Integration with theoretical frameworks

Taken together, the findings extend the TAM by demonstrating that perceived usefulness and ease of use are inseparable from equality, cultural responsiveness, and infrastructural feasibility in African contexts. Equity Theory is strengthened by the experts' insistence that AI should function as an equalizer, not a divider, while CHAT illuminates the significance of anchoring AI systems in indigenous knowledge and Ubuntu values. Finally, the Digital Divide Theory is vividly illustrated by worries regarding offline capabilities, pricing, and linguistic variety. These theories, when synthesized, provide a robust lens for driving AI deployment in Africa.

6.7 Study limitations

While the study provides interesting insights, certain limitations must be acknowledged. First, the sample size of 11 individuals, though sufficient for topic saturation, restricts generalizability across Africa's diverse educational systems. Second, participants were senior academics, which prioritizes expert opinions but excludes the voices of frontline teachers, students, and politicians, whose experiences may differ. Third, the reliance on self-reported data introduces the possibility of bias, particularly in forecasting the next decade.

Fourth, language hurdles were a constraint, as interviews were conducted predominantly in English and French, thus restricting nuance for those more versed in Indigenous languages. Fifth, technological restrictions hindered several online interviews due to unstable internet connections, reflecting the fundamental infrastructural issues under debate. Finally, the study provides a temporal snapshot rather than longitudinal shifts, making its predictions uncertain. These limitations, however, do not negate the study's contributions but rather suggest opportunities for future investigation.

6.8 Future directions

Building on these findings, various prospective study possibilities arise. Longitudinal studies are needed to observe how experts' forecasts unfold over the next decade, providing empirical proof of AI's actual impacts on African education. Quantitative studies with larger, more representative samples could complement qualitative insights, offering generalizable data on attitudes, adoption rates, and learning outcomes.

Implementation studies should focus on unique African contexts, testing AI solutions in rural, multilingual, and low-resource environments to determine practicality and equity implications. Cross-cultural comparative studies between African and Global North contexts could reveal how cultural frameworks impact AI adoption.

Expanding the study beyond specialists to involve teachers, kids, and parents would deepen awareness of AI's everyday consequences and equity concerns. Policy analysis is also vital, particularly investigating how African governments and regional agencies interpret AI within national education strategies [11]. Finally, collaborations between African scholars and technology developers should prioritize culturally sensitive AI design, ensuring African languages, values, and pedagogies inform future discoveries.

7. Conclusion

This chapter has investigated African educational technology experts' perspectives on the future of AI in education over the next decade, with a special focus on equity. Through interviews with 11 experts across six nations, the study has exposed both opportunities and challenges. Five themes emerged: the necessity for age-appropriate AI integration, the inevitability of educational revolution, the centrality of African contextual and cultural realities, the importance of ethical and human-centered methods, and the urgency of teacher capacity building. These findings reflect broader global discussions while foregrounding African-specific factors that are too often absent in international literature.

Theoretically, the study extends the TAM by incorporating equity, culture, and infrastructural elements. It also reinforces the relevance of Equity Theory, CHAT, and Digital Divide Theory in understanding AI adoption in African education. Practically, the findings underline the need for urgent investment in teacher professional development, culturally relevant AI systems, and infrastructural equity to prevent widening disparities. For policymakers, the study underscores the necessity of inclusive methods that integrate indigenous knowledge, multilingualism, and offline capabilities into AI implementation.

Ultimately, the future of AI in African education will be determined not only by technological competence but by how equally and responsibly it is implemented. If led by human-centered, culturally responsive, and equity-driven principles, AI can democratize learning and help Africa's educational reform. Conversely, if deployed without attention to African conditions, AI could exacerbate current gaps and create new forms of exclusion. The next decade is thus a vital opportunity for influencing AI's destiny in Africa. Stakeholders, including governments, educators, technologists, and researchers, must act with haste and foresight to ensure that AI serves as a tool for empowerment rather than division.

Author details

Damola Olugbade
Educational Innovation and Technology, University of South Africa, Pretoria, South Africa

*Address all correspondence to: damola.olugbade@tech-u.edu.ng

References

[1] Holmes W, Tuomi I. State of the art and practice in AI in education. European Journal of Education. 2022;**57**:542–570. DOI: 10.1111/ejed.12533

[2] Kamalov F, Calonge D, Gurrib I. New era of artificial intelligence in education: Towards a sustainable multifaceted revolution. Sustainability. 2023;**15**:12451. DOI: 10.3390/su151612451

[3] Ali A. AI-powered e-learning: Innovations, challenges, and the future of education. International Journal of Information and Education Technology. 2025;**15**:882–890. DOI: 10.18178/ijiet.2025.15.5.2294

[4] Chisom O, Unachukwu C, Osawaru B. Review of AI in education: Transforming learning environments in Africa. International Journal of Applied Research in Social Sciences. 2024. DOI: 10.51594/ijarss.v5i10.725

[5] Hlongwane J, Shava G, Mangena A, Muzari T. Towards the integration of artificial intelligence in higher education, challenges and opportunities: The African context, a case of Zimbabwe. International Journal of Research and Innovation in Social Science. 2024;**VIII**:417–435. DOI: 10.47772/ijriss.2024.803028s

[6] Olugbade D. A systematic review of the role of AI-enabled chatbots in modern education: Benefits, risks, and implementation complexity. In Garcia MB, Rosak-Szyrocka J, Bozkurt A, editors Pitfalls of AI Integration in Education: Skill Obsolescence, Misuse, and Bias. IGI Global Scientific Publishing; 2025. DOI: 10.4018/979-8-3373-0122-8.ch018

[7] Viberg O, Kizilcec R, Wise A, Jivet I, Nixon N. Advancing equity and inclusion in educational practices with AI -powered educational decision support systems (AI – EDSS). British Journal of Educational Technology. 2024;**55**:1974–1981. DOI: 10.1111/bjet.13507

[8] Bulathwela S, Pérez-Ortiz M, Holloway C, Cukurova M, Shawe-Taylor J. Artificial intelligence alone will not democratise education: On educational inequality, techno-solutionism and inclusive tools. Sustainability. 2024;**16**:781. DOI: 10.3390/su16020781

[9] Edwards BI, Olugbade D, Ojo OA. Facilitating cognitive load management and improved learning outcomes and attitudes in middle school technology and vocational education through AI chatbot. Journal of Technical Education and Training. 2024;**16**(3):114–131. DOI: 10.30880/jtet.2024.16.03.009

[10] Yu J, Chauhan D, Iqbal R, Yeoh E. Mapping academic perspectives on AI in education: Trends, challenges, and sentiments in educational research (2018–2024). Educational Technology Research and Development : ETR & D. 2024;**72**:973–996. DOI: 10.1007/s11423-024-10425-2

[11] Maina A, Kuria J (2024). Building an AI future: Research and policy directions for Africa's higher education. 2024 IST-Africa Conference (IST-Africa), 01–09. DOI: 10.23919/IST-Africa63983.2024.10569692.

[12] Olayinka T, Waghid Z, Mataka T, Adegoke O. Demystifying Lesotho, Rwandan and Nigerian educators' viewpoints on smart technologies

supporting AI in higher education. Education and Information Technologies. 2024;**29**:24285–24307. DOI: 10.1007/s10639-024-12820-x

[13] Sanders D, Mukhari S. Lecturers' perceptions of the influence of AI on a blended learning approach in a South African higher education institution. Discover Education. 2024;**3**. DOI: 10.1007/s44217-024-00235-2

[14] Chiu T. Future research recommendations for transforming higher education with generative AI. Computers and Education: Artificial Intelligence. 2024;**6**:100197. DOI: 10.1016/j.caeai.2023.100197

[15] Xu W, Fan O. A systematic review of AI role in the educational system based on a proposed conceptual framework. Education and Information Technologies. 2021;**27**:4195–4223. DOI: 10.1007/s10639-021-10774-y

[16] Almuhanna M. Teachers' perspectives of integrating AI-powered technologies in K-12 education for creating customized learning materials and resources. Education and Information Technologies. 2024;**30**:10343–10371. DOI: 10.1007/s10639-024-13257-y

[17] Shao Z, Zhao R, Yuan S, Ding M, Wang Y. Tracing the evolution of AI in the past decade and forecasting the emerging trends. Expert Systems with Applications. 2022;**209**:118221. DOI: 10.1016/j.eswa.2022.118221

[18] Zhang K, Aslan A. AI technologies for education: Recent research & future directions. Computers and Education: Artificial Intelligence. 2021;**2**:100025. DOI: 10.1016/J.CAEAI.2021.100025

[19] Mustafa M, Tlili A, Lampropoulos G, Huang R, Jandrić P, Zhao J, Salha S, Xu L, Panda S, López-Pernas K, López-Pernas S, Saqr M. A systematic review of literature reviews on artificial intelligence in education (AIED): A roadmap to a future research agenda. Smart Learning Environments. 2024;**11**:59. DOI: 10.1186/s40561-024-00350-5

[20] Opesemowo O, Adekomaya V. Harnessing artificial intelligence for advancing sustainable development goals in South Africa's higher education system: A qualitative study. International Journal of Learning, Teaching and Educational Research. 2024;**23**:67–86. DOI: 10.26803/ijlter.23.3.4

[21] Fawaz M, El-Malti W, Alreshidi S, Kavuran E. Exploring health sciences students' perspectives on using generative artificial intelligence in higher education: A qualitative study. Nursing & Health Sciences. 2025;**27**(1):e70030. DOI: 10.1111/nhs.70030

[22] Toyokawa Y, Horikoshi I, Majumdar R, Ogata H. Challenges and opportunities of AI in inclusive education: A case study of data-enhanced active reading in Japan. Smart Learning Environments. 2023;**10**:1–19. DOI: 10.1186/s40561-023-00286-2

[23] Braun V, Clarke V. Using thematic analysis in psychology. Qualitative Research in Psychology. 2006;**3**(2):77–101. DOI: 10.1191/1478088706qp063oa

[24] Salas-Pilco S. The impact of AI and robotics on physical, social-emotional and intellectual learning outcomes: An integrated analytical framework. British Journal of Educational Technology. 2020;**51**:1808–1825. DOI: 10.1111/bjet.12984

[25] Yılmaz Ö. Personalised learning and artificial intelligence in science education: Current state and future perspectives. Educational Technology Quarterly. 2024;**2024**:255–274. DOI: 10.55056/etq.744

[26] Chiu T. The impact of Generative AI (GenAI) on practices, policies and research direction in education: A case of ChatGPT and Midjourney. Interactive Learning Environments. 2023;**32**:6187–6203. DOI: 10.1080/10494820.2023.2253861

[27] Knopp M, Warm E, Weber D, Kelleher M, Kinnear B, Schumacher D, Santen S, Mendonca E, Turner L. AI-enabled medical education: Threads of change, promising futures, and risky realities across four potential future worlds. JMIR Medical Education. 2023;**9**:e50373. DOI: 10.2196/50373

[28] Alotaibi N. The impact of AI and LMS integration on the future of higher education: Opportunities, challenges, and strategies for transformation. Sustainability. 2024;**16**:10357. DOI: 10.3390/su162310357

[29] Adelana OP, Ayanwale MA, Adeoba MI, Oyeniran DO, Matsie N, Olugbade D (2024). Machine learning algorithm for predicting pre-service teachers' Readiness to Use Brain-Computer Interfaces in Inclusive Classrooms. 2024 IEEE 5th International Conference on Electro-Computing Technologies for Humanity (NIGERCON), Ado Ekiti, Nigeria, pp. 1–10, DOI: 10.1109/NIGERCON62786.2024.10927281

[30] Lim W, Gunasekara A, Pallant J, Pallant J, Pechenkina E. Generative AI and the future of education: Ragnarök or reformation? A paradoxical perspective from management educators. The International Journal of Management Education. 2023;**21**:100790. DOI: 10.1016/j.ijme.2023.100790

[31] Olugbade D, Oyelere SS, Agbo FJ. Enhancing junior secondary students' learning outcomes in basic science and technology through PhET: A study in Nigeria. In Education and Information Technologies. Springer; 2024. DOI: 10.1007/s10639-023-12391-3

[32] Olugbade D. Democratizing education in rural Nigeria through AI and mobile technologies as a transformative pathway to inclusive learning. In: Sanmugam M, Edwards B, Barkhaya NM, Khlaif Z, editors Fostering Inclusive Education with AI and Emerging Technologies. IGI Global; 2025. p. 233–250. DOI: 10.4018/979-8-3693-7255-5.ch010

[33] Paek S, Kim N. Analysis of worldwide research trends on the impact of artificial intelligence in education. Sustainability. 2021;**13**:7941. DOI: 10.3390/SU13147941

[34] Olugbade D, Ojo OA. Immersion technologies: Going beyond textbooks to improve learning in developing nations. In Edwards BI, Tanko BL, Klufallah M, Abuhassna H, Chinedu CC editors. Reimagining Transformative Educational Spaces. Lecture Notes in Educational Technology. Singapore: Springer; 2024. DOI: 10.1007/978-981-97-8752-4_16